CHRISTOPHER HIBBERT

ROME

THE BIOGRAPHY OF A CITY

W. W. NORTON & COMPANY

NEW YORK   LONDON

Photo Acknowledgements
Alinari: 33, 52, 88; Courtesy of the author: 64, 73, 74, 76, 78, 79, 81;
BBC Hulton Picture Library: 1, 17, 22, 24, 25, 32, 39, 43, 44, 47, 58, 60, 66, 67, 71, 82;
British Museum: 8; Cash, J. Allan Ltd: 98; Charmet, Jean-Loup: 11, 29, 55, 65, 70, 83;
Christie's: 57; Deutsches Archäologisches Institut: 3, 5, 6, 10;
Freeman, John & Co: 14, 40, 41, 45, 49, 50, 53, 69;
Mansell Collection: 12, 15, 16, 18, 20, 21, 23, 26, 31, 35, 36, 42, 63;
Mirrorpic: 94; Montreal Museum of Fine Arts: 13;
Moro Giovanna: 9, 19, 37, 38, 51, 61, 75, 80, 85, 87, 89, 91;
Musei Vaticani: 30; Ny Carlsberg Glyptotek: 2, 7;
Osterreichishe Nationalbibliothek: 4; Popperfoto: 90, 92, 93, 95, 96;
Powell Josephine: 27, 28, 46, 68, 72, 97, 98; Scala: 56; Sotheby's: 59.
Printed in Great Britain.

The text of this book is composed in Clowes Dante, with display type set in Clowes Dante
Composition and manufacturing by William Clowes Limited, Beccles and London.
Book design by Jessica Smith

Hibbert, Christopher, 1924—
    Rome, the biography of a city.
    Bibliography: p.
    Includes index.
    1. Rome (Italy)—History. I. Title.
DG808.H52 1985   945′.632   84–22684

ISBN 0-393-01984-5

W. W. Norton & Company, Inc., 500 Fifth Avenue, New York, N.Y. 10110
W. W. Norton & Company Ltd., 37 Great Russell Street, London WC1B 3NU

The frontispiece shows a detail of the Isola Tiberina by G. Vanvitelli (1653–1736) from the Musei Capitolini in
Rome

TO TOM AND ALLYCE

CONTENTS

AUTHOR'S NOTE   ix

PART I

1. MYTHS, MONARCHS AND REPUBLICANS   3

2. IMPERIAL ROME   24

3. BREAD AND CIRCUSES   45

4. CATACOMBS AND CHRISTIANS   64

5. INFAMY AND ANARCHY   81

6. SAINTS, TYRANTS AND ANTI-POPES   97

7. 'THE REFUGE OF ALL THE NATIONS'   113

8. RENAISSANCE AND DECADENCE   125

9. PATRONS AND PARASITES   139

10. THE SACK OF ROME   153

PART II

11. RECOVERY AND REFORM   165

12. BERNINI AND THE BAROQUE   179

13. IL SETTECENTO   200

14. NAPOLEONIC INTERLUDE   227

15. THE RISORGIMENTO AND THE ROMAN QUESTION   244

16. ROYAL ROME   274

17. ROMA FASCISTA   286

EPILOGUE: THE ETERNAL CITY   305

PART III

Notes on Topography, Buildings and Works of Art   315
Sources   371
Index   375

AUTHOR'S NOTE

Although this book is intended to be an introduction to the history of Rome and of the social life of its people from the days of the Etruscan kings to those of Mussolini, I have tried at the same time to make it, in some sense, a guidebook. It cannot pretend to be a comprehensive one, but the notes at the back contain some information about all the buildings and treasures of the city which are mentioned in the text; and I believe that none of the principal sights and delights of Rome has been omitted. The book will, therefore, I hope, not only provide for the general reader an outline of Rome's varied past, as well as character sketches of those who have played their parts in its long history and development, but will also be of practical use to all those who intend one day to visit or revisit this most wonderful of cities.

The book could scarcely have been written without the help of my friend, the Hon. Edmund Howard, formerly Counsellor at the British Embassy in Rome, whose deep knowledge of the city and its people has guided me at every stage of its preparation. He has given me extensive assistance with the notes and, having read the manuscript, has made many suggestions for its improvement. Nor would working on the book have proved such a pleasure without the encouragement of another friend, John Guest, my skilful and trusted editor for over twenty-five years and my companion on numerous walks from one end of Rome to the other.

I am also deeply indebted to Tessa Street who has been both an impeccable typist and a careful reader of the text. And I am also most grateful to yet other friends who have helped me in a variety of ways, to my agent Bruce Hunter; to Peter Carson and Eleo Gordon of Viking; to Thomas Wallace of W. W. Norton; to Peter Hebblethwaite and Father Philip Caraman; to Ben Weinreb and the late Professor Roberto Weiss; to Maria Orsini and Thérèse Pollen; to Valerie Goodier and Nonie Rae, and to the libraries and staffs of the London Library and the Italian Institute of Culture. I am, as always, indebted to my wife for having compiled the comprehensive index.

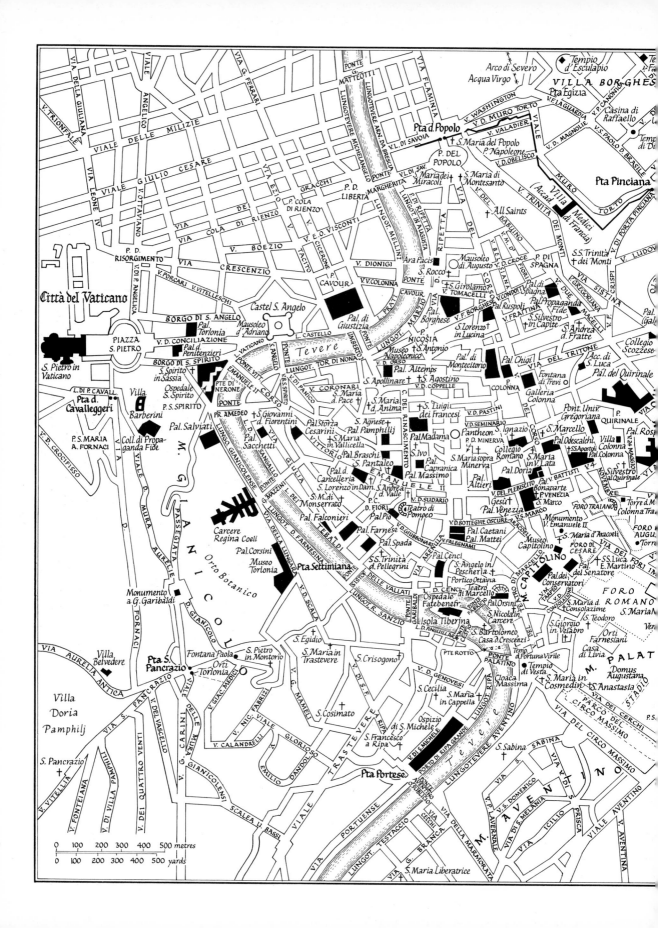

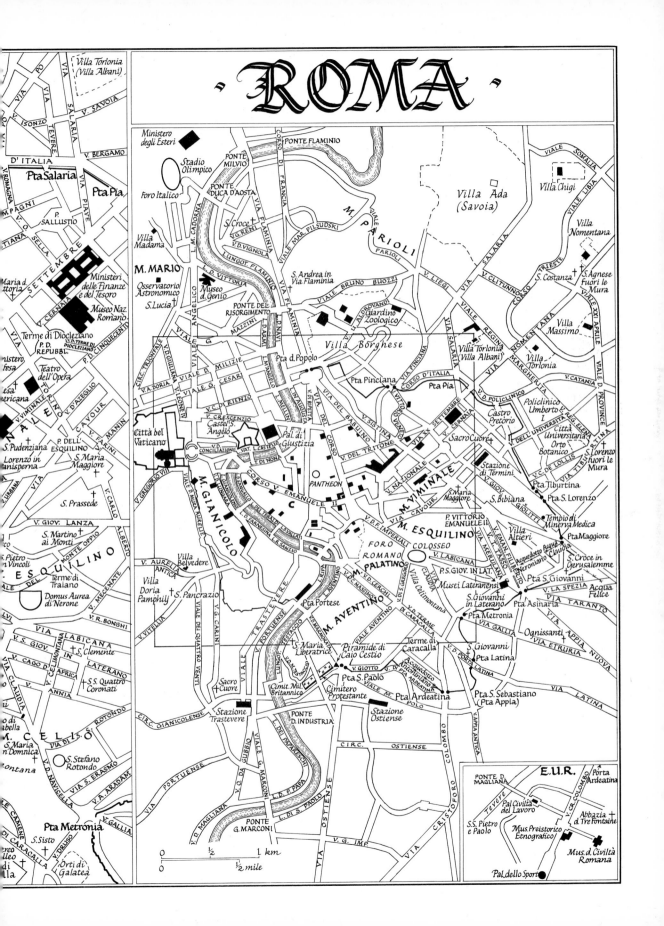

PART ONE

Rome, Capital of the World: a fifteenth-century woodcut proclaims the pre-eminence of the Eternal
City. Romulus and Remus, its mythical founders, appear on the left of the picture.

MYTHS, MONARCHS AND REPUBLICANS

In the days of Augustus, the first of the Roman emperors, a young writer from Padua, Titus Livius, brought to a close the first part of his epic history of the city in which he had come to live. His story had begun in that remote age, seven hundred years before his own birth, in which the origins of Rome were overcast by the mists of romantic legend. Its scene was the high ground overlooking the Tiber some fifteen miles from the salt flats through which the river flowed to the sea. Down the slopes of the hills ran streams which formed swamps and small lakes in the valleys below.[1] And beyond the valleys was the wide expanse of the Roman Campagna, a silent, undulating plain of woodland and pasture that stretched as far as the eye could reach to the surrounding mountains, to the Alban hills in the south, to the Apennines in the east, and, in the north, to the commanding heights of the empire of the Etruscans. Above a bend in the Tiber, where an island lay in midstream like an anchored ship, was the only place for miles at which the river could be crossed with ease. Here rose a hill which was to become known as the Palatine; and it was here, in the eighth century before Christ, that Titus Livius set his story.

He wrote of Romulus and Remus, twin sons of Rhea Silvia, daughter of Numitor, King of Alba Longa in the Alban Hills and a descendant of Aeneas, the hero of Troy. While a virgin attendant in a sacred shrine, Rhea Silvia had been raped by a man she claimed was Mars, god of war. Her twin babies had been left to die in a bucket by the waters of the flooded Tiber but had been saved by a she-wolf which had offered them her teats to suck and had nursed them gently until they were found by a herdsman who took them back to his hut. On reaching manhood, in 753 B.C. the twins decided to establish a new settlement for their tribe on the hills above the river where their lives had been saved; and they asked the gods of the countryside to declare by augury which of them should be its governor. Romulus then climbed to the top of the Palatine, while Remus took up his position on the summit of the nearby hill, the Aventine, to watch for signs in the flight of birds by which the gods made their wishes known. Soon six vultures flew across the Aventine, and Remus understood from this that his claims had been preferred. But then a flight of twelve vultures spread their wings above the Palatine, and Romulus took this as a sign that the gods' favours had fallen upon him. The brothers fell to quarrelling; their supporters began to fight each other; Remus jumped over the half-finished walls which his brother had built on the Palatine, and Romulus killed him in a fit of rage.

Thereafter Romulus's settlement grew and prospered. Yet, whereas there were strong and able men enough, there were too few women, the refugees from other tribes to whom asylum had been given at Rome, in the hope of increasing the population, being mostly male. Romulus, therefore, sent envoys to the surrounding peoples proposing intermarriage. But their offers were insultingly declined. To Romulus the use of force now seemed inevitable, and he set the scene of it with care and cunning. Concealing his resentment, he announced that the forthcoming celebrations of the Consualia, the festival Livy supposed was in honour of the water-deity Neptunus, would be held at Rome that year with particular splendour and that all surrounding tribes would be welcome to attend them. Among the peoples who accepted the invitation and came to inspect the walls and dwellings of the rapidly growing settlement were the Sabines, a well-favoured mountain tribe from the north. When the celebrations were at their height, the men of Rome fell upon the youngest of the Sabine women and dragged them to their homes, while their parents fled through the gates in panic-stricken terror. The fears of the Sabine girls were allayed by Romulus who assured them that as wives of Romans they would thereafter be treated well, sharing in the privileges of the new community and enjoying its coming greatness; they must overcome their present bitterness and give their hearts to those who had taken possession of their bodies.

In due time the Sabine women did learn to live contentedly with their Roman husbands, but the people from whom they had been seized could not forget the humiliation of their rape and planned to avenge it. Their opportunity arose when the daughter of Spurius Tarpeius, commander of the Roman garrison, who had gone outside her father's fortifications to fetch fresh water for a sacrifice, encountered in the valley a party of Sabine soldiers. She fell into flirtatious conversation with them and was persuaded to admit them into the citadel, asking to be given, as a reward for her treachery, 'what they had on their shield arms', meaning the gold bracelets the Sabines then wore from wrist to elbow. The bargain was struck and, on her part, fulfilled, but, once the Sabines had gained access to the citadel, they rewarded her not with the bracelets on their shield arms but with the shields themselves, crushing her to death beneath their weight as a fitting punishment for a traitor. In the ensuing battle with the Romans, the Sabines gained the first advantage; but then Romulus rallied his warriors and seemed on the point of destroying his opponents when the Sabine women, their hair hanging loose and their garments rent, pushed their way in a body between the combatants, begging them, as husbands on the one side and as fathers and brothers on the other, not to shed kindred blood. 'The effect of the appeal was immediate and profound,' so Livy recorded. 'Silence fell. Not a man moved. A moment later Romulus and the Sabine commander stepped forward to make peace. Indeed, they went further: the two peoples were united under a single government, with Rome as the seat of power.'

As the years passed other rival tribes were engaged in battle and were defeated, and these vanquished tribes were allowed to establish their families in the neighbourhood of the victors, thus increasing the heterogeneous population of the settlement. Gradually, the power of Rome spread far and wide, westwards to the sea, eastwards to the Apennines, south towards the lands of the Volsci and north towards the empire of the Etruscans.

Romulus, the inspiration of Rome's victories, disappeared from sight one day when a cloud enveloped him as he was reviewing his soldiers in a thunderstorm on the ground beyond Rome's walls known as the Campus Martius.[2] As the cloud lifted and the sun came out again it was seen that the royal throne was empty. There were those who said that the king had been lifted by a whirlwind back to the domain of the gods whence he had come. Others maintained that he had been murdered and his body had been concealed by some of the hundred senators he had created and who were now jealous of his power. But, after a year's interregnum during which the senators shared the government between them, another king was elected; and he in turn was followed by five others. The first of these six kings, all chosen after the necessary omens had been observed, was a learned Sabine and man of peace, Numa Pompilius. He it was who inspired the Romans with their fear of the gods. He appointed priests with specified religious duties and a high priest with wide authority over them, the Pontifex Maximus; he designated virgin acolytes to serve in the shrine of Vesta, goddess of the hearth and fireside, and to attend to her sacred flame; he introduced twelve Salii or Leaping Priests for the service of Mars, giving them a uniform of an embroidered tunic and bronze breastplate and providing them with sacred shields which they were to carry through the city as they chanted their hymns to the triple beat of their ritual dance. He divided the year into twelve lunar months and stipulated certain days upon which it would be unlawful to carry on public business; he built the Temple of Janus, god of gates and doors, which was to be left open when Rome was at war and closed in time of peace.[3] And he succeeded in bringing peace to the city by securing treaties of alliance with those neighbouring peoples who were not already bound to it.

Upon Numa's death, however, this peace was disrupted by his royal successor, Tullus Hostilius, who won great glory as a soldier in a reign of thirty-two years. The next king, Ancus Marcius, was a grandson of Numa Pompilius whose noble record in the matter of religious observances he was determined to emulate. Yet Ancus was as ready as Tullus had been to fight for the honour and independence of Rome, provided that wars were declared and peace negotiations conducted in accordance with those strict legal formalities and unvarying rites which were later to be supervised by the priestly representatives of the Roman people, the fetials.

During Ancus's reign a clever, ambitious and cunning young man from Etruria came south to settle in Rome. The grandson of an exile from Corinth, he adopted the name of Lucius Tarquinius Priscus and within a few years had gained for himself so eminent a reputation in the city that he was able to secure his election to the throne on Ancus's death. As king, Lucius Tarquinius Priscus planned the Circus Maximus,[4] bringing down horses and boxers from Etruria to entertain the Romans in splendid public games; he enclosed the city within a new, strong wall; he drained the low-lying land where the city's Forum[5] stood, making grants of land around this traditional meeting-place to builders of houses, shops and porticoes; and he laid the foundations for a new temple dedicated to Jupiter on the hill known as the Capitol.[6]

Sometime in about 579 B.C. this first Etruscan king of Rome was murdered by assassins hired by Ancus's sons who hoped to attain the succession for themselves. But, by concealing her husband's murder, the widowed queen was able to persuade the populace to accept her son-in-law, Servius Tullius, as regent, and eventually as king, entitled to wear the white and purple robe of royalty and to be preceded by lictors, members of the now traditional royal escort each of whom bore before him an axe bound with rods, symbolic of the king's power to beat and behead recalcitrant citizens without trial.

Once established in power, Servius Tullius began the great work for which he was always to be remembered, the organization of Roman society according to a fixed scale of rank and fortune. From now on, a census of the population was to be taken regularly, and the people, already divided into *curiae* for voting purposes, were to be further divided into various classes and assigned, according to their means, responsibilities in war and privileges in peace. The richest citizens were required to constitute the cavalry, the *equites*, or, as leaders of the infantry, to equip themselves with sword and spear as well as armour. The rest of the infantry was furnished by four other classes of citizens, the poorer of whom had merely to arm themselves with slings and stones. The poorest citizens of all were exempt from military service, but denied the political privileges which the other classes enjoyed in proportion to their rank.

Having thus organized Roman society in a class system based upon wealth, Servius Tullius then divided Rome into separate administrative areas. He also extended the boundaries of the city, taking in two other hills, the Quirinal and the Viminal, building a rampart around them and, beyond this rampart, distributing land which had been captured in war among ordinary citizens. This distribution much displeased the Senators and, in their discontent, Servius's rival, Tarquin, son of the murdered Lucius Tarquinius Priscus, saw his opportunity to replace him. Encouraged by his wicked and ambitious wife Tullia, Tarquin increased his influence in the Senate by promises and bribery and, when he considered the time ripe, he had Servius murdered. Tullia triumphantly drove over the corpse in her carriage, spattering her dress with blood. And so, in about 534 B.C., the tyranny of Tarquin the Proud began.

Declaring that an idle people was a burden on the state, he inaugurated a massive programme of public works, lavishing the spoils of a successful campaign against the Volscians upon the enlargement and adornment of the magnificent Temple of Jupiter which his father had begun, and setting to work upon it not only builders and craftsmen from all over Etruria but also hundreds of labourers from the proletariat of Rome. Work also began on improvements to the Circus where new tiers of seats were constructed, and upon the excavation of the Cloaca Maxima, the great sewer of the city.[7]

About this time, so Livy wrote, an alarming and ominous event occurred. A huge snake slid out of a narrow crack in a wooden pillar in the royal palace in the Forum. To interpret such omens it was customary to seek the advice of Etruscan soothsayers; but Tarquin felt that, since the portent had been observed in his own royal palace, he was justified in seeking enlightenment from Greece where, at Delphi, the most famous oracle in the world could be consulted. Unwilling to trust so important a mission to anyone else, he dispatched two of his three sons, Titus and Arruns, together with his nephew, Brutus.

At Delphi, having asked the oracle about the snake, the young princes could not resist making another inquiry: 'Who is to be the next king of Rome?' From the depths of the cavern came the answer: 'He who shall be the first to kiss his mother shall hold in Rome supreme authority.' Agreeing to keep this secret from their youngest brother, Sextus Tarquinius, who had been left behind in Rome, Titus and Arruns then drew lots to decide which of them, on return, should kiss their mother first. But, as they did so, their cousin, Brutus, far more astute and ambitious than he liked to appear, pretended to stumble and, falling to the ground, his lips touched the earth, mother of all living things.

Back in Italy the two princes and their brother were drinking together with friends when the conversation turned to the relative merits and faithfulness of their wives. One of the party, Collatinus, strongly maintained that his wife, Lucretia, was without doubt incomparably superior to all other women in Rome, and he undertook to prove it. If they called upon her unexpectedly now, he said, they would be sure to find her, unlike his companions' wives, engaged in some innocent and useful pursuit. And so it proved to be. While the other wives were enjoying themselves in the greatest luxury at a dinner party, Lucretia, surrounded by her maidservants, was hard at work spinning by lamplight. She rose to greet her husband and his friends, the princes; Collatinus, delighted with his success, invited them all to have supper with him.

During the meal the youngest of the princes, Sextus Tarquinius, was much taken with the beauty and proven chastity of his charming hostess; and, as lust rose within him, he determined to debauch her. Some days later he returned to the house when Lucretia was alone and, finding his way to her bedroom, he awakened her by placing his hand on her breast and whispering in her ear, 'Lucretia, not a sound! It is Sextus Tarquinius. I am armed. If you utter a sound, I will kill you.' But Lucretia refused to submit to his threats and blandishments until he said that he would dishonour her for ever in the eyes of the world by killing her first, then cutting the throat of a slave whose naked body he would place by her side. 'Will they not believe,' he asked her, 'that you have been caught in adultery and paid the price?' So Lucretia yielded; Sextus enjoyed her, and rode away, proud of his success.

The next day she told her father and husband, in the company of her husband's friend, Brutus, what had happened. Then she drew a knife from her robe and stabbed herself through the heart. Drawing the knife from her body, Brutus held it before him as he declared, 'By this girl's blood and by the gods I swear that with sword and fire, and whatever else can lend strength to my arm, I will pursue Tarquin the Proud, his wicked wife and all his children, and never again will I let them or any other man be king in Rome!'

At Brutus's passionate bidding the populace of Rome rose up in arms against the tyrant. Tarquin and his two elder sons fled into exile in Etruria; his youngest son, Sextus, was killed. The Kingdom of Rome was at an end. And, in about 507 B.C., with Brutus and Collatinus appointed the first two Consuls in Rome, the days of the Republic began.

Such, then, were the legends of the early history of Rome, legends that clearly indicate the kinds of people and behaviour which later Romans found admirable; and if they were great enough to invent such legends, we at least, as Goethe said, should be great enough to believe them. In fact, behind the fanciful embellishment of the myths, many of them Greek in origin, there lies a basis of truth. There were, indeed, Iron Age settlements on several of the hills above the Tiber where Rome was to be built; and a hut of one of them, known as the House of Romulus, was still preserved as a showplace on the slopes of the Palatine in the days of the Empire. There are, in fact, grounds for believing that the people who lived in these settlements merged with the Sabines and that they were governed by a king and had the kind of class structure and military organization which Servius Tullius is said, on fairly strong evidence, to have imposed upon them. There is also evidence of Etruscan influence in Roman pottery and in the system of land drainage in the Roman Forum from about the time which the legends ascribe to the arrival in Rome of the exile from Etruria who was to become King Tarquinius Priscus.

These Etruscans were a mysterious people who seem to have arrived in Italy either by sea from the Balkans or overland from the north and to have established themselves in the Po Valley and along the western coast in what was to become Tuscany. They were experts in metal-work and in pottery as well as energetic merchants who carried on a thriving trade with the Greek cities of southern Italy. It was natural, therefore, that the Etruscans should be drawn towards Rome whose hills dominated the nearest place to the sea at which the river Tiber could be crossed, and towards the salt beds at the mouth of the Tiber whence the Via Salaria, the Salt Road, led towards Perugia and the other Etruscan towns in the north.

Once the Etruscans were established in Rome, their influence became pervasive and lasting. The kings adopted Etruscan clothes and regalia as well as the ceremonial chair, the *sella curulis*, later to become the symbol of authority of the Roman magistrate; the priests adopted Etruscan religious practices, their methods of divination and augury; the farmers learned Etruscan methods of tilling and draining land. Etruscan sacrifices of men and animals to propitiate the unquiet spirits of the dead were for long to be enacted in the Roman amphitheatre, while the Etruscan lictors' axe and rods were to be revived as part of the trappings of Fascism.

The expulsion of the Etruscan kings and the warfare that soon broke out with rival states led to hard times for the Roman people. Trade was disrupted, agriculture depressed, plagues were persistent. In efforts to placate the gods, new temples were built in the city, temples to Apollo, a god of healing, to Ceres, goddess of corn, to Mercury, a god of trade, to Saturn, a god by whose favours crops were spared from blight. But the days continued dark and pestilential; and the poor grew ever more aware that under the Republic they had as little say in government and as few rights as they had had under the monarchy.

It seems that in 494 B.C. the discontent of the plebeians culminated in revolt against the patrician rule of magistrates and Senate. In the course of this revolt, when Rome was menaced by enemy armies, the plebeians marched out of the city on to the Aventine, threatening to found a separate community. Two Tribunes were consequently elected as representatives of the people, and later a Commission of Ten was established to compile a code of laws. The resultant Twelve Tables, the first landmark in the history of Roman law, were inscribed on bronze plaques and exhibited in the Forum; and for generations to come schoolboys were required to memorize and recite their provisions and to regard them as a cornerstone of the Republic whose greatness was symbolized in the device carried by the Republic's legions, S.P.Q.R. – *Senatus Populusque Romanus*, the Senate and People of Rome. The Tables, while instituting some reforms, were a codification into law of the customs prevailing in what was still essentially a pastoral and highly conservative community. Many of their provisions were harsh but they did combine to go some way towards acquiring equality before the law for all the people of Rome. Punishments were savage: 'Any person who destroys by burning any building or heap of corn deposited beside a house shall be bound, scourged and put to death by burning at the stake . . . If any person has sung or composed against another person a song which is slanderous or insulting he shall be clubbed to death . . . If theft has been done by night, if the owner kill the thief, the thief shall be held lawfully killed . . . Slaves caught in the act should be flogged and thrown from the [Tarpeian] Rock[8] . . . He who shall have roused up a public enemy, or handed over a citizen to a public enemy, must be executed.' Yet 'putting to death of any man who has not been convicted, whosoever he might be' was forbidden; and there were many other clauses designed to protect the weak against the powerful.

For all their vaunted merits, however, the Twelve Tables did not bring the plebeians any closer to sharing authority with the Senate; nor did those theoretical powers they possessed, such as the sole right to declare war in their public Assembly, ever count for much. The Senate remained the effective government of Rome, and the men from those almost invariably rich families who constituted its membership also filled, as though by right, the principal offices of the Republic. The most venerable of these offices was that of the Consuls who wore red sandals with crescent-shaped buckles and leather thongs and a special toga with a wide purple band, and who, like the kings before them, were escorted by twelve lictors carrying the *fasces*, the rods and axe, as an emblem of state. Other, lesser offices, also occupied by patrician families, were the Quaestors, who, after 421 B.C., were

1. Statue of a Vestal Virgin, one of the priestesses who served Vesta, goddess of the hearth. The Vestal wore a sacral dress, otherwise used by brides only.

responsible for financial administration; the Censors, who were established in 440 B.C. to supervise the returns which determined the responsibility of citizens for taxes and military service; the Praetors, who presided in the courts of law; and the Aediles, who were responsible for the streets, temples, sewers and market-places of the city and who organized public displays, games and festivals. In times of crisis a Dictator could be appointed with supreme power and with the right to an escort of twenty-four lictors, though not with the right to ride a horse in Rome, a privilege that might have given him pretensions to regality.

As well as the political offices, there were the religious ones, and these, too, the patricians fought hard to keep out of the hands of the plebeians. They were all of great influence and none more so than the High Priest, the Pontifex Maximus, who, as master of the 'sacred law', presided over the College of Pontiffs. Responsible not only for adjustments in the calendar made necessary by a Roman year of 355 days and for all occasions in life or death, such as marriages, adoptions and burials, in which ritual was involved, the Pontifex Maximus also had charge of the virgins who served Vesta, the goddess of the hearth, whose circular temple, one of the earliest in Rome, was built in the centre of the Forum.[9] These priestesses, free of all bodily defects and chosen between the ages of six and ten, were handed over in the House of the Vestal Virgins[10] in the Forum by their fathers to the Pontifex Maximus who thereafter had full control over them. They were required to remain unmarried for thirty years and to devote that time to offering sacrifices, to performing the ordained rites, and to tending the sacred fire which symbolized the survival of the state. 'And severe penalties have been established for their misdeeds,' in the words of the Greek historian, Dionysius of Halicarnassus. 'Vestals who are guilty of lesser misdemeanours are scourged with rods, but those who have suffered defilement by unchastity are delivered up to the most shameful and the most miserable death [by being buried alive] . . . There are many indications, it appears, when a priestess is not performing her holy functions with purity, but the principal one is the extinction of the fire which the Romans dread above all misfortunes, looking upon it, from whatever cause it proceeds, as an omen which portends the destruction of the city.'

In addition to his other duties, the Pontifex Maximus was responsible for ensuring that the gods were not mocked or displeased and that their wishes were made known. In divining these desires or commands he had the assistance of Augurs who were expert in interpreting the signs by which deities communicated their will to the earthly world in the voice of thunder or by flashes of lightning, by movements in the entrails of sacrificed animals, or by the flight of birds.

Ever since Romulus had seen in the flapping of vultures' wings a favourable omen for his foundation and governorship of the city, the Roman people had set great store by portents and their proper interpretation; and in times of danger, when unnatural events were often witnessed, they heard with alarm the spreading reports of monstrous births, of strange objects in the heavens, of statues pouring blood, of talking animals, of weeping corn, of stones and flesh falling from the heavens. Since the rules of divination were guarded by the Augurs in the strictest secrecy, and since portents could be interpreted in all manner of ways and, of course, invented, the powers of the priestly order of Augurs were immense. To prevent an election they had merely to declare that the time was not propitious to hold it; to block a law they had only to pronounce the omens had signified the gods' opposition to it. Cicero, who was later to confess that the office of Augur was the 'one bait' which could tempt him back into politics, went so far as to say that

the highest and most important authority in the state is that of the Augurs. For what power is greater than that of adjourning assemblies and meetings . . . or that of declaring null and void the acts of these assemblies? . . . What is of greater import than the abandonment of any business already begun after a single Augur has announced, 'On another day'? What power is more impressive than that of forcing the Consuls to resign their offices? What right is more sacred than that of giving or refusing permission to hold an assembly of the people?

The Roman people's readiness to accept the verdict of the Augurs was rarely in doubt; their reverence for the gods was deep and unequivocal, and their offerings to them punctiliously observed, the scrupulous regard for the forms of the rite in Roman religion being held quite as important as the rite itself. The conservative statesman, Marcus Porcius Cato, a rigid upholder of ancestral customs and a large-scale farmer whose treatise on agriculture written in about 160 B.C. is the oldest extant complete prose work in Latin, advised his fellow-farmers:

Before you gather in the harvest you should offer a preliminary sacrifice of a sow pig in the following way. Offer the pig to Ceres before you store away these crops: spelt, wheat, barley, beans, rape seed. First address Janus, Jupiter and Juno with incense and wine before you sacrifice the pig. Offer a sacrificial cake to Janus with these words, 'Father Janus, in offering to thee this sacrificial cake I make good prayers that thou be kind and favourable to me, my children and my house and household.' . . . [Also] make an offering to Mars Silvanus in the wood in the daytime for each head of work oxen. Three pounds of spelt grits, four and one half of lard, four and one half of meat, three sextarii of wine . . . No woman to be present at this sacrifice or to see how it is offered.

Precise instructions are then given of the words to be employed, of the other gods to be honoured with their due sacrifices, and of how they, too, should be addressed.

The Roman gods, indeed, were numerous and to each a proper and precise respect was due in accordance with their known powers. One god looked after the seed when it was underground, others when the grain was growing, yet others when it was stored. The god Nodutus cared for the stem, Volutina for the sheaths, Flora for the crop in flower, Matuta for it in its maturity, Runcina when it was gathered in.

Individual gods had their own specialist priests known as Flamens, but these were offices not so widely sought as those of the Augurs, for the Flamens were subject to numerous taboos. The Flamen of Jupiter, for example, was not permitted to ride a horse or see the army in battle array, to eat or even name certain foods, to pass under an arbour of vines or to go out into the open air without his cap. Additionally, according to the lawyer, Aulus Gellius, 'the feet of the couch on which he sleeps must be smeared with a thin coating of clay, and he must not sleep away from his bed for three nights in succession, and no other person must sleep in that bed . . . If he has lost his wife he must abdicate his office. His marriage cannot be dissolved except by death.'

In the Capitoline temple of the god Jupiter, which this Flamen served, were kept the Sibylline Books, the Books of Fate, which contained the secret key to the destiny of Rome and which were, therefore, as awesomely regarded as the pronouncements of the Augurs. These Books of Fate, containing oracular utterances of the renowned Sibyl of Cumae, a Greek city in Campania, had been purchased and brought to Rome, so it was said, by Tarquinius Priscus. They were carefully guarded in the Temple of Jupiter where they were treated as sacred relics and consulted whenever important decisions were to be made. The texts they contained were framed in the vaguest terms and, as the sceptical Cicero complained, since all specific references to time and place were omitted, they could be interpreted as predicting anything that the Keeper of the Books wanted them to predict. His office, therefore, accorded him great political influence, and it was yet another one which the plebeians were determined to have opened to them.

From time to time the plebeians achieved a success in their struggle for political power. Not long after the promulgation of the Twelve Tables, for instance, in 445 B.C., the marriage of a plebeian with a patrician, forbidden by those laws, was allowed. In 348 B.C. it was agreed that one of the two Consuls should always be a plebeian; and in 338 that the Senate should automatically ratify all measures voted by the People's Assembly. Then, in 287 B.C., when a Dictator, Quintus Hortensius, was in temporary office at a time of national crisis, it was decreed that resolutions of the plebeians' Council should have the force of law without the need for the Senate's concurrence. This appeared a major triumph for the plebeians; but in practice it did not prove so, for not only were the leading and richer members of the plebeians' Council those least interested in upsetting the established regime, but the Tribunes of the People, the Council's guiding lights, were soon persuaded to be less enthusiastic in their support of plebeian rights by the grant of senatorial privileges. So the plebeians failed to take advantage of their victory; the patricians, looking down upon them as their social inferiors, continued to control the Senate, and the Senate controlled the government.

Throughout the struggle between the classes, Rome was gradually extending its dominion. Rival peoples in central Italy were defeated, including the Etruscans whose capital Veii, only ten miles from Rome, was utterly destroyed. Some of the vanquished were granted full Roman citizenship, others lesser privileges; the unmanageable were kept in subjection until they too were considered worthy of joining the growing federation of states. There was, however, a serious setback at the end of the fourth century B.C., when Gaulish nomadic tribesmen from beyond the Alps swarmed down into Italy. 'Terrified townships rushed to arms as the avengers went roaring by,' so Livy recounted. 'The air was loud with the dreadful din of the fierce war-songs and discordant shouts of a people whose very life is wild adventure . . . Men fled from the fields for their lives; and from all the immense host, covering miles of ground with its straggling masses of horse and foot, the cry went up "To Rome".'

North of the city the Roman army was routed, and the Gallic squadrons poured through the city's open gates. All men capable of bearing arms, so Livy said, together with the women and children and the more able-bodied Senators, had withdrawn to the fortress on the Capitol, leaving the aged and useless in the city below. With these remained the oldest of the patricians who, dressed in the ceremonial robes they had been privileged to wear in their days of office, sat waiting for death in the courtyards of their houses upon the ivory-inlaid chairs of the city's magistrates. Here the enemy found them.

They might have been statues in some holy place, and for a while the Gallic warriors stood entranced; then, on an impulse, one of them touched the beard of a certain Marcus Papirius – it was long, as was the fashion of those days – and the Roman struck him on the head with his ivory staff. That was the beginning: the barbarians flamed into anger and killed him, and the others were butchered where they sat. From that moment no mercy was shown; houses were ransacked and the empty shells set on fire.

In Rome today evidence of this conflagration can still be seen in the layer of burnt debris, fragments of roof-tiles and carbonized wood at the edge of the Forum.

The Capitol, however, was held against the Gauls. An assault was made upon it in daylight and driven off. Then one starlit night another attempt was made. The enemy clambered silently up the steep ascent, passing up their weapons from hand to hand. The guards heard nothing; even the dogs were silent.

But they could not elude the vigilance of the geese which, being sacred to Juno, had not been killed in spite of the shortage of provisions. The cackling of these birds and the flapping of their wings woke Marcus Manlius, consul of three years before and a distinguished soldier, who, catching up his weapons and at the same time calling the rest to arms, strode past his bewildered comrades to a Gaul who had already got a foothold on the crest and dislodged him with a blow from the boss of his shield. As he slipped and fell, he overturned those who were next to him, and the others in alarm let go their weapons and, grasping the rocks to which they were clinging, were slain by Manlius. And now the rest had come together and were assailing the invaders with javelins and stones, and presently the whole company lost their footing and were flung down headlong to destruction.

By this time provisions in the Gallic army were running low and disease was spreading fast as choking clouds of dust and ashes from the burned buildings blew across the camp. Corpses were piled in heaps and burned on a spot afterwards known as the Gallic Pyres. An armistice was arranged; and the surviving Gauls, anxious to return home to deal with enemies on their own frontiers, accepted a money payment and withdrew.

For Rome the experience had been both devastating and humiliating, and steps were soon taken to ensure that the city was better defended in future. In place of the rampart of Servius Tullius, a new wall of volcanic stone designed by Greek engineers was constructed to enclose an area of more than a thousand acres, including all the seven hills.[11] From the gates in these walls, large parts of which can still be seen today, legions marched forth in campaign after campaign, against the Aequi, the Hernici and the Volsci, the Samnites, the Umbrians and the Gauls. All were eventually overcome and pacified, and thousands of foreign people were brought to Rome as slaves and many later set free. For the time being the south of Italy remained under Greek dominion; but by 265 B.C. Rome had become master of this area too, and was the supreme power in the Italian peninsula south of the Po.

Sicily, however, remained for the moment outside the sphere of Roman influence; and Rome's interest in this island led her into conflict with Carthage, the north African maritime power whose ships and armies controlled most of the western Mediterranean. The first war with the Carthaginians lasted for over twenty years, during which the Romans lost more than five hundred ships in storms and savage sea battles. But by a treaty of 241 B.C. Rome won control over most of Sicily and later took Sardinia and Corsica as well. A second war with Carthage began in 218 B.C. and brought fearful losses upon the Roman armies at the hands of the brilliant Carthaginian general, Hannibal, who marched across the Alps with his troops and elephants and inflicted defeat after defeat upon the legions, notably at Cannae in southern Italy where over thirty thousand Roman soldiers were killed. The disaster at Cannae was avenged on the Metaurus river where Hannibal's brother, Hasdrubal, was overwhelmed; but Hannibal himself remained undefeated in Italy where his hungry army wreaked havoc in the countryside. Handicapped by a lack of siege equipment, he did not attempt to capture the city of Rome, but on several occasions during the long war the Romans expected him to do so. Once he came within sight of the walls and pitched his camp only three miles away. The Romans, with grand defiance, put up his campsite for auction; and it fetched a high price. On another occasion, fears of an attack were increased by strange portents and by the discovery in unchastity of two Vestal Virgins, one of whom was buried alive in accordance with custom, while the other killed herself. The Sybilline Books were consulted, and by their direction a Gallic man and woman and a Greek man and woman were also buried alive in the market-place. At last, in the summer of 204 B.C., a strong Roman army under a brilliant young general, Publius Cornelius Scipio, sailed across the Mediterranean to Africa. Hannibal was recalled to meet the threat and two years later was decisively defeated at Zama, south-west of Carthage. Carthaginian power was thus destroyed, and in 146 B.C., to prevent it regaining its former dominion, Carthage itself was razed to the ground and its inhabitants massacred in accordance with the persistent demands of Cato who ended his every speech in the Senate, upon whatever subject it might be, with the words, 'And I also think that Carthage must be destroyed.'

By then Roman domination had spread not only across the Mediterranean into north Africa but across the Adriatic into Illyria, into Spain and Syria; and Macedonia had been taken over as a Roman province, a prelude to the incorporation of Greece itself as the province of Actaea.

The influence of Greek thought and culture on life in Rome was profound. Soldiers returning from the wars, officials from eastern embassies and administrators from Greek provinces came back to Rome with admiration for Greek architects and sculptors, for Greek potters and furniture makers, for Greek teachers, philosophers and writers. Soon there was scarcely an aspect of Roman life that was not influenced to a greater or lesser extent by Greek models. Greek teachers came to Rome to instruct the young in all manner of arts and accomplishments, from language and literature, rhetoric and philosophy, to wrestling and hunting, invariably addressing their pupils in Greek which remained the language of higher education long after Latin had come to be adopted as an acceptable tongue for the teaching of grammar. Greek artists also came, and the houses of the well-to-do became filled with Greek sculptures, with copies of Greek statues especially made for the Roman market, and with cameos and jewelled ornaments made by Greek slaves and freedmen. The houses themselves were designed on lines recommended by the architects of Greece. Usually built of the local Roman stone, often faced with stucco, and roofed with flanged tiles of local clay, they consisted of a number of rooms facing on to an interior courtyard, the *atrium*, and had another smaller, quiet courtyard at the back, laid out as a garden, surrounded by a colonnade and known as the *peristylium*, a word derived from the Greek.[12]

Greek gods, too, were imported into the Roman pantheon; existing Roman gods were identified with Greek equivalents, Jupiter with Zeus, for example, Venus with Aphrodite, Juno with Hera, Diana with Artemis, while new cults were introduced. In about 186 B.C. the worship of Dionysus or Bacchus, the Greek god of wine and ecstatic liberation, became widespread in Rome; reports of the orgiastic rites indulged in by the cult's converts alarmed the Roman authorities. 'To the religious content were added the pleasures of wine and feasting, to attract a greater number,' reported Livy, in a highly coloured account of these Bacchanalia. 'When they were heated with wine, and all sense of modesty had been extinguished by the darkness of night and the mingling of men with women and young with old, then debaucheries of every kind began and all had pleasures at hand to satisfy the lusts to which they were most inclined.' It was also reported that the cult was a cover for the conspiracies of revolutionary movements, so it was decreed by the Senate that the rites could not be held without permission and could then be attended by no more than five people at a time.

To most members of the Senate, old-fashioned and respectable, it seemed by the end of the second century B.C. that the Republic was already in decline. The virtues of their ancestors, their patience and resource, frugality and industry, loyalty, discipline and deep sense of responsibility had won them independence and widespread dominion. But the cost to Rome had been great. Plunder and war indemnities had brought great riches to the city; gold and silver had poured in from Spain; from the East had come luxurious curtained beds, rich coverlets, bronze couches and gorgeous furniture of a sumptuousness never before seen in Rome. The booty had been carried, and continued to be carried, in splendid processions down the Via Sacra. The victorious general, his face painted the colour of blood, marched in a gorgeous tunic, a golden crown, too heavy for him to wear, held above his head. Following him, his proud soldiers sang songs full of ribaldry and insults to their leaders, while the long lines of captives stretched back far out of sight, the most important of them, walking for the last time in the open air, soon to be executed in the cells beneath the spurs of the Capitoline hill. Behind them the chariots clattered over the stones, followed by the wagonloads of plunder, of vestments and tapestries, of gold vessels, jewelled scabbards and works of art. Yet, whereas in the past the plunder had been reserved for the city and the honour of the gods, with only a small share for the soldiers, now the army took as much as they could lay their hands on and successful generals became men of astonishing riches.

Nor was it only plunder that came to Rome. The conquest of Sicily had resulted in such vast amounts of wheat being paid in taxes that the whole population of the city could be fed on it for a considerable part of the year; and after 167 B.C. there was no need for Roman citizens themselves to pay taxes. Bakers became commonplace, whereas formerly bread had been made at home; cooks, regarded by the ancients as the lowest sort of slave, were now much in demand, and what had been considered a servile task began to be considered a fine art. With the plunder and grain, slaves had been brought to Rome in their thousands and employed in all manner of tasks both in the workshops of the city, where they deprived free labourers of work, and beyond its walls on the farms and cattle ranches, in the vineyards and olive groves of rich Roman citizens, displacing poor country people who were forced to come to the city in what proved to be a vain search for new employment. Miserable as was the lot of these displaced peasants, that of the slaves was usually far worse. They were frequently ill used: Roman lawcourts accepted their evidence only when it had been extracted under torture; and should a slave, provoked beyond endurance by an intolerable owner, take up arms against him, all his companions in the household might well be killed outright. Cato advised that all slaves, while working, should be kept on an economical diet which excluded meat; those no longer able to do their proper work should be sold for what they would fetch. From time to time slaves seized weapons and broke out into rebellion, but these uprisings were savagely repressed.

In addition to the slaves and the discontented poor, a new class had come into prominence since the end of the wars against Carthage. These were the wealthy businessmen of Rome, known as the Equites because in the past it was they who, sufficiently well off to afford a horse, provided the cavalry of the Roman army. For the most part they did not seek political office. Indeed, to have entered the Senate would have entailed the abandonment of their principal sources of income, since Senators and their sons had to rely for their income on their landed estates, and such activities as brick and tile making, which was conveniently considered a branch of agriculture; they were forbidden to compete for government contracts, to lend money or to own ships large enough for overseas trade.

The senatorial class itself, however, was also changing. A new elite known as the Optimates had emerged. These were the 'best men' who prided themselves not so much upon the distinction and length of their family trees, but upon the number of their ancestors who had achieved high office in the Republic. Their houses were filled with death-masks of distinguished forebears, and with busts and statues to remind themselves and their guests of the part their families had played in the creation of Rome. On ceremonial occasions, and particularly at funerals, these busts were borne aloft by respectful servants, death-masks were worn by actors who also put on the robes and carried the insignia of high office, and orations were made in honour of the family's name, more often perpetuating myths than recounting verifiable fact. Conservative, and in many cases reactionary, the Optimates agreed with Cicero, who had Scipio Aemilianus declare in *The Republic* that 'of all forms of government, there is none which by constitution, in theory or in practice, can be compared with that which our fathers left us and which had previously been left to them by their ancestors'. They firmly upheld the supremacy of the Senate and maintained that the People's Assembly should always follow the Senate's lead and take its sensible advice.

Politically opposed to the Optimates were the Populares, not, as their name might imply, a proletarian group, but mostly men from old senatorial families who were nevertheless in favour of constitutional, judicial and land reforms. They were supported by the Equites who saw much virtue in the proposals for reform advocated by Tiberius Gracchus, a young aristocrat who was elected Tribune for the People for the year 133 B.C. But Gracchus's provocative plans so alarmed the Optimates that soon after his election he was murdered at the door of the Temple of Jupiter Capitolinus. Three hundred of his supporters were clubbed to death and their bodies thrown into the Tiber. Tiberius's brother, Gaius Gracchus, a fine orator, subtle yet passionate, endeavoured to carry on his brother's work as a reformer. For a time he seemed on the verge of success but his plans to grant full Roman citizenship to most Italians, and thus to allow outsiders to share the Romans' free circuses, their cheap grain and the bribes they enjoyed for placing their votes in the People's Assembly, lost him the support of the Roman people. And in 121 B.C. he, too, was defeated. Forced to flee for his life, he reached the wooden bridge across the river and, there, on the point of capture, he presented his throat to a faithful slave who had accompanied him. No less than three thousand of his supporters were afterwards executed without trial.

Political differences in Rome had ended in unprecedented violence. The poor were more deeply antagonistic than ever towards the rich, and the Roman Republic was in its early death throes. At this time there rose to prominence a man from outside the governing class, a tough, crudely outspoken soldier named Gaius Marius who refused to learn Greek on the grounds that it was absurd to use a language which had to be taught by a subject race, and who had grown rich as a businessman and extorter of taxes. He had served with distinction against a royal rebel in north Africa and against German tribes on the northern Italian frontiers; and, by recruiting troops irrespective of their property qualifications, had created a new kind of army, no longer composed of citizens fulfilling a civic duty, but of volunteers without other means of support who, after fighting under the silver eagles, the emblems of Rome, remained loyal to the general who could provide for them rather than to the Senate which distrusted them.

This transference of the legions' loyalty was to have profound consequences in the future; but for the moment the fears of the Senate were concentrated not so much upon the army but upon a war in Italy provoked by the rage of Rome's Italian allies who, after all they had done to secure victory in north Africa and against the German tribes, were still denied Roman citizenship, a privilege which Gaius Gracchus and his followers had attempted to procure for them. This war was known as the Social War (after *socii*, allies); in it Rome had to face not only the armies of her former allies but also of such peoples as the Samnites who, still resenting their defeats so many generations earlier, were demanding not citizenship of Rome but independence from it. The war lasted until 87 B.C. and according to the retired army officer, Velleius Paterculus, it 'carried off more than three hundred thousand of the youth of Italy' before the Senate felt obliged to grant concessions. Even then peace did not come to Rome. Marius had walked off in dudgeon when not given supreme command, allowing his former staff officer, Lucius Cornelius Sulla, a rich patrician of skill and cunning, to enhance a reputation almost as great as that of Marius himself; and when Mithridates VI, a swashbuckling king in Asia Minor, began to expand his kingdom at the expense of Rome's allies, provinces and client states in the East, Sulla was given command of the Roman army. But this appointment was immediately cancelled at the instigation of Marius's supporters who appointed him in Sulla's place. Refusing to accept his supersession, Sulla left Rome to take command of the legions waiting to sail for Asia Minor, marched them back to the city, declared Marius an outlaw and forced him to go into hiding in north Africa. Marius, however, did not remain there long. As soon as Sulla had set sail to fight Mithridates in Greece, Marius returned to Italy to assemble an army from amongst his old soldiers; and, with another ambitious general, Lucius Cornelius Cinna, he marched upon Rome to wreak revenge upon Sulla's supporters there. He did so with the utmost ferocity, slaughtering his principal enemies and allowing his soldiers and slaves to murder, rape and plunder. But in 86 B.C., soon after he had had himself elected consul for the seventh time, he died insane, leaving his colleague, Cinna, to rule alone until he was killed in a mutiny two years later as he was preparing to lead an army against Sulla, who was still in Greece.

In 82 B.C. Sulla appeared in Italy once more and, overwhelming an army which the Senate, now controlled by Populares, had sent out to block his entry into Rome, he stormed into the city, massacring his enemies on a scale which even Marius had not attempted. His personal bodyguard disposed of almost 10,000 citizens, among them forty Senators, as many as 1,600 of the Equites and countless numbers of lesser citizens whose possessions Sulla's men appropriated. Sulla then appointed himself Dictator and rewarded 100,000 of his soldiers with lands taken from the families of the slain.

For the next two years this man, whose complexion was so pitted and blotched that it was said to resemble a mulberry scattered with oatmeal, personally controlled the government of Rome. In the interests of the Optimates, he passed a succession of conservative laws, restoring the power of the oligarchic Senate and destroying that of the Tribunes of the People. He also embarked upon an ambitious programme of public works in the city, sponsoring the construction of a new Senate House[13] and of the Tabularium, the State Record Office.[14] He married his fifth wife, 'a very beautiful woman of a most distinguished family' who, like himself, was recently divorced. Nevertheless, according to Plutarch, 'he still kept company with women who were ballet dancers or harpists and with people from the theatre'.

They used to be drinking together on couches all day long. Those who were at this time most influential with him were the following: Roscius the comedian, Gorex the leading ballet dancer, and Metrobius the female impersonator. Metrobius was now past his prime, but Sulla throughout everything continued to insist that he was in love with him. By living in this way he aggravated a disease which had not been serious in its early stages and for a long time he was not aware that he had ulcers in his intestines. This resulted in his whole flesh being corrupted and turning into worms. Many people were employed day and night in removing these worms, but they increased far more quickly than they could be removed. Indeed, they came swarming out in such numbers that all his clothing, baths, hand-basins and food became infected with the corruption. He tried to clean and scour himself by having frequent baths throughout the day; but it was no use; the flesh changed into worms too quickly.

In 79 B.C. Sulla suddenly retired to Campania where he died a year later. The diseased body was brought back to Rome and laid upon a funeral pyre.

Then a strong wind came up and blew upon the pyre, raising a huge flame. They just had time to collect the bones, while the pyre was smouldering and the fire nearly out, when rain began to fall heavily and continued falling until night. It would seem, then, that his good fortune never left him and indeed actually took part in his funeral. His monument is in the Field of Mars and they say that the inscription on it is one that he wrote himself. The substance of it is that he had not been outdone by any of his friends in doing good nor by any of his enemies in doing harm.

Soon after Sulla's death Italy was racked by another outbreak of savage violence which threatened to cost as many lives as the recent wars. It began in a barracks at Capua where captives, mostly Thracians and Gauls, were kept in appalling conditions and trained as gladiators. One day about eighty of these men broke out, armed themselves, first with spits and choppers from the cookhouse, then with gladiators' weapons from a convoy of wagons on its way to another city, and in the wild country of Lucania, south-east of Naples, defeated a small army of legionaries sent out against them from Rome. Slaves joined the gladiators, as did discontented herdsmen and shepherds, until their leader, Spartacus, a Thracian of high intelligence and some culture, had a formidable and well-armed multitude at his command. Spartacus would have taken them north across the Alps where they could have obtained their freedom. But, having defeated four armies, his men supposed themselves invincible and were content to remain in Italy ravaging the

2. Cnaeus Pompeius Magnus (Pompey The Great), the highly gifted and arrogant statesman and general, who was defeated by Julius Caesar on the plain of Pharsalus in 48 B.C.

countryside. In 71 B.C., however, Spartacus was at last overwhelmed in Apulia, and six thousand of his followers were crucified along the Appian Way.

The Roman general who brought about this defeat was the enormously rich Marcus Licinius Crassus, an ingratiating and avaricious officer, who was assisted in the later stages of the campaign by another gifted and ambitious commander, the arrogant Cnaeus Pompeius, afterwards known as Pompey the Great, who took much of the credit for Spartacus's defeat. Pompey and Crassus might well have come to blows; but, both recognizing the advantages of cooperation, they agreed to demand to be elected consuls for the year 70 B.C. though neither, as commanders of armies in the field, was eligible for election and Pompey was additionally disqualified on the grounds of his youth. After their election, Crassus remained in Rome, increasing his fortunes and political standing, while Pompey sought further glory, first in the Mediterranean where, with a navy of five hundred ships, he stamped out the pirates whose insolent operations were interfering with Rome's grain supply, then in western Asia where, in the process of creating new provinces and dependent states and in founding new cities, he not only redrew the map of Rome's dominions beyond the Ionian Sea but also became even richer than Crassus. When he returned to Rome he was welcomed with a Triumph, the third he had been accorded, more magnificent than any the city had seen. Two whole days were set aside for it, yet even so there was not enough time to include all the spectacles prepared. At the head of the procession were carried placards with the names of the countries which the hero had brought within Rome's orbit, banners indicating the huge amounts of money these lands would bring to Rome in taxes, and standards inscribed with Pompey's victories over the pirates. Then came parades of priests and musicians, dancers and jesters; then sad, straggling lines of manacled prisoners, rows of pirate chiefs, and, as Plutarch listed them, 'the wife and son and daughter of King Tigranes of Armenia, Aristobulus King of the Jews, a sister and five children of Mithridates, some Scythian women, hostages given by the Iberians, by the Albanians and the King of Comnagene. There were also great numbers of trophies, one for every battle in which Pompey had been victorious . . . But what seemed the greatest glory of all and one quite unprecedented in Roman history was that this third Triumph of his was over a third continent. Others before him had celebrated three Triumphs; but Pompey's first had been over Libya, his second over Europe, and now this last was over Asia, so that he seemed in a sense to have led the whole world captive.'

There had been fears in Rome that this great hero might establish an unlimited dictatorship as Sulla had done, and in his absence groups of patricians had intrigued with each other in efforts to prevent it. Among them was a corrupt, charming and devious candidate for the consulship, the radical Lucius Sergius Catilina. So widespread were the suspicions aroused by this shady and unprincipled character that a rival candidate, whose relatively humble origins had proved an insurmountable obstacle to the ambitions of less gifted men, was brought into prominence.

Marcus Tullius Cicero was the son of a retired country gentleman, none of whose ancestors had ever been Consul and whose pretensions to high office would, therefore, normally have been regarded by the Optimates as unbecoming in a so-called 'new man'. But Cicero's gifts as an orator were quite exceptional; and by dint of constant, eager practice in the Forum, where he fluently pleaded cases in his supremely eloquent Latin before the Roman courts and deeply impressed the crowds who came to hear him, he had at the age of twenty-nine been elected Quaestor, and in 63 B.C., before he was forty-four, he had become Consul.

His disappointed, embittered rival, Catilina, endeavoured to gain the consulship the next year by promising all manner of sweeping reforms; but he was again defeated, and now, despairing of gaining power by conventional means, turned his thoughts to an insurrection by the discontented and the seizure of power in a *coup d'état*. When Cicero heard rumours of this plot he acted decisively by ordering the immediate arrest of the conspirators. Catilina himself had fled from Rome and was subsequently killed near Pistoia. But five of his accomplices were brought before the Senate. Cicero argued persuasively and brilliantly for the death sentence and, having got his way, went out to the waiting crowds to announce to tremendous cheers, 'Vixerunt!', 'They are dead!' He had been strongly supported in his arguments by Marcus Porcius Cato, a man as implacable and as rigid in his advocacy of Rome's antique traditions as his great-grandfather. Opposing him had been a young, recently elected Praetor, Gaius Julius Caesar.

TWO

IMPERIAL ROME

Caesar was a tall, handsome, tirelessly energetic man from a family which, while ancient and patrician, was not unduly rich. He wore his clothes with a kind of flamboyant elegance which in a later age would have been considered that of a dandy; and he took great trouble with the arrangement of his hair, which became increasingly scanty as he grew older. His political sympathies seemed to lie with the Populares but whether this tendency was due to conviction, to ambition or to family influences – his aunt had been married to Marius and his own wife was the daughter of Cinna – no one could be sure. Certainly the Dictator, Sulla, had not liked or trusted him, and his family had thought it as well to obtain for him a post away from Rome in Asia Minor where his obvious ambition and the disconcerting gaze of his dark, penetrating eyes would arouse less apprehension. There he had come to the notice of the homosexual King of Bithynia in whose bed, it was widely reported, he had spent many libidinous hours; and this supposed affair was to be held against him by his enemies throughout the coming years.

Yet after his return to Rome on Sulla's death he had soon gained a reputation in the courts as a talented pleader whose rather high-pitched voice was offset by firm, impassioned and eloquent gestures. To improve these oratorical skills he had gone to Rhodes to pursue his studies under a celebrated Greek rhetorician who taught on the island. He had certainly improved his skills; he had also become renowned for his ruthlessness: on the journey out his ship had been attacked by pirates who had held him to ransom. They had treated him well enough and had released him unharmed when the ransom was paid. But he had sworn that he would have his revenge; and, as soon as he could, he went after them with a company of soldiers he had raised for the purpose. He came upon them, captured them, and had them all crucified, their throats cut first by way of mercy.

Back in Rome once more, Caesar had reappeared in the courts. He had become active in the College of Priests to which he had been elected in 81 B.C., and, after a time spent in the army as a junior officer, had come to the fore as a young aristocrat who, while proudly tracing his ancestry back through Romulus as far as the goddess Venus, had no patience with the unyielding conservatism of the established government. He had also, following the death of his first wife, married again, having carefully chosen a bride who could provide him with the ample wealth which was not only demanded by his extravagance and taste for luxury but which was still essential for the pursuit of high political office in Rome.

3. Julius Caesar, who became Dictator for life in 44 B.C. Soon afterwards he was murdered and died at the foot of Pompey's statue.

For the moment the great names in Rome remained Crassus and Pompey; and in order to promote his own ambitions, Caesar was prepared for the moment to further theirs. And so the three men rose together. In 65 B.C. Caesar was appointed Aedile, an office which, since it included responsibility for the provision of entertainments for the people of Rome, as well as for the maintenance of the city's buildings, gave its holder unrivalled opportunities to make himself popular. Eagerly seizing these opportunities, Caesar put on more spectacular circuses, wild beast shows and gladiatorial combats than Rome had ever witnessed before. From the office of Aedile, he quickly progressed to that of Pontifex Maximus, and in 62 B.C. to that of Praetor which took him to Spain where he showed himself to be as gifted a general as an orator and where he extracted so much money from defeated tribesmen that he was able not only to add to his own wealth and to gain the loyalty of his soldiers by lavish rewards but also to secure useful allies in Rome by sending part of the plunder home.

So, step by step, Caesar advanced to power, divorcing his second wife and marrying instead Calpurnia, daughter of a Senator soon to be Consul. The consulship was now almost within Caesar's own grasp. And, following merciless campaigns in Gaul and two invasions of Britain, which won him even greater renown and riches, he was ready to challenge Pompey for supreme power.

Caesar's other former colleague, Crassus, had already been killed in Mesopotamia; but the elimination of Pompey, by 52 B.C. sole Consul in Rome, was not so easily obtained. Caesar had thought at first of strengthening his alliance with him by suggesting that he should divorce Calpurnia and marry Pompey's daughter, while Pompey himself should marry a young relative of Caesar. Pompey chose, however, to marry the daughter of one of Rome's oldest and most distinguished families, the head of which he invited to share the consulship with him. And, after this, Caesar gradually came to the decision that was to lead him in 49 B.C., at the age of fifty-one, to take his army south across the Rubicon, the small stream between Ravenna and Rimini which divided Gaul south of the Alps from Italy, even though this meant defying Rome's law of treason which forbade a provincial governor to lead troops out of his territories. As he approached the Rubicon he said to his officers, 'Even now we might draw back; but once across that little bridge, then the whole issue will be with the sword.'

So it was to be. At first there was little resistance as Caesar marched south through Italy. He was joined at Rimini by Gaius Scribonius Curio, an influential Tribune of the People from Rome, whose support he had bought by paying off his debts. He was also welcomed there by another Roman Tribune, the intelligent, strong and forthright Mark Antony. Together they marched on Rome, while Pompey retreated southwards into Campania, thence to Brindisi and across the Adriatic towards the Balkans to the place where the decisive battle between him and Caesar was to be fought.

Disappointed in his hopes of winning the support of Cicero who, disliking him intensely, went off to join Pompey, Caesar was also disappointed by the half-hearted reception accorded to him in Rome by the Senate. Although distrustful of

4. and 4a. A book illumination based on Mantegna's 'Triumph of Julius Caesar', depicting soldiers carrying booty.

Pompey, most of the senior Senators were equally suspicious of Caesar, particularly after he had appropriated the contents of the state treasury in the Temple of Saturn. But, with or without the concurrence of the old aristocracy, Caesar was determined to rule in Rome; and, since he could not become Consul, as elections for this office had to be supervised by the Senators who currently held the office, both of whom had left the city declaring their support of Pompey, he had himself created Dictator instead. Then, having done what he could to deal with the financial crisis in Rome precipitated by these disturbances, he set off to fight his rival.

Overwhelming Pompey's forces on the plain of Pharsalus, Caesar pursued him to Egypt where Pompey was murdered by officers of the boy King Ptolemy XIII who offered his head to Caesar as a peace offering upon his landing at Alexandria. Caesar was not, however, to be so easily persuaded to re-embark. He needed to raise money in Egypt, and he made up his mind not to leave until he had it. To remain, indeed, became not so much a necessity as a pleasure once he had met King Ptolemy's 21-year-old half-sister, the joint-ruler of the country, Cleopatra VII. Driven into exile by Ptolemy's regency council, she now returned secretly and was brought to see Caesar in the palace where he was staying in Alexandria, smuggled into his presence tied up in a sleeping-bag. Caesar was immediately enchanted by her, and she was intrigued by him. They became lovers, and she had a child whom she called Caesarion. This liaison with the young and captivating Cleopatra, whose beautiful voice was 'like an instrument with many strings', brought Caesar into conflict with the Egyptian army which supported Ptolemy XIII. But the army was defeated, Ptolemy was killed, Egypt became a client state, and Cleopatra was confirmed as queen, with her surviving half-brother, Ptolemy XIV, as joint sovereign for mere convention's sake. Then, after further victories in Asia Minor and in Africa, Caesar returned to Rome to celebrate his glorious successes in four Triumphs which eclipsed even the magnificence of those of his dead rival Pompey.

The immense cost of the spectacular Triumphs of Caesar, which were to be commemorated in the canvases of Mantegna, would have exhausted the fortunes of most other generals. But Caesar still had money to spare for more lasting celebrations of his victories, and he decided upon a complete reconstruction and enlargement of the Forum,[1] that traditional meeting-place, the heart of all the public life of the city, the scene of speeches and elections, of funeral services and sacrifices to the gods, of Triumphs and religious processions, sometimes of executions and of gladiatorial combats, often of celebrations such as the banquet Caesar himself gave here in 45 B.C. to 22,000 guests. Not content with the reconstruction of the Forum, Caesar also spent huge sums of money upon the restoration of the meeting-place of the Senate, the Curia,[2] upon building a new Rostra,[3] or orators' platform, at the Forum's Capitoline end, and upon the erection of the Basilica Julia[4] to the south of the Via Sacra.[5]

This magnificent Basilica was entirely faced with marble. Its central hall, marked out with squares for games, was surrounded by a gallery supported by thirty-six columns. Here the lawyers held their courts, and the Centumviri tried important suits in civil law. These drew crowds of spectators who showed a passionate interest in the legal processes and rhetorical flights of oratory with which they were conducted. The acoustics were notoriously bad: when the four 'chambers' into which the Centumviri were divided were all trying separate cases at the same time the confusion was appalling, and the noise made all the more tremendous by the supporters whom some advocates paid to accompany them to the Basilica in order to cheer at appropriate intervals. It sometimes happened that the speech of an advocate with a particularly strong voice would resound through the building so loudly that no other speakers could be heard; on one occasion, a powerful and moving plea delivered in the thunderous tones of Galerius Trachalus was vigorously applauded not only by the crowds of people in his own chamber but in all the others as well.

North of the Basilica Julia, built as an integral part of the Forum of Caesar, was the Temple of Venus the Mother, Venus Genetrix,[6] from whom Caesar's family claimed to be descended. Outside the temple stood an equestrian statue of Caesar himself, the horse, by Lysippus, taken from a monument of Alexander the Great; and inside was a statue by Arcesilaus of Venus with her breasts adorned with pearls. Beside it was a gilt-bronze statue of Cleopatra.

The Egyptian queen had come to Rome with her son, Caesarion, ostensibly to ratify a treaty of alliance, but in reality to be with her lover, who installed her in great luxury in a house on the east bank of the Tiber beneath the Aventine hill. Her 'insolence' while she was staying there enraged Cicero who confessed to his friend, Atticus, that he detested her; and Cicero was far from being alone in his intense dislike of her and in his distrust of the man upon whose protection she relied. Those who attributed to her influence Caesar's plans to establish public libraries on the Egyptian model in Rome, and his appointment of an Egyptian astronomer to supervise the revision of the dislocated Roman calendar, could not complain that her influence was malign; but other innovations, such as religious rituals practised in Alexandria where rulers were worshipped as gods, seemed to many of Caesar's critics clear evidence of his desire to become a godlike ruler himself.

Caesar's achievements could not be denied. For instance, by resettling the workless destitute of Rome, as well as former legionaries, in foreign colonies he did much to alleviate the problems of poverty and unemployment in the city; and by increasing the number of Senators and widening the areas in Italy from which they could be chosen, he made the Senate a far more representative body than it had formerly been. Yet he contrived at the same time alarmingly to increase his own personal power. He had a law passed enabling him personally to choose candidates for high office; he adopted the title *Imperator*, signifying his supreme command of the armed forces of Rome; he then had himself appointed Dictator in Perpetuity, the letters signifying his elevation to this new office being stamped around his profile on the coinage of Rome, which for the first time bore the image of a living citizen. His striking features were also to be seen in numerous portrait busts, fine examples of an art form in which the Romans now excelled; and these were displayed throughout the city and its surrounding provinces. It was whispered that he would soon revive the kingship; and the rumours were intensified when two staunchly Republican Tribunes of the People, who had removed a diadem from the head of the Dictator's statue and had arrested the ringleaders of a crowd which hailed Caesar as king, were deposed by the servile Senate.

In the hope of putting an end to these reports of his unbridled ambition, Caesar arranged with Mark Antony to make a public display in the Forum of his loyalty to the Republic. The occasion, so Plutarch related, was the festival of the Lupercalia held in February in honour of the fertility god Faunus: 'At this time many of the magistrates and young men of noble families run through the city naked; and in their jesting and merry-making strike those whom they meet with thongs. And many women of high rank purposely stand in their way, holding out their hands to be struck like schoolchildren, believing that they will be granted an easy delivery if pregnant or become fertile if barren.' Caesar, sitting on a golden throne above the Rostra and wearing a triumphal robe, watched this ceremony; and Antony, who was the Dictator's fellow-Consul and one of the priests of the Lupercalia, took part in the sacred running. When he came to the Forum the crowd made way for him. He was carrying a diadem with a wreath of laurel round it, which he held out to Caesar, who twice ostentatiously pushed it away.

Caesar's action was cheered by the crowds in the Forum. But the stories about his ambitions persisted; and, when it became known that he was to embark upon an expedition against the Parthians and had appointed his own political supporters with plenipotentiary powers to represent him while he was away, the opposition against him crystallized. At the centre of the plot to dispose of him were Gaius Cassius Longinus, a proud and hot-tempered soldier who was bitterly disappointed in not being given a command in the Parthian expedition; an impoverished follower of Cassius, Publius Casca; and Cassius's brother-in-law, Marcus Brutus, a former devoted protégé of Caesar and, so some people claimed, his illegitimate son. A fervent Republican, he was inordinately proud of his supposed descent from that Brutus who had deposed the last of the Etruscan kings of Rome.

Caesar, while recognizing well enough that he was far from universally admired or liked, seemed to discount all warnings that he might be in danger. Indeed, he disdainfully remained seated when one day a delegation of Senators came to present him with various laudatory decrees, and he went so far as to disband his personal bodyguard.

On 15 March 44 B.C., shortly before he was due to leave for his campaign against the Parthians, he attended a meeting of the Senate in the Curia Pompeia, an assembly hall attached to the Theatre of Pompey.[7] As Caesar approached the hall a man pushed a note of warning into his hand, but he did not trouble to read it. He entered the building alone and defenceless, Mark Antony, who had accompanied him thus far, being detained at the door in conversation by one of the conspirators. Other conspirators crowded round him as he walked towards his chair, pretending to support a petition made to him by one Tullius Cimber on behalf of an exiled brother. Suddenly Tullius took hold of Caesar's toga with both hands and pulled it from his back as a signal for the attack. The first blow was struck by Casca who missed his aim and merely scratched Caesar just below the throat. Caesar jumped away, dragging his toga free and, grabbing Casca's knife with one hand, used the other to stab him in the arm with the point of his metal pen.

So it began. And, as the other conspirators crowded around Caesar, baring their daggers, those who were not in the conspiracy were so horror-struck that they stood transfixed while the victim, driven this way and that, was stabbed time and again until the white of his tunic was reddened with blood.

Some say that Caesar fought back against all the rest [wrote Plutarch], darting about to avoid the blows and crying out for help, but when he saw that Brutus had drawn his dagger, he covered his head with his toga and sank down to the ground. Either by chance or because he was pushed there by his murderers, he fell down against the pedestal on which the statue of Pompey stood, and the pedestal was drenched with his blood, so that one might have thought that Pompey himself was presiding over this act of vengeance against his enemy, who lay there at his feet struggling convulsively under so many blows.

Brutus stepped forward as though he wished to make a speech. But the Senators, unwilling to wait for him, rushed out of the building and fled to their homes, their excitement and terror infecting the Roman people, some of whom bolted their doors while others ran from their homes and shops to see where the assassination had taken place.

As Antony went into hiding, Brutus and his collaborators, 'still hot and eager from the murder', marched to the Capitol, holding up their daggers in front of them, calling out that liberty had been restored and inviting distinguished people whom they met to join their procession. The next day Brutus made a speech which was listened to in complete silence, indicating, so Plutarch thought, that the people both pitied Caesar and respected Brutus. And, as though in recognition of this popular feeling, the Senate voted that there should be no alteration made in any of the measures passed by Caesar while in power, yet at the same time Brutus and his friends were given honours and high rewards. 'Everyone thought, therefore, that matters were not only settled but settled in the best possible way.'

Matters, however, were far from settled. 'The state of things is perfectly shocking,' one of Caesar's associates reported. 'There is no way out of the mess. For if a man with Caesar's genius failed, who can hope to succeed?' The Dictator was dead; but the Republic was not restored: power remained in the hands of those who could command the support of the legionaries and it could be seized by any man who, assured of this support, could force the Senate to accept an autarchy.

Mark Antony, still Consul, saw himself as that man. When Caesar's body was brought back to the Forum from Pompey's Theatre, he made a moving funeral oration which Shakespeare's imagination has rendered unforgettable. Antony's words, the sight of Caesar's lacerated body and the rumoured contents of the dead man's will which was said to have bequeathed a legacy to each Roman citizen, combined to arouse the people to frenzy. They tore down railings, they smashed benches and tables to make a pyre upon which Caesar's body was burned; they then rampaged through the city with blazing brands, setting fire to the houses of

5. (opposite) Augustus, Julius Caesar's adopted son and heir, the first of the Roman emperors, who claimed to have transformed Rome from a city of brick into one of marble.

his assassins. Brutus and Cassius escaped from Rome, and Antony later allowed them to assume commands in the East.

Antony's general policy was, indeed, one of appeasement. He issued orders in Caesar's name, having taken possession of his papers, and he erected a statue in the Forum dedicated to Caesar, 'Glorious Father of the Country'; but he stamped out a rapidly developing cult of Caesar's divinity and abolished for ever the title of Dictator. In his endeavours to take over control of the state, Antony was, however, at a serious disadvantage, for Caesar had nominated as his personal heir his great-nephew and adopted son, a brilliant, astute, calculating soldier, not yet nineteen years old, who now took the name Gaius Julius Caesar Octavianus. For a time Antony ruled in conjunction with the young Octavian and Marcus Aemilius Lepidus, an aristocratic former deputy of Caesar who had proposed him for the dictatorship. These three men defeated a Republican army at the battle of Philippi after which both Brutus and Cassius killed themselves. Cicero was put to death; and, despite Antony's earlier objections, Caesar was declared a god, and Octavian was thus elevated to the status of a god's son.

Octavian made much of this relationship; and when he and Antony, having disposed of Lepidus, divided the Roman empire between them, coins in the western part of the empire, whose capital was at Rome, described Octavian, its ruler, as 'Son of the Divine Julius'. At the same time, in the eastern empire Antony, now Cleopatra's lover, endorsed her claim that Caesarion was Caesar's son and rightful heir. The inevitable and final clash between the two rival parties came at Actium outside the Gulf of Ambracia. Here in 31 B.C. Octavian's fleet, commanded by his friend, Marcus Vipsanius Agrippa, overwhelmed the ships of Antony and Cleopatra who fled to Egypt where, the next year, they both killed themselves at Alexandria.

Vastly enriched by Cleopatra's treasure, Octavian returned to Rome where by gradual and cautious degrees, shrewdly and carefully placating Republican sentiments and skilfully taking advantage of the Roman people's desire for peace after civil strife, he established himself as the leading man of the state. Short of stature, often ill and more often believing himself to be ill, he did not possess the personal magnetism of Julius Caesar. Nor did he possess Caesar's great gifts as a general; but he chose his deputies with well-judged discrimination, kept strict discipline within the legions and retained the loyalty of his friends, as well as the support of some of the greatest poets and writers who flourished in his time. Ovid, immoral and self-indulgent, offended him and was exiled to Romania; while Livy's reservations about Julius Caesar and his admiration for Caesar's enemies led Octavian to refer to him as a 'Pompeian'. But Virgil expressed his approval of Octavian and so did Horace who became his friend, though he had fought against him under Brutus and Cassius at Philippi.

Octavian could be ruthless, not only with his opponents but also with those members of his family who offended his taste for a simple and well-regulated life: he banished his daughter, and then his granddaughter, when they fell into company of which he disapproved. Yet he was never a tyrant, and his adoption of

6. Figures in the frieze of the Altar of Augustan Peace, which was consecrated on 4 July 13 B.C.

the grave and exalted name Augustus, signifying a man who enjoyed the divine gift of carrying out his enterprises under favourable auspices, and later the title of *Pater Patriae* was accepted by the Romans who recognized his firm sense of duty and who welcomed his reforms and the lasting peace which accompanied them. This peace was commemorated in Rome by that beautiful monument of white marble, the Ara Pacis Augustae, the Altar of Augustan Peace, which was consecrated in 13 B.C. in a ceremony attended, as the frieze depicts, by great officers of state accompanied by lictors with their rods, by priests and by Flamens in their strange spiked skull caps, by members of the imperial family and by Augustus himself.[8]

35

The *Pater Patriae* kept the people of Rome content with liberal supplies of food and lavish entertainments. He established an effective police force, a fire-brigade and a strong, permanent bodyguard, the Praetorian Guard. He also inaugurated a building programme which was more ambitious by far than Julius Caesar's and by which, so he proudly declared, he transformed a city of brick into one of marble. With the help of a team of architects, mostly no doubt Greek, he constructed a new Forum to the north and at right angles to his adoptive father's, flanking it with immense colonnades and two large side apses between a temple filled with treasures and dedicated to Mars the Avenger,[9] in commemoration of his victory at Philippi where retribution for Caesar's murder was exacted. Another splendid new temple was raised in honour of his deified father,[10] and, nearby, a new Rostra. Augustus also ordered the reconstruction of the Basilica Julia which had been burned down, as well as of the ancient shrine of the Lares and Penates, household gods of the Roman state, and of the ancient Basilica Aemilia which had been used for generations as a meeting-place and as a centre for money changers, remains of whose copper coins fused into the stone by the heat of fire during a Gothic invasion of the declining Empire can still be seen in the green stains in the Basilica's pavement.[11] At the same time, various members of Augustus's family and friends were responsible for the restoration of the Temple of Saturn,[12] the treasury of the Roman state, the Temples of Concord[13] and of Castor and Pollux,[14] and the official house of the Pontifex Maximus.[15]

On the Capitol, Augustus himself restored, at what he proudly described as 'great expense', the fine temple of Jupiter; and, in fulfilment of a vow he had made after having escaped being struck by lightning in Spain, he built a new temple to Jupiter Tonans.[16] On the Palatine hill he erected a huge new temple to Apollo with fine porticoes and libraries at the side,[17] and he converted the Lupercal, the cave in which Romulus and Remus had been suckled by the wolf, into an ornamental grotto.[18] On the Quirinal he reconstructed the temple of Quirinus where Romulus was worshipped as Mars;[19] on the Aventine he restored the ancient Temples of Diana[20] and of Juno Regina.[21] Below them he built a huge circular Etruscan mausoleum with a steeply pitched conical roof of earth planted with cypress trees.[22] And, downstream from this, opposite the island in the Tiber reached by the Ponte Fabricio, he completed the Theatre of Marcellus which, named after his nephew, was later to be transformed into one of Rome's grand Renaissance palaces.[23]

After the death of Augustus in A.D. 14, his strong-willed widow, Livia, continued to live on the outskirts of Rome in a fine villa at Prima Porta. The exquisitely decorated plaster of one of the rooms, painted with birds and flowers in a *trompe-l'œil* manner that makes the representation of a little bird-cage astonishingly real, has been preserved in the Museo delle Terme.[24] Livia also had a smaller house on the Palatine, perhaps the one now known as the Casa di Livia;[25] and this, too, had walls beautifully painted with fruits and flowers and with mythological scenes set amidst temples and porticoes. It was here on the Palatine that Livia's wary and grimly sarcastic son, Tiberius, who succeeded Augustus, built himself the palace

7. Livia, the strong-willed wife of the Emperor Augustus, whose house on the Palatine was probably that now known as the Casa di Livia.

8. A coin of the reign of the Emperor Nero (A.D. 54–68). He had 'fair hair', Suetonius said, 'a handsome though not attractive face, blue myopic eyes and a thick neck'.

known as the *Domus Tiberiana*, the first of those grand imperial buildings which were soon to spread all over the hill.[26] But grand as it must have been, this palace, whose floors disappeared in the sixteenth century beneath the Orti Farnesiani,[27] was almost modest compared with the fantastic Golden House of the Emperor Nero.

Nero was the great-grandson of Tiberius's wife, Julia, Augustus's daughter, who had formerly been married to Agrippa, commander of the Roman forces at Actium. By Agrippa, Julia had had five children, the youngest of whom had given birth to Caligula, Tiberius's successor. Caligula had spent much of his youth on the island of Capri, where Tiberius had spent the last ten years of his life in secluded retirement, and when he came to the imperial throne was still only twenty-four years old. Arrogant, profligate and mentally deranged, Caligula had no taste for the business of government and ruled through his secretaries, in the same way as Tiberius had governed through such deputies as Sejanus, whose overweening ambition had led to his execution in the ancient water cistern later converted into the dark dungeons of the Mamertine prison.[28] But Caligula was not emperor for long. At the beginning of 41 he and his wife and daughter were all murdered by officers of the Praetorian Guard. Increasingly influential in imperial affairs, they had secured his succession less than four years previously and now arranged for the throne to pass to his well-meaning, though eccentric and probably spastic uncle, Claudius.

Claudius was married to Messalina, a lascivious and malevolent woman whom he was persuaded to have killed after she had taken part in a form of public wedding ceremony with her lover. He then married his niece Agrippina, a great-granddaughter of Augustus who was widely suspected of being responsible for poisoning him with a dish of deadly mushrooms. Nero was Agrippina's son by a previous and very rich husband.

He was sixteen when he became emperor, and he gave good grounds for hope that he would be a generous and discerning ruler. He was described as handsome with an imposing manner, though completely under the dominance of his formidable mother whom he both loved and feared. Yet it was not long before he displayed those characteristics of monstrous cruelty, abandoned profligacy and insane vanity described in the pages of Tacitus and Suetonius. 'His body was blotchy and repulsive,' Suetonius said. 'He had blue myopic eyes and a thick neck. He had a paunch and his legs were excessively thin. He enjoyed good health. In spite of the immoderate luxury of his habits, he was ill on only three occasions in the fourteen years of his reign, and even then he never gave up drinking or changed his indulgent way of life . . . or the manner of his entertainments.'

The most notorious and profligate of these entertainments [according to Tacitus] were those given in Rome by Tigellinus [his unpleasant Sicilian principal minister and joint commander of the Praetorian Guard]. A banquet was set out upon a barge on a lake in the palace grounds. This barge was towed about by vessels picked out with gold and ivory and rowed by debauched youths who were chosen in accordance with their proficiency in libidinous practices. Birds and beasts had been collected from distant countries, and sea monsters from the ocean. On the banks of the lake were brothels filled with ladies of high rank. By these were prostitutes, stark naked, indulging in indecent gestures and language. As night approached the groves and summer-houses rang with songs and were ablaze with lights. Nero disgraced himself with every kind of abomination, natural and unnatural, leaving no further depth of debauchery to which he could sink.

Having arranged for the death of his mother who, after escaping murder by drowning, was battered to death by a gang of sailors, Nero then ordered the execution of his 19-year-old wife who died in a hot bath, bound with cords and with all her veins cut. Afterwards he married his mistress who died after a vicious kick from him when she was pregnant. Yet, depraved and monstrously cruel as he was, Nero did have artistic gifts and worked hard to develop them. He wrote poetry; he spent long hours practising on the harp; he endeavoured to improve his singing voice by lying with lead weights on his chest in painful attempts to strengthen his diaphragm; he studied Greek literature and sought to introduce Greek games and Greek contests in the arts, going so far as to perform himself in

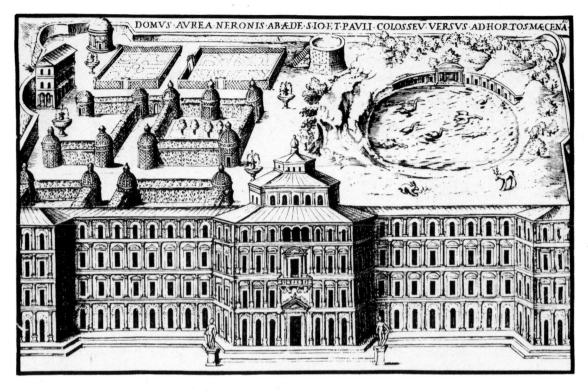

9. An imaginative reconstruction of Nero's Golden House, which was opened to the public by his successors. The Colosseum was built on the site of the lake.

public, to the horror of the upper classes, not only as musician, poet and actor but even as charioteer. Nero also had pretensions – and talents – as an amateur architect, and seems to have taken the deepest interest in the construction in 61 of the gymnasium and baths known as the Thermae Neroniae.[29]

The Emperor's opportunities as a builder were spectacularly increased when, during the moonlit night of 18 July 64, a fire broke out in some shops near the Palatine and, fanned by the wind, soon spread uncontrollably throughout the city.

> Furiously the destroying flames swept on [wrote Tacitus], first over the level ground, then up the heights, then again plunging into the hollows, with a rapidity which outstripped all efforts to cope with them, the ancient city lending itself to their progress by its narrow, tortuous streets and its misshapen blocks of buildings. The shrieks of panic-stricken women; the weakness of the aged, and the helplessness of the young; the efforts of some to help themselves, of others to help their neighbours; the hurrying of those who dragged their sick along, the lingering of those who waited for them – all added to the scene of utter confusion.

Nero was at Antium when the fire began. He hurried back to Rome to help direct the fire-fighting and to supervise the provision of shelter for the homeless.

But any credit he might have been given for this was dispelled by a well-founded rumour that when the flames were at their height he had mounted a stage in his palace and had likened modern calamities to ancient disasters by singing a tale of the sack of Troy.

The fire, which had burned fiercely for six days, left most of Rome in smouldering ruins. Of the fourteen regions into which the city was then divided, only four remained intact. Three had been burned to the ground, and little had escaped in the other seven. The Emperor's palace, the *Domus Transitoria*, had been utterly destroyed. Nero set to work with a will, ordering the reconstruction of the city on more regular lines than had been possible in the haphazard, piecemeal building of the past, widening the streets, creating open spaces and providing tall apartment blocks for the workers who had lost their homes. Most of the Emperor's energies, however, went into the planning with his architects, Severus and Celer, of what became known as the Golden House, that magnificent palace whose porticoes, pavilions, baths, temples, fountains and gardens sprawled in lavish profusion across a 200-acre park extending from the Palatine hill across the valley to the Esquiline and taking in parts of the Caelian hill as well. In the valley was a large artificial lake surrounded by fanciful grottoes, columns and gazebos; and towering over the colonnaded approach to the golden façade of the palace itself was a colossal gilded bronze statue, 120 feet high, of Nero himself, the hero of the enterprise.

Inside the palace were white, painted rooms from which flowers fell upon the guests through fretted ivory ceilings; walls were inlaid with mother-of-pearl and precious stones; concealed jets in the cornices sprayed fine showers of rose water and scent; the roof of a great dining-hall 'revolved slowly day and night in time with the sky'; streams of water flowed down a staircase over a glistening mosaic floor; water from the sea and sulphur-water from Tivoli poured into the palace's baths; on every side were works of art from Greece including, perhaps, the Laocoön.[30]

Little now remains of this *Domus Aurea*, which Nero's successors converted to public use before it was swept by a raging fire in A.D. 104. But in the fifteenth century some of its rooms, with delicately painted stucco reliefs by the artist known as Fabullus, were discovered buried in the earth beneath the Baths of Trajan; and these rooms, to which artists were lowered by ropes so that they could inspect the work of their great and ancient predecessor, were the inspiration of both Raphael and Giovanni da Udine for their decorations of the open galleries of the Vatican.[31]

When the palace was finished Nero declared, 'Good! Now at last I can begin to live like a human being!' But, in fact, he had only a short time left to enjoy the fantastic setting he had created for himself. Hated by the people of Rome, he was also detested by the Senate whose independence was lost and whose members, in constant danger of being tried for treason, were denied high office by the Emperor's preference for Greeks and orientals. A group of Senators and others conspired to replace him. The plot was discovered, however; the conspirators were hunted

10. The Emperor Vespasian, in whose reign (A.D. 69–79) the Colosseum was begun.

down and executed; and Nero became more tyrannical and megalomaniacal than ever. Identifying himself with several gods, including Apollo, god of the sun and of the arts, he claimed to be above the natural laws that governed mortal man. When news of fresh revolts reached him, he merely laughed, ordered another banquet, and composed more songs, proclaiming that he had only to appear and to sing to bring the world to his feet.

Then one night in 68 the Emperor awoke from a troubled dream and found the palace strangely quiet. His guests had fled and even his guards had gone. He ran through the empty rooms and, returning to his bedroom, discovered that a golden box of poisons which he kept there had been removed. He shouted for the gladiator, Spiculus, who could, if the occasion demanded, kill him with a single, painless blow of his sword. But Spiculus had fled with the others. At length Nero came upon an attendant who offered him refuge in his house beyond the city walls.

He mounted a horse just as he was, 'barefooted and with an old faded cloak thrown over the tunic,' Suetonius recorded. 'His head was covered with a handkerchief across his face . . . All of a sudden there was an earth tremor, and lightning flashed right in his face. Terrified, he heard soldiers in a nearby camp cursing him, and he heard a passer-by say, "These men must be after Nero."' His horse took fright and shied at the stench of a corpse which had been left on the road, and the jolt pulled the handkerchief from his head. A veteran of the Praetorian Guard, recognizing him, saluted out of habit.

Outside the house he waited while a tunnel was dug so that he could enter it unobserved. He scooped up some water from a pond, murmuring, 'This is Nero's iced water now.' He crawled on all fours through the tunnel into the nearest room where he lay down on a thin mattress covered by his old cloak. He was offered a piece of coarse brown bread but, although he was hungry, he refused to eat. Abandoning all hope, he ordered that a trench be dug just large enough to take his fat body, and that wood and water should be fetched so that the last rites could be properly observed. He burst into tears as the materials were gathered, crying out again and again, 'What a great artist dies in me!'

A message was brought to the house: the Emperor had been declared a public enemy by the Senate and, as soon as he was discovered, was to be executed as criminals had been in the days of his ancestors. He asked what kind of death that was, and was told he would be stripped naked, tied to a stake and flogged to death. He picked up a dagger and tried its edge, but he lacked the courage to use it. Asking for someone to set him an example of suicide, he reproached himself for his lack of resolution. 'It is a disgrace for me to go on living like this,' he said in Greek. 'It is unworthy of a man like Nero.' But it was not until he heard the clatter of horses' hooves outside that he summoned the courage to strike the blow. Whispering a line from Homer in a trembling voice – 'and in my ears there rings the beat of swift-footed horses' – he seized the dagger and, with help, pushed it into his throat.

After the death of Nero, the last of the emperors from the family of Augustus, the Empire, which for all the many failings of the imperial court had been governed well in his reign, was torn by civil war. Emperor followed briefly upon emperor. First Galba, the rich governor of Nearer Spain, was hailed by his soldiers and marched on Rome, but he was soon murdered. Then Otho, his successor, was driven to commit suicide. And Vitellius, who followed Otho, was lynched in a Roman street. Quietly waiting his opportunity, however, was a 60-year-old man whom Nero, having once disgraced for falling asleep during one of the imperial song recitals, had appointed to crush a revolt in the province of Judaea. This was the wary, hard-working, autocratic yet amiable Vespasian, whose simple tastes befitted the son of an honest Sabine tax-collector. Proclaimed Emperor in Egypt, where he had served after leaving Judaea, Vespasian declined to leave for Rome until he had consulted the oracles. But these being favourable, he entered the city, and under his rule, which lasted for ten years from 69, Rome slowly recovered from the damage which the months of civil disturbances and the wild extravagance of Nero and Vitellius had inflicted upon it. His financial measures were unconventional but effective; his solid, approachable character, his unaffected love for the simple, country life to which he had grown accustomed as a child in a village in the Sabine hills, and his rugged, bluff good humour endeared him to the Roman citizens. Maintaining a regular daily routine, Vespasian rose early, received friends and deputations as he dressed, attended conscientiously to affairs of state, drove out for a ride in his carriage, went to bed with one of his mistresses, had a bath, then enjoyed an ample though never exotic dinner, often making a crude joke as he ate. His jokes were celebrated, and one in particular was cited as characteristic. It concerned a tax which he had levied on the ammoniac urine that the Roman fullers collected from the city's public urinals to use in the dyeing of cloth. Vespasian's son regarded this tax as unseemly and voiced his objections to his father. Vespasian held a coin under his son's nose, urging him to notice that gold had no smell.

With the money that he raised, Vespasian was able to restore the buildings which had been damaged or burned in the reigns of his predecessors and to construct so many new ones that he felt himself justified in inscribing on his coinage the legend, *Roma Resurgens*. Appearing on building-sites with a basket of masonry on his shoulder, he gave personal encouragement to the redevelopment of the Capitol and the Forum; he lavishly restored a sanctuary dedicated to Claudius;[32] he erected in a new Forum[33] the now vanished Temple of Peace to house treasures looted from Jerusalem;[34] and he began, on the site of Nero's drained lake, that most famous of Rome's ancient monuments, the Colosseum.

THREE

BREAD AND CIRCUSES

'Rome has been restored to herself,' wrote the Spanish poet Martial when the 'far-seen amphitheatre' was nearing completion. 'What was formerly a tyrant's delight is now the delight of the people.' The tyrant's colossal column, the figure on the summit replaced by that of the sun-god, still stood nearby and it was possibly this, rather than the vast size of the Colosseum itself, that gave the amphitheatre its name. The measurements were daunting. Its oval ground area, 617 feet long by 513 feet wide, enclosed an arena 282 feet by 177 feet. The surrounding walls rose in four storeys to a height of 187 feet. The top floor, an enclosed, colonnaded gallery, was reserved for women and the poor, who sat on wooden seats; the floor immediately below this, also enclosed, was reserved for slaves and foreigners; beneath this were tiers of exposed marble seats, the higher for the middle class, the lower for more distinguished citizens. Just above the level of the ringside were the boxes of the Senators, magistrates, priests, Vestal Virgins and members of the Emperor's family. High overhead on the roof of the topmost gallery, were sailors expert in the handling of canvas whose duty it was to pull across a coloured awning to protect the spectators from rain or the heat of the sun.

In all about fifty thousand spectators could be accommodated. They approached the amphitheatre across a precinct cobbled with lava and then a smooth pavement bounded by stones. Above them loomed the plain exterior of the building, faced with the local limestone known as travertine and relieved by statues standing in the arches between the columns of the arcades. They entered through seventy-six entrances, each of which was numbered to correspond with the admittance tickets which also bore the number of a seat. There were four other unnumbered entrances, two for the Emperor's entourage, and two for the gladiators, through one of which, the Porta Sanivivaria, the survivors returned to their barracks and through the other, named after Libitina, goddess of death, the corpses of the defeated were taken out.[1]

The gladiatorial combats, adopted by the Romans from the Etruscans, had lost most of their religious, sacrificial significance and had become part of that system by which the authorities placated the people of Rome, a large proportion of whom were always unemployed, by providing them with regular entertainment as well as with free distributions of food. Relics of their religious past lingered on, however: the games, for instance, were also known as *munera*, offerings; and the

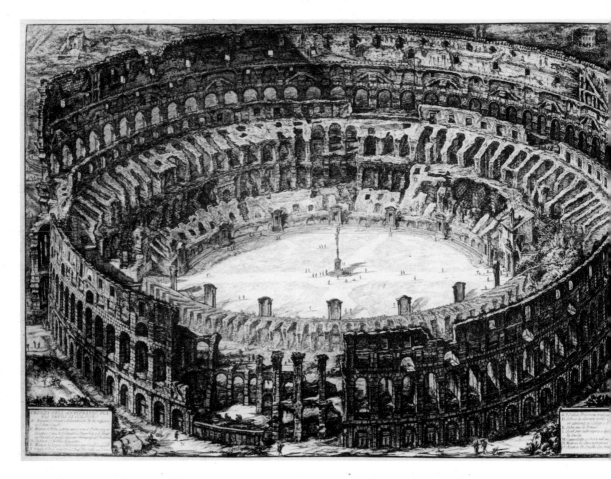

11. 'The Colosseum' by Piranesi, who executed more than two thousand engravings of Rome and its monuments.

attendant who made sure that a fallen gladiator was dead by delivering a *coup de grâce* to the head was usually dressed as Charon, ferryman of the souls of the dead across the river Styx from the upper world into Hades. Yet these were mere trappings. Great men vied with each other in the presentation of more and more spectacular games, not so much as sacrifices to the spirits of the dead as for their own glory and to gain the gratitude of the people, while the imperial court valued them as a vital social bond bringing the Emperor closer to the populace.

The games usually began early in the morning with a parade of gladiators, dressed in purple and gold cloaks, driving round the arena in chariots. The gladiators then marched around on foot, followed by slaves carrying their weapons, shields and plumed helmets, and ended in front of the Emperor's box where they thrust their right arms forward from their naked chests, shouting, 'Hail Emperor!

We men who are about to die salute thee!' They then marched off to await their turn to fight, for the spectacle was generally opened not by them but by comic turns in which clowns and cripples, dwarfs and obese women pretended to fight each other with wooden swords and threw themselves to the ground in extravagant representations of paroxysmal death.

The gladiators reappeared to the cheers of the crowd and the blast of trumpets. Some carried heavy swords or lances and wore armour on their arms and legs; others, with little protection apart from a shoulder piece, had nets in which they hoped to be able to entangle their opponents before dispatching them with the thrust of a spear. When the fighting began the shouts of the crowd grew louder and more excited: 'Habet, he's got him!' 'Lash him!' 'Strike him!' 'Burn!' 'Kill!' 'Whip him to fight harder!' 'Why does he meet the sword so timidly?' 'Why doesn't he die like a man?' But soon individual voices and cries were lost in the wild and deafening uproar. A wounded gladiator who fell to the ground could appeal for mercy by casting aside his shield and raising his left hand. His opponent could, in the absence of the Emperor, kill or spare him as he chose. If the Emperor were present, the choice was his. As the spectators screamed their preference he made his decision known, either by raising his thumb as a sign of reprieve or by turning it down as a verdict of death.

Successful gladiators were the heroes of the day; and there were those, unlike the impressed criminals and prisoners of war, who chose the precarious existence in the hope of achieving fame and the admiration of women. It was a hard life, though, as well as a dangerous one. The training was long and exacting; and, if the medical attention and the meals supplied in the gladiatorial schools were adequate, the quarters in which the men were lodged were usually cramped and foul.

Fights between gladiators were but one of the spectacles that the Colosseum had to offer. There were boxing matches, archery contests, women swordsmen, fights between charioteers, all of them often accompanied by the music of bands and hydraulic organs. Above all, there were wild beast shows in which thousands of animals were slashed to death. For these, the arena would be planted with trees and scattered with rocks, and from the labyrinth of cells beneath would emerge hundreds of roaring, bellowing, howling animals – leopards and bears, lions, tigers, camels, giraffes, ostriches, crocodiles, deer and chamois. As they came out and ran confused and frightened about the arena, they were engaged and baited, wounded and finally slaughtered with expert *crudelitas* by the skilled *venatores*, professional beast slayers who knew by constant practice how best to taunt an animal to fury without much danger to themselves, and how to satisfy the passions of the bloodthirsty crowd. The experiences of Alypius, a young law student, well illustrate how even the squeamish and kind-hearted could be affected by the general hysteria. Alypius was dragged unwillingly into the amphitheatre by some fellow-students on their way home from a dinner party. At first he shut his eyes but the wild excitement of all around him, their shouts of encouragement and furious imprecations, induced him to look upon the bloodshed from which he then found it impossible to take his fascinated eyes. He began to experience a savage thrill of

12 and 12a. A fourth-century mosaic of gladiators and *venatores*.

pleasure, to shout and jump like the rest; and thereafter he never missed a *venatio* if he could help it and dragged in others initially as reluctant to witness the cruelty as he himself had been.

A few condemned these spectacles. Nero's tutor Seneca, visiting the amphitheatre one day at noon when the shows were exceptionally savage, afterwards voiced his disgust. He had expected 'some fun and wit' but discovered 'just the reverse':

> It is pure murder. The men have no protective clothing. Their entire bodies are exposed to the blows, and no blow is ever struck in vain. The spectators call for the slayer to be thrown to those who in turn will slay him, and they demand that the victor should be kept for another butchering. The outcome for the combatants is death; the fight is waged with sword and fire . . . And when the show stops for an interval, they shout, 'Let's have men killed meanwhile! Let's have something going on.'

But protests such as Seneca's were rare. Neither Horace nor Pliny expressed disapproval of the amphitheatre. Indeed, most leading Romans commended the gladiatorial games as exemplifying the qualities which were traditionally most admired in the Roman character, courage in the face of death, endurance, respect for ancient customs. Even Cicero, who condemned the cruelty of the wild beast hunts, saw virtue in the gladiators' fights which were object-lessons in discipline and self-sacrifice. 'See how men who have been well trained prefer to receive a blow rather than basely avoid it,' he wrote. 'How frequently it is shown that there is nothing they more highly estimate than giving satisfaction to their owner or to the people! . . . What gladiator of ordinary merit has ever uttered a groan or changed countenance?'

As revered as successful gladiators were the charioteers of the circus, where performances were staged before audiences as enthusiastic if not as large as those in the Colosseum. There were several circuses in Rome, the Circus Flaminius which had been built in the days of the Republic,[2] the Circus Gaius inaugurated by Caligula,[3] and, most splendid of all, the Circus Maximus which, in use perhaps since the time of the kings, had been improved and enlarged by Julius Caesar and could accommodate well over 150,000 spectators.[4] Here, in the immense arena eventually measuring 1,800 feet by 600 feet and surrounded by shops and eating places, by taverns and the booths of prostitutes and fortune-tellers, horse races and chariot races took place in an atmosphere of noisy excitement, betting frenzy and amorous intrigue.

> Many are the opportunities that await you in the circus [Ovid advised in his *Art of Love*]. No one will prevent you sitting next to a girl. Get as close to her as you can. That's easy enough, for the seating is cramped anyway. Find an excuse to talk to her . . . Ask her what horses are entering the ring and which ones she fancies. Approve her choices . . . If, as is likely, a speck of dust falls into her lap, brush it gently away; and, even if no dust falls, pretend it has done and brush her lap just the same. If her cloak trails on the ground gather up the hem and lift it from the dirt. She will certainly let you have a glimpse of her legs . . . The deft arrangement of a cushion has often helped a lover . . . Such are the advantages which a circus offers to a man looking for an affair.

The sport was opened by a purple-robed state official wearing a heavy wreath of gilded laurels and holding an ivory baton surmounted by an eagle. He raised up a white napkin to the crowd and dropped it on to the freshly raked yellow sand that covered the arena. At first there might be displays of equestrian skill, the performers always riding without stirrups or standing on their heads or lying upon the horses, jumping from one mount to the next, engaging in mock sword fights with each other, or leaning down to snatch a trophy from the sand. Next came the horse races; then the chariots thundered round the track, as many as twelve emerging at once from the stables as soon as the rope, which was extended between the twin statues of Mercury, was pulled away. Sometimes the chariots were drawn by two horses, more often by four (*quadrigae*), occasionally by as many as ten. They raced round the circuit for seven laps, enveloped in clouds of sand thrown up by the wheels and the horses' hooves, the completion of each lap being signalled to the crowd by the movement of large wooden eggs and later of dolphins on the high embankment in the centre of the course. The chariots bore the colours – red, white, blue and green – of the *factiones* or stables from which they came; the horses were bedecked with pearls in their manes; their breastplates were studded with charms and medallions; the coloured ribbons of their *factio* were tied round their necks and in their knotted tails. The charioteers, leaning back against the reins, whips in their hands, helmets on their heads, their legs bound with leather straps, daggers sheathed by their thighs in case they had to cut themselves loose, also proclaimed the identity of their *factio* by the colour of their tunics. As the chariots hurtled towards the posts where they had to turn, consummate skill was needed to guide the horses into just the right position, for horses that turned too close to the post might swing the chariot crashing into it, while those that gave it too wide a berth lost positions that might never be regained.

The excitement of the displays in the Circus Maximus and the Colosseum attracted far larger audiences than did the theatres of Rome, even though the plays which were presented frequently offered scenes as violent and far more lubricious than those to be seen in the more popular places of entertainment. There were three principal theatres in Rome at this time, none of them offering anything like the accommodation afforded by either the Colosseum or the Circus Maximus, yet all of them enormous when compared with the largest theatres which have succeeded them. The Theatre of Pompey had about 27,000 seats, the Theatre of Marcellus some 10,000 and the smaller Theatre of Balbus which had been built in 13 B.C. had 8,000.[5] But long gone were the days when such theatres could be filled by dramatists like Livius Andronicus, one of the founders of Roman drama, or Plautus and Terence who had adapted the content and style of the Greek masters for the stages of Rome. Plays were now written not so much for public performance as for private declamation; and the theatres presented productions more notable for the impressiveness of their effects than for the beauty of their language, the interest of their plots or the delineation of character. Playing to huge auditoria, actors wore easily identifiable masks and brightly coloured costumes, often merely making stylized gestures or dancing while a chorus spoke or loudly sang the accompanying words. Audiences, coarsened and degraded by the spectacles in the amphitheatre, demanded as much violence and sensationalism, rape, incest, pillage and cannibalism as the plot could be made to support. Women appeared naked on the stage, Leda making love to the swan, Pasiphae with the white bull of Minos; and when blows were exchanged real blood was shed and wounds inflicted. Before the end of the first century, convicted criminals were substituted for actors in the final scene and actually executed; bandits died on crosses; and a convict forced to take over the part of Hercules was wrapped in a poisoned cloak and burned on a funeral pyre.

Although the worst excesses were enacted in the times of the less humane emperors, even in those of the more kind-hearted the savageries continued apace. In the reign of Titus, when the Colosseum was inaugurated, no less than 5,000 animals, so it was calculated by Suetonius, were slaughtered there in a single day.

Titus had become Emperor in 79 when his father Vespasian, before suffering a fatal stroke, alluded to the customary apotheosis of an emperor in the last of his famous jokes: 'Goodness me! I think I am about to become a god.'

Titus had proved a vengeful conqueror of the Jews whose rebellion he had suppressed, slaughtering prisoners wholesale after the sack of Jerusalem, throwing them to wild animals, setting up the Roman eagle in the Holy of Holies and carrying off to Rome the sacred treasures of Herod's temple. These included the silver trumpets and the seven-branched candelabrum, the menorah, which are shown being carried through Rome in a relief on the Arch of Titus erected across the end of the Via Sacra in 81.[6] Titus had also been renowned for his profligate ways, his riotous parties, his fondness for young homosexuals and his lust for the Jewish princess, Berenice. Once established in power in Rome, however, he sent Berenice back to her people; he saw no more of his pretty boys, and he proved himself a generous, affable and charming ruler who displayed a sincere concern for the welfare of the city when first it was attacked by plague and then by yet another fire. His reign, though, was short. He died in 81, to be succeeded by his brother, Domitian, a lonely, introverted man of twenty-nine who had always been jealous of Titus's success and who had affected to be more interested in poetry and music than in politics. According to Suetonius, Domitian spent much of his time at the beginning of his reign by himself, catching flies and impaling them with deadly accuracy on the point of his pen. When his wife fell in love with an actor and had to be dismissed from the imperial household, he was more lonely than ever and before long found an excuse to call her back to him. The older he grew the more isolated and suspicious he became. And, since he had deeply offended the Senate by appointing himself Censor for life so that he had permanent control over its membership, by adopting titles of unprecedented grandeur such as *Dominus et Deus*, and by seeming bent upon a course leading to complete absolutism, he had good cause to fear the dagger of an assassin. It was said that in his palace on the

Palatine he paced up and down the principal courtyard glancing apprehensively at the images of the gardens reflected in the polished Cappadocian marble surfaces, in dread of catching sight of a lurking enemy.

This immense palace, largely financed by confiscations of property from Senators accused of treachery, rivalled in splendour Nero's *Domus Aurea*. Designed for Domitian by Caius Rabirius, it comprised his official residence the *Domus Flavia*, his private palace the *Domus Augustana*, and a vast stadium, surrounded by double porticoes, where horse races were probably held. To clear the site for this extensive development, rows of houses were demolished and tons of earth were carted away to level the ground. Fifteen years passed before the new complex of cloisters and peristyles, fountains and pools, sunken gardens and colonnades, temples and decorated apartments was completed. The remains of the dining-hall still bear witness to the palace's vanished magnificence, to the pleasures enjoyed by the Emperor's guests who, reclining on cushioned couches beneath pink marble walls, could see through windows overlooking gardens in which brightly plumaged birds fluttered in cages beside sparkling fountains.[7] But the obsessively paranoiac Domitian seems to have derived little pleasure himself from the luxury of his palace. And in 96, the year of its completion, the death he had long expected overtook him. He was stabbed to death by several assailants encouraged by his wife Domitia, various palace officials and the commanders of the Praetorian Guard.

The elderly and pliable lawyer, Marcus Cocceius Nerva, undoubtedly one of the conspirators, was chosen to succeed him. But the fury of the army, whose pay Domitian had considerably increased, and of the rank and file of the Praetorian Guard, forced Nerva to adopt a son and heir from outside his own family. And so, in 98, a gifted provincial official, well liked by both the army and the Senate, Marcus Ulpius Traianus, became Emperor upon Nerva's death.

Trajan had been born near Seville in 53. His mother was Spanish, his father a descendant of Roman settlers. He himself had served with distinction as Governor in Upper Germany and after two highly successful campaigns in the Kingdom of Dacia (in what is now Romania), the immense sums seized from this rich land enabled Trajan to undertake a programme of public works in Rome on a scale of unparalleled grandeur. On the site of Nero's Golden House he built the city's finest baths.[8] He constructed a new Forum, the last of its kind, to the designs of the great architect from Damascus, Apollodorus, whose marble colonnades, temples, libraries and grand Basilica Ulpia, surrounding an open space with marble statues and bronze reliefs, were long considered amongst the most wonderful marvels of the ancient world.[9] He built commodious markets, the Mercati Traianei, whose shops, originally built in three tiers, can still be seen off the Via IV Novembre.[10] And most remarkable of all, to the west of the markets, Trajan erected in 113 the monumental column whose summit about 140 feet above the ground marks the height of the ridge that once separated the Forum from the Campus Martius. Designed by Apollodorus and constructed of eighteen blocks of marble four feet high and eleven and a half feet in diameter, it is decorated with exquisitely executed reliefs which spiral up around it, containing 2,500 figures and constituting

13. Roman Senators on their way to the Forum. A painting by Jean Lemaire (1598–1659).

a detailed and uniquely informative narrative of Trajan's Dacian campaigns. At the top of the column stood a statue of the victorious Emperor, and a spiral stone staircase inside led to a platform from which extensive views could be enjoyed over the rooftops of the city.[11]

The population of Rome at this time was probably about a million, their buildings covering an area of almost eight square miles. But there were so many large public basilicas, temples, circuses, baths and theatres, so many acres of imperial gardens, so much land that could not be inhabited for fear of offending the gods that most people were compelled to live in tall apartment blocks, *insulae*, which towered, as many as six storeys high, over the narrow lanes.[12]

In the more solid and pleasant of these *insulae* the whole of the ground floor was occupied by a single tenant and the accommodation was nearly as spacious as that in a house; but the apartments over it were small and cramped and became increasingly less desirable on each successive floor, the highest and cheapest floors being overcrowded with tenants and sub-tenants, their families and dependants. From the outside, the *insula* might well present an attractive appearance, its façade decorated with tiles and mosaics, with balconies of wood or brick projecting from each storey and with potted plants and flowers to be seen behind their railings. Inside, however, the apartments were for the most part dark and comfortless, lit by windows covered with parchment or sheets of cloth, or by wooden shutters which might keep out the rain or the glaring sun but which plunged rooms into a darkness that a candle or smoky lamp did little to alleviate. Furniture was sparse, limited to a few stools and beds, though the beds were frequently part of the structure, shelves or bunks fitted against the wall. Heat was commonly provided by movable braziers and cooking done on open stoves, so that the flimsily built structures were as likely to catch fire as they were to collapse.

Water supply and sanitation were almost as primitive as they had been in the time of the kings. By Trajan's day more than 200 million gallons of water were brought into Rome every day by eight aqueducts; but while the occupants of some of the ground floors of the *insulae* benefited from this, those who lived above them did not. Water had to be fetched in buckets from fountains in the streets or brought up the stairs by notoriously lazy and ill-natured water-carriers. Similarly, while the drainage system of the city, started seven centuries before, had since been regularly extended and improved, the upper floors of the *insulae* were not connected to it. Their occupants had to take their receptacles downstairs to empty them into a pit in the basement or into nearby cess trenches. Those who could not or would not do this hurled their contents from the windows into the street.

Despite Nero's reconstruction of the city on a more regular plan after the fire of 64, many of the streets of Rome were as narrow, tortuous and dark as they had ever been, the widest being scarcely more than twenty feet and, in the centre of the city, the Via Sacra and the Via Nova were not even as wide as this. Not all of them were paved or had sidewalks and, although a decree had been passed in the time of Domitian prohibiting shopkeepers from displaying their wares in the streets, the decree seems not to have been too strictly observed. The lower floors of many *insulae* were divided into shops and booths, taverns and warehouses; and, since the traders' families lived in poky little lofts approached by ladders, it was natural that they should wish to spend their lives in the streets when the weather allowed and to bring out their goods to catch the attention of the passers-by. As well as shopkeepers, barbers carried on their business in the street, cutting hair with iron scissors in the fashion favoured by the reigning Emperor or some idolized charioteer, curling the locks of the young, dyeing those of the old, shaving chins with iron razors which were often painfully blunt despite frequent recourse to the whetstone, and, when their arms were jogged by the crowd, staunching the consequent flow of blood with spiders' webs soaked in oil and vinegar.

Craftsmen, too, worked in the street; itinerant vendors shouted their wares; jugglers, snake charmers and acrobats collected audiences; beggars thrust forward their bowls and cans; and even schoolmasters attempted to teach their pupils in the persistent din. The passage of carts and baggage animals in the streets during the hours of daylight had been forbidden by law by Julius Caesar, and the prohibition had remained in force; but horsemen were allowed, and so were the wagons of demolition and building contractors, litters and chairs borne by slaves; on the frequent days when public games were held, so were chariots bound for the amphitheatre, and, on the days of religious festivals, the carriages of priests and Vestal Virgins. The embargo on other vehicles did little, therefore, to lessen the confused congestion of the daytime streets, while the nights were disturbed by the shouts of wagoners and drovers, and the cries of night watchmen in the unlit alleys. 'Most sick men die here from insomnia,' Juvenal who was living in Rome at the end of the first century wrote in one of his satires:

> Rest is impossible. It costs money to sleep in Rome.
> There is the root of the sickness. The movement of heavy wagons
> through narrow streets, the oaths of stalled cattle drovers
> would break the sleep of a deaf man or a lazy walrus.
> On a morning call the crowd gives way before the passage
> of a millionaire carried above their heads in a litter,
> reading the while he goes, or writing, or sleeping unseen:
> for a man becomes sleepy with closed windows and comfort.
> Yet he'll arrive before us. We have to fight our way
> through a wave in front, and behind we are pressed by a huge mob
> shoving our hips; an elbow hits us here and a pole
> there, now we are smashed by a beam, now biffed by a barrel.
> Our legs are thick with mud, our feet are crushed by large
> ubiquitous shoes, a soldier's hobnail rests on our toe . . .
> Newly mended shirts are torn again. A fir-tree
> flickers from the advancing dray, a following wagon
> carries a long pine: they swing and threaten the public.
> Suppose the axle should collapse, that axle carrying
> Ligurian stone, and pour a mountain out over the people –
> what would be left of the bodies? The arms and legs, the bones,
> where are they? The ordinary man's simple corpse
> perishes like his soul.

The life of the rich was in sharp contrast to that of the poor whose life was passed in these dark, noisy and noisome alleys. The houses of the classes from which the Senators were chosen were not elaborately furnished, but the furniture they did contain was of the most exquisite quality and made in a variety of beautifully fashioned materials, bronze and maple wood, ivory and tortoiseshell, terebinth and porphyry with inlays of silver and gold. Statues, busts, water-clocks and curios, strange and valuable objects collected during tours of duty in the Empire's far-flung provinces were all carefully arranged in the small rooms which led one into another around courtyards shaded by trees, bright with flowers and filled with the sounds of singing birds and splashing fountains.

In the bedroom the master of the house would wake early, usually at dawn, and, while slaves with brushes and sponges, buckets of sand and water set about their daily tasks, he would throw aside the covers of his bed and begin to dress. The operation was not a lengthy one, for he wore no special clothes at night, content to sleep in the undergarments he had worn by day. Over his loincloth he wore a belted tunic of linen or wool, in cold weather two or even three of these, and then the *synthesis* or, for more formal occasions, the white toga whose folds could not be arranged without much practice or the help of an experienced slave. On his feet he wore sandals or boots of soft leather reaching half-way up the calves like those worn by soldiers.

The toilet of his wife was necessarily a more lengthy process. It did not take long for her to dress, since, like her husband, she wore her underclothes in bed and over her shift she had only to don her *stola* which reached to the ground, covering her feet, and her *palla*, or shawl, which she could if she wished pull over her head. But the dressing of her hair, which was combed up and twisted into elaborate shapes by her *ornatrix*, or the arrangement of her wig, which was usually blonde, took quite as long as the application of her make-up: the whitening of her forehead, the reddening of her lips, the outlining of her eyes with antimony and the painting of her eyebrows with dampened ash. For the conditioning of her skin she would have used some kind of unguent, such as that described by Ovid which consisted of barley-meal and wheat-flour, ground pulse and ground antlers, beaten eggs, narcissus bulbs, gum and honey. Sprayed with scent, with jewels fixed in her braided hair, glittering studs in her ears, a necklace round her throat, rings on her fingers and bracelets on her arms, she was now ready to be helped on with her brightly coloured cloak and to go forth into the morning sun carrying perhaps a feathered fan and followed by a servant with a parasol.

In earlier times women had been at the mercy of their husbands, who had been selected for them by their parents and to whom they had usually been married at a very early age, sometimes as young as twelve years old, often at fourteen. As the fifth of the Twelve Tables of 449 B.C. had decreed, 'Females shall remain in guardianship even when they have reached their majority.' In those days a woman had no right in law to divorce her husband, though he could, without undue difficulty, get rid of her on the slenderest pretext, and even though himself an acknowledged adulterer, could kill his wife for her own unfaithfulness. But since then women, although very rarely to be found practising a profession, had gradually liberated themselves and had come to have interests and influence in what had formerly been considered male preserves. This was much to the consternation of many old-fashioned conservatives who expressed their disapproval of modern wives, strongly condemning them for practising birth-control, for attempting to rival men in learning and seeking to share in their games and sports. 'What modesty can you expect of a woman who wears a helmet, abjures her own sex, and delights in feats of strength?' Juvenal asked indignantly. 'Who . . . with spear in hand and breasts exposed takes to pig-sticking?' Juvenal was equally appalled by women who, instead of eating by themselves as in the past, or demurely sitting at their husbands' feet, now reclined beside them, drinking, eating and joining the male conversation on those couches for three people from which the *triclinium*, the dining-room, derived its name.

In most families the main meal was eaten in the evening, breakfast and the midday meal being little more than snacks. The *triclinia*, arranged around low tables, were furnished with cushions upon which the bare-footed diners rested their elbows. When children were present, they sat on stools. The table was usually covered with a cloth and on this were placed knives and spoons and toothpicks. Forks were unknown. Anything which could not be carried conveniently to the mouth in a spoon was picked up in the fingers. Servants were consequently in attendance with bowls of warm, scented water and napkins. Slaves carried the food to the table, the dishes for a banquet filled with such delicacies as had long been enjoyed and would still be relished for centuries to come, oysters, lobsters and mullet, goose's liver and capons, sucking-pigs and roasted veal, asparagus, truffles, mushrooms, fruits and cakes. Wine, in labelled amphorae with wooden or cork stoppers, was decanted through strainers into mixing-bowls and then cooled with snow or mixed with warm water before being poured into drinking-bowls.

The meal was a leisurely one. Seven courses were common, and between them the guests might be entertained with music or with dancers and acrobats. In houses renowned for gluttony and vice, dinner might last for as long as ten hours, the guests gorging themselves while watching the dancing of naked Spanish girls or staggering out from time to time to be sick in a room set aside for this purpose. Sometimes they drank so much that they could not stand and had, like the rich and vulgar host described by Martial, to summon a slave with an amphora into which they could 'remeasure the wine [they] had drunk from it, relying upon the slave to guide the stream'. But such crapulous behaviour was far from common. At the dinner tables of most well-to-do families in Trajan's Rome, a modern observer might consider the appetites of the guests healthy rather than Gargantuan and the behaviour decorous, even though spitting on the floor was commonplace and belching a polite indication of enjoyment.

Before his meal the Roman would have had his bath. The rich had bathing-rooms in their own houses where slaves scraped, washed and massaged them, but all citizens had access to the public baths. Just as the latrines were recognized places to meet, gossip and exchange the news of the day, so were the *thermae* with which successive Consuls and Emperors had provided the people in every quarter of the city. Most of them offered the full range of halls and chambers – *apodyteria* where the people undressed; *sudatoria* where they sat and sweated; *calidaria* where, in an atmosphere slightly less hot, they could splash themselves with water from tubs or fountains and cleanse their skins with scrapers; *tepidaria* where they could cool themselves before diving into the cold baths of the *frigidaria*. In some less reputable establishments men and women bathed naked together; but most baths had either staggered opening hours or separate chambers, generally adjoining, so that the same heating system could be used for both, and the sexes segregated. The men sometimes wore leather trunks, more often nothing at all; most women wore a loincloth.

In many baths there were promenades lined with works of art, reading-rooms and libraries, exhibition halls and gymnasia. All manner of ball games were played in the baths and all sorts of sports were practised, particularly wrestling matches in which both men and women took part. The women's baths had beauty parlours, and outside both men's and women's were cafés and small shops.

The baths closed at sunset. Thereafter, however, there were many other places in which the Roman could enjoy himself when the circus and the amphitheatres were silent. There were, for instance, the brothels outside which prostitutes displayed themselves on benches. Many, if not most, of them were foreigners, often Egyptian or Syrian. They wore far more startlingly bright clothes than respectable women would choose, short tunics and togas and bangles round their ankles. Taxed by the authorities on the basis of the fees they charged their customers, they were allowed to parade the streets and were a common sight on the Via Sacra and in the Subura, the noisy, crowded area of the city which Juvenal called the 'boiling Subura'. To be seen with these prostitutes occasionally was not considered reprehensible in a young man of good family. Venereal disease seems to have been known but was far from widespread.

The authorities regulated the opening hours of brothels, but tavern-keepers were not so circumscribed and a cooling drink was always available. So, too, was a game of chance; for, despite the prohibitions regularly imposed, gambling was a common pastime with most Roman citizens and an obsession with many. Bets were placed on games of backgammon, chess and draughts as well as on those simpler games played with marbles and dice, nuts and knuckle-bones. Stakes were high and passions ran hot. 'When was gambling so reckless?' Juvenal wondered. 'Men now come to the gaming tables not with purses but with a treasure chest.' For those with a taste for less risky and less exciting pursuits there were the lovely walks beyond the city walls, amidst the temples and porticoes, the statues and frescoes of the Saepta Julia,[13] the shady cypress groves and olive trees of the Campus Martius.

By the time of Trajan's death the Roman people, whose city he had so enriched, had learned to address him as *Optimus Princeps*, the best of all rulers. They had even more cause to be grateful to his adopted son who succeeded him in 117, the restless, homosexual and complex Hadrian. Of Spanish extraction, Hadrian seems to have spent most of his early life in Rome where he became known as a young man of highly cultivated tastes and strong, if often irrational, opinions. As Emperor he did not care to have his artistic opinions questioned and he quarrelled so violently with Apollodorus over the designs for the Temple of Venus and Rome that he had him banished from the city and possibly had him executed too. This temple, designed by Hadrian himself and dedicated by him in 135, was but one of several buildings, original in conception and skilful in execution, for which the

14. An early-nineteenth-century view of the Pantheon, which was described by William Thomas in 1549 as 'the perfectest of all the antiquities'.

Emperor was responsible in Rome.[14] His love of Greece, apparent in his beautiful villa at Tivoli,[15] is also evident in the Pantheon, that wonderfully well-preserved Roman monument which, even in Hadrian's day, was the admiration of the civilized world.

The original Pantheon had been built between 27 and 25 B.C. by Agrippa to whom credit is still given in the inscription above the portico. But whereas Agrippa's building was renowned for its exterior, Hadrian's is remarkable for the huge circular hall behind the grey and red granite columns of the pedimented porch. Inside this hall, beneath the vast dome which, covered with sheets of gilded bronze, remained the largest in the world until modern times, stood statues of the gods covered with jewels, that of Venus, so Pliny said, wearing in the ears the two halves of the pearl which Mark Antony took from Cleopatra after she had drunk its twin dissolved in vinegar to win a bet.[16]

Having rebuilt the Pantheon as a suitably magnificent temple for all the gods, Hadrian began to construct his own memorial, the mausoleum which in the later history of Rome became that awesome state fortress and prison known as Castel Sant' Angelo.[17] The mausoleum was not finished at the time of Hadrian's death in 138 and was completed by his adopted heir, Antoninus, who, because of his devotion to his country, his gods and his father, became known as Antoninus Pius.

For over twenty years Antoninus ruled over a largely peaceful Empire; but the long frontiers of this Empire were coming under ever more persistent attack and, after his time, emperors intent upon survival were increasingly preoccupied with its defence. Antoninus Pius's successor, the conscientious and idealistic Marcus Aurelius, spent most of his reign fighting the German tribes of the north, and the column which towers above the Piazza Colonna commemorates his triumphs.[18] Yet Marcus Aurelius, who seems still to ride with noble purpose across the Capitol in the equestrian bronze statue which so impressed Michelangelo, was the last of the four good emperors of Rome's triumphant age.[19] His cruel and arrogant son Commodus was possessed by so wildly consuming a passion for gladiatorial contests that he took part himself in almost a thousand combats, arriving in the amphitheatre wearing a gold crown studded with jewels and preceded by an attendant bearing the club and lion skin of Hercules with whom he had identified himself. In Hercules's honour he slaughtered animals in the arena with insensate relish before appearing in his role as gladiator. The Senators dutifully watched his performances, shouting their approval of his bloodlust, although as one of them, Dio Cassius, recorded, their overriding emotion was one of fear, since it was rumoured that Commodus, in celebration of Hercules's killing of the Stymphalian birds, had made up his mind to round off an invigorating display of his prowess by massacring a few spectators.

On one occasion, Dio Cassius said, 'having killed an ostrich and decapitated it, he came up to where we Senators were sitting, holding the head in his left hand and raising aloft his bloody sword; and, without uttering a word, he wagged his head with a grin as though to threaten he would treat us in the same way.' Frightened as they were, the Senators could scarcely restrain their laughter at the antics of their crazy master, yet knowing that any sign of amusement would have resulted in their being killed on the spot, they stuffed their mouths with the laurel leaves from their garlands.

The strangulation of the megalomaniacal Commodus on the orders of a commander of the Praetorian Guard inaugurated a period of intermittent civil war in which a succession of imperial reigns were brought to a violent end, usually at the instigation or with the cooperation of these powerful household troops. Commodus's successor, Pertinax, the son of a freed slave who after distinguished military service had become Prefect of the City of Rome, was murdered within three months. Then the rich Senator, Didius Julianus, who had bought the throne at an auction organized by the Praetorian Guard, was killed after nine weeks on the orders of the resolute and forceful north African, Septimius Severus, who had been proclaimed Emperor by his legions on the Danube. Severus died a natural death in Britain, reputedly bequeathing to his sons the advice to get on well with each other, to be generous to their armies and not to bother with anyone else. But

Caracalla, the violent and emotional son who followed him, having had his brother murdered, was himself assassinated by Macrinus, the Praetorian Prefect, in 217. Macrinus himself became Emperor for a short time until he, too, was killed in a rebellion planned by the Syrian sister-in-law of Septimius Severus, Julia Maesa, who replaced him with her grandson. This new 14-year-old Emperor was a devotee and high priest of the Syrian sun-god, El-Gabal, who was worshipped in the town of his birth in the form of a conical black stone which was said to have fallen there from heaven. The boy was known as Elagabalus after this deity whose cult he brought to Rome without any attempt to assimilate it into Roman institutions.

As the attention of the new emperor was diverted by the most trifling amusements [wrote Edward Gibbon in a characteristic passage], he wasted many months in his progress from Syria . . . and deferred till the ensuing summer his triumphal entry into the capital. A faithful picture, however, which preceded his arrival, and was placed by his immediate order over the altar of victory in the senate-house, conveyed to the Romans the just but unworthy resemblance of his person and manners. He was drawn in his sacerdotal robes of silk and gold . . . his head was covered with gems of an inestimable value. His eyebrows were tinged with black, and his cheeks painted with an artificial red and white. The grave Senators confessed with a sigh, that, after having long experienced the stern tyranny of their own countrymen, Rome was at length humbled beneath the effeminate luxury of Oriental despotism . . .

In a solemn procession through the streets of Rome the way was strewed with gold dust; the black stone, set in precious gems, was placed on a chariot drawn by six milk-white horses richly caparisoned. The pious emperor held the reins, and, supported by his ministers, moved slowly backwards, that he might perpetually enjoy the felicity of the divine presence. In a magnificent temple raised on the Palatine Mount, the sacrifices of the god Elagabalus were celebrated with every circumstance of cost and solemnity. The richest wines, the most extraordinary victims and the rarest aromatics were profusely consumed on his altar. Around the altar a chorus of Syrian damsels performed their lascivious dances to the sound of barbarian music, whilst the gravest personages of the state and army, clothed in long Phoenician tunics, officiated in the meanest functions with affected zeal and secret indignation.

To the temple of his deity, for his greater honour, Elagabalus transported all the most holy objects in Rome, including the Palladium, a small figure of Pallas Athene which had been brought from Troy by Aeneas. Shocked as they were by this blasphemous impiety, the Senators were even more horrified by the orgies which now took place in the imperial palace where the most exotic and extravagant meals were served at all hours of the day and night, where concubines and catamites disported themselves upon cushions stuffed with crocus petals and where the Emperor himself, dressed as a woman, made mockery of high Roman offices by bestowing them upon his various lovers and offended against the most sacred laws of Rome by violating a Vestal Virgin.

For fear lest his outrageous behaviour might result in her own ruin, his grandmother disowned him. Experiencing no difficulty in persuading the Praetorian Guard to assassinate both him and his mother, she had another grandson,

Severus Alexander, declared emperor in his place. For thirteen years he and his mother ruled the Empire between them until in 235 both were killed in a mutiny of their troops.

Thereafter emperor followed emperor with bewildering frequency, there being six different rulers in Rome in the one year 238. Many were usurpers; most were army officers; nearly all died violent deaths, usually at the hands of soldiers supporting the claims of a rival. One of them, Philip the Arab, son of a desert chief, who reigned for five years from 244, celebrated the thousandth anniversary of the foundation of Rome with exceptionally savage wild beast hunts in the Colosseum, with shows and entertainments which 'dazzled the eye of the multitude', with mystic sacrifices and with music and dancing on the Campus Martius which was 'illuminated with innumerable lamps and torches'. But such celebrations could not divert attention from the sad plight of Rome, the decline of the Senate much of whose authority was being assumed by the army, the slow disintegration of the Empire's frontiers and the recurrent financial crises within the city.

Little building of note had taken place in Rome since the time of Septimius Severus who restored the Portico d'Ottavia[20] and the Temple of Vesta, who made the fine terrace known as the Belvedere on the Palatine[21] and in whose honour were erected both the Arco degli Argentari[22] near the Circus Maximus and the grand Arch of Septimius Severus in the Forum.[23] Septimius Severus also began the huge and splendid baths which bear the name of his son Caracalla who inaugurated them in 217. They were the most luxurious in Rome, as the remains of them to be seen in the fountains of the Piazza Farnese, in the Salon d'Hercule of the Palazzo Farnese and in the baptistery of S. Giovanni in Laterano still testify.[24] They were also the largest baths in the city, being able to accommodate 1,600 people at a time. Not until the reign of Diocletian were larger baths to be built.[25]

Diocletian, a man of humble origins from Dalmatia, came to the throne in 284. Before his accession there had been a brief recovery in Rome's fortunes. Valerian, who had become emperor in 253 and his co-emperor and successor, his son Gallienus, had led strong forces against the Persians and Germans. Gallienus, after reorganizing the army, had inflicted a decisive defeat upon the Goths in what is now Yugoslavia in a battle that cost them no less than fifty thousand lives. And Aurelian, who succeeded Gallienus's successor, Claudius Gothicus, had been equally successful against Rome's enemies in northern Italy, and had built the defensive walls round the city which enclosed those parts of it that had spread far beyond the walls of the Republic.[26] So, as the fourth century approached, the Empire, although still in financial chaos, was no longer on the verge of disintegration; and Diocletian, an administrator of exceptional ability, gave it the firm government it now needed. He enlarged the army; he overhauled the system of collecting taxes from the greatly increased number of Roman citizens who had become liable to pay them by the *Constitutio Antoniniana* of 212–13; and he increased the number of imperial provinces, removed their governors from military commands and, under his ultimate authority, created three other rulers whose capitals were established at Milan, Trier and in Salonica. His own capital was at Izmir on the Sea of Marmara, though the Senate remained in Rome, which was still the inspiration of the Empire, an ideal to be worshipped as a god.

Diocletian's reforms answered their purpose: the Empire was more orderly and united than it had been for generations. But the Emperor saw a threat to its unity and to the cult of the worship of Rome in that spreading, foreign, unpatriotic cult, Christianity. And he determined to stamp it out once and for all.

FOUR

CATACOMBS AND CHRISTIANS

One Sunday afternoon towards the middle of the fourth century a group of Roman schoolboys went out through a gate in the Aurelian Wall and walked along the Via Appia. 'We went down into the catacombs,' one of them, Eusebius Hieronymus, recorded. 'These are caves excavated deep in the earth, and contain, on either hand as you enter, the bodies of the dead buried in the walls. It is all so dark there . . . Only occasionally is light let in to mitigate the horror of the gloom, and then not so much through a window as through a hole. You take each step with caution, as though surrounded by deep night.'

For generations these mazelike, subterranean galleries and passages, dug out of the soft tufa rock around Rome, had been used by a religious sect which, in Tacitus's words, 'were detested for their abominations and popularly known by the name of Christians after one Christus who was put to death in the reign of Tiberius by the Procurator, Pontius Pilate'. The Christians had at first interred their dead in tombs above ground as well as below, but as land for burial became scarce and expensive and as persecution increased, they had taken to excavating cemeteries below ground where burials could take place without so much notice by the authorities or interference from hostile pagan crowds. The largest of them were dug on land belonging to such well-to-do converts as the Flavian relatives of the Emperor Domitian who gave permission to their fellow-Christians to use their villas for meetings and worship and their gardens as burial grounds. And so beneath the cypress trees along the Via Appia, and on other roads leading out of the city, warrens of dark tunnels were dug through the rock, some of them on four different levels like the Catacombs of St Calixtus, named after a former slave who, having served a sentence of hard labour in the Sardinian quarries, had been placed in charge of them before becoming leader of his sect. On the walls of the chambers were painted Christian symbols – the fish, the lamb, the shepherd – and scenes from the Bible, and in the recesses were placed not only the bodies of the dead, wrapped in lime-coated shrouds, but also precious objects such as lamps and vessels of golden glass, and relics of holy men, martyrs and saints.[1]

Among the bodies of saints placed here were, it is believed, that of St Sebastian, traditionally said to be a member of Diocletian's bodyguard who was condemned to be shot to death with arrows when his religion became known, and, for a time, those of two earlier saints, Paul, the great Jewish missionary from the Greek city of Tarsus, and Simon, the fisherman from the shores of the Sea of Galilee whose

15. Part of the catacombs on the Via Appia dating from the reign of the Emperor Tiberius.

16. Michelangelo's 'Crucifixion of St Peter'. According to tradition the saint asked to be nailed to the cross head-down so that his execution would not resemble too closely that of Christ.

Aramaic title *Kepha* (Peter), meaning rock, was given to him by Christ himself with the words, 'And on this rock I will build my Church, and the powers of death shall not prevail against it. I will give you the keys of the kingdom of heaven.' In fulfilment of this mission Peter is believed to have come to Rome where both he and Paul were executed in the persecutions ordered by Nero.

These persecutions followed the fire of 64 for which the Emperor himself was widely held to be responsible and for which scapegoats were consequently needed.

To put an end to the rumours he shifted the charge on to others [Tacitus recorded]. First those who acknowledged themselves of the [Christian] persuasion were arrested; and upon their testimony a vast number were condemned ... Their death was turned into a diversion. They were clothed in the dress of wild beasts, and torn to pieces by wild dogs; they were fastened to crosses, or set up to be burned, so as to serve the purpose of lamps when daylight failed. Nero gave up his own gardens for this spectacle.

As it was in Nero's time, so it was in the reigns of Domitian and Marcus Aurelius, of Decius and Valerian. There were emperors who were more merciful. Trajan, for instance, ordered, 'Christians are not to be hunted out. Any who are accused and convicted must be punished. Yet if a man denies being a Christian and corroborates his denial by such acts as worshipping our gods, he should be pardoned, however suspect he may have been in the past.' But throughout the second and third centuries the Christians were more often persecuted than not; and, even when the authorities were prepared to tolerate them, the common people – suspicious of their exclusiveness, their rites and their supposed 'abominations' which included cannibalism – regarded them as alien troublemakers and revolutionaries, a danger to the state and a blasphemy against the ancient gods of Rome. Their deaths in the amphitheatre accordingly became one of the fiercest thrills that the shows there could afford. Christians were eaten by half-starved lions, burned alive before images of the sun-god, shot down by flights of arrows, hacked to death with axes and swords. In the reign of Diocletian alone, when the congregation of Christians was forbidden, when their clergy were arrested unless they sacrificed to the recognized gods, and their places of worship destroyed together with their sacred objects and holy books, there were probably as many as three thousand martyrs. Yet their religion could not be suppressed; and while those arrested were torn to pieces in the Colosseum, the survivors were joined by convert after convert until by the time of Diocletian's death there were perhaps thirty thousand Christians in Rome, meeting together for worship, occasionally in halls reserved especially for the purpose but usually in villas or 'houses of the Church' known as *tituli* after the original title holders of the building.

By then there had already been thirty-three bishops, or popes, in Rome, all holding that position of divine, unique authority within the Christian community which, so they believed, had been granted to St Peter by Christ. A minority of them had been born in Rome; several came from the East; one at least from Africa. Some were of humble birth, others noblemen. This evident capacity of Christianity to attract converts from all peoples and classes in the Empire was one of the main reasons why it appealed to the man who emerged as the strongest contender for the imperial throne after the confusion caused by the abdication of Diocletian.

This man was Constantine. The son of an army officer and an experienced officer himself, Constantine had been born in about 285 in what is now Yugoslavia and had spent most of his youth in the eastern part of the Empire which Diocletian had divided to protect its borders. His mother, Helena, a former serving-girl from Asia Minor, was at some uncertain date converted to Christianity and, on a visit to the Holy Land, was credited with having discovered the cross upon which Christ was crucified. Her son, so it was alleged, had the nails melted down and made into a charmed bit for the bridle of his horse. Having married the stepdaughter of one of Diocletian's fellow-Emperors, Maximian I, Constantine had invaded Italy in 312 and at the Mulvian Bridge near Rome had defeated his brother-in-law, Maxentius, Maximian's son, to become undisputed ruler of the Empire in the West. At this battle he had fought under a banner bearing the insignia of the faith to which he had been converted from sun-worship and to which he was drawn not only by political considerations but also by his own need for a personal, divine intercessor. Thereafter, in those battles in which he won and consolidated his rule over the whole of the Empire, East and West, he claimed to be fighting in Jesus's name and to be the champion of His faith against the forces of evil. By imperial edicts he granted freedom of worship to all Christians and restored to them the property, both personal and corporate, of which they had been deprived during the persecutions.

In Rome, Constantine contrived to benefit the Christian community without giving too much offence to the rich and influential classes who were still mostly, and in many cases devoutly, pagan. He gave the Christians buildings in which they could meet and worship their God, bury their dead and revere their saints and martyrs. But he ensured that the sites were well away from the centre of the city and that, while the interiors of the buildings might be splendid, they displayed little of this splendour to the passers-by in the streets outside.

South-west of the Porta Maggiore[2] stood a palace which had formerly belonged to the rich Laterani family and which had formed part of his wife's dowry.[3] This he gave to the Pope who established in it the surviving private chapel, the Sancta Sanctorum,[4] now approached by the Scala Sancta, the holy stairs which, so tradition firmly held, Jesus ascended in Pontius Pilate's palace in Jerusalem and which were brought to Rome by Constantine's mother.[5] Helena, as Empress-Dowager, had a palace near to the Lateran, the Palatium Sessorianum; and here the great hall was converted into a basilica which became known as S. Croce in Gerusalemme in commemoration of the holy Cross, its most precious relic.[6] North of S. Croce in Gerusalemme, Constantine himself is believed to have built a basilica, the first Basilica di S. Lorenzo fuori le Mura.[7] This was constructed over the catacomb where lay the bones of St Laurence, one of the deacons of the early Christian community in Rome. St Laurence, it is said, was burnt to death on a grill in 258 when, having been ordered to hand over the sect's valuables, he collected together the city's destitute and sick and presented them to the authorities with the words, 'Here is the Church's treasure.' Certainly, beside the Lateran Palace on the site of what is now St John Lateran, Constantine did build the Constantinian basilica which, since it contained the *cathedra*, or official seat of the bishop, became and has always since remained Rome's cathedral.[8] A large rectangular hall with a nave flanked by double aisles and terminating in an apse, this basilica seems to have been conceived by Constantine, internally at least, as a splendid Christian rival to the monumental public meeting-halls of the imperial city.

The same inspiration is evident also in the other great basilica which Constantine built on the slopes of an imperial estate on the Vatican hill. This basilica was as massive as the Constantinian basilica; but between the apse and the nave, which was covered with graves, a transept changed the longitudinal shape into that of a cross. Beneath this crossing, surmounted by a baldacchino supported on twisted marble columns, was the shrine of St Peter whose remains, brought here from the catacombs, were reburied in the basilica which was for ever to bear his name.[9] At about the same time, above the catacombs, yet another large basilica was built as a kind of enclosed and roofed-in cemetery, its floor, like that of St Peter's, covered with graves. Dedicated to the Apostles, it was later known as the Basilica of San Sebastian in honour of the Christian soldier who, his body pierced by arrow shafts, survived death only to be executed.[10]

Basilicas, churches, covered cemeteries and mausolea were not the only fine buildings to be erected in Rome in the time of Constantine. In the Forum he completed, to modified designs, a secular basilica begun by Maxentius, the Basilica Nova, an immense structure, the last of ancient Rome's law courts and meeting-places, three of whose huge coffered vaults still remain.[11] In one of its apses Constantine had placed an immense seated statue of himself, the body of wood, the robe of gilded bronze and the head of marble. This colossal head, six feet high and weighing nine tons, can still be seen in the courtyard of the Palazzo dei Conservatori on the Capitoline hill where the deeply cut pupils of the large and penetrating eyes stare out, above the huge hooked nose, like those of a commanding god.

Like most of his great predecessors, the Emperor Constantine built baths for the city. He may well have been responsible for the Arch of Janus Quadrifons,[12] the huge structure in the Forum Boarium, the ancient cattle market by the banks of the Tiber.[13] And he was, of course, the inspiration for the Arch of Constantine which was erected in 315 by the Senate and people of Rome to commemorate the Emperor's triumph over Maxentius at the Mulvian Bridge.[14]

Splendid as Constantine found Rome, however, and magnificent as were the new buildings he gave to the city, he had to accept Diocletian's view that it could no longer serve as the Empire's capital, being too far removed from the northern and eastern frontiers. He had also to recognize that he had failed to make Rome fully Christian, that the deep-rooted pagan beliefs of most families were as strong as ever. So the Emperor removed his court to Byzantium on the Bosphorus strait and there founded the new Christian capital which was to become known as Constantinople.

Yet, although Rome was no longer the seat of imperial power, the city remained the *caput mundi*, '*Invicta Roma Aeterna*', as its coins declared. The centre and showplace of the civilized world, with a population of about 800,000, it was still the home of those incalculably rich families whose political influence was still paramount in the Senate, whose members still filled many of the most important posts in Italy and the Empire, whose businesses were still run from Rome, whose villas still stood beyond its walls and whose ancestors' mausolea lined the roads leading out of it. Visitors to the city still stood in awestruck admiration as they looked across the Forum to the Colosseum, or gazed up at the temples, tiled with gilded bronze, on the Capitoline hill, or wondered at the number and size of the basilicas and triumphal arches, the statues, obelisks and fountains, the baths and libraries, the circuses and theatres.

Eight bridges crossed the river.[15] Nineteen aqueducts carried water to the city on row upon row of arches stretching in seemingly endless lines across the countryside beyond the walls.[16] The Roman poet, Rutilius Namatianus, expressed his pride in the indestructible glory of his city:

> No man will ever be safe if he forgets you;
> May I praise you still when the sun is dark.
> To count up the glories of Rome is like counting
> The stars in the sky.

There were still many powerful men in Rome who believed that this glory could only be preserved by a return to the old traditions and the old gods, by a rejection of the new Christianity with its foreign, plebeian origins, its internal feuds and its unfamiliar art. There were men like Quintus Aurelius Symmachus, the noble, upright, rich and cultivated leader of the Senate who, while numbering many Christians among his friends, constantly upheld the superior virtues of the pagan tradition and even supported the gladiatorial games, arranging for lavish entertainments to be given when his son was appointed Praetor and expressing disappointment when the German prisoners he had imported chose to strangle each other in their chains rather than fight before a Roman crowd. Symmachus was naturally appalled by an imperial order from Constantinople that the winged statue of Victory should be removed from the Senate House. 'The Great Mystery cannot be approached by one avenue alone,' he protested on behalf of his fellow-Senators. 'Leave us the symbol on which our oaths of allegiance have been sworn for so many generations. Leave us the system that has given prosperity to the State.' But his words were in vain; in 382 the statue was taken away. And a few years later in 392, shortly before Symmachus's death, an imperial decree, sterner and more effective than previous edicts, forbade all forms of pagan sacrifice and banished flowers and incense from the altars of the household gods. 'They who were once the gods of the nation,' wrote St Jerome, 'dwell now with the owls and bats under their lonely roofs.' In 408 a further decree provided that all temples should be put to other than religious uses. The gladiatorial games had already been abolished in 404 by imperial decree after a Christian monk, Telemachus, had been stoned to death by furious spectators in the arena of the Colosseum when he had tried to separate two fighting gladiators.

Up till the close of the fourth century, pagan shrines had been restored and kept in repair and use beside the places of Christian worship. A few years after Constantine's death in 337, new pagan statues had been erected along the Sacra Via; and since then the Temple of Vesta had been renovated. But now the struggle was over. Christianity had triumphed and Christian buildings were to dominate the city. No longer were they to be relegated to the outskirts of Rome and made as discreet as their size would allow. They were henceforth to appear as conspicuous and monumental witnesses to the faith, some of them being built in the very heart of the city and most, displaying increasingly classical emphasis, designed with high naves, approached through a porch or narthex, flanked by aisles and terminating in semicircular apses.

Powerful support for this new style of church building came from St Damasus, a rich and well-born prelate of strong Roman sympathies who was elected Pope in 366 and strove hard to identify the Christian Church more closely with Rome's long classical past. He and his immediate successors, many of them Roman and most of them upper class, treasured their classical heritage, revered the great Latin writers, admired the architecture which had developed in their times and saw the Kingdom of God as a sanctified successor to the Empire of the Caesars. The religious buildings which now appeared in Rome clearly reflected both this new philosophy and the growing confidence of the Church. Among these buildings, in which columns and other features from classical buildings were incorporated, were the grandly imposing S. Paolo fuori le Mura, begun in 384, to replace the modest basilica that Constantine had built over the grave of St Paul;[17] the church of San Lorenzo in Damaso, now part of the fabric of the Palazzo della Cancelleria;[18] and the church of S. Pudenziana which is dedicated to the daughter of the Senator who was believed to have been one of St Peter's first converts in Rome and in which the magnificent mosaic in the apse depicts Christ surrounded by the Apostles wearing the togas of Roman Senators.[19] In about 400 building began north of the Colosseum upon the church of S. Pietro in Vincoli as a shrine for the chains which had bound St Peter.[20] Soon afterwards work started to the south of the Colosseum on the basilica of SS. Giovanni e Paolo which was dedicated to the two Christian martyrs who were beheaded in 361 for refusing to sacrifice to pagan gods.[21]

But while all this building was in progress within the city, beyond its walls the Roman Empire was crumbling into ruins. Invasion succeeded invasion, defeat followed defeat. In 378 the German people known as Visigoths overwhelmed an imperial army at Adrianople; and in 408 they invaded Italy and marched south upon Rome under their leader Alaric, a nobleman by birth who had once commanded the Gothic troops in the Roman army. When the Visigoths first appeared before the Aurelian Walls, which had recently been strengthened and raised to almost twice their original height, they were kept at bay with payments of money. But in 410 when they reappeared, the gates were opened by traitors within the city, and for the first time in eight hundred years a foreign force occupied Rome.

A ferocious sack had been expected when the fearful sound of the Gothic war trumpets had been heard; but the tall, rough-looking troops of Alaric, mostly Arian Christians like their commander, were not malevolent. Some buildings were burned down, including the Palace of Sallust,[22] many houses and churches were plundered, a few citizens were roughly treated, and pagan temples were ransacked with exceptional venom. But after three days, the Visigoths withdrew, having respected the sanctity both of St Peter's and of St Paul's. Yet, while the fabric of the city had not been badly damaged, the people of Rome had suffered a deep emotional shock. 'It is the end of the world,' lamented St Jerome, as Christians blamed pagans for their humiliation and disgrace, and pagans blamed Christians for having deserted the gods who had in the past afforded the city protection. 'Words fail me. My sobs break in . . . The city which took captive the whole world has itself been captured.'

Confidence soon returned, however. The Pope at the time of Alaric's invasion was Innocent I, a man of strong will and high ability who at every opportunity stressed the supreme authority of the papacy and its importance as a political and spiritual force. And in 440 a man of like determination, energy and force of character was elected Pope. This was the Roman-born Leo I who insisted that the powers which he had inherited had come to him through his predecessors directly from St Peter and that Peter alone had been granted that power by Christ.

Fortified by the faith, Pope Leo went out himself when Rome was next endangered to confront the barbarians in the north. The enemy now was the restless, savage-tempered Attila, the squat and swarthy leader of the Huns, who 'felt himself lord of all' and took pride in the title that had been bestowed upon him, 'the Scourge of God'. In 452 Attila's forces crossed the Alps and, having sacked and pillaged various northern towns including Milan, Padua and Verona, were preparing to advance south when Pope Leo arrived at his headquarters. He demanded and obtained a meeting with Attila and, while no one knew what passed between them, the Huns soon withdrew, persuaded perhaps that famine and pestilence in Italy would destroy them should they move south towards Rome.

A few years later Pope Leo was faced with another threat, this time from the Vandals, fierce Germanic warriors who attacked by night, blackening their faces and their shields. In 455, having poured across Spain and ravaged north Africa, they invaded Italy and, led by their gifted chieftain, Gaiseric, they advanced upon Rome. Leo could not prevent them breaking into the city which they pillaged far more thoroughly than Alaric's men had done. They remained for two weeks during which they stripped most of the gilded tiles from the roof of the Temple of Capitoline Jupiter, rampaged through the mansions of the rich, invaded the Christian churches, and then marched down to their ships at Ostia with thousands of captives and wagons piled high with plunder, including the menorah and other sacred objects which the Emperor Titus had brought to Rome from Jerusalem.

Yet brutal and rapacious as the Vandals had proved to be, the damage they did to Rome was not as widespread as it would have been had not Pope Leo interceded so forcefully for the city and obtained undertakings from Gaiseric to restrain his men from murder, rape and indiscriminate incendiarism. Gaiseric did not keep all his promises, but at least the ancient basilicas were spared; and life in Rome was soon restored to normal. Indeed, in the years that had passed since the first barbarian incursion into the city, the moral force of the Christian faith had grown ever stronger. The Church was still rich, and the papacy had become recognized as a decisive factor in European affairs. In the proud words of Pope Leo, Rome was once more 'the head of the world through the Holy See of St Peter'.

Interrupted though it had been, the building of churches in Rome continued apace, as thousands of converts were admitted into the faith. The most magnificent of all early Christian churches in Rome and one that most clearly exemplifies the continuing taste for classical forms so evident in the late fourth century was, indeed, started soon after the invasion of Alaric and finished in 432. This is S. Sabina on the Aventine which has survived largely unchanged to this day.[23] In the year of its completion the church of S. Maria Maggiore had been begun on the Esquiline and had been decorated with some of the most beautiful fifth-century mosaics that have come down to us.[24] Soon afterwards Pope Sixtus III, who took a deep interest in the architecture of the city, had undertaken a reconstruction of the Lateran Baptistery as well as of San Lorenzo fuori le Mura. And one of Sixtus III's successors, Simplicius, who was chosen Pope in 468, built the lovely S. Stefano Rotondo on the Caelian hill whose unusual circular design may have been inspired by the church of the Holy Sepulchre in Jerusalem.[25]

During the papacy of Simplicius, while bitter doctrinal disputes divided Christendom in the East, the Roman Empire in the West approached its final disintegration. When the boy Emperor Romulus Augustulus was deposed in 476 by the German warrior Odoacer, no successor was appointed and Odoacer became ruler of Italy. Yet building continued in Rome as though these events in the outside world were of little concern to a city whose prestige as the home of the papacy had been much enhanced by the death of imperial power in the West. Old structures were renovated and extended, while new ones – monasteries, mausolea, chapels, shrines and baptisteries – appeared both inside the walls and beyond them where suburbs were developing beside the graves of the martyrs and where hostels, shops and taverns catered for the ever-growing number of pilgrims who flocked to Rome from all over the Christian world.

Pilgrims to Rome in these years discovered a city surprisingly little changed by the passing troubled years. In 467 the Bishop of the Auvergne described the jostling, affable crowds and the convivial atmosphere in the circus and the markets. The rich still entertained visitors with traditional Roman hospitality in their houses; orators still practised their art in the Forum; wrestling matches and wild beast shows were still held in the Colosseum, whose massive walls remained untouched by building contractors who were later to use it as a quarry; chariots still careered in clouds of dust around the Circus Maximus to the roars of the excited crowd; statues were still to be found in all quarters of the city. Indeed, Odoacer's successor as King of Italy, the Ostrogoth Theodoric maintained that the bronze and marble population of Rome was almost equal to its natural one: ten years after his death there were an estimated 3,785 statues still standing in the city. Anxious to preserve these 'precious monuments left in the streets and the open spaces of Rome', Theodoric, a persistent advocate of racial harmony, instructed his representatives in Rome to guard them carefully and at night to listen for the ringing sound which should warn the watchmen that a thief might be attempting to remove an arm or leg. Theodoric also gave orders for the repair of the Colosseum after it had been damaged by an earthquake in 508 and for the restoration of the imperial palaces on the Palatine, setting aside for the purpose the proceeds of a tax on wine.

But after the death of Theodoric in 526, there were further catastrophic upheavals in Italy which were to precipitate ancient Rome's decay. The Byzantine Emperor Justinian I determined to drive the Arian Ostrogoths out of the peninsula and to re-establish direct imperial rule and the true faith. During the war that followed, Justinian's general Belisarius occupied Rome, which was three times besieged, its defenders on one occasion smashing the statues on Hadrian's mausoleum and catapulting the fragments at the enemy. The city was eventually captured by the new Ostrogothic leader, Totila, who demolished long sections of the Aurelian Wall, burned the Trasteverine district and threatened to raze the rest of the city as a pasture for cattle. Belisarius addressed a passionate appeal to him to remember that 'trespass against Rome's greatness would be justly regarded as an outrage':

Beyond all cities on earth Rome is the greatest and most wonderful. For neither has she been built by the energy of a single man, nor has she attained to such greatness and beauty in a short time. On the contrary, a long succession of emperors, many associations of illustrious men, countless years and wealth . . . have been required to gather together all the treasures she contains. She remains a monument to the virtues of the world . . . Destroying Rome, you will lose not the city of another but your own. Preserving her you will enrich yourself with the most splendid possessions of the earth.

Influenced by such pleas as this, Totila held his hand in Rome where the population had been reduced by the sieges to perhaps as few as 30,000. But the city was not long to remain his capital. In 552 he was defeated and killed in a battle in the Apennines against the eunuch Narses, formerly commander of the imperial bodyguard, who had succeeded Belisarius as general of the Byzantine forces.

Once the Ostrogoths had been finally defeated, however, Italy had other invaders. The Lombards, a Germanic people, began to move down from the north in 568 and then to lay waste the countryside outside Rome, driving farmers and peasants, monks and clergy to seek safety in the city where a series of disasters – fires, floods, food shortages and plague – made life miserable for all those inside the walls.

As the sixth century drew to its close, Rome's decay was pitiable. Eyewitnesses painted a desolate picture of a city in which buildings were crumbling into ruins; aqueducts and sewers were in urgent need of repair; public granaries had long since collapsed; monuments were dismembered, legally if deemed to be 'beyond repair'; statues were looted and violated; the Tiber carried along in its swollen, yellow waters dead cattle and snakes; people were dying of starvation in hundreds and the whole population went about in dread of infection. Those with sufficient money had forsaken their city for the relative comforts of Constantinople. Their large country villas had been abandoned for use as quarries or as living quarters for poor monks. The surrounding fields, undrained, had degenerated into swamps, and mosquitoes infested the plain of the Campagna.

In 590 a long procession of supplicants and penitents, numbering almost the entire population of Rome, could have been seen walking with bowed heads through the streets of the city. Some, already dying, fell down and expired by the way. The survivors marched slowly on until they came to the Mausoleum of Hadrian where, so the faithful reported, the Archangel Michael, captain of the heavenly host and guardian of the sick, appeared in the sky sheathing his sword as a sign that the plague would soon be over. In gratitude for this heavenly deliverance, a chapel was afterwards built above the mausoleum and dedicated to St Michael, and thereafter the fortress which the mausoleum had already become was to be known for all time as the Castel Sant' Angelo.

Leading the penitents that day in 590 was a man from a rich patrician family who had been born in Rome some fifty years before, the great-grandson of Pope Felix III. Strongly drawn to monasticism, he had resigned his position as Prefect of the city, had converted his family's palace on the Caelian hill into St Andrew's Monastery, and had sold the rest of his estate for the foundation of other monasteries elsewhere, all of them, like St Andrew's, governed by rules similar to those established by St Benedict. After taking Holy Orders he had gone to Constantinople as papal nuncio and, a few weeks before the march of the penitents, he had been elected Pope. Complaining that he had never wanted such preferment, Pope Gregory I proved himself not only one of the most saintly men who had held this high office but also an administrator, statesman and diplomat of exceptional gifts, the creator of the medieval papacy. Declaring that he did not intend to have 'the treasury of the Church defiled by disreputable gain', he devoted himself to the relief of the poor, reorganizing the system of food distribution which the papacy had taken over from the imperial authorities, and establishing or improving several relief centres, known as *diaconiae*, which were later to be converted into churches as, for example S. Giorgio in Velabro[26] and S. Maria in Via Lata.[27] He also took care of the needy among the pilgrims whose numbers were constantly increasing throughout his pontificate.

Dedicated to the conversion of unbelievers, Pope Gregory sent missions from Rome in every direction, into Lombardy, Spain and England, then into Germany, the coastlands of France and the Low Countries. Before long, Christian pilgrims from all these places were arriving in Rome, some of them bringing great wealth, others walking in penniless, several with iron collars round their necks or arms indicating that they were criminals upon whom a pilgrimage to Rome had been imposed as an expiation of their misdemeanours. They crowded into the basilicas, filed through the catacombs, worshipped at the shrines, deposited gifts, made endowments, dropped coins in the bowls of mendicants, or flocked to the *diaconiae* for food and shelter. Soon guidebooks were provided for them, instructing them what routes to follow, what to look out for, where to see the grill upon which St Laurence had been burnt, or the arrows which had pierced the body of St Sebastian, or the chains with which St Peter had been bound. Pope Gregory himself found the trade in relics distasteful and absurd. He had once discovered some Greek monks digging up 'martyrs' bones' in a graveyard where most burials had, in any case, been pagan; and he warned those anxious to purchase relics, like the Byzantine empress who had made inquiries about the head of St Paul, that removing sacred objects and disturbing bones were highly dangerous activities, adding that a group of workmen who had broken into St Laurence's tomb accidentally during building operations had all died within days. Pope Gregory insisted that the strips of linen lowered into graves were as worthy of veneration as the bones they contained.

During St Gregory's pontificate no new churches were built in Rome for the crowds of visitors to the city and its growing resident population. But several existing buildings had already been, or were soon to be, appropriated for Christian use, and others were reconstructed so as to admit more worshippers, to facilitate their movement past the holy places or to keep them at a safe distance from valuable relics. In the days of Felix IV (526–30), the audience hall of the city Prefect on the Via Sacra had been converted into the church of SS. Cosma e Damiano and decorated with mosaics;[28] about half a century later, probably in the pontificate of Benedict I (575–9), a former ceremonial hall at the foot of the Palatine, had been transformed into the church of S. Maria Antiqua;[29] in the time of Boniface IV (608–15), for the first time a pagan temple was made over to the Christians when the Pantheon became the church of S. Maria ad Martyres;[30] and in 625 Pope Honorius I turned the Senate House in the Forum into the church of S. Adriano.[31] Pope Gregory's predecessor Pelagius I (556–61) had reconstructed S. Lorenzo fuori le Mura so that the martyr's grave could be seen by pilgrims; and, perhaps at Gregory's own suggestion, an annular crypt, one of the earliest of many, was constructed in St Peter's to ease the flow of pilgrims and to allow them to see relics without being close enough to touch or damage them.

The flood of pilgrims into Rome from Europe, Asia Minor and north Africa was soon to be much increased by thousands of refugees from the Muslim Arabs who were carrying the banner of the Prophet far north and west from their homelands into Syria, Palestine, Egypt, Mesopotamia and Persia, into eastern Europe and across the southern shores of the Mediterranean and into Spain. These refugees settled in Rome where they established their own communities: Greeks, for example, in the area between the Circus Maximus and the Tiber where they built a church, later to be known as S. Maria in Cosmedin but then called S. Maria de Schola [or foreign colony] Graeca.[32]

In the years to come, refugees from the east and their descendants, several of whom, Greeks and Syrians, were elected Pope, were to exercise a profound influence over the Roman Church. They established monasteries in and around Rome of which there were no less than twenty-four by 680. And they brought to Rome their sacred relics, including the head of the Persian martyr, Anastasius, and the manger of the baby Jesus which, from the time of the Palestinian Pope Theodore, could be seen in the church of S. Maria Maggiore. They helped to ensure that icons became commonplace in Rome, that the decoration and furnishing of many Roman churches followed eastern patterns and that the eastern practice of moving martyrs' bones from one place to another, so strongly resisted by Pope Gregory I, became generally accepted.

17. A portrait from a twelfth-century manuscript of Pope Gregory the Great, who was born in Rome in about 540 and died there in 604.

Pope Gregory died in 604. He left the papacy efficiently administered, fully capable of managing its own affairs as well as those of the temporal government, rich enough not only to maintain its buildings and to see to the wants of the clergy but also to care for the poor, to pay officials to govern the State and for troops to defend it, and to represent Rome in her uneasy relations with Byzantium, still theoretically her overlord.

Long after Gregory's death the influence and authority of Constantinople and of the Hellenistic world was still felt in Rome. In 667 the disagreeable Byzantine Emperor Constans II came on a state visit to the city, was received with punctilious ceremony by Pope Vitalian, by the clergy and notables, and behaved as though Rome were his own personal property. He removed many of its bronze statues, stripped the gilded bronze tiles from the roof of the Pantheon and left behind his name scratched on both the Janus Quadrifons and inside the Column of Trajan.

During his stay Constans occupied rooms in one of the old imperial palaces on the Palatine hill where most of the buildings were now in ruins, roofless and with grass and weeds growing between the cracks in walls and pavements. Much of imperial Rome below the Palatine was in the same forlorn state. But, since Pope Gregory's time, Christian Rome had been much embellished. Honorius I, a member of a noble family long settled in the Roman Campagna, who had been Pope from 625 to 638, had spent a great deal of money on restoring and converting old buildings, and in constructing new ones. On the southern outskirts of the city, he is thought to have rebuilt the church of SS. Vincenzo e Anastasio;[33] near the Porta S. Pancrazio on the Janiculum he had been responsible for the restoration of the splendidly decorated S. Pancrazio;[34] and on the site of the grave of the martyr, St Agnes, he had completely reconstructed the basilica of S. Agnese fuori le Mura[35] which the Emperor Constantine the Great's granddaughter, Constantia, had raised to the young Christian girl who, consecrating her virginity to Christ, had offered herself to martyrdom when she was no more than twelve years old.

When the Emperor Constans came down from the Palatine on the last day of his visit and sailed away with his plunder to Sicily, he had only a few months left to live. In September 668 he was murdered by a slave in Syracuse. After his death, Rome grew increasingly independent of Byzantium – itself beleaguered by the Arabs and later, once more, by the Lombards – and, while certain papal patrons still displayed a taste for eastern forms of art, these forms were absorbed into those traditionally associated with Rome which remained, as it always essentially had been, a city of the West.

Rome's independence was sharply demonstrated in the early eighth century during a heated controversy over iconoclasm. The Byzantine Emperor, the Syrian Leo III, condemned the veneration of religious pictures and relics as sacrilegious and ordered their removal and destruction. Immediately the Romans, led by Pope Gregory II and then by Gregory III, rose up in determined resistance. Gregory II, whom Byzantine agents in Rome attempted to murder, warned the Emperor: 'The whole West has its eyes on us . . . and on St Peter . . . whom all the kingdoms of the West revere . . . We go out to the most distant corners of the West to seek those who desire baptism . . . and they and their princes wish to receive it from ourselves alone.'

In 753, when the Lombards, having captured Ravenna, capital of the Byzantine governors of Italy, laid siege to Rome, the Pope, Stephen II, ignoring Byzantine instructions and advice, entered into negotiations with the enemy on his own account. Having persuaded them to lift the siege, he travelled north across the Alps and made his way to Saint-Denis near Paris to the Christian ruler of the Franks, a Germanic people who had invaded the Western Roman Empire in the fifth century and had now established their rule over a vast territory between the Pyrenees and the Rhine, including the land to which they were to give their name, France. Their king was Pepin the Short, last of a line of hereditary officials whose supreme influence over the corrupt and degenerate Frankish monarchs of the Merovingian dynasty had passed from father to son, generation after generation. Pepin had deposed the weak and sickly Merovingian King, Childeric III, and, with papal acquiescence, had packed him off to a monastery, having cut off his long, flowing hair, the age-old symbol of royalty among the Franks. At Saint-Denis, Pope Stephen confirmed his predecessor's approval of Pepin's usurpation, and on the understanding that the Romans would be granted Frankish support against the Lombards, anointed him in the abbey as King of the Franks and 'Patrician of the Romans'. Soon afterwards, the Lombards were defeated and forced to restore to Rome the Patrimony of St Peter, those large tracts of land acquired by the Church, which they had seized in central Italy and which, together with former Byzantine territory, were collectively to be known as the Papal States.

In 774 Pepin's son and successor, Charlemagne, came to Rome. A tall, fair, masterful young man, he was met outside the city by a delegation of magistrates and nobles sent to welcome him by Pope Hadrian I. The processional route along the Flaminian Way was lined with young Romans under arms, with children carrying palms and olive branches and chanting the praises of the Deliverer and Protector of Rome. Representatives of the national communities stood under their banners, among them the Saxons, the name of whose *schola*, the *burgus Saxonum*, survives in Rome today as the Borgo, the quarter around Castel Sant' Angelo. At the sight of the holy crosses and the emblems of the saints, Charlemagne dismounted from his horse, and proceeded the rest of the way to St Peter's on foot, kissing the ground before entering the Basilica.

Already overlord of nearly all that is now France, Belgium and the Netherlands, as well as parts of Germany and Switzerland, Charlemagne was inspired by this visit to Rome to conceive of an even greater empire, a Christian empire to replace that of the Caesars, an empire which would stretch beyond the Rhine to the Vistula, and south of the Alps to encompass Italy.

A quarter of a century later, Charlemagne, *Rex Pater Europae*, set out upon a lengthy progress of his dominions, a progress which was to culminate in another visit to Rome and the realization of his long-cherished ambition. Grieving at the loss of the last of his five wives, the beautiful Liutgard, who had died on the way, he arrived in the city in November 800. At Christmas Mass in St Peter's, where

Pope Leo III placed the imperial crown upon his now grey-haired head, the congregation rose to acclaim him with shouts that rang round the walls: 'Long life and victory to Charles Augustus, crowned by God, the great and pacific Emperor of the Romans!' The Roman Empire of the West had been revived.

FIVE

INFAMY AND ANARCHY

During the Lombard invasions, aqueducts had been destroyed, churches had been looted, and catacombs had been broken into and bones and sacred relics carried off. Several times the Tiber had burst its banks and the swirling waters had flooded over the fields and into the streets. Pope Hadrian I, a Roman aristocrat by birth, had raised a large labour force in the countryside and had set about repairing the damage, restoring Rome's water supply, extending the city's welfare system, rebuilding the Aurelian Walls and their fortified towers, improving agriculture on the large estates of the Church beyond them, and clearing the debris out of the catacombs from which cartloads of bones and relics were drawn into Rome to be re-buried in consecrated ground. Numerous churches were renovated and several were adorned with rich furnishings, curtains and candelabra; silver paving was installed at St Peter's, together with a chandelier with over a thousand lights.

Helped by generous gifts from Charlemagne and by the increased landed wealth of the Church, Pope Leo III, a Roman priest of humble stock, was able to continue the work undertaken by his predecessor, and add to the glories of the city, now once again an imperial capital. At the Lateran Palace a grand dining-hall was constructed which rivalled the Hall of the Nineteen Divans in the great palace of the Emperors in Constantinople. Around St Peter's, a wall, to be known as the Leonine Wall,[1] was begun by Leo III and completed in 854 by Leo IV, also a Roman, who, attended by barefoot, chanting clergy with ashes strewn in their hair, consecrated it with prayers and holy water. By the time of Paschal I, yet another native of Rome, the concern of church builders to make the new imperial city a noble reflection of both the early Christian Rome of the Emperor Constantine and of the Rome of classical antiquity had become apparent. Exemplified in S. Prassede[2] and its annexed Chapel of St Zeno,[3] both of which contain magnificent mosaics, this intention is also apparent in the splendid churches of SS. Quattro Coronati,[4] S. Martino ai Monti,[5] S. Maria Nova (now S. Francesca Romana),[6] S. Maria in Domnica[7] and in the rebuilt S. Cecilia in Trastevere[8] to which were brought from the catacombs the bones of the virgin martyr who is said to have been sentenced to death by suffocation in the steam of her own bathroom and, surviving both this and attempts at decapitation by a soldier, to have lingered for three days, softly singing hymns to the glory of God and converting many by her example.

When Pope Leo IV died in 855, however, this brief Carolingian renaissance in

18. A bronze statuette of Charlemagne, first Holy Roman Emperor, believed to be a contemporary likeness.

Rome was already at an end. Charlemagne himself had died forty years before and his successors had found their involvement with Rome as complicated and often as unwelcome as the papacy and the Romans had found their subjection to the Empire. Disagreements and quarrels over the relative authority of Pope and Emperor had been exacerbated not only by the interference of influential Roman families but also by the failure of the imperial forces to protect Rome adequately against Saracen pirates, who came up the Tiber in 846 and plundered both St Peter's and S. Paoli fuori le Mura. As the alliance between the Carolingian dynasty and the papacy disintegrated, these rich families and their supporters became ever more powerful, making and breaking popes at will and presuming to speak for the city as the patricians of the ancient past had done. Theophylactus, one of the richest and most masterful of the aristocrats, assumed full control of Rome at the beginning of the tenth century, styling himself Senator and Consul and considering himself ruler of the papacy as well as of the city. His daughter, Marozia, became the wife of Prince Alberic of Spoleto; and their son, Alberic the Younger, ruled Rome for over twenty years as *Princeps atque omnium Romanorum Senator*. On his deathbed in 954 he made arrangements for his dissolute 18-year-old son, who had been christened Octavian after the Roman emperor, to be elected Pope as John XII.

John XII's pontificate was disastrous. Having summoned King Otto I from Germany to support him against Berengar, the ruler of northern Italy, and having crowned Otto as Emperor in St Peter's, John immediately regretted his action and, upon the new Emperor's departure, opened negotiations with Berengar instead. Otto then returned to Rome, deposed John XII, appointed his own nominee, a layman, as Pope Leo VIII, and made it clear to the Romans that he regarded both the city and the papacy as his to have and to hold. Deeply resentful of this, the Roman aristocracy, who had long since regarded the papacy as theirs, refused to submit and, appealing to the people to support them, time and again rose up in revolt.

The first of these revolts erupted in January 964 when at the sudden ringing of the alarm bells, the Romans flew to arms and attacked the German Emperor Otto's forces in the Borgo, the area enclosed by the Leonine Wall across the river. Repulsed, they fled to Castel Sant' Angelo where the imperialists broke down the barricades, and would have slaughtered all the fugitives had not Otto himself intervened. The next day the Roman leaders of the rebellion appeared before the Emperor to beg for mercy. They were required to swear allegiance both to him and to Pope Leo. A hundred of them were kept as hostages; the rest, humiliated, were permitted to depart. 'Otto left the city in anger, leaving the Pope like a lamb amongst wolves,' in the words of Ferdinand Gregorovius. 'The blood which had been shed on 3 January never dried in Rome. Hatred of the foreigner found nourishment therefrom, and the Romans who had been repressed by force, scarcely saw their prisoners at liberty and the Emperor at a distance, when they hastened to give vent to their desire for revenge.'

They recalled the deposed Pope, John XII, who arrived back in the city with a host of friends and vassals to drive his rival out of it. Excommunicating Leo VIII, Pope John took a savage revenge upon those clergy who had supported him, ordering one to be flogged, another to lose a hand, a third to have two fingers and his nose cut off and his tongue torn out. He would, no doubt, have ordered further punishments had not he died on 14 May, murdered, so it was reported, by the enraged husband of his mistress.

In his place the Romans, without reference to the Emperor whom they had sworn to obey, elected the learned Benedict V, an impertinent presumption which aroused the fury of Otto I who descended once more upon Rome to ensure the reinstatement of his creature, Leo VIII. The imperial army arrived before the walls at the beginning of June. The surrender of Benedict was peremptorily demanded. It was immediately refused, and the first assault upon the city was launched. At the beginning resistance was stubborn. Benedict was persuaded to mount the walls to encourage the defenders by his presence. But plague broke out in the city, and food supplies ran low. The gates were opened on 23 June. Benedict was handed over, his vestments were torn off by Leo VIII, his pallium was cut in two, his ferule broken in half, and he was sentenced to perpetual exile. The leaders of the resistance again swore obedience to the Emperor beside St Peter's grave and undertook never again to interfere in papal elections.

For the moment, the Romans were spared further punishment. But upon the death of Leo VIII, and the nomination by the Emperor of John XIII as his successor, they rebelled once more; and this time the Emperor was merciless. He banished to Germany several leading citizens who had assumed the title of Consul; twelve *decarones*, representatives of the districts or *rioni*[9] into which the early-medieval city was divided, were hanged or blinded; the city Prefect was handed over by the Emperor to Pope John XIII who ordered that he be hanged by his hair from the equestrian statue of Marcus Aurelius, stripped naked, placed backwards upon an ass whose tail, furnished with a bell, he had to grasp as reins, and then driven through the streets with a sack of feathers on his head and other sacks fastened to his thighs, before being exiled beyond the Alps. The bodies of two other rebels who had died were dug up and thrown outside the city walls.

The Romans were provoked rather than subdued by these humiliations. And for the rest of the century and well into the next the disturbances and intermittent violence in the city continued unabated, while the papacy was beset by repeated scandals and the rivalry of anti-popes. Already one pope, Stephen VI, had ordered the exhumation of the body of Pope Formosus, a predecessor who had offended him. The corpse was clothed in pontifical vestments, seated upon a throne and put on trial. Found guilty of all the offences with which it was charged, it was stripped of its vestments; the three fingers of the right hand with which papal benediction was customarily bestowed were torn off; and the remains were then thrown into the Tiber. Some months later the pope who had presided over this gruesome tribunal was thrown into prison and strangled. His successor was violently deposed, the next pope murdered, and by 904 when Pope Christopher was executed, having murdered his predecessor, Leo V, there had been eight popes in as many years. It had long since become customary for the servants of a dead or deposed pontiff to overrun his private apartments and the public rooms in the Lateran Palace, with as many of the populace as could gain admittance, and for them to carry off everything that came to hand, clothes and money, furniture and hangings, pictures, gold and silver. Yet the Lateran was soon filled with treasures once more, since popes who did not find means to enrich themselves were few. So were lesser prelates whose pleasure-bent lives were passed in what Gregorovius described as 'sumptuous dwellings, resplendent in gold, purple and velvet'.

They dined like princes on vessels of gold. They sipped their wine out of costly goblets or drinking horns. Their basilicas were smothered in dust, but their commodious wine goblets were resplendent with decoration. As at the banquet of Trimalchio, their senses were gratified with the spectacle of beautiful dancing girls and the 'symphonies' of musicians. They slept on silken pillows and on beds artificially inlaid with gold, in the arms of their paramours, leaving their vassals, servants and slaves to look after the requirements of their court. They played at dice, hunted and shot with the bow. They left the altar, after celebrating Mass, with spurs at their ankles, daggers at their sides to mount their horses – furnished with gold bridles – and to fly their falcons. They travelled surrounded by swarms of parasites, and drove in luxurious carriages which no king would have scorned to possess.

The death of Pope John XIII in 972 and that of his protector, the Emperor Otto I, the next year did nothing to end the rivalry between the Roman nationalists and the imperialists. John XIII's successor, an imperial nominee, Benedict VI, was dragged into Castel Sant' Angelo and strangled in 974 in an insurrection led by the powerful Roman family, the Crescenzi, who installed Boniface VII, a Roman, in his place. The anti-Pope Boniface VII was then expelled from Rome by the Emperor's young heir, Otto II, and replaced by Benedict VII; and the Romans, led by the Crescenzi, were thereafter continually at odds with successive emperors. Otto II died in 983, and since his heir, Otto III, was a child of three whose throne was in danger of usurpation, Boniface VII thought it safe to return to Rome from Constantinople where he had fled with the papal treasury. In Rome he had Pope Benedict's successor, John XIV, arrested, imprisoned and killed, either by starvation or poisoning. Boniface himself was then murdered by the fickle mob and his corpse was thrown under the statue of Marcus Aurelius. Thus it went on. Boniface's successor, a Roman antagonistic to the Crescenzi, was followed by a pope of pure German descent, Gregory V, whom the Crescenzi and their adherents drove out of Rome, offering the papal tiara for a large sum of money to a rich Greek who accepted it and thus became the anti-Pope, John XVI. As soon as he heard of these insults to his imperial authority, Otto III, now seventeen, marched south upon Rome with a large army and discovered the anti-Pope hiding in the Campagna. He cut off his nose, tongue and ears, tore out his eyes, and dragged him back to Rome where he was thrown into the cell of a monastery to die. The Emperor then advanced towards Castel Sant' Angelo where the Romans were holding out, took it by assault on 29 April 998, and captured the head of the Crescenzi family whose eyes were snatched from his skull and whose limbs were mutilated before he was dragged through the streets on the skin of a cow, decapitated on the battlements and finally displayed on a gallows on the Monte Mario beside the corpses of twelve other leading Romans who had taken part in the revolt.

'Woe to Rome!' lamented a monkish chronicler at about this time. 'Oppressed and downtrodden by so many nations! Thou art taken captive; thy people are ruled by the sword. Thy strength is become as naught . . . Thou wert too beautiful . . . Thy gold and thy silver are carried away in the sacks of thine enemies. What thou didst possess thou hast lost!'

Yet there were even worse times still to come. Power in Rome now passed from the Crescenzi to another influential family whose estates looked down upon Rome from the heights of Tusculum. In 1032, the Tuscolani, several members of whose family had already held the office, arranged for another of their kin, though a mere boy, to be elected Pope Benedict IX; and in his time the papacy reached the utmost depth of moral degradation. The young Pope lived like a Turkish sultan in the palace of the Lateran, while his brother ruled the city as 'Senator of the Romans'. Their family filled Rome with robbery and murder, according to Gregorovius whose lurid account does not seem to have been unduly exaggerated. 'All lawful conditions had ceased . . . Only an uncertain glimmer, however, falls on these days when the Vicar of Christ was a pope . . . more criminal than Heliogabalus. We dimly see the leaders of Rome conspiring to strangle the youthful delinquent at the altar on the feast of the Apostles, until terror, produced perhaps by an eclipse of the sun, allowed Benedict time to escape.'

In 1044 a conspiracy to rid Rome of Benedict IX was more successful. But the anti-Pope who bribed his way to the succession, after savage fighting during an earthquake, was scarcely an improvement. Grossly sensual and corrupt, he was said to be closer to Satan than to Christ, to consort with devils in the woods, to attract women to his bed by spells, to conjure up demons with the help of books of magic which were afterwards found in the Lateran. He occupied the palace for less than two months. Driven out by the Tuscolani, he sought safety in the Sabine hills; and Benedict IX returned to the palace, only to sell his holy office to his godfather.

It seemed by now that the whole structure of the papacy was in danger of dissolution. But as at other times in its history when it seemed in the greatest peril, a man was found to save it. On this occasion its saviour was an obscure monk from the Cluniac monastery of St Mary on the Aventine hill.

Hildebrand, the son of a Tuscan labourer, had left his monastery to continue his education at the Schola Cantorum at the Lateran. Here his character earned him the high regard of one of the masters, the future Pope Gregory VI, who took him into his service. He later worked for Leo IX and Alexander II, two popes who in the middle part of the eleventh century concerned themselves with the reform of the medieval Church. The reform movement had begun in the monasteries of northern Italy and France from which attacks had been made on all manner of abuses in the Church from the sale of offices to the concubinage of the clergy. The reformers had then extended their programme to demand freedom from political and foreign interference and the right of the Church to be solely responsible for the election of popes and the investiture of bishops.

As papal adviser, Hildebrand was closely identified with the formulation of the Church's demands, and in 1073 he was elected by acclamation to succeed his former master, Alexander II, as Pope Gregory VII. Stern and autocratic, Gregory was determined to maintain the momentum of the reformist movement. Emphasizing the need for ecclesiastical and spiritual renewal, he made it clear that he would brook no opposition from either the Emperor or the aristocracy of Rome. He was soon in trouble with both. At Christmas 1075 he was reading midnight Mass in the crypt of S. Maria Maggiore when shouts and the clash of arms were heard outside and a party of men broke into the church brandishing arms. One of them seized the Pope by the hair and, dragging him wounded from the altar, threw him on to a horse and galloped off with him through the dark streets to a fortified tower belonging to a nobleman, Cencius de Praefecto. The city was soon in uproar. Alarm bells clanged, militia barred the gates, men paraded with torches throughout the *rioni* and priests veiled their altars. The next day, when it became known where the Pope was held, the tower of Cencius was stoned by the populace and the prisoner was released. He returned immediately to complete the interrupted Mass at S. Maria Maggiore.

Not in the least intimidated by this episode, Pope Gregory now repeated in even stronger terms his demands for a more powerful and autonomous Church, going so far as to claim that the Pope had not only the right to overrule Church councils and to dethrone bishops, but to depose emperors and to wear a red cloak as a sign of imperial rank as well as a high papal tiara as symbolic of his government of the world by ordinance of God. These assertions of the Church's authority naturally led to a fierce quarrel with the German Emperor, Henry IV, who, as self-styled 'Emperor by the pious ordination of God', took to addressing Gregory as 'no longer Pope but false monk'. Gregory quickly responded by excommunicating Henry and declaring him deposed. The excommunication was so effective in depriving the Emperor of support north of the Alps that he felt obliged to come south as a penitent, to beg for forgiveness and for reacceptance into the Church. On hearing of his approach, and not yet knowing its purpose, the Pope, who was on his way to Germany for a conference at Augsberg, withdrew to Canossa, the fortress home of his friend and supporter, the Countess of Tuscany. Outside the triple walls of the fortress the Emperor begged for forgiveness, clothed in a penitential shirt. For three cold January days the Pope kept him waiting. Then the gates of the castle were opened and the Emperor, after receiving absolution, was required to give up his crown into the Pope's hands, to agree that he would remain a private person until the decision of a council was made known and that, if he were to be restored to the throne, he would swear obedience to the Pope's will.

This humiliating submission was, however, not a lasting one. By virtue of his absolution, Henry regarded himself once more the rightful King of Germany with his authority undiminished. And so the quarrel flared up afresh. Henry, excommunicated and deposed for the second time, refused to accept the verdict; and, marching south, he laid siege to Rome. He persuaded his German bishops to depose Gregory in turn and to replace him by the Archbishop of Ravenna who took the title of Clement III. Set upon resistance, Gregory appealed for help to Robert Guiscard, the Norman Duke of Apulia and Calabria, and prepared for war.

Rome paid a dreadful price. In June 1083 Henry's troops broke through the Leonine Wall and, after fierce fighting, took possession of St Peter's. Gregory occupied Castel Sant' Angelo and from this commanding stronghold succeeded in preventing the Germans from crossing the Tiber into the city. But over the next few months the Pope lost the support of most of the Roman people who, tired of war and unwilling to have their homes destroyed in a fight between the opposing factions, agreed to open the gates. On 21 March 1084, therefore, several regiments of German soldiers marched through the gate of St John, and surrounded the Lateran Palace, where Henry took up residence with his anti-Pope, Clement III, who later crowned him in St Peter's. Gregory, still holding out in Castel Sant' Angelo, refused to submit. And a large proportion of the noble families of Rome and their vassals, including the Corsi and the Pierleoni, continued to support him against the foreign interloper. So, too, did the Normans under Robert Guiscard.

When the mansions of the Corsi and Pierleoni had been stormed and reduced to ruins, and when Septimius Severus's colonnaded Septizonium[10] on the Palatine, which Gregory's nephew, Rusticus, bravely defended, had also been shattered by the German siege machines, the Normans, accompanied by thousands of Saracens from Sicily and gangs of rapacious Calabrian peasants, advanced to Gregory's relief in Castel Sant' Angelo. At news of their approach the Emperor hastily decamped along the Via Flaminia with his outnumbered forces, taking his anti-Pope with him. A week later, the vanguard of Robert Guiscard's forces entered the Flaminian gate and advanced across the Campo Marzio towards Castel Sant' Angelo, brushing aside the resistance of those Romans who still supported the Emperor. Having released the Pope, whom they escorted to the Lateran, they then inaugurated a pillage of the city which was to last for several days.

The Romans, sinking their differences, made repeated attacks upon the common enemy, but their leaders were cut down mercilessly. Those who sought safety in flight were captured and held to ransom, their houses looted and then set on fire. Medieval chroniclers depict a fearful scene of sack and rape, of robbery and murder, of huge areas of the city laid to waste or destroyed by fire. And while due allowance must be made for the woeful exaggeration of such disasters by imaginative monks, the reality was appalling enough. Men, women and children were carried off into captivity and slavery with ropes round their necks; many churches were wrecked and some, like those of the Quattro Coronati, S. Clemente, S. Silvestro and S. Lorenzo in Lucina, were burned to the ground. Whole districts in the most densely populated parts of the city were reduced to rubble, numerous monuments were damaged beyond repair, and if little was plundered this was because previous pillagers had left little which was considered worth the trouble of carrying off.

Pope Gregory, now hated by the Romans who blamed him for the catastrophe, went wearily away with his deliverers. Although he retained his breadth of vision, he never recovered from his ordeal and within a few months, on 25 March 1085, he died at Salerno.

For the whole of the next century, Rome remained intermittently a battleground over which popes fought anti-popes, supporters of the papacy attacked adherents of the Emperor, while both sides hired mercenaries and bribed their rivals' retainers and vassals. Popes were kidnapped, denied admission to the city, like Urban II, driven out of it, as Paschal II was by the Emperor Henry IV, forced to flee from it for their lives, like Gelasius II. And all the time the arguments about the relationship between the temporal and the spiritual power raged unabated,

19. In this early drawing of the city, the Colosseum can be distinguished on the far left, the Pantheon in the centre, Castel Sant' Angelo on the far right and beyond it the Borgo leading to St Peter's.

from time to time changing emphasis, once seeming to be partially resolved by the agreement known as the Concordat of Worms, by which Pope Calixtus II and the Emperor Henry V came to an uneasy compromise over the investiture of bishops and abbots, only to flare up again, intensified and complicated by the eternal concept of Rome as 'queen of all other cities' and 'head of the world', and by the refusal of the Roman people to accept either Pope or Emperor as master of their affairs.

The Romans had been dominated for a long time by the mighty families whose castellated and battlemented mansions, many of them built into and over the city's ancient monuments, towered above the roofs of every *rione*: the Corsi, the Crescenzi and the Pierleoni, the Tuscolani and the Frangipani, the Colonna, the Normanni and the Papareschi, the Tebaldi, the Savelli, the Caetani, the Annibaldi and the Orsini. All of them were rich; many of them claimed descent from the great families of imperial Rome; and several had recently provided or were soon to provide candidates for the papacy. Innocent II, for example, was a Papareschi, Anaclete II a Pierleoni, Clement III an Orsini. Yet these families no longer indisputably controlled the *rioni*. For in Roman society a new force was developing, composed of craftsmen and skilled artisans, now organized into guilds, of entrepreneurs, financiers and traders, of lawyers, lesser clergy and officials employed in the administration of the Church. And it was largely due to the growing influence of such groups as these that in 1143, during the pontificate of the Papareschi Pope, Innocent II, the Roman people rose in revolt, demanding the banishment of all nobles from the city, looting their palaces as well as those of the cardinals, and proclaiming the establishment of a Republic, the restoration of the Senate and the appointment of a head of government known as the *Patricius*. Encouraged by the revolutionary fervour of Arnaldo da Brescia, the austere radical religious reformer who came to Rome soon afterwards, the Senate pursued their demands for the Pope's abdication to the *Patricius* of his temporal power and for his income to be limited to those tithes and gifts which had satisfied the priests of Rome in the distant past.

At the height of the dispute between the Senate and the papacy, Innocent II died. His successor, Celestine II, unable to come to terms with the Republicans, also died within five months. Lucius II, equally unsuccessful, resolved to suppress them by force, launched an attack upon their stronghold on the Capitol, was apparently wounded in this assault by a rock that struck him on the head, and died as his predecessors had done with the argument unresolved. It was now left to Eugenius III, the first Cistercian pope, to attempt to settle the crisis. Denounced by Arnaldo da Brescia as 'a man of blood' whose Curia was 'a den of thieves', and barred from entering St Peter's for his consecration by lines of unyielding Republican Senators, Eugenius was driven out of Rome in February 1145 when he declined to renounce the civil power of the papacy. He fled to Viterbo where he set about collecting troops for the suppression of the Republic. But both sides,

20. The cloister of S. Paolo fuori le Mura, which was begun at the end of the twelfth century and completed in 1214.

exhausted by the struggle, were now prepared to compromise; the Republicans agreed to dismiss the *Patricius*, while the Pope undertook to recognize the Republic.

It was an unsatisfactory compromise which could not last. And the arguments, occasionally breaking into violence, continued for a further forty years, during which time both parties invoked the help of the Germans; and the Emperor, having decided to support the Pope, immediately afterwards resumed the old disputes, while joining with him in denying the demands of the Roman citizens. At last, in 1188 a final solution was achieved by Pope Clement III, who had been born in Rome. He agreed to recognize the city as a commune with rights to declare war and make peace, to appoint Senators and a Prefect. He also undertook to make over a proportion of the papal income for the maintenance of the city walls and the payment of officials. In exchange, the Senators, among whom members of great families rubbed shoulders with those less nobly born, swore loyalty to the Pope, recognized his temporal powers and restored to him the property of the Church which had been seized in the troubles. Thereafter, while the aspirations of the citizens had been largely satisfied, the popes gradually regained and extended the influence which they had enjoyed in the days of Gregory the Great. Under Innocent III and his successor, Honorius III, from 1198 to 1227, the medieval papacy, having for the time being thrown off the claims of the German Empire and become master of its own affairs, was the ultimate spiritual authority in Europe and a force which had to be respected in the continent's political and international affairs. In spite of recurrent moral weakness and almost constant lack of physical force, it was now a dominant force in western Europe.

With stability restored to the city, the popes turned their attention to its material improvement. Church building had not been entirely suspended in the previous troubled century. In its first decades the grandly ornate new churches of Quattro Coronati, S. Clemente,[11] S. Maria in Trastevere,[12] S. Bartolomeo in Isola[13] and S. Crisogno[14] had all been completed, and others had been rebuilt, several of them with tall *campanili* as at S. Maria in Cosmedin. Later, S. Giovanni a Porta Latina[15] and SS. Bonifacio e Alessio[16] had been consecrated; and at the end of the century a large new basilica had been started at S. Lorenzo fuori le Mura. Innocent III, however, was less concerned with ecclesiastical than with secular buildings. He renovated the Lateran Palace; he began the construction of a large fortified mansion for the papacy on the site of the present Vatican;[17] he and his brother, Riccardo, built an immense tower, the Tor de' Conti near the Forum of Nerva, as a fortification for this part of the city,[18] and, as though in extenuation of such a display of pride and extravagance, he commissioned and endowed S. Spirito in Sassia as a hospital and hostel for poor pilgrims across the river in the Borgo between St Peter's and Castel Sant' Angelo.[19]

This part of Rome within the Leonine Wall had by now become as crowded with buildings as the *rioni* on the other bank of the Tiber and contained a large proportion of the city's 35,000 or so inhabitants. Around St Peter's, the magnet of Christianity, were huddled monasteries and lodging-houses, small churches and oratories, the houses of clergy, taverns and hermits' cells, a foundlings' home, an orphanage and a poor-house, a home for penitent prostitutes and all kinds of shops that made the *civitas Leonina* a city in its own right, a community at once part of and separate from Rome, *regina urbium*. Money changers thronged beneath the walls of the basilica, calling the rates of exchange and ringing coins on the tops of their tables. Standing before their booths or crying their wares in the streets were vendors of candles, of souvenirs and bits of relics, of rosaries and icons, of phials of oil and holy water, of strips of linen that had touched the tomb of St Laurence and of dried flowers that had grown near the grave of St Sebastian. Men sold straw for bedding; cobblers repaired the soles of shoes worn into holes by long pilgrimages; fishmongers and fruiterers shouted above the din of the crowds; and booksellers, renting space from the canons, offered their goods for sale within the walls of the basilica where mendicants and would-be guides wandered about in search of the charitable, the curious and the gullible.

Below them the Tiber wound its way beneath the Ponte Sant' Angelo, its banks littered with nets and pots and fishing-baskets, ancient grain mills floating on the surface, water-carriers lowering their buckets at the river's edge. Beyond the river bank, through the gloomy tortuous streets, past the outside staircases of the cramped houses, beneath overhanging balconies and brick arches just high enough to admit the passage of a woman with a bundle on her head, the Romans strolled and pushed and jostled, avoiding as best they could the beasts of burden and the laden porters, stepping over the rubbish and ordure flung upon the earth and the cobblestones, and jumping across the streams of blood and filthy water from the butchers' and tanners' shops which flowed unchecked despite the authorities' ordinances. The houses on either side were constructed of brick and other materials usually plundered from ancient ruins, their roofs sometimes tiled or shingled, more often thatched. Their occupants spent much of the day in the streets, sitting in front of the doors or on the lower steps of the exterior staircases, working at some craft, cooking, washing clothes or talking to each other as though oblivious of the busy yet familiar scene. High above their heads loomed the numerous *campanili* and the burnt-brick fortified towers of the mansions of the rich which could be seen rising as though in threatening menace in every *rione* and clustering together closely on the higher ground of the Esquiline, Caelian and Aventine hills. Near at hand were the markets – the meat market at the Theatre of Marcellus, the fish market at S. Angelo in Pescheria,[20] and the market on the Capitol. And beyond them to the east and north and south, stretched the *disabitato*, that expanse of open land, of fields and vineyards, farms and ruins, scrub and pasture between the built-up areas and the Aurelian Walls. On the inner edge of it, the houses were more spacious, with gardens in which fig trees and vines cast a welcome shade, seeming a world away from the dark, cramped dwellings of the teeming, dirty Trastevere; and in the distance to the west, near the place where the Porta S. Giovanni now stands, were the groups of buildings lying in the shadow of the renovated Lateran.

Many of the monuments of imperial Rome lay crumbling and apparently disregarded, a tempting invitation to foreign princes, bishops and other rich visitors who went about the city, collecting interesting pieces, as the half-brother of King Henry IV of England did in 1430 when he visited Rome as Bishop of Winchester. Other ancient monuments had, however, been preserved by their being made over to churches or private individuals by the popes. In this way, the Triumphal Arch of Septimius Severus, for example, was saved by its being allocated to two proprietors, one of them the Church of SS. Sergio e Bacco, whose priests built beside and over it.[21] Both the Arch of Titus and the Arch of Constantine had been appropriated by the Frangipani family who, confirmed in possession of them, assured them a kind of rough protection by turning them into fortresses. This family also built a series of bristling towers around the Circus Maximus.

Yet, despite the casual manner in which the inhabitants treated a large part of their heritage, no visitor to Rome could be unaware of the influence which the ancient city had had upon the medieval, nor, despite depredation and neglect, how much of imperial Rome remained. A celebrated guidebook, the *Mirabilia*, written in these years by a canon of St Peter's, draws the stranger's attention not only to the Christian treasures of the city but also, with a sense of awe and wonder, to its pagan

93

antiquities. A number of these were displayed outside the Lateran Palace where, beside groups of now unidentifiable classical bronzes, could be seen the equestrian statue of Marcus Aurelius; the head and hand of the colossal image of Constantine placed upon high columns,[22] a bronze tablet upon which was incribed part of a decree by which the Roman people transferred Augustus's imperial authority to Vespasian;[23] the bronze sculpture of a boy picking a thorn from his foot;[24] and the *lupa*, the she-wolf, symbol of early Rome, which had been struck by lightning in 65 B.C. when it stood on the Capitol.[25] Moreover, while most ancient monuments had been pilfered for building materials, and while parts of others, including even statues, had been thrown into the lime kilns, many antiquities had been saved by the Church or the Senate from further damage or appropriation. Trajan's Column, for example, had been preserved by the Senate who decreed that it should 'never be mutilated or destroyed, but should remain as it stands to the honour of the Roman people, as long as the world endures. Anyone daring to injure it shall be punished by death and his property shall fall to the Treasury.' Similarly, the monks of S. Silvestro in Capite,[26] who had acquired the Column of Marcus Aurelius, declared that 'anyone taking the column by force from our convent shall be eternally damned as a spoiler of the Temple, and shall be encompassed by the everlasting anathema. So be it.'

Other monuments, dilapidated and collapsed, had been repaired and re-erected, like the obelisk which is now at the Villa Mattei on the Caelian.[27] This was restored and placed on the Capitol near the Palazzo del Senatore[28] which itself, like the earlier Casa di Crescenzio,[29] was a medieval structure reflecting a deep reverence for classical antiquity. And those responsible for these repairs were proud to inscribe their names, in the manner of their ancient forebears, upon the works for which they had been responsible: on walls and bridges can still be read such inscriptions as that of 1191–3 on the Pons Cestius, 'Benedictus [Benedict Carushomo], Chief Senator of the Illustrious City, restored this almost entirely ruined bridge.'

When Honorius III died in 1227 to be succeeded by Francis of Assisi's friend, Gregory IX, the quarrel with the German Emperor, now Frederick II, over papal authority broke out afresh and was still unresolved on the death of the Emperor in 1250. At the same time, the city of Rome became more aggressive in its demands, particularly its financial demands, upon the papacy. These were most forcefully and successfully expressed after the appointment of the Bolognese Brancaleone di Andalò as a professional and highly paid Senator in 1252. Brancaleone, a tough and resolute personality, as well as subduing the power of the papacy in the city, also succeeded in keeping the meddlesome Roman families in order, demolishing no fewer than 140 of their fortified towers and hanging two pugnacious Annibaldi. But after the death of Brancaleone, whose head was placed in an antique vase and displayed as a valuable relic on a marble pillar on the Capitol until removed by the Church, Rome once again became an intermittent battleground with the Pope's supporters fighting his rivals in the streets, and the controversy over papal supremacy raging more fiercely than ever. And it was not until Charles of Anjou, a grim younger brother of the King of France and since 1283 himself King of Naples and Sicily, came to the protection of the Pope that some sort of order was restored. For the papacy, however, and ultimately for Rome, order was bought at a high price. Once the authority of the French king was established in Rome, Charles, who had had himself appointed Senator, tried to ensure that the popes thereafter elected were either sympathetic to France or, like Innocent V, were actually French. But the consequences of this foreign dominance did not at first become apparent. In 1277 an Italian of noble birth, Giovanni Gaetano Orsini, was elected; and although he was followed by a Frenchman, his subsequent successors, up till Boniface VIII, were all Italian: Honorius IV was a Savelli, Nicholas IV a Masci of Ascoli and Boniface VIII a Caetani of Anagni.

Under these Italian popes the Church increased its wealth, as legal fees and bribes, payments for benefices and offices, tithes and donations poured into Rome, and as pilgrims showered handfuls of money upon the holy shrines. Bankers, innkeepers and traders prospered too, particularly in 1300, which Boniface VIII proclaimed the first Holy Year.

The profits made by the people of Rome that year were incalculable. One visitor 'saw so large a party of pilgrims depart on Christmas Eve that no one could count the numbers. The Romans reckon,' he continued, 'that altogether they have had two millions of men and women. I frequently saw both sexes trodden underfoot, and it was sometimes with difficulty that I escaped the same danger myself.' Day and night the streets were packed with people, lining up to pass through the churches; to see the shrines and the most famous relics; to gaze with reverence upon the handkerchief with which St Veronica wiped the sweat from Christ's face on his way to Calvary and which still bore the image of his features; to throw coins upon the altar of S. Paolo fuori le Mura, where two priests remained constantly on duty with rakes in hand to gather up the scattered offerings; to buy the relics, amulets, mementoes and pictures of saints whose sale brought such profits to the street-vendors of Rome.

Also prospering in these last decades of the thirteenth century were the artists and craftsmen at work in the city, helping to fulfil the ambitions of the popes and their families who hoped to make Rome worthy of her past, a place which would rival and even surpass in beauty Florence and the other cities of Tuscany, while remaining within a conservative tradition that looked warily upon the Gothic innovations in architecture spreading south from beyond the Alps. Numerous churches were completely redecorated at this time. St Peter's, S. Paolo fuori le Mura and S. Maria Maggiore were remodelled and the Lateran Palace and Basilica reconstructed. Splendid tombs and sepulchral monuments were created. Painters, sculptors, jewellers, goldsmiths and workers in mosaics and marble were all kept busy, as clergy and laity alike displayed their taste in extravagant and ostentatious rivalry. Cimabue and Arnolfo di Cambio came down from Florence. Giotto was sent for to work at St Peter's and at the opulent new palace at the Vatican which took the place of the more modest residence built by Innocent III. Artists born or long resident in Rome were fully employed as well. Pietro Cavallini worked at the Lateran and St Peter's, at S. Paolo fuori le Mura, S. Cecilia, S. Giorgio in Velabro and S. Maria in Trastevere. Jacopo Torriti was employed on the mosaics at the Lateran Basilica and at S. Maria Maggiore where he was helped by Filippo Rusuti.

But soon this brief flurry of artistic activity came to an abrupt halt, for the supposed financial and political security of Rome proved to be illusory. Charles of Anjou was dead and the Angevin influence in Rome eliminated. Yet France was still unwilling to accept the claims made for the papacy by Boniface VIII who, repeating those of Innocent III, declared in his bull *Unam Sanctam* that 'if the earthly power err it shall be judged by the spiritual power'. Dispensing excommunication after excommunication to gain obedience to his demands, Boniface enraged the monarchs of the West, and in particular King Philip IV of France. He was about to excommunicate Philip when the French legate in Italy, abetted by the Colonna family whose estates the Pope had appropriated, invaded the papal palace at Anagni and carried him off into captivity. Humiliated and ill treated, Boniface was allowed to return to Rome where he died soon afterwards. He was briefly succeeded by the inadequate Italian, Benedict XI, but in 1305, through the manipulation of the French king, the Frenchman Bertrand de Got became Pope as Clement V and secured a succession of subsequent French popes by creating a majority of French cardinals. Required by his master, Philip, to annul Boniface's bull *Unam Sanctam*, Clement abandoned Rome in 1308 and moved the papal residence to Avignon. For sixty-eight years French popes were to conduct the affairs of the Church from their new centre in the south of France, in what became known as the Babylonian Captivity; and Rome, abandoned also by the artists whose patrons had deserted them, sank once more into anarchy.

SIX

Saints, Tyrants and Anti-Popes

'My longing to see Rome, even now when the city is deserted and a mere shadow of its former self, is scarcely to be believed,' Francesco Petrarch wrote to a friend a few days before Christmas 1334. 'Seneca rejoiced in his fortune at having seen it. And if a Spaniard was capable of these feelings, what do you think I, an Italian, feel? Rome has never had, and never will have an equal.'

Petrarch was then living at Avignon in the household of Cardinal Giovanni Colonna. His father, a Florentine lawyer, had gone to Avignon with the intention of obtaining employment at the papal court and had sent his son to study at the nearby town of Montpellier in the hope that he would follow in the family profession. But Petrarch had little interest in law, and as soon as his father died he gave up his studies to satisfy what he described as 'an unquenchable thirst for literature'. Passionately devoted as he was to the classical Latin poets, his longing to see Rome intensified with the passing years, and in 1337, when he was thirty-three and already a distinguished poet, his ambition was satisfied at last.

Rome was by then, as Petrarch had envisaged, a sad shadow of the city of the Caesars, withered and decayed, 'a rubbish heap of history'. Within weeks of the Curia's departure for Avignon, the Lateran basilica had been destroyed in a raging fire, and ever since then, while rebuilding desultorily continued, the city had been torn by violence. Rome's patrician families, bereft of any master, fought each other in the streets. The Colonna waged war on the Orsini; the Conti and the Savelli, the Frangipani and the Annibaldi joined one side then the other; retainers and mercenaries camped amidst dusty ruins and in the deserted houses of cardinals; and priests, many of them related to the belligerent factions, joined in the quarrels and paraded through the streets with daggers and swords. Lawlessness was unbounded. Houses were invaded and looted by armed bands; pilgrims and travellers were robbed; nuns were violated in their convents. Long lines of flagellants filed through the gates, barefoot, their heads covered in cowls, claiming board and lodging but offering no money, scourging their naked backs, chanting frightening hymns outside churches, throwing themselves weeping, moaning, bleeding before the altars.

Petrarch had been warned what to expect. His patron, Cardinal Colonna, had urged him to go to Rome if only to have a romantic illusion dispelled by dismal reality. Yet, walking through the ruins in the company of various members of the

21. Francesco Petrarch, who was crowned as poet laureate on the Capitol in 1341.

Colonna family who described the city as it had been in the days of their forefathers, Petrarch was profoundly and lastingly impressed. He lamented the decay; he was distressed by the lack of knowledge and even of interest that most Romans had in their heroic past. But he told Cardinal Colonna that he found the city, despite its present neglect, even more beautiful than he had anticipated. He begged the Pope, Benedict XII, to return from Avignon and to help Rome to be recognized once more as the *caput mundi*. He resolved to write an epic poem in the manner of Virgil, extolling one of ancient Rome's most renowned heroes, Scipio Africanus. And he conceived an ambition to be crowned as poet on the Capitol in a ceremony reminiscent of those performed, in the manner of the ancient Greeks, in the time of the emperors.

Three years later, in September 1340, he received the hoped-for invitation to be granted the laurel crown both from the Chancellor of the University of Paris and from the Roman Senate. He did not hesitate in his choice for long. Paris had become Europe's seat of learning; but Rome, though now abandoned, had been the centre of a high culture and a remarkable civilization when the French capital had been a rough riverside settlement. Petrarch went to Rome and on 8 April 1341, in the great hall of the Palace of the Senate on the Capitol, he was summoned by a herald to appear before the people. He delivered an address in Latin, knelt to have the wreath of laurel placed upon his head, then advanced in procession to St Peter's where he laid the crown upon the tomb of the Apostle. Soon afterwards he left Rome but, as though to remind him that even poets laureate are not immune from the trials of ordinary men, he was robbed on the way and obliged to return to the city for an armed escort.

Among those who acclaimed Petrarch that day upon the Capitol was a good-looking young notary, Cola (Niccolò) di Rienzo, as ardent a votary of ancient Rome as Petrarch himself, an enthusiast who was later to boast that he was the natural son of the Holy Roman Emperor, Henry VII, but who was in fact the child of an obscure tavern keeper and a washerwoman. Eloquent, vehement and emotional, Cola was well known in the city as an excitable connoisseur of ancient monuments and inscriptions over which he would declaim with much enthusiasm and some learning. He was a demagogic champion of the people's rights and a vociferous critic of the patrician families in one of whose violent squabbles his brother had been murdered. When, therefore, in 1343 a delegation left Rome for Avignon to request the recently elected Pope, Clement VI, to return and exercise his authority in the unruly city, it was inevitable that Cola, although not yet thirty, should accompany it. Indeed, in Avignon he emerged as the emissaries' leader, impressing the Pope with his vivid and moving account of the plight of Rome and of its people whose lives the aristocrats were making so miserable. Clement declared that he would at least visit Rome as soon as he could, and issued a bull providing for another Holy Year in 1350 and thereafter every half century. Taking personal credit for what he represented as the complete success of the mission, Cola reported

NICOLO DI LORENZO DETTO COLA
DI RENZO, *Tribuno del Popolo Romano.*

22. Cola di Rienzo, the messianic demagogue of the fourteenth century, who tried to restore Rome's greatness in her days of decadence.

his triumph to the Romans in a letter in which *folie de grandeur*, later to be a pronounced characteristic of his unbalanced nature, was already evident.

On his return to Rome, where he proposed that a splendid statue of the Pope should be erected in the Colosseum or on the Capitol, Cola enhanced his reputation as a champion of the people and began to see himself in the role of their deliverer from the thrall of the nobles, and as the instigator of a revolution that would restore to them the glory and the grandeur of the days of ancient Rome. The nobility treated him as a joke rather than a threat, inviting him to dinner and laughing at his grandiloquent talk and his prophesies of nemesis. But when he spoke in public, as he did one day in the Lateran basilica, wearing a kind of toga and a white hat decorated with strange symbols of gold crowns and swords, the populace listened and wondered.

Allegorical scenes depicting shipwrecks, fires and like catastrophes now appeared on the walls of the city. Notices were posted on the doors of churches with such announcements as that which appeared on S. Giorgio in Velabro: 'In a short time the Romans will return to their good ancient government.' Support for Cola among the people and in the guilds grew day by day: it was felt that with the help of his ally, the Pope, he might well destroy the arrogant power of the nobles who were still the unscrupulous masters of the Senate. And in May 1347 Cola was ready to strike.

On the morning of Whit Sunday he left the church of S. Angelo in Pescheria after Mass and, surrounded by his adherents and accompanied by the evidently nervous papal vicar, he marched towards the Capitol to summon a parliament. His head was bare but he was otherwise in full armour. Armed guards had been placed at intervals along the route. The ringing of church bells and the fluttering of banners above the heads of the marchers gave the procession a celebratory rather than a conspiratorial air. At the Capitol, Cola made an inspiring speech, assuring the thousands of people who had gathered there that he was prepared to die out of love for the Pope and for the salvation of the people. A lieutenant then read out a programme of revolutionary reform directed against the nobles. All the edicts were accepted by acclaim; and the powers of a dictator were conferred upon Cola who announced that he would exercise them in conjunction with the Pope's representative. He later bestowed upon himself the title of 'Niccolò, by the authority of our most merciful Lord Jesus Christ, the Severe and Clement, the Tribune of Freedom, of Peace and Justice, and the Illustrious Redeemer of the Holy Roman Republic'.

The sudden and unexpected success of the self-styled Tribune threw the nobles into confusion. At first they condemned the illegal usurpation of authority, Stefano Colonna, commander of the militia, going so far as to declare that he would 'throw the young fool from the windows of the Capitol'. But they did not maintain that attitude for long. A mob appeared in arms before the Colonna palace; its master fled to Palestrina; all other nobles were confined to their estates or fortresses, and then summoned to do homage at the Capitol. Intimidated, they obeyed. The Colonna and Orsini, the Savelli, Annibaldi and Conti joined with the College of

Judges, the notaries and guilds of Rome in swearing loyalty to the new Republic and to its 'Illustrious Redeemer'.

Having enlisted a large military escort of both cavalry and infantry and appointed a personal bodyguard, Cola and his colleagues issued a series of decrees on all kinds of political, judicial and financial matters. Exiles were recalled to Rome; the poor received generous assistance; nobles were ordered to remove the fortifications from their palaces and to take down the coats of arms from their walls. Opponents of the regime were severely punished alongside malefactors, adulterers and gamblers. Corrupt judges were exposed in the pillory with their crimes inscribed on mitres placed upon their heads; a criminal monk was beheaded; so was a recalcitrant noble of the house of Annibaldi. A former Senator, Jacopo Stefaneschi, found guilty of expropriation, was hanged on the Capitol.

Cola was not content, however, with the restoration of a stern though just Republic in Rome. His hazy vision extended to an Italian confederation with Rome as its capital, a national brotherhood of the whole of 'Sacred Italy' which would bring peace and order to the entire world. He sent out envoys with silver wands to all the principal cities and rulers in the peninsula, inviting them to send representatives to a national parliament in Rome. And so strong was the hope for a transformation in the melancholy state of spiritual and political affairs in Italy, so powerful the influence which the very name of Rome still inspired, that Cola's pretensions were taken seriously and in many cases with enthusiasm. Respectful replies were received from Milan and Venice, from Florence and Siena, from Genoa, Lucca, Spoleto and Assisi. Twenty-five cities agreed to send delegations to the parliament in Rome. The Pope sent a silver casket engraved with his own arms as well as with those of Rome and of Rome's new Tribune. From Avignon also came warm encouragement from Petrarch: 'Prudence and courage be with you . . . Everyone must wish Rome good fortune. So just a cause is sure of the approval of God and of the world.'

Cola himself was convinced that he was under the personal protection of the Holy Spirit. His behaviour became increasingly flamboyant. He rode about the city clothed in gold-trimmed silk on a white horse, a banner bearing his assumed coat of arms flying over his head. On the festival of Saints Peter and Paul he rode to St Peter's on a charger, clad for this occasion in green and yellow velvet, carrying a steel sceptre in his hand. Fifty men with spears guarded him. The sword of Justice was borne before him. Blaring trumpets and ringing cymbals announced his approach, while an attendant scattered among the people pieces of gold and coins engraved for the Tribune by Florentine masters. On the steps of St Peter's the clergy greeted him with a rendering of *Veni Creator Spiritus*.

The festival of 1 August, the day chosen for the opening of the national parliament and the celebration of the unity of Italy, was marked by the most extravagant ceremonies. Customarily upon this day the chains of St Peter were displayed to the faithful; but before this solemnity was observed, Cola di Rienzo had himself created a knight in the Lateran, appearing in front of the assembled congregation cleansed by immersion in the ancient green basalt basin in the

Baptistery where the Emperor Constantine was said to have washed away his paganism. The next day, now clothed in scarlet, Cola presented himself to the people as 'Candidate of the Holy Spirit, the Knight Nicholas, the Severe and Clement, the Zealot for Italy, the Friend of the World, the Tribune Augustus'. He announced by decree that the Roman people now held jurisdiction over all other peoples as they had done in the ancient past; that Rome, the foundation of Christendom, was once more the head of the world; that all the cities of Italy were free cities with the rights of Roman citizenship, and that, since he and the Pope were now arbiters of the world, the rival claimants to the Holy Roman Empire must appear before him and a papal representative to have their fates decided. Raising his sword in the air and pointing it dramatically in three directions, he then called out, 'This is mine!' Although not clear as to the exact purport of these words, the populace cheered loudly as a flourish of trumpets brought the proceedings to a close.

Enthusiasm for the Tribune's policies was, however, already waning fast. The Pope, disconcerted by Cola's grandiose claims, expressed regret at his earlier support. The cities of Italy, fearing the loss of their independence, began to reconsider their endorsement of a national brotherhood under so flamboyant and perhaps deranged a leader. Men who had worked with him and had at first been fascinated by his Messianic pronouncements doubted his ability to put his visionary theories into practice. The Roman people regarded their former hero with growing uneasiness, as he had himself crowned with wreaths of plants from the Arch of Constantine and, on the day of the Assumption of the Blessed Virgin Mary, compared himself to the Virgin's son. A monk, who had been among his most fervent admirers and who now broke down and wept, expressed the general disappointment and disillusionment.

Encouraged by the Pope who dispatched a legate to Rome to take proceedings against Cola, the Roman nobles now prepared for revenge. Cola struck first by inviting several of the Colonna and Orsini to a grand banquet on the Capitol, and then arresting them after one of the guests, Stefano Colonna, had made a sardonic reference to the gorgeous attire of their host. But Cola shrank from further punishment. While the populace waited for news of their execution, and the bells in the *campanili* above the prison walls tolled in mournful expectation of their death, Cola pardoned them on condition that they swear loyalty to the laws of the Republic.

On their release the nobles immediately broke their oath and within a month they and the troops they had raised were rampaging throughout the countryside beyond the walls of the city. Inside Rome, the Pope's legate had arrived at the Vatican Palace where he summoned Cola to appear before him. The Pope's anger with the presumptuous Tribune had been inflamed by Cola's recent announcement that the whole of 'Sacred Italy' must reconstitute itself as a new Roman Empire and by his evident ambition to become Emperor himself. Neither the French Pope nor the French cardinals had any wish to see the restoration of the Roman Empire which would threaten the independence of the papacy and might well entail the return of the Curia to Rome from Avignon. The papal legate was consequently enjoined to be uncompromising with Cola.

But Cola was not to be intimidated. He arrived at the Vatican wearing chain-armour and a silver crown. In his hand he carried a sceptre and, to the astonishment of the legate, over his mail he had put on a pearl-embroidered dalmatic such as Emperors wore at their coronation.

'You have sent for me,' he is reported to have announced with haughty curtness. 'What do you want?'

'I have a message from our Lord, the Pope.'

'What message?'

The impatient arrogance of Cola's demeanour so flustered the legate that he apparently lost the power of speech, and stood dumbfounded in the hall. So the Tribune 'contemptuously turned his back and left the palace with a curious smile'. At the foot of the steps he mounted his horse and galloped off to fight the aristocrats.

On the cold morning of 20 November 1347, in torrential rain, the opposing forces advanced upon each other outside the gate of San Lorenzo. Cola's troops, mostly infantry still staunchly loyal to his Republic, were commanded by scions of noble houses who had quarrelled with their families. The aristocrats' army of some four thousand infantry and six hundred horsemen was led by old Stefano Colonna, his sons and grandsons and various members of the Orsini, Caetani and Frangipani families in unaccustomed alliance. The clash was short and vicious. At first it seemed that the aristocrats would triumph as they rushed upon Cola's men, incensed by the deaths of the 20-year-old Giovanni Colonna, whose horse fell into a pit, and of his father who was thrown from his saddle. Cola himself, shivering with fear at the onslaught and at the sight of his banner sinking into the mud, cried out in terror, 'O God! Hast Thou deserted me?' But his men soon rallied, and before long the nobles' forces were in headlong flight. They left behind them no less than eighty once-feared and respected aristocrats whose bodies, stripped naked, lay on the field until the afternoon, to be insulted by the Roman mob.

Cola, his confidence restored, an olive wreath on his head, led his troops in triumph to the Capitol where, with a theatrical gesture, he wiped his clean and naked sword upon his surcoat before returning it to its sheath and addressing his victorious soldiers. The next day he went out with his young son beyond the gate of San Lorenzo and there, with bloody water from the pool where Giovanni Colonna had fallen, he christened him 'Knight Lorenzo of the Victory', obliging his cavalry leaders to dub the boy with their swords.

This heartless act and his craven behaviour on the field of battle lost Cola much of his remaining support. It was said that his character had entirely changed, that he lived in his palace in the greatest luxury, surrounded by wastrels who fawned upon him, flattering his insane vanity, and that he was spending money like water. Certainly he raised taxes to an almost unprecedented height to pay his troops. Yet even this might have been forgiven him for the sake of his past, had not the Pope issued a bull against the Roman people, detailing numerous charges against Cola as a criminal and a heretic, and instructing them to depose him. With the Holy Year so close they dared not offend the Pope and risk losing the profits the pilgrims would bring. And so, bereft of popular support, plagued by terrifying dreams, by fainting fits and giddiness, Cola decided to abdicate. On 15 December 1347 he came down from the Capitol in tears. Some of the people who watched him depart cried too; but no one came forward to prevent his leaving or even to wish him well. Soon afterwards the papal legate made his formal entry into the city, took possession of it in the name of the Church, and announced that the Jubilee of 1350 would take place as planned.

For weeks before this Holy Year began, the roads leading into Rome had been crowded with pilgrims who camped on the verges, importuned by those hundreds of pedlars and tricksters, mendicants and guides, pickpockets, acrobats and musicians who always materialized in Rome when strangers with money appeared. According to Pope Clement VI's biographer, as many as five thousand people entered the city every single day and were lodged and fed there, complaining of the cupidity of the Romans but finding plenty to eat, at a price. The Pope himself remained at Avignon; so whereas the pilgrims of 1300, including the Florentine chronicler, Giovanni Villani and, perhaps, Dante, had been able to receive the papal blessing from Boniface VIII standing in the loggia of the Lateran, those of 1350 had no such gratification. Nor were they able to admire the Lateran itself which was again collapsing in ruins. Indeed, most of the great Christian as well as the imperial monuments of Rome were now in a deplorable condition, neglected, scarred by war, or shattered by earthquake. The Black Death which had ravaged western Europe two years before, and had killed well over half of the inhabitants of Florence, had not taken so dreadful a toll in Rome as in other large cities in Italy, a mercy commemorated by the marble steps leading to the church of S. Maria d'Aracoeli.[1] But the earthquakes of 9 and 10 September 1348 had rocked the city. St Paul's had tumbled in ruins, as had the basilica of the SS. Apostoli.[2] Several towers had collapsed; the gable of the Lateran had crashed to the ground; blocks of masonry had fallen into the arena from the upper floors of the Colosseum. And little of this damage had been repaired. 'The houses are overthrown,' wrote Petrarch, appalled by the state of the city. 'The walls tumble to the ground, the temples fall, the sanctuaries perish . . . The Lateran lies on the ground, and the Mother of all churches stands without a roof and exposed to wind and rain. The holy dwellings of St Peter and St Paul totter, and what was until recently the temple of the Apostles is a shapeless heap of ruins to excite pity in hearts of stone.'

The laws of the city, Petrarch added, were 'trodden underfoot'; and pilgrims took care to go about in groups, for isolated visitors were in constant danger of robbery and even of murder. One cardinal, in a far from uncommon instance, was shot at from a window as he made his way to St Paul's, the arrow piercing his hat, and thereafter he never ventured out without a helmet and a coat of mail under his habit. Once the Jubilee was over the lawlessness became more scandalous than ever. Nobles, employing brigands as household troops, took possession of their *rioni* and ruled them as petty tyrants. The papal vicar was driven out of the city, and any pretence of central government was at an end. A group of citizens, encouraged by the Pope, assembled in S. Maria Maggiore on the day after Christmas 1351 and decided to insist upon the appointment of an elderly and respected Roman as Rector. This man, whose installation was ratified by the Pope, was Giovanni Gerroni. But he had not exercised his wide-ranging powers for long when, beset by conspirators plotting his downfall, he declared himself unequal to his task and left Rome, taking the contents of the public treasury with him. Once more the great families, the Orsini and Colonna prominent among them, took control; once more the populace rose in revolt, driving one Senator, Stefanello Colonna, from the city, and burying another, Berthold Orsini, beneath a heap of stones which were hurled at him as he came down the stairs from the Capitol; and once again a popular leader was elected to save the Republic. But the new dictator, Francesco Baroncelli, was no more effective than Giovanni Gerroni had been. And the Romans began to regret the fall of the Tribune, Cola di Rienzo, who, for all his faults, had once brought order to their lives and a hope, if brief, of renewed glory.

After escaping from Rome, Cola had spent two years high up in the fastnesses of the Abruzzi mountains east of Rome, living as a penitential hermit with an austere and conservative sect of Franciscan anchorites known as the Fraticelli. From the Abruzzi he had wandered further north across the Alps and had made his way to the court of Charles IV, King of Bohemia, whom he had pressed to go to Rome as the city's saviour, undertaking to return there first himself as imperial vicar, in the way that John the Baptist had prepared the way for Christ. Elaborating upon this theme, Cola enjoined King Charles to picture himself being crowned Holy Roman Emperor by the Pope, to envisage Cola as being created Duke of Rome, and to imagine the three of them, Emperor, Pope and Duke, as representing the Holy Trinity on earth. Wary of his strange visitor and his 'fantastic dreams', the King reported Cola's arrival in Prague to the Pope, who instructed the Archbishop of Prague to detain him in the strictest custody. In July 1352 the Archbishop declared that Cola was guilty of heresy and must be handed over to the papal plenipotentiary. The next month Cola arrived in Avignon where, soon afterwards, Pope Clement died.

Clement's successor, Innocent VI, a former professor of civil law at Toulouse, regarded Cola in a more favourable light than his predecessor had done. He thought that his return to Rome, demanded by Petrarch and now also by the Romans themselves, might be used to the Church's advantage. Cola's experience of Roman affairs might well be of assistance to Cardinal Gil Alvarez Carrillo de Albornoz, a Castilian grandee, who had recently been appointed Vicar-General of Italy. Pope Innocent, therefore, ordered Cola's release from prison where he had lain excommunicated and under sentence of death. And so it was that on 1 August 1354 immense crowds thronged the streets of Rome to welcome back their former Tribune. From windows and rooftops decorated with banners and with flowers, he was cheered by excited people as he advanced towards the Capitol.

But Cola was no longer the handsome figure who had left Rome seven years before. Now pale and fat, he had lost his gift of fiery eloquence; his enthusiastic fervour had given way to dreamy introspection, occasionally broken by fits of hysteria in which laughter alternated with uncontrollable tears. Once established in power, he behaved with that tyrannical excess that had characterized his last months as Tribune in 1347, raising money by arbitrary taxes and every other means at his command, even seizing citizens and selling them for the ransoms which could be extorted from their families. Soon not only the nobles but the people, too, were bent upon his downfall.

One morning in October, through the window of his bedroom overlooking the Piazza Mercato, came the shouts of the mob: 'Popolo! Popolo! Death to the traitor who has imposed the taxes!' Finding that the guard and his servants had all fled, Cola hastily put on his armour and the splendid clothes he had worn as Tribune, snatched up the banner of Rome and went out on to the balcony. At first, he tried to address the people but their shouts carried his words away. Then, unfurling the banner, he pointed to the gold letters, Senatus Populusque Romanus. But the shouts grew louder and more insistent: 'Death to the traitor!' Stones were hurled and an arrow pierced his hand. Then the mob set fire to the wooden fortifications surrounding the palace. As the flames took hold, Cola, having hurriedly shaved off his beard, donned an old cloak and blackened his face, rushed down the stairs through the smoke into the courtyard. Shouting 'Death to the traitor!' like the rest, he tried to escape unrecognized in the crowd. But he had forgotten to remove his rings and bracelets, and, catching the glint of these, someone shouted, 'This is the Tribune!' as he grabbed the fugitive by the arm. Cola was dragged towards the bottom of the steps by the statue of the Madonna where Berthold Orsini had been stoned to death, and the crowd fell silent. Cola crossed his arms upon his chest. He was now a pathetic figure, the edges of his magnificent grey silk, gold-trimmed dress clearly visible beneath his tattered cloak, his legs still clad in purple stockings. For a time that seemed so protracted that his medieval biographer described it as a full hour, no one moved against him. Then one of his own former officials came forward with a sword and thrust it through his body. His head was cut off, his body stabbed, and his mangled corpse dragged away to the rione of the Colonna where it was strung up outside a house near the church of S. Marcello.[3] For two days it was left dangling there, to be stoned by street-boys.

Almost every day in these years, sitting by the door of the convent of S. Lorenzo in Panisperna,[4] could be seen a fair-skinned elderly woman begging for the poor and gratefully raising to her lips the offerings that were made to her. The daughter of a Swedish judge and widow of a Swedish nobleman to whom she had borne eight children, Birgitta Godmarsson, foundress of the Brigittines, had felt herself drawn to Rome by a vision in which Christ had appeared before her, commanding her to leave immediately for the city and to remain until she had seen both Pope and Emperor there. As she went upon her spiritual and charitable rounds in Rome from church to crumbling church and hospital to ruinous hospital, she had further visions: both Jesus and His Mother spoke to her, strengthening her faith in the eventual salvation of the city and the return of the Pope to it. Around the house where she lived, in what is now Piazza Farnese, stretched the charred shells of burned-out buildings, piles of rotting refuse, deserted palaces, stagnant swamps, fortresses abandoned by their wealthy owners who had gone to live on their estates in the Campagna, hovels occupied by families on the verge of starvation, churches rendered derelict by the long absence of the Curia. Pilgrims took home with them stories of a gloomy, quiet city whose silence was broken only by the howling of dogs and the occasional shouts of a mob.

In Avignon the popes remained deaf to the calls which the Romans made to them, heedless of the prayers which the saintly Birgitta Godmarsson uttered so fervently and of the letters which Petrarch continued to write into his old age. In 1362, however, Guillaume de Grimoard became the sixth of the Avignon popes as Urban V. Encouraged by Charles IV, now Holy Roman Emperor, who offered to accompany him, he recognized the need to return to Rome, not only for the sake of the neglected and decaying city but also for the papacy itself which was now in danger at Avignon both from the mercenary bands roaming throughout western Europe and from the English who were fighting the French in wars which were to last for a hundred years. Pope Urban also hoped to bring about a reunion of the Eastern and Western Churches and considered that negotiations with the patriarch of Constantinople could be conducted more satisfactorily if he were in Rome. In 1367, therefore, Pope Urban travelled across the Alps, knelt in prayer before the grave of St Peter and took up residence in the stuffy, dismal rooms of the Vatican which had been prepared for him. His visit, though, was brief. He found the city oppressive and even more dilapidated than he had feared. The clergy did not encourage an understanding with Constantinople, and he felt that he could more easily carry on the role of mediator between England and France from Avignon. So, having supervised the removal of the Apostles' heads to the Lateran and seen them enclosed in the silver busts he had ordered as reliquaries, he went back to France in 1370, ignoring St Birgitta's warning that he would die if he abandoned Rome and fulfilling her prophecy by expiring at Avignon within a few months of his return.

Six years later, his successor, Gregory XI, the last of the Avignon popes, fearing that the Church and her estates in Italy would be lost to the papacy for ever were he not to return, made up his mind to take the Curia permanently back to Rome. He was encouraged and strengthened in his decision by a remarkable young woman who was to become patron saint of Italy.

Caterina Benincasa was the youngest of the several children of a dyer from Siena. A spirited, pretty girl, she at first surprised and then dismayed her parents by showing no disposition to marry and by resisting all efforts, including beatings, to change her mind. She insisted upon becoming a Dominican nun, a member of the tertiary order who take simple vows and may continue to live at home. She spent long hours in prayer, experienced a succession of ecstatic raptures and ultimately

23. Pinturicchio's painting of the canonization of St Catherine of Siena, in 1461.

the pain of the stigmata. Her holiness, her asceticism, the long letters and prayers which she dictated, being unable to write, attracted wide attention and a group of faithful followers, the Caterinati, who were to accompany her on her travels. The first of her fateful journeys took her to Avignon where, passionately devoted to the cause of peace within the Church and Italy, and urgently preaching a crusade against the Muslims, she begged Pope Gregory to fulfil his intention of leaving France and returning to Rome. Towards the end of 1376 he made up his mind to follow her advice and the dictates of his own conscience.

Pope Gregory sailed up the Tiber by night and came ashore by St Paul's on the morning of 16 January 1377 to the cheers of the crowd and the sound of trumpets. As recorded on the reliefs decorating his tomb in the church of S. Francesca Romana he was accompanied by numerous cardinals on magnificently caparisoned horses. The artist has depicted him riding beneath a baldacchino with St Catherine by his side and with Rome in the form of Minerva coming forward to meet him. Above the Porta S. Paolo, which is shown as a tottering ruin, the papal chair drifts through the clouds and an angel bears the papal tiara and the keys of St Peter. The scene so charmingly evoked marks, however, not the end of a sad period in the history of Rome, but the beginning of an age of even more bitter discord. For Pope Gregory, though not yet fifty, was already an elderly-looking and dying man. He survived for little more than a year, and his death provoked a papal election of extraordinary animosity.

The Roman people had made it clear, through deputations, addresses and speeches in the various *rioni*, that the next pope must be an Italian and preferably a Roman; and when the cardinals entered the hall of conclave in the Vatican a large crowd shouted menacingly, '*Romano o Italiano lo volemo!*' To protect the cardinals, militiamen had been ordered to surround the Vatican, and the Borgo had been barricaded. As a warning against violence, a block and headsman's axe had been placed in St Peter's; and the treasures of the Church had been removed to Castel Sant' Angelo.

The precautions seemed well justified to the nervous cardinals who were informed before entering the curtained compartments into which the hall had been divided that the building had recently been struck by lightning. It was now invaded by the captains of the *rioni* who reminded the cardinals of the Romans' demands. One cardinal, braver than the others, replied that the conclave must be left undisturbed to reach its own decision. As though provoked by this, the shouts from the mob outside grew louder and more threatening. Meanwhile the floor of the hall splintered as lances were pushed up between the beams from below where firewood and tinder were being piled so that the whole place could be burned down should the voting prove unfavourable.

The first ballot showed a majority in favour of Bartolomeo di Prignano, the Archbishop of Bari, who, although an Italian, was a Neapolitan, a subject of the House of Anjou which still reigned in Naples, and a candidate, therefore, not unacceptable to the French. But a rumour spread abroad that the Roman Cardinal Francesco Tibaldeschi had been chosen. Shouting their congratulations, hundreds of people burst into the conclave to greet their supposed new pope who was persuaded by his fellow-cardinals to act the part to save them all from being hurled out of the windows. And so, while the aged Tibaldeschi sat trembling in the papal chair with mitre and mantle, apprehensively acknowledging the vociferous plaudits of his supporters, the other cardinals escaped to a nearby chapel where the election of the Archbishop of Bari was confirmed. At length Tibaldeschi admitted the imposture, and the uproar in the hall grew more tumultuous than ever. But when it became known that the new pope, who took the title of Urban VI, was at least an Italian if not a Roman, the protests quietened down, and the people grudgingly accepted the election.

The French cardinals, however, did not. Exasperated by Urban, who behaved in so high-handed and yet confused a manner that some of them maintained his elevation had driven him mad, they protested that his election was invalid, since it had been conducted under duress, and declared, on behalf of a majority of the Sacred College, that he was deposed and that Robert, Cardinal of Geneva, was Pope instead. The Great Schism had begun.

The new anti-Pope, the lame and wall-eyed Clement VII, returned to Avignon. The rough and energetic Neapolitan, Urban VI, remained in Rome. And Catherine of Siena, broken-hearted by the division of the Church and by her failure to reform its degenerate clergy, died in April 1380 in Via S. Chiara and was buried in S. Maria sopra Minerva.[5]

One of those who mourned her comforted himself with the thought that she had been spared the sight of the further degradation of Rome and of the Church which, under Urban's successor, another Neapolitan, the clever and avaricious Boniface IX, celebrated a third Jubilee in 1390. A monetary expedient rather than a holy festival, this Jubilee was financed by the dispensation of indulgences on an unprecedented scale and brought to Rome a stream of pilgrims. But the corruption of the Church was no less distressing to them than the sight of the city, now little more than a decayed provincial town. Goats nibbled amongst the weeds of the piazzas and in the overgrown rat-infested ruins of the Campo Marzio; cattle grazed by the altars of roofless churches; robbers lurked in the narrow alleys; at night wolves fought with dogs beneath the walls of St Peter's and, with their paws, dug up corpses in the nearby Campo Santo. 'O God, how pitiable is Rome!' an English visitor lamented. 'Once she was filled with great nobles and palaces, now with huts, thieves, wolves and vermin, with waste places; and the Romans themselves tear each other to pieces.'

Abandoning in despair their attempts to form a strong and stable political state, the Romans allowed the grasping Boniface to assume full control of the city, to turn the Vatican as well as the restored and enlarged Castel Sant' Angelo into a stronghold, to rebuild the Senatorial Palace as a papal fortress, and to appoint his relations and their friends to positions of power and profit. On his death, fear of the King of Naples led to the election of yet another Neapolitan pope, Innocent VII, against whom the Romans roused themselves to revolt in an uprising that ended in humiliating retreat. And after the death of Innocent VII, the election of the Venetian, Gregory XII, who seemed disposed to try to come to terms with the Pope in Avignon, led to the invasion of Rome in 1413 by the King of Naples who was determined not to lose his influence through the ending of the Great Schism.

At about this time a fresh attempt to end the Schism, which was dividing Europe into rival camps, was made by a council of the Church at Pisa. The council's solution was to depose both the Avignon and the Roman pope and to elect in their place the Cretan, Petros Philargos, who took the title of Alexander V. He promptly adjourned the council whose decision was, in any case, not recognized by either of his rivals. There were now three popes instead of two, each of whom excommunicated the others.

A renewed attempt to disentangle the imbroglio was now made by the Emperor Sigismund who summoned another Church council at Constance. By this time a new pope had appeared upon the scene in the unlikely person of Baldassare Cossa, successor of the pope chosen at Pisa, Alexander V, whom he was widely supposed to have murdered. Sensual, unscrupulous and extremely superstitious, Baldassare Cossa, who took the title of Pope John XXIII, came from an old Neapolitan family and had once been a pirate and then a dissolute soldier.

In mutually suspicious alliance with the King of Naples, Pope John established himself in Rome where, in breach of their understanding, the King attacked him on 8 June 1413, driving him out of the city. He fled with his court along the Via Cassia beside which several prelates died of exhaustion and the rest were robbed by their own mercenaries. Yet again, the city behind them was plundered. The Neapolitan soldiers, unchecked by their commander, set fire to houses, looted the sacristy of St Peter's, stabled their horses in the basilica, ransacked sanctuaries and churches, and sat down amidst their loot to drink with prostitutes from consecrated chalices.

Pope John XXIII, who had fled to Florence, went on to the council at Constance where he found himself accused of all manner of crimes, including heresy, simony, tyranny, murder, and the seduction of some two hundred ladies of Bologna. After escaping from Constance in the guise of a soldier of fortune, he was recognized, betrayed and brought back to face the council which deposed both him and the Avignon Pope Benedict XIII and which, once the Germans and English had united with the Italians to keep out the French, elected a new Italian Pope, Martin V.

He came from the Roman house of Colonna which, for all its power over the past three centuries, had not before produced a pope. And he returned to Rome in 1420 under a purple baldacchino, jesters dancing before him, the people shouting their welcome long into the night as they ran through the streets with flaring torches. He was to reign in Rome for over ten years, and was to be succeeded by two other Italian popes of rare qualities, the Venetian Eugenius IV and the Ligurian Nicholas V. There was hope that at last a new age was dawning.

SEVEN

'THE REFUGE OF ALL THE NATIONS'

Patron and advocate of Rome's new age, Nicholas V appeared peculiarly ill suited for his role. Small, pale and withered, he walked with bent shoulders, his black eyes darting nervous glances around him, his large and prominent mouth pursed as though in disapproval. Yet no one doubted his generosity and kindliness, just as all who knew him praised his learning, his determination to reconcile the Church with the secular culture of the burgeoning Renaissance and to make Rome once again worthy of its past as the glory of the ancient world and the focus of Christianity. The son of a Ligurian doctor, he had been forced by poverty to abandon his studies at the University of Bologna and to go to work as a tutor in Florence. Amiable and witty, he had made many friends and impressed them with the breadth of his knowledge. 'What he does not know,' said one of them, his fellow humanist, Aeneas Silvius Piccolomini, 'is outside the range of human understanding.' He had become Pope in 1447.

Both his predecessors, Martin V and Eugenius IV, the austere, dignified and extremely tall son of a rich merchant, had done what they could to restore the ravaged city. Pope Martin had revived the ancient office of Overseer of the Public Thoroughfares with a view to clearing away the rubbish and filth that filled the streets and poisoned the air. He had restored several churches and other public buildings; reconstructed the aqueducts which were in such a ruinous condition that many citizens had no idea what their original purpose had been; and, after rebuilding the Acqua Vergine, he had erected a fountain facing the Piazza dei Crociferi which was to be transformed in the eighteenth century into one of Rome's most celebrated sights, the Trevi Fountain.[1] Pope Martin had also summoned to Rome the great Tuscan master, Masaccio, and had brought from Ostia the relics of St Augustine's mother, St Monica, whose tomb can now be seen in the church of S. Agostino.[2] Yet when Pope Eugenius had returned to Rome in 1443, having been driven from it after quarrelling with his predecessor's family, the Colonna, the city was still in the most parlous condition. S. Maria in Domnica and S. Pancrazio both remained on the verge of collapse; S. Stefano had no roof, and many other churches were in as bad or worse a state. Several lanes in the Borgo were avoided by the prudent citizen because of the ever-present danger of tumbling masonry. The streets, filthy as ever, still resembled those of a country village in which cattle, sheep and goats, driven by their owners in long country capes and knee-boots, wandered from wall to wall.

24. Pope Nicholas V, founder of the Vatican Library, who died in Rome in 1455.

You must have heard of the condition of this city from others, so I will be brief [wrote a visitor, Alberto de' Alberti, in March 1444]. There are many splendid palaces, houses, tombs and temples, and other edifices in infinite number, but all are in ruins. There is much porphyry and marble from ancient buildings, but every day these marbles are destroyed by being burnt for lime in scandalous fashion. What is modern is poor stuff, that is to say, the new buildings; the beauty of Rome lies in what is in ruins. The men of the present day, who call themselves Romans, are very different in bearing and in conduct from the ancient inhabitants. *Breviter loquendo*, they all look like cowherds.

Other visitors wrote of moss-grown statues, of defaced and indecipherable inscriptions, of 'parts within the walls that look like thick woods', caves where forest animals were wont to breed, of hares and deer being caught in the streets, of the daily sight of heads and limbs of men who had been quartered being nailed to doors, placed in cages or impaled on spears.

Eugenius had continued Martin's work of restoration. He had repaired the Hospital of the Holy Spirit, renovated the Lateran Palace, carried out extensive works at Castel Sant' Angelo, restored walls and bridges as well as numerous churches. He had ordered the removal of piles of rubbish and wooden shanties from around the Pantheon, forbade the extraction of masonry from the Colosseum and other ancient monuments under the severest penalties, paved streets, constructed a mint near St Peter's, and commissioned the imposing bronze doors from the Florentine Filarete which are still to be seen in the central portal of the present basilica and which were among the first examples of Renaissance work in Rome.[3]

Yet, despite all the work that his predecessors had done, Nicholas V found that Rome was still for the most part a crumbling, dirty medieval city, bitterly cold in winter when the *tramontana* blew across the frozen marshes, unhealthy in summer and autumn when malaria was rife. The inhabitants, a large proportion of them foreigners and most of the rest born outside the city, numbered now no more than about forty thousand, less than a twentieth of the population in the days of Nero and ten thousand less than the Florence of the Medici. Had it not been for the pilgrims who came to Rome each year and provided the city with its one highly profitable trade, there would have been fewer inhabitants even than this.

The Pope set about his task with characteristic resolution, in accordance with his belief that if the faith of the people was to be strong, they must have visual encouragement, 'majestic buildings, lasting memorials, witnesses to their faith planted on earth as if by the hand of God'. Several more churches were, therefore, repaired, including S. Stefano Rotondo and S. Teodoro.[4] The Senatorial Palace was again rebuilt, as was the Vatican Palace, which thereafter became the principal papal residence. Work also began on a new basilica to replace old St Peter's whose southern wall, now leaning outwards almost five feet from its base, was in danger of collapse. Having consulted Leon Battista Alberti, whom he had known in Florence, Pope Nicholas decided upon a domed basilica with a nave and double aisles, and, disregarding his predecessor's prohibition, had no less than 2,500 wagonloads of materials from the Colosseum carted across the Ponte Sant' Angelo.

By the beginning of 1449 Pope Nicholas considered that the restoration of Rome and the peaceful state of the Church justified his declaring that the year 1450 would be a Universal Jubilee. Plenary indulgences – remission of punishments due for past sins – were to be given to all who came to Rome and paid daily visits over a specified period to the city's four principal churches, St Peter's, St Paul's, the Lateran Basilica and S. Maria Maggiore. Italians had to remain in Rome for fourteen days to qualify; those who came from beyond the Alps for eight. Romans had to make the peregrination of the churches every day for a month.

Tens of thousands of pilgrims consequently made their way to Rome from all over Europe. 'Countless multitudes of Frenchmen, Germans, Spaniards, Portuguese, Greeks, Armenians, Dalmatians and Italians were to be seen hastening to Rome as to the refuge of all the nations of the earth,' wrote one who made the journey. 'They were full of devotion and chanting hymns in their different languages.' Another eyewitness compared the thronging multitudes to a flight of starlings or a swarm of ants. From Danzig (Gdánsk) in Germany alone as many as two thousand men, women and children took the road to the south.

A greater crowd of Christians was never known to hasten to any Jubilee [recorded an enthusiastic chronicler from Brescia]. Kings, dukes, marquesses, counts and knights, people of all ranks in Christendom, daily arrived in such huge crowds in Rome that there were millions in the city. And this continued for the whole year, excepting in the summer on account of the plague which carried off innumerable victims. But almost as soon as the epidemic abated at the beginning of the cold season the influx again began.

All the most popular shrines were crowded to the doors. At all hours of the day hundreds of pilgrims jostled and pushed and craned their necks in the catacombs beneath the church of St Sebastian, in St Peter's, where the Pope, who was frequently seen walking barefoot between the stations, gave his benediction every Sunday, and in those other sacred places where the heads of the Apostles, the handkerchief of St Veronica and the other precious relics of Rome were displayed. There was a special attraction this year, the canonization of St Bernardine of Siena, the Franciscan friar and 'people's preacher'. This took place on Whit Sunday in St Peter's, where a lofty throne was installed for the Pope beneath two hundred wax-lights. Surrounded by fourteen cardinals and twenty-four bishops, all magnificently arrayed in the richest vestments, he carried out the rite with the 'greatest exactness, solemnity and splendour'.

The surge of pilgrims to Rome in 1450 brought immense profits to the Church, enabling the Pope to deposit 100,000 golden florins in the Medici bank alone and to continue confidently with his restoration of the city. Huge sums were also made by numerous Roman citizens, particularly money-changers, apothecaries, inn-keepers and artists who painted pictures of the holy handkerchief and other relics. But the numbers of pilgrims were far too great for the authorities to cope with adequately. The additional food brought into the city from the Papal States proved utterly insufficient for the thousands of mouths to be fed. Millers ran out of grain, bakers out of flour, dealers out of wine and cheese, fruit and salted meat. Prices rose steeply. Many hungry pilgrims were forced to depart before their obligations had been completed. The Florentine pilgrim, Giovanni Rucellai, estimated that there were 1,022 inns in Rome – though a census of 1527 records no more than 236 – but they were soon all full, 'and every house became an inn'.

Pilgrims begged for the love of God to be taken in on payment of a good price, but it was not possible. They had to spend the nights out of doors. Many perished from cold; it was dreadful to see. Still such multitudes thronged together that the city was actually famished. Every Sunday numerous pilgrims left Rome, but by the following Saturday all the houses were again fully occupied. If you wanted to go to St Peter's it was impossible on account of the masses of men that filled the streets. St Paul's, St John Lateran, and S. Maria Maggiore were filled with worshippers. All Rome was filled, so that one could not go through the streets. When the Pope gave his solemn blessing, all spaces in the neighbourhood of St Peter's, even the surrounding vineyards, from which the loggia of the benediction could be seen, were thick with pilgrims, but those who could not see him were more numerous than those who could, and this continued until Christmas.

After Christmas there was a slight lull, but then in Lent the crowds surged in again to such an extent that many of them had to camp out in the vineyards, there being no other sleeping-places left.

In Holy Week the throngs coming from St Peter's or going there were so enormous that they were crossing the bridge over the Tiber until the second or third hour of the night [wrote the contemporary Roman chronicler, Paolo di Benedetto di Cola dello Mastro]. The crowd was here so great that the soldiers of Sant' Angelo, together with other young men – I was often there myself – had frequently to hasten to the spot and separate the masses with sticks in order to prevent serious accidents. At night many of the poor pilgrims were to be seen sleeping beneath the porticoes, while others wandered about in search of missing fathers, sons, or companions; it was pitiful to see them. And this went on until the Feast of the Ascension, when the multitudes of pilgrims again diminished because the plague came to Rome. Many people then died, especially many of these pilgrims; all the hospitals and churches were full of the sick and dying, and they were to be seen in the infected streets falling down like dogs. Of those who with great difficulty, scorched with heat and covered with dust, departed from Rome, a countless number fell a sacrifice to the terrible pestilence, and graves were to be seen all along the roads, even in Tuscany and Lombardy.

After the plague there was another fearful disaster on 19 December when a larger crowd than ever had assembled to see the holy handkerchief and receive the papal benediction. About four o'clock it was announced that, due to the lateness of the hour, the benediction could not be given that day. So all the people hurried away over the Ponte Sant' Angelo which was encumbered with shopkeepers' booths. At the far end of the bridge a number of horses and mules took fright, blocking the passage of the pedestrians. Unaware that the bridge was for the moment impassable, other pilgrims pushed forward on to it, pressing those in front of them into the now struggling mass of bodies, several of whom fell and were trampled underfoot. Soon panic broke out. People were squashed to death or pushed screaming through the booths and over the railings into the river. For a whole hour the confusion continued as people struggled to get off the bridge, while others forced their way on to it to drag away the dead and wounded. Soon over 170 bodies were laid out in the nearby church of SS. Celsoe e Giuliano[5] and a further thirty lay drowned in the Tiber. People who escaped had their clothes torn to pieces.

Some were to be seen running about in their doublets, some in shirts, and others almost naked [a Florentine pilgrim reported to Giovanni de' Medici]. In the terrible confusion all had lost their companions, and the cries of those who sought missing friends were mingled with the wailing of those who mourned for the dead. As night came on, the most heartrending scenes were witnessed in the church of San. Celso which was full of people up to 11 o'clock; one found a father, one a brother, and another a son among the dead. An eyewitness says that men who had gone through the Turkish war had seen no more ghastly sight.

The disaster did, however, have one good outcome: to prevent such accidents in future Pope Nicholas ordered a row of houses in front of the bridge to be cleared away, the demolition of the ruinous Arch of Gratian, Valentinian and Theodosius[6] and the creation of an open space, the Piazza di Ponte Sant' Angelo.

As well as endeavouring to make Rome architecturally worthy of her position as the focus of Christianity, Pope Nicholas tried to make her worthy of it artistically, too. He made it a leading centre for goldsmiths and silversmiths and for tapestry makers, calling upon Renaud de Maincourt to come from Paris and to open a tapestry workshop in the city. He also employed Fra Angelico, the small and saintly friar from Florence who knelt to pray before starting to paint each morning, who was so overcome by emotion when depicting Christ upon the cross that tears poured down his cheeks, and who was so modest and unworldly that when Nicholas asked him to dinner he excused himself from eating meat without the permission of his prior, it never occurring to him that the Pope's authority in the matter might suffice. For Nicholas, Fra Angelico decorated the lovely private chapel in the Vatican as well as the Chapel of the Blessed Sacrament, and painted the altarpiece of the high altar of S. Maria sopra Minerva. He died in Rome in 1455 and was buried in this church.

With works of art came books. Agents were sent all over Europe in pursuit of manuscripts and volumes, and generously rewarded humanist scholars came to Rome to translate and copy ancient texts. At the Pope's desire Homer, Herodotus and Thucydides, Xenophon, Polybius, Ptolemy and Diodorus were all translated into Latin. And at his death this librarian manqué, himself a gifted calligrapher, was able to bequeath over a thousand volumes to the Vatican Library, his own foundation.[7]

In the short pontificate of Pope Nicholas's successor, the Spaniard Alfonso de Borgia who became the first of the Borgia Popes as Calixtus III in 1455, the vigour of artistic and scholarly life in Rome diminished. An elderly, gouty compromise between candidates backed by the Colonna and the Orsini, Calixtus III condemned his predecessor for spending so much money on restoration, works of art and books when he should have been concentrating on a crusade against the Saracens. He himself sold works of art and even pawned his mitre to fight the Turks and raised a pontifical fleet to free various Aegean islands from their control. But most of his time was spent as an invalid in the Vatican, surrounded by relations who passed in and out of his candle-lit bedroom and who invited other Spaniards to come to Rome to share their good fortune. To the undisguised relief of the Romans, exasperated by the invasion of those they called 'the Catalans' and by the Spanish accents and fashions to be seen and heard in the streets, Pope Calixtus died three years after his elevation. So, once again, cardinals from all over Europe converged upon Rome to play their parts in a conclave which was to elect a pope in whom the papacy and Rome, by now indissolubly interwoven, could both take pride.

One of the cardinals making his way to Rome that hot summer of 1458 was Guillaume d'Estouteville, the rich and wily Archbishop of Rouen who, intent upon being elected himself, began promising positions of honour and profit immediately upon his arrival. In the latrines of the Vatican, recognized as the safest places in which to conduct intrigues, his supporters gathered, discussing ways by which their candidate could be assured of the necessary two-thirds majority. Confident as they were at first, it soon became clear that most of the eighteen cardinals present favoured another candidate, the equally ambitious Bishop of Siena, who described in his autobiography the dramatic scenes in the conclave when the time for the second scrutiny drew near, the first vote having proved inconclusive.

The cardinals assembled in the Chapel of St Nicholas where, upon the altar, was the golden cup into which they were to place their slips of paper. The cup was guarded by three cardinals, one of them d'Estouteville who was trembling with excitement. Into the cup, in order of seniority, the cardinals dropped their votes, and when all had done so the cup was emptied. The papers were unfolded and the names read out. D'Estouteville then declared the result. But the Bishop of Siena, who had been prudently making notes of the names as they had been announced, objected that his rival had miscounted the number of votes cast for him. And so he had. But even so the Bishop of Siena had not acquired the sufficient majority; and it was decided that the Sacred College would have to resort to the method known as *per accessum* by which, during discussion, it could be discovered whether or not any of the voters might be prepared to transfer their support to another candidate for the sake of agreement.

'All sat in their places, silent, pale, as though they had been struck senseless,' recalled the Bishop of Siena in his account of the final stages of the conclave. 'No one spoke for some time, no one so much as moved a muscle apart from his eyes which glanced this way, then that. The silence was astonishing.' Suddenly the young Rodrigo Borgia, who had been appointed cardinal (at the age of twenty-five) by his uncle, Calixtus III, stood up to announce, 'I accede to the Bishop of Siena.' But, after this declaration, all fell into silence once more. Two cardinals, afraid to vote in this open manner, hurriedly left the room, 'pleading the calls of nature'.

Then another cardinal rose to announce his support of the Bishop of Siena. Yet even this did not secure the two-thirds majority: one more vote was wanted. Still no one spoke. At length the aged Prospero Colonna unsteadily rose to his feet and 'would have given his voice solemnly [in favour of the Bishop of Siena] but he was seized about the waist [by d'Estouteville] who rebuked him harshly. And when he persisted in his intention d'Estouteville tried to drag him out of the room. Provoked by this indignity, Colonna called out in loud protest, "I also accede to Siena and I make him Pope!"'

In Rome there were rejoicings that night that an Italian had been chosen. 'Everywhere was laughter, joy, voices crying, "Siena! Siena! Oh, fortunate Siena!" ... Bonfires blazed at every crossroads ... Neighbour feasted neighbour. There was not a place where horns and trumpets did not sound, not a quarter of the city that was not alive with public joy. The older men said they had never seen in Rome such popular rejoicings.'

The Pope, who chose the title Pius II, was disappointed only by the Roman mob who had, as custom allowed, ransacked his apartments. Some of the looters, mistaking the name announced from a high window of the palace, had rushed away to the house of the rich Archbishop of Genoa where they were delighted with their plunder. Those who burst into the real Pope's rooms, however, found little of value, though they took away everything they could carry, even the marble statues.

The Pope had been born poor. The son of an impoverished nobleman who farmed his own land beyond the yellow stone walls of the small Tuscan village of Corsignano, he was the eldest of eighteen children. Before his birth, his mother had had a startling dream that she was bringing into the world a baby with a mitre on his head. And since miscreant clerics were made to wear paper mitres while being tortured or executed, since *miterino* ('worthy of a mitre') was rudely applied to those whom such a fate might be expected to befall, his mother naturally feared that her son would come to some disgraceful end. Indeed, although he turned out to be a good child, willing to help his father till the grey and stony soil, and to be a conscientious, though amorous and high-spirited student, it was not until he became Bishop of Trieste that she felt able to place a more favourable interpretation upon her vision. Attractive, clever, witty and eloquent, her son advanced rapidly in the world. Already a diplomat of exceptional persuasiveness when he entered the Church, as well as a renowned orator, poet and conversationalist, he had become a bishop a mere two years after taking holy orders. He had entered the conclave with quiet confidence that he would be elected; and, while prepared to promote the interests and indulge the whims of his friends and family in the manner of so many of his predecessors, he was also determined to become a worthy occupant of his holy office and to bear always in mind the words he had spoken to a friend when he was ordained deacon and accepted that the chastity he confessed to dread must now replace his former licentiousness, 'I do not deny my past. I have been a great wanderer from what is right, but at least I know it and hope that the knowledge has not come too late.'

ÆNEAS SYLVIUS

Obyt Anccia Anno 1564.

Coronat A° 1500 Nat Pont Max.

PICOLOMINEUS, dictus PIUS II

Ut pius Æneas, ut et alter Sylvius esset,
Ductor & Oenotriæ Pastor in urbe fuit.

25. The humanist Pope Pius II (1405–64), who did his best to protect the city's monuments from spoliation.

Steeped as he was in classical literature and moved as he was by beauty in architecture as well as in nature, Pius II had a deep and abiding interest in the antiquities of ancient Rome; and he frequently inspected these remains and described them with enthusiasm. While yet a cardinal he had composed the well-known epigram:

> Oh Rome! Your very ruins are a joy,
> Fallen is your pomp; but it was peerless once!
> Your noble blocks wrench'd from your ancient walls
> Are burn'd for lime by greedy slaves of gain.
> Villains! If such as you may have their way
> Three ages more, Rome's glory will be gone.

He did his best to protect the city's monuments from further spoliation, and in a bull of April 1462 forbade the breaking down of ancient buildings in Rome and in the Campagna even on private property. In his *Commentaries* he describes himself overcome by rage on seeing a man digging up stones from the Appian Way, 'smashing large boulders into small pieces with which to build a house at Genzano'. He reproved the man angrily, and gave orders that the road must never again be plundered in this way. Yet Pius himself was not above pillaging a monument when a building of his own inspiration needed good pieces of stone. Thus marble slabs from the Colosseum and the Forum were used for the steps leading up to the new tribune for the Papal Benediction which the Pope constructed at St Peter's.

These steps and the tribune were one of the few ambitious enterprises which Pope Pius undertook in Rome, for he had in mind a great crusade, and the resources of the Church, even though pilgrims and jubilees were so highly profitable, were severely limited. The Papal States made the Pope a sovereign prince, but they did not produce much revenue; Rome itself produced far less; while the taxes of Church property outside Italy and the first year's revenues, known as annates, which holders of benefices had been required to pay to the papacy since the beginning of the fourteenth century, had been severely reduced by what was known as the Pragmatic Sanction of Bourges. This decree, issued by the French clergy in 1438, upheld the right of the French Church to administer its temporal property independently of the papacy and reduced annates by four fifths. It was not superseded until 1516 when the papacy and the French king agreed to the Concordat of Bologna. Throughout his pontificate, therefore, Pius II had financial worries. The Curia as the repository of the Church's archives, the administrator of her justice, the superintendent of her finances, diplomacy and policies, and Christendom's final court of appeal, was an extremely expensive organization to run, even though there were steady fees and charges to support its organization and officials. The Pope was alone responsible for the payment of the magistrates and the costly administration of Rome which, although there was still a Senator who paraded about the city clothed in crimson gown and brocaded cloak, carrying an ivory sceptre and attended by four servants, His Holiness now ruled monarchically with the help of a Governor.

There were still occasional revolts against this rule. There had been one in 1436 when Pope Eugenius had been forced to flee and to restore order, first through his crafty, cruel, awesome representative, Giovanni Vitelleschi, Bishop of Recanati, and then through the equally worldly and despotic Cardinal Lodovico Scarampo, in whose time various priests found guilty of theft were exposed for several days in a cage in the Campo dei Fiori. The ringleader, a canon, was seated on an ass and, wearing a mitre decorated with figures of devils, was hanged on a tree in the Piazza S. Giovanni; and two of his principal accomplices were burned to death. Again, in the reign of Nicholas V, there had been disturbances when an arrogant citizen, Stefano Porcari, in emulation of Cola di Rienzo, had attempted to overthrow papal rule and establish a Republic; he had been executed together with his brother-in-law, Angelo de Maso, and Angelo's eldest son. And now, in Pius II's time, while the Pope and most members of the Curia were out of Rome, having gone north to a congress at Mantua, Angelo de Maso's two younger sons, Tiburzio and Valeriano, rose up against papal rule and, collecting a gang of three hundred young men, mostly from noble families, rampaged about the city, forcing the intimidated Senator to flee from his palace in the Campo dei Fiori and seek safety in the Vatican. Thereafter citizens were seized and held to ransom; women were violated and then drowned; the houses of supporters of papal rule were ransacked. One of the gang kidnapped and raped a girl on her way to her wedding. This so outraged the citizens that the Governor felt obliged to take strong action. Tiburzio de Maso was induced to quit the city which he left for one of the castles of his relations, the Savelli, 'swaggering like some great prince through the streets', saluting the crowds who had gathered to see him depart.

When Pope Pius returned to Rome, the de Maso brothers, encouraged in their revolt by the Colonna family and the *condottiere* leader, Giacomo Piccinino, were stirring up further trouble. And Pius knew that in order to restore order and firm papal government in the city they would have to be destroyed. Tiburzio, who had made his way back into Rome through a gap in the walls near the Baths of Diocletian, was arrested and, with several of his companions, sentenced to death. The Senator, Cardinal Tebaldo, proposed that men guilty of 'such atrocious crimes' should be tortured before they were executed. But the Pope intervened: death was punishment enough, and priests could accompany the condemned men to the scaffold. He wept from pity when they were hanged.

He was now fifty-five years old. Persistent gout, stone and a constant cough had long since aged him prematurely. His hair was almost white, his small frame bowed and shrunken; and he was quickly roused to anger, though the outbursts were soon controlled. He worked as hard as ever, rising at daybreak and saying or hearing Mass before attending to his papers. Audiences and interviews with cardinals and officials of the Curia occupied his time before a scanty midday meal followed by a brief siesta. Dictation, literary work and more audiences took up the afternoon until supper-time. Before going to bed he said the remainder of his office, and when in bed he called his secretaries for further dictation before five or six hours' sleep.

Preoccupied with the threat to Christendom from the Turks – who had captured Constantinople in 1453, pushed their frontiers as far as the Danube, and in 1480 were to establish a bridgehead in southern Italy by capturing Otranto – Pope Pius had been bitterly disappointed by the failure of the Congress he had called at Mantua to discuss a great crusade. He had returned to Rome and, standing on the steps of St Peter's, had displayed pieces of the skull of the Apostle Andrew to the assembled multitude as he vowed to deliver the Christian world from its enemies. In the summer of 1464, racked with gout and fever, he had set out for Ancona where the forces of Christendom were to assemble for a Holy War. But once again his hopes were not to be realized. When he arrived at Ancona there were only two ships in the harbour; and by the time a few others sailed down the Adriatic from Venice he had but a few hours left to live. No sooner was he dead than the Venetian galleys set sail for home; and the cardinals, thankful to be spared the discomfort of a crusade, returned to Rome to elect his successor.

EIGHT

RENAISSANCE AND DECADENCE

Sitting in the loggia of his new palace overlooking the Via Lata the Pope watched the races that were one of the highlights of the Roman carnival. From the palace to the Arch of Domitian, first Jews raced against each other, then there were races between young Christians, between middle-aged men, old men, asses and buffaloes, and at last the eagerly awaited contest of the *barberi*, the riderless Arab horses, tightly swaddled in white cloth and with nail-encrusted saddles to make them run 'like mad creatures'. They came thundering past to be halted in mid-gallop by an immense white sheet hung across the street. The crowds, dressed in all manner of fantastic costumes as nymphs and gods, heroes and fairies, paraded up and down beneath the decorated buildings from which foliage and garlands, ribbons and flowers dropped down towards the rows of benches and daises. At the end of the day, the Pope entertained the citizens at tables spread with delicious food in front of his palace, and then from his windows cast handfuls of money to the crowds who were permitted to finish the remains of the banquet.

The palace stood next to the Basilica di San Marco,[1] which the Pope had carefully restored. Known in his day as the Palazzo San Marco, some of its windows can still be seen in the façade of the Palazzo Venezia into which the smaller palace eventually developed.[2] Having moved into the palace in 1466, the Pope had decided that the carnival should be held near by in the Via Lata instead of on the Capitol or Monte Testaccio; and so Rome's principal thoroughfare, the Corso, which takes its name from the carnival races or *corse*, came into being.

The Pope, who had assumed the title of Paul II on his election as Pius II's successor in 1464, was a charming and open-handed Venetian, vain and sensual. Devoted to pleasure and to spectacle, he was also possessed of a strong and resolute will. He revised the statutes of Rome and took forceful action against the *brigosi*, those who fought in the merciless family vendettas which were still the scourge of Rome as of so many other Italian cities, depriving them of civil rights and even pulling their houses down. And although widely blamed by the stricter clergy for imparting a pagan nature to the festivities of the carnival, he acted firmly against the Roman Academy, a semi-secret society founded to revive classical ideals and the celebration of old Roman rites, and to promote antiquarian and archaeological pursuits. He had its members, including its founder, Julius Pomponius Laetus, arrested on various charges and one of their number, Bartolomeo Platina, was put to the torture.

Yet Paul II, himself a Christian humanist, was a patron of scholars as well as an insatiable collector of objects of art, of jewels, intaglios, cameos, vases, cups inlaid with precious stones, of gold and silver plate and those tapestries and brocades with which the Palazzo San Marco was filled. His extravagance, harshly condemned by some of his contemporaries, was later to be seen as a relatively harmless foible when compared with the nepotism of his successor, Sixtus IV, who, in his efforts to promote the interests of his family, embroiled the papacy in the tangles of Italian politics.

A large, ambitious, gruff and toothless man with a huge head, a flattened nose and intimidating expression, Francesco della Rovere had been born into an impoverished fishing community in Liguria. He had been unremitting in granting offices, money and profitable lordships in the Papal States ever since it had been in his power to do so. Six of his young relations, nephews or illegitimate sons, were made cardinals. These included Pietro Riario, who, having been appointed Bishop of Treviso, Patriarch of Constantinople and Archbishop of both Florence and Seville as well as Mende, died before he was thirty, worn out by excess and heavily in debt, having squandered 200,000 gold florins in his short life as cardinal. His cousin, Giuliano della Rovere, the 28-year-old Bishop of Carpentras, was also appointed a cardinal, as was the son of the Pope's niece, Raffaele Riario, though he was only seventeen. Giuliano's nephew, Lionardo della Rovere, was made Prefect of Rome, while Pietro Riario's brother, the fat, noisy and vulgar Girolamo Riario, was granted the lordship of Imola, a small town between Bologna and Forlì, for the purchase of which a loan was requested from the Medici bank.

This request led to a serious quarrel with the Medici, since the head of the bank and of the Florentine state, Lorenzo de' Medici, was anxious himself to purchase the strategically placed town of Imola and determined at all costs to keep it out of the hands of the Pope. He accordingly made excuses for not granting the loan; so the Pope turned to the Medici's leading rivals as Florentine bankers in Rome, the Pazzi, who eagerly took the opportunity of obtaining the valuable Curial account. Encouraged by this coup, Francesco de' Pazzi, the young manager of his family's bank in Rome, conceived a plan for taking over from the Medici as rulers in Florence. In this he sought the help of Girolamo Riario, whose ambitions were far from satisfied by the lordship of Imola, and of a *condottiere*, Gian Battista Montesecco, who had worked for the papacy in the past. Montesecco promised help, provided he could be assured by the Pope himself that the enterprise had papal blessing. It was agreed, therefore, that he should be granted an audience. He was accompanied to the Vatican by Girolamo Riario and by Francesco Salviati, the disgruntled Archbishop of Pisa who had been denied access to Tuscany, being unacceptable to Lorenzo de' Medici.

'This matter, Holy Father, may turn out ill without the death of Lorenzo and [his brother] Giuliano, and perhaps of others,' Montesecco said, according to his own account of the subsequent conversation.

'I do not wish the death of anyone on any account, since it does not accord with our office to consent to such a thing. Though Lorenzo is a villain, and behaves ill towards us, yet we do not on any account desire his death, but only a change in the government.'

'All that we can do shall be done to see that Lorenzo does not die,' Girolamo said. 'But should he die, will Your Holiness pardon him who did it?'

'You are an oaf. I tell you I do not want anyone killed, just a change in the government. And I repeat to you, Gian Battista, that I strongly desire this change and that Lorenzo, who is a villain and a *furfante* [scoundrel], does not esteem us. Once he is out of Florence we could do whatever we like with the Republic and that would be very pleasing to us.'

'Your Holiness speaks true. Be content, therefore, to let us do everything possible to bring this about.'

'Go, and do what seems best to you, provided there be no killing.'

'Holy Father, are you content that we steer this ship? And that we will steer it well?' Salviati asked.

'I am content.'

The Pope rose, assured them of 'every assistance by way of men-at-arms or otherwise as might be necessary', then dismissed them.

The three men left the room, convinced as they had been when they entered it that they would have to kill both Lorenzo and Giuliano if their plan was to succeed, and that the Pope, despite all that he had said to the contrary, would condone murder if murder were necessary.

Murder, indeed, was committed, though not condoned by the Pope. The assassination took place on Sunday 26 April 1478 during Mass in the Cathedral in Florence. Giuliano de' Medici was slashed to death before the High Altar, but his brother, Lorenzo, escaped with a wound in the neck. The Florentine people, rallying to the family's help, sought out the murderers and, having stripped Francesco de' Pazzi naked, hanged him at the end of a long rope from the machicolation of the Palazzo della Signoria.

The Florentines' fierce reprisals after the failure of the conspiracy aroused intense anger in Rome where Girolamo Riario, at the head of three hundred halberdiers, stormed off to arrest the Florentine ambassador and would have cast him into the dungeons of Sant' Angelo had not the Venetian and Milanese ambassadors protested against this violation of diplomatic immunity. Riario's uncle, the Pope, ordered the arrest of all Florentine bankers and merchants in Rome, though he felt obliged to release them when reminded that his great-nephew, Cardinal Raffaele Riario, a student at the University of Pisa, was then on a visit to Florence where, though not involved in the plot, he had been thrown into prison and threatened with hanging.

Having excommunicated 'that son of iniquity and foster-child of perdition, Lorenzo de' Medici, and those other citizens of Florence, his accomplices and abettors', the Pope declared war upon them and persuaded the King of Naples as well as Siena and Lucca to do the same. On this occasion conflict was averted by Lorenzo de' Medici's astute diplomacy. But the Pope's attempts to involve Italy in quarrels that might be turned to the advantage of his greedy family later did result in wars; and Count Riario's quarrel with the Colonna and his involvement with the Orsini led once more to fighting in Rome between these two rumbustious families.

Yet, for all his persistent nepotism and its expensive and bloody consequences, Sixtus IV was a great benefactor to Rome and to the Roman people to whom in 1471 he 'restored' the ancient bronzes which had stood outside the Lateran for generations and are now in the Capitoline Museum. Indirectly, the Pope could also take credit for that most splendidly majestic of all Rome's palaces, the Palazzo della Cancelleria, which was built by his nephew, Raffaele Riario, with the vast profits of a single night's gambling.[3] Largely by means of the heavy taxation of foreign churches and the sale of ecclesiastical offices, Pope Sixtus himself was able to carry out numerous public works. Streets were paved and widened, including the Via Papalis, the Via dei Coronari and the Via dei Pellegrini. More churches were rebuilt, notably SS. Nereo e Achilleo,[4] S. Maria del Popolo[5] and S. Maria della Pace;[6] a foundling hospital was established; and in preparation for the Holy Year, 1475, the Pope laid the foundation stone of the Ponte Sisto,[7] standing up in a boat as he dropped some gold coins into the water. Pope Sixtus's finest bequest to Rome, however, is the Sistine Chapel which was built for him by Giovannino de' Dolci and decorated by some of the most gifted artists of his time, including Botticelli and Ghirlandaio, Pinturicchio, Signorelli and Perugino.[8]

Patron of letters as well as of art and architecture, Pope Sixtus reformed the University of Rome, the Sapienza.[9] A 'Universal School' for the study of law and the liberal arts had been founded by Charles of Anjou in 1265, and Thomas Aquinas, summoned to Rome by Urban IV, had taught here for a time. But he, like others before and after him, had found that the Romans – men of a legal turn of mind and of practical inclinations – were not drawn to scholasticism and the abstractions of philosophy. He had felt more at home in Paris, as the medieval theologian, St Bonaventure had also done. Rome's 'Universal School', accordingly, had not thrived; and the Sapienza, founded by Boniface VIII in 1303, had fared little better. The university, as re-established by Eugenius IV and reformed by Sixtus IV, proved more lasting, however, although on more than one occasion the professors' pay was stopped when the demands of the Pope's soldiers seemed more pressing. One of these professors was Julius Pomponius Laetus, founder of the Roman Academy and now restored to papal favour, who continued with his work in collecting ancient Roman inscriptions.

Meanwhile, the Pope himself was collecting books and manuscripts to add to the Vatican Library. He constructed a new building in which these books could be housed and studied by scholars, and, from Melozzo da Forlì, he commissioned a picture of himself in it with his librarian, Bartolomeo Platina, the member of the Roman Academy who had been tortured in the time of Paul II. Also in the picture, almost it seems as a matter of course, are three of his nephews, Girolamo Riario and Giovanni and Giuliano della Rovere.

The Pope was still obsessed by the fortunes of these young men in whose interests he had quarrelled with several Italian states other than Florence. In 1483 he had gone so far as to place Venice under interdict; and when he heard that the

TEMPLA DOMVM EXPOSITIS:VICOS FORA MOENIA PONTES:
VIRGINEAM TRIVII QVOD REPARARIS AQVAM.
PRISCA LICET NAVTIS STATVAS DARE COMMODA PORTVS:
ET VATICANVM CINGERE SIXTE IVGVM:
PLVS TAMEN VRBS DEBET:NAM QVAE SQVALORE LATEBAT:
CERNITVR IN CELEBRI BIBLIOTHECA LOCO.

26. The creator of the Sistine Chapel, Pope Sixtus IV, who laid the foundation stone of the Ponte
Sisto in preparation for the Holy Year 1475. Melozzo da Forlì's fresco shows him at the inauguration
of the Vatican Library with three of his nephews and his librarian, Bartolomeo Platina.

Venetians had done well out of the war which he had hoped would profit his family he was so angry that at first he could not speak. Then he burst out furiously that he would never countenance such terms. The next day he collapsed and within a few hours was dead.

The Romans' immediate reaction was one of rejoicing that the power of the Pope's avaricious relations was at an end. The mob ransacked the Riario palace[10] and, for good measure, plundered the granaries and broke into the banks of the Genoese money-lenders. Girolamo Riario marched south to salvage the possessions and authority of the family. But the Colonna mustered their forces to prevent him, and Florence and Siena both offered the Colonna their support. As barricades were erected in the streets and the citizens were mustered on the Capitol, civil war appeared inevitable. The speedy election of a new Pope, the genial, easy-going and unexceptionable Innocent VIII, delayed the outbreak of violence but could not prevent it. One of Lorenzo de' Medici's agents referred to Innocent as 'the Rabbit' and there was something undeniably *conigliese* about the slant of his doleful eyes and his unassertive manner. Strongly supported in the election by the late Pope's nephew, Giuliano della Rovere, under whose influence he remained, he was also said to be the tool of Lorenzo de' Medici whose daughter, Maddalena, was married to one of the several sons of the Pope, who complacently acknowledged them as his own.

Whether or not prompted by advisers, Innocent's policies, often unscrupulous, were almost invariably unsuccessful; and during his pontificate Rome relapsed into the kind of anarchy that had been all too familiar a century before. Armed gangs roamed through the city at night, and in the mornings the bodies of men who had been stabbed lay dead and dying in the streets; pilgrims and even ambassadors were robbed outside the gates; the palaces of rival cardinals became fortified strongholds with crossbowmen and even artillery at the windows and on the castellated roofs. Justice became a commodity to sell like any other. A man who had murdered his two daughters was permitted to buy his liberty for 800 ducats. Other murderers purchased pardons from the Curia and safe conducts which allowed them to walk the streets with armed guards to protect themselves from avengers. The Vice-Chamberlain, when asked why malefactors were not punished, answered with a smile in the hearing of the historian, Infessura, 'Rather than the death of a sinner, God wills that he should live – and pay.'

As Innocent lay dying, unable to take any nourishment other than women's milk, the Sacred College discussed the choice of a suitable successor. No scholar was needed now, still less a saint, but a man who could bring order to Rome, who could protect the Papal States against their rivals and enemies, who was, in short, a capable administrator and diplomat, a man of strong personality rather than of moral worth. And, at a cost, such a man was found. In the early morning of 11 August 1492 the window of the Hall of Conclave was opened, the Cross appeared from it and the election of Rodrigo Borgia of Valencia as Pope Alexander VI was announced.

27. The Borgia Pope, Alexander VI (1431–1503), depicted praying to the Risen Christ, a detail of Pinturicchio's 'Resurrection', in the Borgia Apartment of the Vatican.

28. In this detail from his 'The Disputation of St Catherine of Alexandria', in the Hall of the Saints in the Borgia Apartment, Pinturiccio probably used Pope Alexander's beloved daughter, Lucrezia, as a model.

Pope Alexander had lived in Rome for several years in the palace now known as the Palazzo Sforza-Cesarini[11] where, to celebrate the arrival in Rome of the skull of St Andrew, tapestries had been draped from the windows and objects of art from the Borgia collections had been displayed in the loggia. It was known that Rodrigo Borgia was extremely rich, having inherited fortunes from both his brother and his uncle, Pope Calixtus III, and having acquired the revenues of various convents in Spain and Italy as well as those of three bishoprics. It was also known that he had numerous mistresses and at least six illegitimate sons, three of them by Vanozza Cattanei who was also the mother of his beloved daughter, Lucrezia, and by now a respected and respectable woman. Yet Pope Alexander was not considered particularly corrupt or vicious in an age in which, as the Florentine statesman, Francesco Guicciardini, put it, 'the goodness of a pontiff [was] commended when it [did] not surpass the wickedness of other men'. Charming, energetic, unabashedly enthusiastic in his pursuit of pleasure, he soon induced women to overlook the plainness of his features and the ungainliness of his corpulent body. Women and men alike were impressed by his intellect. 'He is of aspiring mind,' a contemporary wrote of him, 'of ready and vigorous speech, of crafty nature but above all of admirable intellect where action is concerned.'

Certainly the Roman people greeted his election with enthusiasm, believing his tastes and the joviality of his nature augured well for them. He was borne through the streets to the sound of cheers and trumpets to the Lateran where, the excitement proving too much for him, he fell fainting into the arms of Cardinal Riario. At first the enthusiasm seemed justified: the Pope was not as generous with his money as the Romans had hoped, but flagrant abuses in the administration of justice were ended, prices in the markets became more reasonable and stable and the streets, in which murders had been commonplace, were no longer splashed nightly with blood. Yet men looking to the future had cause to fear that the Pope's passionate devotion to his children and, in particular, his determination to advance the interests of his son, the sinisterly beguiling Cesare, might have dreadful consequences.

On the day of his father's coronation Cesare, then aged twenty-seven, was appointed Archbishop of Valencia. Soon afterwards, though his interests were exclusively secular, he became a cardinal. Thus was launched a notorious career which was to take Cesare, through bribery, aggression and murder, to the Dukedom of the Romagna and the command of the armies of the Church. Pope Alexander's ambitions for his son, however, were threatened in the early stages of this career by the equally insistent aspirations of the unprepossessing but romantic and adventurous King Charles VIII of France. In 1494 Charles announced his claim to the Kingdom of Naples as inheritor of the rights of the House of Anjou, and in September led his huge and lumbering army across the Alps and down into Lombardy.

As the French approached Rome, having occupied Florence, the Pope was forced to realize that his refusal to allow them free passage through papal territory would

29. A view of Castel Sant' Angelo by Piranesi.

be ignored. For the first time in his life he seemed utterly irresolute. He called in Neapolitan troops only to dismiss them; he brought his valuables, together with arms and ammunition, to Castel Sant' Angelo, yet at the same time considered flight. He repeated his refusal to allow the French free passage, then rescinded it.

The vanguard of King Charles's army entered Rome at about three o'clock in the afternoon of the last day of December 1494. The last troops did not pass through the Porta del Popolo until long after darkness had fallen. By flickering torchlight and the gleam of lanterns, the men and horses marched through the narrow streets, Swiss and German infantry in brightly coloured uniforms, carrying broadswords and long lances, Gascon archers, French knights, artillerymen with bronze cannon and culverins, and, surrounded by his bodyguard, the King himself, a short, ugly young man with a huge hooked nose and thick fleshy lips, constantly open. He dismounted at the Palazzo S. Marco from which Lorenzo Cibò, Archbishop of Benevento, hurried forth to meet him and to conduct him inside. He entered the dining-room and sat by the fire in his slippers while a servant

combed his hair and the wispy, scattered strands of his reddish beard. Food was placed upon a table; a chamberlain tasted every dish before the King ate, the remains being thrown into a silver ewer; four physicians likewise tested the wine into which the chamberlain dangled a unicorn's horn on a golden chain before His Majesty raised it to his lips.

During the next few days, while the King visited the churches of Rome, while the Pope took shelter in Castel Sant' Angelo, and while three of his cardinals entered into negotiations with a French delegation, the occupying forces wreaked havoc in the city. Houses were occupied; banks attacked; palaces, including that of Vanozza Cattanei in the Piazza Branca, were ransacked. At length a treaty was concluded, and on 28 January 1495 Charles left Rome, having recognized Alexander as Pope but established himself for the moment as master of the Pope's domains. He was soon master, too, of Naples; and although a Holy League of Italian states was formed to expel him from the peninsula, when the mercenary troops of the League engaged him in battle on his homeward journey by the banks of the River Taro, they were unable to prevent his withdrawal with his plunder to France. Since he was left in possession of the field and had captured the French baggage train – which included a piece of the Holy Cross, a sacred thorn, a limb of St Denis, the Blessed Virgin's vest and a book depicting naked women 'painted at various times and places . . . sketches of intercourse and lasciviousness in each city' – the Italian commander, the Marquis of Mantua, claimed the victory. But the French army, though battered and weary, was still a powerful force. Accompanied by mules – one to every two men – loaded with treasure, it moved north towards the Alps and reached France in safety. The Italians were shocked by the realization that for all their virtues, talents, wealth, past glory and experience, they had been unable to withstand the ruthless men from the north, just as Pope Alexander, so proud of his stamina and prone to comparing his strength to that of the bull in his family's coat of arms, had been unable to withstand the shock of meeting the French King. Recognizing the power of France in the little, short-sighted figure who limped towards him, his head and hands twitching, Alexander had fallen fainting to the ground.

As though to exacerbate the humiliations which the city and Italy had undergone, the Roman people had now to contend with other adversities. Syphilis, probably brought to Europe in 1494 either from Africa or the West Indies, or from America by Christopher Columbus's sailors, was spreading fast. French soldiers had contracted it in Naples, and called it the Neapolitan disease; Italians referred to it as the *morbo gallico*. In Rome it was so virulent that seventeen members of the Pope's family and court, including Cesare Borgia, had to be treated for it within a period of two months. With venereal disease came the worst inundation that the city had known for many years. In December 1495 the waters of the Tiber gushed through the streets, surging into churches and swirling round the walls of palaces that collapsed into the flood. A number of people were drowned, including the prisoners in the Tor di Nona.[12] The cost of the damage was incalculable.

The disaster was ascribed to the hand of God and interpreted as a punishment for the follies and corruption against which the ascetic and fervent Dominican friar, Girolamo Savonarola, was preaching so vehemently in Florence. Warning of even worse disasters to come, he condemned the Church as a satanic institution for the promotion of whoredom and vice, speaking of visions of plague and tempests, famine and catastrophe, and of a black cross, rising from Rome, inscribed with the words, 'The Cross of God's Anger'. The Pope forbade Savonarola to preach, then, when he persisted, offered him a cardinal's hat, which was refused with the words that another sort of red hat would suit him better, 'one red with blood'. Finally the Pope excommunicated him. But the attacks continued until the Florentines themselves took action against the inconvenient fanatic and had him tortured, hanged and burned.

Thereafter, the corruption of the Pope and of most of the cardinals, who owed their elevation to him, became more outrageous than ever. 'The Pope is seventy years old,' wrote Paolo Capello in September 1500. 'He grows younger every day; his cares do not last a night; he is of cheerful temperament and does only what he likes; his sole thought is for the aggrandizement of his children; he troubles about nothing else.' His adored daughter, Lucrezia, who was married to Alfonso of the proud house of Este, was entrusted with the care of the Vatican Palace and with papal affairs and correspondence while her father was absent. His son, Cesare, was indulged in every whim, granted titles and immense sums of money which were raised by the sale of offices, including cardinalates, to his relations and to such intimate friends as Adriano Castellesi da Corneto who built the fine palace in the Borgo later to be called the Palazzo Giraud-Torlonia.[13] No favour was denied Cesare whose word became law in Rome: those who stood in his way were strangled, poisoned, thrown into the Tiber or into the dungeons of Castel Sant' Angelo, or, as in the case of a daring lampoonist, punished by the loss of a hand and his tongue, which were nailed together.

When Cesare's brother, Giovanni, who had been created Duke of Gandia, Prince of Tricario, Count of Claromonte Lauria and Carinola, and Duke of Benevento, disappeared in Rome, Cesare was immediately suspected of having killed him. A charcoal-dealer who lived beside the Ripetta[14] was seized and questioned.

About one o'clock [he said], I saw two men come from the street on the left of the Slavonian Hospital to the Tiber, close to the fountain where people throw rubbish into the river. They looked round and then returned. Soon after two more appeared, looked round likewise and made a sign. Then came a man on a white horse, a dead body behind him, whose head and arms hung on one side, his feet on the other. He rode to the spot indicated, when his attendants with all their might threw the corpse into the river. The horseman asked: 'Have you thrown him well in?' They replied, 'Yes, sir.' He looked into the river, and the attendants, seeing the cloak of the dead floating on the surface, threw stones to make it sink.

Questioned as to why he had not informed the authorities, the charcoal-dealer replied, 'In my time I have probably seen a hundred corpses thrown into the river at night and no one has ever troubled about them.'

The river was dragged by scores of fishermen and the body pulled ashore. The wrists were tied together and there was a deep wound in the neck as well as others in the head and thighs. The Pope was overwhelmed with grief. 'I know the murderer,' he declared, weeping in his room. 'Had I seven papacies, I would relinquish them all for the life of my son.' Announcing that he would henceforth think only of the reform of the Church, he appointed a commission of six cardinals to make recommendations towards that end. But when they did so, the Pope decided that nothing could be done which might diminish papal authority, and the inquiries into the murder were soon quietly dropped. The Duke of Gandia's precious furniture and jewels were consigned to Cesare's trust for the dead man's little heir.

Cesare Borgia may or may not have murdered his brother, but he certainly killed his brother-in-law, the Duke of Bisceglie, second husband of his sister, Lucrezia, for whom he had a more profitable marriage in mind. The Duke was stabbed on the steps of St Peter's on his way home from the Vatican, then strangled in his bed where he lay recovering from the wound. This was in September 1500, another Holy Year.

The pilgrims who came to Rome that year had no need to be told the stories with which this murder was embellished, nor those that surrounded the death of the Duke of Gandia and the stabbing by Cesare Borgia of the Pope's chamberlain whose blood was spattered in his master's face, to realize how right Savonarola had been to call Rome the 'sink of iniquity'. Everywhere the evidence was there for them to see. Cardinals flaunted their riches in the piazza as openly as in their palaces, where banquets were held of a richness that would have been regarded extraordinary even on the tables of Lucullus. The Pope's daughter, gorgeously dressed and surrounded by scores of other women as flamboyant as herself, rode her bejewelled horse through the streets to the Vatican. The Pope's son, on the festival of S. Giovanni, sat on horseback on the steps of St Peter's, hurling lances at bulls, which had been collected for the purpose within a wooden enclosure, before advancing to one of the animals whose head he severed at a single stroke. The corpse of the physician to the Hospital of the Lateran – whose practice it had long been to shoot passers-by with arrows at dawn before robbing them, and to poison rich patients whose wealth had become known to the hospital's confessor – swung from a gallows on the battlements of Sant' Angelo next to the bodies of other hanged men.

Yet the pilgrims still offered money at the sacred shrines; indulgences were still bought with faith and hope; and the crowds still knelt in front of St Peter's – an estimated 200,000 on Easter Sunday – to receive the blessing of the Pope. And while there was much to condemn in Alexander, there were grounds, too, for gratitude. Andrea Bregno's splendid altar, now in the sacristy of S. Maria del Popolo, was commissioned by him; the area around Castel Sant' Angelo was transformed by him; the piazza in front of it was enlarged and paved; a street, the Via Alexandrina, now the Borgo Nuovo, was built to lead from it to the Vatican; the fortress itself was reconstructed inside and given a far more imposing external appearance. The Vatican Palace was also enhanced for all future generations by the work Pope Alexander commissioned for his new Borgia Tower, the decorations by Bernardino Pinturicchio and his assistants of the rooms, among them the Sala del Credo and the Sala delle Sibille, in the Borgia Apartment.[15]

A year before this work was finished in 1495, an artist of genius came to live in Rome. Although he was over fifty and had already executed several distinguished designs in Milan where he had collaborated with Leonardo da Vinci, his first four years in the city where he was to spend the rest of his life were passed in tireless study, examining and measuring the classical monuments of the city, preparing himself for the days when he should make himself known to the world as Donato Bramante, innovator and master of the High Renaissance style of architecture which was to spread from Rome throughout Europe.

NINE

PATRONS AND PARASITES

Three years after the body of Pope Alexander VI, already decomposing in the August heat, had been carried out of the Vatican, Giuliano della Rovere, who had detested his predecessor, that 'Spaniard of accursed memory', led a procession to St Peter's basilica as Pope Julius II. Accompanied by cardinals, prelates and dignitaries of the Curia, he walked behind the Cross to a wide hole, twenty-five feet deep, to lay the white marble foundation stone of the new building which was to rise above the crumbling structure of the old. He climbed down into the hole, around the edges of which the spectators crowded, kicking earth over his mitre so that he called out crossly to them to move back. There he was handed an earthenware vase containing gold and bronze medals on one side of which was stamped his own likeness and on the other a representation of the intended church with domes and towers and portico. The vase was placed in a small cavity beneath the stone on which was inscribed: 'Pope Julius II of Liguria in the year 1506 restored this basilica which had fallen into decay.' The Pope then scrambled out hastily, leaving the stone slightly askew, evidently concerned that the sides of the hole might collapse before he had reached the safety of the pavement.

It was a rare display of anxiety. The Pope was a tall, thin, good-looking man, rough and irascible, talkative, restless and overbearing. He had a fiercely commanding expression and a very quick temper. He always carried a stick with which he would strike irritating subordinates, and he would hurl anything at hand, including his spectacles, at messengers who brought him unwelcome news. He had had many mistresses in the past, from one of whom he had contracted syphilis, and as a cardinal had fathered three daughters. But his sensual appetites had since then been concentrated on Greek and Corsican wine and on good food, in particular caviar, prawns and sucking pig. 'No one has any influence over him, and he consults few or none,' the Venetian ambassador reported. 'Anything that he has been thinking about during the night has to be carried out immediately . . . It is almost impossible to describe how strong and violent and difficult to manage he is . . . Everything about him is on a magnificent scale, both his undertakings and his passions.'

The grandson of a poor fisherman, he often spoke of the poverty of his childhood and was proud to claim that he was 'no schoolman'. He sometimes said that he ought to have been a soldier; and certainly when he personally led his armies out of Rome to compel the obedience of rebel cities in the Papal States and to recover

30. Donato Bramante, who came to Rome in 1499 and was later principal architect to Julius II, who laid the foundation stone of the new St Peter's in 1506.

lost territories for the Church, he displayed a taste for hard campaigning that dismayed the less robust cardinals whom he obliged to accompany him. Unwilling to rely upon capricious and often irresolute mercenaries, he decided to form a professional papal army; and this decision led in 1506 to the creation of the Swiss Guards who remained a fighting force until 1825 when they became a smaller domestic bodyguard, though still retaining their old uniform of slashed doublets, striped hose and rakish *berrette* as well as their pikes and halberds.

Strong-willed, purposeful and resolute, Pope Julius was as determined to recreate in Rome a monument worthy of the everlasting glory of the Church as he was to re-establish the Church's rule in the Papal States and to restore the temporal power of the papacy which he believed to be essential to its authority. This monument to papal prestige was to be the new Church of St Peter's whose foundation stone he had laid on that Low Sunday in the spring of 1506.

His immediate predecessors had merely tinkered with the old basilica. Nicholas V, after restoring much of the decaying fabric, parts of which, so he was warned by Leon Battista Alberti, were in danger of collapsing, had come to realize that it was really past repair. He commissioned designs for a new building from the Florentine sculptor, Bernardo Rossellino, who was probably advised by Alberti. But work had not progressed far by the time of Nicholas's death; and it had not seriously been resumed by Calixtus III, who was more concerned with the Turkish menace than the arts of the Renaissance. Patching and minor improvements, rather than complete rebuilding, had been the policy of Pius II and Paul II as well as of Sixtus IV, all of whom recoiled from the momentous undertaking that so much appealed to Pope Julius's taste for the grand, irrevocable gesture.

His decision was regarded in Rome with deep misgiving by cardinals and citizens alike. It was tantamount to sacrilege, they protested, to destroy a sacred basilica, more than a thousand years old, a holy place venerated, generation after generation, since the very dawn of Christianity. Around the pedestal of the antique and mutilated statue of Menelaus known as Pasquino[1] were displayed innumerable protests about the Pope's decision. But Julius was undeterred. He had made up his mind, and nothing would alter it. He considered Rossellino's design, and rejected it as too old-fashioned; he considered, with more sympathy, another plan proposed by Giuliano da Sangallo, but this too he thought insufficiently ambitious. And so, for an edifice which, as he put it, would 'embody the greatness of the present and the future', he turned to Bramante who had already displayed his exceptional gifts in the design of the enchanting Tempietto in the cloister of S. Pietro in Montorio.[2]

Encouraged by the Pope, Bramante set to work with a will, directing hundreds of workmen in demolishing the decaying walls of Constantine's basilica and discarding everything inside it for which he had no use, statues and mosaics, candelabra and icons, tombs and altars, earning himself the title of 'il ruinante'. Load after load of Carrara marble and that volcanic ash known as pozzolana were carted on to the site, together with travertine from Tivoli and lime from Montecelio. One day the Pope came to watch the work in progress and remarked proudly to a foreign envoy to whom he introduced his architect, 'Bramante tells me he has 2,500 men on this job. One could hold a review of such an army.'

The cost mounted month by month. By the beginning of 1513 well over 70,000 gold ducats had been spent. But money was not an acute problem, even though the municipality of Rome had to be supported, the poor of the city cared for, the military forces of the papacy paid and its architectural heritage constantly sustained. The papacy was receiving a good share of the riches being derived from the discovery of America; numerous indulgences were being granted; loans were being raised from, among others, the astonishingly rich banker, Agostino Chigi, who retained as security the papal tiara which he kept in his counting-house behind the Arco dei Banchi[3] in the Via del Banco di S. Spirito;[4] and gifts were

31. Michelangelo's patron, Pope Julius II (1447–1513), depicted at prayer not long before his death, in a detail of Raphael's 'Mass of Bolsena' fresco, in the Vatican's Stanza d'Eliodoro.

being solicited from all over Europe. The King of England sent tin for the roof and was rewarded with wine and Parmesan cheese.

Money was needed not only for St Peter's. Pope Julius had spent and continued to spend huge sums on the Vatican Palace where an extensive and lovely garden, the first great Roman pleasure-garden since the time of the Caesars, was laid out beneath its walls, and where the Cortile del Belvedere was formed between the Vatican offices and the formerly isolated Palazzetto del Belvedere which was itself converted into a sculpture gallery.[5] To this gallery were carried the Pope's two masterpieces of classical sculpture, the Apollo del Belvedere[6] which had formerly stood in the garden of his cardinalate mansion beside the church of S. Pietro in Vincoli, and the Laocoön which had been discovered in January 1506 by a man digging in his vineyard near the Baths of Trajan.[7] The Pope had immediately sent Giuliano da Sangallo to inspect this. And as Giuliano's son, then nine years old, had recorded, 'We set off together, I on my father's shoulders. As soon as my father saw the statue, he exclaimed, "This is the Laocoön mentioned by Pliny." The opening had to be enlarged to get the statue out.' There were, of course, many rich collectors anxious to acquire it. But Julius managed to obtain it by promising the finder and his son a large annuity. The statue was carried through streets bedecked with flowers to the peal of church bells and the singing of the choir of the Cappella Giulia which the Pope himself, a lover of music as well as of sculpture, had founded.

While money was being lavished upon the Vatican Palace and St Peter's, work was continuing on the widening and restoring of Rome's streets. The Via delle Botteghe Oscure, the Street of the Dark Shops, the Via S. Celso, the Lungara and the Judaeorum were all transformed, as was the Via Magistralis which became, and remains, the Via Giulia, one of Rome's most handsome thoroughfares. The Pope also expended immense sums on the church of S. Maria del Popolo which was decorated by several of those artists whom his largesse drew to Rome and in which Julius placed the magnificent tombs of Cardinals Girolamo Basso della Rovere and Ascanio Sforza, designed for him by Andrea Sansovino.[8]

The erection of a fine marble tomb for himself had long been one of the Pope's most cherished ambitions. As a first step in its realization he sent for a young sculptor from Florence, Michelangelo Buonarroti. The son of a poor Tuscan magistrate of aristocratic stock, Michelangelo was a gloomy, laconic young man of twenty-nine, self-absorbed, quarrelsome and quickly offended. The Pope found him an infinitely more difficult artist to deal with than the amenable Bramante and the sweet-natured, charmingly polite and unobtrusive Raffaello Sanzio who was also working for him in the Vatican on the rooms to be known as the Raphael *Stanze*.[9] But Michelangelo was already recognized as a genius of astounding power and versatility, and it was inconceivable that the Pope, one of the most enlightened and discriminating patrons that Rome had ever known, should not wish to employ him.

At first all went well. Michelangelo was paid a hundred crowns for the expenses of his journey to Rome where the Pope was delighted with the designs that were shown to him. He asked the sculptor to go to the quarries in the mountains of Carrara; and here Michelangelo spent eight months choosing and helping to excavate the blocks of marble, weighing in all over a hundred tons, for a monument which promised to surpass 'every ancient or imperial tomb ever made'.

After he had chosen all the marble that was wanted [so his fellow-Tuscan and contemporary, Giorgio Vasari, recorded], he had it loaded on board ship and taken to Rome, where the blocks filled half the square of St Peter's ... In the castle [Castel Sant'

Angelo] Michelangelo had prepared his room for executing the figures and the rest of the tomb; and so that he could come and see him at work without any bother the Pope had ordered a drawbridge to be built from the corridor to the room. This led to great intimacy between them, although in time the favours Michelangelo was shown . . . stirred up much envy among his fellow craftsmen.

The easy intimacy between the Pope and Michelangelo did not last long, however. The sculptor did not like being watched at work, normally choosing to have his studio locked; nor did he like being asked questions about his probable rate of progress. Touchy and irritable, he began to resent what he took to be his patron's bossy interference, and was then offended by the casually offhand manner in which his request for interviews and money were refused by the papal officials. After one such rebuff, Michelangelo lost his temper, told his servants to sell all the contents of his studio and rode out of the city to Florence. He was eventually persuaded to return to the Pope's service, but not to work on the tomb as he had hoped. First of all, though he protested it was 'not his kind of art', he was required to make a monumental bronze statue of Julius fourteen feet high, which was to be erected on the façade of the Church of S. Petronio in Bologna and, after a revolution some years later, was melted down for a cannon by the Pope's enemy, the Duke of Ferrara. He was then asked to undertake a task for which he felt even more ill qualified, the painting of the ceiling of the Sistine Chapel. 'He tried in every possible way to shake the burden off his shoulders,' Vasari said. 'But the more he refused, the more determined he made the Pope, who was a wilful man by nature . . . Finally, being the hot-tempered man he was, he was all ready to fly into a rage. However, seeing His Holiness was so persevering Michelangelo resigned himself to doing what he was asked.' He was given an advance payment of 500 ducats and began work on 10 May 1508.

Immediately he regretted that he had given way. There was trouble over the scaffolding which Bramante constructed for him: initially it hung down from the ceiling on ropes but Michelangelo wanted it supported by props from the floor. There was trouble with his assistants whom he had sent for from Florence and whom he considered so incompetent that he scraped off everything they had done and decided to paint the whole area, all ten thousand square feet of it, himself. He locked the chapel door, refusing admittance to his fellow-artists and to everyone else, thus provoking another quarrel with the Pope who was himself told to go away. And then there was trouble with a salty mould which, when the north wind blew, appeared on many areas of the ceiling and so discouraged Michelangelo that he despaired of the whole undertaking and was reluctant to go on until Giuliano da Sangallo showed him how to deal with it.

The labour was physically as well as emotionally exhausting. He had to paint standing, looking upwards for such long periods that his neck became stiff and swollen; he could not straighten it when he climbed down from the scaffold and had to read letters holding them up with his head bent backwards. In hot weather it was stiflingly hot and the plaster dust irritated his skin; in all weathers the paint dripped down upon his face, his hair and his beard. 'The place is wrong, and no

32. An engraving after a self-portrait of Michelangelo, who began work on the ceiling of the Sistine Chapel in 1508.

painter I,' he lamented in a sonnet he wrote describing his exhausting work. 'My painting all the day doth drop a rich mosaic on my face.' 'I live in great toil and weariness of body,' he wrote to his brother. 'I have no friends . . . and don't want any, and haven't the time to eat what I need.'

He was plagued by his patron who insisted upon being let into the chapel to see what he was paying for. The Pope kept asking when it would be finished, as he clambered up the scaffold with his stick, impatient to have the chapel opened before he died. 'How much longer will it take?'

'When it satisfies me as an artist,' Michelangelo replied on one occasion, eliciting from Julius the angry reply, 'And *we* want you to satisfy *us*, and finish it soon.'

Later Michelangelo refused to commit himself further than to say he would finish it when he could. 'When I can! When I can!' the Pope, infuriated, shouted back at him. 'What do you mean? When I can. I'll soon *make* you finish it!' He hit him with his stick, then threatened to hurl him off the scaffold if he did not get on more quickly. After these outbursts came apologies. The Pope's chamberlain would call at Michelangelo's house with presents of money, with excuses and apologies, 'explaining that such treatment was meant as a favour and a mark of affection'.

At last, after nearly four years' work, the scaffolding was removed. But the artist was still not satisfied; there were touches that he wanted to add, backgrounds and draperies he wanted to enliven with ultramarine, details to enrich with gold. But the Pope would wait no longer. Even before the dust had settled after the dismantling of the scaffolding, he rushed into the chapel to look at the astonishing achievement of more than three hundred figures, many of them painted three and even four times life-size. On the morning of 31 October 1512 he celebrated Mass inside the chapel and afterwards, in Vasari's words, the whole of Rome 'came running to see what Michelangelo had done; and certainly it was such as to make everyone speechless with astonishment'.

Now over seventy and in the last year of his life, the Pope thought once more of his uncompleted tomb to which Michelangelo returned 'most eagerly'. And, although the tomb never was finished as originally intended, out of its grand conception came one masterpiece that can still be seen in Rome, the vibrant statue of Moses in S. Pietro in Vincoli.[10]

News of the death of Pope Julius II on 20 February 1513 was received in Rome with the utmost sorrow. Women were seen weeping in the streets as they waited their turn to kiss the pontifical feet which were left protruding from the grille of the mortuary chapel; men told each other that they would not live to see another pope who was at once so staunch a patriot and so munificent a patron. The city was thronged with mourning crowds so numerous that the dead man's Master of Ceremonies had never known the like in forty years' residence in the city. 'All knew him to be a true Roman pontiff,' declared the Florentine statesman and historian, Francesco Guicciardini. 'Although full of fury and extravagant conceptions, he was lamented above all his predecessors and . . . held in illustrious remembrance'.

Yet sorrowful as the Romans were that winter, the election of Giovanni de' Medici, son of the great Lorenzo, as Pope Leo X, was greeted with an enthusiasm as extravagant as their recent grief. Delighting in pageantry, the new Pope took pains to ensure that the *Sacro Possesso*, the formal entry into the Vatican, was as splendid an occasion as money and the ingenuity of the Master of Ceremonies could provide. Every house on the route of the procession was bedecked with wreaths of laurel and ilex, with rich brocades and velvet draperies; the streets were strewn with box and myrtle; ornate inscriptions in Latin welcomed and glorified the new Pope, son of a Roman mother, Clarice Orsini, greeting him as the 'Paragon of the Church' and 'Ambassador of Heaven'. Altars had been set up at several corners; heraldic devices and Medici and Orsini emblems were displayed on rooftops and over doorways; fountains ran with wine instead of water. Triumphal arches, erected by rich merchants and bankers seeming to vie with one another in opulence and inventiveness, spanned the streets and contained in their niches effigies of Christian martyrs in close proximity to antique statues of pagan gods; and, in the arch erected by Agostino Chigi, there were real people dressed as gods.

The procession left the piazza in front of the Vatican, led by men-at-arms. There followed scarlet-clad members of the cardinals' households and of the prelates of the papal court; standard bearers; mounted captains of the *rioni*; milk white mules from the Papal States; equerries in red robes fringed with ermine, bearing papal crowns and jewelled mitres; Roman noblemen with escorts of liveried attendants, among them the heads of the Orsini and Colonna families walking side by side and hand in hand; merchant princes of Florence, several of them related to the Pope; foreign ambassadors and their suites; pages with silver wands, escorting a palfrey on which was carried the Holy Sacrament beneath a canopy of cloth of gold; priests, clerks, lawyers in black and violet; bishops and cardinals on horses with trailing white draperies; and, last of all, men of the Swiss Guard in their parti-coloured uniforms, armed with halberds, marching before His Holiness who, astride a white Arab stallion, was shaded from the sun by a baldacchino of embroidered silk carried by eight Roman citizens of patrician rank.

The figure of the Pope was scarcely equal to the magnificence of his escort. Excessively fat and flabby, he looked much older than his thirty-seven years. His mouth hung open; his face was almost purple in the heat; the sweat ran down his short neck and the folds of his chin. He appeared to be sinking under the weight of his jewelled cope and his triple tiara as he rode along, unconcernedly breaking wind. Yet he found the energy to smile with benign satisfaction upon the people who lined the way, to nod complacently when an attendant read out some flattering inscription which his own purblind eyes could not discern; to raise his plump hands, encased in perfumed gloves sewn with pearls, to bestow the papal benediction. He murmured a few words of pleasant encouragement when his chamberlains threw out handfuls of silver coins from their capacious money-bags. Indeed, his geniality and obvious enjoyment of the spectacle, his pride and exalted contentment were disarming. The people renewed their shouts of welcome: 'Leone! Leone! Leone!'

33. Raphael's portrait of Leo X (1475–1521), in which the Medici Pope is shown with his cousin Giulio, the future Pope Clement VII, on his right and Cardinal Luigi de' Rossi standing behind the chair.

At the Ponte Sant' Angelo the Jews, as custom required, were assembled to request permission to continue living in Rome and, in the person of the Rabbi, to offer a copy of their Law. The Pope allowed the volume to fall to the ground as he uttered the prescribed words rejecting their faith, but it was noticed that as he confirmed their privileges there was only the slightest diminution of his graciousness.

Having traversed the Via Papale and reached the statue of Marcus Aurelius which then still stood outside the Lateran, the Pope dismounted and entered the hall of the palace, exhausted but evidently well prepared to do justice to an ample and delicious banquet.

'In thinking over all the pomp and lofty magnificence I had just witnessed,' mused a Florentine physician who recorded every detail of that splendid *Possesso*, 'I experienced so violent a desire to become Pope myself that I was unable to obtain a wink of sleep or any repose all that night. No longer do I marvel at these prelates desiring so ardently to procure this dignity. I really believe that everyone would rather be made a Pope than a Prince.'

Inside the Lateran the Pope was relishing his meal with all the enthusiasm, though less of the gross appetite, that he had displayed for good food and drink ever since, at his father's urgent insistence, he had been created a cardinal at the age of sixteen. He is reported to have murmured to his brother Giuliano soon after his election, 'God has given us the papacy. Let us enjoy it.'

Enjoy it he certainly did, and at prodigious cost. It was estimated that within a single year, despite his creation of no less than 1,200 offices for sale, his disposal of bishoprics and abbeys and his lavish creation of expensive cardinalates, he had spent not only all the savings of his predecessor but also the entire revenues of himself and his successor. 'He could no more save a thousand ducats,' so Macchiavelli's friend, Francesco Vettori, thought, 'than a stone could fly through the air.' Although soon deeply in debt to almost every banking-house in Rome, some of which charged him interest at 40 per cent, he made not the slightest attempt to economize in any way, raising the number of the papal household to 683, continuing to bestow purses of gold upon guests who sang with him and to squander money at the gaming-table where he would cheerfully pay his losses at the simple game of *primiero* without demur and throw the winnings over his shoulder. He paid enormous sums for French hounds and Icelandic falcons and for the preservation of whole districts of the Campagna where he abandoned himself to the pleasures of hawking and hunting, to the slaughter of penned animals, some of which, entangled in nets, Leo himself would kill, holding a spear in his right hand and a glass to his weak left eye, complacently acknowledging the congratulations of his attendants.

Wagonloads of carcasses were brought back to Rome where scores of chefs prepared them for the Pope's tables to accompany the delicacies and surprises, the peacocks' tongues and lampreys cooked in cloves and nuts in a Cretan wine sauce, the pies of nightingales. And the bankers and merchants, the prelates and nobles of Rome rivalled the Pope and each other in the sumptuousness of their banquets.

The meal was exquisite [wrote the Venetian ambassador of a characteristic dinner at the palace of Cardinal Cornaro]. There was an endless succession of dishes, for we had sixty-five courses, each course consisting of three different dishes, all of which were placed on the table with marvellous speed. Scarcely had we finished one delicacy than a fresh plate was set before us, and yet everything was served on the finest of silver of which his Eminence has an abundant supply. At the end of the meal we rose from the table both gorged with rich food and deafened by the continual concert, carried on both within and without the hall and proceeding from every instrument that Rome could produce – fifes, harpsichords and four-stringed lutes as well as the voices of a choir.

Banquets at the riverside palace of Agostino Chigi, whose bathroom fittings were all of silver and gold, were even more pretentious. This inordinately rich banker was said to have had his servants cast the silver dishes upon which each course of dinner had been served into the Tiber in a gesture indicative of his indifference to such trifles, though it was also said that he had taken the precaution of having a net placed beneath the surface of the water so that they could be dragged out again at night. He had also given a dinner at which the food was served on plates engraved with the armorial bearings of his guests, and at which the walls of the banqueting hall were covered with the finest tapestries. At the end of the meal the Pope, as honoured guest, congratulated his host on the excellence of the food and the magnificence of the setting. Chigi then gave a signal for the cords supporting the arras to be released. The tapestries fell to the floor, revealing empty stalls and mangers. 'Your Holiness!' he said, 'this is not my banqueting hall. It is merely my stable.'

The Pope's own table was renowned for its entertainments, for the antics of jesters, of dwarfs and buffoons, of the vulgarly witty Dominican friar, Fra Mariano Fetti, who could eat forty eggs or twenty chickens at a sitting and pretended to enjoy ravens complete with feathers and beaks, of half-starved morons who gobbled up carrion covered with strong sauce in the fancy that they were being privileged to consume a papal delicacy.

The most successful of all Pope Leo's practical jokes was deemed to be that played upon one Baraballo, an old priest who was persuaded to believe that his absurd attempts at verse demanded comparison with the great poems of Petrarch and that he, too, was worthy of being crowned with laurel on the Capitol to which he would be granted the honour of riding on a white elephant which had recently been presented to the Pope by the King of Portugal and was now housed in the Belvedere. On the appointed day the windows of the Vatican were crowded with smiling faces as the poor, deluded priest walked forth in scarlet toga fringed with gold to be lifted into an ornately decorated howdah. 'I could never have believed in such an incident if I had not seen it myself and actually laughed at it,' wrote Paolo Giovio, the Pope's biographer: 'the spectacle of an old man of sixty bearing an honoured name, stately and venerable in appearance, hoary-headed, riding upon an elephant to the sound of trumpets.'

Yet the Pope who took such pleasure in this kind of farce, who enjoyed bullfights and who would sit for hours myopically watching cardinals and their ladies dancing at masked balls, was by no means entirely occupied with trivialities. Certainly he preferred broad comedies and more or less indecent farces to the more serious dramatic performances which were also staged in his palace; and certainly he was indiscriminate in his literary and musical patronage, being as inclined to reward the most frivolous poetaster or satirist as he was to grant his patronage to such leading writers as Ariosto and Guicciardini, while virtually disregarding the claims of Erasmus. 'It is difficult to judge,' remarked Pietro Aretino who had cause to be grateful for the Pope's open-handedness, 'whether the merits of the learned or the tricks of fools afforded most delight to His Holiness.' But, even though his own tastes were questionable, the Pope was an estimable patron all the same. He brought the most accomplished European choristers to the Sistine Chapel; he conferred considerable benefits upon the Sapienza, increasing the number of professors and the range of faculties; he granted his protection to the Roman Academy and positively encouraged the study of Latin and Greek, offering his friendship to Marco Girolamo Vida as well as Ariosto, bringing Giano Ascaris to Rome and suggesting that he should edit the Greek manuscripts in his possession, and inviting Markos Musuros to come to the city with at least ten young men to teach Italians the Greek language. He also brought his extensive and valuable family library from Florence to Rome where, until it was returned by his cousin for the Biblioteca Laurenziana, it was made freely available to those scholars and writers who were offered numerous inducements to come to Rome to fulfil the Pope's ambition of making it the most cultured city in the western world.

Pope Leo was anxious to play his part in making it a most beautiful city, too. He commissioned Sansovino to design the church of S. Giovanni dei Fiorentini[11] in the Piazza dell' Oro, then the centre of the Florentine colony in Rome. He built the Via Ripetta to provide a new way out of the congested old town towards the Piazza del Popolo.[12] He restored the church of S. Maria in Domnica, providing it with its splendid porticoed façade which is attributed to Baldassare Peruzzi. He found money to continue the reconstruction of St Peter's and the decoration by Raphael of the Vatican Palace, commissioning from Raphael cartoons for ten tapestries to hang on the walls of the Sistine Chapel.

He could not, however, bring himself to tolerate the disturbing presence of Michelangelo. He claimed to have the deepest affection for him and would even tearfully tell stories of their childhood together in the Medici Palace in Florence where, as Vasari said, the young Michelangelo, whose gifts had been recognized by the Pope's father, had lived as one of the household. But the Pope, while recognizing his genius, did not really get on with Michelangelo. 'He is an alarming man,' he said, 'and there is no getting on with him.' He persuaded him to turn to architecture and to go back to Florence where a new façade was required for Brunelleschi's Church of S. Lorenzo.

Michelangelo was kept at work in Florence by Pope Leo's cousin, Giulio de' Medici, who succeeded to the papal throne after the short and uneventful intervening reign of the obscure and parsimonious ascetic, the Flemish Adrian VI, who spent more time in prayer and private study than on the problems of the Church. As a young, rich cardinal, the new Pope, who took the title Clement VII, had lived in Rome in the Palazzo della Cancelleria which had been confiscated from Cardinal Raffaele Riario because of his involvement in a plot against Pope Leo X. Tall and handsome with black hair, sallow complexion and deep brown eyes, one of which had a slight squint, Giulio de' Medici bore no resemblance to his cousin. Nor did his manner – cold, aloof and dismissive – give grounds for hope that he would be as generous and hospitable. In an unflattering, though not unjust sketch of his character, Francesco Guicciardini described him as 'rather morose and disagreeable than of a pleasant and affable temper; by no means trustworthy and naturally disinclined to do a kindness; very grave and cautious in all his actions; perfectly self-controlled and of great capacity, if timidity did not sometimes warp his better judgement'. Yet, saturnine as he appeared and reserved as he undoubtedly was, he had proved himself a most bountiful as well as discriminating patron of artists and musicians. He was a liberal contributor to all kinds of charitable causes, as his cousin had been, and a generous, though not ostentatious host. By nature disinclined to be either gregarious or open-handed, he was well aware of the advantages of hospitality and munificence; and when he became Pope, after the exchange of numerous bribes during the longest conclave in human memory, he continued to lavish invitations upon the influential and commissions upon the talented. He brought to a successful conclusion an ambitious scheme for cleaning and improving the streets of Rome, taking a particular interest in the Via Trionfale, the Flaminia, the Via Lata which led from the Piazza del Popolo to the Piazza Venezia and the streets around Piazza Navona.[13] And he continued to employ Raphael in Rome and asked him to design a villa, later to be known as the Villa Madama, on the cypress-covered slopes of Monte Mario above the bend of the Tiber at the Ponte Molle.[14] He brought Raphael's favourite pupils, Giulio Romano and Gian Francesco Penni, to work in the Vatican. He encouraged the Polish astronomer, Nicolaus Koppernigk, known as Copernicus, in his controversial researches, attending his lectures when he came to Rome and requesting him to publish his findings. And he bought several works of art from the vain and cantankerous Benvenuto Cellini.

But the Pope had little time to spare for the contemplation of the works he commissioned or, indeed, for the musical evenings and the theological and philosophical discussions that he had enjoyed as a cardinal, since foreign affairs and the growing schism in the Church preoccupied his waking hours. His cousin had tried to dismiss from his mind all thoughts of German demands for reform in the Church, hoping that the problems would eventually resolve themselves in the pettifogging arguments of German monks. But there was one tiresome Augustinian friar in particular who would not be satisfied.

TEN

THE SACK OF ROME

Martin Luther had come to Rome in 1510 on business for his Order. Shocked by what he saw, he was confirmed in his belief that the Church must be radically reformed. The city itself disappointed him: it was hard to recognize 'the footprints of ancient Rome, as the old buildings were now buried beneath the new, so deep lieth the rubbish, as is plain to see by the Tiber, since it hath banks of rubbish as high as twice the length of a soldier's spear'. He found the Renaissance atmosphere of the city thoroughly distasteful. He loathed Aristotle, yet here men considered him almost on a par with the Fathers of the Church; and they seemed to consider such ornamentations as those in Raphael's *Stanze*, in which Christian and pagan themes mingled in outrageous harmony, as worthy of regard and study as Holy Writ. They equated beauty with goodness; they supposed the pursuit of happiness on earth could be reconciled with the hope of eternal salvation. While the Pope went 'triumphing about with fair-decked stallions, priests gabbled Mass'. 'By the time I had reached the gospel,' Luther complained, 'the priest next to me had already finished and was shouting, "Come on, finish it, hurry up!"' He had been thankful to return to Germany.

Pope Leo had eventually excommunicated Luther and had hoped that the supremely powerful Emperor Charles V, who was also King of Spain and Naples as well as ruler of the Netherlands, would, as a good Roman Catholic, bring the heretic to trial and have him executed. Although there would have been strong opposition in Germany to such a drastic move against the Reformation, the Emperor was prepared to act against Luther provided he obtained something in exchange: he asked for the support of the papacy in his intended attack against France's remaining possessions in Italy, including Milan which King Francis I had seized in 1515. A bargain was struck. The Emperor's army marched against the forces of Francis I, Milan was occupied and the French were obliged to retreat towards the Alps. The French King, however, had never supposed that once papal affairs were in the hands of the suspicious and hesitant Medici, Clement VII, the understanding between the papacy and the Emperor would remain secure; and he was right. After repeated changes in his vacillating and convoluted policies, the Pope did decide to ally himself with France; but this naturally antagonized Charles V who, having defeated the French once more, took action to forestall the threatened anti-imperial league.

As a first step he instructed his envoy, Ugo di Moncada, to approach the unruly Cardinal Pompeo Colonna, who had vociferously opposed Clement VII's election in the hope of becoming pope himself. Colonna was easily persuaded to raise a strong force of mercenaries and retainers, to march through the Borgo and to attack and pillage the apostolic palace as a self-styled deliverer of Rome from papal tyranny. Driven to seek safety by flight into Castel Sant' Angelo, Pope Clement was further humiliated by being compelled to sign a treaty abandoning the anti-imperial alliance and pardoning Colonna. But as soon as he could, he broke the treaty, sent papal troops to ravage the Colonna estates, declared the family outlaws and all their titles forfeit. In a rage so intense that he trembled at the very mention of Pope Clement's name, Cardinal Colonna offered the services of all the men he could muster to Charles V's viceroy at Naples.

These were not the only enemies that Clement's faithless and irresolute policies had raised up against the papacy. For a huge army of German *Landsknechte*, mostly Lutherans, assembled by the Emperor's brother, Ferdinand of Austria, had marched across the Alps, declaring their determination to wreak vengeance upon the Roman anti-Christ. Led by the fat old veteran, Georg von Frundsberg, and undeterred by torrential rain and blinding snowstorms, they advanced into Lombardy, and defeated and killed the skilful *condottiere*, Giovanni delle Bande Nere, head of the junior branch of the House of Medici. Joined in February 1527 at Piacenza by the main body of the Emperor's army of Spaniards, Italians and an international force of lancers under the renegade Constable of France, Charles, Duke of Bourbon, the German *Landsknechte* converged upon Rome.

Warned by his secretary, Gian-Matteo Giberti, that they were 'on the brink of ruin', the Pope tried to come to terms with the commanders of the advancing armies, now well over 20,000 strong. The prospect of a large indemnity tempted them; but the *Landsknechte* refused to be denied the opportunities of pillage. They rounded upon their leaders, shouting that they would not go back until they had had their way with Rome; and in the tumultuous uproar Georg von Frundsberg was seized with a fit of apoplexy and had to be carried off helpless to Ferrara. The march then continued under the nervous direction of the Duke of Bourbon who was as much the servant as the master of the undisciplined, heterogeneous forces he commanded. These forces, half-starved, their ragged uniforms soaked by torrents of rain and the swirling waters of the mountain streams through which they stumbled, holding hands in gangs of thirty, drew ever nearer to Rome, excited by thoughts of plunder.

Rome was certainly an easy prey to any large band of marauders. The sprawling walls, constantly repaired but never now formidable, still enclosed the huge area occupied by the capital of the ancient Empire. Unlike other large early-sixteenth-century towns in Italy, within the city walls were vineyards and gardens, waste grounds and thickets in which deer and wild boar sought shelter, villas and shapeless ruins covered with ivy and eglantine from whose dense foliage pigeons clattered out in their hundreds. The wooded hills of the Palatine, the Caelian and

34. Imperial troops parody a papal procession and blessing during the Sack of Rome.

the Aventine were dotted with farmhouses and convents and with those crumbling monuments that had served as quarries for many generations. West of the immense bulk of the Colosseum sprawled the long, marshy, scrub-covered expanse of the Campo Vaccino with only a few columns of antique temples to indicate that this cowherds' pastureland had once been the classic Forum. The Capitol, bristling with towers and battlements, and the fortified ruins in the valley below were awesome reminders of the lawlessness and family feuds of the recent medieval past. Indeed, Rome was still essentially a medieval city. Since the dawn of the Renaissance many fine new churches had been built in Rome, among them S. Maria del Popolo, S. Agostino, as well as S. Giovanni dei Fiorentini and S. Pietro in Montorio. Splendid new palaces and villas had been built in the city too, apart from the Palazzo della Cancelleria, the Venezia, the Farnese and the Villa Madama. In the Borgo were the Palazzo Soderini, the Penitenzieri[1] and the Palazzo Castelli

(Giraud-Torlonia). Across the river in the Ponte Rione were the Palazzo Lante ai Caprettari,[2] the Palazzo Cicciaporci[3] and the Palazzo Cenci.[4] In the nearby district of Parione were the palaces of the Massimi.[5] And in the area, at that time open, between the Porta S. Spirito which led into the Borgo and the Porta Settimiana which was the entrance into Trastevere, Baldassare Peruzzi had built a splendid villa for Agostino Chigi.[6]

Yet the Rome which lay between the Corso and the Tiber and in the transpontine quarter of Trastevere, the Rome in which most of its people still lived, was the Rome of the Middle Ages, a Rome of alleys and dark lanes, a maze of courts and passages with the occasional church and fortress rising above the little houses that crowded down to the river where they overhung the muddy waters and could be entered by boat.

In this part of Rome, and in the Ponte Rione where could be found the houses of the bankers and merchants, jewellers and silversmiths, booksellers and courtesans, lived and worked most of the fifty to sixty thousand people of Rome. A large proportion of these inhabitants were foreigners, many of them Jews living in the *rioni* of Regola, Ripa and Sant' Angelo; about seven thousand of them were Spaniards; and some were French, several of these congregating in the streets leading off Piazza Navona where they carried on business as pastrycooks and confectioners. There was also a numerous German community working in inns and butchers' shops and in the printing industry which had been originated in Rome by their fellow-countrymen in the previous century.

Foreigners and natives alike were mostly occupied in making or supplying the ordinary needs of life; few were now craftsmen. Many, about three in every hundred, lived by prostitution, either by the arts and skills of a courtesan such as the lovely Clarice Matrema-non-Vuole who could recite by heart all Petrarch and most of Virgil and Ovid, or by the earthier charms of girls like the one who gave Benvenuto Cellini syphilis.

The cosmopolitan nature of Rome's population added to the problems of the city's defence. Many citizens believed that they might just as well be ruled by the international Emperor as by the Italian Pope who had, in any case, made himself extremely unpopular by the financial measures which his circumstances had forced upon him. Indeed, the *caporioni* had such difficulty in persuading the able-bodied men of their districts to turn out in obedience to the tapping of the drum that only six out of the thirteen *rioni* could produce a muster at all; and many of those on parade were of doubtful use, the most trustworthy having already been appropriated for the protection of private property. Even to close the bridges proved an impossible task, for Renzo da Ceri, the experienced *condottiere* appointed to lead the defence, was prevented from doing so by Roman people whose business interests required them to be left open.

The Pope seemed as paralysed by indecision as the Roman people were indifferent to his fate. The imperialist army was almost within sight of the gates before he asked for financial help from the Commune – and was told that he could have it only if he raised twice as much elsewhere. It was not until a week after this that he raised money himself by selling cardinalates to six rich men – and making more fuss over this, so Francesco Guicciardini, his lieutenant-general, said, 'than over ruining the papacy and the whole world'. And it was not until 4 May, when the enemy were advancing up Monte Mario and his villa there was being taken over for officers' quarters, that he summoned the Great Council of Rome to a meeting in the Church of S. Maria d'Aracoeli where he assured them unconvincingly that the crisis would be over in a few days but that in the meantime the citizens must do their best to defend themselves.

His commander, Renzo da Ceri, had already reinforced the weakest parts of the Leonine Wall and had erected defensive works inside the Vatican; but with so few troops at his disposal, he had little hope of keeping the enemy out of a city whose delegates would have attempted to negotiate a separate peace had he allowed them to leave it. With only 8,000 armed men, including 2,000 Swiss Guards and 2,000 former members of Giovanni de' Medici's Bande Nere, he awaited the arrival of the inevitable herald from the imperialist camp as the bell on the Capitol rang the tocsin throughout the night.

The herald's demand for surrender and the payment of a huge indemnity was recognized by both sides as nothing more than a customary preliminary to the assault which Bourbon could not have prevented his hungry, half-naked men from launching even had he wanted to. When he spoke to them before the attack, 'he had not even reached the end of his oration', so one of his officers recorded, 'before an excited and joyful murmur began to fill the camp, from which it could be guessed that for that multitude every hour to be endured before the assault would seem like a century'.

The inevitable attack began at about four o'clock in the morning of 6 May 1527 with an outburst of harquebus fire on both sides. An assault on the wall between Porta del Torrione and Porta S. Spirito and two diversionary feints were made at the same time upon the Belvedere and Porta Pertusa. This first assault was repulsed with heavy losses; but then a thick mist arose from the Tiber, and the defenders, their artillery now virtually useless, were reduced to throwing rocks, shouting at their unseen enemy, 'Jews and infidels, half-castes, Lutherans', and to letting off the occasional shot.

One of these stray shots from a harquebus hit the Duke of Bourbon who was carried away dying to a nearby chapel by the Prince of Orange, an adventurer in the Emperor's service. The news of Bourbon's death caused elation among the defenders, who left their posts and dashed through the streets of the Borgo crying, 'Victory! Victory!' It also caused momentary despondency in the imperialist ranks. But the Germans and Spaniards soon rallied and, having mounted scaling-ladders made from vine poles under cover of the thick mist, they were soon clambering over the breaches and, vastly superior in numbers, were pushing the defenders back. The Swiss Guards fought bravely and so did some of the Roman militia, the Bande Nere and the students of the Collegio Capranicense[7] who had dashed to the defence of the walls and had all been killed. But many of the papal troops either deserted to the enemy or joined the crowds struggling to escape across the Tiber over the bridges, on which scores of people were crushed to death, or in overloaded boats that capsized, throwing many more into the river.

The Pope ran for safety along the stone corridor that led from the Vatican to Castel Sant' Angelo, glancing down through the apertures at the havoc below, his skirts held up by the Bishop of Nocera so that he could run the faster. 'I flung my own purple cloak about his head and shoulders,' the Bishop said, 'lest some Barbarian rascal in the crowd below might recognize the Pope by his white rochet, as he was passing a window, and take a chance shot at his fleeing form.' Thirteen cardinals and some three thousand fugitives also reached the castle; but others, desperately trying to reach safety before it was too late, were caught on the drawbridge as it was raised and fell into the moat.

Rome was now at the mercy of the imperialist troops. Gian d'Urbina, the cruel and arrogant commander of the Spanish infantry, infuriated by a pike wound in the face inflicted by a Swiss Guard, rampaged through the Borgo, followed by his men, killing everyone they came across. 'All were cut to pieces, even if unarmed,' wrote an eyewitness, 'even in those places that Attila and Genseric, although the most cruel of men, had in former times treated with religious respect.' The Hospital of S. Spirito was broken into, and nearly all those who were cared for there were slaughtered or thrown into the Tiber alive. The orphans of the Pietà were also killed. Convicts from the prisons were set free to join in the massacre, mutilation and pillage.

The imperialists stormed over the Ponte Sisto and continued their savagery in the heart of the city. The doors of churches and convents, of palaces, monasteries and workshops were smashed open and the contents hurled into the streets. Tombs were broken open, including that of Julius II, and the corpses stripped of jewels and vestments. The Sancta Sanctorum was sacked; the Host stamped and spat upon; relics and crucifixes ridiculed or used as targets by harquebusiers. The head of St Andrew was cast contemptuously to the ground and that of St John kicked about the streets as a football. The Holy Lance that had speared Christ's side and had been presented to Innocent VIII was paraded through the streets of the Borgo on the spear of a German soldier; St Veronica's handkerchief was offered for sale in an inn; the Emperor Constantine's golden cross was stolen and never recovered; so were the tiara of Nicholas I and the Golden Rose of Martin V. Romans who took shelter in churches were slaughtered out of hand. 'Even on the high altar of St Peter's,' according to one contemporary account, 'five hundred men were massacred, as holy relics were burned or destroyed.'

Men were tortured to reveal the hiding-places of their possessions or to pay ransoms for the sparing of their lives, one merchant being tied to a tree and having a fingernail wrenched out each day because he could not pay the money demanded.

Many were suspended for hours by the arms [wrote Francesco Guicciardini's brother, Luigi]; many were cruelly bound by the genitals; many were suspended by the feet high above the road or over the river, while their tormentors threatened to cut the cord. Some were half buried in the cellars; others were nailed up in casks or villainously beaten and wounded; not a few were branded all over their persons with red-hot irons. Some were tortured by extreme thirst, others by insupportable noise and many were cruelly tortured by having their teeth brutally drawn. Others again were forced to eat their own ears, or nose, or their roasted testicles and yet more were subjected to strange, unheard-of martyrdoms that move me too much even to think of, much less describe.

The Spaniards were the most brutal, it was generally agreed. 'In the destruction of Rome the Germans were bad enough, the Italians were worse, but worst of all were the Spaniards.' They practised 'unheard-of tortures to force their victims to disclose where they had hidden their treasures'. And they were not always successful, it seems; years afterwards casks and vessels of buried money were discovered, suggesting that the owners had died before they could recover them.

Those who professed to support the imperial cause suffered with the rest, and none was safe from capture and demands for ransom. Neither S. Giacomo,[8] the Spanish church in the Piazza Navona, nor the church of the Germans, S. Maria dell' Anima,[9] was spared. Nor was the palace of the imperial ambassador, where two hundred refugees were hidden, nor the Palazzo dei SS. Apostoli,[10] which was occupied by the mother of one of the imperial commanders, Ferrante Gonzaga. Over two thousand people, more than half of them women, who had been given refuge in the Palazzo dei SS. Apostoli, were made to pay ransom. Most officers had little authority over their men and stood by helpless when they did not condone, encourage or even participate in the atrocities: one German commander boasted his intention of eviscerating the Pope once he had laid his hands on him.

Some priests were, indeed, eviscerated. Others were stripped naked and forced to utter blasphemies on pain of death or to take part in profane travesties of the Mass. One priest was murdered by Lutherans when he refused to administer Holy Communion to an ass. Cardinal Cajetan was dragged through the streets in chains, insulted and tortured; Cardinal Ponzetti, who was over eighty years old, shared his sufferings and, having parted with 20,000 ducats, died from the injuries inflicted upon him. Nuns, like other women, were violated, sold in the streets at auction and used as counters in games of chance. Mothers and fathers were forced to watch and even to assist at the multiple rape of their daughters. Convents became brothels into which women of the upper classes were dragged and stripped. 'Marchionesses, countesses and baronesses,' wrote the Sieur de Brantôme, 'served the unruly troops, and for long afterwards the patrician women of the city were known as "the relics of the Sack of Rome".'

As the invaders grew exhausted by their excesses, Cardinal Pompeo Colonna rode into Rome with two thousand followers on 7 May. Moved to tears by the sight of Rome, he opened his palazzo as a place of refuge, and did what he could to control his men – but they too were uncontrollable. They ran through the city, eager to plunder anything which the imperialists had disregarded, 'carrying away even the ironwork of the houses' and, so the Duchess of Urbino was told, 'raking together the chattels of the poor'. 'They were peasants, dying of hunger,' the Cardinal of Como said, 'and they sacked and robbed all that the other soldiers had not deigned to harvest.'

The number of people killed in the Sack of Rome was never determined. 'We took Rome by storm,' one of the German invaders reported laconically, 'put over six thousand men to the sword, seized all that we could find in the churches and elsewhere, burned down a great part of the city, tearing apart and destroying all copyists' works, all letters, registers and state documents.' A Spanish soldier claimed that he had helped to bury almost ten thousand corpses on the north bank of the Tiber and that a further two thousand had been thrown into the river. A Franciscan friar confirmed that twelve thousand people had been killed, and added that many lay unburied. In places they were piled so high they blocked the streets.

By the beginning of June, when St Peter's had been turned into a stable, the church of the Florentines into a barracks and the oratory of the nunnery of S. Cosimato[11] into a shambles, when palaces had been stripped bare, the Villa Madama had been almost destroyed and many other houses burned to the ground, when the Sapienza had been ruined and precious libraries and pictures lost for ever, Rome was a city of despair. Through it the stench of ordure and of decaying corpses was wafted by the early summer breeze and, mingling with the noxious smell of open drains and sewers, aggravated an epidemic of plague.

In Rome, the chief city of Christendom [a Spaniard wrote], no bells ring, no churches are open, no Masses are said, Sundays and feast-days have ceased. Many houses are burned to the ground; in others the doors and windows are broken and carried away; the streets are changed into dunghills. The stench of dead bodies is terrible; men and beasts have a common grave and in the churches I have seen corpses that dogs have gnawed. In the public places tables are set close together at which piles of ducats are gambled for. The air rings with blasphemies fit to make good men – if such there be – wish that they were deaf. I know nothing wherewith I can compare it, except it be the destruction of Jerusalem. I do not believe that if I lived for two hundred years I should see the like again.

From the windows of Castel Sant' Angelo which Benvenuto Cellini, according to his own fantastic account, saved virtually single-handed by his own 'unimaginable energy and zeal', Pope Clement looked out repeatedly for some sign that the army of the anti-imperial league was on its way across the Campagna to his relief. But each day he was disappointed, for the army, commanded by the Duke of Urbino, a general of unsurpassed prudence, remained rooted in Isola Farnese about ten miles north of Rome; and by 7 June the Pope had made up his mind he must capitulate. Required to surrender large areas of papal territory, he was not permitted to leave the castle until an immense ransom had been paid, and months passed while wearisome negotiations were conducted. In December the imperial troops, driven out of the city by plague and hunger, returned after plundering the Campagna. They threatened to hang their captains and cut the Pope to pieces if they did not receive their arrears of pay. When he heard this the Pope decided he must try to escape without delay; and on 7 December, with the connivance of an imperialist commander, he managed to do so. Disguised as a servant in a cloak and hood with a basket over his arm and an empty sack on his shoulder, he made his way to the episcopal palace at Orvieto, where an embassy from Henry VIII of

England, which had sought him out to obtain his authority for the King's divorce from Catherine of Aragon, found him 'in an old palace of the bishops of the city, ruinous and decayed . . . the chambers all naked and unhanged and the roofs fallen down'.

Beset by worry, pitiably thin and shrunken, almost blind in one eye, his liver diseased and the pale skin of his bearded face tinged with yellow, the Pope remained at Orvieto, while the imperial troops continued to occupy Rome. It was not until 11 February 1528 that, their arrears paid at last, they moved out; and not until October that the Pope rode back to the Vatican.

It was a devastated city that he saw. 'Rome is finished,' decided Ferrante Gonzaga the day after the Pope's return. 'Four fifths of it is quite uninhabited.' It was estimated that over 30,000 houses had been destroyed – almost as many as remained – and those that did still stand faced out upon streets filled with rubble and, even now, with the stench of putrefaction. The population had been reduced by half, and most of those who still lived in the city were compelled to live on charity. Trade had come to a halt; shops were deserted. Only three of Rome's more than a hundred apothecaries and herbalists still carried on business and it was believed that as many as 12,000,000 gold ducats had been lost. Much had been saved, of course. Philip of Orange, who had taken up quarters in the Vatican (where he was robbed by *Landsknechte*), managed, by posting reliable guards, to ensure that the Vatican Library and Raphael's *Stanze* were kept from harm. The body of the Duke of Bourbon which was laid in the Sistine Chapel helped to protect the paintings there. Many relics were preserved by being buried in secret places. But the catalogue of losses, which included the Raphael tapestries in the Vatican and the stained-glass windows of Guillaume de Marcillat in St Peter's, made mournful reading. So did the list of scholars and artists who had left Rome for other cities.

Parmigiano had fled to Bologna where he was joined by the philosopher Lodovico Boccadifferro and the engraver Marcantonio Raimondi. Giovanni da Udine, who had helped Raphael with the Vatican Loggie and the Villa Madama, had returned to Udine. Vicenzio da San Gimignano had returned to Florence; and Giovanni Battista Rosso Fiorentino settled in Perugia before moving to France. Polidoro da Caravaggio had fled, only to be murdered in Messina. Jacopo Sansovino had left Rome for Venice where he was appointed City Architect. Fabio Calvo, the translator of Vitruvius, Paolo Bombace, the Greek scholar, Paolo Bombasi, the poet and Mariano Castellani, the writer, had all perished in the sack. The grammarian, Julianus Camers, had committed suicide. The poet, Marcantonio Casanova, had been seen begging for bread in the streets before dying of the plague. Peruzzi had been tortured, forced to paint the dead Duke of Bourbon, released, recaptured, tortured again and robbed, before escaping to Siena where he became Architect to the Republic.

The man blamed and vilified for this disastrous dispersion lingered on in the Vatican, ill and almost blind, until, in the late summer of 1534, he contracted a fatal fever. Few mourned for him. He had, so Francesco Vettori said, 'gone to a great deal of trouble to develop from a great and respected cardinal into a small and little respected pope'. Indeed, his death, so a Roman correspondent informed the Duke of Norfolk, was 'the cause of rejoicing' in the city. In St Peter's, where his body lay, intruders transfixed it with a sword and his temporary tomb was smeared with dirt. The inscription beneath it, '*Clemens Pontifex Maximus*' was obliterated and in its place were written the words '*Inclemens Pontifex Minimus*'. Had it not been for the intervention of his nephew, Cardinal Ippolito de' Medici, the body would have been dragged round the streets on a meat-hook. Rome seemed once more to have returned to the barbarity and desolation of the Dark Ages.

PART TWO

ELEVEN

RECOVERY AND REFORM

Less than ten years after the Sack of Rome, the city prepared to welcome the Emperor under whose banners the plunderers had invaded it. Charles V, now revered in Rome for his crusade against the Ottoman admiral Barbarossa, and crowned in 1520 as Holy Roman Emperor, was to enter Rome through the Porta S. Sebastiano which was to be extravagantly decorated with frescos and stucco work. He was to be escorted past the Baths of Caracalla and the Septizonium, under the Arch of Titus and across the Forum by a specially constructed road to the Arch of Septimius Severus, then down the Via di Marforio to the Piazza di S. Marco and over the river to the Piazza of St Peter's. All buildings which stood in the way of the Emperor's path were to be demolished: there was to be no impediment to the progress of the five hundred horsemen, the four thousand foot-soldiers marching seven abreast, and the fifty young men from Rome's leading families, all clad in violet silk, who, with cardinals, dignitaries and resplendent bodyguards, were to accompany the Emperor through the city. François Rabelais, who was then living in Rome as physician to Cardinal Jean du Bellay, calculated that over two hundred houses had been pulled down as well as three or four churches. The whole route was decorated under the supervision of Antonio da Sangallo the younger, assisted by Battista Franco, Raffaelo da Montelupo and Maerten van Heemskerck.

The pope responsible for this grand display was Alexander Farnese whose coronation as Paul III in 1534 had been celebrated by tournaments and pageants as if to assure the people that the sad days which had followed the Sack of Rome were now at last over. Soon afterwards the Pope had revived the Roman Carnival and had subsequently attended the traditional spectacle in which a herd of swine were driven with oxen off the summit of Monte Testaccio and were stabbed to death by mounted men with lances as they thudded to the ground.

Shrewd, clever and cunning, Pope Paul was also amiable and courteous. He spoke quietly, slowly and at length. Yet there was a sharp gleam in his small eyes, a hint of impatient combativeness that made men wary in his presence. He was feared as well as liked. His grandfather, a highly successful *condottiere*, had extended the already considerable possessions of his family around Lake Bolsena; his father had married an heiress of the powerful Caetani family; his beautiful sister, Giulia, had married an Orsini and had become the mistress of the Borgia Pope, Alexander VI. With the help of this useful connection, Alexander Farnese had prospered in the Church. As a cardinal, he had become its Treasurer, and he had much enlarged

35. Titian's portrait of Allesandro Farnese (1468–1549), Pope Paul III, with his grandsons, Alessandro and Octaviano. Pope Paul helped to restore Rome after its devastation in 1527.

his fortune by the acquisition of numerous benefices. He had become rich enough to begin the building of that most splendid of High Renaissance palaces, the Palazzo Farnese,[1] which cost so much that even his resources were for a time exhausted by it and work had to cease, a misfortune advertised to passers-by in the Via Giulia by a placard inscribed with the words, 'Alms for the building of the Farnese'.

In those days Alexander Farnese had been renowned for his worldly ways. He had four illegitimate children and was as unscrupulous in promoting their interests as any of his predecessors had been in promoting theirs: two of his grandchildren were created cardinals while still in their teens. But, although he never lost his faith in astrologers, consulting them before embarking upon any transaction or journey and rewarding them liberally when their prognostications proved well founded, he abandoned his most questionable secular habits before becoming Pope. As Pope, he displayed a real concern for Church reform, supporting new religious orders, confirming the militant Jesuit Order, founded by Ignatius Loyola, and calling the Council of Trent, thus encouraging the Counter-Reformation which the Sack of Rome had made imperative.

In Rome he was often to be seen walking about the streets inspecting the building projects which were at last beginning to make the city whole again after its devastation. Although his finances were sometimes so strained that he had to resort to a renewed sale of indulgences and even to appropriate money contributed by Spain for a crusade against the Turks, he kept Antonio da Sangallo and numerous other architects and craftsmen busy in reconstructing the Belvedere and the buildings on the Capitoline hill, in renewing the city's fortifications, in forming the Sala Regia[2] and the Cappella Paolina[3] in the Vatican, and in resumed work upon St Peter's. He restored the University of Rome and increased the subsidies of the Vatican Library. He had himself painted three times by Titian and, determined to enlist the services of Michelangelo, he set out with ten cardinals for the great man's house on the Macel' de' Corvi.

Michelangelo had returned to Rome, aged fifty-nine, at the request of Clement VII who had asked him to decorate the altar wall of the Sistine Chapel. He had not wanted to accept this commission, since he was desperately anxious to get back to work on Julius II's tomb. And in the time of the ill and weary Pope Clement he had been able to work on the tomb in secret while progressing slowly with cartoons for the Sistine Chapel wall. With the forceful Pope Paul III, however, Michelangelo could not prevaricate. The Pope was determined to have Michelangelo working for himself alone. 'I have harboured this ambition for thirty years,' he is reported to have said to Michelangelo. 'And now that I am Pope I shall have it satisfied. I shall tear the tomb contract up. I am quite set upon having you in my service, come what may.' One of the attendant cardinals, looking around the sculptor's studio, observed that the statue of Moses was alone worthy to do honour to the memory of Pope Julius. Another suggested that the remaining statues could be made by assistants from Michelangelo's models. The Pope, having seen the cartoons for the Sistine Chapel wall, became more insistent than ever. So Michelangelo gave

36. A detail from the 'Last Judgement' in the Sistine Chapel, which Michelangelo completed in 1541.

way. He was appointed Chief Architect, Sculptor and Painter to the Vatican and began work on *The Last Judgement* in 1535.

When the fresco was revealed on All Hallows' Eve 1541, 'it was seen', so Vasari said, 'that Michelangelo had not only excelled the masters who had worked in the chapel previously but had also striven to excel even the vaulting that he had made so famous. For *The Last Judgement* was by far the finer since Michelangelo imagined to himself all the terror of those fearful days.'[4]

The Pope himself was evidently so overwhelmed with emotion that he fell to his knees, crying 'Lord, charge me not with my sins when thou shalt come on the

Day of Judgement.' So enthralled was he, indeed, by Michelangelo's genius that he would give him no respite from his labours, instructing him to start work now on frescos for the Cappella Paolina. Already he had interrupted his work on *The Last Judgement* by asking him to consider the problem of there being in Rome no impressive central square in which so great a state visitor as Charles V could be received. The Capitol was the natural place for such a square; and Michelangelo was required to construct one on the summit of the hill, and to design a suitable grand approach to it, the Cordonata.

Michelangelo began by designing a new base for the statue of Marcus Aurelius which the Pope decided should be the centre of the new piazza, the Piazza del Campidoglio. He then proposed that an oval shape, decorated with a complicated geometric design, should be inscribed around it. Opposite the Cordonata, beyond the statue and its oval surround, was to be a restored Palazzo del Senatore; on either side of this, opposite each other at a slightly canted angle, were to be a reconstructed Palazzo dei Conservatori and a new palace, the Palazzo Nuovo, now the Capitoline Museum. The whole design was not to be realized until the middle of the next century, but successive architects were careful to follow the master's plans.[5]

As it was with the Capitol, so it was with the Palazzo Farnese which, left unfinished at the time of Antonio da Sangallo's death, was completed by Giacomo della Porta who incorporated in it Michelangelo's designs for the cornice and the upper storey of the courtyard. So it was also with the Porta Pia which, designed by Michelangelo in 1561, was not finished until 1565, the year after he died. And so it was with St Peter's upon which, as *capomaestro* in unwilling succession to Antonio da Sangallo, Michelangelo spent his last unhappy years.

Still vigorous in old age, he could work almost as concentratedly as he had when carving one of St Peter's most treasured possessions, the Pietà.[6] Even now he continued his labours far into the night, a heavy paper cap of his own devising serving as a holder for a candle. 'He can hammer more chips out of very hard marble in fifteen minutes than three young stonecarvers can do in three or four hours,' a French visitor to Rome recorded. 'It has to be seen to be believed. He went at it with such fury and impetuosity that I thought the whole work would be knocked to pieces. He struck off with one blow chips three or four inches thick, so close to the mark that, if he had gone just a fraction beyond, he would have ruined the entire work.'

But these bursts of almost frenzied activity were now succeeded by bouts of illness, of cantankerous depression, of moods of bitterness in which he felt that the work on St Peter's had been imposed upon him as a penance by God. There were differences with the members of the *Congregazione della Fabbrica di San Pietro*, the works committee, whom the Pope's high regard allowed him to dominate. There were quarrels, too, with the assistants and followers of Sangallo who had hoped to carry on their master's plan. Michelangelo disapproved of this plan. He had never liked Bramante, but he conceded in a letter to a member of the *Fabbrica* that he was 'as skilful in architecture as anyone from the time of the ancients up to now', and he condemned Sangallo's plan on the grounds that it deprived Bramante's

37. Michelangelo's Coronata, leading up to his Piazza del Campidoglio on the Capitol; and on the left, the steeper slope of 122 steps to S. Maria d'Aracoeli.

design 'of all light'. 'And that's not all,' he added in a passage that illustrates the hazards of life in sixteenth-century Rome. 'It has no light of its own. And its numerous hiding-places, above and below, all dark, lend themselves to innumerable knaveries, such as providing shelter for bandits, for coining money, ravishing nuns, and other rascalities, so that in the evening when the church is to be closed, it would take twenty-five men to seek out those who are hiding inside, and because of its peculiar construction, they would be hard to find.'

Michelangelo put forward a new design, closer in spirit to Bramante's, though proposing a dome of a different shape and dispensing with the corner towers. A wooden model of this design was offered to the Pope in 1547 and was eagerly accepted. So the work proceeded under Michelangelo's directions. But it proceeded slowly. Money was short, the members of the *Fabbrica* were hostile; in 1549 Paul III died and was succeeded by Julius III who was sympathetic towards the *capomaestro* yet less willing to support him unreservedly. Michelangelo himself was growing very old and was often ill, suffering from stone which made it difficult for him to urinate, gave him intense pain in his back and side and prevented him from going to St Peter's as often as he should have done. The *Fabbrica*, increasingly dissatisfied with him, appointed one of his leading critics,

38. The view from the Palatine over the Forum. According to Livy, it was on the Palatine that the first Roman settlement was built by Romulus.

Nanni di Baccio Bigio, as Superintendent of the Basilica. This indifferent artist was dismissed by the Pope, who disposed also of another rival, Pirro Ligorio, by giving him the post of Palace Architect, in which capacity he created the delightful Casino di Pio IV in the Vatican Gardens.[7] But Michelangelo, approaching ninety, was now too aged to cope with the multiple difficulties and frustrations that daily beset him. He was rumoured to be in his dotage, and he confirmed the stories himself. 'I've lost my brains and my memory,' he told Vasari; and to his nephew, Lionardo, he wrote, 'I am so ill in body so often that I cannot climb the stairs and the worst is that I am filled with pains ... I did not acknowledge the *trebbiano* [white wine] ... Writing, being old as I am, is very irksome to me ... But thank you ... It's the best you've ever sent me ... I'm sorry, though, you put yourself to this expense, particularly as I've no longer anyone to give it to, since all my friends are dead.'

Michelangelo himself died on 18 February 1564. He was followed to the tomb, in Vasari's words, by a great concourse of artists and 'was buried in the Church of SS. Apostoli in the presence of all Rome'.[8] Florence claimed his remains, however, and his body was 'smuggled out of Rome by some merchants, concealed in a bale, so that there should be no tumult'.

The final months of his long life had been clouded by disappointment that the last of the popes he had served, Paul I V, had had no real sympathy for Renaissance art and had been so disgusted by the nudes in Michelangelo's *The Last Judgement* that he was with difficulty dissuaded from having the whole fresco destroyed. His predecessor, Julius III, on the other hand, while also a dedicated reformer who reopened the Council of Trent and supported the Jesuits, was much more enlightened and far more responsive to beauty. He built the enchanting Villa Giulia,[9] whose gardens, planted with nearly forty thousand trees – cypress, pomegranates, myrtles and bays – contained a beautiful fountain by Bartolommeo Ammanati. He bought the so-called 'statue of Pompey',[10] against which Caesar was supposed to have been murdered and which was discovered in the 1550s in the Via dei Leutari, and he arranged for it to be placed in the Palazzo Spada,[11] then the home of Cardinal Capodiferro. And he appointed the greatest of Italian Renaissance composers, Giovanni Pierluigi da Palestrina, director of the Cappella Giulia in St Peter's.

Pope Paul I V, in striking contrast, declined to concern himself with such activities. Austere, uncompromising and rigidly orthodox, he was a member of the noble Neapolitan Carafa family and an unquestioning supporter of the Roman Inquisition. Preoccupied with Church discipline and international affairs, with the detested Spanish monarchy, with the excommunication of Elizabeth of England, the threat from the Muslims and the suppression of the heretics of the Netherlands, he insisted that virtue, not beauty, should be the concern of popes. He had the statuary taken out of the Villa Giulia and would have removed it also from the Cortile del Belvedere had he not been persuaded to content himself with stripping the reliefs from the walls and closing it to the public.

Paul I V would, indeed, have liked to destroy all the ancient monuments in the city on the grounds that they were the work of pagans. During his reign, sexual misconduct was punished with the most savage ferocity and sodomites were burned alive. Jews, confined in the ghetto, were made to wear an identifying badge and excluded from many occupations and all honourable positions. The Pope made himself so detested in Rome that upon his death the head of his statue upon the Capitol was struck off, dragged through the streets and thrown into the Tiber, while the monastery of the Dominicans, blamed for the excesses of the Inquisition, was stormed by a furious mob.

The former Dominican friar who became Pope Pius V in 1566 was quite as austere and ascetic a man and as severe a reformer as Paul I V. The son of poor parents and a shepherd himself until he was fourteen, he had achieved high office in the Inquisition, even though he had displayed such excessive zeal in pursuing and punishing the unfaithful during his first appointment in Como that he had been recalled. He had been promoted Commissary General of the Roman Inquisition and afterwards Grand Inquisitor. After his election as Pope, the Curia, the Church and the city were alike subject to disciplines which satisfied all but the most rigorous proponents of the Counter-Reformation. Members of religious orders were subjected to far stricter rules; bishops were required to spend much longer periods in their sees; nepotism was suppressed and the granting of indulgences and dispensations restricted. The powers of the Inquisition were increased and its scope widened so that none was safe from its grasp. The Congregation of the Index drew up a list of prohibited books, and obliged several printers to flee from Rome. Prostitutes were driven out of the city or required to live in restricted areas. Jews, expelled from the Papal States, were permitted to remain in Rome only in conditions even more humiliating than those to which they had been subjected in the days of Paul IV. Their traditional race during the Carnival was no longer allowed to take place along the course between S. Lucia[12] and St Peter's which it had followed for many years, but was moved to the Corso 'out of respect for the Apostles'.

Pius V's two successors, Gregory XIII and Sixtus V, both continued the process of reform which had followed upon the Sack of Rome, and both on occasions appeared excessive in their zeal: Gregory, who was responsible for the Gregorian Calendar in 1582 and for promoting the world-wide missionary activity of the Church, went so far as to celebrate the massacre of the Huguenots in France on St Bartholomew's Day with a Te Deum, while Sixtus, who reformed the Curia and limited the number of members of the Sacred College to seventy, had had to be recalled from Venice because of his extreme severity there as Inquisitor General. But both these popes were also dedicated builders and both enriched Rome. Pope Gregory founded the Collegio Romano[13] and gave large sums of money to the Jesuit Church, the Gesù,[14] as well as to S. Maria in Vallicella.[15] This last was the church of the Oratorians, the congregation founded by St Philip Neri, whose stress on beauty in worship, especially on good music, and whose advocacy of visual imagery as an aid to devotion helped to make them not only one of the greatest religious orders of the Counter-Reformation but also a pervasive influence on the artistic life of Rome. Their patron, Gregory XIII, also built the conduits from which the Via Condotti takes its name and had fountains constructed throughout the city such as those in Piazza Nicosia and Piazza Colonna.[16] He founded the Accademia di S. Luca;[17] and in 1574, as a summer residence for the popes, he began the Quirinal Palace.[18]

It was the strong-willed Sixtus V, however, who left his mark upon Rome more indelibly than any other pope of the Counter-Reformation. An ambitious, not to say ruthless, town-planner, he achieved so much in his short reign from 1585 to 1590 that men supposed him to have been considering the transformation of the city long before his election. Certainly it seems that, although he was the son of the poorest parents and had spent his early years as a swineherd in the bleak mountains of the Marche, he had for long believed that he, Felice Peretti, would one day rise to supreme authority in the Church. Sixty-four at the time of his election, in poor health and suffering from persistent insomnia, he undertook the task he had set himself as though he had no time to lose. He first restored the city's water supply, mending Alexander Severus's aqueduct, the Acqua Alessandrina – renamed after himself the Acqua Felice – as well as the underground pipes which led from Palestrina, thus providing an ample source for the houses and gardens and the twenty-seven fountains of Rome. He then turned his attention to the

Sixte V. elu Pape
le 24 avril 1585. né de pauvres parens au
Village de la Marche d'Ancone, mourut a Rome
le 27. aoust 1590 age de 69. ans

Se Vend a Paris chez E. Desrochers rue du foin pres la rue S. Jacq.

39. Sixtus V, Pope from 1585 to 1590, the austere reformer of the Curia.

building of new bridges across the Tiber, and to the construction, widening and rerouting of streets, determined to extend Rome beyond the congested older parts of the city, northwards and eastwards up to and beyond S. Maria Maggiore and Trinità dei Monti, these two churches themselves being connected by a new street, the Via Sistina. Other streets were planned to radiate from S. Maria Maggiore to link together the major basilicas. Obelisks were re-erected at important crossings, such as the obelisk which was brought from Heliopolis by Augustus and, formerly standing in the Circus Maximus, was placed in 1589 in the centre of the Piazza del Popolo.[19] 'In three years,' wrote the Venetian ambassador admiringly, 'all this area will be inhabited.'

Praiseworthy as this town-planning was deemed to be, the Pope's treatment of ancient buildings horrified many Romans. It was considered perfectly acceptable to place statues of Saints Peter and Paul on the columns of Trajan and Marcus Aurelius; but his demolition of the remains of the Septizonium and his intention, unrealized, to turn the Colosseum into a wool factory aroused widespread condemnation. So did the destruction of large parts of the Lateran Palace which he ruthlessly carried out, insisting that, in time, he would deal with other 'ugly antiquities' in the same way. He did not live long enough to execute his threat, even had he meant it to be taken seriously. But, before he died, additions to the Lateran, the Vatican and the Quirinal Palaces had all been begun or completed. Pius V's library had been extended across the Court of the Pine-cone[20] at the Vatican, while the Court of St Damasus[21] had been completed by adding on to the papal apartments. The Sistine Loggia[22] had been built at St John Lateran and the Cappella Sistina[23] in S. Maria Maggiore. Most gratifying of all, the work on St Peter's dome was almost finished at last.

For some years after the death of Michelangelo, little progress had been made at St Peter's. His successor as Chief Architect, Pirro Ligorio, had been dismissed in favour of Vignola who in 1573 had been succeeded by Giacomo della Porta. This *Capomaestro* had completed the Cappella Gregoriana[24] for his patron Gregory XIII; but it was not until the advent of Sixtus V that he was provided with the steadfast encouragement and, above all, with the funds, to press on with the dome as fast as he could. Financial reforms and traditional malpractices provided the money for over eight hundred workmen to be kept constantly employed not only by day but also at night so that the Pope might live to see the dome, as designed by Michelangelo, though modified into an ovoid rather than hemispherical shape by della Porta, soar triumphantly above the church.

At the same time, the Pope was determined to realize an ambition which others had set aside as too daunting – the removal to a more commanding setting of the great Egyptian obelisk,[25] for ages a major landmark of Rome, which was believed to have stood in the circus where the Christian martyrs were slaughtered in the days of Nero. It now rose to the south of the basilica, adjoining the chapel of St Andrew.[26] The Pope wanted it moved to the middle of the piazza in front of St Peter's and, having had erected there a wooden replica to see how the original

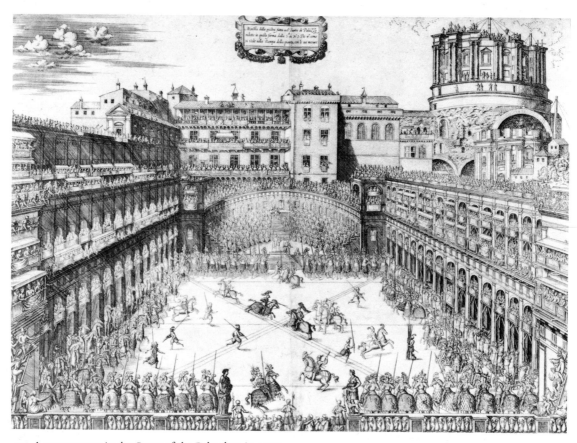

40. A tournament in the Court of the Belvedere in 1565.

would look, he advertised for a Leonardo da Vinci to undertake an operation that Michelangelo had said was impossible. Hundreds of plans were submitted from all over Europe, from mathematicians and engineers, from natural scientists and master masons, from philosophers and necromancers and, so it was said, from more than five hundred architects. Some were ludicrous, others ingenious, but none seemed practicable as a means of moving a solid stone monument eighty feet high and weighing five hundred tons through a densely built-up area. Bartolommeo Ammanati said that he could not at the moment think of a solution but that if the Pope would wait a year he was sure he would come up with the answer by then, a suggestion calculated to try His Holiness's limited patience to the utmost. Then, assuming a confidence he was far from feeling, Domenico Fontana, assistant *Capomaestro* at St Peter's, claimed that he could undertake the task and produced a little wooden model which lifted a leaden obelisk without difficulty. The Pope watched the operation approvingly and told Fontana to go ahead immediately and waste no further time.

As the days went by, Fontana became increasingly apprehensive. He was a small, self-satisfied man, loquacious, didactic, opinionated and pedantic. Several of his colleagues found him so irritating that they could not help hoping that his career would end in disaster. As he looked down into the huge hole which had been dug around the base of the obelisk, whose weight over the centuries had sunk it deep below the surface of the ground, he had forebodings of disaster himself. He thought it as well to order a relay of post-horses to be held in readiness in case he had to fly from the Pope's fury. But though an uninspired architect, Fontana was a most meticulous and methodical engineer. He had made all his calculations with the utmost care.

At two o'clock on 30 April 1586 the operation began. Every window and rooftop from which it could be observed was crammed with expectant faces. Below them the 800-strong St Peter's work-force, who had heard Mass at dawn, stood waiting by the ropes and windlasses for Fontana, standing on a raised platform, to give the signal for the obelisk to be raised from its pit. Protected by straw mats and by planks encircled with iron bands, it stood motionless and, so some of the crowd declared, immovable in its pyramidal scaffolding of stout poles and cross-beams.

41. The Piazza di S. Pietro during a papal blessing in 1567, showing the drum of the dome completed.

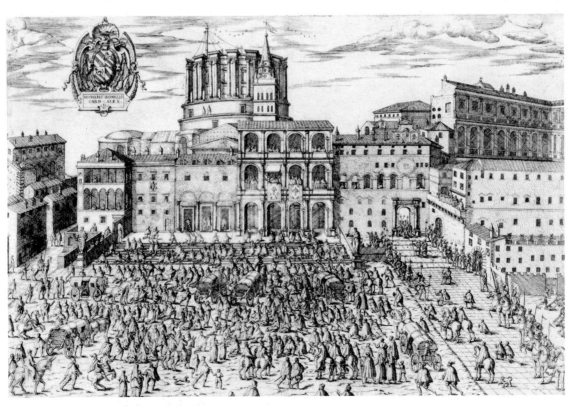

And then as Fontana lifted up his hand, as trumpets blared and the workmen and 140 cart-horses pulled with all their strength upon the ropes, the windlasses creaked into motion and, to the cheers of the spectators, to the thunder of the guns of Castel Sant' Angelo and the pealing of bells, the immense monolith rose slowly out of the earth. It was later laid horizontally to the ground upon rollers.

An even larger crowd than had witnessed the raising of the obelisk gathered in the piazza of St Peter's to watch its re-erection on the Feast of the Exaltation of the Cross. They did so, however, in breathless silence, for the Pope had ordained that anyone uttering the slightest sound that might endanger the operation would be instantly executed: a gallows was erected in the piazza to lend fearsome authority to his order. Even so, as the obelisk was raised and for a moment seemed in danger of thudding back to the ground, a man's loud voice called out in Genoese dialect, '*Aigua ae corde!*', 'Water on the ropes!' It was a sailor from Bordighera who had seen that they were about to burn and split with the heat of friction. His brave disobedience to the Pope's demand was rewarded by his being asked to name a favour he would like His Holiness to grant. He is said to have asked that his home town should be allowed to supply palms for St Peter's on Palm Sunday every year thereafter. The request was willingly granted and for centuries observed.

That night, as the obelisk stood firmly in position, resting on the backs of the four satisfied-looking bronze lions which still support it today, there were happy rejoicings in Rome, banquets, fireworks and dancing. The golden ball on the summit of the needle, long supposed to contain the ashes of Julius Caesar, was removed and found to be solid. It was replaced with a bronze cross, in one of whose arms was later placed a piece of the Holy Cross; and on the base of the obelisk were inscribed the words, '*Ecce Crux Domini Fugite Partes Adversae*', the challenge of the Counter-Reformation.

Other pieces of the Holy Cross, contained in a lead casket, were placed within the crowning cross raised above the dome of St Peter's, which was finally completed on 21 May 1590. Together with these fragments were inserted relics of St Andrew, of St James the Great, of Popes St Clement I, Calixtus I and Sixtus III and seven Agni Dei – medallions of the Lamb of God, made of wax from paschal candles and dust from the bones of martyrs and blessed by the Pope in the first year of his pontificate and every seventh year afterwards.

Pope Sixtus V had lived to see the dome completed; but it was left to the pious Florentine, Pope Clement VIII, to have it covered with lead and to see the cross installed above the lantern. In 1594 Pope Clement celebrated his first Mass at the new high altar in St Peter's where della Porta had built for him the Cappella Clementina[27] opposite the Cappella Gregoriana by the entrance to the crypt. Soon afterwards, della Porta died and Fontana's nephew, Carlo Maderno, was appointed to succeed him. The age of the Baroque had begun.

TWELVE

BERNINI AND THE
BAROQUE

'A little before my Comming to the Citty,' wrote the English diarist, John Evelyn, during his visit to Rome in 1644, 'Cavaliero Bernini, Sculptor, Architect, Painter & Poet . . . gave a Publique Opera (for so they call those Shews of that kind) where in he painted the Seanes, cut the Statues, invented the Engines, composed the Musique, writ the Comedy and built the Theater all himself.'

Gian Lorenzo Bernini, then at the height of his astonishing powers, had been brought to Rome as a child by his father, a sculptor who had come from Naples to work in the Cappella Paolina[1] in the Church of S. Maria Maggiore. A precociously gifted and industrious boy, he had spent long hours studying in the Vatican, copying paintings and, as his own son was later to testify, making 'so many sketches you wouldn't believe it'. By the age of eight he had already, with expert skill, carved a head in marble. The painter Annibale Carracci, who had been summoned to Rome to work at the Farnese Palace, said of him that he had arrived in childhood where others would be proud to be in their old age. He may have been as young as fifteen when he finished the assured *Martyrdom of St Laurence*, having put his own leg in the fire to study in a looking-glass the features of torment. Within a year or so he had completed the *Martyrdom of St Sebastian* and had long since gained the admiration of the Pope who, having commissioned a portrait bust from him, had expressed the hope that the young artist would 'become the Michelangelo of this century'.

Camillo Borghese had been elected Pope and had chosen the title of Paul V in 1605. Tall, strong, healthy and vigorous with a neat moustache, triangular beard and myopic eyes that rendered his peering gaze disconcerting, he had the appearance of a shrewd and successful merchant; and he certainly made sure that his family, to whom he was devoted, enjoyed all the benefits that riches could bestow. Yet he was a devout man, most assiduous in prayer: he made his confession and said Mass every day; and, when celebrating, was 'the ideal of the priesthood'. He was believed to have preserved his baptismal innocence. Charitable to the poor, he was also cultivated and indefatigably industrious. While he lavished money upon building and works of art, and indulged his nephews in their every whim, creating Marcantonio Borghese Prince of Vivaro, and loading Scipione with ecclesiastical offices and revenues, it was generally felt that such extravagance might be excused in one so conscientious, pious and chaste.

There was also a political motive behind his artistic patronage. The Roman

42. A self-portrait of Gian Lorenzo Bernini, who worked in Rome from his boyhood until his death there at the age of 81 in 1680.

Church which had evolved from the Counter-Reformation could not afford to be complacent: constantly assailed by its enemies, it was still vulnerable to attack, still beset by problems. There was trouble with the Venetian Republic over papal jurisdiction and ecclesiastical immunity; there was trouble, too, with England where the Protestant King James I had required Roman Catholics to take an unacceptable oath of allegiance; there were disturbances in Germany where differences between Catholics and Protestants were soon to lead to the Thirty Years' War. Yet, while there was no cause for complacency, the Church could now afford to present – and, so its leaders henceforth believed, *should* present – a less formidable aspect to the world, to offer exhilaration rather than repression, to welcome rather than exclude, to enlist a less austere art in the service of the faith, to replace the cold mannerism into which the High Renaissance classicism had degenerated with that enthusiasm of feeling, that exuberant style later to be known as Baroque.

The many monumental fountains which Paul V created in Rome were harbingers of the wonders to come. In the days of the Emperor Trajan, as the Pope was fond of reminding visitors, there had been as many as 1,300 fountains in the city supplied by eleven aqueducts. And modern Rome, while it could not expect to have so many, deserved far more than it had. To provide an abundant supply of water for his new fountains, the Pope repaired the aqueduct of the Emperor Trajan, renamed the Acqua Paola, which carried water from the lake of Bracciano as far as the Trastevere; and to celebrate the completion of the restoration in 1612 he built the grandiose Fontanone dell' Acqua Paola on the Janiculum.[2] Other fountains were erected in the Cortile del Belvedere, in the Piazza Scossa Cavalli, in the Piazza di Castello (destroyed in the revolution of 1849), in the Piazza di S. Maria Maggiore, in that of the Lateran, in the Via Cernaia 'for the thirsty country people and the dust-covered carriers', and, for the Jews, in the piazza of the synagogue. Three magnificent fountains were built in the Vatican gardens, the Fontana degli Specchi, the Fontana delle Torri and the Fontana dello Scoglio, all designed by Carlo Maderno who also built the fine fountain on the north side of St Peter's piazza, later to be matched on the south side by a fountain by Bernini.[3]

While these fountains were being erected all over Rome, the Pope was busy supervising the construction of the Borghese Chapel in S. Maria Maggiore, the removal of the huge classical pine-cone to the Cortile della Pigna at the Vatican, the restoration and decoration of several churches and the building of the new Church of S. Maria della Vittoria.[4] He was also actively occupied in the enlargement of the Quirinal Palace, the embellishment of the Vatican, the paving of streets, and the adornment of his family's three palaces. These were the palace which had been built for Cardinal Adriano Castellesi da Corneto in the Borgo and which later became known as the Palazzo Giraud-Torlonia; the Borghese Palace which, designed for the Spanish Cardinal Deza by Martino Longhi the elder, had been bought by the Pope in 1605 and soon afterwards presented to his nephew, Marcantonio;[5] and the palace, later to be known as the Palazzo Pallavicini-Rospigliosi, which was designed by Giovanni Vasanzio and Carlo Maderno for the Pope's nephew, Scipione Borghese.[6]

234

PAVLVS V. Camillus Burghesius Ro=
manus, creat? die 17. Maij an. 1605. Sedit
an. 15. mens. 8. dies 12 Obijt die 28 Ia=
nuarij an. 1621. Vac Sed. dies 12.

43. Camillo Borghese, Pope Paul V (1552–1621), who expressed the hope that the young Bernini
would 'become the Michelangelo of this century'.

Scipione, the extravagant, sybaritic and amiable cardinal whose expressive features have been captured for all time in Bernini's extraordinary lifelike bust,[7] was as prodigal a patron as his uncle. He not only paid for the restoration of the Basilica of S. Sebastiano and for the construction of Giovan Battista Soria's magnificent façades for S. Gregorio Magno[8] and S. Maria della Vittoria, but he also assembled one of the finest private collections of art and antiquities that the world has known. It contained some of the most impressive of Bernini's early works, including the *Apollo and Daphne* and the *David*, which were displayed – and can still be seen – in the villa that the Cardinal built for his own pleasure and the entertainment of his friends in the large park he had created beyond the Church of Trinità dei Monti.[9]

John Evelyn went to see this park one November day and thought that, from a distance, its wall, 'full of small turrets and banqueting houses', gave it the appearance of 'a little Towne'.

Within is an Elysium of delight [Evelyn continued] . . . The Garden abounds with all sorts of the most delicious fruit, and Exotique simples: Fountaines of sundry inventions, Groves & small Rivulets of Water. There is also adjoyning it a Vivarium for Estriges, Peacocks, Swanns, Cranes, etc; and divers strange Beasts, Deare & Hares. The Grotto is very rare, and represents among other devices artificial raines and sundry shapes of vessells, Flowers & which is effected by changing the heads of the Fountaines. The Groves are of Cypresse and Lawrell, Pine, Myrtil, Olive etc. The 4 Sphinxes are very Antique and worthy observation. To this is a Volary full of curious birds . . . The prospect towards Rome & the invironing hills is incomparable, cover'd as they were with Snow (as commonly they continue even a greate part of summer) which afforded a sweet refreshing. About the house there is a stately Balustre of white Marble, with frequent jettos of Water & adorned with statues standing on a multitude of Bases, rendering a most graceful ascent. The walls of the house are covered with antique incrustations of history as that of . . . Europe's ravishment & that of Leda. The Cornices above them consist of frontages and Festoons, betwixt which are Niches furnished with statues, which order is observed to the very roofe. In the Lodges at the Entry are divers good statues of Consuls etc. with two Pieces of Field Artillery upon Carriages (a mode much practiz'd in Italy before the Greate Men's houses) which they looke on as a piece of state more than defence.

Inside the villa Evelyn was shown a wonderful collection of art and curiosities, of antique statues, oriental urns, 'Tables of Pietra-Commessa' and vases of porphyry, looking-glasses, clocks, 'Instruments of Musique', Bernini's sculptures, which he considered 'for the incomparable Candor of the stone & art of the statuary, plainely stupendious', and a 'World of rare Pictures of infinite Value & of the best Masters'. 'In a word nothing but magnificent [was] to be seene in this Paradise.' Among the curiosities were a toy satyr 'which so artificially express's an human Voice with the motion of eyes & head that would easily affright one who were not prepared for that most extravagant vision', and a chair 'which Catches fast any who sitte downe in it, so as not to be able to stir out of it, by certaine springs conceiled in the Arms and back thereof, locking him in armes & thighs after a true tretcherous Italian guize'.

44. Maffeo Barberini, Pope Urban VIII (1568–1644), in whose pontificate Bernini executed much of his finest work.

Beyond the walls of the villa the gardens were fully worthy of the horticultural centre which Rome had now become. There were *giardini segreti* in which the fragrance of orange blossom mingled with that of rare herbs; a sunken garden planted with anemones, hyacinths and narcissi, herbaceous borders, beds of carnations and tuberose; a tulip garden surrounded by roses; rows of strawberries hedged with jasmine. And at the approach to these delights the visitor was welcomed by a large marble tablet inscribed with the words, 'Whoever thou art, so long as thou art a free man, fear not here the bonds of the laws! Go where thou wilt, ask whatever thou desirest, go away whenever thou wishest ... Let seemly enjoyment be the guest's only law ...'

At first all were freely admitted to the grounds, Romans and foreign visitors alike; but when a staid tourist was shocked by some of the pictures in a summer-house, the Pope, sympathetic to such aversions, took the opportunity of ordering that the park should be closed to strangers. And thereafter he could retire to the villa in perfect peace to contemplate the view across the green park to the Campagna, while his more gregarious nephew could entertain his many friends without disturbance.

Throughout the life of Paul V, Bernini remained on excellent terms with the Pope and his family, his principal and generous patrons. But when Cardinal Maffeo Barberini came to the papal throne as Urban VIII in 1623, he required the exclusive services of the great sculptor and allowed him no time for other patrons, making only one exception in the case of Scipione Borghese who had helped him in his election. Otherwise Bernini was now a Barberini man; and when Cardinal Mazarin attempted to persuade him to go to work in France, the Pope was adamant in his refusal. 'Bernini was made for Rome,' he said, 'and Rome was made for him.'

Maffeo Barberini was fifty-five at the time of his election, a good-looking, accomplished, masterful and highly intelligent man, a scholar and a poet. The son of a rich Florentine, he had both the means and taste to ensure that Rome derived the fullest benefits from Bernini's genius. He had known him well for long. Indeed, while Bernini was working on his *David* he supposedly held a looking-glass to the sculptor's face to provide a model for the hero's look of tense concentration. And as soon as he became Pope he sent for Bernini, then aged twenty-three, and said to him, 'It is your great fortune, Cavaliere, to see Maffeo Barberini made Pope; yet our fortune is even greater, since Bernini lives in our pontificate.'

The friendship between the two men now deepened. The Pope was devoted to the younger man, as he might have been to a beloved son. 'He is a rare man,' the Pope declared, 'a sublime artist, born by Divine Disposition and for the glory of Rome to illuminate the century.' He gave instructions that the sculptor should be allowed to enter his room whenever he chose to do so, and begged him to have no reserve in his presence now that he was Pope. He asked Bernini to sit and talk to him while he was having dinner, and to stay until he fell asleep. And Bernini, a small, spare man who ate little apart from fruit, did what he was told. Whereas

45. St Peter's in the pontificate of Paul V (1605–21), after the erection of the obelisk but before the piazza was enclosed by Bernini's colonnade.

with others he was renowned for his independence and fiery temper, with the Pope, himself liable to bouts of excessive irascibility, Bernini was always pliable and patient, equable and polite.

Although the sculptor's earlier works in the new pontificate were relatively minor – a new façade for the Church of S. Bibiana,[10] for example, and a statue of the saint to be placed inside it – the Pope had great plans for him in mind. And in the summer of 1626 Bernini was given the most important commission of his career so far, a monumental work for St Peter's which was to occupy him and numerous assistants, including his father, for nearly ten years.

The appearance of St Peter's had changed dramatically since the death of Michelangelo. The confused clutter of buildings of all periods and styles, mostly dilapidated and some dangerous, which still clustered beneath the dome when it was finished in 1590, had all been swept away. For, one stormy day in 1605, a big block of marble had fallen to the pavement during Mass, narrowly missing those members of the congregation who were standing by the altar of the Madonna della Colonna and driving them screaming from the church. The *Fabbrica* had been forced to conclude that the whole of the old, tottering remaining parts of the basilica must be demolished, and the Pope had reluctantly agreed, despite the protests from various cardinals and conservative Romans who reiterated the protests which Julius II and Bramante had had to face a hundred years before. Far more respect had been shown for the monuments and relics, however, than '*il ruinante*' and Julius had had the patience to grant them. Records had been kept; corpses had been reverently disinterred and reburied with full honours elsewhere; treasures had been carefully packed and taken away, in many cases to the lasting benefit of other churches.

As della Porta's successor, and an architect whose work was much admired by Paul V, it had fallen to Carlo Maderno to build the new nave. He was then fifty-one years old, good-natured and amenable. He had worked with his uncle, Domenico Fontana, in erecting obelisks for Sixtus V; he had subsequently worked for another uncle whose studio specialized in the design of fountains; and he had himself designed several fountains, other than the one in St Peter's piazza, as well as a new façade for the Church of S. Susanna.[11] He watched work begin on digging the foundations for his new nave at St Peter's on 8 March 1607, and he remained chief architect until his death over twenty years later, having provided the basilica with a nave which has been severely criticized for blocking the view of the dome from the piazza and a façade which has been as strongly condemned for being too wide in relation to its height.[12]

Appointed to succeed Maderno, Bernini proposed improving the façade by providing it with towers at either end as Maderno had originally intended. Pope Urban agreed to this and work began. Soon the first two stages of the south tower were finished, and a wooden and painted canvas model of the third stage had been placed in position above them. This addition to the basilica's façade was admired by all except Bernini's most jealous rivals. But then, to the architect's horrified mortification, cracks began to appear not only in the tower but also in the façade to which it was attached. Bernini's structure, hastily built while the unreliable members of the *Fabbrica* still approved of its design, was evidently much too heavy for Maderno's foundations which had not been intended for such a weight. Orders were immediately given for the tower to be demolished before further damage was done. Humiliated and castigated by the *Fabbrica* and even by the Pope, Bernini retired to his house where he was reported to be ill in bed, while other architects were commissioned to propose plans in place of the *capomaestro's* disastrous enterprise.

Fortunately for Bernini's reputation, he had already begun work on the great canopy under the dome, the baldacchino over St Peter's grave[13] which, followed by the nearby statue of Longinus[14] and the tomb beneath which Pope Urban was to be buried,[15] ensured that his failure with the towers was ultimately eclipsed. The construction of the baldacchino also nearly ended in failure, since the erection

CÆLORVM + TV ES PETRVS

46: The crossing of St Peter's, showing Bernini's baldacchino (1624–33) beneath the dome.

of so massive a bronze monument, as high as the Farnese Palace, required extensive foundations; and the digging of these beneath the pavement of St Peter's necessitated the disturbance of many holy graves and relics. Protests against such sacrilege were vociferous; and when several men engaged upon the work died in mysterious circumstances and others refused to carry on, fearing the whole project was accursed, there were demonstrations in the piazza and marches of angry objectors throughout the Borgo. But the Pope, although himself seriously ill – an additional sign of God's disfavour – was determined that the baldacchino should be completed. He authorized the payment of additional wages to the workmen, and he even sanctioned the stripping of the bronze revetment from the portico of the Pantheon, an act of vandalism which gave rise to the celebrated pasquinade, attributed to the Pope's physician:

> *Quod non fecerunt barbari,*
> *Fecerunt Barberini.*
> What the barbarians did not do,
> the Barberini did.

So long as the Barberini Pope lived, Bernini was secure in his position as the recognized artistic director of Rome. But he was still only thirty-four when the baldacchino was completed; and the especial esteem in which he was held by the Pope aroused the deepest resentment among his older rivals, a resentment which his manner did little to alleviate. Increasingly moody and unpredictable, he was at times friendly and amenable, at others arrogant and dismissive. His sardonic sense of humour was always unsettling: it was difficult to be sure when he was making a joke. He maintained with all apparent seriousness, for example, that the dilapidated Hellenistic 'Mastro Pasquino', was the finest of all antique statues. Also, while he never spoke ill of his rivals, it was felt that he regarded their work as decidedly inferior to his own on which he was always careful to place a high price; and, being acquisitive, he became extremely rich. Deeply religious, he went every day to the Church of the Gesù for vespers and was most exact about confession. And his enemies declared that he had much to confess. It was believed that he had contracted the *morbo gallico* and this may, indeed, be why the Pope, paying the compliment of visiting him when he was ill, suggested that he should settle down, marry when he recovered and have children. He replied that his statues were his children. But soon afterwards he did marry and he did have children, eleven of them; and the marriage seems to have been a very contented one.

Bernini's professional career, however, suffered a severe setback on the death of his patron in 1644 and the election of Cardinal Giambattista Pamphilj as Innocent X. The new pope was a dour, uncommunicative and distrustful man, without close friends and much influenced by an astute, grasping and interfering sister-in law, Donna Olimpia Maidalchini. Tall, gaunt and excessively unprepossessing, with a furrowed brow, ugly chin, bulbous nose and bilious complexion, he made the sad, resigned comment when shown the remarkable portrait of him by Velasquez, which hangs in the Palazzo Doria picture gallery, '*Troppo vero*, too true, too true.'[16]

Recognizing that there was no trace of beauty in his own form, he had a horror of displays of nudity in art. And parsimonious though he was, he paid for fig leaves and metal tunics to cover the genitals and breasts of numerous offending statues in Rome. He was even said to have required Pietro da Cortona to clothe a nude figure of the child Jesus by Guercino. With Bernini and with Poussin, who had become one of the leading painters in Rome, he had as little as possible to do. 'Things in Rome have greatly changed under the present papacy,' wrote Poussin to a friend in Paris, 'and we no longer enjoy any special favour at Court.' Associating them with the family of his detested Barberini predecessor, whose extravagance and largesse towards his family had left the papacy almost bankrupt, Pope Innocent turned to other artists instead, to the sculptor, Alessandro Algardi, one of whose early commissions was the huge statue of S. Filippo Neri in S. Maria in Vallicella, to Girolamo and Carlo Rainaldi, and to an architect a few months younger than Bernini, Francesco Borromini.

A gloomy, solitary man, often depressed, usually irascible and always difficult, Borromini was bitterly conscious of his humble origins, of his early years as a stonemason in the studio of his relative, Carlo Maderno, and he was inordinately jealous of Bernini's easy success and self-assurance. His own dealings with his clients were constantly disrupted by quarrels and often ended in acrimony, while with his assistants he was a demanding, rarely satisfied and sometimes violent master. On one occasion he had a workman beaten so savagely for a misdemeanour that he died of the wounds inflicted upon him. Disdainful of the smart clothes that Bernini wore, Borromini dressed like a workman, deriding his rival's concern about money and fashionable living, and finding it impossible to forget that his smart contemporary had been hailed as a genius long before his own exceptional talents had been recognized. When his chance to overtake Bernini came with the accession of Innocent X, Borromini lost no opportunity of blackening his rival's name and of bringing up the errors that had led to the demolition of the tower on the façade of St Peter's.

Yet Innocent was a man of taste and discernment. While appreciating Borromini's exceptional gifts, he could not be blind to Bernini's, however predisposed he was to dislike him personally. When the tomb of Urban VIII was unveiled in 1647, he was heard to declare, 'They say bad things about Bernini, but he is a great and rare man.' It was not long before he was persuaded to take him into his own employment.

The Pope's family, the Pamphilj, had originally come from Umbria; but in the sixteenth century they had settled in Rome where they had an unpretentious palace on Piazza Navona. Pope Innocent determined to rebuild this palace on a much grander scale and to make its surroundings as distinctive and imposing a memorial to his own family and reign as the neighbourhood of the Palazzo Barberini[17] was to that of Urban VIII. He commissioned Girolamo Rainaldi to undertake both the new palace[18] and, assisted by Carlo Rainaldi, a new church beside it, S. Agnese in Agone.[19] Borromini was later called in to help with both these buildings and had already been consulted about a fountain which was to be created in the piazza around an obelisk that the Pope had noticed, lying broken in pieces, by the Via Appia.

Artists other than Borromini had also been asked to submit designs for this fountain, but Bernini had not been one of them, although his Triton fountain[20] in the Piazza Barberini was an acknowledged masterpiece and the Fountain of the Barcaccia[21] in the Piazza di Spagna[22] had shown how ingenious he was in solving any problems which might be presented by a lack of pressure in the water supply. It seems, however, that a friend of his, Prince Niccolò Ludovisi, who had married a niece of the Pope, persuaded Bernini to submit a model and arranged for it to be placed in a room where His Holiness could not fail to see it. Another story, related by the Modenese ambassador, has it that a silver model of Bernini's design was presented to the Pope's bossy and influential sister-in-law who told him he need look no further. In any event, the Pope was enchanted by Bernini's model. 'We must indeed employ Bernini,' he said. 'The only way to resist executing his works is not to see them.' And so the splendid Fountain of the Four Rivers came into existence and Bernini was restored to papal favour.[23]

He remained in favour throughout the pontificate of Innocent X, making two fine busts of him, designing the Fonseca Chapel in the Church of S. Lorenzo in Lucina[24] for the Pope's doctor, Gabriele Fonseca, and building the Church of S. Andrea al Quirinale[25] for the Jesuit novices living on the Quirinal hill with money provided by Cardinal Camillo Pamphilj. Bernini was also on excellent terms with the Chigi Pope, the devout and intellectual Alexander VII who, on the very day of his election in 1655, sent for him to ask for his services. And it was in Alexander VII's pontificate that St Peter's piazza was transformed into the most dramatically realized public space in Europe by Bernini's colonnades,[26] that the beautiful staircase connecting the Vatican palace with the basilica, the Scala Regia,[27] was built, and that the basilica itself was enriched by the Cathedra of St Peter, the grand frame for the throne of St Peter which Bernini created in the apse.[28]

It was also in the reign of Alexander VII that Rome welcomed that most extraordinary of exiles, the former Queen of Sweden. Vivacious, witty and unconventional, Queen Christina had given up her throne eighteen months before at the age of twenty-seven, and had been received into the Roman Catholic Church. Regardless of the impression she created, she seemed to take delight in shocking people and once introduced her intimate friend, Ebba Sparre, to the staid English Ambassador as her 'bedfellow', assuring him that her friend's mind was as lovely as her body. She often wore men's clothes and, although short in stature, spurned the high heels that women usually favoured and wore men's flat shoes instead.

Her voice and nearly all her actions are masculine [wrote the Duc de Guise who had seen much of her during a visit to France]. She has an ample figure and a large bottom, beautiful arms, white hands, but more like those of a man than a woman; one shoulder is higher than the other [she had been dropped as a baby], but she hides this defect so well by her bizarre dress, walk and movements . . . Her face is large but not to a fault, also all her features are marked: the nose aquiline, the mouth big but not disagreeably so, teeth

47. Queen Christina of Sweden, who lived in Rome from 1655 and died in the Riario Palace in 1689.

passable, her eyes really beautiful and full of fire; in spite of some marks left by chicken-pox her complexion is clear ... The shape of her face is fair but framed by the most extraordinary coiffure. It's a man's wig, very heavy and piled high in front ... She wears her skirt badly fastened and not very straight. She is always heavily powdered over a lot of face-cream ... She loves to show off her mastery of horses ... She speaks eight languages, but mostly French and that as if she had been born in Paris. She knows more than all our Academy and the Sorbonne put together, understands painting as well as anyone and knows much more about our court intrigues than I do. In fact she is an absolutely extraordinary person.

In Rome she was to be judged so, too. At first, however, she behaved with the utmost discretion, obviously delighted with the respect and honour shown to her. She was received in private audience by Pope Alexander who arranged for her to sit beside him, even though a chair had to be specially designed for her by Bernini, since only a ruling sovereign could sit in His Holiness's presence in a chair with arms and no chairs without arms which were sufficiently imposing could be found. She was invited to occupy apartments in the Torre dei Venti above the Cortile del Belvedere which had been beautifully furnished for her and provided with a blazing fire and a silver bed-warmer. She was presented with a splendid carriage and six horses, a litter and two mules, an exquisitely caparisoned palfrey and a sedan chair, designed, like her bed, by Bernini, with sky-blue velvet upholstery and silver mountings. She was invited to a banquet by the Pope, although protocol did not allow him to eat in the presence of a woman; and upon the table, fabricated by Bernini's assistants, were all manner of concoctions in gilded sugar, allegorical compliments to the Queen's character and attainments. The orchestra played; the choir of St Peter's sang; a sermon was preached by a Jesuit priest; and after the meal was over the Queen was accompanied by a procession of distinguished guests to the Palazzo Farnese, which a less favoured convert, Frederick of Hesse-Darmstadt, had been required to vacate for her benefit.

From the Palazzo Farnese, which had been redecorated and refurnished for her, the Queen set out to see the sights of Rome under the direction of the charming and amusing Cardinal Azzolino. She was escorted everywhere, from St John Lateran to St Peter's, from the Sapienza where she was given over a hundred books, to the Propaganda Fide[29] where she was welcomed in over twenty languages, from the Collegio Romano where she was shown an apparatus used for making antidotes to poison, to Castel Sant' Angelo, where, having a meagre appetite and little taste for alcohol, she was not tempted by the offer of refreshments comprising the richest wines and huge mounds of crystallized fruits, nougat and sugared almonds. That year the Carnival was known as 'the Carnival of the Queen'; and at the end of February a magnificent pageant, the *Giostra delle Caroselle*, was presented especially for her benefit. She was serenaded in her box as Cavaliers fought Amazons in the arena below and a fierce dragon, rockets issuing from its nostrils and flames from its mouth, was slain in her honour.

But by now the Queen's eccentric behaviour and the depredations of her unpaid servants, who went so far as to chop up the doors of the Palazzo Farnese for

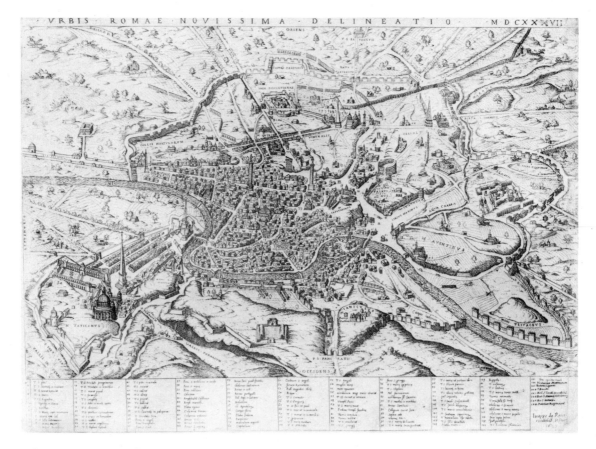

VRBIS ROMAE NOVISSIMA DELINEATIO · MDCXXXVII

48. A bird's-eye view of Rome in 1637.

firewood, were causing widespread annoyance in Rome. Having given up male attire for the moment, the Queen now wore the most provocative dresses, even when receiving cardinals. She hung some extremely indelicate pictures on the walls of the palace and had fig leaves removed from its statues; and when the Pope was persuaded to remonstrate with her both about this and her refusal to make public displays of her conversion, she merely replied that she was not in the least interested in 'considerations worthy only of priests'. It was rumoured that she was enamoured of a nun whom she had met in a convent in the Campo Marzio; and it was also said, with good reason, that she had fallen in love with Cardinal Azzolino. The news that Queen Christina was to leave Rome for a time was accordingly greeted with relief by the papal Court.

Missing the pleasures of power and hoping to solve her financial problems, she had decided to have herself made Queen of Naples. But her schemes foundered; and, having ordered the execution of her equerry, the Marchese Gian Rinaldo Monaldeschi, on the grounds that he had betrayed them, she returned to Rome, much to the annoyance of Pope Alexander who expressed the opinion that she was 'a woman born a barbarian, barbarously brought up and having barbarous thoughts'. He was, however, slightly mollified when Cardinal Azzolino obtained the Palazzo Riario for her at a modest rent; she would not, therefore, be living so close to him as she had been at the Palazzo Farnese.

Soon her new palace was filled with treasures, despite her irregular allowances. Pictures and furniture from Stockholm, books and more pictures from Prague, carpets from Persia, musical instruments, marbles, sculptures and an extraordinary variety of other works of art, including one of the finest collections of paintings of the Venetian school ever assembled, were arranged in profusion in the rooms. In the garden exotic and beautiful flowers and shrubs appeared with each passing season; during the spring of 1663 alone 275 orange and lemon trees and 200 jasmine plants were passed in her name through the Roman customs. She remained as unpredictable as ever. One grand visitor who tediously complained of his solitary life, received the reply, 'Better three days by oneself than half an hour with you.'

With the death of Pope Alexander VII in 1667, however, Queen Christina entered upon a more tranquil and less contentious stage of her life. The new Pope, Clement IX, in whose election her friend, Cardinal Azzolino, had played a critical role, was a kind-hearted, modest man, well disposed towards a highly intelligent woman who shared his love of pictures, music and the theatre. Anxious to make her feel at home in Rome, he came to visit her at the Palazzo Riario and gave a public banquet in her honour. At this banquet he provided a chair for her at his own table, a privilege no one could remember ever having seen granted by a pope to a woman before; and after Christmas he gave her a liberal pension.

Her finances now in more satisfactory condition, she added to her collections both at Palazzo Riario and at another palace which she leased, Palazzo Torlonia. The Queen also became a patron of archaeology, having obtained the Pope's permission to excavate the ruins of Decius's palace near the church of S. Lorenzo in Panisperna. She interested herself in alchemy and astronomy, providing a meeting-place at Palazzo Riario for the Accademia di Esperienza founded by Giovanni Giustino Campini; she granted her patronage to the oceanographer, Marsigli, and to the scientist, Borelli, and she took up writing, compiling books of maxims and essays in autobiography. She founded her own Academy, the Accademia Reale, forerunner of the celebrated Arcadia, at which distinguished scholars gave lectures, read papers and held seminars; and she gave her warm support to the theatre which was built on the site of the Tor di Nona prison[30] and in which many of the finest performances were given by singers in her service, such as Antonio Rivani, known as Cicciolino, whose departure from Rome for the court of the Duke of Savoy prompted an imperious letter to her French agent:

I want it to be known that [Cicciolino] is in this world only for me, and that if he does not sing for me he won't be able to sing for long for anyone else, no matter who they are . . . Get him back at any price. People are trying to make me believe that he has lost his voice. That doesn't matter. Whatever has become of him, he shall live and die in my service, or ill will befall him!

49. The Piazza Navona, built on the site of Domitian's athletics stadium. The Fountain of Four Rivers, designed by Bernini, rises in the centre beyond his Fountain of the Moor.

Cicciolino obediently returned and was still in her service when he died in 1686. Some years before, Alessandro Scarlatti, whose great gifts the Queen had been one of the first to recognize, had also entered her service as her *Maestro di Cappella*. Arcangelo Corelli was the director of her orchestra. She had long since acquired the services of Bernini who had created for her the lovely looking-glass which stood behind one of her most precious possessions, the bronze head of a Greek athlete of about 300 B.C.

Bernini still lived on, working hard. He survived the reign of Clement IX for whom he supervised the disposition of the angels on the Ponte Sant' Angelo, carving the full-size models of two of them himself;[31] and he worked on through the reign of Emilio Altieri, the Roman who became Pope Clement X in 1670 and for whose relation by marriage, Cardinal Paluzzi degli Albertoni, he decorated the Altieri chapel in S. Francesco a Ripa.[32]

He was in his mid-seventies when he set to work upon the deeply moving *Death of the Blessed Ludovica Albertoni* in this chapel, but his faculties were little impaired. On a visit to France a few years earlier, he had been described by Paul Fréart, Sieur de Chantelou:

He is of modest height, but well proportioned . . . with a temperament that is all fire.

His eyebrows are long, his brow large, with slight projections over the eyes. He is bald, and the hair that remains is curly and white . . . He is vigorous for his age and always wants to go on foot as if he were thirty or forty. One could say that his mind is one of the most beautiful ever made by nature, since, without having studied, he has most of the advantages that knowledge can give a man. He has, as well, an excellent memory, a quick and lively imagination, and his judgement seems clear and precise. He is a very acute conversationalist, and has a very special gift of expressing things in words, with his face, and by gesture to make you see as easily as the greatest painters do with their brushes. This is doubtless why he has been so successful putting on his own plays . . .

More than ever devout and fully conscious of the imminence of death, he set little store by his secular works, by such palaces he had designed in Rome as the Palazzo di Montecitorio[33] and the Palazzo Chigi-Odescalchi,[34] and by such conceits as the charming little elephant that carries the obelisk in the Piazza S. Maria sopra Minerva.[35] Once, when driving past the spectacularly theatrical Fountain of the Four Rivers, he pulled down the blinds of his carriage in distaste, exclaiming, 'How ashamed I am to have done so poorly.' What did satisfy him, at least, were his major religious works, his *Ecstasy of St Teresa* in S. Maria della Vittoria, which he thought the best thing he had ever done, and his Sant' Andrea al Quirinale. Towards the end of his life he was discovered by his son, who had gone to say his prayers in this church, wandering about in it, as though he were a tourist. Domenico approached his father and asked him what he was doing there 'all alone and silent'. 'My son,' Bernini replied, 'I feel special satisfaction at the bottom of my heart for this one piece of architecture. I often come here as a relief from my duties to console myself with my work.'

He went on working to the end. In the last months of his life he was still as busy as ever, restoring the Palazzo della Cancelleria; and it was this activity, his doctors suggested, that resulted in paralysis in his right arm: it deserved a rest, he said resignedly, after all the hard labour it had performed. He died on 28 November 1680. Nine days later it would have been his eighty-second birthday. His last completed work had been an over life-size bust of Christ carved for Queen Christina.

The Queen had been bitterly disappointed by the election of Innocent XI in 1676, for this new Pope was a severely economical reformer, stern and austere. He strictly limited the festivities of the Carnival, refused favours asked of him with such regularity that the Romans called him 'Papa No', ordered the private parts of statues not already concealed by Innocent X to be decently covered, and the breast of Guido Reni's Madonna to be painted over. He had the public theatres closed, and banished women from every stage. Queen Christina's Tor di Nona became a granary. Yet, for all her regret for the lost pleasures of the past, the Queen was as entertaining as ever, and as obliging as she had always been to those who did not bore her, willingly allowing visitors to see her collections as though they were contained in a public museum, and sometimes inviting sightseers to come to see her, too. She was now, after all, as she herself liked to admit, an ancient monument, one of the sights of Rome.

50. Bernini's architectural masterpiece, the Piazza di S. Pietro, was completed in the pontificate of the Chigi Pope, Alexander VII (1655–67).

She is exceeding fat [wrote one French visitor in 1688]. Her complexion, voice and face are those of a man . . . She has a double chin from which sprout a number of isolated tufts of beard . . . a smiling expression and a very amiable manner. Imagine, as regards her costume, a man's knee-length black satin skirted coat, buttoned all the way down . . . men's shoes. A very large bow of black ribbons instead of a cravat. A belt drawn tightly round the coat over the lower part of the stomach revealing its rotundity.

She died a year after this description of her was written. She had expressed the wish that she should be buried quietly in the Pantheon, the church of the Rotonda, where the bones of Raphael lay. But this was considered an unsuitable resting-place and, in the 'pomp and vanity' she had wished to avoid, her body was carried to St Peter's and placed in the crypt where the remains of only four other women had previously been placed. Some years later, when the seventeenth century was nearly over, Carlo Fontana was asked to design a monument for her.

The Rome in which she died had changed out of all recognition from the city to which Michelangelo had been summoned. The gentle shapes of domes and cupolas beneath the greater dome of St Peter's had replaced the bristling towers of the medieval nobles. The forbidding fortresses of earlier ages, when swordsmen fought each other through the streets, had given way to fine palaces and splendid villas in spacious, flower-filled gardens. And the travertine stone, so extensively used by the architects of the Baroque, had begun to predominate over the marble of the Renaissance. This was the Rome which the travellers of the eighteenth century now came south to enjoy.

THIRTEEN

IL SETTECENTO

'I would rather describe the rest of Italy four times over than give one account of Rome,' the French magistrate, Charles de Brosses, wrote home to a friend in the early years of the eighteenth century. 'Rome is beautiful – so beautiful that all the rest of Italy seems to me little in comparison.'

He had been enchanted from the beginning, for he thought that no other city he had ever seen had 'such a fine approach as Rome'. Having crossed the Tiber by the Ponte Molle, he passed through the Porta del Popolo which

forms the entrance of a quadrilateral space, in the centre of which rises an obelisk of granite that stood formerly in the great circus. At the base of this obelisk is a fountain. Opposite the gate the square is pierced by three long and narrow streets, like crow's feet, the ends of which are separated from each other by the porticoes and colonnades of two handsome, domed, twin churches [S. Maria di Montesanto and S. Maria dei Miracoli]. Of these three streets, the one on the left side [the Via del Babuino] leads to the Piazza di Spagna; the other to the port of the Tiber, called Ripetta [the Via di Ripetta]; the one in the middle, and by far the longest [the Corso] runs as straight as the letter I as far as the Palace of St Mark [the Palazzo Venezia], nearly in the centre of the town . . . Nothing can give a finer idea of the grandeur of Rome than this first sight of the city.

Later travellers agreed with him, even Tobias Smollett, the cantankerous Scottish writer who was ready to find fault with everything and was certainly exasperated on his visit in 1765 by the touts in the custom-house, formerly the hall of Antoninus Pius, where baggage was opened and its contents strewn about the floor, as a search was made for contraband goods until the customary bribes had changed hands. Smollett's coach was 'surrounded by a number of *servitori di piazza*, offering their services with the most disagreeable importunity'. Although he told them several times he 'had no occasion for any, three of them took possession of the coach, one mounting before and two of them behind'. Yet, once he had overcome his exasperation, Smollett had to agree with Charles de Brosses that the 'noble' Piazza del Popolo was such an 'august entrance' into Rome that it could 'not fail to impress a stranger with a sublime idea of this venerable city'. And this first sight was but a foretaste of the delights to come.

De Brosses found that the Corso was 'much too narrow for its length and was made still more so by the *trottoirs* for the use of pedestrians'. And he had to confess that he could not bear the everlasting drive of carriages along it, the tiresome

51. The Ripetta, the river port of the Tiber, which stood where the Ponte Cavour now crosses the river.

'fashion of the Italians of promenading' in their coaches in the midst of a town 'suffocated by the heat and dust'. Yet there were fine buildings on both sides, and finer ones still as one approached the heart of the city and then crossed over the river again towards St Peter's.

St Peter's itself was 'the finest thing in the universe . . . all is simple, natural, and august, consequently sublime . . . You might come to it every day without being bored. There is always something new to observe and it is only after many visits that one gets to know it at all . . . It is more amazing the oftener you see it.' As for the fountains in the piazza, nothing had ever given de Brosses so much pleasure as these 'two watery fireworks which play night and day without ceasing'. Indeed, like Smollett, he was more enraptured by the fountains of Rome – 'this profusion of water and rushing streams' – than by all the other wonders of the city, even the view from the Janiculum at sunset when one could look down upon 'that stupendous panorama of domes, towers, and golden cupolas, churches, palaces, green trees and sparkling waters'.

The Roman people, too, were so pleasant and civil, 'full of good breeding and more obliging than in any other part of Italy'. 'In short, to tell you in one word my impression of Rome,' de Brosses concluded, 'it is this – that it is the most beautiful city in the world . . . and the most agreeable and comfortable in Europe. I would sooner live here even than in Paris.'

There were certain drawbacks, of course, a principal one being the extraordinary indolence of the population, the greater part of whom spent their time avoiding work, doing 'absolutely nothing', living on charity and the money which found its way to Rome from all over Christian Europe. There was 'no agriculture, no commerce, no manufactures'; and it was not in the least uncommon to be told in a shop, with complacent equability, that the goods required were available but were rather awkward to get at, so would the customer please come back another day.

The population of the city, which had numbered about 80,000 in 1563 and 118,356 in 1621, had now risen to about 150,000, according to a census taken in 1709, and was to rise again to 167,000 before the century was over. The residents were almost outnumbered by the tourists and pilgrims. It was estimated, on the basis of the extra bread baked in the city's ovens, that there were some 100,000 visitors in 1700. And a census kept by the large hospice of S. Trinità dei Pellegrini[1] indicates that in the Holy Year of 1750 no less than 134,603 pilgrims stayed at that hospice alone. Many of Rome's residents were officials, many more were priests: the 1709 census listed 2,646 priests and 5,370 monks, nuns and other religious; and there seemed more than this, since it was fashionable for men to dress as though they were in holy orders even when they were not. 'Everyone in Rome,' said Casanova, himself persuaded to adopt the attire, 'was either a priest or trying to look like one.' Nor did it seem, great though their numbers were, that there were too many ecclesiastics to serve the extraordinary number of religious houses in Rome. There were 240 monasteries, 73 convents, 23 seminaries and nearly 400 churches including those used by foreigners, the Germans' church of S. Maria dell' Anima, the Poles' S. Stanislao,[2] the Spaniards' S. Maria in Monserrato,[3] the Portuguese S. Antonio[4] and the French S. Luigi dei Francesi.[5]

To most visitors it seemed astonishing that so many of those who were evidently not priests appeared to be quite content to pass their lives in utter idleness, thanks to the official Board of Charities and the sustenance provided by religious foundations and the richer families. If homeless, they could enter papal workshops where, between meals, they 'sat with their arms folded', or they could seek shelter in one of the city's many refuges where, provided they moved on after one night, their clothes were mended and their shoes cobbled. If ill, they would be visited, nursed and brought food by the Fatebenefratelli of S. Giovanni di Dio,[6] or they would be given a bed in one of Rome's numerous hospitals, perhaps the vast S. Spirito where, beside walls hung with paintings, they would be entertained with

52. The Basilica of S. Maria Maggiore, whose sixteenth-century portico by Martino Longhi the Elder was destroyed when Fuga built the present façade for Pope Clement XII in 1741. The column was brought from the Basilica of Maxentius by Pope Paul V.

musical concerts. If leprous, they would be cared for at S. Gallicano in Trastevere,[7] if mad at S. Maria della Pietà,[8] if too young or too old to look after themselves at the Ospizio di San Michele, where orphaned girls were given a dowry when they left.[9] Injured children were looked after at S. Maria della Consolazione,[10] pregnant women at the S. Rocco where their names would be kept secret if they so wished.[11]

The unemployed could always earn ample pocket-money by begging, particularly in the streets around Piazza di Spagna where foreigners could most easily be waylaid. Mendicants, supplied with begging-letters by the scriveners who could be seen sitting beneath umbrellas in every square, were constantly to be observed hovering at the doors of palaces, sitting on the steps of churches ready to act as unwanted and incompetent guides, waiting in the streets at dusk with lanterns for the hesitant passer-by. The least service, from the opening of a door to the unnecessary brushing of a coat and the imparting of unsolicited information, was considered worthy of reward; a man could live well in Rome from the *buona mancia* elicited from pestered tourists and from the commissions received as touts, pimps and middlemen.

Servants in private houses and palaces were as ready to ask for a tip from their masters' guests as they would have been from some stranger in the street. 'You go to see a man,' Montesquieu complained. 'Immediately his servants come to ask you for money, often even before you have seen him.' This was to a certain extent understandable, Charles de Brosses thought, since the palaces were more like hotels or picture galleries than homes.

All these great apartments which are so vast and so superb are only there for foreigners [he wrote of the Borghese Palace]. The master of the house cannot live in them, since they contain neither lavatories, comfort nor adequate furniture; and there is hardly any of the latter, even in the upper-storey apartments which are inhabited . . . The sole decoration in the rooms consists of pictures with which the four walls are covered from top to bottom in such profusion and with so little space between them that, to tell the truth, they are more tiring than attractive to the eye.

Romans who did work never worked hard. The hours of the siesta were long; and during those hours, so Father Labat said, the only living creatures to be seen in the streets were dogs, lunatics and Frenchmen. Even before and after the siesta, the seven hundred workshops of the masons and smiths, the painters and engravers, wood-carvers and potters were frequently closed and shuttered. Feast days and festivals were so common that almost every other day was a holiday; there were 150 religious festivals at the beginning of the century and only thirty less than this by 1770. There were, in addition, occasional pageants, such as the *Sacro Possesso* in which, after Pope Clement XIV had fallen off his palfrey in 1769, the Pope took part by riding in a coach; annual events like the incursion in December of peasants from the Abruzzi who, dressed in sheepskin coats and brigandish hats, would parade through the streets, playing bagpipes before the shrines; weekly summer festivals including the naumachia – the water jousts and mock sea-battles in the

53. The Piazza S. Maria della Rotonda with the Pantheon in the background. Despite the dedicatory inscription on the trabeation of the portico – M. AGRIPPA L. F. COS. TERTIUM FECIT (Marcus Agrippa, son of Lucius, Consul for the third time, built this) – the Pantheon was built in the reign of the Emperor Hadrian (A.D. 117–38).

flooded Piazza Navona; local processions, fêtes and fairs in which each *rione* bid to outdo the next in the magnificence of its decorations, the loudness of its band, the originality of its floats and fancy dresses, and the brilliance of its fireworks; and, as a climax to the Feast of St Peter, there was the world-famous illumination of the basilica by the 365 marvellously agile and expert technicians of the *Fabbrica* who, clinging to ropes, leaping across the leads but remaining always out of sight, miraculously outlined the building with six thousand paper lanterns and flaring fire-lamps.

Every year, just before Lent, came the eight days of the Roman Carnival, a wild, tumultuous celebration that ended on Ash Wednesday. The festivities, heralded by the ringing of a bell on the Capitol which was otherwise sounded only for the death of a pope, were opened with a ceremony in which the Jews of Rome, excused by Clement IX from their former customary races, handed over a payment to meet the cost of the prizes to be awarded to the winners of the horse-races and were thanked by a pretended kick in the small of the Chief Rabbi's back. The lay and

54. A panoramic view of Rome in 1765 by Giuseppe Vasi.

ecclesiastical authorities of Rome, escorted by halberdiers in black and violet uniforms, then proceeded down the Corso which was decorated with banners, foliage and flowers and thronged with people in masks and strange disguise. They were dressed as Cossacks and English sailors, Chinese mandarins and Barbary pirates, Scottish Highlanders, giants on stilts, and characters in the *commedia dell'arte*. There were men dressed as women, and women disguised as boys or army officers. In fact every conceivable costume was to be seen. Confetti and paper streamers, darts and pellets made of *pozzolana* and plaster, handfuls of flour and showers of water flew through the air as the people sang and danced, shouted and hugged each other, jumping out of the way of carriages, or clambering up on to their running-boards and shouting greetings through the windows.

There were parades of extravagantly decorated floats drawn by gaily caparisoned horses with silver bells, flowers and gorgeous plumes, the most admired often fabricated by the inventive students of the French Academy;[12] there were tournaments in palace courtyards; and every afternoon there was the longed-for race of the Barbary horses which began in the Piazza del Popolo. Filled with oats and often with stimulants, the excited animals had cords laid over their backs covered with sharp nails or rowels to act as spurs. Often they were only with difficulty prevented from jumping over the barriers. When all was ready, a party of dragoons rode down the sand-covered Corso making sure that all carriages had been moved off into side streets; then other cavalrymen rode at breakneck speed down the street, the crowds of spectators pressing against the walls on either side. As the horses thundered past towards the Piazza Venezia, sand spattering at their hooves, blood running down their backs, fireworks exploding around them, the noise of cheering was tumultuous. The owner of the winner was presented with a prize of money and a *palio*, a banner of gold brocade embroidered with the emblem of a galloping horse and fixed to a brightly painted pole.

On the last night of the Carnival the revellers poured out into the streets, carrying tapers, jostling and pushing, trying to blow out each other's flickering flames while keeping their own alight, climbing on to the tops of carriages to keep their lights out of reach, or holding them aloft on long sticks, crying the traditional threat, 'May he who does not carry a candle be knocked senseless!' On this night, as on others, there were dances in the palaces, in the theatres, in assembly rooms, and in the streets, where music and laughter filled the air until the sun came up.

On Sundays during the Carnival the churches, lit by brilliant candles and tapers, were decorated with flowers and velvet hangings, their statues and ubiquitous effigies of the Madonna bedecked with ornaments. Their naves and aisles, filled with the music of orchestras and the hubbub of the congregation, seemed more like theatres than places of worship; and so in a sense they were.

During Lent, services in the churches took on a more sombre note, with queues of women dressed in black outside the confessionals. But when Easter came, all was cheerfulness once more. Fireworks exploded in the sky and there was dancing in the streets. The religion of Rome, indeed, was much more characteristically reflected in the midnight revels around the porphyry obelisk in the Lateran piazza on the Festival of St John than in the services held amidst representations of suffering in San Stefano Rotondo on the anniversary of the martyrdom of St Stephen. Many of these festivals were of pagan origin as, for instance, the *Rappresentazione dei Morti* in All Saints, where wax models of the dead were propped against corpses from the hospitals, and the Festival of the Madonna of the Hams when the windows of the food shops were stuffed with cooked meats, pies

55a. A view of the Forum, then known as the Campo Vaccino (the cow field), by Piranesi. The submerged Arch of Septimius Severus is in the left foreground.

and strings of sausages arranged in fantastic and often gruesome displays. But, whether pagan or Christian in origin, most festivals were celebratory rather than penitential, and all were designed to please the eye as much as to stir the soul. It was entirely in the tradition of Roman religion that a preacher should conclude his sermon on the virtues of fasting with a recipe for grilled cod.

Saints were honoured in the Roman calendar and given credit for such particular powers as had been accorded to the gods of the ancient past. Just as in the days of the old Republic, Rumina was looked to for the protection of farms and Matuta for watching over those in childbirth, so now sufferers from headaches sought the intercession of Santa Bibiena, while sore throats were the responsibility of San Biagio. Portents, too, were regarded with the same deep foreboding as they had been in the days of Augustus, and while statues in the temples had then shed tears and blood so now did the Madonnas and crucifixes of papal Rome.

Yet superstitious as they were, going in dread of the evil eye and imagining all manner of disasters consequent upon such portents as the netting of a two-headed sturgeon in the Tiber, the Romans were essentially a cheerful, easygoing people, happy to abide by their proverb, *Chi si contenta gode*, 'The contented man enjoys himself', apparently without envy of the rich with whom they mixed upon the most familiar terms. In the palaces of the cardinals and the nobility there was a constant procession of callers going in and out without hindrance. Fishmongers or

55b. Another of Piranesi's views of the Campo Vaccino, looking towards the Arch of Titus with the Orti Farnesiani in the background.

fruit-sellers would set up their stalls beside the front doors without asking permission or requiring it, making themselves at home in the rooms where servants talked to their masters as though they were the most intimate of friends and where one might see a monk gratefully accept a pinch of snuff from a cardinal's proffered box. Even at the Vatican washing was hung out to dry from the windows; while at the Quirinal, relations of the Pope's numerous servants came to meals and sometimes even to live, and hawkers carried their wares along passages and into the crowded saloons. Yet the easy informality did not preclude the observation of the most elaborate protocol when the occasion arose. Ceremonies at the papal Court were regulated by the strictest rules; and few cardinals, however humble their personal tastes, would appear in the streets without a cavalcade of liveried attendants to accompany the black and gilded carriages drawn by horses with red silk ribbons in their manes. If, while driving, a cardinal met a fellow-prelate on foot, he was expected to alight and to greet him with due ceremony. A visitor to Rome once observed this *ceremonia* and described how 'after many bows, gracious smiles, and protestations of attachment, the cardinals took leave of one another. But the one who had been in the coach had to walk on some distance instead of re-entering it, and keep turning back and bowing to the one on foot. He for his part did the same and so they continued until each was out of sight.'

The cavalcades of Cardinal de Bernis were particularly impressive, for he was the French ambassador and rarely appeared without an immense retinue including thirty-eight footmen, eight couriers, eight valets and two chaplains. At his palace a splendid banquet was given every year on 13 December in commemoration of King Henri IV's conversion to Roman Catholicism. One year Charles de Brosses was invited and discovered that the feast was a 'real field-day for masters and servants alike, conducted in the boldest and most shocking manner'.

No sooner was food placed before us [de Brosses continued] than a horde of strange footmen bore down carrying empty plates and demanding this and that for their masters. There was one in particular who attached himself to me as the most promising member of the party. I gave him a turkey, then a chicken, a cut of sturgeon, a partridge, a slice of venison, some tongue, some ham, and always he came back. 'My friend,' I said to him, 'we are all getting the same. Why doesn't your master eat what is before him?' Detroy, sitting not far from me said, 'Don't be silly. All he asks for his master he's taking for himself.' And I could see that . . . lackeys were vying with one another in the amount they could stuff into their pockets, even wrapping the truffled poultry in napkins . . . for the linen was worth taking too. The cleverest ones were whisking the dishes away. You could see them filing out of the room and taking them home under their *ferriacuoli*, the big cloaks they wear.

Some servants had wives and children waiting on the staircases to carry the plunder off to their 'miserable abodes'. And Charles de Brosses 'was told as a fact' that their masters indulged in pilfering as well. If any Italian gentleman fancied anything he simply sent his servant home with it, thus appropriating dish and contents together. The ambassador confided in him that he lost between twenty-five and thirty valuable pieces every year at least and, 'even more annoyingly', pieces he had borrowed.

Other rich men in Rome spared themselves this annoyance by not giving banquets at all and by contenting themselves with *conversazioni*, at the best of which the guests could not only enjoy good talk on all manner of subjects, but also an orchestra and singers or a game of cards. On these occasions only the lightest snacks were provided, often no more than dishes of ice-cream which was eaten in enormous quantities in Rome at all hours of the day and night, even in church, by rich and poor alike.

Apart from this indulgence, the Romans were not greedy, though foodstuffs were cheap enough. At the tables of those who could afford far more, a meal of pasta and salad, poached fish, cheese and fruit would be deemed quite adequate and, by the poor, ideal. The poor rarely cooked at home, fetching what they needed from the *cucina* or the *pasticceria*, going to those places in and around the city where food was prepared in the open, to the Piazza Colonna where cabbages were cooked, to the steps of the Church of S. Marcello where tripe simmered in huge pans, to the big market in Piazza Navona where peasants who had come in from the country with their produce could be persuaded to do a little cooking if pressed, or to the column of Marcus Aurelius in Piazza Colonna where the coffee-sellers roasted their beans, the only place in Rome where they were allowed to do so, the smell being considered offensive.

Indeed, the poor of Rome spent as little time as possible at home except in excessively cold weather when, rarely having fireplaces or even charcoal stoves, they would huddle together, their feet in muffs, passing *caldini*, pots filled with embers, from hand to hand. They preferred to gossip and gamble in the streets; to dance; to watch their version of football, a rough game with teams of up to thirty on each side, which was accompanied by constant shouts of encouragement and abuse and often ended in fights; to wander up to Monte Testaccio to enjoy the white Castelli wines kept cool in the cellars of the hill; and in the evenings, if they could afford it, to go to the theatre, to the Teatro delle Dame[13] near the Piazza di Spagna or the Argentina,[14] to the *operette* at the Capranica,[15] the comedies at the Tor di Nona or the marionettes in the Piazza Navona. The performances, however, were not the only attraction – perhaps not even the main attraction: people went to meet their friends, to eat ice-cream, have a picnic, or to gamble. 'It is the fashion here to regard the theatre as a place for meeting people and paying social calls,' wrote an English visitor. 'Instead of listening to the music they all laugh and talk as though they were at home.' This naturally did not encourage a happy relationship between the audiences, who armed themselves with rotten fruit in the expectation of having to pelt the performers, and the cast who were always ready to retaliate, as the actors at the Capranica did more than once, with broken tiles and stones. In the boxes where the chairs were set around gaming tables and servants stumbled about with wine and refreshments, the uproar was often as continuous as it was in the pit where the audience sat on benches, shouting to each other, eating, drinking and knocking over the candles by which those few who had come for the performance vainly tried to follow the score. But usually when arias began, the whole house fell into silence as the voices of the principal singers filled the theatre. The voices of the singers playing female parts were always those of *castrati*, for, although actresses had been seen briefly on the Roman stage in the middle of the sixteenth century and, again briefly, under the protection of Queen Christina, they had been banished by Innocent XI. The most popular of the *castrati*, though, were almost indistinguishable from women. 'They have hips, buttocks, bosoms and plump round necks,' a French visitor wrote. 'You could mistake them for real girls.' And, according to Montesquieu, an Englishman did mistake one of them, a transvestite *castrato* from the Capranica, for a girl and fell 'madly in love' with him. Emasculated when children in such surgeries as that near the Vatican whose services were advertised by a signboard proclaiming, 'The Pope's Chapel Singers Castrated Here', *castrati* were to be found in many a fashionable café where, so one English tourist thought, 'they looked as pretty and tempting as may be'.

For those who could not afford to enter a theatre there were excitements and drama enough in the streets. In the Piazza Navona where mountebanks and acrobats performed their turns, astrologers told fortunes and barbers and tooth-drawers carried on their trades for all to see, in the Corso where the rich paraded in their carriages and on the Quirinal where they strolled in their gardens, in the tortuous streets of the Campo Marzio where grand palaces loomed over tiny houses squeezed into vacant plots, and in the dark, cramped, garlic-flavoured alleys of Trastevere, the life of Rome could be observed in all its wonderful variety. Shop signs hung on every side, so that tailors could be recognized by pairs of scissors or a cardinal's red hat, barbers by a shaving plate, surgeons by a bleeding arm or foot, and tobacconists by a man, usually a Turk, smoking a pipe. And this, combined with the convenience of being able to find most trades concentrated in certain areas – the clock-makers, for instance, in and about Piazza Capranica, the cabinet-makers between Via Arenula and Piazza Campitelli, the booksellers around the Chiesa Nuova, the hatters in Via dei Cappellari, the rosary makers in Via dei Coronari, the carriage-repairers in the Via delle Carrozze, and the locksmiths in Via dei Chiavari – made amends for there being, at least until 1744, no names on the streets or numbers on the houses, nor until 1803, when marble slabs were erected, any indication of *rioni* boundaries.

Since food was prepared and cooked in the open, and since shopkeepers, artisans and workmen pursued their crafts and labours out of doors, since rubbish was piled against the walls to wait for the highly irregular attention of the refuse-collectors, and since all classes of citizens were as ready to relieve themselves against any convenient wall as they were on the relative privacy of a cardinal's staircase, the streets, choked with dust in summer and clogged with mud in winter, were as filthy and noisome as may well be imagined. They were 'badly paved and extremely dirty', wrote Father Labat in 1715. In the evening a few carts were trundled about followed by a man who swung from side to side a leather tube attached to a water barrel. But the Romans did not really 'know what sweeping means, they leave it to Providence. Heavy rain showers act as brushes in Rome.' They were to do so for many years to come, and occasioned many a sour and wide-ranging condemnation of Rome in general, as for instance that by Hazlitt in his *Notes of a Journey through France and Italy*:

It is not the contrast of pigstyes and palaces that I complain of, the distinction between the old and new; what I object to is the want of any such striking contrast, but an almost uninterrupted succession of narrow, vulgar-looking streets, where the smell of garlick prevails over the odour of antiquity. A dunghill, an outhouse, the weeds growing under an imperial arch offended me not; but what has a greengrocer's stall, a stupid English china warehouse, a putrid trattoria, a barber's sign, and old clothes or old picture shops or a

56. The Piazza and Palazzo Montecavallo by Kaspar van Vittel (Gaspare Vanvitelli, 1653–1736), who emigrated to Rome and painted views of the city and Campagna in a classicizing, idealized manner.

Gothic palace, with two or three lacqueys in modern liveries lounging at the gate, to do with ancient Rome?

Yet most foreign visitors in the eighteenth century wrote home not so much to complain of the squalor of the city as to commend its delightful vistas, such as those to be enjoyed from the Piazza delle Quatro Fontane to the Porta Pia and the obelisks on the Quirinal, the Pincio and the Esquiline, and the romantic impression created by Rome's pastoral setting, by the animals that wandered to graze amongst the lichen-covered ruins, by the oxen drawing haycarts across the Forum and the shepherds resting in the shade of ruins, the scenes evoked in the tranquil, nostalgic engravings of Piranesi.

From time to time these peaceful scenes were shattered by violence. The Romans remained a fierily contentious people, quick to flare up in anger and slow to forgive. Murders were frequent, both crimes of passion and premeditated killings carried out in pursuit of revenge or in exasperated impatience with the cumbersome processes of antiquated laws. 'What astonishes all foreigners and is the talk of the

57. A group of travellers in Rome on the Grand Tour, by Nathaniel Dance. The seated figure, Thomas Robinson, later 2nd Lord Grantham, is shown holding an elevation of the Temple of Jupiter Sator.

town again today,' wrote Goethe on 24 September 1786, 'are the murders. Four people have been murdered in our quarter within three weeks.'

The culprits frequently escaped justice, usually with the help of sympathetic friends or bystanders who helped them to reach one of the city's many places of sanctuary; and, when they *were* condemned, the spectators at their execution regarded them with pity rather than distaste. In some of Rome's prisons there were mechanical crucifixes from which the figure of Christ reached forward with arms outstretched to give the condemned man comfort before his ordeal. And on the scaffold he was expected to play his part in the dramatic ceremony of beheading with heroic fortitude. A drama it certainly was. Describing an execution such as those carried out in Rome, Lord Byron wrote that 'the ceremony, including the *masqued* priests; the half-naked executioner; the bandaged criminals; the black Christ and his banner; the Scaffold; the soldiery; the slow procession, and the quick rattle and heavy fall of the axe; the splash of blood, and the ghastliness of the exposed heads – is altogether more impressive than the . . . dog-like agony of affliction upon the sufferers of the English sentence.'

During the Carnival the drama became a grotesque comedy with the headman disguised as *Pulcinella* and the audience expected to play their parts as at a pantomime. These Carnival executions usually took place in the Piazza del Popolo where criminals could also be seen undergoing the punishment of the *cavalletto*, a machine in which the miscreants were held face downwards while being flogged with a bull's penis, or being forced to parade through the streets with the nature of their offence and its punishment placarded on their backs. For the most heinous offences, the condemned might still be punished with the *martello* which 'is to knock the malefactor on his temples with a hammer while he is on his knees, and almost at the same time to cut his throat and rip open his belly. Lesser crimes are frequently punished by the gallies [which, since the Roman authorities had no galleys, meant working, not too laboriously, in a chain-gang] or the *strappado*: the latter is hanging the criminals by the arms tied backwards, and thus bound they are drawn up on high, and let down again with a violent swing, which, if used with vigour, unjoins their backs and arms.'

But while punishments, when inflicted, could be savage, and murders, both committed and planned, were as common as the weapons still hanging in S. Maria in Trastevere and other churches even now testify, foreign visitors to Rome were rarely themselves in danger. Even on the darkest night they stood little chance of being robbed, not so much because the streets were patrolled by watchmen armed with long, hooked poles as because it was generally recognized that money, when required, could always be extracted in less troublesome ways from the unwary, particularly from the English.

The English swarm here [wrote Charles de Brosses] and they are the people who spend most money. The Romans like them on account of their open-handedness, but at heart they prefer the Germans, and this is the case all over Italy. I perceive that no nation is so thoroughly detested as ours and this comes from our foolish habit of lauding our manners to the detriment of other nationalities, and finding especial fault with everything that is not done in the French manner.

The money the English spend in Rome, and the custom they have of making this journey a part of their education does not seem to do them much benefit. There are a few who are intelligent and profit by their stay in Rome, but these are the exceptions. Most of them have a carriage ready harnessed stationed in the Piazza d'Espagna, which waits for them all day long, while they play at billiards, or pass the time in some such fashion. There are numbers of these people who leave Rome without having seen anything in it except their countrymen, and do not know where the Colosseum is.

It was certainly true that Rome abounded with English gentlemen on the Grand Tour known to the Romans as '*milordi pelabili clienti*' ('a soft touch as customers'),

58. Edmund Gibbon (1737–94), who conceived the first thought of his great history 'while musing on the Capitol in the gloom of an October evening'.

whose interest in the art and architecture of the city was as severely limited as the young man of Dr John Moore's acquaintance who considered two or three hours a day far too much time to spend 'on a pursuit in which he felt no pleasure, and saw very little utility'. After six weeks, however, this young man did not want to admit that he had not seen all that his fellow-tourists had seen. So 'he ordered a post-chaise and four horses to be ready early in the morning, and driving through churches, palaces, villas, and ruins with all possible expedition, he fairly saw, in two days, all that we had beheld during our crawling course of six weeks. I found afterwards, by the list he kept of what he had done, that we had not the advantage of him in a single picture, or the most mutilated remnant of a statue.'

An equally impatient tourist was the inordinately rich Lord Baltimore, 'proprietor of all Maryland and Virginia, with an annual income of £30,000'. He travelled about with a doctor, two Negro eunuchs and eight women; and when asked by an official to point out which of the ladies was his wife, he replied that he was an Englishman, and it was not his practice to discuss his sexual arrangements: he would settle the matter with his fists. In Rome, so his guide wrote, he 'went through the Villa Borghese in ten minutes . . . Nothing pleased him but St Peter's and the Apollo Belvedere . . . He thinks he has too much brain . . . and has wearied of everything in the world.'

There was another young tourist in Rome at this time, however, who was far more conscientious. This was James Boswell. He arrived in the city in March 1765 and guided by a fellow Scotsman, Colin Morison, a Jacobite refugee, he immediately embarked upon 'a study of antiquities, of pictures, of architecture and of the other arts which are found in such great perfection at Rome'. He viewed the Forum and 'experienced sublime and melancholy emotions' as he thought of all the great scenes which had been enacted there, and 'saw the place, now all in ruins, with the wretched huts of carpenters and other artisans occupying the site of that rostrum from which Cicero had flung forth his stunning eloquence'. From the Forum he went to the Colosseum which he was shocked to find full of dung and rented out as sheds for animals; but even so it was 'hard to tell whether the astonishing massiveness or the exquisite taste of this superb building should be more admired'. He climbed the Palatine hill on which the cypresses seemed to mourn for the ruin of the imperial palaces, and there he saw a statue which so resembled Cicero that he began to talk Latin to Morison with whom he resolved always to speak the language thereafter, throughout his tour. The next day he climbed the Capitoline where, from the roof of the modern Senate, Morison pointed out ancient Rome on its seven hills and read a clear summary of the growth of the city; and he visited San Pietro in Carcere and saw inside it the remains of the 'famous Tullia prison of which Sallust gives so hideous a picture'. He went over the Baths of Diocletian; studied the antiquities of the Campus Martius; admired the oriental marble columns in S. Maria Maggiore; walked round the Belvedere, the Borghese Palace and the Vatican Library; judged Michelangelo's Moses 'superb', though the beard was too long and the 'horns, though sacred, ludicrous as like a satyr'; and he deemed the Laocoön 'supreme'. He was struck by the sight of 'a strange fellow sitting in the sun reading Tasso to a group of others in rags like himself'; and by a procession of Roman girls 'who had received dowries from a public foundation, some to be married, others to become nuns. They marched in separate groups, the nuns coming last and wearing crowns. Only a few of them were pretty and most of the pretty ones were nuns.'

At Santa Maria sopra Minerva on the Feast of the Annunciation of the Blessed Virgin Mary, Boswell saw the Pope, Clement XIII, being carried round the church 'on a magnificent chair decorated with a figure of the Holy Ghost'. The whole congregation knelt in front of His Holiness who gave them his blessing before

59. Jean Lemaire's painting of the Piazza del Campidoglio, with the statue of Marcus Aurelius standing between the large statues of Castor and Pollux which were found in the theatre of Pompey and placed here in 1583.

taking his place upon a sort of throne so that they could kiss his slipper. At St Peter's on Maundy Thursday, Boswell was present at another, more celebrated ceremony, the *mandatum*, or washing of the feet. This ceremony began with Mass in the Sistine Chapel followed by a procession to the Pauline Chapel, the Pope carrying the Sacrament; then His Holiness pronounced the benediction from the loggia of St Peter's before washing the feet of twelve priests of various nations. He performed these traditional ablutions with 'great decency', Boswell thought, and afterwards, when serving the priests their customary meal, he 'mingled grandeur and modesty', looking like 'a jolly landlord', and smiling when he offered them wine.

In the midst of his sightseeing and studies Boswell naturally 'indulged in sensual relaxations', as he confessed to Jean Jacques Rousseau: 'I sallied forth of an evening like an imperious lion, and I had a little French painter, a young academician, always vain, always alert, always gay, who served as my jackal. I remembered the rakish deeds of Horace and other amorous Roman poets, and I thought that one might well allow one's self a little indulgence in a city where there are prostitutes licensed by the Cardinal Vicar.'

After 'much enjoyment' with a *fille charmante*, the sister of a nun, who cost him fourteen *paoli* (about seven shillings), Boswell resolved to have a girl every day and seems to have succeeded in doing so, taking particular pleasure in the girls employed in a small brothel run by three sisters named Cazenove and indulging himself also with older women, with one of whom, a 'monstre' who charged five shillings, he was 'quite brutish', until, as Rousseau had warned him he well might, he contracted a venereal disease.

Most tourists found Roman women accommodating as well as deeply attractive, as Goethe did the tavern-keeper's daughter who wrote her name in spilled wine on the table-top, intertwining it with his own and the hour of the night at which they should meet. These Roman girls were renowned for their lovely complexions, their dark and glossy hair, their brilliant eyes and – the result, so it was said, of the clear and sparkling water – their healthy, white teeth. They were also famous for the boldness of their glance: the French writer, Jean Baptiste Dupaty, found it impossible to get them to 'drop their eyes before yours'. Another French visitor, Auguste Frédéric Louis Viesse de Marmont, wrote in his memoirs, 'The freedom of the women passes all belief and their husbands permit it, speaking cheerfully and without embarrassment of their wives' lovers. I have heard M. Falconniere talk of his wife in a quite incredible way . . . In my role of young man and foreigner I was only too glad to benefit by the consequences.' Husbands, indeed, generally asked of their wives only that they should not be openly promiscuous and that they should not disgrace themselves with their *cicisbei*.

Apart from whoring and sightseeing and writing those long accounts of his activities which were essential to his enjoyment of them, Boswell spent hours in Rome in the company of those other Scots and Englishmen who were to be encountered everywhere in the city. He had long conversations with Lord Mountstuart, son and heir of George III's friend, the Earl of Bute, and with John Wilkes, the entertaining demagogue exiled for his libel upon the King. He fell 'quite in love' with the 'modest and amiable' Swiss painter, Angelica Kauffmann, and he saw a good deal of three other painters then living in Rome, Nathaniel Dance, George Willison and Gavin Hamilton. He called upon Peter Grant, a member of the Scots College,[16] who acted as his guide in St Peter's. And, although he was anxious not to be suspected of talking politics with traitors, he called at the Palazzo Muti-Papazzurri,[17] home of the Old Pretender, the titular King James III, to see the old man's secretary, Andrew Lumisden, who became a close friend.

Boswell does not, however, mention Gibbon who was also in Rome at this time

60. Johann Winckelmann (1717–68), the Prussian cobbler's son, who was appointed Chief Superintendent of antiquities in 1763.

and who could 'never forget nor express the strong emotions which agitated [his] mind as [he] first approached and entered the Eternal City'. After a sleepless night, Gibbon wandered amidst the ruins of the Forum, 'each memorable spot where Romulus stood, or Tully spoke or Caesar fell, was at once present to [his] eye; and several days of intoxication were lost or enjoyed before [he] could descend to a cool and minute investigation'. Then, in the gloom of one October evening, as he sat musing on the Capitol, while barefoot friars were chanting their litanies in the church of S. Maria d'Aracoeli, he 'conceived the first thought' of his great history.

Few English gentlemen, so Charles de Brosses maintained, shared Gibbon's excited enthusiasm, although other observers contended that it was the young French tourists who were least interested in what they had come, or been sent, to see. In any event, after they had collected a few antiquities to take home with them, picking them up on the site, buying them in dealers' shops, or acquiring them from one of the numerous *cognoscenti* who hawked marble fragments as well as more modern 'masterpieces' about the streets, many of these young French and English gentlemen decided they had had enough of ruins. Those who set out with maps and guidebooks, magnifying glasses and sketch-pads, mariner's compasses and quadrants, usually expressed themselves as disappointed by what they found: the arches of the Theatre of Marcellus were filled in and occupied by poor families; the Palatine was overrun with weeds; the Arch of Septimius Severus was half-buried and the part that could be discerned was used as a barber's shop. Almost all that could be seen of the Tabularium were the capitals of three columns; the Baths of Caracalla were smothered in foliage, and 'a few tattered ropemakers working in the shade of a foot or two of ancient wall' were the only live creatures whom one visitor found on the deserted Palatine. The Caelian hill looked like an abandoned quarry. Twice a week there was a market in the Forum; and animals, as Boswell discovered, also occupied the Colosseum in which the visitor had to pass through a hermitage to reach the crumbling, ivy-clad seats.

Even so, there was still much of interest to be enjoyed by those more conscientious tourists who avoided the charlatans and self-styled antiquarians against whom John Northall warned his readers in his *Travels through Italy*, and who took the trouble to find a competent guide – preferably Johann Winckelmann.

A Prussian cobbler's son who became Europe's leading authority on classical art, Winckelmann had arrived in Rome in 1755 and had soon afterwards been appointed librarian to the papal Secretary of State and had been given rooms in the Palazzo della Cancelleria. He later became librarian to Cardinal Albani, moving to an apartment in the Palazzo Albani, now the Palazzo del Drago;[18] and he helped his patron with the arrangement of his treasures in the Villa Albani, now Villa Torlonia.[19] In 1763 he was appointed Chief Supervisor of all antiquities in and around Rome. Openly homosexual and infectiously enthralled by his subject, he was, in John Wilkes's opinion, 'a gentleman of exquisite taste and sound learning'. He was also extremely tactful. When showing Wilkes and his beautiful mistress, Gertrude Corradini, round Rome, Winckelmann pretended not to notice their absence when, overcome by lust, Wilkes and Corradini, a woman who 'possessed the divine gift of lewdness', disappeared for a few moments to make love behind a convenient ruin. 'This was the more obliging,' Wilkes commented, 'because he must necessarily pass such an interval with the mother of Corradini who had as little conversation as beauty.'

Even when guided by Winckelmann, many young tourists soon lost interest in Rome's ruins and preferred to visit the convent of the Capuchins where visitors were shown a cross made by the Devil, a painting by St Luke, and macabre grottos decorated entirely with knuckles, kneecaps, ribs, grinning skulls and crossbones.[20] In each compartment, standing erect against the wall, were – and still are –

skeletons in Capuchin habits, the skin dried tight upon the bones, long beards hanging to the girdles, rosaries clutched in spindly fingers. The monks who conducted visitors through these gruesome caverns cheerfully pointed out the skeletons of former friends and the niches where their own bones would shortly be displayed.

A pleasurable *frisson* was also to be enjoyed in the catacombs which had altered little since the day when John Evelyn had crept into them on his belly from a cornfield, 'guided by two torches', and had descended 'a good depth in the bowells of the Earth, a strange & fearefull passage for divers miles'.

That which renders the passages dreadfull [Evelyn recorded] is the *Skeletons* & bodies, that are placed on the sides, in degrees one above the other like shelves, whereof some are shut up with a Course flat Stone, & *Pro Christo* or ⚒ & Palmes ingraven on them, which are supposed to have been Martyrs . . . As I was prying about I found a glass phiole as was conjectured filld with dried blood, as also two *lacrymatories*. Many of the bodies, or rather bones (for there appeard nothing else) lay so intire, as if placed so by the art of the Chirugion, which being but touch'd fell all to dust. Thus after two or 3 miles wandring in this subterranean Meander we return'd to our Coach almost blind when we came into the day light againe, & even choked with smoake. A French bishop & his retinue adventurring it seemes too farr in these denns, their lights going out, were never heard of more.

Like Rubens and so many other foreign travellers before and after him, Evelyn had been advised to look for accommodation in the neighbourhood of the Piazza di Spagna, so called since the establishment of the Spanish embassy there in the early seventeenth century, and he eventually settled for rooms with a Frenchman who, after bargaining, agreed to accept twenty crowns (just over twenty-five pence) a month. It was in this area, in a room in the Palazzetto Zuccari,[21] that Winckelmann lodged when he first came to Rome. Salvator Rosa lived nearby in Via Gregoriana; Piranesi in Via Sistina. The early neo-classical painter, Anton Raphael Mengs, was also a near neighbour, so was Carlo Goldoni in Via Condotti in which stood, and still stands, the Caffè Greco,[22] frequented in these and later years by Casanova, Goethe, Leopardi, Schopenhauer, Bizet and Berlioz, Gogol and Keats (whose rooms are preserved at the foot of the Spanish Steps),[23] Wagner, Liszt, Mendelssohn, Rossini, Stendhal, Balzac, Byron, Thackeray, Tennyson, Hans Andersen and countless other artists and writers, who came to Rome either to study, like the Scottish architects, Robert Adam and Robert Mylne, or to work, like Fragonard, Vernet, Claude Lorrain, Canova, Houdon and William Kent who had the unique distinction for an Englishman of frescoing the ceiling of a Roman church, S. Giuliano dei Fiamminghi, the national church of the Belgians.[24] There were few good hotels apart from the Albergo Londra and the Monte d'Oro where Charles de Brosses did not mind being fleeced because the puddings were so delicious. There were, however, a number of comfortable inns, including the Eagle, the Falcon, the Golden Lion and the Five Moons. Most visitors, in any case, moved into furnished rooms as soon as they found a set that suited them, if possible in the elegant Casa Guarneri. 'These apartments are generally commodious

61. A young 'grand tourist' arrives in Rome at the Villa de Londres, opposite the Caffè degli Inglesi. The Piazza di Spagna was then known as the 'English ghetto'.

and well furnished,' wrote Tobias Smollett who was directed to the 'open, airy and pleasantly situated' Piazza di Spagna, known in his day as 'the English ghetto', as soon as he arrived in Rome. 'And the lodgers are well supplied with provisions and all necessaries of life . . . The *vitella mongana* . . . is the most delicate veal I ever tasted . . . Here are the rich wines of Montepulciano, Montefiascone and Monte di Dragone; but what we commonly drink at meals is that of Orvieto, a small white wine of an agreeable flavour.'

Quick as he was to complain of them elsewhere on the Continent, Smollett had to admit that prices in Rome were very reasonable. For a 'decent first floor and two bed-chambers on the second' he paid 'no more than a scudo [twenty-five pence] per day' and his landlord plentifully supplied his table at a price which was quite as reasonable. A whole house could be secured for no more than six guineas a month; and Robert Adam enjoyed a pleasant apartment as well as the services of a cook, valet, coachman and footman for little more than £4 a week.

Delighted by the cheapness of their accommodation and of their excellent meals, foreign tourists were predisposed to enjoy themselves in Rome and there were few

223

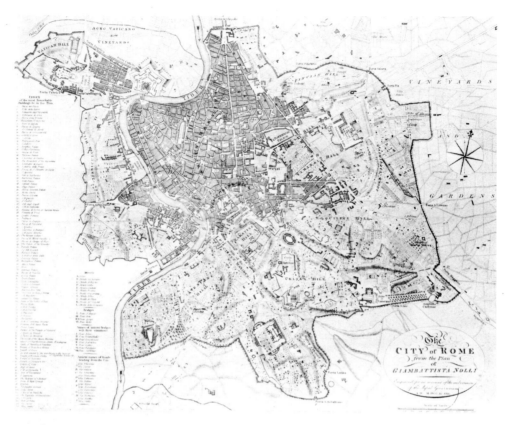

62. The city in 1748, from the plan of Giambattista Nolli, revised in 1798.

who did not. In earlier times Protestants had found it advisable to enter Rome in disguise and to leave before Easter to avoid the house-to-house search for non-communicants supervised by the Inquisition. Sir Henry Wotton, who began his travels in 1587, came disguised as a German Catholic with 'a mighty blue feather' in his black cap, explaining the reasons for the feather as follows: 'First, I was by it taken for no English. Secondly, I was reputed as light in my mind as in my apparel (they are not dangerous men that are so). And thirdly, no man could think that I desired to be unknown, who, by wearing of that feather, took a course to make myself famous through Rome in a few days.'

But by the eighteenth century, although Sir Thomas Nugent in his *The Grand Tour* warned his readers to beware of what they said in front of servants, the Inquisition was no longer a threat to the tourist, provided he did not actually practise black magic. Indeed, the Roman Inquisition, even at its most strict, had never been as uncompromisingly severe as the Spanish or the Languedocian. Admittedly, the philosopher, astronomer and mathematician, Giordano Bruno, had been held for seven years in one of the prisons of the Sant' Ufficio and, declining to recant the heresies of which he was accused, had been taken with his tongue in a gag to be burned alive in February 1600 at the stake in the Campo dei Fiori.[25] But after Galileo, whose writings about the laws of the universe were deemed by the Jesuits to be as dangerous to the Church as 'Luther and Calvin put together', had been brought to face trial by the Inquisition in Rome, he had been allowed to live in a comfortable apartment. And when the Congregation of the Holy Office had insisted upon sentencing him despite the more sympathetic attitude of the Commissary General, the sentence had been immediately commuted by Pope Urban VIII and Galileo had been allowed to return to his estate at Arcetri near Florence. A hundred or so years after Galileo's death the Inquisition's prison in Castel Sant' Angelo held only four men, and the possibility of a traveller being required to join them was extremely remote. Travellers who kept their heretical views to themselves had little to fear from the authorities even when they loudly expostulated, as some did, at ceremonies in which girls took the veil in convents and had their dresses, ornaments and hair cut off. At one of these ceremonies, so

63. Goethe in Italy in 1787. 'Only now do I begin to live', he exclaimed on entering Rome, and confessed that he had not spent an entirely happy day since he left it.

Catharine Wilmot, Lady Mount Cashell's Irish companion, wrote, 'not only the women, but many of the young Englishmen were in indignant tears'.

One Englishman instinctively layed his hand upon his sword, swearing that such heart-rending superstitious cruelties ought to be extirpated from off the face of the earth [Miss Wilmot continued]. All was in a moment silent as death, and everyone was obliged to see, and everyone obliged to hear, the snapping of the scissors, which separated a hundred glossy braids and curls from [the girl's] head, which fell amongst her bands of Roses at the feet of the Abbess, who continued with unrelenting piety to strip her of every ornament, and then bound her temples with sackcloth and threw over her the black austerities of her holy order, placing a crown of thorns upon her head, a branch of white lilies in her hand, a large crucifix by her side, and all the insignia of a heavenly office.

But, as another Protestant visitor observed, one was not obliged to witness such heart-rending scenes, and the popery of Rome seemed inspiriting rather than oppressive. A Scottish Presbyterian who came to Rome to convert Pope Clement XIV in the 1770s and – by way of preparation for his task – shouted insults at him in St Peter's, calling him a seven-headed beast of nature and mother of harlots, was arrested by the Swiss Guards. But the Pope intervened on the man's behalf, maintaining that he had acted with the best intentions, paying for his return passage to Scotland, and expressing an obligation to him for undertaking such a long journey with a view to doing good.

In Lent it was easy enough to obtain a licence to eat meat; and there were in any case plenty of taverns and butchers' shops prepared to sell or serve meat without bothering about the licence. Rome, in fact, was an easy, friendly place where the foreigner was soon made to feel at home and where some foreigners felt so much at home that their own countries thereafter seemed somehow strange to them. One of these was Goethe who exclaimed as he entered the city, 'Only now do I begin to live!' and who lamented after he had left it, 'I have not spent an entirely happy day since I crossed the Ponte Molle to come home.'

FOURTEEN

NAPOLEONIC INTERLUDE

On the death of Pope Clement XII in 1740, Charles de Brosses went to the pontifical palace where he saw 'a sad image of human grandeur. All the rooms were open and deserted.' He passed through them 'without seeing a cat' until he came to the chamber of the Pope 'whose corpse lay on a bed, watched by four Jesuits, who were reciting, or pretending to recite, prayers'. The Cardinal Camerlengo, the official who held supreme authority in Rome between the death of a pope and the election of his successor, came

at nine o'clock to do his duty which consisted of tapping with a small hammer several blows on the brow of the defunct and calling him by his name, Lorenzo Corsini. Finding that he gave no answer, he said, 'This is why you are mute,' and taking off the fisherman's ring, he broke it, according to custom . . . As the Pope's corpse has to remain a long time exposed in public, the face was shaved and the cheeks rouged to hide the pallor of death. He certainly looked better than when he was alive.

The Pope, who came from a princely Florentine family, had been blind for the last few years of his life, and had struggled in vain to halt the decline in the political role of the papacy which had been shrinking ever since the Peace of Westphalia had ended the Thirty Years' War in 1648. Neither he nor his immediate predecessors had been men well chosen to exert with force and conviction the authority of the Holy See. Clement XI had had to face a scandal in the early years of his pontificate when, in 1703, young girls and widows had been offered shelter in the palaces of prelates after an earthquake, and disease had added to the damage and suffering caused by a catastrophic flood that had brought the waters of the Tiber cascading through the streets of the city. It was rumoured that many of the women rendered homeless had received offers of more than shelter, and the Pope had had to order that they be removed to other homes and cared for at the expense of the Roman authorities. The Pope, a good and charitable man, had had thereafter to face a succession of further troubles and difficulties which were said to have reduced him to a state of perpetual tears.

Benedict XIII, Pope from 1724 to 1730, had been equally ill qualified to reassert the authority of the papacy. A Dominican of the most simple tastes, he had left affairs largely in the hands of the grasping Cardinal Niccolò Coscia who had made the most of the opportunities for self-aggrandizement which had been offered him. After the death of Benedict and of his successor Clement XII, it had been

64. A view of the Janiculum from the rooftops of Rome. The Villa Corsini is on the skyline on the far right.

hoped for a time that Benedict XIV would provide the Church with the firm leadership his predecessors had failed to give. Benedict XIV was an intelligent, witty, sociable man, noted for his moderation, restraint and engaging manners. Rome was fortunate to have so able an administrator, so sympathetic a pontiff and so liberal a patron. He turned the financial deficit which he found on his accession into a credit balance; he wandered about the streets of the city visiting his parishioners, sometimes incognito, wearing a wig and a tricorne hat; he provided paintings for St Peter's, mosaics for S. Maria Maggiore and manuscripts for the Vatican Library. During his pontificate, for the first time, signs and tablets were fixed to indicate the names of streets. But while the Romans had good cause to be grateful to him, the enemies of the Church had good cause also to be grateful for the elevation of so indulgent an adversary. And just as Benedict XIV found it impossible to counter firmly the argument of the *philosophes*, so Clement XIII and Clement XIV were unable to protect the Jesuits from the attacks made upon them by the Jansenists and the Roman Catholic powers alike. Clement XIII died suddenly in 1769 – the result of poison, it was inevitably alleged – after having witnessed the expulsion of the Jesuits from France and being faced with international demands, for their total destruction. His successor, Clement XIV, felt obliged to concede the demands and suppress the Society; and, having reluctantly signed the decree of suppression, an act which failed to secure an improvement in the papacy's relations with the European powers, the Pope fell

228

into a decline and died in misery the next year. It was now left to Giannangelo Braschi, who in 1775 became Pope Pius VI, to face the challenge presented to the papacy, now bereft of power and influence, by the coming revolution in France.

In appearance the new Pope seemed ideally suited to his task. Tall, healthy and extremely good-looking, he had a dignified bearing, a commanding presence and an exceptional fluency of speech. Although his hair was white, his fresh complexion and very dark eyes made him appear much younger than he was. One contemporary said of him that he 'seemed to be a born ruler'. Another, Prince Heinrich of Reuss, wrote, 'I know of no sovereign with more noble a bearing than Pius VI. He has an impressive manner and in all his gestures there is something noble . . . His manners captivate everyone.'

The eldest of the eight children of Count Marcantonio Braschi, he was born in the Romagna and had been educated by the Jesuits. Intent upon a legal career, he had studied at the University of Ferrara, and had afterwards advanced rapidly in his profession. Offered a canonry of St Peter's when he was thirty-six, he had at first declined it, as he was engaged to be married. But with the consent of his fiancée who became a nun, he entered the Church in which he received as rapid a preferment as he had done in his lay career. Very conscious of his own qualities, he was also extremely vain of his personal appearance, and 'in order to heighten its effect,' so Ludwig von Pastor wrote, 'he paid particular attention to the snow-white hair that framed his countenance. Some went so far as to suggest that he elegantly raised his long robe to one side so as to show his shapely foot. This betokened a serious flaw in his character which fitted ill with his desire for fame. These weaknesses were severely criticized and exaggerated by the satiric Romans.'

The Romans also criticized him for his evident desire to enrich his family in the manner of his predecessors. For one of his nephews he built the vast Palazzo Braschi[1] which still dominates the Piazza S. Pantaleo, the last palace to be built in Rome for the family of a pope. Pius VI was, however, intent not only upon promoting the fortunes of his family and restoring the Holy See to its former reputation, but also upon enhancing the appearance of Rome. From Carlo Marchionni, designer of the Villa Albani, he commissioned a sacristy for St Peter's,[2] which Alexander VII, Clement XI and Clement XII had all intended and failed to do, laying the foundation stone himself in September 1776 and thereafter frequently visiting the site, where numerous antiquities were unearthed. He presented St Peter's with a huge bell, the Campanone, weighing 28,000 lbs., as well as the two clocks at the ends of the attico of the vestibule. He provided mosaics for twenty-five altars in the basilica, and had the ceiling of the nave regilded, ordering that the arms of Paul V should be replaced by his own. The restoration of the ceiling of the Lateran Basilica was commemorated in the same way.

Pope Pius also built an orphanage and workshops on the Janiculum, and a school for poor boys in the Piazza S. Salvatore in Lauro. He extended the Hospital of S. Spirito; laid out the Giardino della Pigna in the Vatican; enlarged the Vatican Museums and added to their collections;[3] decorated the Hall of the Muses in the Museo Pio-Clementino where he built a fine staircase as well as the Gabinetto delle

Maschere.[4] He erected obelisks near Trinità dei Monti,[5] in the Piazza di Montecitorio[6] and in the Piazza del Quirinale[7] beside the colossal statues of the horse-tamers.[8] And he inaugurated a massive programme of public works in the Pontine marshes where 1,500 acres of land were reclaimed, and the Via Appia, unearthed in the process, was repaired and repaved.

Yet, while a patron and public benefactor of vigour and discernment, Pope Pius was far from being a statesman, and was to show himself quite incapable of dealing effectively with the problems presented to the Roman Church by the Revolution in France. When the French Assembly issued a document known as the Civil Constitution of the Clergy which required the popular election of both bishops and priests and the severance of those ties that had traditionally bound them to Rome, the French Clergy appealed to the Pope to authorize them to accept the Constitution and thus avoid the schism its rejection would entail. The Pope hesitated before replying to their request. So the Assembly demanded an oath of loyalty to the Constitution by them all. Some complied with the Assembly's demand, others did not; and the French Church was consequently split between *constitutionnel* priests who were prepared to obey the Assembly and recalcitrant priests who refused to do so. The Pope's eventual condemnation of the Civil Constitution led to violent disturbances in Paris where anti-clericalism was fostered both by political clubs and by the theatres which presented plays about the horrors of the Inquisition, the tribulations and hypocrisy of monastic and convent life, and the alleged greed and dissipation of the leaders of the Roman Catholic Church. Effigies of the Pope were set alight on bonfires, revolutionary slogans were plastered on church doors, convents were invaded and nuns assaulted, and a severed head was hurled through the windows of the Papal Nuncio's carriage. After the King had himself been beheaded, the Pope decided that protests were useless. 'I see terrible misfortunes coming,' he said, 'but I shall have nothing to say. To speak in such times of trouble and disturbance can only make bad worse.'

The Roman people had at first been inclined to regard the French Revolution with either indifference or derision. But as the months went by and the émigrés who remained in the city were less and less hopeful of an early return home, the mood of the Romans became increasingly antagonistic towards the 'assassins of Paris'. The nationalization of Church property in France, the confiscation of papal territories, the dwindling of contributions and the paucity of tourists and pilgrims all contributed to an exacerbation of this antagonism. When the French Convention, determined to gain international recognition for the Republic, dispatched envoys to Rome, the people turned upon them in fury.

Even those in sympathy with the Revolution, such as the Jacobin students at the French Academy, had to admit that the envoys behaved with excessive provocation. They strode about with tricolour cockades in their hats, supervised the removal of the portraits of popes and cardinals from the walls of the Academy and replaced them with pictures of Republicans; and, on the afternoon of 13 January 1793, having taken down the fleurs-de-lis from the façade of the French Embassy to make room for the Convention's emblems, they appeared in their carriage on the

Corso, the very epitome of revolutionary fervour, tricolour badges in their hats, a tricolour flag flying above their heads. Imprecations and insults, then stones and rocks were hurled at the carriage whose driver, in evident fear for his life, whipped his horses into the Piazza Colonna and made at breakneck speed along the Vicolo dello Sdrucciolo for the courtyard of the Palazzo Palombara, the mansion of a French banker. The carriage hurtled through the gates; but, before they could be closed, the mob chased after it. One of the envoys managed to escape but the other received a fatal wound in the stomach from a razor. As he was carried away, the stones still raining down upon his body, a large part of the mob dashed off to smash the windows of houses of people supposed to be Francophiles – including those of Torlonia, the banker – to sack the Palazzo Palombara and the French post office, and to attack the French Academy whose door was set on fire. Throughout the night the streets rang with shouts of 'Long live the Pope!', 'Long live the Catholic religion!' while carriages were stopped and their occupants invited to join in the cheering. 'The revolution which was to have started in Rome has misfired,' the Venetian ambassador reported. 'There were no supporters of it anywhere.'

And so, for the moment, papal Rome was spared. The French Convention, beset by other problems on every side, contented itself with the threats of vengeance and acclaimed its murdered envoy as a martyr of the Republic. But in 1796 Napoleon Bonaparte was appointed commander-in-chief of the army in Italy with the unanimous support of the Directory, all of whose members recognized in him a man who would not scruple to replenish the country's empty coffers with treasure looted from his defeated enemies. And, after his brilliant victories over the forces of the King of Sardinia and the Emperor of Austria in Italy, Bonaparte certainly did not hesitate to impose extortionate terms of surrender in obedience to the Directory's orders to carry everything out of the country that could be transported and was of use. From the papacy he took Ferrara, Bologna and the port of Ancona; and when the Austrians showed signs of recovery in northern Italy and the Pope misguidedly refused the peace terms of the Directory, Napoleon received orders to march towards Rome.

'We are the friends of every nation,' Bonaparte declared, 'especially the descendants of Brutus and the Scipios. Our intention is to restore the Capitol, to set up there in honour the statues of the men who won renown, and to free the Roman people from their long slavery.' In fact, it did not suit him to depose the Pope, as the Directory wanted him to do. For, if Pius were to be deposed, Naples might well then seize central Italy; and Naples, whose neurotic Queen was a sister of Marie Antoinette, would then be a greater threat to France than Rome. So Bonaparte decided to leave the Pope where he was and to impose upon him the terms of the Treaty of Tolentino. 'My opinion,' Bonaparte reported to Paris, 'is that Rome once stripped of Bologna, Ferrara, Romagna and thirty millions can no longer exist. The old machine will fall to pieces by itself.'

As it happened, Rome lost far more than thirty millions. Palaces, galleries and churches were stripped; antique sculptures, Renaissance paintings, tapestries, and precious stones and metals were packed up and loaded on to wagons. The Laocoön, the Belvedere Apollo, and countless other masterpieces were piled up with the works of Raphael, Caravaggio and Bernini. On one day gold and silver bars worth 15,000,000 *scudi* were carried off; on another 386 diamonds, 333 emeralds, 692 rubies, 208 sapphires and numerous other precious stones and pearls, many of them prized off papal tiaras, were sent to Paris. A few weeks later over 400 valuable manuscripts followed them. A procession of 500 horse-drawn wagons under a strong guard of soldiers took further bundles and cases of plunder along the Via Flaminia. Soon afterwards 1,600 horses were seen being led away to the headquarters of the French army.

As the treasures left Rome, representatives of the French government moved in. Bonaparte's brother, Joseph, arrived as ambassador with a salary of 60,000 francs a year and established himself with a large French household in Palazzo Corsini. French officers came on leave, and French agents, accompanied by Italians from the north sympathetic towards the Revolution, came to encourage the Republican groups that existed in Rome. On the night of 27 December 1797, after a sharp rise in food prices, these groups combined to stage a demonstration on the Pincio in protest against papal rule. On this occasion the demonstrators were dispersed by papal troops who shot and killed two men; but the next day a crowd of Jacobins appeared before Palazzo Corsini, shouting, 'Long live the Republic! Long live Liberty!' Joseph Bonaparte received their leaders whom he reproved for causing such a commotion. He was about to go out to address the crowd gathered at the palace gate when there was a discharge of guns from a papal cavalry picket which had entered the embassy precincts. The frightened crowd now swarmed into the courtyard and up the palace stairs, while Bonaparte ordered the cavalry picket to withdraw from French territory. As the papal troops retreated, the mob inside the palace took courage, and ran out towards them. The troops turned to open fire again, wounding several of the demonstrators. In the ensuing mêlée a young French general named Duphot, who had been having lunch with the ambassador and had rushed out upon the papal soldiers with drawn sword, was shot through the neck.

His death afforded the Directory the excuse they needed for sending in their army to occupy Rome. And so on 11 February 1798 General Berthier, who had succeeded Bonaparte as commander-in-chief, marched into Castel Sant' Angelo, billeting his officers in Roman palaces and his soldiers in Roman convents. The Pope's troops were disarmed, and several of his cardinals arrested. Others were expelled or deposed, while the Pope himself was abruptly informed on 17 February that he would have to leave Rome within three days. He was then eighty years old, very frail and mortally ill. He asked if he might be allowed to spend the few remaining days of his life in the city of St Peter, but the officer to whom the request was made, a Swiss Protestant, replied, 'People die anywhere.'

Pius, soon to be referred to by French officials as 'Citizen Pope', entered the travelling carriage that awaited him in the Cortile di San Damaso with two priests and a doctor. The Blessed Sacrament was enclosed in a small case hanging round his neck. His eyes filled with tears as he peered into the darkness through the

65. The end of the race of the riderless Arab barbs in the Roman Carnival.

carriage window towards St Peter's basilica. A detachment of dragoons escorted him to the Ponte Molle where people knelt in the snow to receive his blessing as he left. Five days later he arrived in Siena where he was given a room in the convent of the Hermits of St Augustine. At daybreak on 29 August the following year, the crucifix slipped from his hand as he lay dying on his bed in the French fortress of Valence. He had reigned for twenty-four years, six months and two weeks, the longest pontificate since the twenty-five years ascribed to that of St Peter.

In Rome, so it was reported in France, the establishment of a Roman Republic had been greeted with enthusiasm. Trees of Liberty were planted in the Forum and beside the statue of Marcus Aurelius on the Capitol, and citizens danced around them with tricolour cockades in their hats. But French observers actually living in Rome noticed no such signs of popular rejoicing. General Berthier, after his ceremonial entry into the city, had gone to the Capitol where the Tree of Liberty had been hoisted. He had made a speech invoking the shades of the ancient heroes of the first Roman Republic, but declared that he had 'seen nothing but the most profound dismay'. There was 'no trace of the spirit of liberty at all'.

There were those, of course, who welcomed the change of government or were at least prepared to give the impression of doing so for the sake of peace or profit. The Sforza, Santa Croce and Borghese families entertained the French in their palaces; women of other families were seen with French officers walking in gardens and riding in carriages; certain bankers and merchants increased their wealth by collaborating with the occupying forces; certain cardinals gave up their caps and one even signed himself 'Citizen Somaglia'.

Some of the measures introduced by the new government, as directed by the Directory's three civil commissioners, were welcomed by the people or at least regarded as just, such as the regulations providing for the lighting of streets at night, when formerly the only lamps to be seen were those small *lampioncini* that burned before representations of the Madonna. But many of the Republican government's other measures were far less well received: the Romans complained angrily of the renaming of their streets and *rioni*, of the adoption of the Republican calendar which abolished Sunday and provided for only one day's holiday in ten. They objected to the withdrawal from circulation of familiar coins and their replacement with foreign *assignats*, resulting in a further rise in the cost of living. At the same time the attempts of the French authorities to foster Republican enthusiasm by the introduction of the *carmagnole*, a dance popular in revolutionary France, in place of the traditional dances of the Carnival; by the insistence on *voi*, in imitation of the French *vous*, instead of *lei*; by the decoration of ancient statues with revolutionary favours; and by the replacement of religious feast days with such celebrations as the Fête of the Federation, and the Fête of the Perpetuity of the Republic, in which enthusiasts disguised as Roman senators honoured the memory of early martyrs in the cause of liberty, were all alike regarded with derision or contempt.

Other activities of the French were bitterly resented. There were outcries of protest when the bronze angel on the summit of Castel Sant' Angelo was painted in the colours of the Revolution, provided with a cap of liberty and transformed into 'the Liberating Genius of France'. The people were also outraged when the authorities refused to allow the revered statue of St Peter[9] to be decorated with its traditional emblems on the Apostle's feast day. Far more widely resented, however, were the government's depredations: its forcible seizure of Church property, its monetary exactions from families who could afford to pay them, and its use of the money thus acquired not for the relief of the poor but for the extravagance of its own members and for the maintenance of the French army of occupation.

Despite these wholesale appropriations, the Roman Republic was soon close to bankruptcy; and while officials, profiteers and speculators, their wives and hangers-on flaunted their new-found riches in the streets, parading about in the latest Parisian fashions, the men with hair cut *à la Titus*, the women in those *outré* and revealing dresses which Madame Tallien wore at Frascati's, the poor of Rome went hungry. At first the protests were limited: men joined dogs in urinating against the Trees of Liberty and delighted in seeing them knocked over by donkeys, until guards were mounted over them. But in February 1798 there were riots in Trastevere; and the suppression of these, with the execution of twenty-two of the ringleaders in the Piazza del Popolo, was followed by demonstrations, outbreaks of violence and assassinations elsewhere.

At the end of November help came from an unwelcome deliverer. Taking advantage of the partial withdrawal of French troops for other Napoleonic enterprises, the soldiers of the King of Naples marched into Rome through the Porta S. Giovanni on the south side of the city, while the French, greatly outnumbered, withdrew through the Porta del Popolo on the north, leaving a garrison in Castel Sant' Angelo to fire their cannon on the Neapolitans as they encamped in St Peter's Square. The cannonade soon ceased, however; and during the course of the next few days the Romans grew accustomed to the sight of King Ferdinand riding around the city with an escort of resplendently uniformed dragoons. But the proud liberators did not remain long. Defeated by the French north of Rome, the Neapolitans withdrew from the city, taking with them as much plunder as they could conveniently carry and leaving more awaiting shipment in Roman warehouses. On 11 December King Ferdinand rode hastily after his retreating troops; four days later the French reoccupied Rome.

That winter was a hard one. Despite the severely repressive rule of the French Civil Commissioner, Bertolio, who assumed the powers of a dictator, there were riots in the city as food shortages became acute and the price of fuel rose week by week. Almost every day there was a rattle of gunfire in the Piazza del Popolo as criminals and troublemakers were executed; and gangs of brigands, in virtual control of the countryside around the city, entered the gates with impunity. Although the anniversary of the fall of the Bastille was celebrated with great pomp in the Forum in July 1799, and officials made promises of better times soon to come, there had been little alleviation of the crime and distress with the advent of

66. Pope Pius VII (1742–1823), Napoleon's adversary.

the warmer weather. In September the French garrison in Rome, bereft of the support of the rest of their army which had now been largely withdrawn from the peninsula, were obliged to discuss a capitulation. On the last day of the month, after their commander had issued a proclamation exhorting the Romans to maintain their tranquillity, they marched out of the city, while the Neapolitans entered it once more from the south.

But, as before, the Neapolitans were not to remain for long; and when Napoleon's victory over the Austrians at Marengo gave him mastery over Italy again, his troops were ready to return. He now, however, had a different adversary to face, in the person of Gregorio Barnaba Chiaramonti who had been elected Pope in March 1800 at a lengthy conclave held in Venice and who entered Rome as Pope Pius VII in July.

A cultured, sensitive and learned man with a pleasantly ironical sense of humour, Pope Pius was supposed by the more rigidly conservative cardinals to be in sympathy with many of the ideas of the Revolution. As Archbishop of Imola he had agreed to style himself 'Citizen-Cardinal' and to have the baldacchino over the throne in the cathedral removed; his writing-paper had borne the superscriptions 'Liberty' and 'Equality'. Yet those closest to him knew that his desire to reconcile the Revolution with the Church had not prevented him from taking a stand against the authorities when he felt the Church to be threatened. He would prevaricate, feign forgetfulness, ignore an unwelcome order. He came to terms with Napoleon by negotiating, through Cardinal Consalvi, the Concordat of 1801 and he presided over Napoleon's coronation as Emperor in Nôtre Dame in 1804. But when Napoleon decided to destroy the temporal power of the papacy, and ordered General Miollis to occupy Rome once more, the Pope recognized that there could be no further reconciliation.

The French dragoons who rode into Rome through the Porta del Popolo at dawn on 2 February 1808 were supposed at first to be on their way to Naples; but as they took over Castel Sant' Angelo and, one after another, occupied the different *rioni*, having disarmed most of the papal troops, it was realized that they had come to stay. Indeed, Napoleon, whose favourite bedside books were Plutarch's *Lives*, dreamed of founding a second Roman Empire; and, determined not to repeat the mistakes that had been made during the previous French occupation of Rome, he saw to it that only the most efficient and scrupulous officials were employed in the administration of the city.

General Miollis himself was a cultivated man, courteous and placatory. At his headquarters in Palazzo Doria he gave superb dinner-parties at which the nobles and prelates of Rome were not only provided with exquisite meals but also persuaded to believe that, while the Emperor had no reason to question the religious authority of the Pope, his role as a secular prince was no longer acceptable in the new Europe. Many of the nobles acquiesced in this view and raised no objection when the rest of the papal troops were disarmed, the papal printing-presses closed down and papal officials brought increasingly under French control. But the clergy were less amenable; and when it became known that the Pope disapproved of the parties at Palazzo Doria, they began to refuse the General's invitations. The Romans in general shared the Pope's distrust of French motives. Angered by the abolition of the lottery, they were further provoked when the French authorities, ignoring the Pope's decision that the annual Carnival ought not to take place while a foreign garrison was in occupation of the city, seized the stage properties and decorations by force and decreed that the celebrations should take place as usual. The shopkeepers and tavern-owners consequently closed their doors and shutters, and the people turned their backs upon the Corso.

As the French hold upon the city tightened, the Pope's resolve hardened. 'The Pope is not a man whom one may hope to persuade by persistent argument,' the French chargé d'affaires reported. 'He is firm and immovable in his attitude. Once he has made up his mind, anything you say will not persuade him to change it. He does not prevent you from speaking, but after you have finished talking yourself he just lowers his head on his breast and allows you to leave in silence.'

In the hope that the Pope might be more pliant if his advisers were removed, Miollis ordered the expulsion from Rome of the Dean of the Sacred College and the Pro-Governor of the city, and sent two officers to arrest Cardinal Bartolommeo Pacca, the uncompromising Pro-Secretary of State. Pacca, however, had been warned of their coming and arranged for the Pope to be with him when they arrived. The Pope upbraided them furiously, so angrily, in fact, that Pacca observed a phenomenon he had believed to be imaginary: a man's hair standing on end. His Holiness ordered the officers to tell their General that there must be an immediate end to these outrages, that Cardinal Pacca was under his protection, and that if the French wanted him they would have to break into the innermost chambers of the Quirinal to find him. The Pope then stormed out of the room followed by Pacca; and, as he returned to his own private apartments, the keys were turned in the seventeen doors through which they passed.

Napoleon decided that the time had now come to issue a decree formally annexing the Papal States to the French Empire and creating Rome a 'free imperial city'. The decree was read by a mounted herald on the Capitol; then, as trumpets blared, the papal flag was lowered from the summit of Castel Sant' Angelo and the French tricolour was hoisted in its place. The Pope, watching the scene from a heavily curtained window in the Quirinal, said to Cardinal Pacca, 'Consummatum est!' He then walked over to a table on which lay a document he had long threatened to issue, the bull of excommunication. After a prayer and words of encouragement from Pacca, he picked up a pen and signed it. Later that day, copies of the bull and of an order requiring the Romans not to give their support to the new régime were posted on the doors of St Peter's, St John Lateran and S. Maria Maggiore.

General Radet, the young and headstrong chief of the Roman police, now seized his opportunity to come to the attention of the Emperor as an officer of initiative and daring. He asked General Miollis for signed warrants authorizing him to arrest Cardinal Pacca and to abduct the Pope. Miollis readily granted him the warrant for

67. (opposite) Napoleon with his son, styled King of Rome. Born in 1811, the son of the Empress Marie-Louise, the king who was proclaimed Napoleon II after Waterloo, inherited his mother's tendency to consumption and died at the age of twenty-one.

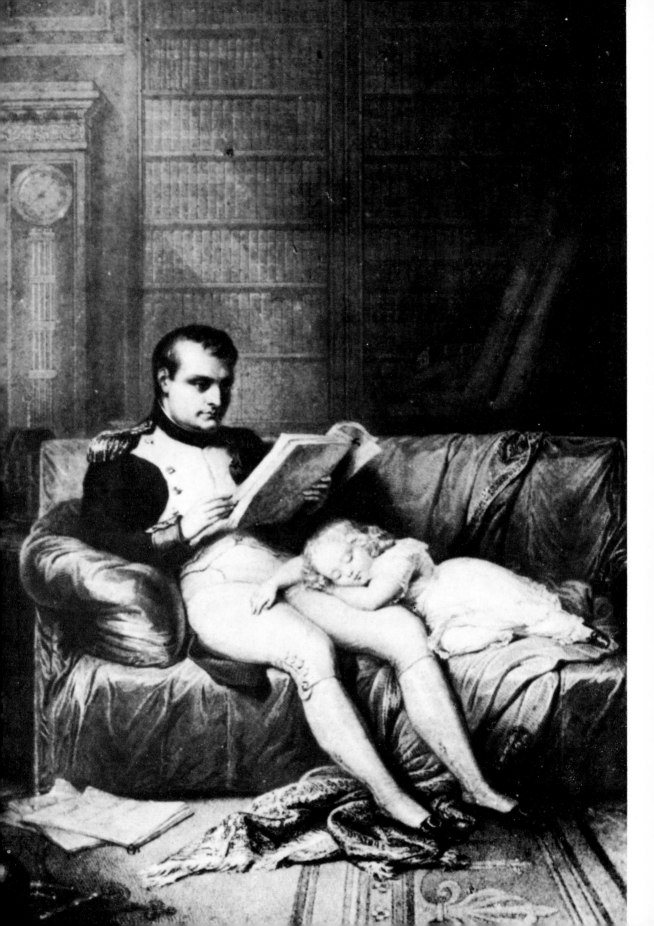

Pacca's arrest, but considered that his instructions from the Emperor did not allow him to take any action against the Pope other than placing a guard upon the Quirinal. But with or without written authority, Radet was determined to act; and in the early hours of the morning of 6 July he led an assault on the Pope's apartments. His plan was to scale the wall of the Quirinal by rope-ladders and, with a party of forty men, to gain access to the papal apartments from the roof, while other parties crept through the gardens and forced windows at the back of the palace. This plan miscarried when a rope-ladder broke and the cries of the falling men alerted the palace guards. But Radet, undeterred by the lights now shining from the palace windows and the tolling of the palace bell, attacked the main door with a hatchet and was raining blows at the lock when it flew open, the bolts withdrawn by the soldiers who had gained access to the hall from the back. Radet rushed for the staircase followed by his men, axes and crowbars in their hands. They disarmed the Swiss Guards who had been ordered not to resist French soldiers, and battering their way through locked doors, at about half-past three they came upon the Pope in the Hall of Audience. He was sitting fully clothed in soutane, stole and *mozzetta* between two cardinals. At sight of him, Radet, a pious man who composed canticles to the Madonna, came to a sudden halt and ordered his men back. 'On the roof and mounting the stairs, it all seemed splendid,' he later confessed. 'But when I saw the Pope, in that instant, I also saw myself at my first Communion.'

'Why have you come?' the Pope asked him.

'Most Holy Father, to repeat to your Holiness, in the name of the French Government, the proposition that he should renounce his temporal power.'

'We cannot yield what does not belong to us. The temporal power belongs to the Church.'

'Then I am under orders to take you away.'

'Those orders, my son, will assuredly not bring divine blessings upon you.'

The Pope felt obliged to obey the orders, though. Allowed half an hour to collect what he needed, he asked for his ciborium, breviary and rosary, and then, without money or even a change of clothes, he followed Radet down the staircase and stepped into the coach which was waiting for him in the courtyard. The door was locked behind him and the coach rattled away towards the Porta Salaria.

The Rome from which the Pope was exiled until the fall of his adversary was governed by the occupying power with efficiency rather than with understanding of the character of the Roman people. Among the aristocracy, the French had a number of supporters, several of whom dined regularly in the gilded salons of the Palazzo di Montecitorio with the amusing and scholarly Prefect of Rome, Baron de Tournon. But even these Francophiles were disillusioned when their sons were conscripted into the Napoleonic armies. They, like other Roman parents, urged their children not to present themselves for enrolment or, if forced to enrol, to desert. Many did desert and found refuge with the brigands in the nearby mountains, so that the drive for conscripts did as much to strengthen the bands of outlaws around Rome as to increase the imperial levies.

68. Pius VII enters Rome on 24 May 1814, his carriage drawn by the sons of noble Roman families.

While the brigands outside the city grew in numbers, so did the poor within it. The dissolution of the religious orders by the Napoleonic régime and the sequestration of their property led thousands of monks and nuns, expelled from monasteries and convents, to join those mendicants to whose needs they had formerly ministered. The number of indigents in Rome rose from 12,000 in 1810 to 30,000 in 1812.

As the lands of the Church were expropriated, as taxes were vastly increased to the level of those levied in France, as more and more Romans were deported and confiscations of their property grew more widespread, the French administration of Rome became ever more detested. And, after Napoleon's defeat at the Battle of Leipzig in October 1813, it also became impracticable. With no hope of further help from France, with the British navy landing raiding-parties along the coast and brigands scouring the countryside beyond the city walls, it was now but a matter of time before the whole structure collapsed. The *coup de grâce* came, however, in an unexpected way.

Five years before, one of Napoleon's most brilliant marshals, Joachim Murat – the innkeeper's son who became a dashing cavalry leader, husband of Napoleon's youngest sister, Caroline, and Grand Duke of Berg and Cleves – had been further rewarded with the Kingdom of Naples. A man of limitless ambition and vanity, he had conceived a plan of uniting southern and central Italy into one kingdom under his sway; and, after the disaster of Leipzig, he made up his mind to break with Napoleon and to make common cause with the Allies in order to further his ends. On the pretext of moving his army north for the defence of Italy against Austria, he filled Rome with troops who appeared to be in transit but of whom many had come to stay. By the end of January 1814 the Neapolitans were in virtual possession of the city. It was only on Castel Sant' Angelo that General Miollis, still loyal to Napoleon though his cause was now lost, continued to fly the French flag. It was to fly there for only a few weeks more. On 10 March 1814 the last French troops marched out of Rome, with drums beating and flags flying, past the silent Roman crowds whom they had governed for almost six years.

In April Pope Pius returned, his carriage, drawn by the sons of noble families, passing slowly down the Corso beneath triumphal arches. He re-entered the Quirinal whose rooms the French had filled with Empire furniture and ornaments, and on whose walls they had painted the figures of classical gods and goddesses. Most of the French ornaments were removed to make room for the crucifixes and religious statues which they had replaced, but not all the goddesses were painted over: the Pope observed that those whose dresses were not diaphanous might make very nice Madonnas. Indeed, the Pope decided not to do away with anything merely because it was French. He retained many of the reforms carried out by the Napoleonic administration and adopted the Napoleonic Civil Code. He offered a home to Napoleon's widowed mother, Letizia, who went to live at the Palazzo Falconieri[10] with Cardinal Fesch, whose father had married her as his second wife. Napoleon's brother Lucien, who had been made Prince of Canino, a little town north of Rome, came to live in a palace there. Asylum was also granted to Napoleon's other brother, Joseph Bonaparte, to his sister, Elisa, formerly Grand Duchess of Tuscany, and even to Napoleon's Inspector-General of Gendarmerie, the Duc de Rovigo.

When the Duc died in 1833, the French occupation of Rome had been largely forgotten and little evidence of their rule remained. In their time the Vatican Library and Museums had been reorganized; further areas of the Pontine Marshes had been drained; the first expert excavations of the Trajan Forum had been carried out; and the charming gardens overlooking the Piazza del Popolo from the Pincian hill had been laid out by the Roman landscape architect, Valadier. But more grandiose conceptions, such as an immense imperial palace stretching from the Piazza Colonna to the Colosseum, were never realized, and Rome appeared to foreign visitors much as it had done when Charles de Brosses had arrived a hundred

69. The Piazza del Popolo from the Pincio Gardens, by the poetical landscape painter, Samuel Palmer, who spent part of his long honeymoon in Rome in 1838.

years before. The population still numbered only about 135,000; and Stendhal, writing in 1827, noted that the inhabited area remained bounded on the south by the Capitol, on the west by the Tiber, and on the east by the Pincian and Quirinal hills. Three quarters of the city inside the Aurelian Walls – the Viminal, the Esquiline, the Caelian and the Aventine hills – he described as being silent and solitary. 'La fièvre y règne,' he wrote, 'et on les cultive en vigne.' He saw an Englishman ride his horse through the Colosseum; and, though he considered the Corso the most beautiful street in the universe, he found, as others had done for centuries past, that it stank of cabbages.

As an English visitor observed, 'One can walk from one end of the city to the other without seeing a single thing to suggest that you are not still in the eighteenth century or to remind you that the French were once masters here for several years.' Most of the looted works of art had been returned; and the Papal States, which the Allies had denied to the faithless Murat, had been given back to the Pope. Rome, like the rest of Europe, as one of the diplomats who had attended the Congress of Vienna chose to put it, 'was as it might have been had the tragedy of the Revolution never occurred'. The old world could not be restored, however: there were more upheavals soon to come.

FIFTEEN

THE RISORGIMENTO AND THE ROMAN QUESTION

'There is storm in the air,' Pope Gregory XVI said to a friend shortly before his death in 1846. 'Revolutions will soon break out.' Revolutions had, indeed, been likely ever since the Congress of Vienna had set about the task of undoing the work of Napoleon and of breaking up Italy into its former small components so that the pieces could be handed back, wherever possible, to their former masters. The watchword of the Congress had been 'legitimacy', a doctrine invented by Talleyrand to express the advantages of the Bourbon restoration in France. In pursuit of 'legitimacy' in Italy, the Bourbons had been re-established in Naples, the House of Savoy recovered Piedmont and Sardinia, whose territories were extended to include Savoy and Nice as well as the former Republic of Genoa, and the Pope had been returned to power in the Papal States. This fragmentation of Italy suited the Austrian Foreign Minister, Prince Metternich, very well. To him Italy was *'ein geographischer Begriff'*, a mere geographical expression; so long as it remained divided, Austria would be able to maintain her hold over Lombardy and Venetia. At Vienna he succeeded not only in acquiring these two valuable territories for his country, but he also arranged for Tuscany to be accorded to an Austrian archduke and for Parma to be ceded to the daughter of the Austrian Emperor. And in the Kingdom of Naples the wife of the restored monarch, Ferdinand IV, was an Austrian. Austria was thus restored to the dominant position she had enjoyed in Italy at the end of the eighteenth century; and over those large areas which she controlled, the clouds of reaction gathered and darkened. So they also did in most of the rest of Italy where police spies, clerical privileges and press censorship became commonplace.

In the Papal States all the officials who had served the French were dismissed from their posts; the French codes of law were destroyed; education was limited while taxes were increased; and power was concentrated in the hands of the Cardinal Secretary of State and of those other ecclesiastics appointed to direct the various departments of the Government. In the time of Pius VII some reforms had been effected by Cardinal Consalvi, his Secretary of State; but these had been nullified by Pius's successor, Leo XII; while Pope Gregory XVI, an obscurantist of the most extreme persuasion, went so far as to prohibit the building of railways – he called them *'chemins d'enfer'* – in the Papal States, fearing that they might 'work harm to religion' and lead to the arrival in Rome of deputations of malcontents from restless provinces beyond the Appenines. He set his mind firmly against reform. In Cardinal Lambruschini he had an adviser who, though more personally attractive than himself, was no less uncompromising. And in Giuseppe Gioacchino Belli, the Roman dialect poet, whose sonnets are a vivid memorial of the lives and conversations of the Romans of the period, he had an adversary who delighted in satirizing his views. 'I really liked Pope Gregory,' Belli wrote, 'because it gave me so much pleasure to speak ill of him.'

In the Papal States, as elsewhere in Italy, there were occasional demonstrations, disturbances and uprisings. But the demands of the rebels, beset by economic pressures and social discontents, were for independence, constitutions and reforms rather than, as yet, for national unity. The main causes of complaint were the failure of the papacy to restore municipal liberties or to allow laymen to play any significant part in government.

There were, however, various secret organizations in the peninsula whose members looked forward to the day when, at some unspecified date and by vaguely suggested means, Italy would attain freedom from foreign domination and achieve

70. Dancing in the Frastevere during the Carnival.

the ultimate unity of its separate states. One such secret society was the Carbonari who took their name, symbolically, from *carbone* (coal) which, black and lifeless, burns brightly when it is kindled, and who used charcoal-burners' shops as covers for their activities. Another was Young Italy, whose motto, '*Dio e popolo*', expressed the religious foundation of the national cause, and whose oath required its members to work 'wholly and for ever to constitute Italy one, free and independent'. Both organizations took heart when, on the death of Pope Gregory XVI, Cardinal Mastai Ferretti, the 54-year-old Bishop of Imola, was elected to succeed him; for the new Pope, who took the name of Pius IX, was a kindly, polite, good-looking man who was believed to have pronounced liberal tendencies. His election certainly distressed the reactionary Cardinal Lambruschini, who had hoped to become Pope himself, and Cardinal Bernetti, Lambruschini's predecessor as Secretary of State, who, when the Bishop of Imola appeared on the point of fainting at the prospect of his likely election, murmured in his neighbour's ear, 'Well, after the policemen come the ladies.'

In Rome, where he was little known, Pope Pius was greeted at first with some distrust; but by the time his carriage had been driven away from the Quirinal to the Vatican his handsome face, calm expression and gentle gestures had impressed all who saw him. '*Ah!*' the women said. '*Ah! Che bello!*' The reports that subsequently emanated from the Vatican were highly favourable: the new Pope was a charming man, sensitive and generous, simple and devout, with a most endearing self-deprecating humour. He was also evidently not prepared to tolerate his predecessor's regressive policies. He formed a council to watch over all branches of the administration and to investigate proposals for modernization and change. He appointed a commission on railways and on the civil and penal codes; he granted an amnesty for political offences; planned gas lighting in the streets, and the introduction of laymen into the government. Metternich was appalled by these signs that the Pope was prepared to align himself with liberal Europe. 'We were prepared for everything but a liberal pope,' he said. 'And now that we have one, who can tell what may happen?' It was 'the greatest misfortune of the age'.

Metternich was also deeply concerned by Pius's evidently genuine feeling for Italy, by his apparent attraction to the idea that the papacy should play a vital role in the regeneration of the nation, and that the Pope should preside over a confederation of Italian states. Yet Pope Pius was not really in sympathy with the motives behind the liberal movement; nor did he in his heart believe that representative government could be reconciled with papal authority. He doubted that he was capable, even if willing, to lead a national movement to fulfilment. They wanted to make a Napoleon out of him, he complained, when he was really nothing but a priest. And it was undoubtedly true that despite his fine voice and commanding presence, he did not have the strength of character to fulfil the hopes and control the enthusiasm of the applauding thousands who followed him through the streets of Rome shouting '*Evviva!*' and waving the scarves and handkerchieves which were made in his colours. He enjoyed the acclaim, his enemies said, but he was nervous of its consequences, of the repeated cry, '*Viva Pio*

71. Pope Pius IX (1792–1878), whose pontificate, marked by a transition from liberalism to conservatism, was the longest in history.

72. Pius IX acclaimed at the Quirinal Palace on the night of 16 July 1846 for having granted amnesties to some four hundred political offenders imprisoned by his predecessor, Gregory XVI.

Nono, solo! Solo!' He saw that he was being held up for popular acclaim not so much as a reforming pope but as one who had 'sided with the revolution against tradition'. His cautious and sensible early reforms were now dismissed as unworthy of the times; he was presented no longer as a saint, but caricatured as a tortoise.

All over Italy there were feelings of hopes unfulfilled, expectations unrealized, opportunities missed; and the desires awakened were surging beyond control. At the beginning of 1848, in fulfilment of Pope Gregory's prophecy, revolutions broke out from Sicily and Naples to Florence, Venice and Milan. News of these

uprisings and of the war of liberation against Austria was received in Rome with the greatest excitement. But on 29 April Pope Pius felt it his duty as Pope to deliver an Allocution separating himself once and for all from the nationalists and indeed from the Risorgimento – the campaign for a united Italy itself: 'We assert clearly and openly that war with Austria is far from our thoughts, since we, however unworthy, are the Vicar of Him who is the author of peace and the lover of concord.'

This unequivocal announcement aroused a storm of protest, and led to the temporary appointment of the liberal Count Terenzio Mamiani della Rovere as head of the administration which the Pope had been forced to accept under the terms of a constitution granted the previous March. In the middle of September, however, after the resignation of Mamiani followed by that of his liberal successor, Count Eduardo Fabbri, neither of whom felt capable of controlling the political situation or the extreme demands of the revolutionary clubs, the government was placed in the hands of the ex-revolutionary conservative Count Pellegrino Rossi, a tall, pale, thin scholar of strong character and varied gifts. His books were on the Index, he had a Protestant wife and he was intensely disliked in the Curia. Yet the Pope trusted him, for Rossi saw in the papacy 'the one great thing that was left to Italy'; and he was determined to preserve its temporal power, not by making concessions to the democrats but by wise economic reforms and enlightened administration. But he was a proud, aloof and provocative man who took no trouble to hide his contempt for his opponents, whether Republican or conservative, and made many enemies among them by his cruel sarcasm.

The bitterness of his enemies' hatred was demonstrated on 15 November when he dismounted from his carriage outside the Palazzo della Cancelleria for the new session of the Council of Deputies. A small crowd shouted insults as he approached the broad stone steps of the palace: 'Abbasso Rossi! Abbasso Rossi! Morte a Rossi!' He took no notice. His expression was one of scorn and distaste, emphasized some observers said, by a slight contemptuous smile. Suddenly a man struck him, then another stabbed him in the neck, severing the carotid artery, before escaping into the crowd, his head hidden in the folds of a cloak.

The next day Rome was in uproar. Armed gangs paraded through the streets shouting slogans and singing songs in praise of the assassins. A large crowd of soldiers, policemen and well-known citizens surged about the Quirinal demanding a democratic programme; and, when it seemed that the Pope was unwilling to give way, they attacked the palace, firing through the windows, trying to set fire to the doors and killing the Latin Secretary. Protesting that he did so only under duress, the Pope surrendered to the radicals and agreed to the formation of a cabinet sympathetic towards them. Soon afterwards, virtually a prisoner in his own palace, he left Rome for Gaeta in the Kingdom of Naples disguised as an ordinary priest, his features partially concealed behind large spectacles. And from Gaeta, advised by Cardinal Antonelli, an ambitious, clever and devious politician, he demanded the submission of the rebels. He denounced as 'a monstrous act of unconcealed treason' the proposal that a constituent assembly be elected in Rome

73. Count Pelligrino Rossi (1787–1848), who was murdered outside the Palazzo della Cancelleria.

on the basis of universal suffrage, and threatened anyone who so voted with the 'Greater Excommunication'. His condemnations, however, had little effect. It was impossible now to check the enthusiasm in Rome by so uncompromising a stand. The American Margaret Fuller, a former schoolteacher from Boston, now mistress of the Marchese Ossoli, expressed a common sentiment when she wrote that she thought she could never have heard of a violent death with satisfaction but that Rossi's assassination seemed to her 'one of terrible justice'.

In spite of papal condemnation, the representatives of a constituent assembly were elected in due course and these, on 9 February, voted the end of the papal state and its replacement by the Roman Republic. This fired the imagination of liberals all over Italy, but it also aroused the anger of Catholic Europe to which the Pope appealed for its suppression. He appealed to King Ferdinand of Naples who

74. Cardinal Antonelli (1806–76), Pope Pius IX's artful, able and sensual Secretary of State.

lost no time in moving his army up to the frontier; he appealed to the Austrian Emperor whose forces, having defeated those of Piedmont, also marched towards Rome; and, most ominously for Rome, he appealed to France where the nephew of the Emperor Napoleon I, Louis Napoleon – whose election the year before to the French Assembly had been compared by a journalist to the sudden and unexpected appearance of the demon king in a pantomime – had recently been proclaimed President. Although personally sympathetic towards the Italian nationalists, Louis Napoleon had good reasons for responding to the Pope's call: he needed the support of the French clergy to achieve the destiny he already envisaged for himself as creator of the Second Empire. He could not afford to allow the Austrians to extend their influence in Italy, nor did he want to be eclipsed by the King of Naples, the choice of whose kingdom as a place of exile by the Pope had been interpreted as a diplomatic defeat for France. Besides, there was a strong feeling in France that the Pope had been disgracefully ill used, and the mounting of an expedition to restore him would not, therefore, be unpopular. So a French army also advanced upon the Roman Republic which prepared itself to fight for its existence by creating on 29 March a Triumvirate to dictate its policy during the imminent emergency. The members of this Triumvirate were Carlo Armellini, a respected Roman lawyer, Count Aurelio Saffi, the leader of the liberals from the Romagna, and Giuseppe Mazzini, a man whose fame and genius were to ensure that he was to be the inspiration of the Republic's defence.

The son of a doctor from Genoa who had become professor of anatomy at the university, Mazzini had been born in 1805. He had thought of becoming a doctor himself, but after fainting at the sight of his first operation, he had turned to law. He had little taste for this either and, although he did well enough in his examinations, he was a troublesome and argumentative student, restless, impatient, moody, slow to make friends and quick to take offence. He remained a difficult personality throughout his life. When he was well and happy he could be generous, charming and lively, but in the moods of dispirited tiredness which often overcame him he was irritating, exacting and didactic. He dressed always in black and allowed himself no luxuries other than expensive writing-paper and scent. He ate the simplest food and for days on end would exist on a diet largely composed of bread and raisins. He had a beautiful voice and striking features. His eyes were dark and flashing, the only eyes that one man who knew him had ever seen that 'looked like flames'. His skin was smooth and olive, his hair black and long; he walked quickly with a feline grace, holding his head forward.

The suppression of a revolt in Genoa when he was sixteen had brought the Carbonari to his admiring notice and he had later joined the society. The unification of Italy was a cause which he had thereafter embraced with passionate intensity, and he gave up his whole life to its realization with single-minded stubbornness. 'Mine is a matter of deep conviction,' he would say dogmatically. 'It is impossible for me to modify or alter it.' And this very refusal to compromise, this blind dedication to an ideal that allowed him to disregard the obstacles in the way of its realization, this intolerance of views other than his own, formed his unique and essential contribution to the birth of his country.

75. Giuseppe Mazzini (1805–72), inspiration of the Roman Republic. 'Rome was the dream of my young years,' he wrote, 'the religion of my soul.'

For him there could be no other capital of Italy but Rome, 'the natural centre of Italian unity'; and Rome became for him, in the words of the Countess Martinengo Cesaresco, 'a talismanic obsession'.

'Rome was the dream of my young years, the religion of my soul,' Mazzini wrote. 'I entered the city one evening, early in March [1849], with a deep sense of awe, almost of worship ... I had journeyed towards the sacred city with a heart sick unto death from the ... dismemberment of our Republican party over the whole of Italy. Yet nevertheless, as I passed through the Porta del Popolo, I felt an electric thrill run through me – a spring of new life.'

Inspired by the hope that the liberation of Italy would be accomplished by a pure, spreading fire set off by a spark in Rome, he addressed the Assembly with brilliant eloquence:

There are not five Italies, or four Italies or three Italies. There is only one Italy. God, who, in creating her, smiled upon her land, has awarded her the two most sublime frontiers in Europe, symbols of eternal strength and eternal motion – the Alps and the sea ... Rome shall be the holy Ark of your redemption, the temple of your nation ... Rome, by the design of Providence, and as the People have divined, is the Eternal City to which is entrusted the mission of disseminating the word that will unite the world ... Just as to the Rome of the Caesars, which through action united a great part of Europe, there succeeded the Rome of the Popes, which united Europe and America in the realm of the spirit, so the Rome of the People will succeed them both, to unite Europe, America and every part of the terrestrial globe in a faith that will make thought and action one ... The destiny of Rome and Italy is that of the world.

As undisputed leader of the Republic, Mazzini, brooking no arguments nor any rival, made many enemies in Rome. He 'thinks he is Pope and infallible,' wrote one of them. Another, Luigi Carlo Farini, was soon to say, 'He is pontiff, prince, apostle, priest. When the clerics have gone he will be thoroughly at home in Rome ... He has the nature of a priest more than a statesman. He wants to tether the world to his own immutable idea.'

To the Romans at large, however, he was an inspiring figure who infected them with his own feverish, almost hysterical enthusiasm. He went to live in a small room in the Quirinal from which he emerged each morning to walk about the streets 'with the same smile and warm handshake for all', radiating confidence in the destiny of the Republic, in the unique greatness of the city of its birth in whose air could be felt 'the pulsations of the immense eternal life of Rome, the immortality stirring beneath those ruins of two epochs, two worlds'. The city might fall if no further help arrived, he had to concede, but even in its fall the people would regain their 'Religion of Rome' and from the ashes of its defeat would arise a new spirit, fierce and purified.

To outsiders its collapse seemed inevitable. A leader in *The Times* referred dismissively to the 'degenerate remnant of the Roman people' preparing to fight in the mistaken belief that they were heroes; and foreign residents in Rome did not disguise their belief that the Triumvirate would soon be dismissed, that the defenders of Rome would run away at the first shot, and that the people were only too anxious for the French to arrive and for the suppression of the Republic. Certainly, the forces which the Triumvirs had been able to assemble for the defence of Rome offered little ground for hope that the French could be kept out. There were only about a thousand men in the National Guard and these were scarcely a match for the well-trained troops of the French army. Admittedly, they had shouted their readiness for war when addressed by Mazzini; but their officers, some timid and many unsure that the Republic's cause was one worth dying for, expressed among themselves far less bellicose sentiments. There were some 2,500 regular papal troops who had declared their readiness to support the new government against the allies of their former master; but most of them were believed to be activated not so much by faith in the Republic as by jealousy of the Swiss Guards who, they believed, had been more favoured than themselves in the past. There was also, however, a strong force of irregular troops, seasoned and fervent, who had entered Rome on 27 April under the leadership of a bearded Messianic-looking figure in a flamboyant black felt hat decorated with a plume of ostrich feathers. He had ridden a white horse, darting keen glances to right and left, his long brown hair falling to his broad shoulders, his deeply set eyes divided by a long, aquiline nose with a very high bridge.

'I shall never forget that day,' wrote a young artist who left his studio to fight beside this imposing newcomer. 'He reminded us of nothing so much as of our Saviour's head in the galleries. Everyone said so. I could not resist him. I went after him. Thousands did the same. He only had to show himself. We all worshipped him. We could not help it.'

Giuseppe Garibaldi, then aged forty-two, was a guerilla leader of outstanding gifts. The son of a sailor, he had been born in Nice, which had been taken by Napoleon from the Kingdom of Piedmont, and he had been brought up to speak the Ligurian dialect as his first language and French as his second. Italian did not come easily to him, therefore, and his accent betrayed his frontier origins. Like his father, he had been born to the sea and had become a cabin-boy apprentice before he was seventeen. A year later he had sailed down the coast of the Papal States and then up the Tiber in a small boat drawn by oxen, with a cargo of wine for Rome. 'The Rome that I then beheld with the eyes of my youthful imagination,' he wrote, 'was the Rome of the future – the Rome that I never despaired of even when I was shipwrecked, dying, banished to the farthest depths of the American forests – the dominant thought and inspiration of my whole life.'

He had gone to South America after having been condemned to death in an ill-fated insurrection planned by Young Italy, and while living there he had, as he put it, 'served the cause of nations' by fighting in various revolutions. Returning to Italy in 1848 he found that he had arrived by chance in a year of ferment, a year in which his dream of a united Italy, with Rome as its capital, might be realized. The appearance of his followers did not, however, inspire confidence in the Roman people. With their long, unkempt hair, their matted beards and dusty, high-crowned, black-plumed hats, they looked more like bandits than soldiers. Some carried muskets, others lances, all wore daggers in their belts. They did have a kind of uniform: dark blue tunics for the men, and for the officers and orderlies red smocks of the kind that Garibaldi's Italian troops had worn in South America ever since a stock of them had been acquired in Montevideo where they had been awaiting export for use in the slaughterhouses of the Argentine. 'They rode on American saddles,' an Italian regular officer recorded disdainfully, 'and seemed to pride themselves on their contempt for all the observances more strictly enjoined on regular troops.' They were indeed, a 'parcel of brigands', as an English resident in Rome told a visitor; they were not in the least likely to enhance the reputation of the Republic. Yet such was the enthusiasm which their leader aroused that their numbers were soon swelled by hundreds of volunteers, artists and clerks, schoolboys and boatmen, Romans and foreigners – Englishmen, Dutchmen, Swiss and Belgians. Students and young lecturers from the University formed a special Students' Corps. Soon even the most conservative and sceptical observers had to admit that, as excitement mounted, hopes for the Republic increased and that there was little to complain about in its declared programme of 'no war of classes, no hostility to existing wealth, no wanton or unjust violation of the rights of property; but a constant endeavour to ameliorate the material condition of the classes least favoured by fortune'. Church property was to be nationalized; the offices of the Inquisition turned into apartments; ecclesiastical estates partitioned into smallholdings to be let at nominal rents. Yet the government decreed that there was to be no persecution of priests, even of those who preached against its policies. And there was, indeed, very little anti-clerical violence in Rome. *The Times* correspondent, who was not there at the time, accepted the most lurid reports that came out of the city and wrote of priests who had the courage to appear in the open being cut into pieces and thrown into the Tiber. But, in fact, so friends of Arthur Hugh Clough, the English poet, were informed, priests walked about 'in great comfort'. 'Be assured,' Clough continued, 'the worst thing I have witnessed has been a paper in manuscript put up in two places in the Corso, pointing out seven or eight men for popular resentment. This has been done by night. Before the next evening a proclamation was posted in all the streets, from (I am sure) Mazzini's pen, severely and scornfully castigating such proceedings.'

It was true that rumour of a cell in the dungeons of the Inquisition being found stuffed with bones and human hair had led to a violent riot. It was also undeniable that, after the siege had begun, several priests, some, though not all of whom had fired at soldiers, were all murdered, together with three peasants who had been mistaken for spies; and that in May a furiously anti-clerical terrorist from Forlì, who had been placed in charge of a volunteer regiment of provincial customs officers, was responsible for a number of savage crimes in Trastevere. But it was generally agreed that the Pope's claim that Rome had become 'a den of wild beasts . . . who infringe the personal liberty of decent people and expose their lives to the daggers of cut-throats' was quite unjustified, and that the Republic's maxim, 'Firmness in principles, toleration to individuals', was being widely observed.

Yet, despite the brief enthusiasm aroused by the arrival of the Garibaldini, there was continued scepticism among the foreign colony in Rome as to the ability of

76. Giuseppe Garibaldi (1807–82), defender of the Roman Republic in 1849. 'He reminded us of nothing so much as of our Saviour's head in the galleries,' said a young artist who left his studio to become one of his soldiers. 'We all worshipped him. We could not help it.'

the Republic to withstand the powerful enemies it had raised up against itself. William Wetmore Story, the American sculptor and writer, watched the barricades going up at Porta San Giovanni and 'voted the workmen too lazy to live'. Another day he went to Porta Cavalleggeri and Porta Angelica

to see the barricades, or rather earth mounds, ramparts, stockades, which the Romans are building in the event of a French attack. They had been working at these some thirty hours and in some places had gone three feet. Bunker Hill ramparts were thicker. Here nothing is right earnest. The labourers were leaning picturesquely on their spades, doing nothing, and everything was going on as leisurely as if the enemy were in France instead of a few hours' march of the city.

The next day Story heard the commander of the Guardia Civica haranguing his men in the Piazza SS. Apostoli. He asked them if they were prepared to defend Rome with their lives. '*Si!*' they shouted, '*Si!*' holding up their caps on their bayonets, 'making the Piazza ring with huzzas. But the enthusiasm did not seem of the right stuff – it was rather a *festa* demonstration.'

Emilio Dandolo, who entered Rome with a battalion of *bersaglieri* from Lombardy on 29 April, formed the same impression. He felt that the applause which greeted his men from the windows on every side might well have been welcoming the last scene of some absurd comedy.

There was the same superabundance of standards, of cockades, of badges of party that had characterized the last few months of Milan's liberty [before the Austrians resumed control], the same clanking of swords along the public streets, and those various and varied uniforms of the officers, not one matching the other but all seeming more suitable for the embellishment of the stage than for military service . . . This array of warriors in glittering helmets with double-barrelled guns and with belts full of daggers reconciled us but little to the scanty numbers of real, well-drilled soldiers.

Behind the flourish and the bombast, however, work *was* progressing rapidly upon the defences of Rome, Story's caustic comments notwithstanding. Ramparts were being raised, loopholes made in walls; the trees in the gardens of the Villa Borghese were being cut down for barricades; the covered way from the Vatican to Castel Sant' Angelo was being demolished. In every *rione* men were appointed to take command of the citizens when the bells of the Capitol and Montecitorio summoned them to arms; platforms were erected in the squares so that the most accomplished of the Republic's orators could address the people; priests and nuns were asked to pray for victory; pensions were promised to those who might be killed; hospitals were organized by Princess Belgioso who could rely upon the help of nearly six thousand volunteers.

Garibaldi was seen everywhere. It had been decided not to appoint him commander-in-chief, since accusations that the city had been taken over by outsiders were already common enough. But he was regarded by all as the natural military leader and whenever he appeared, accompanied by a gigantic and outlandishly dressed Negro orderly who had followed him from South America, he was greeted with loud cheers. His own men, strengthened by some 1,300

77. A Garibaldian lancer carrying a message through the streets.

volunteers from Rome and the Papal States and supported by troops of the Papal Army and the National Guard, were given the formidable task by the Republic's Minister of War, General Avezzana, of defending the most dangerous part of the front. This was the high ground of the Janiculan hill, south of St Peter's between the Porta Cavalleggeri and the Porta Portese. It was protected by a line of walls stretching south from Castel Sant' Angelo which had been either built or extended by Urban VIII after the development of gunpowder had revolutionized the art of siege warfare. They were much more capable both of being used offensively by artillerymen and of resisting bombardment than the ancient walls of Aurelian; but they had a serious disadvantage in that the open ground beyond them was as high as the defences and in one place even higher. It was here that the French were likely to concentrate their batteries so that they could fire upon the fortifications by the Porta San Pancrazio, the gate between the Porta Cavalleggeri and the Porta Portese which led directly into the Trastevere quarter. On the high ground beyond this gate were the gardens of two villas, the Villa Corsini[1] and the Villa Pamphilj.[2] It was in the exposed Villa Corsini that Garibaldi established his headquarters, while, out of sight, north of the vineyards in the valley, the French army marched through a deserted countryside.

Assured by their commander, General Oudinot, that the Romans considered them as liberators from the papal yoke and that no resistance would be offered them, they marched with confidence in the warm April sun, without siege guns or scaling-ladders, their scouts only a short way in front of the resplendently uniformed columns. Oudinot's intention was to enter Rome either by the Porta Angelica between the Vatican and Castel Sant' Angelo or by the Porta Pertusa which, in fact, had been walled up. As his leading troops in their white coats and heavy shakos approached the Porta Pertusa shots were fired from two cannon on the Leonine Wall. This was taken to be the customary signal for midday. But when further shots were fired, the French were forced to conclude that the Romans were, after all, prepared to offer a token resistance and orders were given to unlimber the artillery and make an assault upon the walls.

The assault, however, was not so easy an undertaking as the more sanguine French officers had supposed. A succession of infantry attacks upon the Vatican and the Borgo were repulsed by heavy artillery and musket fire from the walls, to whose defence men from the poorest quarters of the Trastevere had rushed with guns and knives; and the French troops were sent scurrying for cover behind the mounds and in the dykes that cut across the valley beneath the Vatican hill. Watching these preliminary operations from the terrace of the Villa Corsini, Garibaldi decided that the moment had come for his men to move. Few of the French had yet been engaged, and their initial repulse was a minor set-back rather than a defeat; but if his men were to attack now while the enemy were reorganizing and considering how best to proceed, he would catch them at a serious disadvantage. So, sending forward about three hundred of his young volunteers as an advance guard, he prepared to follow them with his own Garibaldini.

The volunteers went forward down the slope beyond the Pamphilj gardens towards a deeply sunken lane, the Via Aurelia Antica, that led from the Porta San Pancrazio towards the road to Palo. And here, beneath the arches of the Pauline Aqueduct, the volunteers, most of them untrained students, came suddenly upon eight companies of the well-disciplined *20me de Ligne*. The students dashed recklessly forward, firing their muskets, brandishing their bayonets, shouting patriotic slogans, and, to their excited surprise, driving the French regulars back. But the *20me* soon recovered their composure. The students' headlong charge was halted, the French advance was resumed, and within minutes both the young volunteers and the men of Garibaldi's legion who had come forward to support them were being pushed back towards the walls of the city.

Garibaldi himself then appeared, a commanding figure in a poncho riding his white horse. He had called up reserves of papal troops and *bersaglieri* from Rome; and with the help of these and the men of his legion who had not yet been

78. Garibaldian staff officers outside the headquarters at the San Silvestri convent in Rome.

engaged, he rallied his forces and rode forward to counter-attack, shouting encouragement. Responding to his call, the Italians rushed across the gardens against the French, cheering wildly as they raced past the fountains and the statues which were already covered by a pall of smoke, stabbing at the enemy in their heavy uniforms, splashing the flowers and the grass with blood, 'savage as dervishes,' so one French officer recalled, 'clawing at us even with their hands.'

Unable to withstand so ferocious an assault for long, the French fell back towards the aqueduct, and then across the vineyards and over the Palo road as far as Castel di Guido, some twenty miles from Rome, leaving behind them about five hundred killed and wounded and almost as many prisoners. And at the news of the wonderful victory, the Romans, 'all elated and surprised at themselves', as Story described them, took to the streets in joyful celebration. Far into the night the city was ablaze with lights from the uncurtained windows of the houses and the crowded cafés and restaurants. The streets and piazzas were full of happy people congratulating each other on the bravery of the Romans and their faithful friends.

'The Italians fought like lions,' Margaret Fuller said. 'It is a truly heroic spirit that animates them. They make a stand here for honour and their rights . . .'

Garibaldi pressed Mazzini to take advantage of this spirit and of the victory of 30 April to pursue the enemy and attack him again. But Mazzini was anxious for a settlement with France and refused to consider any action which might make a *rapprochement* difficult to achieve. 'The Republic is not at war with France,' he insisted, 'merely in a state of defence.' French prisoners were to be entertained as guests of the city, provided with meals, wine and cigars before being returned to their army. Their wounded were to be treated with all the care that an Italian officer might hope to receive. Such considerations, however, had little effect upon the French President, Louis Napoleon, who considered the army's repulse a disgrace which could not be tolerated. 'Our military honour is in peril,' he told General Oudinot. 'I will not allow it to be compromised. You can be certain of being reinforced.' In the meantime he sent Ferdinand de Lesseps to Rome to enter into negotiations for a settlement so as to gain time for these reinforcements and for General Vaillant, France's greatest military engineer, to join the French army in Italy.

Garibaldi could never forgive Mazzini for what he took to be an appalling error of judgement on what was, and remained, 'a burning question' between them. 'If Mazzini had been willing to understand that I might possibly know something of war . . . how differently things would have turned out,' he wrote caustically years later. Mazzini had always had 'an urge to be a general, but he did not know the first thing about it.'

Garibaldi's own limitations as a general, as well as his consummate skill as a guerilla leader, were shown in operations which the Roman Republic's defenders had now to undertake against the Neapolitan army of King Ferdinand of the Two Sicilies. The Neapolitans were satisfactorily dealt with near Palestrina; but soon after Garibaldi's return to Rome, the expected French reinforcements also arrived outside the city and there was a far more dangerous enemy to face.

'My government's orders are positive,' General Oudinot now informed the Roman Republic. 'They require me to enter Rome as soon as possible . . . I have abrogated the verbal armistice which, at the instance of M. de Lesseps, I agreed to grant for the time being. I have warned your outposts that either army has the right to reopen hostilities. Solely to give time for any of our French residents to leave Rome . . . I am deferring the attack upon the place until Monday morning.'

Taking 'the place' to mean not only the city itself but all the outposts, including the Corsini and Pamphilj villas which were essential to its defence, the Roman generals concluded that all their men could relax on Sunday. But by 'the place' Oudinot afterwards claimed that he had referred only to the city itself and, having rejected the idea of an assault on the other side of Rome which might involve prolonged street fighting, he prepared to take the two vital villas as a necessary preliminary to an assault from the west. Accordingly, in the early hours of Sunday morning 3 June, the villas were attacked; and, since the defenders were fast asleep in their bivouacs at the time, they were captured without much difficulty, together with another smaller house, the Villa Medici del Vascello,[3] at the foot of the slope.

Rome was soon in uproar. All over the city bells were pealing in the *campanili*, drums beating, crowds collecting in the piazzas. Soldiers ran shouting through the streets to their posts, cab-drivers drove at full tilt through the narrow streets of the Trastevere to help with the wounded who were being carted through the Porta San Pancrazio in wheelbarrows. An orderly burst into the lodgings in Via delle Carrozze near Piazza di Spagna where Garibaldi was ill in bed with rheumatism and a month-old, still festering wound. He leapt out of bed, buckled on his sword-belt and hurried off to the Porta San Pancrazio as the roar of the cannon on the Janiculum thundered in his ears. Outside the gate he looked up towards the ornate, four-storeyed Villa Corsini, strongly occupied now by the French whose sharpshooters, crouching behind a low wall on which were rows of large earthenware pots containing orange trees, covered with their fire the entire slope between the villa and the Porta San Pancrazio. In front of the villa a narrow drive, flanked by high box hedges, led down from the bottom of an outside staircase to a gate in the garden wall. The place might have been designed to repel a frontal attack. And even if it were to be captured, behind it the grounds of the Villa Pamphilj afforded ample space for troops to reform for a counter-attack on a wide front supported by artillery. Yet, having considered the difficulties presented by the ground for an outflanking movement, Garibaldi considered that he had no alternative other than an attack from the front. This would inevitably entail a dreadful loss of life as his men, under constant fire from the well-entrenched enemy, debouched from the narrow Porta San Pancrazio, ran across the open ground to the villa's boundary walls, and closed up again to pass through the garden gate and along the narrow, high-hedged drive beneath the many windows of the villa.

Time and again the attempt was made, and on every occasion it failed. Shouting 'Long live the Roman Republic!' soldiers and volunteers charged across from Urban VIII's wall to fall dead or wounded in the sweltering sun. And all the while behind the walls a band played the 'Marseillaise' at full blast in the vain hope that this might induce the French, fellow-Republicans after all, to throw down their arms in shame. Once or twice a group of desperate Italians, running through the dust and smoke, reached the steps, gained access to the entrance hall and toppled the defenders from the windows; but always the French counter-attacked successfully before other Italians could reach the villa. One brave assault by some four hundred *bersaglieri* was described by one of their officers: men fell to the ground around him on every side, yet, rather than turn back, the survivors knelt to fire, as though they had come to a wall which afforded them some protection. Many more had died before the bugler was ordered to sound the retreat. As the rest ran back, so many of them fell that the officer thought 'they had stumbled in their haste over the roots of the vines. But their motionless bodies soon showed [him] the truth.'

After hours of pounding from the Roman batteries, the Villa Corsini, occasionally bursting into flames, began to collapse into ruins. From the walls of Rome men could see the floors give way and the French defenders clinging to the ends of the shattered beams. Garibaldi, who had spent the morning shouting encouragement as he sent one assault party after another across the open ground, had himself escaped injury, though his poncho and huge hat had been torn in many places by musket balls and scraps of flying metal. He now decided to make one last assault upon the villa and to take part in it himself. The attempt almost succeeded: the ruined villa was captured and the French driven out of its grounds into those of the Villa Pamphilj. Civilian spectators, overcome with excitement, poured out of the Porta San Pancrazio and began to run up the hill to congratulate the victors. But their rejoicing was premature. The French counter-attacked yet again; they retook the villa, and many more Italians fell to join the littered dead.

Among those officers who survived there was much criticism of Garibaldi's crude handling of the forces at his command. He 'had shown himself,' wrote one of them, Emilio Dandolo, 'to be as utterly incapable as a general of division as he had proved himself an able and efficient leader in the skirmishes against the Neapolitans.' In Rome that night, however, few voices were raised against him. Men spoke instead of the treacherous conduct of the blackguardly French, of the heroism of the Italian soldiers and volunteers, of the young men who had bravely died in answer to the call 'Roma o morte!'

Romans! [Mazzini declared in a proclamation to the people] You have sustained the honour of Rome, the honour of Italy . . . May God bless you, guardians of the honour of your forefathers, as we, proud of having recognized the greatness within you, bless you in the name of Italy.

Romans! This day is a day of heroes, a page of history. Yesterday we said to you, be great. Today we say to you, you are great . . . We say with perfect trust . . . that Rome is inviolable. Watch over her walls this night. Within those walls is the future of the nation . . . Long live the Republic!

The defenders of Rome responded to these moving words with what appeared to the French to be tireless energy. The guns in the batteries maintained a regular fire; companies of *bersaglieri*, Garibaldini, papal troops and volunteers rushed out with bayonets whenever the French launched an attack upon an exposed part of the line; men worked bravely under fire to repair emplacements and dig new defences. Arthur Hugh Clough, on a visit to the Monte Cavallo hospital, saw Italian soldiers recovering from their wounds and formed the impression that 'they would fight it out to the last'. Certainly the civilians, although the explosions were increasing and getting nearer to the heart of the city, were taking it all 'coolly enough'. In the Trastevere, the most endangered part of Rome, the people seemed wholehearted in their support of Mazzini and, 'recently so Catholic', now cursed the Pope and clergy 'in whose names they saw this carnage and these horrors committed'. '*Ecco un Pio Nono!*' they would shout when a cannon-ball flew over; and, when one landed among them and did not explode, they would run forward to pick it up and throw it in the river. Even when, towards the end of June, many

79. French troops attempting to enter Rome through the Porta Cavallegheri on 30 April 1849.

of them had to abandon their ruined homes, their determination to resist appeared unbroken.

Clough thought, however, that middle-class Romans were less enthusiastic in their defence of the Republic. He fancied they considered it 'rather useless work', though they did not 'feel strongly enough on the matter to make them take active steps against a government which [had] won their respect alike by its moderation and its energy'. As the days passed, the feeling that the cause of the Republic was doomed grew even more widespread. It became increasingly difficult to maintain vigilance and discipline in the fortifications. Gunners in the batteries began to fire shots at random, as though it did not much matter where they landed; and civilians were so reluctant to help with the digging that on one occasion they had to be driven up to the walls at the point of the bayonet.

Remorselessly and skilfully, General Vaillant's engineers advanced their siege-works closer and closer to the city. The French batteries on Monte Verde and in the grounds of the Villa Corsini ceaselessly pounded the defences around Porta San

Pancrazio, while night patrols ensured that the defenders could never rest in peace. It was still expected that the attack would come from the west, and Garibaldi insisted that he must have more men to defend the Janiculum. But Pietro Roselli, the Roman professional officer who had been placed in supreme command, could not neglect other parts of Rome's defences, particularly in the south where there were large numbers of French troops around S. Paolo fuori le Mura and in the north where they had captured Ponte Molle. So Garibaldi adopted an even more independent line than usual. He appropriated soldiers who had been allocated to other duties; and when, after a ferocious bombardment, the French threatened to dominate the city from S. Pietro in Montorio, he refused to obey an order to counter-attack on the grounds that it would be better to establish an inner line of

80. The attack on the Villa Corsini on 3 June 1849. On the left, Angelo Masina, the rich young democrat who raised a squadron of lancers to serve under Garibaldi, is seen dying.

defence on the Aurelian Wall and that his men were in no condition to counter-attack anyway.

His disagreements with the Roman High Command exacerbated the uneasiness of Garibaldi's relationship with Mazzini. It had never seemed likely that the two men, both obstinate, self-willed and headstrong, would be able to cooperate without friction. They were, it was often suggested, jealous of each other. Garibaldi, envious of Mazzini's acknowledged intellect, described him as 'a doctrinaire' whose followers were 'learned academics, accustomed to legislate for the world from their studies'. Mazzini, who did not enjoy Garibaldi's influence and standing as a man of action, considered his rival 'weak beyond expression', 'the most easily led of men'. If 'Garibaldi has to choose between two proposals,' Mazzini complained, 'he is sure to choose the one that isn't mine.' 'You know the face of a lion?' he once said to a friend. 'Is it not a foolish face? Is it not the face of Garibaldi?'

Mazzini considered now that 'Rome had already fallen', but that if its fall was to have any significance in the future it must die in great suffering and self-sacrifice so that it should provide an inspiration to Italy. His feeling for Rome was more obsessive than ever and the suggestion that the defenders should abandon it and fight the French outside the walls appalled him. He himself was prepared to die within the city, and he called upon the people, in the last resort, to follow him to the front and throw back the enemy with their bare hands. 'God grant that they will assault,' he said, 'and then we could have a noble defence of the people at the barricades. My mind is overwhelmed with grief that so much bravery, so much heroism should be lost.'

The assault that Mazzini had prayed for came at about one o'clock in the morning on the last night of June. The day before had been celebrated as usual as the Feast of St Peter and St Paul; and, encouraged by the government, who thought that they might serve as a demonstration of the Romans' defiance of their enemies, the people had let off fireworks and rockets into the darkening sky, and coloured lanterns had been hung up in the streets. Before midnight a heavy summer storm had sent rain pouring in torrents upon the city, so that when the bombardment began cascades of mud spattered the ruins. The subsequent fighting under the moonless sky was savage and bitter; but it was also brief. The French attack, carefully planned, was swift and determined. One column stormed through a breach in the wall built by Urban VIII, while another burst upon the Aurelian Wall and then fanned out to the left towards the battery near the Porta San Pancrazio and to the right to surround the Villa Spada where Garibaldi, having withdrawn from the Villa Savorelli, had established his headquarters.

Summoned to an emergency meeting of the Republican Assembly, Garibaldi left for the Capitol convinced that further resistance in Rome was pointless and that the government must now be forced to accept the alternative he had long pressed upon them – a guerilla campaign against the French outside the city walls. His Negro orderly was dead; his chief-of-staff was dying; he had often barely escaped death himself. He entered the Capitol, the sweat pouring from his face, his clothes covered with mud and drying blood, his bent sword sticking out of its scabbard. The members rose to cheer him. He reiterated his belief that the struggle must now be carried on outside the city. '*Ovunque noi saremo,*' he said, '*sarà Roma*' – 'Wherever we go, there will Rome be.'

'I am going out of Rome,' he declared later from the saddle of his horse to the crowds collected around the obelisk in St Peter's piazza. 'Whoever is willing to follow me will be received among my people. I ask nothing of them but a heart filled with love for our country. They will have no pay, no provisions and no rest. I offer hunger, cold, forced marches, battles and death. Whoever is not satisfied with such a life must remain behind. He who has the name of Italy not only on his lips but in his heart, let him follow me.' Those who were prepared to go with him must meet that evening by the Lateran, ready to leave Rome by the Porta San Giovanni.

About four thousand volunteers gathered there at the appointed hour, soldiers and civilians, men and boys, patriots, politicians and several criminals who were leaving Rome in order to escape the law or in the hope of loot. Garibaldi's pregnant wife, a short, dark, masculine, South American woman of mixed Portuguese and Indian descent was also there, having come to Rome to share his dangers with him. They filed out slowly through the gate in their civilian clothes and motley uniforms, followed by a single cannon.

Mazzini had never considered going with them: never a man to follow anyone happily, to follow Garibaldi would have been intolerable. At the meeting of the Assembly he had resigned his office as Triumvir in protest against its decision to capitulate. Afterwards, he had walked about the streets of Rome in order, so it was alleged, to offer himself to the knife of an assassin and, by surviving, to demonstrate that the Catholic press was lying when it claimed that the Romans wished him dead for having forced a tyranny upon them. 'In two short months he had grown old,' wrote Margaret Fuller who saw him that evening. 'All the vital juices seemed exhausted. He had passed all these nights without sleep; his eyes were all bloodshot; his skin orange. He was painfully thin; his hair was flecked with white; his hand was painful to the touch.' He was still in Rome on 3 July when the French made their formal entry into the city. Their arrival was described by A. H. Clough:

I stood in the Corso with some thirty of the people and saw them pass. Fine working soldiers, indeed dogged and business-like, but they looked a little awkward while the people screamed and hooted and cried, '*Viva la Repubblica Romana,*' etc. When they got past, some young simpleton sent a pail after them; four or five raced down with bayonets presented, while my young friend cut away up the Corso double-quick. They went on. At this moment, some Roman bourgeois as I fancy, but perhaps a foreigner, said something either to express his sense of the folly of it, or his sympathy with the invaders. He was surrounded and I saw him buffeted a good deal . . . I was told he got off. But a priest who walked and talked publicly in the Piazza Colonna with a Frenchman was undoubtedly killed . . . Poor man, he was quite a liberal ecclesiastic, they tell me; but certainly not a prudent one. To return to my own experience: After this, the column passed back by another street in the Corso, and dispersed the crowd with the bayonet point . . . An English acquaintance informed me that in passing by the Café Nuovo, where an Italian tricolour hung from the window, Oudinot plucked at it and bid it be removed. The French proceeded to do this but the Romans intervened. Cernuschi, the Barricade Commissioner, took it down and kissed it, and, as I myself saw, carried it in triumph amidst cheers to the Piazza. I didn't follow; but on my bolder friend's authority I can state here the French moved up with their bayonets and took it from Cernuschi, stripping him moreover of his tricolour scarf.

P.S. The priest is not dead and perhaps will survive. But another I hear was hewed to pieces for shouting, 'Viva Pio IX, a basso la repubblica!' . . . The French soldiers showed excellent temper. At the same time some faces I have seen are far more brutal than the worst Garibaldian and we have hitherto seen nothing so unpleasant in the female kind as the vivandières.

The Times correspondent agreed that the occupying forces behaved themselves well, though they were hissed and groaned at as they passed the Caffè Nuovo, 'one of the strongholds of the Ultra-Liberals',[4] and, outside the Caffè delle Belle Arti, assailed with repeated cries of 'Death to Pio Nono! Death to the priests! Viva the Roman Republic! Death to the Cardinal Oudinot!' 'The General's staff, who had borne with the good humour of French soldiers the first part of these insults, became furious on hearing the Commander-in-Chief personally vituperated and without a moment's hesitation they charged the crowd.'

The occupying forces, however, were rarely thus provoked. In the first few days the cafés and restaurants which they patronized were boycotted by the Romans, and some, such as the large Caffè Nuovo where 'unmistakable disgust was evinced', were closed down. But generally, as at the Bon Gout in Piazza di Spagna, the French were treated with 'polite indifference'; and gradually the insults decreased. Search parties were sent out for leaders of the now defunct Republic, but they were conducted with so little thoroughness that they were seen as a matter of mere form. Most of the so-called 'revolutionaries' were allowed to escape with the help of sympathetic foreign consuls, the British consul, for example, issuing so many hundreds of diplomatic passes that Lord Palmerston was constrained to reprove him. With the assistance of the American chargé d'affaires, Mazzini got away to Civitavecchia and eventually to England, without interference from the authorities.

Nine months after Mazzini's departure from Rome, Pope Pius returned in state through the Lateran gate, escorted by French troops. He rode to the Vatican, where he had chosen to live instead of at the Quirinal; and from the Vatican he presided over the restoration of his authoritarian and paternalistic papal rule. Soon the hotels and lodging-houses of Rome were again filled with foreign tourists and the workshops of the city were busy once more.

One visitor who had spent three months in Rome almost twenty years before found it 'scarcely changed at all': her favourite restaurant had the same owners, the same cooks and the same waiters. The Romans she met were as friendly as ever. She felt no sense of that repression which enemies of the régime were later to describe. Nor did Jean-Jacques Ampère, the French historian and philologist, who

81. Pope Pius IX blessing the victorious French army drawn up in the piazza of St Peter's on 18 April 1850.

was in Rome at the same time and who thought that there was more liberty in Rome than anywhere else in Italy – that the priests were quite prepared to abide by a policy of *laissez-faire* outside the sphere of their special requirements.

In one way, however, Rome had changed: it was no longer the centre of the art world, which was gradually moving to Paris. Jacques-Louis David, who had come to Rome with Comte Joseph-Marie Vien, a pioneer of the neo-classical style, when Vien had been appointed Director of the French Academy, had long since returned to Paris. Antonio Canova, the sculptor whose studio was in Palazzo Venezia and whose monument to the Stuarts in St Peter's[5] and sculpture of Pauline Bonaparte in the Borghese Gallery[6] are among several of his works which can be seen in Rome, had gone home to Venice. The Icelandic sculptor Bertel Thorwaldsen, in whose studio in Rome there were at one time no less than forty assistants, had returned to Denmark in 1838. And the Nazarenes, who were among the first primitives of the nineteenth century and had come from Germany to occupy an abandoned monastery, had begun to break up even before the completion of the frescos for the Casino Massimo.[7]

Yet if Rome was no longer the art centre it had formerly been, interest in its classical monuments and early Christian art was now more intense than ever. For

270

this the archaeologists Luigi Canina and G. B. de Rossi were largely responsible, Canina by his excavations of the Appian Way and his etchings of reconstructions of hundreds of Roman antiquities, de Rossi by his digs in the Colosseum, the Forum and in the early churches of Rome and his discoveries of the catacombs of St Calixtus and St Agnese.

Pope Pius took the greatest interest in de Rossi's work and his eyes filled with tears when the archaeologist took him down to show him the fragments of inscriptions he had found in the Crypt of the Popes in the Catacombs of St Calixtus. 'Are these really,' he asked in wonderment, 'the tombs of my predecessors who repose here?' The Pope was also deeply interested in those modern inventions which in the 1850s and 1860s were beginning to transform life in Rome and the Papal States, in hydraulics and telegraphs, in steam power, machinery and railways, taking particular pride in his own special train with its white and gold painted coaches which included a chapel on bogie wheels. He frequently walked out to watch progress on these wonders of science and to bless them when they were completed. He blessed the first train which left Rome for Frascati in 1860 and which, travelling at thirty miles an hour, arrived there to be welcomed by a band which made puffing, grinding and whistling sounds in imitation of mechanical locomotion. Lord John Manners, Chief Commissioner of Works in the British government, was present when in 1863 the Pope attended the opening of the steel drawbridge across the Tiber near Porta Portese and was embarrassed to be presented to His Holiness, since he was wearing an old straw hat and carrying an umbrella. But he was soon made to feel at ease as the Pope said to him, 'I am very glad to see you, especially at this moment. You will be able to tell them, when you return to London, that the Roman pontiff is not always at prayer, surrounded with incense and monks. You will be able to tell the Queen that Her Majesty's Minister of Public Works one day surprised the old Pope in the midst of his workmen, attending the opening of a new bridge over the Tiber, and himself explaining pretty well the mechanism of the new invention.'

Yet interested as he was in scientific progress, the Pope closed his mind firmly to proposals for a united Italy of which Rome would be the capital and to which the temporal estates of the Church, held in trust from God and for centuries an instrument for the preservation of the papacy's spiritual independence, would have to be surrendered. But the Risorgimento was gaining a momentum that made the Pope's stand irrelevant. Cavour, the King of Sardinia's brilliant and unscrupulous chief minister, was elaborating those policies which were to enable his master to expand his territories from Piedmont into Lombardy and south across Parma, Modena and into Tuscany. Garibaldi was preparing the forces which would seize Sicily and Naples from the Bourbons. In September 1860 the Piedmontese army invaded the Papal States; and by the end of the year King Victor Emmanuel II, by a series of well-manipulated plebiscites, had gained control of all Italy with the exception of the Veneto and Rome.

On 17 March by a unanimous vote of the Parliament in Turin, Victor Emmanuel was proclaimed King of Italy and ten days later, although it was still in the hands

82. Victor Emmanuel II (1820–78), first King of the United Italy, the only Knight of the Garter the Duchess of Sutherland had ever seen who 'looked as if he would have the best of it with the dragon'.

of the Pope, Rome was declared the capital of the new kingdom. At the Vatican the Pope was assured by the French Ambassador, the Duc de Grammont, that France would oppose any aggression on Rome with 'force of arms'. At first the Pope believed that France would do so, convinced by the protestations of the Ambassador who, in the opinion of his British counterpart, Odo Russell, was 'an amiable humbug . . . affecting, like all French diplomatists in Italy, the greatest contempt for Italian aspirations, wishing to hang Cavour and shoot Garibaldi'. And so, advised by his Secretary of State, Cardinal Antonelli, the Pope refused to make any concessions on what had become known as the Roman Question. He told Odo Russell that the crisis would pass, that one day soon the Church would triumph over her enemies; and, in the meantime, there were 6,000 French troops in Rome as well as an international force of volunteers in the pay of the papacy. As though in defiance of his enemies, in 1864, the Pope issued his Syllabus of Errors which stigmatized as an error the view that 'the Roman pontiff can and should reconcile himself to and agree with progress, liberalism and modern civilization'; and on 18 December 1869, the Feast of the Immaculate Conception, he opened the Vatican Council at which the dogma of Papal Infallibility was defined.

But then in 1870 France declared war on Prussia, and by the time the battle of Sedan had deprived Louis Napoleon of his empire, nearly all the French soldiers had been withdrawn from Rome in a vain attempt to avert a catastrophic defeat. Immediately King Victor Emmanuel's troops prepared to take their place. On 16 September the Pope went to S. Maria d'Aracoeli to pray before the Santo Bambino, the figure, so revered in Rome, which is said to have been carved out of wood from one of the olive trees in the Garden of Gethsemane. Three days later, for the last time, he crossed Rome in his carriage from the Vatican to St John Lateran to review the troops assembled in the piazza. Slowly, the frail, white-haired old man of seventy-eight climbed the Scala Santa on his knees and at the top, after praying aloud, he stood up to bless the soldiers below him.

In the early hours of the morning of 20 September, the King's cannon opened fire upon the city gates. In the Vatican the windows rattled in their frames. But the Pope had given orders that no more than a token resistance should be offered, a resistance sufficient to demonstrate that he was yielding to the usurpation of Rome by force. Soon the firing died away as a white flag was hoisted from the cupola of St Peter's.

Next year Italy transferred her capital to Rome, the King established his court at the Quirinal and the Pope withdrew into the Vatican, where he died, a self-styled prisoner, in 1878, having reigned for longer than any other pontiff in the history of the papacy. The King also died in 1878. He had never settled contentedly in Rome, seeming happy only at the Villa Ludovisi[8] which he leased from the Duke of Sora for his morganatic wife, Rosina Vercellina. Homesick for Turin, he much disliked the gloomy Quirinal, where for several years foreign royalty, Catholic and Protestant alike, were unwilling to stay the night for fear of offending the Pope. For many years to come, indeed, the Pope and the new regime were to remain unreconciled; and Roman society was to be torn by conflicting loyalties.

SIXTEEN

ROYAL ROME

'Rome is quite unchanged since you and I were here forty years ago,' Henry Wadsworth Longfellow had told a friend a few months before the Piedmontese invasion. 'I said as much to Cardinal Antonelli the other day, and he answered, taking a pinch of snuff, "Yes, thank God."' The new inventions which had intrigued his master, Pope Pius IX, had scarcely altered at all the essentially pastoral nature of life in the city. There was still no industry and no stock exchange; the main source of wealth was still agriculture. To Edmond About, the French writer and traveller, Rome was like an immense farm in the middle of a great plain of wheat. Each year, before the onset of malaria made the Campagna so perilous, this wheat was brought into store in Rome. It was, even in the 1860s, a common sight to see cows, sheep and goats herded through the streets. As late as 1865 twelve cows were burned to death in a fire in a byre in Via delle Vite, in the very heart of the city.

This aspect of Rome was slow to change, but Cardinal Antonelli could not feel so contented about other differences in the appearance and atmosphere of the city. The papal zouaves had been replaced by regiments of *bersaglieri* who marched at their rapid pace through the streets in theatrical-looking uniforms and wide-brimmed hats crowned with dark green feathers. Bookstalls were far more numerous and, as well as the familiar *Osservatore Romano* and *Voce della Verità* approved of by the Vatican, passers-by were now offered a variety of other Italian and foreign newspapers and journals. Prelates made far less of a show in the streets, the cardinals' coaches being painted black and draped as though in mourning; and monks and white-cowled friars, once described as 'picturesquely poor', were also far less often to be seen.

These changes were remarked upon and condemned by the Roman-born Augustus Hare whose *Walks in Rome* was published in 1871.

The absence of Pope, cardinals and monks [Hare wrote]; the shutting up of the convents; the loss of the ceremonies; the misery caused by the terrible taxes and conscription; the voluntary exile of the Borghese and many other noble families; the total destruction of the glorious Villa Negroni[1] and so much else of interest and beauty; the ugly new streets in imitation of Paris and New York, all grate upon one's former Roman associations. And to set against these, there is so very little – a gayer Pincio, a live wolf on the Capitol, a mere scrap of excavation in the Forum, and all is said.

Henry James also remarked upon the changes wrought in Rome since the advent of the men from the north. James, who had paid his first visit to Rome in 1869 and, after his first walk through the city, had then decided, like Goethe, that he was fully alive for the first time in his life, returned in 1872 and was sad to find that the cardinals no longer walked on the Pincio and were only occasionally to be seen around the Lateran where they descended from their dismal-looking coaches to exercise their legs. These limbs now alone still testified to the traditional splendour of the Princes of the Church: 'For as they advanced, the lifted black petticoat reveals a flash of scarlet stockings and makes you groan at the victory of civilization over colour.' The throngs of smartly dressed young men, James thought,

scarce offered compensation for the monsignori, treading the streets ... followed by solemn servants who returned on their behalf the bows of the meaner sort; for the

83. Floods in the Piazza Navona. The Church of S. Agnese in Agone is on the left adjoining the Palazzo Pamphilj.

mourning gear of the cardinals' coaches that formerly glittered with scarlet and swung with the weight of the footmen clinging behind; for the certainty that you'd not, by the best of traveller's luck, meet the Pope sitting deep in the shadow of his great chariot with uplifted fingers like some inaccessible idol in his shrine. You may meet the King indeed who is as ugly, as imposingly ugly, as some idols.

Visitors might also come across various members of the King's family, as James himself did, without being in the least impressed:

Yesterday Prince Humbert's little *primogenito* [the future King Victor Emmanuel III] was on the Pincio in an open landau with his governess. He's a sturdy little blond man and the image of the King. They had stopped to listen to the music, and the crowd was planted about the carriage-wheels, staring and criticizing under the child's snub little nose. It appeared bold cynical curiosity without the slightest manifestation of 'loyalty' and it gave me a singular sense of the vulgarization of Rome under the new régime. When the Pope drove abroad it was a solemn spectacle; even if you neither kneeled nor uncovered you were irresistibly impressed. But the Pope never stopped to listen to opera turns, and he had no little popelings under the charge of superior nurse-maids whom you might take liberties with.

Yet James conceded that the essence of Rome, 'this Paradise of exiles,' as Shelley had described it, remained immutable. He could still enjoy the lovely view from the top of the Lateran and ride from there down the tree-lined lane to the Church of S. Maria Maggiore, or wander through the cork woods on Monte Mario and the fields towards S. Paolo fuori le Mura. Although artists' models had been banished from the Spanish Steps, foreign artists still gathered in the cafés around Piazza di Spagna, in the Via Condotti where the Caffè Greco was more crowded than ever, and in such good cheap restaurants as the Trattoria Lepri where fifteen years before Herman Melville's dinner had cost him fifteen cents. Teams of oxen were still driven through the streets with fruit and casks of wine from the Campagna; pigs still snuffled about for acorns outside the Flaminian Gate; and guides still conducted their groups of tourists around the familiar sights to which were now added the Protestant Cemetery[2] which Shelley, when his little son was buried here, thought was so beautiful 'it might make one in love with death', and the house by the Spanish Steps in which Keats had died in the arms of his friend, Joseph Severn. And everywhere, as George Gissing complained, tips had still to be given, 'sometimes as much as five in a morning's walk through the rooms' of the Vatican.

George Gissing had come from Naples by a train in which the ticket collector went 'along from door to door outside', while the other passengers in his carriage repeated excitedly to each other throughout the journey, 'A Roma! A Roma!' For them Rome had not lost its fascination, as it never did for Gissing. He returned in 1897 and decided that he preferred it to both Naples and Florence: 'Florence is the city of the Renaissance, but after all the Renaissance was only a shadow of the great times, and like a shadow it has passed away. There is nothing [in Florence] that impressed me like the poorest of Rome's antiquities.' There was, as there was for the young artist, Phil May, 'no place like Rome'.

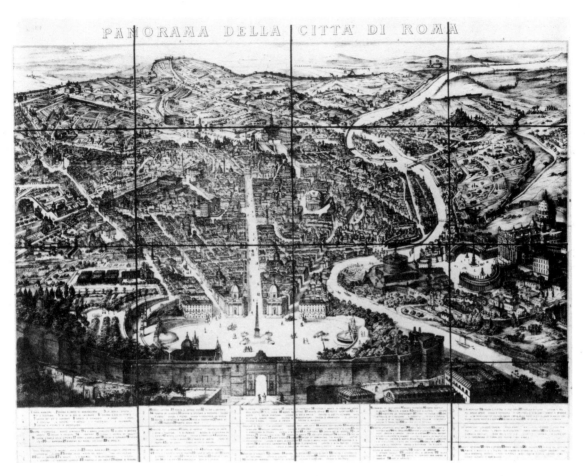

84. A panoramic view of Rome in about 1870.

Few visitors could stay in Rome long, however, without being aware of the problems caused by the dissensions among the leading families, the quarrels between those who were prepared to accept the King as their sovereign and those who claimed that their loyalty to the Pope prevented them from doing so. Some of these families were as ancient as the Massimo; others, the Orsini, Colonna and Caetani among them, had come to prominence in the Middle Ages. Yet others, including the Farnese, the Boncompagni, the Borghese, the Barberini and the Doria, were descendants of the relations of popes and prelates of the Renaissance and Counter-Reformation. A few owed their wealth to more recent good fortune or endeavour, such as the Torlonia, descendants of a travelling salesman, whose riches came from banking. Prince Torlonia, the head of the family in 1870, changed his servants' livery so that they should no longer bear the colours of the King, though he contrived thereafter to maintain a comfortable neutrality. Another Torlonia, Duke Leopold, as Mayor of Rome, called upon Cardinal Parocchi

277

to offer civic congratulations to Pope Leo XIII on reaching the fiftieth anniversary of his ordination and was promptly dismissed from office by the Prime Minister.

Some families were more consistent and open supporters of the new régime. These included the Doria, the Boncompagni-Ludovisi, the Ruspoli and, most prominent among them, the Caetani, whose head, Michelangelo Caetani, the liberal Duke of Sermoneta, was a learned Dante scholar, sculptor and craftsman. Having lost his sight when he insisted that his local doctor instead of a specialist should operate upon his eyes for cataracts, he became a deputy in the new Parliament for the plebeian district of Trastevere. At the Caetani Palace in Rome,[3] ministers of the new government were as welcome as artists, writers and distinguished foreigners, though a request to visit the family's house in the Pontine Marshes, Sermoneta Castle, was greeted by a response worthy of a Massimo: 'Pray go by all means. But I am afraid I cannot offer you luncheon there. Our cook at Sermoneta died towards the end of the sixteenth century.'

Although Michelangelo Caetani was an unequivocal advocate of the new regime, he remained on quite friendly terms with several cardinals. But there were some families among the 'black' or 'Guelph' nobility who refused to have anything to do with the King's government. The Barberini and Chigi, the Borghese and the Aldobrandini, the Sacchetti and the Salviati all turned their backs upon the House of Savoy, and the Lancellotti refused to open the main gates of their palace once the royal family had taken possession of the Quirinal. It was not until 1896, on the grounds of his great age of eighty-six, that Pope Leo XIII abandoned his practice of granting separate audiences for all the 'black' families of Rome; and even then they were compensated for this deprivation by being asked to a grand reception once a year. When Oscar Wilde visited Rome in 1900 the divisions in society were as marked as ever. Having obtained a ticket from the hall porter at the Hôtel de l'Europe to see the Pope on Easter Day, he managed to catch a glimpse of his 'supernatural ugliness' as he was carried past on a throne, a wonderful figure, 'not of flesh and blood but a white soul robed in white'. Wilde had never seen anything 'like the extraordinary grace of his gestures, as he rose, from moment to moment, to bless – possibly the pilgrims, but certainly me'. But then he saw King Victor Emmanuel II's successor, King Umberto I, drive past the Caffè Nazionale where Wilde was drinking coffee: 'I at once stood and made a low bow, with hat doffed – to the admiration of some officers at the next table. It was only when the King was passed that I remembered I was *Papista* and *Nerissimo*! I was greatly upset. However, I hope the Vatican won't hear about it.'

While a proportion of the rich and ancient families of Rome refused to recognize the new regime, the people as a whole welcomed it. Victor Emmanuel had been cheered upon his arrival in the city; and both King Umberto and Queen Margherita were extremely popular. A plebiscite held by the new government revealed that, of those entitled to vote, 133,681 approved of the incorporation of Rome into the Kingdom of Italy and only 1,507 disapproved. But invasion by the army was followed by an invasion of bureaucrats and officials; and this the people welcomed no more than did the officials themselves who had been comfortably housed in Italy's temporary capital, Florence.

To meet the needs of these civil servants the government requisitioned several large convents in the centre of Rome, including San Silvestro in Capite,[4] which was occupied first by the Ministry of the Interior and then by the Central Post Office, and the Minerva which was allocated to the Ministry of Finance. The government also took over various palaces, the Montecitorio for the Chamber of Deputies, the Braschi Palace for the Ministry of Agriculture and the Palazzo

85. Milkmen with goats in the Piazza Flaminio. Rome retained its pastoral atmosphere throughout the nineteenth century.

Madama[5] for the Senate. The Villa Madama was allocated for the use of distinguished visitors.

The requisitioning of large buildings, however, provided not nearly enough space for the men from the north. The municipality of Rome was requested to find 40,180 additional rooms for the use of the government; and the city council was able to offer only 500, of which a considerable number were converted haylofts. For, while many churches had been repaired in the long pontificate of Pius IX, very few other buildings had been constructed, apart from the developments around the Ospizio di San Michele in Trastevere[6] and the Termini railway station.[7] The Pope's enterprising Minister for War, the Belgian Monsignor François-Xavier de Mérode, had, however, foreseen that the open country between the Termini Station and the Quirinal was a likely development area. He had bought large tracts of it, and subsequently built several large houses on it. Much of the rest he now sold, at a handsome profit, to building speculators. The wide street which passed through it was known as Via Mérode before being renamed Via Nazionale.

The development of this area was soon after followed by that of several others, the first decade after 1870 witnessing a great expansion of housing from the Colosseum up to Via XX Settembre, the next seven years, until 1887, a further expansion from Via XX Settembre up to the Villa Medici. In 1887 overproduction in the building industry and overextension of credit resulted in a spectacularly sudden crash and numerous bankruptcies: the number of apartments under construction in 1888–9 was only a fifteenth of the number being built in 1886–7. But the damage, in the eyes of many foreign observers, had already been done. For them the new houses and offices, the consulates and embassies, the apartment blocks, hotels and lodging-houses had ruined the appearance of Rome. 'Twelve years of Sardinian rule have done more for the destruction of Rome, with its beauty and interest, than the invasions of the Goths and Vandals,' Augustus Hare considered. 'The whole aspect of the city is changed, and the picturesqueness of the old days must now be sought in such obscure corners as have escaped the hand of the spoiler.'

George Gissing agreed with him, as he surveyed the construction work in progress around Castel Sant' Angelo where 'great ugly barrack-like houses' were rising thick and fast. 'Indeed, modern Rome is extremely ugly . . . its streets are monotonous and wearisome to an incredible degree.'

The crash of 1887 only temporarily disrupted work on public buildings in Rome. The florid and massive Palace of Justice[8] was started in 1889, soon after the completion of the ministries of War and Finance in Via XX Settembre.[9] The complex of hospitals called the Policlinico[10] was built in 1887–9; the vast and cumbersome monument to Victor Emmanuel II[11] in 1885–1911; and by the time the river embankments had been finished at the turn of the century, the new district of Prati del Castello had begun to fill in the meadows on the right bank of the river in the space between Castel Sant' Angelo and Monte Mario. All this building was carried out without proper planning or control, so that many lovely

villas with their surrounding gardens and parks were swallowed up by the remorseless advance of brick, stone and mortar. The Villa Borghese and the Villa Doria were spared; but the Villa Ludovisi, which Henry James thought the most beautiful in Rome, vanished, together with the Villas Giustiniani-Massimo,[12] Montalto,[13] Albani, Altieri[14] and Negroni.

86. The Via Condotti seen from the bottom of the Spanish Steps looking across the Fountain of the Barcaccia. Lemonade sellers congregated here, as well as children hoping for work as artists' models.

No proper provision was made, either, for the immense number of peasants who were attracted to Rome by the building boom and who, together with the officials and their families, helped to raise the population of the city from 200,000 in 1870 to over 460,000 by the end of the century. The families of these labourers were to be seen sleeping on the steps of churches, under arches or in makeshift shelters, the beginnings of those shanty towns which were to disgrace many Italian

87. The building of the Tiber embankments near the Passegiata di Ripetta in about 1890.

cities in the next century. Their poverty-stricken way of life was rendered all the more pitiable by contrast with that of the relatively affluent bureaucrats and army officers and their wives who enjoyed the *ora del vermouth* in the cafés of the Via Nazionale and the Corso, who frequented the smart new shops and the *trattorie* which seemed to spring up like mushrooms overnight, who spent their evenings at the opera in the fine Teatro Costanzi, now the Teatro dell' Opera,[15] and who mingled with the foreigners who continued to gather in the Piazza di Spagna.

88. Women in the vegetable market.

89. One of the city's numerous shops selling curios and antique oddments.

The number of foreigners who flocked to Rome increased year by year: despite the new building which so many tourists condemned, Rome had lost little of its appeal for the visitor as the nineteenth century drew to its close and the twentieth began. There were those, like the young and poor James Joyce, an ill-paid employee of an Austrian bank living in rooms in Via Frattina, who were unhappy in the city, which seemed to him like a man who made a living 'by exhibiting to travellers his grandmother's corpse'. He longed for someone to talk to about Dublin. But such sentiments were rare. Far more representative were the reactions of Henry James's brother, William, who found Rome 'just a *feast* for the eye from the moment you leave your hotel door to the moment you return', and of Sigmund Freud who went every day to S. Pietro in Vincoli to study Michelangelo's Moses, which he thought was the finest work of art in the world, and who told a friend that Rome had been 'an overwhelming experience' for him, 'one of the summits' of his life. For Rome, as Hilaire Belloc wrote in 1914 on a return visit to the city to which he had walked years before, Rome goes on, in defiance of building speculators and developers, 'astonishingly the same'.

SEVENTEEN

ROMA FASCISTA

'Either the government will be given to us or we shall seize it by marching on Rome!' The challenge was issued at a Fascist congress held in Naples towards the end of 1922, and was greeted by repeated cries of 'Roma! Roma! Roma!' from a crowd of delegates and supporters, 40,000 strong. The speaker was Benito Mussolini, a 29-year-old former socialist who, as an influential journalist, had been expelled from the party for strongly advocating Italy's intervention in the Great War. He had fought in the war with the *bersaglieri*; and, after being wounded, had returned to journalism. As early as February 1918 he had been pressing for the appointment of a dictator in Italy, 'a man who is ruthless and energetic enough to make a clean sweep'. Three months later, in a widely reported speech at Bologna, he hinted that he himself might prove such a man.

His supporters were a strange rag-bag of discontented socialists and syndicalists, republicans and anarchists, unclassifiable revolutionaries, conservative monarchists and restless soldiers many of whom had been *arditi* (the impetuous commandos of the Italian army) and some of whom were wanted by the police. They formed themselves into what were known as *fascii di combattimenti*, fighting groups, bound by ties as close as those that secured the *fasces* of the lictors, the symbols of Roman authority. The Fascists had not at first been successful at the polls: in 1919 as candidates for the Chamber of Deputies they received no more than 4,795 votes. But the failure of successive governments to deal with Italy's social unrest and manifold problems allowed the Fascists to put themselves forward as saviours of their country, the only force by which Bolshevism could be checked and strangled. Protesting that violence could be met only by greater violence, squads of armed Fascists, known as *squadristi*, attacked socialist workers' organizations, rival parties' and trade union headquarters, newspaper offices and all those whom they deemed Bolshevik sympathizers with a ferocity and regularity that led almost to civil war. Shouting patriotic slogans, singing nationalist songs and wearing the black shirts which the labourers of the Marche and Emilia had adopted as the uniform of the anarchists, the *squadristi* obtained the support of thousands who were prepared to condone their methods, their violence, their revolting practice of filling their opponents with castor oil, in the belief that only by such means could Bolshevism be wiped out and order restored. So, by the end of 1922, having taken over Ravenna, Ferrara and Bologna, and encouraged by the occasional complicity of certain government officials, the frequent help of the police and the probable acquiescence of the House of Savoy which Mussolini had said could still play an important role in the nation's history, the Fascists were ready to seize Rome by force.

In four converging columns, 26,000 strong, they closed in upon the city on 28 October. The government proclaimed its intention of declaring martial law, but the King refused to sign the decree; and, once it was known that he was prepared to accept Mussolini, the army and the police stood aside and the blackshirts approached the capital, by train, by bus or on foot. Mussolini himself, a superb opportunist and flexible *agitatore*, for the moment remained in Milan. He had already been asked to form a government, so that the March on Rome was, in fact, unnecessary. But the March was required by the myth of Fascism, as were the fictitious 3,000 Fascist martyrs who were supposed to have died in the insurrection that brought Mussolini to power. He arrived in Rome by train at half-past ten on the morning of 30 October.

Once in power, as the youngest prime minister the Italians had ever had, Mussolini showed how shrewd a politician he was. Although from the beginning determined to become a dictator and, in personal control of the police, to have all his leading opponents arrested, he presented to the King a list of ministers calculated to demonstrate that he was a national rather than a party leader. And it was as a national leader that the Italians were prepared, indeed anxious, to welcome him. They were tired of strikes and riots, hungry for the flamboyant techniques, the medieval trappings of Fascism. Thus it was that there were spontaneous demonstrations of support for Fascism after the March on Rome, and thus it was that Mussolini's immense popularity survived the sporadic violence in Rome on the night of the Fascists' triumphant entry, the undoubtedly fraudulent elections of 1924, and even the murder of the brave and gifted socialist leader, Giacomo Matteotti, in which Mussolini was widely believed to have been implicated.

He had set to work with the most enthusiastic determination, getting up early, performing a variety of violent exercises, then eating a breakfast which a stomach ulcer required should be as sparse as all his other meals, and reading with astonishing speed several Italian and foreign newspapers before arriving in his office at eight o'clock. He had no pleasures, he said, other than his work; and although there was to come a time when he scarcely worked at all, in these early years of power the claim was largely true. He fenced and boxed, he swam, played tennis and rode a horse; but his object was not so much pleasure or relaxation as the banishment of fat from his body and his massive but already slightly sagging jaw, the acquisition and maintenance of a hard strong physique, the proof that years of treatment for a persistent venereal disease had not taken toll of his constitution as his enemies maintained. He did take pleasure in sexual encounters, but these were hurried and impatient. Women who came to his office, or his hotel room, or to the flat he later took in the upper floor of a palazzo in Via Rasella, were ravished, usually on the floor, and then hastily dismissed while he, not having bothered to remove either his trousers or his shoes, returned to his desk. Generally ill dressed, he was frequently unshaved and often unwashed, being accustomed to splashing eau-de-Cologne over himself when he got up in preference to wasting

90. Mussolini, in October 1922, standing with a group of leading blackshirts who led the March on Rome.

time in a bath. He could not be bothered to tie up shoelaces, so he had elastic laces made with bows. He did not see why he should not wear spats with evening dress if they kept his feet warm, nor a black tie with tails if he could not find a white one, and he often did so, frequently also wearing yellow shoes. He appeared at his office in a morning suit, as the striped trousers and cut-away black coat appealed to him, but he was constantly wriggling his huge neck in the butterfly collar and shaking back the cuffs of his starched shirt.

At first Mussolini occupied offices both in the new Palazzo del Viminale, the Ministry of the Interior,[1] and in the old Palazzo Chigi, the Ministry of Foreign Affairs.[2] But finding these inadequate, in 1929 he moved to Palazzo Venezia where he occupied the biggest of the spacious halls on the first floor. Almost seventy feet long and forty wide, it occupies two storeys of the original building and has two rows of windows, the upper row originally belonging to the floor above. The tall, wide centre window of the lower row opens on to a balcony and from here Mussolini made many of his celebrated speeches, hands on hips, legs splayed apart, jaw thrust out, falling into silence from time to time to gaze down at the crowds below him, to receive the benediction of their frenzied roar, *'Duce! Duce! Duce!'*, his expression as motionless as the symbol of his regime, the axe and the lictors' rods carved in stone on the wall beside him.

The room from which this commanding figure appeared was known as the Sala del Mappamondo from the old map of the world displayed there. It was unfurnished apart from a large desk placed sixty feet from the door, a lectern and three chairs arranged in front of a huge fireplace decorated, like the wall outside, with the emblem of Fascism. Some visitors whom the Duce wished to intimidate were required to walk across the bare floor towards the fireplace while no notice was taken of them, their feet ringing on the coldly echoing polished marble mosaics, the dark figure beneath the towering candlestick on the table still immersed in his papers. But others found him friendly and courteous, walking towards them quickly, holding out his hand. Even when he gave the impression, as he did to Lord Vansittart, of a man who 'took such obvious pleasure in his own company' that he was 'reminiscent of a boxer in a flashy dressing-gown shaking hands with himself', he managed to give pleasure to his visitors as well as to himself, although he was quite humourless and essentially misanthropic. He spoke fluently in a low voice, displaying a brilliant flair for unusual yet apt allusions and striking neologisms. 'When the Duce starts to talk,' his Foreign Secretary once said of him, 'he is delightful. I know nobody who uses such rich and original metaphors.' But he was not a good listener. He found it difficult to keep still in his chair, and would sometimes stand up abruptly to carry on the conversation, distractingly striding up and down the room. As the years passed, he grew increasingly restless during tiresome interviews and in the day-to-day conduct of government. He gave the impression of being always occupied with business, and at night left the light burning in the Sala del Mappamondo to bolster the illusion of ceaseless industry. In fact, he had no taste for organization, no patience with difficult work, such a horror of making decisions that he would write the word 'approved' on two conflicting memoranda emanating from two different ministries and then go through the door to his private apartment where his mistress lay waiting for him, or go home to his family in Villa Torlonia,[3] the large graceful house in Via Nomentana which Prince Giovanni Torlonia had placed at his disposal for as long as he wanted it for one lira a year.

A skilful journalist and propagandist as well as artful politician, he was much happier when manipulating the masses by the written and the spoken word than when engaged in administration. He envisaged government as a series of dramatic headlines, *'La Battaglia del Grano'*, 'The Battle to Reclaim the Marshes', 'The Demographic Campaign'. And he loved to be seen and photographed conducting these operations, reviewing troops and party members in the choreographic displays of Fascism, speaking to farm-workers at harvest time, his hairy, barrel-shaped chest bare to the sun, acting as host to those delegations which were regularly brought to Rome such as the ninety-three most prolific women in the country. These black-shawled progenitors of over thirteen hundred children were taken on a tour of the city on Christmas Eve 1933, visiting the Exhibition of the

Fascist Revolution, where, in the Shrine of the Fascist Martyrs, they knelt to kiss the glass case containing the bloodstained handkerchief that the Duce had held to a bullet wound in his nose after an attempted assassination, placing a wreath by the altar in the Fascist Martyrs' Chapel, receiving medals and scrolls in the offices of the National Organization for the Protection of Mothers and Children, and being presented to the Duce at Palazzo Venezia before attending the closing ceremony in the Augusteum.

The Rome they saw was gradually being transformed under the personal direction of the Duce who could be seen from time to time surveying the progress of the work from the balcony of the Sala del Mappamondo and who sent down occasional messages to encourage the workmen in their labours.

In five years [he told the City Council], Rome must appear wonderful to the whole world, immense, orderly and powerful as she was in the days of the first empire of Augustus. The approaches to the Theatre of Marcellus, the Campidoglio and the Pantheon must be cleared of everything that has grown up round them during the centuries of decadence. Within five years the hill of the Pantheon must be visible through an avenue leading from Piazza Colonna . . . The third Rome will extend over other hills, along the banks of the sacred river, as far as the shores of the Tyrrhenian Sea.

He envisaged a city vastly increased in size and population, dominated by those huge buildings and skyscrapers which so much appealed to him. It would have, towering above the Forum, an immense Palace of Fascism which would be one of the largest and most impressive structures in the world. And to make way for this new Rome all that was 'filthy and picturesque', all that smelled of the Middle Ages would be destroyed.

The threatened wholesale destruction of medieval Rome was never carried into effect, but much of it did vanish, as did fifteen ancient churches, to be replaced by those monuments of Fascist architecture in many, though by no means all, of which the realization of sheer size and ostentation seems to have been the guiding principle of their design. A promised wide thoroughfare linking the Colosseum and the Piazza Venezia did appear as the Via dei Fori Imperiali;[4] a wide avenue leading from the river to St Peter's Square, the Via della Conciliazone,[5] was begun to commemorate that real achievement of the Fascist regime, the 1929 agreement with the Vatican known as the Lateran Pact which brought to an end the 80-year-old division between Church and State; and, on the southern outskirts of Rome, the huge complex, known as E.U.R. and built for a proposed Roman exhibition to celebrate the twentieth anniversary of the March on Rome, remains as an example of planning on the grand scale.[6]

But in Rome, as elsewhere in Italy, Fascist achievements never matched Fascist promises and boasts. The success of various land-reclamation schemes could not be denied, and the draining of the huge areas of the Pontine Marshes, the partial eradication of malaria there, the building of canals, new roads, towns and hydroelectric power stations, gave land, homes, work and opportunities to thousands of poor people from all over Italy, while a widespread improvement in working conditions was achieved. Yet despite the boasts of Fascist statisticians that never less than 100,000 labourers were engaged on public works and that between 1922 and 1942 the government spent no less than 33,634 million lire on such enterprises, performance fell far below both intention and claims. Archaeological work in Rome included excavations and reconstructions in Caesar's and Trajan's Forum, in the Piazza Venezia and on the Capitol, the rebuilding of the Curia and the uncovering of temples in the Largo di Torre Argentina dating back to the time of the Roman Republic, and the repair of both the Ara Pacis and the Augusteum which Mussolini intended, so rumour had it, for his own tomb. While much was undoubtedly accomplished, only a fraction of the work planned was actually undertaken. Work begun was often left unfinished, and immense sums of money disappeared on impossibly ambitious schemes or drifted into the pockets of corrupt officials and high-ranking Fascists anxious to make their fortune while they could. A huge Forum of Mussolini, for instance, was planned to cover an immense area between Monte Mario and the Tiber. It was, so the Duce ordered, to dwarf both St Peter's and the Colosseum and to have as its centrepiece a marble obelisk 118 feet high and weighing nearly 800 tons, 'the largest monolith in the world'. But then it was decided that even this was not impressive enough. Instead, there must be a statue of Hercules 263 feet tall, its right hand raised in a Fascist salute, its features resembling those of Mussolini himself. After 100 tons of metal had been expended, part of a gigantic head and a foot as large as an elephant's had been cast, this project progressed no further.

The Duce himself was rarely blamed for Fascism's shortcomings. There were many anti-Fascists in Rome, but few anti-Mussolinians. He was not only a dictator, he was an idol. Photographs of him were stuck on the walls of countless homes, slogans in praise of him – *Duce! Duce! Duce! Il Duce ha sempre ragione* – were splashed in white paint everywhere; objects that he had touched were prized as sacred relics. Skilfully presented to the people as Italy's man of destiny, he was accepted as such; and millions fell under the sway of that proudly jutting jaw, those black, wide-open eyes, those wonderfully expressive gestures, that strangely emotive voice. When, on the night of 9 May 1936, he announced from the balcony of the Palazzo Venezia that victory had been achieved in Abyssinia and Italy had 'her empire', the last words of his speech were lost in a wild torrent of cheers, in the screams of hysterical women, in shouts of adoration and protestations of loyalty until death.

Yet Mussolini was by then already on the road which was to lead to his downfall, set upon a course for a war for which his forces were utterly unprepared. The victim of his own propaganda, convinced of his infallibility, closing his mind to unwelcome evidence, he chose to believe that alliance with Hitler in the Rome–Berlin Axis would 'bring Italy the true greatness of which Fascism had made her worthy'.

When Hitler came to Rome in May 1938, with the expressed intention, so a secretary at the Italian Embassy in Berlin reported, of flattering the Italians' pride and of demonstrating that the Axis was a living reality, Mussolini was determined that his visitor should be deeply impressed.

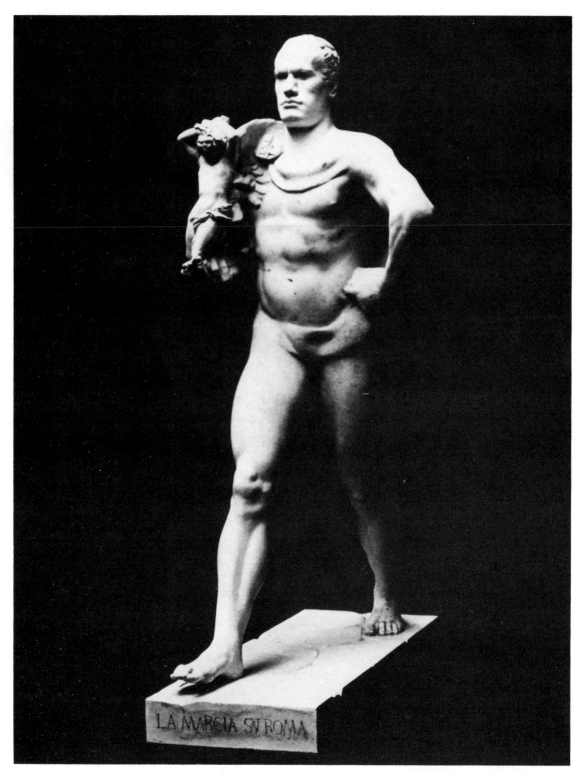

91. The hero of the March on Rome.

The planning had begun six months before; and all along the railway line to Rome houses had been repainted and stations redecorated. The streets of the city itself, through which the parades were to pass, were made splendidly welcoming; and although many shopkeepers refused to display portraits of the Führer, they allowed banners and flags to be flown from their windows. The Italian soldiers who were to take part in the parades and who had been chosen for their height and prepossessing appearance were drilled endlessly, issued with new uniforms and equipped with weapons which they had not yet been trained to use in war. The resultant military pageants were, indeed, magnificent, so Count Ciano, Mussolini's son-in-law, said. 'The Germans, who may have been a little sceptical on this point, will leave with a very different impression.'

Hitler certainly seemed to be impressed. And he himself had a 'great personal success', Ciano thought. 'He has succeeded in melting the ice around him . . . His personal contacts, too, have won sympathy, particularly among women.' His reluctant host at the Quirinal, the diminutive King Victor Emmanuel III, however, disliked him on sight. He told Mussolini that on his first night in the palace Hitler had asked for a woman. This request caused the utmost commotion in the Royal Household until it was explained that the Führer could not get to sleep until he had seen a woman remake his bed. Was the story really true? Ciano wondered. Or was it malice on the part of the King, who also insinuated that Hitler injected himself with stimulants and narcotics? The whole atmosphere of the palace, Ciano decided, was 'moth-eaten'.

The antipathy between the King and Hitler was as marked as the cordiality which existed between the two dictators. On first meeting Hitler, Mussolini had decided that the 'silly little clown' was 'quite mad'. But he had now changed his mind about him. At the station when they said good-bye, both of them were moved and Hitler was seen to stare at Mussolini with an almost dog-like devotion. 'From now on,' the Duce told him, 'no force on earth will be able to separate us.' The Führer's eyes filled with tears.

Neville Chamberlain's eyes also filled with tears when he left Rome the following year to the strains of 'For He's a Jolly Good Fellow', sung rather tunelessly by a group of English residents. Chamberlain's visit had not been a success, and Mussolini had not intended that it should be. 'These men are not made of the same stuff as the Francis Drakes and the other magnificent adventurers who created the British Empire,' he decided after the Englishmen had gone. 'They are the tired sons of a long line of rich forefathers.' But then what could you expect of a people, he asked later in a speech in which his misconceptions of English life were so grotesque as to be appealing, who changed into dinner-jackets for their afternoon tea?

On 10 June 1940, after many hesitations and doubts, Mussolini declared war upon these degenerate people, persuaded by the surrender of the Belgian Army that he could wait no longer. That night in Rome an atmosphere of gloom hung over the dreadfully quiet city. Going home dejectedly to his flat to pack, the correspondent of *The Times* passed down Corso Umberto and across Piazza di

92. The Duce appeals for 90,000 more young Fascists to bring the Fascist Militia up to its required strength.

Spagna and saw not a single flag hung out. Italian friends came to wish him farewell, walking past the policeman on watch near his front door and the people muttering anxiously in the doorways, and they shook hands with him with a kind of sad apology. 'I feel miserable,' Count Ciano recorded in his diary. 'The adventure begins. May God help Italy!'

Ciano's fears were well justified. The course of the war proved disastrous for Mussolini; and in Rome, by the summer of 1943, Fascists and non-Fascists alike constantly discussed ways and means of getting rid of him. The King, in almost daily contact with various dissident groups, had been deeply distressed and alarmed by an Allied air raid on Rome on 19 July in which hundreds of people had been killed and the basilica of S. Lorenzo fuori le Mura very badly damaged, and he had been persuaded after weeks of hesitation to order the arrest of Mussolini when he called for an audience either at the Quirinal or at the Villa Savoia.[7] At the same time a group of prominent Fascists had themselves been plotting their leader's overthrow which, it was planned, should be arranged at a meeting at Palazzo Venezia of the Fascist Grand Council, the supreme authority of the state. Informed of this plot, the King was confirmed in his resolve to act, since a vote of no confidence in Mussolini by the Council would give him the constitutional authority he felt he needed to dismiss him. Although forewarned that Count Dino Grandi, a former ambassador in London and one of the most influential members of the Council, was to present a resolution calling for the Duce's resignation, Mussolini strode with his usual confidence into the Sala del Pappagallo where the meeting was to be held, not looking at any of them. He was wearing the greyish-green uniform of the Supreme Commander of the Fascist Militia as though to distinguish himself as a man apart from the others who were all, at his orders, clothed in the black bush-shirt known as the *Sahariana*. 'Salute the Duce!' the Secretary of the Party called out. They all obediently jumped to their feet and gave the traditional response, 'We salute him!' Glowering, Mussolini sat down at a table on a dais raised above the level of the table at which the others sat. On their way into the room they had noticed that the courtyard was filled with Fascist militiamen. Other militiamen were patrolling the corridors, stairs and apartments of the palazzo itself. One senior member of the Council had murmured apprehensively to Grandi, 'This is the end for us.'

The Duce began to speak. He spoke for two hours, rambling on inconclusively, inconsequentially, disingenuously, blaming everyone other than himself for Italy's predicament, remarking in one aside, so outlandish and irrelevant that his listeners wondered if it were some obscure joke, that he had foreseen the English attack at El Alamein on 23 October 1942 because he knew they wanted to spoil the twentieth anniversary of the March on Rome during the following week.

For a long time after these extraordinary pronouncements had been drawn to a close, no one spoke. In the uneasy silence they were all conscious of an appalled disillusionment, so the Italian ambassador to Berlin considered. They had never heard Mussolini speak to such ill effect. Twenty years of power were at an end. As

93. Mussolini standing beside his writing-table in the vast Sala del Mappamondo at Palazzo Venezia. Contrary to rumour, visitors were rarely required to walk across the sixty feet of mosaic from the door. 'He met me at the door,' wrote Duff-Cooper of an interview in 1934, 'and accompanied me to it when I left . . . I was favourably impressed.'

other members began to speak, abusing each other, the Germans and the Allies in turn, and as Ciano rose to make an unprecedented attack upon the Duce, Mussolini leant in a cramped position over the table as though he were in pain, occasionally pressing his hands against his stomach or lifting them to shade his eyes from the glaring light of the chandeliers. His pale face was covered with sweat. After six and a half hours, Mussolini adjourned the meeting. When he came back and the debate resumed, he appeared to have recovered. He spoke with calm confidence and it seemed, so Grandi said later, that 'he had regained at one stroke all that he had lost'. But it was too late. At a quarter-past two in the morning the resolution was put to the vote. Nineteen of the twenty-eight members of the Council voted in its favour. Mussolini gathered his papers together and stood up abruptly. 'Salute the Duce!' the Secretary called out once more. But Mussolini cut short the muffled response by snapping, 'I excuse you from that.' At the door he paused for a moment and announced accusingly, 'You have provoked the crisis of the regime.'

94. Mussolini with his family at Villa Torlonia. From the left are his wife, Rachele, holding the baby, Anna Maria, the Duce with his younger son Romano, and in front of Edda, the two elder boys, Bruno and Vittorio.

The next morning, however, he went to his office as usual and carried on with his work as though nothing unusual had occurred. He brushed aside the advice of close colleagues and members of his family to have the members of the Council who had voted against him arrested. When the Secretary of the Party telephoned to say that some of the nineteen were now having second thoughts, he accepted the news as though he had expected it and had already decided how to deal with the traitors. 'Too late,' he answered with one of those enigmatic threats which had once been heard with alarm but had long since ceased to carry any weight.

It was arranged that he would go to see the King that afternoon. He went home to Villa Torlonia to change into the civilian suit which the royal staff had specified for the audience. This seemed ominous to his wife, since he had always worn a tailcoat for official audiences in the past, and she warned him, 'Don't go. He's not to be trusted.' But Mussolini had no sense of danger. He conceded to the Chief of Staff of the Fascist Militia that the King might want to take over from him as

297

Commander-in-Chief of the Armed Forces but there would be nothing more important than that. He had had a royal audience once or twice a week for over twenty years; the King had always been solidly with him.

Accompanied by his secretary, he stepped into his car which drove off towards the Via Salaria and the Villa Savoia. It was a quiet Sunday, suffocatingly hot; the streets were almost deserted. The papers that morning had announced the fall of Palermo.

The car stopped outside the portico and the driver was surprised to see the King standing at the entrance to the villa in the uniform of a Chief Marshal of the Empire. He had never seen the King greet the Duce in that way before; nor had he ever seen so many *carabinieri* as there were in the grounds that day. But the Duce at first remained quite unperturbed, maintaining that the vote of the Grand Council was not legally binding. And even when informed by the nervous King of his dismissal he seemed unable at first to understand what was being said to him. Then he sat down suddenly and heavily and, so it seemed, feeling faint. The King went on talking, but Mussolini interrupted him to murmur, 'Then it's all over.'

The interview had lasted for a mere twenty minutes. The Duce came out of the villa looking bemused as he walked down the steps to his car which had been moved across to the other side of the drive. As he approached it a captain in the *carabinieri* came up to him and said, 'His Majesty has charged me with your protection.' Mussolini objected, but the captain was insistent. 'No, Excellency, you must come with me.' He took him by the elbow and led him to an ambulance the back doors of which were open. Mussolini, followed by his secretary, stepped inside, pulling his rather rumpled brown felt hat over his eyes. The captain, another officer and three *carabinieri* climbed in after him, as well as three police officers in plain clothes carrying machine-pistols. The doors were loudly slammed shut. It never occurred to him even now that he had been arrested.

No one spoke as the ambulance sped away to the *carabinieri*'s Podgora barracks in Via Quintino Sella, where Mussolini stepped down and stood scowling about him, his jaw thrust out, leaning forward slightly with his legs apart and his hands on his hips, as though he had come on a tour of inspection. He was shown to the officers' mess where he was left alone for about an hour before being taken on in the ambulance across the river to the barracks of the *carabinieri* cadets in Via Legnano. For the rest of that day and for the whole of the next he was kept here, for most of the time lying on a camp-bed in the commandant's office, looking through the window at the cars driving in and out and at the cadets marching in front of the wall on which, painted in huge white letters were the slogans of his régime: '*Credere! Obbedire! Combattere!*' On the evening of 27 July he was driven out of the barracks and taken into exile on the island of Ponza.

In the streets of Rome on the night of his arrest, the people had gathered to ask each other what was happening. There were squads of soldiers armed with machine-guns in the squares, but what they had been called out for no one knew. There were rumours of an Allied parachute landing in the south; stories that the

Duce had resigned and gone home to the Romagna, that he had flown to Germany, that he had been assassinated. It was known that the Grand Council had met and that the meeting had been prolonged; but its decisions had not been made public. When wireless sets were turned on there were no sounds but hum and crackle. Even the gramophone records which were usually brought into use when programmes did not run to time had not been played. And then at last the announcer had come on to the air with news of the resignation of Cavaliere Benito Mussolini and the nomination as Head of the Government of Marshal Pietro Badoglio.

The information was greeted with the wildest excitement which even the subsequent announcement that the war would continue failed to dampen. It was believed that this was merely a formula, a meaningless declaration made to give the new government time to negotiate a peace without interference from the Germans. Crowds rushed through the streets shouting that the war was over. They broke into the offices of the Fascist newspaper, *Il Messaggero* and threw furniture, files, telephones and enormous portraits of the fallen Duce out of the windows. They hurled a bronze bust out of an office into the Corso and dragged it by ropes through the streets. They hacked Fascist emblems off buildings and tore Fascist badges out of the lapels of anyone foolhardy enough to wear them. Few badges, however, were still worn. Almost everyone, it seemed, had suddenly become anti-Fascist. Hooligans looking for victims could find none. The houses of a few known Fascists were broken into, but their owners could not be found. A gang of demonstrators burst into Palazzo Venezia, shouting that they wanted the man who had oppressed them for so long, but they did not attempt to break down the locked door of the Sala del Mappamondo and they contented themselves by waving a red flag.

Elsewhere there was little violence. The mood in the city was one of gaiety rather than revenge. People ran to the Quirinal to cheer the King and to Via XX Settembre to cheer Badoglio. In Via del Tritone, Piazza Colonna, Via Nazionale and Piazza del Popolo they sang and danced as at a *festa*. 'Fascism is dead,' they called happily to one another. It was true. Not a single man died that night in an effort to defend it, though one, the head of the Stefani News Agency, committed suicide. Fascism had collapsed in Rome without a struggle. Even Mussolini's own newspaper, *Popolo d' Italia*, quietly recognized his dismissal and where his photograph had previously appeared inserted one of Badoglio instead.

Most Romans remained at home. They had heard the announcer on the wireless say, 'The war goes on.' And they rightly feared that it might continue for a long time yet. The British and Americans and their allies had overrun Sicily and were now ready to invade the mainland. But the Germans were far from being beaten; and they would surely take steps to protect themselves from the consequences of an armistice signed by the Italians without their knowledge.

After a month of furtive negotiations, on 3 September, in an army tent near Syracuse in Sicily the Italian surrender was signed. On the same day Badoglio assured the German ambassador in Rome that Italy would fight alongside 'her ally

Germany to the end'. On the evening of 5 September, the Allies having landed at Salerno, the armistice was revealed. Immediately the German High Command ordered its troops in the neighbourhood of Rome to close in upon the capital. After a brief, bravely conducted but badly commanded resistance, the Italian defences of Rome crumbled. The King and the General Staff of the Armed Services fled to southern Italy, and the Nazi occupation of Rome began.

Rome was declared an open city, not to be defended even if attacked, and was allowed to have an Italian commander, subordinate to Field Marshal Kesselring, the German commander-in-chief. The administration of Rome was, however, kept strictly under the control of the Germans who watched even more closely over the activities of the various government departments than they did over those of the new Fascist government in northern Italy which had been set up at Salò on Lake Garda under the presidency of Mussolini after his rescue by the Germans from his Italian captors. The activities of the Fascist Party, which had been allowed to reopen its General Headquarters in Palazzo Wedekind,[8] were also carefully watched, as were those of the Roman branch of the Party, the Fascio Romano, in Palazzo Braschi. The German forces stationed in Rome were placed under the command of General Stahel, an officer whose tight lips and glinting spectacles lent him a far more intimidating aspect than General Kurt Maeltzer who was soon to succeed him. Yet Maeltzer's ready smile, his roistering habits and buffoonery belied a harsh and callous nature.

It was, indeed, immediately made clear to the Romans that the Germans intended to rule their city with a firm, relentless hand. A proclamation was issued by Rome radio, which had of course been taken over by the occupying forces, ordering all Italians to surrender their arms on pain of being executed. A curfew was established; and it was eventually decreed that anyone seen on the streets after five o'clock in the afternoon would be shot on sight. A series of man-hunts resulted in the arrest of numerous men whose presence in Rome was considered a threat to the new regime. And to the fears of house arrest were added those of being rounded up in a cordoned-off street and pushed into a lorry for shipment to a German factory, farm or mine, or to those defence lines which were to prove so formidable an obstacle to the Allied advance and which were already being constructed. At the same time men of military age were in danger of being called up by the Fascist authorities. Hundreds of young Romans consequently disappeared from their homes every day. It has been calculated that of a total wartime population of 1,500,000 in Rome, some 200,000 were being hidden by the rest, many of them in churches and religious houses, others in the Vatican, yet others in such warren-like structures as Palazzo Orsini where the partly English and outspokenly pro-Allied Duchess of Sermoneta managed to disappear when the Germans came to arrest her.

Jews were naturally at particular risk. Granted full rights as Roman citizens in 1870, they had not since been persecuted with anything like the cruelty practised in Nazi-occupied Europe. In speeches and conversation Mussolini had often ranted against them and under German influence had endorsed a programme of racial legislation which was, however, never very rigorously enforced. Several Jews had thought it as well to go abroad; others had been expelled. But most of their faith had continued until now to live contentedly in Rome without undue interference from the authorities. On 26 September, however, Colonel Kappler, the head of the Gestapo in Rome, suddenly demanded fifty kilos of gold from the Jewish community. This was followed by an attack on the synagogue by Gestapo agents and by threats of attacks on shops run by Jews and houses occupied by them. About 8,000 found refuge in Catholic convents and institutes which held extra-territorial status; but over 2,000 were arrested in raids and deported to Germany in conditions of terrible brutality. Many others, given due warning, were able to escape from Rome, like the half-Jewish writer, Alberto Moravia, who fled to a peasant's cottage at Fondi.

Escaped prisoners of war, many of whom had converged upon Rome hoping to find sanctuary in the neutral Vatican, were also hounded by the Gestapo and the Fascist police. Thousands of them managed to get back to their units, however, many of them through an organization and escape line formed by one of their number, Major S. I. Derry, who was assisted by a resourceful and intrepid Irish priest, Monsignor Hugh O'Flaherty. Risking their lives, numerous Romans broke the curfew and evaded the nightly patrols to bring food and money, clothes and medical help to the large number of apartments all over the city where escapers were hidden while waiting to be moved on. Several Italian helpers in the escape line were caught and shot; but a fugitive was hardly ever refused assistance, even though helping him might well result in a visit to one of the Gestapo interrogation centres in Via Tasso or to the Pensione Jaccarino in Via Romagna where Pietro Koch, a former wine-merchant and officer in the Italian regiment of the *Granatieri*, was, with the assistance of his two Italian mistresses, employed as a freelance interrogator by Colonel Kappler. In these notorious places, captured Resistance fighters were forced to undergo such fearful tortures that some died, while others broke down and revealed what secrets they knew.

Clandestine resistance in Rome had begun a week after the announcement of Badoglio's surrender when, on 9 September, a group of politicians representing the Socialist, Christian Democrat, Communist and Action Parties had met under the chairmanship of the former Prime Minister, Ivanoe Bonomi, and had founded the first Committee of National Liberation in Italy. Subsequently, numerous other committees and groups were established to form an Italian Resistance movement which, by the end of the war, had endured losses greater than those suffered by the Allied Fifth Army during the entire Italian campaign. In Rome there were military groups, formed by Colonel Giuseppe Montezemolo from members of the Italian armed services, which provided an excellent network of communications with army contacts all over Italy and which proved extremely useful to Allied Intelligence. And there were groups, formed out of adherents to one or other of the political parties, which also maintained intermittent communication with Allied Force Headquarters through secret wireless stations established by Allied agents in Rome and which, in the case of the Socialist and Communist groups, organized acts of sabotage, attacks on German troops and assassinations of SS and Fascist police.

The most celebrated of these exploits was the attack by a Communist group on a detachment of soldiers from a German police regiment on their way to mount guard at the Ministry of the Interior. As they marched up Via Rasella a large bomb concealed in a rubbish cart exploded, killing thirty-two Germans and wounding many more, as well as a child and several other civilians. All the partisans involved got away, but the Germans took terrible reprisals. When Hitler heard of the killings he demanded that thirty or even fifty Italians should be shot for each German killed. And after Field Marshal Kesselring had managed to have the ratio reduced to ten to one, the main prison of Regina Coeli⁹ and other detention centres for partisans were ransacked for victims, five more than were required being produced because of some miscalculation after a further ten had been added to the list by Kappler when another victim had died in hospital. Among them were anti-Fascist officers of the Italian army and the *carabinieri*, activists from the political parties, a few Allied prisoners of war, seventy-five Jews, a priest and a diplomat. They were all shot in the caves along the old Ardeatine Way.

A surge of hope had swept through the people of Rome when news had come through that the Allies had landed north of the city at Anzio on 20 January 1944. But this was followed by a mood of despair as it became clear that the invasion had not been a success and that, pinned down in their bridgehead, the Allies were in danger of being forced back. Conditions in Rome began to deteriorate fast. Water, like gas and electricity, was frequently cut off; water-sellers appeared in the streets, as in the days of the Middle Ages; and a bottle of clear water became a precious possession. Prices soared as food became scarce; the black market flourished; people offered their possessions in the streets – books, gramophone records, clothes – in order to get money for bits of beef or packets of salt or extra bread. The poor verged upon starvation, despite the charitable work of the Vatican which, according to Sir D'Arcy Osborne, the British Minister to the Holy See, was eventually supplying 100,000 meals a day at one lira a head. In the parks, trees were cut down and benches chopped up for firewood. Men walked about in constant apprehension of arrest or deportation; and one day a pregnant woman, the mother of five children, was shot in the face and killed as she ran screaming towards her husband who had been rounded up for forced labour. Thereafter women had their heads shaved for sleeping with Germans.

Yet the graffiti scrawled on the walls did not attack the Germans alone. The papacy, fearful of exacerbating the plight of the Romans in general and the Jews in particular, was blamed for its refusal to condemn outright the excesses of the occupying force. The Allies, as careless in observing Rome's status as an open city as were her enemies, were attacked for their negligent air raids on the city which, while directed at such targets as railway lines, frequently damaged buildings and killed people in the surrounding areas. One raid in the Testaccio district left many dead; another on the Castro Pretorio barracks cost nearly a hundred civilian lives as well as those of several patients in the nearby Policlinico hospital.

Then, at last, at the end of May, as the roar of heavy guns could be heard in the distance, reports that the Germans were preparing to withdraw from Rome spread throughout the city: the luggage of their officers was seen being carried into the street from the big hotels on the Via Veneto. Yet even now there were fears that the Germans would defend the city as Mussolini wanted them to do. Remembering only too well how the Romans had greeted his downfall the year before, he insisted that there must be a battle for Rome, that the city must be fought for, street by street. On 2 June, however, the Pope issued a warning: 'Whoever raises a hand against Rome will be guilty of matricide to the whole civilized world, and in the eternal judgement of God.' And, on that same day Kesselring sought permission from Hitler to evacuate the city. Hitler, describing Rome as 'a place of culture' which must 'not be the scene of combat operations', granted it, ignoring Mussolini's protests.

So the German evacuation began. For fear lest it might lead to a Roman uprising, it was set in motion as discreetly as possible. Kesselring told General Maeltzer to attend a performance the following evening, 3 June, by Gigli in Verdi's opera *Un ballo in maschera*. Soon after the curtain fell, however, the general exodus started; and by dawn German troops could be seen streaming out of the city, on foot, in vehicles, on bicycles, their artillery drawn by horses, their baggage piled up on Rome's horse-drawn cabs which they had commandeered. The Romans watched them depart with relief but without rancour: some of the troops in the bedraggled, dejected columns were offered drinks and cigarettes. 'Continuous files of German soldiers, tired, sweaty but armed to the teeth, passed along the Lungotevere, between people standing in rows, people in shirt-sleeves, dirty and silent,' recorded Mario Praz. 'They don't laugh, they don't jeer, they don't show pity. The ancient Roman crowd, among the ancient monuments, sees once more an army in retreat, understands and is silent.'

On the outskirts of the city, German rearguards, shelled and dive-bombed, fought to delay the enemy advance; but by the middle of the afternoon Allied troops had passed beneath the walls of S. Paolo fuori le Mura and were advancing towards Porta S. Paolo, while American tanks were soon grinding their way slowly through Porta S. Giovanni. Families came out on to balconies and into the streets, cheering and clapping their hands, holding up flowers and jugs of wine; and, as the tanks and trucks continued to rumble through the streets in the gathering darkness, they lit candles in their windows in celebration of the end of their long trial.

95. General Mark Clark, commander of the 5th Army, talking to a priest in St Peter's Square after his troops' liberation of Rome in June 1944.

EPILOGUE:
THE ETERNAL CITY

As bells rang in the *campanili* on the morning of 5 June 1944, the American commander of the victorious Fifth Army, Mark Clark, climbed the steps of Michelangelo's *cordonata* towards the Piazza del Campidoglio on the Capitoline hill. Here, where Brutus, 'still hot and eager' from Caesar's murder, had come to address the people, where Augustus had made sacrificial offerings in the lovely Temple of Jupiter, where Greek monks had prayed in the church of S. Maria d' Aracoeli in the Dark Ages, where Petrarch had received the poet's laurel crown, where Cola di Rienzo had fled down the stairway to his death, and where Gibbon had been inspired to write his great history, the leader of the men who had delivered Rome from the last of her foreign masters looked down upon the city which the Allies were now to control.

The tasks facing them were daunting. They had to feed a population swollen by a mass of refugees to almost 2,500,000; they had to restore electric lighting and repair the water supply; above all they had the problem of keeping order while introducing democratic freedoms to a people quite unused to them. Given the difficulties, they succeeded well enough. Although rationed except for use by the army and the hospitals, electric lighting was restored on 6 June. The telephone service began to operate again the next day. Before the end of the month the bread ration had been doubled to 200 grams a day, and banks, schools, the university, some libraries and even a few theatres had reopened. The postal services returned to normal on 1 July. Three months later the water supply, gravely disrupted by German sabotage of the main aqueducts, had been fully restored. Law and order were maintained with the help of the *carabinieri* and Finance Guards who had entered Rome with the Allies, and the offices of the new administration on the Capitol were handed over to the new mayor, the popular and consistently anti-Fascist Prince Filippo Doria Pamphilj.

Nevertheless, there were widespread complaints in Rome that repairs and reforms were not being carried out quickly enough, that the Allies were not living up to their promises to end the people's hardships as soon as the Germans were driven north. A popular song of the time was directed against the head of the Allied administration of the city, Colonel Poletti, an American of Italian extraction, who gave radio talks on current problems:

Charlie Poletti, Charlie Poletti,
Meno ciarla e più spaghetti.
[Less of the talk and more spaghetti]

Certainly the people, particularly the old and the pensioners, had grounds for complaint. The black market, which had flourished under the Germans, continued to prosper; yet the innumerable regulations and restrictions concerning food which were so irksome to the poor were continually extended. Buildings and vehicles were requisitioned without apparent necessity; Allied officials were often found to be intransigent or dismissive, while Allied soldiers were compared unfavourably with German troops who had usually been better behaved. Yet unprejudiced Romans had to admit that they enjoyed far greater freedom both of expression and of movement under the Allied occupation than they had done under the Germans, that the fear and oppression which had formerly overshadowed Rome had been lifted, and that the occupying forces seemed genuinely anxious to hand back the government of the city and the country to Italians as soon as possible. A more broadly based Italian government, replacing Badoglio's and deriving its authority from Crown Prince Umberto following the retirement of King Victor Emmanuel, had been formed immediately after the liberation of Rome; and on 15 August the city and its surrounding provinces were handed over to this government for direct administration under the supervision of the Allied Control Commission.

So, slowly Rome became the city of the Romans once more. Past wrongs were gradually forgotten, and the people recovered their natural good humour. While tribunals dismissed some Fascists from their posts and detained others responsible for serious crimes, while a few notorious figures of the former regime, like the deputy governor of the Regina Coeli gaol, had been lynched by the mob, and while the windows of some shops owned by Fascists had been stoned and smashed, there was an evident desire to look to the future rather than to resent the past. By a referendum in June 1946 the country voted for a Republic instead of the discredited monarchy. Parliament reopened in May 1948 after elections which returned the Christian Democrats with an absolute majority; and so, under the inspiring leadership of Alcide De Gasperi, and with Allied economic aid, Italy was able within a short time to take its respected place among the nations of the West, and Rome was soon to give her name to the treaty which inaugurated the union that binds so many of them together.

Six and a half centuries after Pope Boniface VIII had declared that 1300 would be the first of the Holy Years of the Church, Pope Pius XII presided over another Holy Year in Rome, pronouncing his blessing over the crowds as his predecessor had blessed the crowds in which Dante had stood. The Church's great traditions continued from century to century, yet the Church was gradually changing. In 1962 Pope John XXIII called the Second Vatican Council, and over two thousand mitred bishops gathered in the huge central nave of St Peter's to take part in the deliberations which were to give authority to the Church's renewal.

96. Pope John XXIII (1881–1963), sitting in his gestatorial chair, blesses the crowds in St Peter's Square during the celebrations for the seventieth anniversary of the Rerum Novarum in 1961.

In these years the appearance of Rome and the life of the city were being transformed too. An economic boom in Italy, which was to lead to the production of one and a half million motor vehicles in 1967, ensured that the traffic in Rome's streets became more congested and frequently more chaotic than ever. Outside the city walls new suburbs sprawled to the south down the left bank of the Tiber, to the north along the old road to Florence, east and south-east towards the Sabine and Alban hills and westward on either side of the Via Aurelia. The population, which had reached two million by the early 1960s, had grown to 2,830,569 by 1983.

It was an increasingly cosmopolitan city. The establishment of the headquarters of the Food and Agriculture Organization of the United Nations in Rome in 1950

97. The Palazzo della Civilta Romana.

98. The Palazzo dei Congressi.

was followed by that of several other international bodies; by an increase in the two diplomatic corps, one accredited to the Republic, the other to the Pope; by an influx of students to the several academies maintained by most of the European nations and by America; by the construction of large new hotels; by the expansion of the film industry, centred upon Cinecittà[1] and the consequent arrival of numerous technicians, writers, actors and actresses – pursued by intrusive *paparazzi* – to swell the number of artists and musicians who had found Rome so congenial in the past.

In politics the former authority of the Christian Democrats as a unified party had crumbled. During the economic depression which followed the affluence of the 1960s, while allegations of corruption against ministers caused a crisis in public confidence, the Communist Party, which had gained ground under the leadership of Palmiro Togliatti, made further advances. And in 1976, for the first time in its history, Rome had a Communist mayor. Many Communists, however, remained devout Roman Catholics. When Togliatti died, thousands of the mourners who lined the route between the Piazza Venezia to St John Lateran made the sign of the cross as the cortège passed, several of them after having first saluted it with a clenched fist. But to the left of the Communists and far to the right were such organizations as the Red Brigade and the Armed Revolutionary Nuclei. These were responsible in the late 1960s and 1970s for a succession of outrages in Rome, one of the most notorious of which was the murder of the Christian Democratic leader and former Prime Minister, Aldo Moro, whose body was found in the boot of an abandoned car not far from his party's headquarters on 9 May 1978.

Yet the subsequent reign of terror which some newspapers predicted never occurred. Rome was once again, in Belloc's phrase, 'astonishingly the same'; and the city was seen to retain the lustre and the fascination which had held men and women in thrall for so many centuries. Throughout those ages poets and patriots, artists and historians, philosophers and statesmen have fallen under the spell of Rome, 'mother of kingdoms, the world's capital, the mirror of cities'. To Virgil she seemed the beauty of the world, the natural ruler of the nations. To the twelfth-century Englishman, Master Gregory, the first visitor from his country to provide a detailed account of the city, she appeared 'most wonderful'. Nothing could equal the beauty of Rome, 'Rome even in ruins'. For Hildebert of Blois also, Rome was incomparable: 'No other city can be compared to you, O Rome, even though you are almost a total ruin: in your destruction you teach us how great you were when you were whole.' Dante called Rome life-giving and the Romans the people of God. For Milton she was the Queen of the Earth. Emperors considered her the pre-ordained centre of authority. The Czars (Caesars) of Russia spoke of their capital as the third Rome, just as the ancient emperors had made of Constantinople the second Rome. Byron was repeating an ancient belief when he wrote:

> While stands the Coliseum, Rome shall stand;
> When falls the Coliseum, Rome shall fade;
> And when Rome falls – the World.

Napoleon was obsessed by its spell and dreamed of Rome as the capital of his empire, creating his young son King of Rome. Mazzini too was obsessed by Rome. Garibaldi's cry of '*Roma o morte!*' became one of the inspirational sentiments of the Risorgimento. Cavour could not envisage the Italian Kingdom without Rome as its capital. Mussolini sought to revive the Roman Empire. And his adversary, Churchill, in pressing for the capture of Rome by Allied forces declared, 'He who holds Rome holds the title-deeds of Italy.'

In a far distant age Rutilius Namatianus wrote a moving panegyric of the city in which he claimed that Rome 'has united all peoples into one nation and made all the world one city'. It is this universal element in the history of Rome which is the secret of its perennial vitality, which made it Shakespeare's 'high and palmy state' and which makes it still today the Eternal City.

PART THREE

NOTES ON TOPOGRAPHY, BUILDINGS AND WORKS OF ART

Since they are so capricious, no attempt has been made to indicate the opening times of the numerous museums, galleries, palaces, monuments and churches of the city. The use of an ordinary guidebook, such as Georgina Masson's excellent *Companion Guide to Rome*, is essential. In the preparation of these notes, we have found invaluable Ernest Nash's *Pictorial History of Ancient Rome* (2 vols., Zwemmer for the Deutsches Archaeologisches Institut, 1961), Anthony Blunt's *Guide to Baroque Rome* (Granada, 1982), Richard Krautheimer's *Rome: Profile of a City 312–1308* (Princeton University Press, 1980) and the indispensable *Guida d'Italia: Roma e Dintorni* (Milan, 1965).

In these notes buildings, etc. in capitals are those which have a note to themselves: bold figures in the index will guide the reader to the relevant note.

1. MYTHS, MONARCHS AND REPUBLICANS

1. The SEVEN HILLS OF ROME are usually taken to be the Palatine, the Esquiline, the Viminal, the Quirinal, the Capitol, the Caelian and the Aventine. The Pincio and the Janiculum are omitted from the traditional list because they were never part of the ancient city. The heights are as follows: Capitol and Aventine, 47 metres; Palatine and Caelian, 50 metres; Janiculum, 85 metres. The Esquiline, Viminal and Quirinal rise to a plateau which, at the eastern end, near the PORTA PIA, reaches 63 metres, but without any steep escarpment. The hills nearer the Tiber were, however, more steeply sloping in ancient times than they are now.

2. Originally an open plain, enclosed by the great loop made by the Tiber on its way through Rome, the CAMPUS MARTIUS, or Field of Mars, was used principally for military exercises. It was redesigned by Agrippa between 27 and 25 B.C. with temples,

baths and public gardens. The buildings were restored by Hadrian who made the area one of the great monumental centres of the city. The Greek geographer, Strabo, wrote in 7 B.C.: 'Superior to all is the Campus Martius. The greatness of the plain itself is wonderful, all open for horse and chariot racing and for the great multitudes who take part in ball games and in gymnastics. The ground is covered with grass, which is green all the year round, and is surrounded by buildings and hills that reach to the river's edge. It presents a scenic effect from which it is difficult to tear oneself away.' The area had lost its idyllic appearance by the end of the sixth century. Seven feet below the Piazza di Campo Marzio, which takes its name from the nearby church originally founded in the eighth century, part of a pavement of the ancient Campus Martius was discovered in 1822.

3. The site of Ancus's TEMPLE OF JANUS is not known for certain. It may have stood where the ARGILETUM, Rome's ancient shopping street, entered the FORUM (see note 33, Chapter 2). A temple dedicated to the same god was built in the FORUM OLITORIUM opposite the THEATRE OF MARCELLUS during the First Punic War (264–241 B.C.) and was restored by Tiberius in A.D. 17. A TEMPLE OF HOPE and a temple dedicated to JUNO SOSPITA were also built nearby in the third century B.C. Parts of these temples were incorporated into the church of S. NICOLA IN CARCERE. This church, which takes its name from an eighth-century prison, has been in existence since at least 1128. It was restored in 1599. The façade is probably by Giacomo della Porta.

4. See note 4, Chapter 3.

5. See note 1, Chapter 2.

6. The imposing TEMPLE OF JUPITER OPTIMUS MAXIMUS, MINERVA AND JUNO, known for short

as the TEMPLE OF JUPITER CAPITOLINUS, was the principal shrine of ancient Rome. It covered a large area of the south-west summit of the Capitoline hill near the TARPEIAN ROCK. It was consecrated in 509 B.C. The Senate held its first session here each year; and it was here that a Roman general, celebrating a Triumph, went to offer a sacrifice to Jupiter after the procession. The temple was rebuilt several times, principally by Quintus Lutatius Catulus in 69 B.C. when use was made of white Corinthian columns from Athens. Martial then referred to it as the 'ugly temple made uglier by Catulus'. Afterwards restored by Augustus and Domitian, it was still a showplace when the Emperor Constantius II visited Rome in 357; but it was plundered by the Vandals in 455, and by the Middle Ages had disappeared beneath the houses, gardens, market and fortresses on the Capitoline hill. The site is now covered by the PALAZZO DEI CONSERVATORI.

7. Although Tarquin initiated its construction, the CLOACA MAXIMA, the largest of Rome's sewers, was not completed with its vaulted roof until 33 B.C. In Tarquin's time there was probably an open canal which ran from the ARGILETUM – the area of low ground on which the streams descending from the Quirinal, the Viminal and the Esquiline hills converged – across the FORUM, which it also served to drain, to debouch into the Tiber near the site of the cattle market – the Foro Boario – at a spot which is just below the Ponte Rotto (PONS AEMILIUS, see note 15, Chapter 4). This canal remained uncovered at least till the end of the third century B.C. and the vaulted roof made of the porous rock known as tufa cannot be earlier than the second century B.C. The semicircular arch of its opening, five metres in diameter, can still be seen in almost perfect condition.

8. The TARPEIAN ROCK on the Capitol was named after Spurius Tarpeius, commander of the Roman garrison in the Sabine War, whose daughter, Tarpeia, let the enemy into the city. It was the traditional place of execution for traitors. It is commemorated by the Via del Monte Tarpeo.

9. The remains of the TEMPLE OF VESTA which can still be seen in the FORUM are those of the reconstruction of Septimius Severus which was carried out after the fire of 191. The original round temple, probably built of rushes and covered with a thatched roof, had already been rebuilt a number of times after previous fires. Despite changes in building

materials, it continued to retain the circular form of the primitive huts used by the founders of Rome.

10. The HOUSE OF THE VESTAL VIRGINS was rebuilt by Nero after the fire of A.D. 64 and later restored and enlarged. The remains are those of a second-century reconstruction. The house was built around a large central courtyard enclosed by a two-storied portico. There were ponds and gardens in the centre and possibly a small clump of trees. At the east end was a large hall with side rooms for storing the sacred furnishings. Along the north and south sides of the courtyard were living quarters. Although there were originally no more than four virgins, and later only six, their quarters were extremely spacious and may have extended to as many as four floors. Among the statues of the Vestals, who survived until 394, is one from which the name has been erased: this is thought to be of Claudia, who was converted to Christianity in 364.

11. It has now been clearly established by archaeological research that the wall commonly known as the SERVIAN WALL after King Servius Tullius was not, in fact, built during his reign in the sixth century B.C. but after the burning of Rome by the Gauls in 387 B.C. The earlier wall, which may well have followed primitive fortifications of mounds of earth with stakes, was built of blocks of the soft grey stone known as *cappellaccio* which is found in the subsoil around Rome above a layer of Pliocene clay. The wall which replaced it after the Gallic fire was built of the more solid yellowish grey tufa, *grotta oscura*, from quarries near Veii north of the city. Stones from Servius Tullius's wall have been found embedded in the parts of the later wall which can still be seen on the Capitoline hill.

12. In addition to *cappellaccio* and *grotta oscura*, another tufa, a darkish grey stone from the Alban hills known as *peperino*, was used in Rome as a building material from the third century B.C. It was strong enough to be used for the beams of architraves. Rome's first prison, the TULLIANUM, from which Via del Tulliano takes its name, was built of *peperino* after the Gallic invasion of 387 B.C. Another stronger, slightly rougher building material which came into use in the third century B.C. was *sperone*, a stone from a quarry in the volcanic crater of the Gabine lake. During the second century B.C. experiments were made with brown tufas from various quarries near

Rome at Monte Verde, south of the Janiculum, and near the River Anio. The Anio tufa is to be seen in more than half the ruins of the FORUM. Also during the second century it was found that *pozzolana*, a volcanic ash, could be mixed with lime to make a strong cement which, combined with tufa fragments, produced concrete. This concrete was used in the foundations of the restored temples of CONCORD (120 B.C.) and of CASTOR AND POLLUX (117 B.C.). Concrete walls with marble facings became common a hundred years later. Also becoming familiar before the end of the Republic was travertine, a calcareous limestone found in large quantities near Bagni on the road to Tivoli. Soft when quarried, it hardened quickly and is a lovely white or light yellowish colour. The colonnade of ST PETER'S was to be built of this. Brick was not used in wall construction until the days of the Empire, but brick tiles were used in roofing for six centuries B.C.

13. See note 2, Chapter 2.

14. See note 1, Chapter 2.

2. IMPERIAL ROME

1. The FORUM, an area of under five acres, had become too restricted for all the meetings and public activities of the Romans which were conducted there. Sulla had planned substantial changes in its layout; and in

78 B.C. the TABULARIUM, or State Record Office, had been built to close the north-west end of the area at the foot of the Capitoline hill. A large building of greyish, volcanic *peperino* with Doric columns, the Tabularium now forms the base of the PALAZZO DEL SENATORE on the side overlooking the Forum. It was Julius Caesar, however, who formed the most ambitious project for the enlargement of the area. His new Forum enclosed the SACRA VIA on the northern side beyond the BASILICA AEMILIA, and was to be bounded on the southern side by the BASILICA JULIA.

2. The ancient Senate House of Rome, the CURIA, was traditionally founded by Tullius Hostilius, the third king of Rome. This first building, known as the Curia Hostilia, was restored in 80 B.C. and later by Caesar who realigned it along its present site. Burned down in A.D. 283, the Curia was rebuilt by Diocletian (284–305). In the seventh century it was converted into a church by Pope Honorius I. This church was demolished in the 1930s and the Curia reconstructed as it was left by Diocletian, a brick building of severe simplicity. As the Curia could accommodate only three hundred senators, who sat above the president's podium on the wide shallow steps, meetings were often held in other places to provide room for the growing number of senators, which had risen to nine hundred in Caesar's time. By the podium stood a pedestal with a golden statue of the Goddess of Victory. This was removed by imperial decree in A.D. 357 but was returned after a protest by pagan Senators in 392. It finally disappeared two years later.

3. The ROSTRA took its name from the prows of ships which were captured at the battle of Anzio in 338 B.C. and which were used to decorate the platform. It had originally stood below the COMITIUM, the open space in front of the CURIA where the earliest assemblies of the people took place and where foreign ambassadors sat when the Senate was in session. Caesar moved the Rostra further towards the centre of the FORUM at the Capitoline end, where its remains can be seen today. The crowds that gathered round the Rostra and in the space surrounding it in Caesar's day were much like those described by Plautus a century and a half earlier. The whole area, to quote Ward Perkins's translation of Professor De Ruggiero's paraphrase, was thronged with lawyers and litigants, bankers and brokers, shopkeepers and strumpets, fortune-tellers and dancers, gossips and

scandal-mongers, 'good-for-nothing parasites waiting' for a tip from the rich, serious-minded gentlemen in the lowest part of the Forum, the sick drinking the waters beside the fountain of Juturna', and 'nearby, in the fishmarket, the *bon viveurs*. And everywhere a rabble of idle vagabonds, the men about town, the type that are either deep in gaming or spreading false rumours and passing pompous judgements on affairs of state. And with them those credulous and simple-minded people who crowd the Forum and the Comitium in times of crisis, when fantastic portents are being reported, to hear exactly where a rain of blood and milk has fallen.'

4. The BASILICA JULIA was mainly built by Julius Caesar between 55 and 44 B.C. and completed by Augustus. Partially destroyed by fire in A.D. 283, it was restored by Diocletian. It was flanked by two streets leading into the FORUM from the riverside, the Vicus Jugarius on the north-west and the Vicus Tusculus, the centre of the Etruscan shopkeepers, on the south-east. Only the foundations now remain.

5. The SACRA VIA extended for a distance of five hundred metres in a westerly direction from the ridge called the Velia, where the ARCH OF TITUS was to be built across it, to the foot of the Capitoline hill, bending here and there to pass by some monumental building. It ran along the middle of the FORUM, passing the BASILICA JULIA and the Temples of VESTA, of CASTOR AND POLLUX and of SATURN. Successful Roman generals passed along it on their triumphant processions through the Forum to the TEMPLE OF JUPITER CAPITOLINUS.

6. Built as a votive offering for Caesar's victory at Pharsalus, the TEMPLE OF VENUS GENETRIX was dedicated in 46 B.C. and restored by Trajan. Part of the fourth-century reconstruction of the porticoes survives. Originally an Italian goddess of horticulture, Venus came to be identified with the Greek goddess of love, Aphrodite. As the supposed ancestress of Julius Caesar, her cult became widespread in the days of the Empire.

7. The THEATRE OF POMPEY, Rome's first stone theatre, was built by Pompey in 55 B.C. in the style of the Greek theatre on the island of Lesbos where he had been honoured for his victory over King Mithridates. A temple to Venus Victrix was incorporated in the theatre and inaugurated with concerts and wild beast hunts in which eighteen elephants

and five hundred lions were slaughtered. The building, which according to different writers could seat from 12,000 to 27,000 people, followed the curve of Via di Grottapinta. It was gilded by Nero in A.D. 66 for the reception of King Tiridates of Armenia and later restored by Theodoric the Goth. The bronze Hercules, now in the VATICAN MUSEUM, was discovered on the site in 1864. The theatre was acquired by the Orsini in the early Middle Ages. The RIGHETTI PALACE was later built over its ruins by the Condulmer family of Pope Eugenius IV (1431–47). It passed to the Orsini, then to the Pio family, who added the imposing façade, before coming into the hands of the Righetti.

8. The ALTAR OF AUGUSTAN PEACE was discovered in the fifteenth century beneath the PALAZZO FIANO. Parts of it were acquired by the Grand Duke of Tuscany; others, after passing through various hands, found their way into museums in Rome and into the Louvre. The reconstructed altar, those fragments not recovered being represented by facsimiles, is now displayed in a glass building between the AUGUS-TEUM and the Tiber.

9. The TEMPLE OF MARS THE AVENGER was completed in 2 B.C. Set between the colonnades of the FORUM OF AUGUSTUS, it had a wide façade with eight supporting columns and was faced with white Carrara marble on a podium reached by a single flight of steps. Parts of the steps and some of the columns are still visible. A high wall enclosed both the Temple and the Forum on the north-east side, dividing it from the populous Subura district of Rome between the Viminal and Esquiline hills.

10. The TEMPLE OF CAESAR was raised by Augustus in 29 B.C. to the memory of Caesar on the spot in the FORUM where his body was cremated and where Antony made his famous oration. It had six Ionic columns in front. The new ROSTRA was constructed in front of the temple's façade, looking towards the Capitol.

11. Built in 179 B.C. by the Censors, M. Aemilius Lepidus, after whom it was named, and M. Fulvius Nobilior, the BASILICA AEMILIA was one of the oldest and finest basilicas in Rome. After its restoration a century later by members of the Paullus family and its complete reconstruction by Augustus following a fire, Pliny the elder considered it one of

the most beautiful buildings in the world. It had a double set of porticoes on two floors overlooking the FORUM. The great hall, where business was transacted and justice administered, covered an area of 94 metres by 24 metres, the whole building being 10,000 square metres in area. The hall was divided into three naves separated by columns of African and Italian *cipollino* marble. The basilica was situated in an area formerly occupied by butcher's shops and later by the stalls of moneylenders. The moneylenders remained after the building was finished, carrying on business alongside the outer wall looking on to the Forum. The ruins visible today are those of Augustus's reconstruction.

12. Inaugurated during the Republic in 497 B.C. when the festival of the Saturnalia was instituted as a public holiday, the TEMPLE OF SATURN was one of the earliest of Rome's temples and one of the Republican city's principal monuments. Rebuilt in 30 B.C. by one of Caesar's generals with booty from a campaign in Syria, and again after a fire in the fourth century, it was for many years used as the State Treasury. It rose at the foot of the Capitoline hill on a majestic podium. Eight of the impressive columns of the vestibule have survived.

13. According to ancient tradition, the TEMPLE OF CONCORD was originally a sanctuary erected in 367 B.C. to commemorate the agreement between the patricians and plebeians. Restored in 121 B.C., it was rebuilt by Tiberius in A.D. 7–10. It was often used for meetings of the Senate. It stood at the foot of the Capitoline hill just below the TABULARIUM. A rough rubble platform, partly faced with stone, is all that survives.

14. The TEMPLE OF CASTOR AND POLLUX was built in *c*.430 B.C. after a battle won by the Roman dictator, Aulus Postumius, who had vowed to the Dioscuri, sons of Zeus, to honour them for victory. There was a legend that the sons had taken part in the battle and had brought tidings of their success to Rome where their white horses had been seen watering at the FOUNTAIN OF JUTURNA, the principal fountain in Rome around which the citizens gathered to hear the latest news and to drink the supposedly curative waters. The temple was built close to this fountain by Aulus Postumius's son after his father's death. It was restored in 117 B.C., and again in 6 B.C. by Augustus. It had eight frontal and eleven lateral

columns of which three remain standing on the east side. These are of white Parian marble and date from the restoration carried out by Augustus.

15. The HOUSE OF THE PONTIFEX MAXIMUS or REGIA was, traditionally, the residence of Numa Pompilius and the later kings of Rome. It was situated east of the TEMPLE OF CAESAR. From the beginning of the Republic it became the residence of the chief religious authority of the Roman State, the Pontifex Maximus, and contained his archives. It was rebuilt in marble in about 36 B.C. after a fire, and was restored by the Emperor Septimius Severus towards the end of the second century. Julius Caesar spent the last months of his life here, and it was from here that he went to his death at the Curia Pompeia.

16. The TEMPLE OF JUPITER TONANS was completed in 22 B.C. Shown on a coin with six frontal columns, it was probably, like many other temples, flanked by a row of columns on either side.

17. The TEMPLE OF APOLLO on the Palatine was built by Augustus after the naval battle of Actium in 31 B.C. when he defeated the fleet of Mark Antony and Cleopatra. It was famed for its beautiful colonnades of yellow marble, its sculptures and paintings by Greek masters. The two colonnades in front of the temple housed the Latin and Greek libraries. The remains of the temple are on the south-west side of the Palatine near the ancient plain of the Velabro.

18. The LUPERCAL, or Wolf's Grotto, was a cave at the north-western corner of the Palatine where the rites known as Lupercalia were performed in honour of the god Faunus or Pan. A goat was sacrificed, its hide cut off and divided into strips with which naked youths ran about on the Palatine, flicking women who approached them in the belief that to be struck in this way would ward off infertility. The grotto was connected from the earliest times with the legend of Romulus and Remus and the wolf. The church of S. ANASTASIA was built nearby, perhaps in accordance with the Church's ancient practice of substituting Christian for pagan celebrations. Certainly the foundation of this church at the southern end of Via di S. Teodoro, between the CIRCUS MAXIMUS and the Palatine, is a very old one. It probably existed in the early fourth century. It was completely rebuilt from 1606 onwards. After the portico had been destroyed by a cyclone in 1634, the façade, which bears the arms of Urban VIII, was

reconstructed in 1636, probably to the designs of Domenico Castello. The interior was restored in 1722.

19. The TEMPLE OF QUIRINUS was built in 293 B.C. on the Quirinal hill. Quirinus was a very ancient deity whose Flamens ranked third after those of Jupiter and Mars. In classical times his functions seem to have been forgotten and became identified with those of Mars. Later Romulus was identified with Quirinus.

20. The TEMPLE OF DIANA on the Aventine is traditionally assigned to the reign of King Servius Tullius. It was restored, with encouragement from Augustus, by the general, Agrippa, who married his daughter, Julia. Diana was probably in origin a woodland deity who became a fertility goddess. Her cult was soon identified with that of Artemis, the virgin huntress and goddess of childbirth.

21. The TEMPLE OF JUNO REGINA on the Aventine was built, according to tradition, in fulfilment of a vow made by Marcus Furius Camillus, the saviour of Rome after the Gallic invasion, during a war against the Etruscans in about 396 B.C. Juno, wife and sister of Jupiter, was one of Rome's principal goddesses. She was the goddess of light and patroness of womanhood. June was consequently considered the most suitable time for marriage. Juno was also patroness of state finances; and under the title Moneta she had a temple on the Capitoline hill, the TEMPLE OF JUNO MONETA. This was dedicated by Lucius Furius Camillus in 344 B.C. and became the first Roman mint. Hence *moneta* came to mean mint and is the derivation of the word money. The temple was on the north-east summit of the Capitol known as the Arx, the citadel of Rome, where the church of S. MARIA D'ARACOELI now stands.

22. Like the mausoleum of Hadrian, the CASTEL SANT' ANGELO, the MAUSOLEUM OF AUGUSTUS was a cylindrical tomb built of travertine in the Etruscan style. The height of the tomb was 44 metres. There was a conical mound of earth adorned with cypresses at the top. Constructed in his lifetime, the tomb held the remains of Augustus himself, of his wife Livia, his sister Octavia, son-in-law Agrippa, and of various other members of the Julio-Claudian family. It fell into disrepair and eventual ruin after the end of Imperial Rome and, in the twelfth century, became a fortress of the Colonna family. Still later it was used

by builders as a quarry of the valuable travertine stone. In the twentieth century it became a concert hall until it was closed in 1936 when restoration of the whole Piazza Mausoleo di Augusto began.

23. Begun by Julius Caesar and finished in A.D. 13 by Augustus, who demolished several temples for the purpose, the THEATRE OF MARCELLUS was dedicated to the son of Augustus's sister Octavia who died as a young man. It was designed to hold 20,000 spectators. Encased in travertine, its solidarity and dominating position overlooking the Tiber island led to its transformation into a fortress in the mid twelfth century by the Fabi family. Throughout the Middle Ages it remained one of the most formidable vantage-grounds in Rome, controlling the bridges to and from the Tiber island as well as the populous district of Trastevere on the other side of the river. In the thirteenth century it was held by the Savelli family who leased the vaults to butchers and craftsmen and who, in the sixteenth century, built the palazzo to the designs of Baldassare Peruzzi. The whole complex was sold to the Orsini in 1712; and the palace is now known as the PALAZZO ORSINI. The family device of a bear, *orso*, can be seen on the gateway in Via di Monte Savello. The small shops that formerly filled the theatre's arches have been cleared away so that the double order of semi-columns is now revealed.

24. The MUSEO DELLE TERME, one of the finest collections of classical sculpture and painting in the world, is housed in the vast remnant of what was once the BATHS OF DIOCLETIAN.

25. On the west side of the Palatine, above a steep escarpment overlooking the Tiber, stand the remains of the sumptuous villa known as the HOUSE OF

LIVIA. It is now considered that the house may have been that of Augustus himself who married Livia in 38 B.C. after her divorce from Tiberius Claudius Nero. Livia probably remained here after the Emperor's death in A.D. 14 until her own death fifteen years later. The house contains the customary *atrium* or forecourt, leading into a dining-room (*triclinium*) with a nearby open saloon (*tablinum*). The charming wall-paintings have survived in a number of rooms.

26. The DOMUS TIBERIANA was built on the north-west side of the Palatine, not far from where Augustus had lived. To the west of it ran the ancient street called the Clivus Victoriae. The palace was restored under Domitian and again under Hadrian. A large platform on still visible arches projected above the FORUM.

27. The ORTI FARNESIANI were designed by Giacomo da Vignola for Cardinal Allesandro Farnese, later Pope Paul III. Large areas of them have now disappeared as a result of archaeological excavations, but enough remains to picture how beautiful they must have been in their heyday when they were among the first botanical gardens in Europe. The view from the terrace is one of the most lovely in Rome.

28. The ancient State Prison of Rome, the MAMERTINE, the name of which dates from the Middle Ages, contained a lower cell inside a water cistern called the TULLIANUM. It could be entered only through a hole in the vault, and the only exit was a drain connected to the CLOACA MAXIMA into which corpses were thrown. Vercingetorix, the defeated Gaul, and Jugurtha, the African, both perished here. A medieval legend that St Peter had been confined here led to the conversion of the building into the chapel of S. PIETRO IN CARCERE beneath the church of S. Giuseppe dei Falegnami. When Charles Dickens came here in 1845 he noticed, with his customary relish for the macabre, that the walls were covered with 'rusty daggers, knives, pistols, clubs, divers instruments of violence and murder, brought here, fresh from use, and hung up to propitiate offended heaven'.

29. The THERMAE NERONIAE in the CAMPUS MARTIUS were rebuilt by the Emperor Alexander Severus at the beginning of the third century. They seem to have been similar to the BATHS OF CARACALLA and DIOCLETIAN.

30. Later displayed in the palace of the Emperor Titus, the Laocoön, whose discovery is described in Chapter 9, is now in the CORTILE DEL BELVEDERE at the VATICAN.

31. The fragments of the DOMUS AUREA or Golden House which remained above ground were finally demolished in 121 by Hadrian for his TEMPLE OF VENUS AND ROME.

32. The TEMPLE OF CLAUDIUS was situated near the COLOSSEUM on the Caelian hill. It was begun by Claudius's widow, Agrippina, the mother of Nero; and after being almost demolished by Nero, was sumptuously rebuilt by Vespasian. It had eight frontal columns and was in the centre of a large enclosure whose perimeter measured 800 metres.

33. VESPASIAN'S FORUM was built athwart what is now the Via dei Fori Imperiali. A huge colonnaded area, it lay north-west of the church of SS. COSMA E DAMIANO which was constructed in its library. The FORUM OF NERVA or the FORUM TRANSITORIUM was to be built adjoining it. This Forum, dedicated in A.D. 97, was constructed over the ancient street, the ARGILETUM, the centre of the booksellers and copyists, which led to the crowded district of Subura. It contained the Temple of Minerva, often to be seen in sixteenth-century views of Rome, which Pope Paul V plundered in 1606 for his FOUNTAIN OF THE ACQUA PAOLA and of which only the ruined podium can now be seen.

34. The TEMPLE OF PEACE, like VESPASIAN'S FORUM, was partly financed by the spoils from the Temple in Jerusalem. It was a rectangular building 130 metres long, with a colonnade all the way round. Dedicated in A.D. 75, it was considered by Pliny, in its setting in the FORUM, as one of the principal sights of Rome.

3. BREAD AND CIRCUSES

1. For centuries the COLOSSEUM remained Rome's most celebrated ancient monument as well as a quarry to be plundered. The PONTE SISTO and the PALAZZO VENEZIA were but two of the buildings for which it provided materials. It was also a delight for botanists. In 1813 Antonio Sebastiani, author of

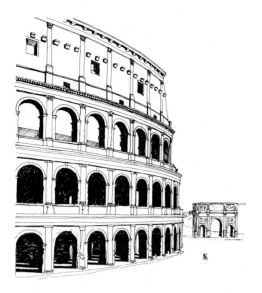

Flora Colisea, listed 261 species that grew there; and in 1855, Richard Deakin added over 150 more. The building was restored at the beginning of the nineteenth century by Pius VII and later by Leo XII, Gregory XVI and Pius IX.

2. The CIRCUS FLAMINIUS, now vanished, was built by the Censor, C. Flaminius, in 221 B.C. It was situated in the area along the Via Catalana between the THEATRE OF MARCELLUS and the huge and sinister PALAZZO CENCI.

3. The CIRCUS GAIUS, built by Caligula and completed by Nero, was somewhere in the area now covered by ST PETER'S. No part of it appears to have survived other than the obelisk which may once have stood in the centre of the dividing wall, but which certainly stood to the south of the basilica before being moved to its present position in the centre of the piazza (see Chapter 11).

4. Situated in the valley between the Palatine and the Aventine, the CIRCUS MAXIMUS was almost half a kilometre long. It was said to have been built by one of the kings, Tarquinius Priscus or Tarquinius Superbus, in the place where the rape of the Sabine women occurred. But, although some of the *carceres*, the chariot enclosures, may have dated from the fourth century B.C., the circus was probably not, in fact, finished until the second century B.C. The imperial tribune was installed on the Palatine side of the arena by Augustus, who also erected the obelisk now in PIAZZA DEL POPOLO. The Circus Maximus was almost entirely destroyed by fire in the days of Nero and again in those of Domitian. It was built anew by Trajan, enlarged by Caracalla and, after a partial collapse during the reign of Diocletian, was restored by Constantine. The last games were held here by Totila the Ostrogoth in 549. There are some remains of the walls around the curve at the south-eastern end. The medieval tower here is all that survives of the fortress which the Frangipani family built on part of the site.

5. Built by Cornelius Balbus, a friend of Augustus, the THEATRE OF BALBUS covered an area between Piazza Margana, Via dei Funari and Via delle Botteghe Oscure. Part of it must have occupied the site of the PALAZZO CAETANI.

6. The ARCH OF TITUS stands on the ridge of the Velia between the Palatine and the Oppian summit of the Esquiline, the SACRA VIA leading through it into the south end of the FORUM. It was erected either by Titus's successor, Domitian, or perhaps by Trajan who succeeded Nerva in 98, and was intended to celebrate the victories of Vespasian and Titus over the Jews. It became part of the Frangipani family fortifications in the Middle Ages. It was restored by Pope Sixtus IV and again by the Roman architect, Giuseppe Valadier in 1821. The view from it was frequently depicted by landscape artists for foreigners in the age of the Grand Tour.

7. The PALAZZO DEI FLAVI and the DOMUS AUGUSTANA were parts of a vast complex of palaces, porticoes and gardens which were built for Domitian on the Palatine and which entailed the destruction of many private houses and the levelling of the hill's original twin crests of the Germalus and the Palatium. It had been the Emperor's intention to leave a monument behind which would eclipse all others; and, according to the poet Statius, the splendid edifices 'rose above the clouds in the full splendour of the sun to kindle the jealousy of Jove himself'. The palace stood on the most prominent site of the Palatine overlooking the FORUM on one side and the CIRCUS MAXIMUS on the other. The building was entered by a magnificent arcaded vestibule which occupied the whole length of the façade. The first great hall was the Emperor's audience chamber or throne room. It was lined with precious marbles and

filled with beautiful statues. To the left was a chapel dedicated to Minerva whom Domitian regarded as his special protectress. To the right was the basilica, a court where the Emperor dispensed justice. The *peristylium* or great central court, surrounded by porticoes, lay beyond. And, still further, was the marvellous banqueting hall or *triclinium*, adorned with the richest marbles and flanked on either side by a *nymphaeum*, rest rooms, fountains and statues of nymphs. Little now remains except fragments of walls and pillars.

8. TRAJAN'S BATHS were worthy precursors of the huge BATHS OF CARACALLA and DIOCLETIAN. Possibly designed by Apollodorus of Damascus, they were built on the usual plan of a large rectangular enclosure containing baths, rest rooms, gymnasia, sports grounds, gardens and libraries. Some remnants of walls and pillars survive in the Parco di Traiano which was laid out around the ruins. Two isolated vaults of brick indicate the baths' approximate limits.

9. The FORUM OF TRAJAN, the last and largest of the imperial fora, measures 118 metres by 89. On either side were two elevated porticoes leading to the immense BASILICA ULPIA which stood at the west side but of which now only numerous broken columns survive. Beyond the basilica were two large libraries between which rose TRAJAN'S COLUMN.

Slightly further west stood the TEMPLE OF TRAJAN which was dedicated to the Emperor and his consort, Plotina, in A.D. 112. It too was designed by Apollodorus of Damascus.

10. The MARKET OF TRAJAN, the well-preserved shopping area of ancient Rome, not only served as a commercial centre but also as a means of supporting the south-west flank of the Quirinal which had been

excavated for the apse of the FORUM. The Via Biberatica, whose name is derived from *piper*, the Latin for pepper, is a street of spice shops. Apart from the restoration of some of the shop doors, the lower two storeys of this street appear much as they did in Trajan's time. The high medieval tower which looms over the market is the TORRE DELLE MILIZIE. Built by Gregory IX (1227–41) as part of the fortifications of the area, it was later acquired by the Annibaldi, then by the Caetani, the family of Boniface VIII (1294–1303). It later passed into the hands of the Conti before being bought by Marchese Cosmo del Grillo who built the adjoining Baroque palace towards the end of the seventeenth century.

11. The sculptures on TRAJAN'S COLUMN were originally coloured and could be inspected from the terraces of the TEMPLE OF TRAJAN and the BASILICA ULPIA.

12. The INSULA OF FELICULA near the PANTHEON was one of the most prominent and celebrated landmarks in the city in the time of Septimius Severus. The

highest of its several storeys towered over the surrounding buildings.

13. The SAEPTA JULIA, planned by Julius Caesar, was built in 26 B.C. by Agrippa with the encouragement of Augustus. It was a vast voting hall about 30 metres long and 95 metres wide. It soon fell into disuse as a voting hall and was subsequently used as a bazaar. It stood between the PANTHEON and the TEMPLE OF ISIS, close to S. MARIA SOPRA MINERVA.

14. Built over the foundations of the vestibule of the DOMUS AUREA, and dedicated in A.D. 135 by the Emperor Hadrian, the TEMPLE OF VENUS AND ROME was once the largest temple in Rome, measuring 110 metres by 53 metres. Its double sanctuaries were placed back to back in an unusual design not before seen in Rome. The tumbled ruins are surrounded by evergreens beside the VIA SACRA between the Piazza di Colosseo and the monastery next to the church of S. FRANCESCA ROMANA. This church, which originated in an eighth-century oratory, was rebuilt in the Baroque style at the beginning of the seventeenth century. The twelfth-century campanile, however, remains. The church contains a fifth-century encaustic picture of the Madonna and Child.

15. The largest and costliest of the Roman imperial villas, HADRIAN'S VILLA at Tivoli was built between A.D. 125 and 134 at the foot of the southern slope of the Tivoli mountain. It is a vast complex of palaces, quadrangles, libraries, picture galleries, pleasure gardens, sports grounds, theatres, baths, *nymphaea*

and storehouses, of which considerable vestiges remain. So as to be reminded of the places which had particularly impressed him during his travels, the Emperor had recreated in miniature, though without exactly copying them, the valley near Alexandria in Egypt where the city of Canopo was situated, the Temple of Serapis, and, from Greece, the Stoa Poikile, the covered colonnade in Athens where Zeno, the founder of the Stoic school of philosophy, used to teach. The palaces and galleries were filled with works of art many of which, excavated at different times, found their way into museums in Rome, in the VATICAN and in England. The Villa was acquired by the Italian Government in 1870.

16. The PANTHEON was built in about 125 over the previous temple raised by Augustus's son-in-law, Agrippa. The bronze roof was rifled by the Eastern Emperor Constans II in 663, while Pope Urban VIII removed the bronze panels in the ceiling of the portico for work in ST PETER'S. The rotunda has often been damaged by fire and flood; but it has as often been restored by emperors and popes alike, by Domitian, Septimius Severus, Caracalla and Popes Gregory III, Alexander VII, Clement IX and Pius IX. It has consequently, despite spoliation, remained structurally almost intact. At the beginning of the seventh century it was given to Pope Boniface IV by the Emperor Phocas (in whose honour the COLUMN OF PHOCAS was erected in the FORUM in 608, the last monument to be placed there). Pope Boniface dedicated the Pantheon in 609 to St Mary and all the Saints and Martyrs. The dome, which has a diameter of 43.30 metres, is nearly a metre wider than the dome of St Peter's. A number of artists are buried here, including Raphael. The tombs of the first two kings of Italy are also to be seen here. The apparent indifference of the Romans to their treasures is evidenced by the holes cut into the columns of the portico. These were used to secure the ends of wooden poles which supported the roofs of a poultry market. This market was moved by Pope Eugenius IV in 1431. But the fish market in the Piazza della Rotonda outside the Pantheon continued until 1847. The obelisk surmounting the Renaissance fountain in the piazza is Rameses II's.

17. Begun in 135 the MAUSOLEUM OF HADRIAN which became CASTEL SANT' ANGELO was completed under Antoninus Pius in 139. It was built in the shape of a cylinder on a marble-covered square base with outer walls of travertine and *peperino* stone and

surmounted by a conical mound of earth planted with trees in the Etruscan style. At the top there was a statue of Hadrian, possibly in the guise of a sun god, driving a four-horse chariot. Around the cylinder was a row of columns with statues at intervals. The mausoleum was used as a tomb for sixty years and held the remains of the imperial families until the reign of Septimius Severus. In 271 it was included in the AURELIAN WALLS and served in the defence of Rome on many occasions from the Gothic siege of 410 to the Sack of Rome in 1527. The conversion of the tomb into a fortress, particularly the alterations carried out by Pope Benedict IX (1033–44) and Pope Alexander VI (1492–1503), transformed its original appearance.

18. The COLUMN OF MARCUS AURELIUS in Piazza Colonna was erected between 176 and 193. It measures 29.60 metres in height and 3.70 in diameter. The Emperor's triumphs over the Quadi and Marcomanni in Bohemia are depicted on the lower part of the column, and his victories over the Sarmatians in what is now the Ukraine on the upper part. An inside staircase leads to the enormous Doric capital at the summit where there stood a statue of the Emperor. In 1589 Pope Pius V placed a statue of St Paul there instead.

19. The STATUE OF MARCUS AURELIUS on the Capitol originally stood in the piazza of the LATERAN. Throughout the Middle Ages it was believed to represent Constantine. This may well have been the

reason for its preservation. In 1538, when it was the only monumental bronze of its kind to survive in Rome, it was moved to the empty piazza before the PALAZZO DEL SENATORE on the Capitol. Michelangelo designed the plinth. In 1981 the statue was removed for repairs and in 1984 was still being renovated in the Restoration Institute of Rome.

20. It was a common practice in ancient Rome to surround a temple with porticoes. In 49 B.C., when Q. Metellus Macedonius built the TEMPLE OF JUPITER STATOR next to the TEMPLE OF JUNO REGINA, he surrounded both with porticoes. These were rebuilt by Augustus in 23 B.C. and dedicated to his sister, Octavia. The PORTICO OF OCTAVIA was of great size, measuring 135 metres by 115. It contained many Greek sculptures and paintings within its double colonnades. In addition to the temples, there were, inside the enclosures, an assembly hall, school and libraries. The remains of the portico are to be seen in Via del Portico d' Ottavia near the THEATRE OF MARCELLUS.

21. The BELVEDERE TERRACE, which was built out on huge supporting arches, stands at the south-east corner of the Palatine not far from the ruins of the BATHS OF SEPTIMIUS SEVERUS and the site of the SEPTIZONIUM. Napoleon's mother, who spent her last years in Rome, delighted in the lovely views that the terrace affords.

22. The ARCO DEGLI ARGENTARI was built in 204 by moneylenders. Richly carved, it portrayed the two sons of Septimius Severus, Geta and Caracalla, offering a sacrifice. After having had his brother murdered, Caracalla had his name and effigy removed from the bas-relief. The arch stands at the north-west end of the Palatine near the portico of the church of S. GIORGIO IN VELABRO.

23. One of the greatest triumphal arches to have been built anywhere in the Empire, the ARCH OF SEPTIMIUS SEVERUS was built in 203 to mark the tenth anniversary of the Emperor's accession. The original inscription indicated that it was erected in honour of Septimius Severus and of his two sons. As with the ARCO DEGLI ARGENTARI, however, the name of Geta was removed by Caracalla after the fratricide. The arch is 28 metres high and 25 wide. The bas-reliefs commemorate some of the Emperor's main battles.

24. The ruins of the BATHS OF CARACALLA, more impressive than those of any other *thermae* in Rome, are to be seen on the south side of Viale delle Terme di Caracalla. The complex of buildings was surrounded by a large enclosing wall. The baths, begun in 206, were extended by Heliogabolus and Alexander Severus and restored by Aurelian. Probably the most lavishly equipped of all Roman baths, they

contained many masterpieces of sculpture. They remained in use until the Gothic invasion of Rome. In the present century performances of opera have been given here on an outdoor stage between the pillars of one of the vaults of the bath-house.

25. The BATHS OF DIOCLETIAN covered an area of 389 yards by 345½ yards , the *frigidarium* alone being 300 feet long, 88 feet broad and 72 feet high, and the swimming pool 3,000 square metres in area. They were begun in 298 by Maximian and completed in about 305 by Diocletian. From the heights of the great arches, Petrarch surveyed the wide expanse of the ruins around him and reflected upon Rome's glorious past, as Gibbon was to do while gazing over the FORUM. The site is now occupied by the MUSEO DELLE TERME, by Piazza Esedra and by the church of S. MARIA DEGLI ANGELI which Michelangelo constructed in the central hall of the *frigidarium*. Although much altered by Vanvitelli in the middle of the eighteenth century, the church still provides a good impression of the interior of a Roman bath. The hemicycle of the stadium attached to the baths can still be traced in the curve of the two buildings of 1896–1902 which form the south-western perimeter of the Piazza della Repubblica.

26. Impelled by his fear of a sudden barbaric invasion, Aurelian raised around the city the finest defensive walls in the Empire. Built between 271 and 275 these AURELIAN WALLS extended for over twelve miles. They had 381 rectangular towers at short intervals and other circular towers at either side of the sixteen gates. Although the wall embraced an area much larger than the inhabited parts of the city, it protected only a small portion of .the crowded Trastevere district.

4. CATACOMBS AND CHRISTIANS

1. The tombstones of the popes who had reigned between 230 and 283 were discovered in 1854 in the CATACOMBS OF ST CALIXTUS. Also discovered were frescos with clear allusions to the early practice by members of the Christian Church of the sacraments of Baptism and the Holy Eucharist. As prescribed by Roman law, and like all other cemeteries, the catacombs were situated in the country outside the city walls and consequently were repeatedly sacked during the successive invasions of Rome by the barbarians. The tombs of the saints and martyrs were ransacked, inscriptions and statuary shattered, precious objects of identification like medallions, cameos, intaglios removed, and the relics of the dead violated. It was concern for the relics which prompted the popes of the seventh to the ninth centuries to remove a vast number of human remains to churches within the walls. The list, which is still extant, of the remains brought into the city by order of Pope Paschal on 20 July 817 records the removal of 2,300 bodies. It was this pope who found the remains of St Cecilia in the Catacombs of St Calixtus. He removed them to the church in Trastevere which he dedicated to her. By the middle of the ninth century the catacombs were completely abandoned and soon entirely forgotten. Their existence came to light again in 1578 through their discovery by a workman digging in a vineyard. But although the exploration of the catacombs from the sixteenth century onwards led to the collection of much valuable information about Christian antiquity, it was responsible for another wave of ransacking and pillaging, perhaps worse than that of the barbarians. Pietro Santi Bartoli, one of the chroniclers of the discoveries made in the catacombs in the last half of the seventeenth century, wrote, 'In a Christian cemetery discovered outside Porta Portese . . . many of the relics of the martyrs have been found, a beautiful set of the rarest medallions, works in metal and crystal, engraved

stones, jewels and other curios and interesting objects, many of which were sold by the workmen at low prices.' After being the object of much attention and devotion during the Counter-Reformation, interest in the catacombs waned in the eighteenth century, to be revived again mainly through the efforts of the archaeologist G. B. De Rossi in the pontificate of Pius IX (1846–78).

2. The splendid PORTA MAGGIORE, formerly the Porta Praenestina, was constructed by the Emperor Claudius in A.D. 52 at the junction of the roads leading to Palestrina and Cassino. Conduits of the Acqua Claudia and the Anio Novus were built into it. Repaired by

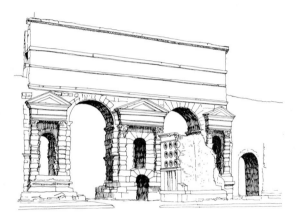

Vespasian and Titus, it was afterwards incorporated into the AURELIAN WALLS. Just outside it is the so-called Baker's Tomb erected at the end of the Republican era in memory of one Marcus Vergilius Eurysaces by his widow. The frieze depicts the various processes of baking bread.

The other principal gates of Rome are listed below, those of which no traces remain being indicated by italics.

Angelica   In the Leonine Wall between Porta Pertusa and Porta Castello near Castel Sant' Angelo. It was built in 1563 and named after Giovanni Angelo de' Medici who became Pope Pius IV in 1559.

Appia   Now the Porta S. Sebastiano (see below).

Ardeatina   In the Aurelian Wall on the south side of Rome at the end of the Viale delle Terme di Caracalla. It originally led into the ancient Via Ardeatina but now gives on to the Via Cristoforo Colombo.

Asinaria   About 200 yards to the west of the Porta S. Giovanni. It has been reopened recently after being

closed since 1409. It gave on to an old road called the Via Asinaria which existed before the building of the wall.

Aurelia   Also known as the Porta S. Pancrazio or the Porta del Gianicolo. Originally part of the Aurelian Wall, it was erected by Pope Urban VIII in the wall which he built around the Janiculum in 1642. It was badly damaged in the defence of the Roman Republic in 1849 and was rebuilt in 1854 by Virginio Vespignani.

Belisaria   Now called the Porta Pinciana. It is flanked by two cylindrical towers which were built by Belisarius to defend Rome against the Goths. Only the central arch is original, the others being modern. The gate stands at the top of Via Vittorio Veneto and leads to the park of the Pincio.

Caelimontana   Part of the old Servian Wall. It has been identified with the Arch of Dolabella on the ancient Via Caelimontana which is now Via S. Paolo della Croce north of the park of the Villa Celimontana. The Arch of Dolabella was built by the Consuls Cornelius Dolabella and Junius Silanus in 10 B.C.

Capena   Part of the Servian Wall, it marked the beginning of the Via Appia. It stood at the east end of the CIRCUS MAXIMUS near the Obelisk of Acsum in what is now the Parco di Porta Capena. The urban stretch of the Via Appia ran from the Porta Capena to the Porta Appia along the Viale delle Terme di Caracalla. Some remains still exist.

Carmentalis   Part of the Servian Wall between the Aventine and the Capitol.

Cavalleggeri   In the wall built by Pope Leo IV (847–55) around the Leonine City. It was situated in the Largo di Porta Cavalleggeri on the south side of ST PETER'S and next to the Palazzo del S. Uffizio. The wall along this side of the basilica, having fallen into ruins, was rebuilt during the pontificate of Pope Nicholas III (1277–80). Only one arch, dating from the time of Alexander VI, now remains. The gate was formerly known as Porta del Torrione.

Collina   A gate in the Servian Wall beside which Hannibal established his camp in 216 B.C.

Esquilina   In the east stretch of the Servian Wall. It was replaced in the time of Augustus by a triple gate later named after the Emperor Gallienus.

Flaminia   Beside S. MARIA DEL POPOLO, from which it took its present name of Porta del Popolo. Built into the Aurelian Wall, it opened on to the Via

Flaminia which leads out of Rome to the north-east, and which was built by the Censor Caius Flaminius in 220 B.C.

Flumentana In the Servian Wall near the Foro Boario between the Palatine and Capitol hills.

Fontinalis In the Servian Wall along a ridge between the Capitol and Quirinal hills. The ridge and gate were removed by Trajan for the building of his forum.

Latina In the Aurelian Wall near the Parco degli Scipioni and beyond the BATHS OF CARACALLA. It opened on to the Via Latina. It was built by Belisarius with a single arch.

Lavernalis Part of the Servian Wall, it was replaced by a bastion by Pope Paul III (1534–49). This bastion is in the Via S. Maria del Priorato which runs down to the river on the slope of the Aventine along the grounds of the Priory of the Knights of Malta.

Metronia In the Aurelian Wall in the Piazza Metronia. The arches still stand but traffic does not pass through them.

Mugonia Said to have been built by Romulus on the Palatine near the ARCH OF TITUS.

Naevia In the Servian Wall on the Aventine.

Nomentana In the Aurelian Wall, just east of the Porta Pia. It gave on to the road to Nomentum (Mentana) to the east of Rome. It was walled up in 1564 by Pope Pius IV.

Honoriana Built in 405 by the Emperor Honorius, it stood in what is now the Piazzale Labicano near the Piazza di Porta Maggiore. It was demolished by Pope Gregory XVI in 1838. It led out on to the Via Casilina, the road to Capua (Casilinum).

Ostiensis In the Aurelian Wall on the old Via Ostiensis. It is now called the Porta S. Paolo since it led to the basilica of St Paul outside the Walls. The gate is situated at the end of the Viale del Piramide di Cestio and is very close to the pyramid which was itself incorporated as part of the Aurelian Wall. The outer façade of the gate was added by the Emperor Honorius at the beginning of the fifth century.

Pertusa In the Leonine Wall. It was blocked up by the middle of the nineteenth century.

Pia The last architectural design by Michelangelo. It was built between 1561 and 1564 near the Porta Nomentana. It closes the upper end of the Via XX Settembre. It is flanked on the right by the gardens of the British Embassy (now the Chancery only) and on the left by the Villa Paolina once owned by Napoleon's sister, Pauline Borghese, and now the French Embassy to the Holy See. It was near this gate that the Italian army of King Victor Emmanuel II under General Cadorna stormed the Aurelian Wall and entered Rome on 20 September 1870. It now houses the Bersaglieri Museum.

Pinciana See Belisaria.

del Popolo See Flaminia.

Portese Built by Pope Urban VIII (1623–44). It stands on the right bank of the Tiber at the south end of the Borgo near the Ponte Sublicio.

Portuensis Built by the Emperors Arcadius and Honorius in the early fifth century near the Porta Portese. It marked the beginning of the Via Portuense which led to Porto, the port of Rome at the mouth of the Tiber established by Claudius in A.D. 42. It was demolished by Urban VIII.

Praenestina See Maggiore.

Praetoria The main entrance into the vast compound of the Castro Pretorio which was built in A.D. 23 by Tiberius's minister, Sejanus, to house the Praetorian Guard and which is still a barracks today.

Querquetulana In the Servian Wall on the Caelian hill.

Quirinalis In the Servian Wall on the north-west slope of the Quirinal hill.

Ratumena In the Servian Wall at the foot of the Capitol. It has been identified with the Porta Fontinalis. It seems also to have been called Porta Pandana.

Raudusculana In the Servian Wall on the Aventine at a point where the Viale Aventino now widens into Piazza Albania.

Romana Said to have been built by Romulus on the Palatine near the Velabro.

Salaria A northern gate in the Aurelian Wall, the outlet for the famous salt way or Via Salaria. It led to the port of Ascoli Piceno (Truentum). It was demolished in 1874 according to Gregorovius's diaries. It was here that Alaric and his Goths broke into Rome in A.D. 410.

Salutaris and *Sanqualis* Two gates in the Servian Wall on the north-western slope of the Quirinal.

S. Giovanni Inserted in the Aurelian Wall close to St John Lateran by Iacopo del Duca in 1574 for Pope

Gregory XIII. It opens on to the Piazzale Appio where the Via Appia Nuova begins.

S. Pancrazio   On the highest point of the Janiculum on the site of the ancient Porta Aurelia. It has also been called Porta del Gianicolo. The scene of fierce fighting during Garibaldi's defence of the Roman Republic, it was rebuilt in 1854.

S. Paolo   See Ostiense.

S. Sebastiano   In the Aurelian Wall on the Via Porta di S. Sebastiano. It was first called the Porta Appia and led on to the old Appian Way. It was rebuilt in the early fifth century by the Emperor Honorius and restored in the sixth century by Justinian's generals, Belisarius and Narses.

S. Spirito   On the right bank of the Tiber, on the south boundary of the Borgo near the Ospedale del S. Spirito. It was built about 1540 by Antonio da Sangallo the younger of Florence for Pope Paul III.

Settimiana   Opened by Alexander VI (1492–1503) in a section of the Aurelian Wall where there had been a postern gate. It is at the south end of the Via della Lungara by the Museo Torlonia.

Tiburtina   Originally built by Augustus on the Via Tiburtina leading to Tivoli (Tibur). It was incorporated in the Aurelian Wall when this was built in 271–5. It was repaired by Honorius in 403.

Torrione   See Cavalleggeri.

Trigermina   In the Servian Wall close to the CIRCUS MAXIMUS and the Aventine.

Viminalis   In the Servian Wall half-way between the Porta Collina and the Porta Esquilina.

3. The Laterani family are known to have owned a palace on the Caelian hill which was confiscated by Nero after their implication in an anti-imperial plot. St Optatus mentions the palace as the property of Fausta, the second wife of Constantine. There is no record of a conveyance or donation of the property to the Church, though there is a very early tradition of a gift by the Emperor to Pope Sylvester I (314–35). It is probable that the first residence of the popes at the LATERAN PALACE was in one of the then existing buildings. Subsequently new buildings were erected and by the time of Pope Damasus (366–84) residence at the Lateran had come to be accepted as a sign of legitimacy.

The first palace at the Lateran erected by a pope as a papal residence was the imposing mass of buildings called the *Patriarchio* of Leo III (795–816) which included a richly decorated banqueting hall of great size. This was destroyed by fire in 1308. When the popes returned from Avignon in 1377 they took up residence at the VATICAN and it was not until 1586, as part of a restoration of the whole Lateran area, that Pope Sixtus V (1585–90) employed Domenico Fontana to build the new papal palace. The BAPTISTERY too is not the original. It appears that, before the Baptistery built by Constantine, there had already been two such buildings on the site. Constantine's Baptistery was replaced by another built by Pope Sixtus III (432–40) which, with later changes, especially by Urban VIII in 1637, is the one we see today. This contains the huge green basalt urn in which Cola di Rienzo immersed himself on the festival of 1 August 1347 (see Chapter 6).

4. The SANCTA SANCTORUM, dedicated to St Laurence, was at first the private chapel of the popes in the LATERAN PALACE. It was restored by Pope Nicholas III (1277–80). The building, which now contains the chapel and the steps leading up to it, the SCALA SANTA, was built by Domenico Fontana for Pope Sixtus V (1585–90).

5. The SCALA SANTA was the ancient main ceremonial staircase of the LATERAN PALACE. Removed by Sixtus V, it now leads to the SANCTA SANCTORUM. Because of the tradition of their origin, the devout have always ascended the stairs on their knees.

6. SANTA CROCE IN GERUSALEMME was renovated by Pope Lucius II who added the Romanesque tower in 1144. In 1743, the church was practically rebuilt by Pope Benedict XIV (1740–58), who gave it the appearance it has today.

7. The present S. LORENZO FUORI LE MURA is the amalgamation of two churches. One of these was Constantine's church which, built in 330 on the site of a shrine dedicated to St Laurence, was reconstructed in the sixth century by Pope Pelagius II. The other was a church, dedicated to Our Lady, which was probably erected by Pope Hadrian I (772–95). The two churches were joined by the demolition of their apses. The campanile dates from the twelfth century and the portico from 1220. The basilica was restored in the fifteenth and seventeenth centuries and again in the nineteenth, when the Baroque accretions were removed. It was badly damaged during an Allied

bombardment of Rome's railway marshalling yards in 1943, but has since been completely restored.

8. Constantine built the original BASILICA OF ST JOHN LATERAN over the site of the barracks of the imperial horse guards (*equites singulares*) who, because they had fought for Maxentius, had had their quarters destroyed during the pontificate of St Sylvester I (314–35). After being sacked by the Vandals, the building was restored by Pope Leo I (440–61), Pope Hadrian I (772–95) and a number of other popes. In

1304 it was badly damaged by fire, but it was fully restored by Urban V in 1368. The greatest change to the basilica occurred, however, during the pontificate of Sixtus V (1585–90) who rebuilt and reorganized the whole area of the Lateran to the designs of Domenico Fontana. The building which we see today is substantially his work, with the exception of the impressive façade which was added by Alessandro Galilei for Clement XII (1730–40). The lovely cloister was completed in 1230. The mosaics here, which rival those in the cloister of S. PAOLO FUORI LE MURA, are the work of the Vassallettos, father and son, masters of the Cosmatesque, the school of mosaic work which flourished in Rome from about 1100 to 1300 and which took its name from two craftsmen called Cosmas whose names are inscribed in the SANCTA SANCTORUM chapel.

9. About the year 200, the priest Gaius wrote, in a refutation of the Montanist heretic Proclus, that he could show him the tomb of St Peter on the Vatican. In the time of Constantine, the tradition that St Peter was buried on the Vatican hill during the Neronian persecution of A.D. 64 was firmly established. It has not been shaken by the recent excavations under the present basilica. But some confusion was created by the existence of evidence of the interment of both St

Peter and St Paul '*ad catacumbas*', that is to say, in the catacombs of St Sebastian on the Appian Way. The mystery has been explained by the transfer of the Apostles' relics to secret tombs for their safeguarding during the vicious persecution of the Christians under Valerian in 258. When Constantine brought peace to the Church, the bones of the Apostles were returned to their original resting-places. St Jerome mentions A.D. 336 as the date of this second translation of St Peter's remains. The first BASILICA OF ST PETER was begun about 320 and finished in 329. Initially it was a covered cemetery where Christians were laid to rest near the tomb of the Apostle. It was built over a pagan necropolis in which a Christian cult centre had gradually developed around the niche (*aedicula*) which marked St Peter's tomb. The ancient church was pillaged during the barbarian invasions of the fifth and sixth centuries and again by the Saracens in 846. It was often restored and embellished. At length, in 1452, Pope Nicholas V decided on the demolition and rebuilding of the edifice whose walls were no longer sound. The task was carried out by Pope Julius II (1503–13) and his successors.

10. The original basilica, built in the first half of the fourth century, was dedicated to the Apostles Peter and Paul whose bodies lay for a time in the adjoining catacombs. The place was already a cult centre when Constantine or his family erected the church. Later, after the body of St Sebastian had been buried there and when, perhaps, the connection of the place with the Apostles had faded from memory, the church became known as the BASILICA OF ST SEBASTIAN. The first church was a basilica with a nave and two aisles. Restored in the eighth and ninth centuries, it was handed over to the Benedictines in the second half of the twelfth century and rebuilt from 1609, at the behest of Cardinal Scipione Borghese, by two successive architects, Ponzio and Vacanzio. From this rebuilding the church emerged with a single nave as we see it today.

11. The last great work of classical imperial architecture, the BASILICA OF MAXENTIUS AND CONSTANTINE or BASILICA NOVA was begun by Maxentius in 306 and completed by Constantine in 312. Rectangular in shape, it measured 80 metres by 60 and had arches as high as 35 metres. The front faced east to the COLOSSEUM. The roof was covered with tiles of gilded bronze which were removed in 626 by

Honorius I to cover the old BASILICA OF ST PETER. The imposing remains of the basilica are in the northeast corner of the FORUM beside the church of SS. COSMAS AND DAMIAN.

12. The ARCH OF JANUS QUADRIFONS is near the river north-east of the Piazza Bocca della Verità (for which see note 32, below). The word Janus indicates a covered passage as well as being the name of the Latin divinity who was represented with two faces, one behind the other. Such arches were used at the crossways of important commercial centres, in this case the roads leading from the FORUM to the cattle and oil markets. The sculptured figures show a considerable decline compared with the sculpture of the best classical period. During the Middle Ages, the arch became for a time a fortified stronghold of the aggressive Frangipani family.

13. The site of Rome's ancient cattle market, the FORUM BOARIUM, coincides more or less with that of the present Piazza Bocca della Verità. It numbered several temples among its sights, including that of Fortune, of the late Republican period, and the erroneously named Temple of Vesta which was built in the time of Augustus or even earlier with twenty fluted Corinthian columns surrounding a circular cell. Both of these still stand. The market was held in the open without, apparently, any installations, the cattle salesmen standing beside their animals, the hay merchants beside their bales. Not far away, between the PONS AEMILIUS and the PONS FABRICIUS by the riverside, was another market, the FORUM HOLITORIUM, the oil and vegetable market which

contained large storehouses and some notable monuments such as the THEATRE OF MARCELLUS, the TEMPLE OF JANUS and the PORTICO OF OCTAVIA.

14. The ARCH OF CONSTANTINE is the best preserved of all the arches still remaining in the city. During the Middle Ages it became one of the strongholds of the Frangipani family. It was restored in the eighteenth century and finally detached from all its accretions in 1804. Of the sculptures, removed from

other monuments to adorn this arch, some, like the eight statues of barbarians and a large battle frieze over the central arch, were taken from one of Trajan's monuments. The medallions portraying hunting and sacrificial scenes are from one of Hadrian's buildings; while an arch built by Marcus Aurelius is thought to have contributed eight of the bas-reliefs of the architrave representing that emperor's wars.

15. The bridges over the Tiber and the Aniene listed in the table on p. 332 were built in Republican and imperial times. Those marked with asterisks no longer existed by the reign of Constantine.

16. The main Roman Aqueducts in the time of Constantine were as follows:

The Acqua Appia was completed in 312 B.C. by the Consul Appius Claudius from springs east of Rome.

The Acqua Anius Vetus (272 B.C.) brought spring water from the upper Anio valley.

The Acqua Marcia (144 B.C.) was built by the Praetor Marcius to supply the Capitol, Caelian and Aventine hills. Its arches later carried the waters of the Tepula (137 B.C.) and the Julia (33 B.C.) aqueducts.

The Acqua Virgo (19 B.C.) was built by Agrippa for

Name	Description and Location	Date
*Pons Sublicius	This was the most ancient of the bridges. Built in Rome close to the FORUM BOARIUM, it was made entirely of wood and was the bridge of the Horatian legend.	The time of the kings
Pons Salarius	This carried the Via Salaria across the Aniene River which joins the Tiber just north of Rome. It was destroyed by the Goths under Totila, rebuilt by Narses and demolished again by the French in 1867 to delay Garibaldi. It was restored in 1874 and enlarged in 1930. It is now the Ponte Salario.	Some time before 361 B.C.
Pons Aemilius	Built by the Censors M. Aemilius Lepidus and M. Fulvius Nobilior and finished by the Censors, P. Cornelius Scipio Aemilianus and L. Mummius, the bridge was supported on stone piers. It collapsed twice when Gregory XIII had it rebuilt in about 1575. It collapsed again in 1598, after which it remained broken and was known as the PONTE ROTTO. A fragment survives just above the present Ponte Palatino.	179–142 B.C.
Pons Milvius	Built or rebuilt by the Censor Marcus Aemilius Scaurus, this bridge was restored by Pope Nicholas V (1447–55) and again in 1805 by Valadier for Pope Pius VII. It was again restored by Pius IX after having been partially destroyed in 1849 when Garibaldi's forces were retreating from the French. It is now the PONTE MILVIO.	End of second century B.C.
Pons Fabricius	Built by the Consul L. Fabricius, it is the oldest bridge in use in Rome today. It joins the left bank of the Tiber to the island. It is now known as the PONTE FABRICIO.	62 B.C.
Pons Cestius	Built from the right bank of the Tiber to the island, it is now the PONTE CESTO.	46 B.C.
*Pons Agrippa	Near the PONTE SISTO (Pons Aurelianus, below).	Reign of Augustus
Pons Neronianus	Built by Nero near the present Ponte Vittorio Emanuele, it was later called Triumphalis and Vaticanus. It fell into decay before the year 403.	A.D. 54–68
Pons Aelius	Built by Hadrian to connect his mausoleum to the city, it is now called Ponte S. Angelo. Its architect was Demetrianus. The bridge is still standing but was altered by the addition of two arches in 1688, one at either end. Pope Clement IX (1667–9) commissioned Bernini to decorate it with statues of angels.	A.D. 136
Pons Aurelianus	This bridge was built by Marcus Aurelius. Destroyed in 792, it was replaced by Pope Sixtus IV in 1474. The first papal bridge to be built in Rome, it came to be known as the PONTE SISTO.	A.D. 161–80

his baths. Its water was mostly carried underground from springs on Lucullus's estate. Pope Nicholas V repaired the channel of the aqueduct, which had remained blocked for eight centuries, and had the final reservoir constructed in 1453. It was the only aqueduct bringing water to the city in the fifteenth century. Further restoration was carried out by Urban VIII. This is the aqueduct that feeds the FONTANA DI TREVI. Its name is supposed to commemorate a young girl who led some thirsty Roman soldiers to the springs.

The Acqua Claudia and Anius Novus were started by Caligula (A.D. 38) and finished by Claudius (A.D. 52). The Acqua Claudia, whose fine arches are a feature of the landscape of the Roman Campagna, carried water to Rome from Subiaco, forty-five miles away. The two aqueducts were joined three miles from Rome.

The Acqua Neroniana was built by Nero to take some of the water from the Claudian aqueduct directly to his palace on the Palatine.

The Acqua Trajana was built by Trajan in A.D. 109 to carry water, mostly underground, to the Janiculum.

The Acqua Alexandriana was built about A.D. 226. It was the last of the imperial Roman aqueducts.

In addition there were no less than ten other aqueducts which together have been estimated to have provided Rome with 350,000,000 gallons daily. The aqueducts suffered damage during the barbarian invasions but were mostly destroyed by neglect in the Middle Ages.

17. The BASILICA OF ST PAUL OUTSIDE THE WALLS, built by Constantine and consecrated by Pope Sylvester in 324, was erected on the spot where, it was believed, the body of the Apostle had been buried by his disciple, Timothy, soon after his execution. This church was destroyed in the time of the Emperor Theodosius in 386 and a much larger basilica, with nave and double aisles and containing eighty columns, was built to replace it and was consecrated in 390 by Pope Siricius, though not completed till 395. In the early seventh century, two monasteries were attached to the basilica and handed over to the Benedictines when united. To protect the church and the monastery from pirate raids, Pope John VIII (d. 882) built a defensive wall round the church and neighbouring buildings. In the course of later centuries the basilica was enriched with works

of art by Pietro Cavallini, Arnolfo di Cambio, the Vassallettos, Benozzo Gozzoli and Antoniazzo Romano. A new campanile was added in 1348. In 1823 the basilica was largely destroyed by fire, but work started almost immediately on a new church modelled on the old one. This was consecrated in 1850 by Pius IX. The beautiful early-thirteenth-century cloister, with its lovely mosaic-encrusted columns of different shapes and styles, which escaped destruction by fire, is perhaps by Pietro Vassalletto.

18. The ancient titular church of S. LORENZO IN DAMASO was founded by Pope Damasus (366–84) on the site of his house, though the present edifice dates only from the time of the PALAZZO DELLA CANCELLERIA into which it was incorporated by Bramante for Cardinal Riario. After being used as a stables by French troops during the Napoleonic occupation of Rome, the church was restored, first by Valadier who provided the façade and more completely in 1880 by Vespignani. A fire in 1944 again caused damage which led to further restoration under Pius XII. Two strong supporters of the papacy have their tombs in this church: Cardinal Scarampo who, when in charge of a papal flotilla, defeated the Turks at Mytilene in 1457, and Pellegrino Rossi, the last of Pius IX's Prime Ministers (see Chapter 15).

19. According to legend, the original church of S. PUDENZIANA was built over the site of the house in which St Peter was said, on no verifiable authority, to have lived for several years, converting its owner, the Senator Q. Cornelius Pudens, and his daughters, Pudenziana and Prassede, who were both diligent in gathering and burying the bones of martyrs. An oratory was certainly built on this spot in the reign

of Pope Pius I (*c.* 140–*c.* 155). It must, therefore, have been one of the earliest church buildings in Rome. In A.D. 384, when the church was restored or rebuilt by Pope Siricius, it was called for the first time *Ecclesia Pudentiana*. Further restoration followed under Popes Hadrian I (d. 795) and Gregory VII (d. 1085). The final reconstruction, which left the church as we see it today, was carried out in 1589 by Alessandro Volterra for Cardinal Caetani. The façade was restored by the only one of Napoleon's family to follow his advice and become a Prince of the Church, Cardinal Luciano Bonaparte, who bore a striking resemblance to the Emperor but was charming, shy and given to good works. The fourth-century mosaic in the apse depicting the Apostles gathered round Christ and looking like Roman senators is an evocation of classical Roman art without the addition of Eastern influences. According to Professor Richard Krautheimer it is 'the earliest figural representation to survive in, and presumably one of the first to be designed for, a Roman church'.

20. The name of s. PIETRO IN VINCOLI first appeared in the time of Pope Symmachus (d. 514) but it was not until the year 1000 that it was commonly used. The chains were said to have bound St Peter when he was a prisoner of King Agrippa I in Jerusalem and miraculously escaped, as recounted in Acts xii, 1–13. They were given by the Empress Eudoxia, wife of the Eastern Emperor Theodosius II, to their daughter, also called Eudoxia, who was married to the Emperor of the West, Valentinian III. Over the fabric of an earlier church, Pope Sixtus III (432–40), with the help of the younger Eudoxia, raised a new church which, to begin with, was dedicated to the Apostles. Sixtus IV (1471–84) rebuilt the church and Pope Julius II (1503–13) radically restored it. It was again restored and embellished by Pius IX on the occasion of his Jubilee. The church contains Michelangelo's statue of Moses. The chains are preserved in a reliquary under the high altar. There is a fine fourth-century sarcophagus in the *confessio* behind the altar.

21. The original BASILICA OF SS. JOHN AND PAUL ON THE CAELIAN was raised by one Pammachius, a friend of St Jerome and Senator, possibly in the pontificate of Pope Damasus (366–84). The church is thought to have suffered damage during Alaric's sack of Rome in 410, but it was soon restored. Further additions and repairs were carried out in the eleventh and twelfth centuries and again extensively from 1948 to 1952.

22. Gaius Sallustius Crispus (86–*c.* 34 B.C.) was a Roman politician and historian who acquired great wealth as Proconsular Governor of Numidia in Africa and was able to purchase an estate near Porta Pinciana, between the Quirinal and Pincian hills. Here he built the SALLUST PALACE or Villa and laid out gardens which became famous as the *Horti Sallustiani*. The remains of the palace can still be seen below street level in the middle of Piazza Sallustio. Sallust spent the rest of his life there in retirement writing history.

23. S. SABINA ON THE AVENTINE was founded by a priest, Peter of Illyria, and was built between 422 and 432 on the property of a Roman matron, Sabina, who was later identified with the Umbrian saint. It stands in a commanding position overlooking the Tiber. In 824 Pope Eugenius II added the *schola cantorum*, the *ambones* (pulpits) and the ciborium. In 1222 the church was handed over to St Dominic by

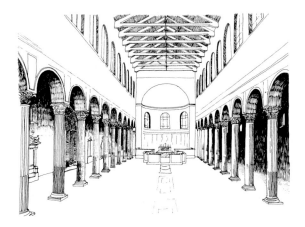

Pope Honorius III and it has been held by the Dominicans ever since. It was very well restored in 1936–8 when the ancient windows with their selenite panes, which had been walled up, were reopened. There are a number of fine frescos by the Zuccaro brothers, Federico and Taddeo. The adjoining monastery was founded by St Dominic in 1220.

24. The fourth of the patriarchal basilicas, after ST JOHN LATERAN, ST PETER'S and ST PAUL'S, S. MARIA MAGGIORE was built on the Esquiline hill where a cult of the mother goddess, Juno Lucina, had been based. When, following the Council of Ephesus which promoted veneration of the Virgin Mary as Mother of God, Pope Sixtus III (432–40) decided to build a basilica in her honour, this obviously seemed a suitable spot. The church, with its splendid classical

columns lining the nave, displays, more than any other in Rome, the striking contrast between its classical origin and its Baroque additions. With most, however, the classical aspect is outside and the Baroque within. Here it is the reverse. The fifth-century mosaics along the walls above the architrave, and those surrounding the high altar, are among the finest treasures of the basilica. There is also a marvellous Cosmatesque pavement. The Renaissance ceiling is believed to have been gilded with the first gold brought from America. The statue of Pope Paul IX kneels before a reliquary containing pieces of wood and metal bands which are traditionally supposed to have formed part of Christ's crib. Nicholas IV (1288–92) rebuilt the apse, Clement X (1670–76) the façade at the rear, and Benedict XIV (1740–58) the front, to the designs of Ferdinando Fuga. The campanile is of 1377 and, at 75 metres, the highest in Rome.

25. S. STEFANO ROTONDO is one of the oldest churches in Italy to have been built on a circular plan. It was once thought that its shape was imposed upon it by its being constructed upon the curve of one of Rome's markets, the Macellum Magnum, which was erected in the time of Nero. It is, in any case, likely that it had been built on an earlier foundation when it was consecrated by Pope Simplicius (d. 483) and dedicated to St Stephen whose cult was already widespread in Rome. The church is entered by a portico with five arches added by Pope Innocent II (1130–43). At the end of the sixteenth century the enclosing wall was frescoed with a series of gruesome paintings of the

tortures of a number of well-known martyrs. One of the chapels which surround the church contains a marble seat said to have been the episcopal throne of St Gregory the Great.

26. The church of S. GIORGIO IN VELABRO probably dates back to the sixth century. It was rebuilt by Pope Leo II (682–3) and completely restored in 1926 when it was freed from its Baroque accretions. The Romanesque tower and the portico are of the twelfth century. The Velabro (Velabrum) is the flat land between the Capitol and Palatine hills and the Tiber. It was originally a swamp, drained by the CLOACA MAXIMA, which became one of the busiest centres of the city. According to Plautus in his play Curculio, it was the meeting-place of bakers, butchers, fortune-tellers and dancers. From the FORUM, the Vicus Jugarius and the Vicus Tuscus led to the river across the Velabro.

27. The Via Lata was the main road running north and south through Rome during the Middle Ages. It followed the urban sector of the ancient Via Flaminia leading to the Porta Flaminia. Its track is now followed by the Corso. A first church, dedicated to S. Siricius who was Pope from 384 to 399, was built by Pope Sergius III (904–11), on the site of the SAEPTA JULIA where one of the earliest diaconiae had been established. This first church was replaced by the present Basilica of S. MARIA IN VIA LATA which was erected by Pope Leo IX (1048–54). That, in turn, was almost entirely rebuilt by Pope Innocent III (1484–92) towards the end of the fifteenth century. Pietro da Cortona (1658–62) designed the façade.

28. The church of SS. COSMA E DAMIANO, which was built in 527 into the remains of Vespasian's Forum of Peace, was dedicated to the two saints, doctors martyred in Syria, whose cult became widespread in the fifth century. The sixth-century mosaic in the apse is one of the earliest and most exquisitely fashioned in Rome. Part of it was restored in the seventeenth century by the Barberini Pope, Urban VIII, the bees of whose coat of arms can be seen in the left-hand corner.

29. S. MARIA ANTIQUA, the oldest church in the FORUM, was rebuilt by Pope John VII (705–7) and embellished by Pope Zacharias (741–52) and Pope Paul I (757–67). The church was abandoned after an earthquake; and in the thirteenth century a new church, dedicated to S. Maria Liberatrice, was built on its ruins. This was demolished in 1902 when work was begun on the restoration of S. Maria Antiqua to its original state. The rare eighth-century frescos are

very probably the work of refugees from the iconoclastic persecution in the Eastern Church.

30. The church of S. MARIA AD MARTYRES, later to be known as S. MARIA ROTONDA, was consecrated in the PANTHEON in 609 as the church of St Mary and all the Saints and Martyrs. (For the Pantheon see note 16, Chapter 3.) Twenty-eight wagonloads of martyrs' bones were brought here from the catacombs by Pope Boniface IV.

31. The church of S. ADRIANO was deconsecrated in 1937 and the building restored as it had been when it was reconstructed by Diocletian after a fire in 289.

32. The church of S. MARIA IN COSMEDIN was originally built in the sixth century on the site of the *Statio Annonae*, the headquarters of ancient Rome's food supply organization, some columns of which were incorporated into the church and can still be seen. The church was enlarged in the eighth century. It had a *diaconia* attached to it as well as a *matroneum*, a gallery for women above the aisles. The Cosmatesque pavement, choir, portico and lovely campanile are all

of the twelfth century. Cosmedin probably recalls the *Kosmidion* of Constantinople. The church was restored in 1899 to its twelfth-century appearance

under the direction of G. B. Giovenale who had Giuseppe Sardi's eighteenth-century façade and other accretions removed. It is now one of the finest early Christian buildings in Rome. In the portico stands the celebrated Bocca della Verità from which the piazza takes its name. This Mouth of Truth, an ancient drain-covering, was used in the Middle Ages in trials by ordeal. Suspects were required to place their hands in the open mouth. If they lied the lips would close, severing their fingers.

33. The church of SS. VINCENZO E ANASTASIO is near the Trappist ABBAZIA DELLE TRE FONTANE south of Rome and just east of the E.U.R. suburb. Its site was, according to tradition, the place of St Paul's martyrdom. Between 561 and 568, in the reign of Pope John III, a monastery and a church were built in this locality and entrusted to Greek monks. These two foundations were originally dedicated to St Paul, but rededicated in honour of St Anastasius when the relics of this Persian martyr were moved there early in the seventh century. The church and monastery were famous throughout the Middle Ages and received donations of land both from the Emperor Charlemagne and from Pope Leo III (795–816). In 1081, Pope Gregory VII replaced the Greek monks by Benedictines who were followed by Cistercians in 1138. In that year Pope Innocent II rebuilt the monastery and restored the church (already known as the church of SS. Vincent and Anastasius) to which he added a portico. The church was again rebuilt in 1221 by Honorius III and finally restored at the end of the nineteenth century. Nearby are the churches of S. PAOLO ALLE TRE FONTANE, a fifth-century foundation rebuilt by Giacomo della Porta in 1559, and S. MARIA SCALA COELI, which was also rebuilt by della Porta and which takes its name from St Bernard's dream of an angel leading a soul up a flight of steps to heaven. There is another Church of SS. VINCENZO E ANASTASIO in Rome. This is near the TREVI FOUNTAIN and was rebuilt by Martino Longhi the younger for Cardinal Mazarin in 1650. It is the parish church of the QUIRINAL PALACE.

34. The BASILICA OF S. PANCRAZIO dates back to the fifth century and possibly to the fourth. It was built near the PORTA S. PANCRAZIO on the Janiculum beside the tomb of St Pancras who, so legend has it, was martyred under Diocletian. After its restoration by Honorius I, and by Hadrian I, the church was completely transformed by the addition of a new

façade in 1609 and an apse in 1675. It was damaged during the French invasion of Rome in 1798, and in the fighting between Garibaldi's troops and the French in 1849. It was repaired in 1934.

35. The BASILICA OF S. AGNESE FUORI LE MURA had been built over the saint's tomb some time before 349 by Princess Constantia who was buried on the site of the nearby Church of S. COSTANZA which was consecrated as a church in 1254 and contains some of the finest mosaics in Rome. The basilica was completely rebuilt by Pope Honorius I and restored by various other popes including Hadrian I (772–95) and Pius IX (1846–78). Yet, as Georgina Masson said, it remains 'one of the rare Roman churches which has best preserved the appearance – and the atmosphere – of a very ancient Christian place of worship'. According to tradition, St Agnes was forced to enter a brothel when her Christianity was revealed, but her hair grew miraculously to cover her nakedness and, awed by her demeanour, the men left her alone. One, however, attempted to rape her, was struck blind in the process and was healed by her with prayer. She was later beheaded under the persecution of the Christians by Diocletian in 314. Over the supposed place of her execution was built the church of S. AGNESE IN AGONE which adjoins the PALAZZO PAMPHILJ. This church was reconstructed in part in 1652 for Pope Innocent X by Girolamo and Carlo Rainaldi, and completed with modifications by Borromini from 1653 to 1657.

5. INFAMY AND ANARCHY

1. When the AURELIAN WALLS were built in 271–5, they did not include the area of the Vatican hill across the river. In 846 the Saracens, after crossing the Mediterranean from Africa, sailed up the Tiber and sacked the churches outside the Aurelian Walls, notably ST PETER'S and ST PAUL'S. The shock of this attack, and the threat of a repetition in 849, induced Pope Leo IV (847–55) to complete the work of enclosing the Basilica of St Peter's and its surrounding buildings within a defensive wall. All the towns and convents in the Papal Estates bore a share of the cost and the Emperor Lothar himself made a notable contribution. The work was begun in 847 and completed in 853, the labouring force being supplied by levies from the *domus cultae*, the great Church farms, and from the churches and monasteries in the Campagna. The LEONINE WALL ran from CASTEL SANT' ANGELO to the foot of the hill behind St Peter's and then turned back until it reached the river again at the south end of the OSPEDALE S. SPIRITO. It included forty-six fortified towers and the area it enclosed came to be known in the Middle Ages as the Borgo, though Leo called it the *Civitas Leonina*. Four gates led into this Leonine City, the first being the PORTA SANT' ANGELO by the castle (known later as the PORTA CASTELLI). The second was the PORTA PELLEGRINI which was near the church dedicated to St Pellegrino on the north side of the Vatican and through which the emperors made their state entry. Next was the SAXON GATE (*Posterula Saxonum*) on the south side of the VATICAN, leading to the TRASTEVERE district where the PORTA S. SPIRITO now stands. The fourth has not been identified.

2. The first church on the site of S. PRASSEDE (which is between S. MARIA MAGGIORE and the LATERAN off the Via Merulana) is mentioned in an inscription of 491. This church was restored by Pope Hadrian I (772–95) and entirely rebuilt in 822 by Pope Paschal I to shelter the relics of the saints taken from the catacombs. It is Pope Paschal's church, with subsequent alterations in the fifteenth, seventeenth and nineteenth centuries, that we see today. It was built as a basilica with a nave and two aisles, recalling on a small scale ST PETER'S with its annular crypt. It is fairly representative of church building in Rome during the Carolingian renaissance. The fine pavement is modern (1914) but in the Cosmatesque manner. There are admirable mosaics over the triumphal arch of the high altar and in the apse dating from the time of Paschal I. The church is said to cover the site of the house where St Prassede sheltered persecuted Christians, twenty-three of whom were discovered and executed in her presence. The church contains one of Bernini's earliest works, completed when he was about nineteen, a small bust of Bishop G. B. Santoni (d. 1593) on one of the columns in the nave.

3. The CHAPEL OF ST ZENO in S. PRASSEDE is the most important Byzantine art work in Rome. It was built by Pope Paschal I (817–24) for his mother, Theodora, who is depicted with a square halo, indicating that she was still alive when the chapel was under construction. It is covered with mosaics of such beauty that in medieval Rome it was called 'the Garden of Paradise'. To the right of the chapel is a fragment of oriental jasper, believed to be part of the

column to which Christ was bound before being scourged.

4. Built in the fourth century, ss. QUATTRO CORONATI was enlarged by Pope Honorius I (625–38) and had its roof repaired under Pope Hadrian I (772–95). Pope Leo IV (847–55) restored the entire building and brought to it the four bodies of the martyrs to whom the church was dedicated. These martyrs were listed in the early Jeromian Martyrology as Saints Severus, Severianus, Carpoforus and Vittorinus and were venerated in Rome on 8 November on the Caelian hill. They were Roman soldiers executed for refusing to sacrifice to a statue of Aesculapius, but in the course of time they were confused with sculptors who were martyred under Diocletian for declining to make a statue of the pagan deity. The church was burned down in 1084 by the Normans under Robert Guiscard and rebuilt by Pope Paschal II between 1111 and 1116. Pius IV (1559–65) redecorated the basilica and gave the adjoining newly rebuilt convent into the keeping of Augustinian nuns. The cloister of this convent is one of the earliest in Rome.

5. S. MARTINO AI MONTI, on the Monte Oppio close to the site of TRAJAN'S BATHS, is one of the oldest foundations in Rome. Originally a titular church ascribed to one Equitius, it was converted into a basilica by Pope Symmachus (498–514) who dedicated it to St Martin of Tours, the great missionary of the Church in Gaul. After restoration by Pope Hadrian I in 772, the church was entirely rebuilt by Pope Sergius II (844–7). It was modernized to designs by Pietro da Cortona from 1635 to 1664 under the Barberini Pope, Urban VIII, and his successors. The façade belongs to this period. And it was at this time that the ancient *titulus Equitii* was discovered among the foundations of Trajan's Baths, and immediately restored to its former use as a chapel. The gilded ceiling was donated by S. Carlo Borromeo. The walls were frescoed by Poussin's brother-in-law, Dughet, between 1645 and 1650.

6. Situated in the FORUM next to the BASILICA OF MAXENTIUS AND CONSTANTINE, the church of S. MARIA NOVA was built in the second half of the tenth century to replace the fifth-century S. MARIA ANTIQUA after its destruction by an earthquake in 896. The old church had occupied a site across the Forum on the slope of the Palatine hill. S. Maria Nova incorporated a chapel to SS. PETER AND PAUL which Pope Paul I (757–67) had built over a portico of the

TEMPLE OF VENUS AND ROME. When S. Francesca Romana established her community of Oblates Regular of St Benedict (apparently the first foundation of a religious community by a Roman since the time of St Gregory the Great), the church was renamed after her. It was given its Baroque appearance in 1600–1615. The façade is by Carlo Lombardi (1615). There is a fifth-century encaustic picture of the Madonna and Child in the crypt, a remarkable example of early Christian art. The beautiful campanile dates from about 1160.

7. The church of S. MARIA IN DOMNICA derives from the first *diaconia* established in Rome. In early Christian times *dominicum* signified a church. It was rebuilt by Pope Paschal I (817–24) and renovated in about 1512 by Cardinal Giovanni de' Medici, later Pope Leo X, who probably employed Andrea Sansovino as architect for the splendid porch which has also been attributed to both Peruzzi and Raphael. The church was restored in 1820. The fine mosaics in the apse are from the time of Paschal I. In Piazza della Navicella is a charming fountain in the shape of a small boat (*navicella*). This was copied, at the desire of Leo X, from a classical model. The church is also called La Navicella.

8. The original church of S. CECILIA IN TRASTEVERE seems to have been built by a Roman woman of rank who was named after the martyred saint. At the end

of the sixth century St Gregory the Great reconstructed it as a basilica which was rebuilt by Paschal I (817–24) who attached a convent. The portico and campanile were added in the twelfth century. The interior of the church has been transformed by successive restoration in 1725, 1823 and 1955. But in the gallery above the entrance enough remains of Cavallini's 'Last Judgement', painted in 1293, to identify it as one of the greatest masterpieces of medieval art in Rome. The statue of the saint is by Stefano Maderno who saw her sarcophagus opened in 1599 and made a sketch of her as she was found and as he afterwards sculpted her, lying on her side in a golden robe with the wounds showing on her neck. The tabernacle over the high altar is by Arnolfo di Cambio. In the apse behind it is a superb ninth-century mosaic made for Paschal I who is shown being introduced by St Cecilia to Christ in heaven. The monumental gateway to the entrance courtyard (1725) is by Ferdinando Fuga who also built the façade of the church. Between S. Cecilia in Trastevere and the Lungotevere Ripa is the delightful small Romanesque church of S. MARIA IN CAPPELLA. Founded at the end of the eleventh century, this has one of the oldest campaniles in Rome. The garden beside it was made by Donna Olimpia Pamphilj, sister-in-law of Innocent X, whose descendants built the surrounding hospice for the aged poor in the nineteenth century. Opposite the west end of S. Cecilia is S. GIOVANNI DEI GENOVESI. The church of the Genoese community in Rome, it was built during the pontificate of Sixtus IV (1471–84), himself a native of Savona near Genoa. It was completely restored in 1864. To the left of the church is the Ospizio dei Genovesi, whose lovely fifteenth-century cloister is attributed to Baccio Pontelli.

9. In the days of the Roman Republic there were four city wards or *regiones*. By 7 B.C. the number had been increased to fourteen; and under Alexander Severus (222–35) fourteen consular *curatores* were instituted under a *Praefectus Urbis*. These, with their approximate locations were:

Porta Capena	Round the Park of Porta Capena
Caelimontium	Caelian hill
Isis et Serapis	Quirinal hill
Templum Pacis	The Subura, Via Cavour, the Viminal
Esquiliae	The Esquiline
Alta Semita	The Gardens of Sallust
Via Lata	The Corso
Forum Romanum	The Forum
Circus Flaminius	Campus Martius
Palatium	The Palatine
Circus Maximus	The area around the Circus
Piscina Publica	The Baths of Caracalla
Aventina	The Aventine
Trans Tiberum	Trastevere

The *rioni* of the Middle Ages gradually evolved out of these *regiones*, though they varied from time to time in number and size as a result of fusions and divisions. In the fifteenth century there were thirteen *rioni* to which, in 1586, a fourteenth was added by the inclusion of the Leonine City or Borgo. These were:

Monti	The high ground on the east side of the city
Trevi	Includes most of the Quirinal hill
Colonna	North from Via del Tritone between the Corso and Via Sistina
Campo Marzo	The most northerly *rione* near PIAZZA DEL POPOLO
Ponte	The area inside the first big river bend
Parione	Around PIAZZA NAVONA
Regola	Along the river from Ponte V. Emanuele on both sides of the Via Giulia
S. Eustachio	Around the church of that name west of the PANTHEON
Pigna	Includes the PANTHEON and borders on the Corso Umberto and the Corso V. Emanuele
Campitelli	Includes the Capitol, FORUM and Palatine
S. Angelo	The area around S. Angelo in Pescheria near the Tiber Island
Ripa	Includes the Tiber Island and the Aventine
Trastevere	The whole urban area on the right bank of the river excluding the Borgo
Borgo	ST PETER'S, the VATICAN

A further eight *rioni* were brought into being by a decision of the Roman Municipal Council on 9 December 1921. These are:

Esquilino	From Quattro Fontane to the LATERAN
Ludovisi	The area south of Porta Pinciana and Porta Salaria
Sallustiano	South-west from Porta Salaria to Porta Pia
Castro Pretorio	Porta Pia to Porta S. Lorenzo
Celio	Porta Metronia to Porta S. Sebastiano
S. Saba	Porta S. Sebastiano to Porta S. Paolo
Testaccio	Porta S. Paolo to the Tiber
Prati	North of CASTEL SANT' ANGELO and the Borgo

Outside the *rioni* the rapidly developing city has been divided into twenty-five *quartieri*.

10. A remarkable and huge construction of large stone blocks, faced with Corinthian columns in three tiers separated by wide architraves, the SEPTIZONIUM or SEPTIZODIUM resembled the *scenae frons* of a Roman theatre. Dedicated by the Emperor Septimius Severus in 203, it was built against the south-eastern slope of the Palatine so that it could be seen by travellers approaching Rome from the south along the Via Appia. It rose from the bottom of the valley to the level of the imperial palaces on the Palatine hill. Substantial parts of it were still standing when Pope Sixtus V (1585–90) had it entirely demolished.

11. St Clement was accounted the third successor of St Peter. He was venerated as a martyr and known as the writer of a famous letter to the Church in Corinth. Built before 385, the church named after him in Via S. Giovanni in Laterano, S. CLEMENTE, is one of the oldest basilicas in Rome. It is made up of two churches, one above the other, resting on several layers of earlier Roman remains including those of a Mithraic shrine and a first-century house, part of which was used as a place of secret Christian worship. The excavated remains of this house and temple are still to be seen deep below the pavements of the modern city. The lower church, mentioned by St Jerome in 392, was restored in the eighth and ninth centuries and then totally destroyed by the Normans in 1084. In 1108 Pope Paschal II built the upper church which was reconstructed by Carlo Fontana during the pontificate of Clement XI (1700–1721). There are fine mosaics in the apse, an outstandingly vivid painting of the Annunciation by

the Florentine artist, Masolino, and a beautiful Cosmatesque pavement. The church has been in the care of Irish Dominicans since 1667.

12. Said to have been founded by Pope Calixtus I (218–22) and completed by Pope Julius I (337–52), S. MARIA IN TRASTEVERE, which stands in the heart of this *rione*, is one of the oldest churches in Rome. Rebuilt by Pope Innocent II (1130–43) of the Trastevere family, the Papareschi, it was restored by Pope Clement XI (1700–1721) who added the portico by Carlo Fontana, and in 1870 by Pius IX. There are outstanding twelfth-century mosaics by Byzantine craftsmen in the apse, and below them other splendid thirteenth-century mosaics by Pietro Cavallini. The lovely mosaics on the façade were probably completed in the thirteenth century.

13. S. BARTOLOMEO IN ISOLA, the church on the Tiber Island, was built by the German Emperor Otto III (980–1002) over the ruins of a Temple of Aesculapius and dedicated to the Emperor's friend, St Adalbert. It was restored in 1113 by Pope Paschal II and again in 1180 after it had been rededicated to St Bartholomew. It was demolished by a flood in 1557 and rebuilt in 1624 by the Roman architect, Orazio Torriani. The campanile is of the twelfth century.

14. The fifth-century church of S. CRISOGNO was rebuilt in 1130 by the Papareschi Pope, Innocent II. It underwent radical restoration in 1626 in the Baroque style of G. B. Soria, but was allowed to retain its splendid Romanesque campanile. Beneath the church, excavations have revealed the hall of a large building of the fourth century which was used as a *titulus* (see note 1, Chapter 8).

15. The fifth-century church of S. GIOVANNI A PORTA LATINA was founded by St Gelasius I (492–6), rebuilt in 722 by Pope Hadrian I and reconsecrated by Pope Celestine III in 1191. Recent alterations have restored its ancient simplicity. The lovely campanile is of the twelfth century.

16. Built before the tenth century, the church of SS. BONIFACIO E ALESSIO on the Aventine hill was largely rebuilt in 1750.

17. The residence of the popes which was originally attached to ST PETER'S on the Vatican hill was a modest mansion erected by Pope Symmachus (498–514) when he was ousted from his palace at the

LATERAN by the Emperor Theodoric the Great. But as the Emperors Charlemagne and Otto II both stayed at the VATICAN during their visits to Rome, Charlemagne in 781 and 800 and Otto in 980, the residence must by then have been imposing enough. Restored by Popes Eugenius III in 1150 and Celestine III in about 1191, it was enlarged by Innocent III (1198–1216) and Nicholas III (1277–80). And since the Lateran Palace had become uninhabitable during the papal transfer to Avignon, Gregory XI, on his return to Rome in 1377, took up residence in the Vatican. His successors expanded the Vatican buildings enormously. Notable were the extensions of Nicholas V (1447–55), who created the Papagallo courtyard; of Sixtus IV (1471–84), who in 1473 built the Sistine Chapel; of Innocent VIII (1484–92) who was responsible for the Palace of the Belvedere; of Alexander VI (1492–1503) who raised the Borgia Tower. Julius II, Paul III, Gregory XIII and Sixtus V all made further extensive additions. The railway station was added in this century by Pius XI.

18. The TOR DE' CONTI, built by the family of Pope Innocent III (1198–1216), was considered one of the marvels of the Middle Ages in Rome. Petrarch thought it 'unique in the whole city'. A violent earthquake in 1348 demolished the upper part, leaving no more than a stump.

19. The hospital, built in 1198 by Pope Innocent III, was put in charge of Guy de Montpellier, the founder of the nursing order of the Holy Spirit in France. The hospital stands on the right bank of the Tiber close to the Porta S. Spirito within the Leonine City or Borgo. The founder of the *Burgus Saxonum*, the quarter from which the Borgo derived its name, was in all likelihood King Ine of Wessex who renounced his kingdom in 726 in order to spend his remaining days in Rome. He had built a church, dedicated to the Virgin, for the pilgrims of the Saxon nation on the site now occupied by the Renaissance church of S. SPIRITO IN SASSIA which was rebuilt after the Sack of Rome in 1527 by Antonio da Sangallo the younger. To King Ine's early church other buildings were attached including a hospice, but the institution had fallen into decay when Innocent III expropriated it in 1198 to found a new general hospital. The existing ARCIOSPEDALE DI S. SPIRITO IN SASSIA was erected by Pope Sixtus IV between 1473 and 1478 after the destruction of the old hospital by fire in 1471.

20. The porch of the PORTICO OF OCTAVIA became the site of a fish market which continued to function until recent times. Parts of the ruins of the portico were transformed into the atrium of the church of S. ANGELO IN PESCHERIA which was probably founded by Pope Stephen III (768–72). It was from this church that Cola di Rienzo set forth to establish the Republic of Rome on the night of Pentecost 1347.

21. Originally a *diaconia*, the Church of SS. SERGIO E BACCO, rebuilt by Pope Innocent III, survived near the ARCH OF SEPTIMIUS SEVERUS until it was demolished to make way for the triumphal procession of Charles V in 1536.

22. The head and hand of the statue of Constantine are now in the courtyard of the PALAZZO DEI CONSERVATORI.

23. The bronze tablet recording the transfer of power from Augustus to Vespasian is now in the Salone del Fauno in the CAPITOLINE MUSEUM.

24. The sculpture of the boy picking a thorn from his foot, a late Hellenistic sculpture of the first century B.C., is in the Sala dei Trionfi di Mario in the PALAZZO DEI CONSERVATORI.

25. The statue of the she-wolf is in the Sala della Lupa in the PALAZZO DEI CONSERVATORI. It is of Etruscan origin and is thought to be the work of Vulca of Veii or his school and dates from the sixth century B.C. or the beginning of the fifth. The twins Romulus and Remus were added by Antonio Pollaiuolo in 1498.

26. Situated in what is now the Piazza S. Silvestro, S. SILVESTRO IN CAPITE was built by Pope Stephen II (752–7) on the ruins of a Temple of the Sun erected by the Emperor Aurelian. The church's most prized relic is the head of St John the Baptist, hence its name. In the Middle Ages the monks made large sums by charging pilgrims for seeing the COLUMN OF MARCUS AURELIUS which was then in their possession.

27. The VILLA MATTEI, built in 1582, was reconstructed in the mock Gothic style by an Englishman at the beginning of the nineteenth century. Parts of the DOMUS AUGUSTANA were incorporated into the structure. Now known as the VILLA CAELIMON-

TANA, its grounds are a public park. The Egyptian obelisk, dedicated to Rameses II, is at the end of the short avenue in front of the entrance. It was probably taken from the Temple of Isis on the Capitol where it had stood at the foot of the Aracoeli steps. It was presented to Ciriaco Mattei by the Senate. The PALAZZO MATTEI DI GIOVE off the Via dei Funari was built by Carlo Maderno in 1598–c. 1611 for the rich Asdrubale Mattei, part of whose collection of antique sculptures can be seen in the courtyard. The palace was extended in 1613–17. Beneath the windows of the palace, in the Piazza Mattei, is the charming FONTANA DELLE TARTARUGHE (tortoises). This was probably designed by Giacomo della Porta and executed in 1585 by Taddeo Landini.

28. The various buildings which were constructed in the early Middle Ages on the ruins of the TABULARIUM included a palace for the Senators. This was built after the revolt of 1143 for the fifty-six Senators then elected. The number of Senators was soon drastically reduced, and after 1358 there was only one. The present PALAZZO DEL SENATORE, designed by Giacomo della Porta and Girolamo Rainaldi, replaced the earlier palace in 1582–1605. The twin flight of steps overlooking the Piazza del Campidoglio was designed by Michelangelo (see note 5, Chapter 11). The clock tower which dominates the piazza is by Martino Longhi the elder (c. 1580).

29. The remnant of a medieval tower known as the CASA DEI CRESCENZI on the corner of the Via del Teatro di Marcello and the Piazza della Bocca della Verità probably belonged to the Crescenzi, one of the most powerful families in Rome towards the end of the tenth century. It dates from the twelfth century and contains fragments of classical monuments embedded in the brickwork.

6. SAINTS, TYRANTS AND ANTI-POPES

1. In the ninth century, the Benedictines took over a monastery formerly occupied by Greek monks on the highest point of the Capitoline hill, the site of the present church of S. MARIA D'ARACOELI. The Benedictines built the original church in 1250, parts of which are preserved in the present structure. In the Middle Ages it became a meeting place such as the FORUM had formerly been. Cola di Rienzo often harangued the people from its steps. Later the Benedictines handed it over to the Franciscans who made it their headquarters in Rome. The fine, steep flight of steps in marble, 122 in number, leading from the Piazza d'Aracoeli to the church, was built in 1348. The statue (by Girolamo Masini, 1887) between the steps and the CORDONATA is of Cola di Rienzo who was, mistakenly, believed to have been the first to mount them at their inauguration. In fact, he had fled from Rome shortly before they were finished. The interior of the church is in the form of a basilica with a nave and two aisles and eleven antique columns on each side. The painting on the ceiling commemorates the great naval battle of Lepanto where Christian forces defeated the Turks in 1571. The church was used as the culminating point of a Triumph offered that year by Rome to the commander of the papal militia, Marcantonio Colonna, who played a leading part in the battle. The church takes its name from an altar – ara coeli – which the Emperor Augustus was supposed to have raised after a vision in which he saw the heavens open and the Madonna and Child appear. This altar was for a long time taken to be the thirteenth-century altar upon which stands the urn that is said to contain the ashes of St Helena, the Emperor Constantine's mother. The magnificent frescos of the life of S. Bernardine of Siena in the Bufalini chapel are by Pinturicchio.

2. The BASILICA OF THE SS. APOSTOLI next to the PALAZZO COLONNA was originally built during the pontificate of Pelagius I (556–61), by Justinian's great general, Narses, to celebrate his victory over the Gothic leader, Totila, in 552. It was restored by Pope Martin V (1417–31), by Pope Sixtus IV (1471–84) and again by Pope Pius IV (1559–65). It was almost entirely rebuilt by Francesco Fontana and his father, Carlo, who finished it in 1714 during the pontificate of Clement XI (1700–1721). Finally it was given a simple, neo-classical façade to a design by Giuseppe Valadier in 1827. The large late-fifteenth-century portico is by Baccio Pontelli.

3. The church of S. MARCELLO is in a small piazza off the Corso on the right going north just after the PALAZZO CHIGI-ODESCALCHI. It was founded in the fourth century. The early church was destroyed by fire in 1519 and rebuilt to the designs of Jacopo Sansovino. The Baroque façade (1682–3) is by Carlo Fontana. It is said to cover the site of the stables of the central post office of imperial Rome where Pope St Marcellus I (304–9) was condemned to work by the Emperor Maxentius.

4. The church of S. LORENZO IN PANISPERNA, dedicated to St Laurence the Martyr, was originally built some time before the sixth century on the traditional site of the saint's martyrdom on the Viminal hill. It was restored in the eighth century and completely rebuilt by Pope Boniface VIII for the Jubilee Year of 1300. Another renovation was carried out in 1575, and nothing is now left of the ancient building. The church stands back from the street behind a court which was surrounded by the convent of the Poor Clares where St Bridget of Sweden begged for alms. The Via Panisperna, which runs like a switchback over the slopes of the Quirinal, the Viminal and Esquiline hills, may possibly have taken its name from the bread (*pane*) and ham (*perna*) that the monks at the church of S. Lorenzo distributed to the poor or, more probably, from two families, the Panis and the Perna, who lived there.

5. The church of S. MARIA SOPRA MINERVA is in the Piazza della Minerva close to the PANTHEON. It was built on the site of a Temple of Isis in about 1280 by the Dominicans, its architects being two of the friars. The adjoining convent was for a long time the headquarters of the order and is still run by them. This is the only ancient church in Rome built in the Gothic style. The burial place of several popes and members of the leading Roman families, it contains beautiful chapels in the classical and early Renaissance styles. Among these is the Carafa Chapel which was commissioned by the Neapolitan Cardinal Oliviero Carafa. This contains Filippino Lippi's superb fresco of the Assumption of Our Lady (1489) and the tomb of the Carafa Pope, the formidable Paul IV. Michelangelo's statue of Christ bearing the Cross is on the left of the high altar. It was carved as a completely nude figure in Florence in 1519–20 and in 1521 was sent to Rome where the finishing touches were inexpertly supplied by Michelangelo's assistant, Pietro Urbano. The gilded drapery and sandals were added later. The relics of St Catherine of Siena are preserved beneath the altar. There is a charming late-thirteenth-century mosaic Madonna and Child beside the fine Cosmatesque tomb of Bishop Durand of Mende (d. 1296) on the left of the Carafa Chapel.

7. 'THE REFUGE OF ALL THE NATIONS'

1. The stupendous FONTANA DI TREVI is set in a small piazza of the same name and can be reached from the Corso by the Via dei Sabini. It was the master

work of Nicola Salvi who began it for Pope Clement XII in 1732. Salvi died before it was finished and Gianpaolo Pannini supervised its completion in 1762. The water from this fountain feeds the fountains of Piazza Navona and Piazza Farnese as well as the *nymphaeum* in the VILLA GIULIA. The fountain probably takes its name from the *tre vie*, the three streets which meet in the piazza. In the nineteenth century it was said that visitors to Rome who drank water from the fountain would come back to Rome. Nowadays tourists throw coins into the basin to ensure their return to the city.

2. Built in 1479–83 near the Ponte Umberto by Jacopo di Pietrasanta for the rich French Cardinal Guillaume d'Estouteville, the church of S. AGOSTINO was constructed of travertine plundered from the COLOSSEUM. Its fine flight of steps flanked by a balustrade and simple façade are among the earliest examples of Renaissance art in Rome. The interior was redecorated in the eighteenth century by Vanvitelli. The church became a favourite place of worship of many of the intellectuals and humanists of the Roman Renaissance and, during their moments of repentance, of their courtesans. Cesare Borgia's mistress, Fiametta, had her own chapel here; and several other fashionable prostitutes were buried here, despite the regulation that required their interment beside the Muro Torto. In the second chapel on the left is a beautiful statuary group of St Anne with the Virgin and Child by Andrea Sansovino. Goritz commissioned the fresco of the Prophet Isaiah by Raphael on the third pilaster on the left of the nave. The famous Madonna and Child, whose foot has been worn smooth by the touch of thousands of mothers, brides and pregnant women throughout the centuries, is

by Jacopo Sansovino (1521). In the first chapel on the left is a remarkable painting by Caravaggio (1604) of the Madonna of the Pilgrims.

3. The central BRONZE DOORS OF ST PETER'S were commissioned by Pope Eugenius IV (1431–47) and completed by Filarete after twelve years of work in 1445. The reliefs on the front, above and below the figures of Saints Peter and Paul, represent scenes from the life of Pope Eugenius including the Council of Florence over which he presided in 1439. On the back of the doors are representations of Filarete and his assistants dancing about happily with tools in their hands beneath an inscription in execrable dog Latin which seems to suggest that, although others got the money for the work, Filarete and his men had the pleasure of executing it. The modern doors to the left of Filarete's are by Giacomo Manzù who, on the back, has provided a relief of the Vatican Second Ecumenical Council showing Pope John XXIII talking to an African cardinal, an allusion to Filarete's depiction of the Ethiopian monks who attended the Council of Florence and afterwards visited Rome. The door on the extreme right is the Holy Door which is opened only during a Holy Year when the Pope knocks on it with a silver hammer.

4. At the foot of the north-west slope of the Palatine hill, in the Via S. Teodoro which leads from the CIRCUS MAXIMUS to the FORUM, stands the ancient circular church of S. TEODORO which was built at the end of the sixth century as one of the *diaconiae*. It was restored a number of times, notably by Pope Clement XI in 1705. A singular Good Friday ceremony is organized here by the Confraternity of the Sacconi Rossi, the members of which appear in their sack-like garb with pointed hoods.

5. The church of SS. CELSO E GIULIANO was consecrated by Pope Celestine I in 432 and wholly rebuilt in 1733–5 by the Roman architect, Carlo de Dominicis.

6. Theodosius was the general who put an end to the Gothic invasion of the Eastern Empire after the battle of Adrianople in 379. He became Emperor of the East that year and sustained the two young half-brothers who inherited the Western Empire – Gratian, aged seventeen, and Valentinian II, aged four. Magnus Maximus tried to usurp the Western Empire and, having taken over the northern provinces in 383, attempted the invasion of Italy in 387.

He was defeated by Theodosius, who restored Valentinian II in 388. The ARCH OF GRATIAN, VALENTINIAN AND THEODOSIUS was erected to commemorate this victory.

7. A papal library had existed in the LATERAN PALACE, but the real founder of the present immense VATICAN LIBRARY was Pope Nicholas V, who increased the collection of books from 340 when he became pope in 1447 to 1,200 when he died in 1455. The library was expanded by Sixtus IV (1471–84) to 3,650 volumes and, after the loss of four hundred during the Sack of Rome, was further enormously increased throughout the sixteenth and seventeenth centuries by the accession of important bequests. By the end of the sixteenth century it had become impossible to house all the volumes, so Pope Sixtus V ordered the construction by Domenico Fontana of the impressive library building which is in use today. This is divided into halls and galleries decorated by various artists working for different popes. The Salone Sistina (1587–9) was built for Sixtus V, the Sala Paolina (1611) for Paul V, the Galleria Urbana for Urban VIII between 1623 and 1644, the Sala Alessandrina (1690) for Alexander VIII, the Galleria Clementina (1730) for Clement XII. The library and archives of the Vatican were opened to the public in 1881. The modernization of the library and the creation of facilities for research by scholars was undertaken in the pontificate of Pius XI (1922–39). Among the most interesting manuscripts to be seen in the collection are the fourth-century Bible (*Codex Vaticanus*); three copies of Virgil's works from the fourth and fifth centuries; Henry VIII's petition for the dissolution of his marriage to Catherine of Aragon; autograph poems by Petrarch and letters of St Thomas Aquinas, Martin Luther, Michelangelo and Raphael.

8. RENAISSANCE AND DECADENCE

1. The BASILICA OF S. MARCO is one of the oldest titular churches in Rome, a titular church being one of the twenty-five Roman churches, administered by priests, whose origins date from early Christian times. From the fourth century these churches were associated with cardinal priests who took their titles from them. The Basilica of S. Marco was founded by Pope Mark in 336 and dedicated to the Evangelist. Pope Hadrian I restored the church in 792 and it was almost entirely rebuilt by Pope Gregory IV in 833. The beautiful mosaic in the apse belongs to this

period. It depicts Christ the Redeemer with the donor, Pope Gregory, being introduced to Christ by St Mark. In the sixteenth century the church was again rebuilt by the Venetian Cardinal Pietro Barbo who was cardinal of S. Marco before becoming Pope Paul II (1464–71). It is this church which we see today. It became the church of the Venetians. The magnificent gilded ceiling (1466–8) by Giovannino and Mario de' Dolci and the grand portico and façade by Giuliano da Mariano and Leon Battista Alberti are among the finest works of the early Renaissance. They were made for Cardinal Barbo. Much of the interior decoration is a Baroque restoration carried out between 1740 and 1750 by Filippo Barigioni for Cardinal Angelo Querini.

2. Built in 1455–68 on the west side of the Piazza di San Marco by Cardinal Pietro Barbo, the PALAZ-ZETTO VENEZIA was originally intended for the reception of ambassadors and other important guests. It was demolished shortly before 1911 to open up the view of the VICTOR EMMANUEL II MONUMENT, and rebuilt on its present site on the west side of the piazza. The huge PALAZZO VENEZIA which is attributed to Leon Battista Alberti, was begun by Cardinal Pietro Barbo in 1455 and completed in 1467 by his nephew, Marco Barbo, who became titular Cardinal of S. Marco. It was the first great non-ecclesiastical building of the Renaissance to be erected in Rome. The Palazzo was retained as a papal

residence until 1564 when it was handed over by the Church to the Republic of Venice for the use of the Venetian ambassadors in Rome and for the titular cardinals of S. Marco who were always Venetian. In 1797 the palace became the property of the Austrian Empire by the Treaty of Campo Formio (by which Napoleon granted Venice and her possessions to Austria in exchange for imperial territories). The

Italian government claimed it in 1916 after the defeat of Austria by the Allies. Mussolini used it as his official headquarters. The palace contains a permanent museum and is now used for temporary exhibitions.

3. The PALAZZO DELLA CANCELLERIA, perhaps the most beautiful of all Roman palaces, was begun in 1483 and completed after several interruptions in 1517. The design of the palace has often been

attributed to Bramante who, however, did not arrive in Rome until 1499 when the building of the palace was well advanced. He may have been responsible for a part of it but the latest opinion is that the original design was by Andrea Bregno. The palace was confiscated from the Riario family by the Medici Pope Leo X (1513–21), who installed in it the offices of the papal chancellery, hence the name *Cancelleria*. The palace later on became the headquarters of the Tribune of the Roman Republic of 1798–9, and of Napoleon's court in 1810. It also housed the first Roman Parliament in 1848. As he entered the building on 16 November of that year Pio Nono's Prime Minister, Pellegrino Rossi, was murdered.

4. Situated in the Via delle Terme di Caracalla, the church of SS. NEREO E ACHILLEO is one of Rome's titular churches. It was also one of the city's *diaconiae*. First mentioned in 337, it was restored by Pope Leo III (795–816) and almost entirely rebuilt by Sixtus IV in the fifteenth century. It was completely redecorated when assigned as a titular church to the famous Oratorian scholar and historian, Cardinal Baronius, in 1597. The mosaic on the arch over the sanctuary representing the Transfiguration is of the time of Pope Leo III. SS. Nereus and Achilleus were,

according to Pope Damasus, two soldiers of the Roman army who, on becoming Christians, refused further service and were consequently martyred, probably during the persecutions of Domitian.

5. Standing just inside the PORTA DEL POPOLO, the church of S. MARIA DEL POPOLO was built as a chapel by Pope Paschal II in 1099. Enlarged as a parish church at the expense of the Roman people – hence the name – it was rebuilt by Sixtus IV in 1474 to the designs of Baccio Pontelli and Andrea Bregno. The side of the church along the piazza has been encased in a neo-classical shell, but the façade still retains its simple early Renaissance elegance. The church contains numerous fine works of art, several commissioned by Sixtus IV himself and other members of the della Rovere family. The most celebrated paintings are those by Pinturicchio in the della Rovere family chapel and those by Caravaggio in the small chapel to the left of the main altar. Other artists whose works are to be seen in the church are Raphael, Sebastiano del Piombo, Sansovino, Bernini and Carlo Maratta. The celebrated thirteenth-century icon of the Madonna on the high altar is traditionally attributed to St Luke. The stained-glass window of 1509 in the main chapel (which was extended for Pope Julius II by Bramante) is by Guillaume de Marcillat. Sansovino's splendid tombs of Cardinals Girolamo della Rovere and Ascanio Sforza behind the altar were commissioned by Julius II. The cardinals, recumbent above beautiful reliefs inspired by classical models, are represented as though asleep rather than lying in state as had formerly been the custom.

6. Attributed by some, though without conclusive evidence, to Baccio Pontelli, the church of S. MARIA DELLA PACE was built by Sixtus IV in about 1480 as a thank-offering for the conclusion of his war with Florence which started after the Pazzi conspiracy. The semicircular portico and the convex Baroque façade were added by Pietro da Cortona for Pope Alexander VII in 1656. Attached to the church is an almost perfect classical Roman cloister, Bramante's first building in Rome. Inside are Raphael's famous frescos of the Sybils of Cuma, Persia, Phrygia and Tibur, painted in 1514.

7. The PONTE SISTO spans the Tiber above the Isola Tiberina at the beginning of a straight stretch of river enclosed by the Lungotevere della Farnesina on the right bank and the Lungotevere dei Tebaldi on the left. Designed by Baccio Pontelli, it was built to replace a Roman bridge of Marcus Aurelius (see note 15, Chapter 4) which had been destroyed in 792. It was completed in 1474. This was more than a thousand years after the last imperial bridge had been thrown across the Tiber. The bridge, which commands a view of ineffable beauty, bears on the parapet the inscription: 'You who pass by here offer a prayer to God so that Sixtus IV, excellent Pontifex Maximus, may be healthy and for long so preserved. Any of you, whoever you are, to whom this request is made, be healthy too.'

8. Intended as a papal chapel for ecclesiastical ceremonies of a semi-public character, the SISTINE CHAPEL was consecrated by Sixtus IV on 15 August 1483. It is in the shape of a parallelogram, 132 feet by 45 feet. The walls on either side are unbroken for two thirds of their height, the windows throwing their light from above. Along each side wall is a set of frescos representing scenes from the life of Moses on the left side and from the life of Christ on the right. These were all painted from 1481 to 1483. In 1506 Pope Julius II called on Michelangelo to fresco the ceiling which till then had been decorated only with a painted blue sky studded with golden stars. From 10 May 1508 to 31 October 1512 the sculptor turned painter worked unremittingly. In 1534, Pope Clement VII persuaded Michelangelo to complete the decoration by painting a gigantic fresco to cover the whole of the great unbroken wall behind the high altar. The subject chosen was the Last Judgement.

9. The SAPIENZA had been re-established by Pope Eugenius IV (1431–47) on the present site of the Palazzo della Sapienza, whose façade conceals Borromini's church of S. IVO. It remained the headquarters of the university until the construction by Mussolini of the University City near San Lorenzo fuori le Mura from 1932 to 1935. The Sapienza was then taken over by the State Archives. The existing building is the work of Giacomo della Porta. Beyond the simple, rather severe façade lies a magnificent courtyard, with a portico and loggias on either side, bounded at the far end by Borromini's tour de force – the church of S. Ivo, built between 1642 and 1660 for the Barberini Pope Urban VIII, the ground plan being derived from the shape of the Barberini family's heraldic bee. The altarpiece, begun by Cortona in 1661, was completed by G. V. Borghesi after 1674. The church was dedicated by the lawyers of the Papal Consistory (the court at which papal

business was conducted) to their patron, St Ivo of Chartres.

The GREGORIAN UNIVERSITY, the pontifical university of Rome in Piazza della Pilotta, and its associated Biblical and Oriental Institutes, originated in the Roman College which was founded in 1551 by Ignatius Loyola as a training ground for laymen as well as priests and missionaries. This attracted so many pupils that it was moved to larger premises in a house belonging to the Frangipani family near the Church of S. Stefano del Cacco, and then to an even larger house of the Salviati near s. MARIA IN VIA LATA. The present university building is by Giulio Barluzzi (1927–30).

10. Built by Domenico Riario and later occupied by Girolamo Riario and his wife, Caterina Sforza, the RIARIO PALACE was renowned for its lovely garden. The property was acquired in the early eighteenth century by the Corsini family who commissioned Ferdinando Fuga to rebuild the palace as the PALAZZO CORSINI (1732–6). In 1797, Joseph Bonaparte moved into the palace as ambassador of the French Directory. It was acquired by the Italian State in 1884 and housed the art collection of the Corsinis which had been gradually expanded and has now

been transferred to the PALAZZO BARBERINI. Another RIARIO PALACE, attributed to Baldassare Peruzzi, was built from 1536 near the church of s. APOLLINARE which was founded by Pope Hadrian in 780 and remodelled by Ferdinando Fuga during the pontificate of Benedict XIV (1740–58). The palace was rebuilt by Martino Longhi the elder about 1580 for the Milanese Cardinal Marco Sittico Altemps of the Italian branch of the von Hohenems family. It is now the PALAZZO ALTEMPS and a Spanish seminary.

11. The PALAZZO SFORZA-CESARINI was built by Cardinal Rodrigo Borgia, later Alexander VI, in about 1462 on the site of the old papal *cancelleria*. It was here that the cardinal held some of his most lavish entertainments. It was rumoured that Borgia ceded it to Cardinal Ascanio Sforza as the price of his vote in the papal election. It was later acquired by the Cesarini family. The palace was completely rebuilt in 1888 to the designs of Pio Piacentini who retained one side of the fifteenth-century courtyard with its portico and loggia.

12. The TOR DI NONA was once part of an Orsini fortification which commanded the ferry crossing over the Tiber upstream of the present Ponte Umberto. For long a prison with a fearsome reputation, it was here that Benvenuto Cellini was held as well as Giordano Bruno.

13. The PALAZZO GIRAUD-TORLONIA in the Via della Conciliazione was built in 1496–1504 by Andrea Bregno for Cardinal Adriano Castellesi da Corneto, papal nuncio in England and a friend of Henry VII. It became the residence of Henry VIII's ambassadors to the Holy See until the Reformation when it passed to the Giraud family and then to the Torlonias, the papal bankers.

14. Along the left bank of the Tiber, at the level of the Ponte Cavour which was built in 1901, was the site of the second main port on the river now marked by the Piazza Porto di Ripetta. Possibly in existence in classical Roman times, the RIPETTA served traffic going down river and was in use until the late nineteenth century. It was built or rebuilt during the early Renaissance with large blocks of travertine which had fallen off the COLOSSEUM during the great earthquake of 1349.

15. The apartment in the VATICAN which Pope Alexander VI prepared for his own use lies below the

STANZE OF RAPHAEL in the part of the Vatican Palace built by Pope Nicholas V (1447–55) and partly in the tower which Alexander himself erected. These buildings are now at the south end of the CORTILE DEL BELVEDERE, which did not exist in Pope Alexander's time, and separate this court from the much smaller Cortile dei Pappagalli. The BORGIA APARTMENT consists of six rooms of different sizes on the first floor decorated by various artists. The superb frescos of Pinturicchio were painted between 1492 and 1495. In the fourth room, the Sala dei Santi, which contains some of Pinturicchio's finest work, the lives of St Paul the Hermit and St Catherine of Alexandria are portrayed, Lucrezia probably having served as a model for St Catherine. On 29 June 1500 Alexander VI was nearly killed when the ceiling of the sixth and largest room, the Sala dei Pontefici, collapsed. It was restored by Pope Leo X and decorated with stuccoes and frescos by Giovanni da Udine and Perin del Vaga. The apartment was used for a period to house the Vatican picture collection and then the printed books of the VATICAN LIBRARY.

9. PATRONS AND PARASITES

1. PASQUINO, the headless marble Greek torso of the third century B.C., which is said to represent Menelaus, stands on the pavement in a small triangular square, the Piazza di Pasquino, outside PALAZZO BRASCHI. It was placed here by Cardinal Carafa in 1501 after being unearthed during the repaving of the nearby Via dei Leutari. The popular pastime of attaching labels to the statue with critical and pungent comments on the activities of those in authority seems to have derived, together with the name, from a fifteenth-century tailor called Pasquino who worked in the neighbourhood, frequently for the papal court, about whose doings he commented with unusual freedom and vehemence. The statue itself was, however, first used for the purpose of protest during the reign of Alexander VI. Pasquino is only one of a number of ancient talking statues which the people of Rome have made the spokesmen of their complaints. Among the others are Marforio, a recumbent statue of Ocean in the courtyard of the CAPITOLINE MUSEUM; Madama Lucrezia, a copious female bust, possibly of Faustina, attached to the wall of PALAZZETTO VENEZIA and perhaps named after the sixteenth-century owner of some nearby houses, whose physical attributes resembled those of the

statue; Abate Luigi, a late classical figure in a toga, to be found in the Piazza Vidoni off the Corso V. Emanuele; the Fontanella del Facchino, a fountain alongside the church of S. MARIA IN VIA LATA which portrays a sixteenth-century water-carrier.

The comments of Pasquino have given a new word to many languages. Pasquinade entered the English language in 1658. An example of a pasquinade is given in translation in Rennell Rodd's *Rome*. It relates to the liberal distribution in Rome of Legion of Honour crosses to Roman collaborators by the Napoleonic administration:

> In fierce old times they balanced loss
> By hanging thieves upon a cross,
> But our humaner age believes
> In hanging crosses on the thieves.

2. The church of S. PIETRO IN MONTORIO was originally built on the Janiculan hill before the ninth century in the place where it was wrongly supposed that St Peter had suffered martyrdom. It was rebuilt, perhaps to designs by Baccio Pontelli, soon after 1481 on the order of Ferdinand and Isabella of Spain. In 1849 it was badly damaged during the fighting between Garibaldi's forces and the French, and was restored soon afterwards. The TEMPIETTO was built in a small courtyard to the right of the church to mark what was still at that time supposed to be the exact spot upon which St Peter was crucified.

3. An inscription on the ARCO DEI BANCHI records the height of a flood of the Tiber in 1276. When the river overflowed its banks near the Ponte Sant' Angelo in the Middle Ages the waters cascaded down the Via del Banco di S. Spirito and its continuation, the Via dei Banchi Novi, which was consequently then known as Canale di Ponte.

4. As well as the ARCO DEI BANCHI, the VIA DEL BANCO DI S. SPIRITO contains the PALAZZO NICCOLINI-AMICI built in the 1530s by Jacopo Sansovino for Roberto Strozzi, and the PALAZZO ALBERINI, later the PALAZZO CICCIAPORCI (see note 3, Chapter 10).

5. The VATICAN GARDENS OF JULIUS II, as laid out by Bramante, were described by an English traveller in 1549 as 'the goodliest thing in the world'. They extended in a northerly direction from the existing buildings of the VATICAN PALACE, which were adjacent to ST PETER'S, to the BELVEDERE over three hundred yards up the slope of the Vatican hill

where Pope Innocent VIII (1484–92) had decided to build a *palazzetto* for himself, well removed from the bustle of the papal palace and offices. The work was carried out by Jacopo da Pietrasanta, perhaps to designs by Pollaiuolo. Bramante planned to use the space between the PALAZZETTO DEL BELVEDERE and the Vatican offices for two long flanking buildings to enclose a large arena for tournaments and a garden. The work was never carried out as designed, though the east side of the enclosure was built and the garden, the GIARDINO DELLA PIGNA, laid out before the death of Julius II. Later, Sixtus V (1585–90) built the VATICAN LIBRARY across the enclosure, thus forming the CORTILE DEL BELVE-DERE and the CORTILE DELLA PIGNA. Later still another court, the CORTILE DELLA BIBLIOTECA, was created by the construction of another transverse wing, the Braccio Nuovo, designed by Raffaello Stern and completed in 1822. This was taken out of the space of the Cortile della Pigna.

The core of the Belvedere Villa survives, but only as part of the buildings which enclose the Cortile della Pigna on the north side, in what is now the MUSEO PIO-CLEMENTINO, built by Pope Clement XIV (1769–74) and his successor, Pius VI (1775–99).

6. The APOLLO DEL BELVEDERE is now in the Gabinetto dell'Apollo in the MUSEO PIO-CLEMEN-TINO at the VATICAN. It is a copy of a Greek original by Leochares, probably in bronze, of the fourth century B.C. It was found in Grottaferrata towards the end of the fifteenth century and formed part of the collection of Pope Julius II when he was still a cardinal. It was placed by him in the garden of his palace and from there transported to the Belvedere garden when he became Pope.

7. See note 30, Chapter 2.

8. See note 5, Chapter 8.

9. The RAPHAEL STANZE were in a part of the VATICAN PALACE which, with the exception of the Borgia tower, was built or restored by Pope Nicholas V (1447–55). In 1492 Alexander VI commissioned Pinturicchio to fresco the six rooms on the first floor of the building, known as the BORGIA APARTMENT. It seems probable that Julius II lived in these apartments as Pope for four years until 1507 when he decided to move into the four rooms on the floor above so as not to be pestered with remembrances of his hated predecessor. These upper rooms were already painted in part by such artists as Piero della Francesca and Andrea del Castagno. Their work was to be completed by another group of painters, including Perugino, Luca Signorelli, Lorenzo Lotto and Raphael, all chosen by Bramante for Julius II. Towards the end of 1508, every one of these artists was dismissed, with the exception of Raphael whose work in the Camera della Segnatura so impressed the Pope that he decided to commission him to paint the entire suite of rooms. In this way it came about that some of the world's greatest thematic paintings were created – a symposium of the learning and beliefs of the Christian Renaissance. In the Sala della Segnatura, the two great frescos represent respectively the Triumph of the Church or of Religious Faith and Truth (commonly called the Disputation of the Sacrament) and the Triumph of Scientific Truth (commonly called the School of Athens). They are to be seen on the opposite walls of the room which the Pope used as a study. In the Stanza di Eliodoro it is Raphael's portrayal of the expulsion of Heliodorus from the Temple in Jerusalem, recorded in the second Book of Maccabees, which has given its name to the room. More justly famous, perhaps, is the painting of St Peter's deliverance from his imprison-ment in Jerusalem. On the other side of the Sala della Segnatura is the Stanza dell' Incendio painted entirely during the pontificate of Pope Leo X between 1514 and 1517 for use as a dining-room. It was Leo who chose the subjects for the paintings. In the fourth room, the Sala di Costantino, apart from some sketches for the painting of the Battle of the Mulvian Bridge, all the work was carried out by Raphael's assistants, chief among them Giulio Romano.

10. Michelangelo's MOSES was installed in the monu-ment to Julius II in S. PIETRO IN VINCOLI in 1544; the whole work, completed by his pupils, was unveiled in 1547. In medieval representations the head of the prophet is shown with horns which were derived from a mistranslation of a Hebrew word. Aware of this error, Michelangelo, nevertheless, retained the horns which, in the ancient world, were often symbols of divinity and power.

11. The church of S. GIOVANNI DEI FIORENTINI, designed by Jacopo Sansovino, was completed by Carlo Maderno in 1614, after both Antonio da Sangallo the younger and Giacomo della Porta had contributed to its construction. The façade was added in 1734 by Alessandro Galilei. The high altar is by Borromini, whose tomb is in the church.

12. The present PIAZZA DEL POPOLO is the work of Giuseppe Valadier, who laid it out between 1816 and 1820, from designs on which he had already started work in 1784. On the south side, opposite the church of S. MARIA DEL POPOLO, are the twin churches of S. MARIA DI MONTE SANTO and S. MARIA DEI MIRACOLI on either side of the CORSO. These were commissioned from Carlo Rainaldi by Pope Alexander VII in 1660.

13. The PIAZZA NAVONA was originally Domitian's Circus Agonalis, or athletes' stadium. In time, the name developed into n'Agona and eventually into Navona. The square remained virtually unchanged as an arena for jousting and sports until the early

Renaissance when Sixtus IV moved a market into it from the Capitoline hill. It was paved in 1485 and as it gradually assumed the character of a public square the seats all around it disappeared. It retained, however, as it still does, its outline of a circus. It acquired its present aspect through the patronage of the Pamphilj Pope, Innocent X. His family palace, PALAZZO PAMPHILJ, was built for him in 1644–50. The church of S. AGNESE IN AGONE was begun by Rainaldi in 1652 and completed by Borromini in 1657. The FOUNTAIN OF THE FOUR RIVERS is by Bernini (see note 23, Chapter 12).

14. The VILLA MADAMA, one of the masterpieces of the Cinquecento in Rome, was begun by Raphael and completed by the Sangallos, who were often associated with him. Work began in 1519 under the supervision of Giulio Romano who, with Giovanni da Udine, was responsible for the decoration of the

interior. The Sack of Rome in 1527 caused some damage to the villa but it is more likely that it was looted than that it was burned as was at one time believed. The story about Pope Clement VII watching the smoke rising from his villa while he was being besieged in Castel Sant' Angelo must be apocryphal since the villa cannot be seen from the castle. Certainly, while many of the statues in the garden disappeared during the Sack, the interior decoration of paintings and stucco remained largely intact. The property passed to the Emperor Charles V's daughter, Margaret of Austria, the Madama whose title gave the villa its name. Her son, Alexander Farnese, inherited it; and from the Farnese it passed to the Bourbons whose heirs sold it in 1913 to a French industrialist and engineer, Maurice Bergès. The villa was by then in a pitiful state of abandonment, but Bergès restored it with the help of the architect Pio Piacentini. In 1925 Bergès sold it to Count Dentice Frasso who, aided by the lavish contributions of his rich American wife, continued the work of restoration. In 1937 the Italian Ministry of Foreign Affairs took a lease of the villa and in 1940 it was bought by the Italian government and is used for entertaining. South of the Villa Madama on Monte Mario is the VILLA MELLINI which was built by Mario Mellini towards the middle of the fifteenth century. Cardinal Giovanni Battista Mellini died here in 1478. The Constable of Bourbon made the villa his headquarters before the Sack of Rome in 1527. It was also used by General Oudinot in 1849. Goethe often went for walks here. The villa is now used as an observatory to which is attached the Astronomical and Copernican Museum founded in 1860.

10. THE SACK OF ROME

1. Built for Cardinal Domenico della Rovere in the 1480s, the PALAZZO DEI PENITENZIERI in Via

della Conciliazione was probably designed by Baccio Pontelli. It is now a hotel.

2. Commissioned by Pope Leo X for his brother, Giuliano de' Medici, the PALAZZO LANTE AI CAPRETTARI was designed by Jacopo Sansovino. It is in the Piazza dei Caprettari: the word means vendors of goats' flesh. The palace was bought by Ludovico Lante in 1533.

3. Designed by Giulio Romano, the PALAZZO CICCIA-PORCI in the Via Banco di S. Spirito was built for a Roman noble, Giovanni Alberini. Started in 1515, it was completed in 1521 after the designs had been modified by the Tuscan architect, Pietro Roselli. After passing through the hands of the Cicciaporci, the palace was acquired by the Senni family.

4. The Cenci were among the richest Roman families and owned a large part of what is now the park of the VILLA BORGHESE until Pope Paul V (1605–21) acquired the estate for his family after its confiscation following the murder of the monstrous Francesco Cenci by his children. Finally completed in 1535 to the designs of Giulio Romano, the PALAZZO CENCI-MACCARANI-DI BRAZZÀ, in Piazza S. Eustachio, was acquired by the Maccarani after the downfall of the Cenci at the end of the sixteenth century and was subsequently sold to the di Brazzà.

5. The original palaces of the Massimi were burned down during the Sack of Rome. A new palace was built for the brothers, Pietro, Luca and Angelo Massimo to the magnificent designs of Baldassare Peruzzi in 1532–6. Its name, PALAZZO MASSIMO ALLE COLONNE, came from the antique columns of the former buildings which were destroyed in the Sack and which seem to have been the inspiration for Peruzzi's columned portico.

6. Completed in 1511, Agostino Chigi's villa was sold in 1580 to Cardinal Alessandro Farnese, a grandson of Pope Paul III, and is now known as the VILLA FARNESINA. It houses the Gabinetto Nazionale delle Stampe (an extensive collection of prints) and provides an elegant setting for receptions of the Accademia dei Lincei. Chigi, inordinately rich, adorned the villa with splendid works by Francesco Penni, Peruzzi, Sodoma, Sebastiano del Piombo, Giulio Romano, Giovanni da Udine and Raphael, whose lovely Galatea is to be seen in one of the loggias. Raphael designed far more work for Chigi

than he completed. The reason, according to Vasari, was Raphael's passionate and distracting love-affair with the Fornarina, the baker's daughter. It seems that Chigi eventually allowed the girl to come to live with Raphael in the villa.

7. The COLLEGIO CAPRANICENSE and the adjoining PALAZZO CAPRANICA, in the Piazza Capranica, were completed in 1457. They were built for Cardinal Domenico Capranica, one of the most eminent cardinals appointed by Pope Martin V. The palace now contains a cinema.

8. The church of S. GIACOMO DEGLI SPAGNUOLI, in Piazza Navona, was the first to be built in Rome after the return of the popes from Avignon. It was founded by Bishop Alfonso Paradinas of Seville for his fellow-countrymen in the Jubilee Year of 1450.

9. Originally intended for the Dutch and Flemish as well as the German community in Rome, the church of S. MARIA DELL' ANIMA in Via S. Maria dell' Anima near Piazza Navona was completed in 1523. The façade is attributed to Giuliano da Sangallo.

10. Adjoining the church of SS. APOSTOLI, the PALAZZO DEI SS. APOSTOLI was probably built in 1478 by Giuliano da Sangallo for Cardinal Giuliano della Rovere who became Pope Julius II.

11. The tenth-century Convent and Church of S. COSIMATO were restored in 1475.

11. RECOVERY AND REFORM

1. Begun in 1514, the PALAZZO FARNESE was designed by Antonio da Sangallo the younger. After the architect's death in 1546, he was succeeded by

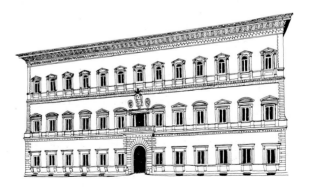

Michelangelo who was responsible for the upper storey of the building. The riverside wing and gardens were completed after Michelangelo's death by Giacomo della Porta in 1574. The palace was inherited in 1734 by the Infante Charles, son of Philip V of Spain, and his wife, Elizabeth Farnese. It afterwards became the Roman residence of the Bourbons of Naples, and early in the nineteenth century was occupied by the representative of Joachim Murat, Napoleon's marshal who became King of Naples in 1806. In 1871 the Italian government leased the palace to the French government for use as the French Embassy for one lira to be paid every ninety-nine years in exchange for the Hotel Galiffet in Paris. The vestibule and courtyard are as impressive as the façade. The first-floor gallery contains frescos of mythological subjects from Ovid's *Metamorphoses* by the Carracci brothers, Annibale and Agostino, assisted by Domenichino and Lanfranco. The nearby charming small Renaissance palace, the PICCOLA FARNESINA, which stands where the Corso widens into the Piazza S. Pantaleo, has no connection with the Farnese family. The lilies which feature in the palace's decorations are those of France, not of the Farnese whose own lilies decorate the fountains in the Piazza Farnese. The Piccola Farnesina was built to the designs of Antonio da Sangallo the younger for the family of the French prelate, Thomas Le Roy, who was granted the right to incorporate the fleur-de-lis into his coat of arms in recognition of his services in negotiating the concordat between François I and Pope Leo X. The palace was purchased by the Roman commune in 1887 and is now the MUSEO BARRACCO which houses a collection of ancient sculpture assembled by Barone Giovanni Barracco.

2. Created for Pope Paul III by Antonio da Sangallo the younger, the SALA REGIA was begun in 1540 but not completed until 1573. Intended for the reception of sovereigns and their diplomatic representatives, it was formed in a wing of the papal apartments which also housed the BORGIA APARTMENT and the STANZE OF RAPHAEL. The frescos of historical subjects are by Vasari, Lorenzo Sabattini, Francesco Salviati and the Zuccaro brothers.

3. The CAPPELLA PAOLINA was begun by Antonio da Sangallo the younger in 1540 and must have been completed before 1542 when Michelangelo began the two great frescos commissioned by Paul III for the side walls. These depict the conversion of St Paul (1542–5) and the crucifixion of St Peter (completed after 1549). They were the last pictorial works of the artist.

4. Michelangelo's LAST JUDGEMENT was widely condemned as being wholly unsuitable for a place of Christian worship. Paul IV (1555–9) referred to it as 'a stew of nudes'. In the reign of Pius IV in 1564 Daniele da Volterra – thereafter known as *il braghettone*, the breeches-maker – was asked to make the figures more decent. Later over-painting was commissioned by Gregory XIII (1572–85) and Clement VIII (1592–1605). Biagio da Cesena, Pope Paul III's master of ceremonies, who criticized the nudity of the figures, is represented in the composition as Minos with the ears of an ass and a serpent around his loins. Other portraits are of Pietro Aretino (as St Bartholomew), Dante, Savonarola, Julius II and the artist's friend, Vittoria Colonna.

5. Michelangelo was at least sixty-three when he began work on the rebuilding of the piazza of the Capitol. He envisaged a new PIAZZA DEL CAMPIDOGLIO to be approached from the Piazza d'Aracoeli below by a ramp known as a CORDONATA from the ribs or cords originally stretched across such ways to give a foothold for animals. The architects who executed

the design after Michelangelo's death were Giacomo della Porta who completed the PALAZZO DEI CONSERVATORI in 1568 and Girolamo Rainaldi who finished the PALAZZO NUOVO or CAPITOLINE MUSEUM, a replica of the Palazzo dei Conservatori, in 1655. These two architects collaborated in the rebuilding of the PALAZZO DEL SENATORE which dominates the piazza and is still the headquarters of the Commune of Rome. They departed slightly from Michelangelo's designs for the façade but retained his double staircase leading to the main entrance which had been built in 1550. Martino Longhi the elder raised the clock tower in 1578–82. The large statues of Castor and Pollux at the top of the Cordonata were found in the THEATRE OF POMPEY in the pontificate of Pius IV and were placed on the Capitol in 1583.

6. Michelangelo's PIETÀ, the only sculpture he ever signed, was commissioned by Cardinal Jean de Bilhères, the French ambassador, in 1498, when the artist was twenty-three.

7. Commissioned by Pius IV's predecessor, Paul IV, the CASINO DI PIO IV was begun in 1558 by Pirro Ligorio assisted by Salustio Peruzzi, son of Baldassare. The Casino is composed of two buildings, the Grande and Piccolo Casino, facing each other across an elliptical piazza which is reached by a double stairway through an arcade.

8. Situated in Piazza dei SS. Apostoli next to the PALAZZO COLONNA, the Church of SS. APOSTOLI was probably first built by Pope Pelagius I (556–61) and was successively restored by the Colonna Pope, Martin V (1417–31), by the della Rovere, Sixtus IV, and the Medici, Pius IV. It was almost entirely rebuilt during the pontificate of Clement XI (1700–1721) by Francesco Fontana and his father. The neo-classical façade is by Giuseppe Valadier; the portico by Baccio Pontelli. The Palazzo Colonna was built by Pope Martin V in about 1427 on the site of a castle belonging to his family. Decorations were complete by the time the palazzo was confiscated by the Borgia Pope Alexander VI. It was restored to the Colonnas by Pope Julius II. In 1620, when the palazzo still looked like a medieval fortress, Filippo Colonna decided to rebuild it with a gallery decorated with marble statues found in an adjoining villa. The wings around the courtyard and the loggia were reconstructed in 1730. The interior salons are richly painted and contain frescos by Pinturicchio, Poussin, Tempesta, il Pomarancio, Cavaliere d'Arpino and Cosmè Tura. Inside the palace is the famous Colonna Gallery founded by Cardinal Girolamo Colonna. This contains family portraits including one of Michelangelo's friend, Vittoria Colonna. There are also fine paintings by Poussin, Veronese and Annibale Carracci.

9. The VILLA GIULIA (or VILLA DI PAPA GIULIO), now a museum of Etruscan art, was built by Vignola for Pope Julius III from 1551 to 1553. It stands in its own park at the southern end of the Valle Giulia close to the GALLERIA NAZIONALE D'ARTE MODERNA. The loggia at the end of the courtyard is by Bartolommeo Ammanati. The villa, as well as its garden and the adjoining *nymphaeum*, was originally adorned with statues, urns and large vases containing orange and lemon trees.

10. The STATUE OF POMPEY is now in the Salone del Trono of the PALAZZO SPADA. It dates from early imperial times and represents a 'nude and noble' captain making an oration. It came to be identified with the statue in the curia of POMPEY'S THEATRE at the foot of which Caesar was supposed to have been murdered. It was discovered in the 1550s during excavations in the Via Leutari and was acquired by Pope Julius III.

11. The PALAZZO SPADA in the Piazza della Quercia was begun, probably by Giulio Merisi da Caravaggio in about 1549 for Cardinal Capodiferro. The decorations were completed in 1559. The elaborate stucco decoration is by Giulio Mazzoni. In 1559 the palace passed to the Mignanelli family and then, in 1632, to Cardinal Spada. Borromini restored the palace after 1632 and added its most notable feature, a *trompe l'œil* perspective in the garden gallery. In 1927 the Spada family sold it to the Italian state for use as the offices of the Consiglio di Stato. The GALLERIA SPADA contains works of art assembled by Cardinal Bernardino Spada and is the only small family collection to have survived in Rome.

12. The church of S. LUCIA DEL GONFALONE in the Via dei Banchi Vecchi was built for the ancient fraternity of the Gonfalone at the beginning of the fourteenth century and rebuilt in the Baroque style in 1764 by the Roman architect, Marco David. It was restored in 1866 by Franco Azzurri.

13. Founded by Pope Gregory XIII, the COLLEGIO ROMANO was built in 1583–5 by Bartolommeo Ammanati as the main centre of study for the Jesuits in whose hands it remained until 1870 when it was taken over by the Italian government and became a state school, now the Liceo-Ginnasio Visconti. The vast building also housed the Biblioteca Nazionale Centrale Vittorio Emanuele II, which was formed out of a number of libraries of various religious communities, including that of the Jesuits in the Collegio Romano, and the library of the Prehistoric

and Ethnographic Museum L. Pigorini which has now been moved to the SCIENTIFIC MUSEUM in the E.U.R. Adjoining the Collegio Romano is the Jesuit church of S. IGNAZIO. This was commissioned by Cardinal Lodovico Ludovisi, whose uncle, Gregory XV, had studied there. Domenichino, among others, was asked to submit a design but the plans of the Jesuit Orazio Grassi were preferred. The wonderful *trompe l'œil* ceiling in the magnificently Baroque interior is the work of another Jesuit, Andrea Pozzo.

14. The church of the GESÙ, which was the model for a type of Counter-Reformation church in what has been called the Jesuit style, was designed by Vignola for the powerful Cardinal Alessandro Farnese who was said to have owned the three most beautiful

objects in Rome, his family palace, his daughter and this church of the Gesù. The façade is generally thought to have been adapted by Giacomo della Porta from Vignola's design, though it has also been attributed to the Jesuit, Giuseppe Valeriani. Begun in 1568, the church was consecrated in 1584 and is the main Jesuit church in Rome. The opulence and colours of the mainly eighteenth- and nineteenth-century decoration are in keeping with Jesuit ideas of attracting worshippers by grand spectacle. The main paintings, by the Genoese Giovanni Battista Gaulli, were executed in 1672–85. The breathtakingly luxuriant tomb of St Ignatius of Loyola is resplendent with lapis lazuli. The globe at the summit is the largest piece of this stone in the world.

15. The oratory and church of S. MARIA IN VALLICELLA or CHIESA NUOVA was begun by that most charitable of mystics, St Philip Neri, with the labour of members of his congregation of Oratorians and

with the help of Pope Gregory XIII. It was built on the site of a twelfth-century church and largely designed by Martino Longhi the elder who replaced Matteo da Città di Castello as architect. Consecrated in 1599, the church was not completed until 1605 by the erection of Fausto Rughesi's façade. Although St Philip wanted the church interior to remain simply whitewashed, Pietro da Cortona was commissioned in 1647 to decorate it with the frescos which took him twenty years to complete. The three paintings on either side of and above the altar are exceptional works by Rubens. The adjoining oratory is by Borromini (1637–62). St Philip Neri found Federico Barocci's altar painting in the Chapel of the Visitation so moving that he 'would sit on a small chair in front of it and all unconsciously be rapt into a sweet ecstasy'. Women gathered to look at him in wonderment and he would then turn upon them crossly and send them away as though embarrassed to be caught in so transfixed a state. Before moving to S. Maria in Vallicella, St Philip Neri had lived with the Arciconfraternita della Carità, a charitable company founded in 1519 by Cardinal Giulio de' Medici, later Clement VII. The company's church, S. GIROLAMO DELLA CARITÀ in Via di Monserrato, which had originally belonged to the Franciscan observants, was rebuilt by Domenico Castello and was finished in about 1660. Here St Philip had attracted a large group of disciples of all classes. So many people came to see him that he had to obtain permission to use the loft over one of the aisles of the church as an oratory, a chapel for prayer without a mass altar. This was the origin of the name which in time became attached to the spiritual exercises which he initiated, the room where they took place, and the congregation which promoted them. From the church St Philip went about Rome, comforting the sick in hospitals and making regular pilgrimages to the seven major basilicas of Rome, accompanied by large crowds of up to a thousand people, with a choir singing litanies and trumpets sounding fanfares.

16. The FOUNTAINS in PIAZZA NICOSIA and PIAZZA COLONNA are by Giacomo della Porta. The one in Piazza Nicosia, made in 1573, was originally in PIAZZA DEL POPOLO.

17. The ACCADEMIA DI S. LUCA, constituted as an academy of fine arts in 1577, was the successor of a much older corporation of artists dating back at least to the fourteenth century and reconstituted in 1478.

In 1588 when Sixtus V gave the sixth-century church of S. Martina to the Academy, the church assumed the name of SS. LUCA E MARTINA and premises were built next door for the use of members of the Academy. These premises, together with the church, were demolished in 1931–3 to make way for the Via dei Fori Imperiali. New premises were found for the Academy in the Palazzo Carpegna in the Piazza dell' Accademia di S. Luca near the TREVI FOUNTAIN.

18. The QUIRINAL PALACE was begun in 1574 on the site of a villa built by Cardinal Ippolito d'Este. A succession of architects contributed to its construction, including Flaminio Ponzio, Domenico Fontana, Carlo Maderno, Bernini and Ferdinando Fuga. Although not finally completed until the pontificate of Clement XII (1730–40), it was used quite regularly by the popes after Clement VIII first occupied it in 1592. The palace was taken over by King Victor Emmanuel II in 1870 and has remained the residence of the heads of the Italian State ever since. The large chapel is by Carlo Maderno.

19. The OBELISK in PIAZZA DEL POPOLO was raised in front of the Temple of the Sun in Heliopolis by the Pharaohs Rameses II and his son Merneptah and was brought to Rome by Augustus for the CIRCUS MAXIMUS. It was moved to its present position in 1589. In 1823 its base was embellished by four marble lions and basins under the direction of Giuseppe Valadier.

20. The CORTILE DELLA PIGNA takes its name from the colossal bronze pine-cone of the imperial era which had been found in the BATHS OF AGRIPPA. Below it is the CORTILE DELLA BIBLIOTECA formed by the construction across the original main courtyard of the Belvedere of two transverse buildings, the LIBRARY, built by Domenico Fontana for Pope Sixtus V from 1585 to 1590, and the Braccio Nuovo, built by Raffaello Stern in 1817–22 for Pope Pius VII. The Braccio Nuovo contains a part of the collection of the MUSEO CHIARAMONTI founded by Pius VII.

21. The COURT OF ST DAMASUS was originally an orchard planted with apple trees by Nicholas V. The construction of the buildings forming the court was begun by Pope Clement VII after the Sack of Rome and completed by Pope Sixtus V.

22. The SISTINE LOGGIA surmounting the roof of the LATERAN PALACE was begun by Domenico Fontana for Pope Sixtus V in 1586.

23. The CAPPELLA SISTINA in S. MARIA MAGGIORE was begun by Domenico Fontana for Pope Sixtus V in 1585.

24. The CAPPELLA GREGORIANA was completed in 1583.

25. The OBELISK in ST PETER'S SQUARE was transported by Caligula from Heliopolis in A.D. 37 for the circus which he built on the Vatican hill. The circus was enlarged by Nero and came to be known as the CIRCUS OF NERO. It was near his gardens where so many Christians were cruelly executed after the fire of A.D. 67.

26. The CAPPELLA DI S. ANDREA was originally the circular tomb of the Emperor Theodosius. It was remodelled by Pope Symmachus early in the sixth century. In the Middle Ages it became the church of S. Maria della Febbre. Its dedication was changed when the head of St Andrew was placed here in the middle of the fifteenth century. It was replaced by the new SACRISTY (see note 2, Chapter 14).

27. Giacomo della Porta's CAPPELLA CLEMENTINA contains Thorwaldsen's monument to Pius VII. Placed here in 1823, it is the only work in ST PETER'S by an artist who was not a Roman Catholic.

12. BERNINI AND THE BAROQUE

1. The CAPPELLA PAOLINA or BORGHESE CHAPEL was completed in 1611 for Pope Paul V by Flaminio Ponzio. Pietro Bernini worked on some of the sculpture for Ponzio's tomb of Clement VIII (1592–1605) which is opposite that of Paul V. Some of the frescos are by Guido Reni. The painting of the Madonna above the altar, which was originally attributed to St Luke, is a work of Roman Byzantine art of the ninth century.

2. The FONTANONE DELL' ACQUA PAOLA, which stands like a triumphal arch overlooking Rome from the Janiculum, was designed by Giovanni Fontana and Flaminio Ponzio, who had also been responsible for reconstructing the aqueduct.

3. Of the fountains created at this time the most noteworthy are:
In Piazza Scossa Cavalli. This was designed by Carlo Maderno between 1613 and 1621. When the piazza was engulfed by the opening up of the Via della

Conciliazione in 1950, the fountain was removed to its present position in front of the church of S. ANDREA DELLA VALLE.

In Piazza S. Maria Maggiore, also by Carlo Maderno and completed in 1614. Its basin lies below the bronze statue of the Madonna and Child by Guillaume Bertholet which crowns the tall fluted column, the only remaining one of eight that stood in the BASILICA OF MAXENTIUS.

In Piazza S. Giovanni in Laterano, finished in 1607. This surrounds the obelisk, the tallest in Rome, which was made for the Temple of Ammon in Thebes in the fifteenth century B.C. and was erected in the CIRCUS MAXIMUS in A.D. 357. The obelisk was removed to its present position under the direction of Domenico Fontana after it had been found lying in three pieces in the circus in 1587. It occupies the site of the equestrian statue of Marcus Aurelius which was transferred to the PIAZZA DEL CAMPIDOGLIO in 1538.

On the north side of St Peter's Square. Built by Carlo Maderno in 1613. This was described by John Evelyn as 'the goodliest I ever saw'. Fed by water from the ACQUA PAOLA, it throws up a powerful jet of water to a height of sixty-five feet.

On the south side of St Peter's Square, a more or less exact copy of its counterpart. Although created later, it appears to be older because it is exposed to the full blast of the *tramontana*, while the other fountain is sheltered by the colonnade. Some authorities doubt the attribution to Bernini and credit its design to Carlo Fontana.

4. Built for Cardinal Scipione Borghese by Carlo Maderno in 1608–20, the High Baroque church of S. MARIA DELLA VITTORIA was originally dedicated to St Paul. It was rededicated to Our Lady of Victory after the defeat by the Habsburg Emperor Ferdinand II's Catholic forces of the Bohemian Protestants at the Battle of the White Mountain near Prague in 1620. The Catholics attributed their victory to a small image of the Madonna found by their troops in the ruins of the Castle of Prague. The façade of the church was added by Soria in 1626. In the Cornaro Chapel, overlooked by statues of various members of the Venetian Cornaro family in what appear to be boxes in a theatre, is Bernini's astonishing sculpture of St Teresa.

5. The work of several architects, probably including Vignola and, later, Martino Longhi the elder, the BORGHESE PALACE was completed for Paul V and his family by Flaminio Ponzio, Vasanzio (Ivan van Santen) and Maderno. Extensive alterations and additions were undertaken in the 1670s by Carlo Rainaldi, who designed the elegant portal and the gardens. The palace housed the Borghese family's famous art collection until it was moved to the VILLA BORGHESE in 1891. Napoleon's sister, Pauline Bonaparte, lived here after her marriage to the radical aristocrat Prince Camillo Borghese in 1803. The palace now houses Rome's most exclusive club, the Caccia or Hunt Club.

6. Completed soon after 1616 on the site of the Baths of Constantine, the PALAZZO PALLAVICINI-ROSPIGLIOSI was later acquired by Cardinal Bentivoglio who sold it to Cardinal Mazarin. It was afterwards purchased by G. B. Rospigliosi, a relation of Pope Clement IX (1667–9). Inside the courtyard is the Casino Pallavicini with Guido Reni's celebrated *Aurora* painted on the ceiling.

7. Bernini's bust of Scipione Borghese, completed in 1632, is in the VILLA BORGHESE.

8. In 575 St Gregory the Great transformed his large house on the Caelian hill into a monastery to which was attached an oratory dedicated to St Andrew. It was replaced, probably during the pontificate of Pope Paschal II (1099–1118) by a church dedicated to St Gregory. This church, S. GREGORIO MAGNO, was completely renovated externally in 1633 for Cardinal Scipione Borghese by Soria, who constructed the impressive flight of steps and the new façade. It was redecorated internally by Francesco Ferrari in 1725–34. The church contains an episcopal chair said to have belonged to St Gregory who is believed to have dispatched St Augustine from here to convert the English. Two English refugees buried here are Robert Pecham, who died in 1569, and Sir Edward Carne, an emissary who was sent by Henry VIII to Pope Clement VII to obtain consent to the annulment of the King's marriage to Catherine of Aragon and who, having also served Queen Mary, prudently decided, after Queen Elizabeth's accession, to remain in Rome as Warden of the English Hospice.

9. The casino of the VILLA BORGHESE was built by the Flemish architect, Ivan van Santen (Vasanzio), in 1613–16. The original grounds were extended by Cardinal Scipione Borghese so that by 1650 the

boundary was about four kilometres long. The house was enlarged in the middle of the eighteenth century when Marcantonio Borghese commissioned Antonio Asprucci and a number of artists to decorate it and provide the existing galleries. Many of the pictures in the Borghese Gallery were sold by Prince Camillo Borghese to Napoleon, while two hundred of the best sculptures were exchanged for an estate in Piedmont. All these works of art are now in the Louvre. Some of the loss was made good when the Borghese family collection was moved here from the BORGHESE PALACE in 1891. The collection was bought by the Italian government in 1902.

10. Originally built in the fifth century, the church of S. BIBIANA was restored in 1220 and again shortly before Bernini was commissioned to make a new façade in 1624. The statue of the saint inside the church was Bernini's first attempt both at a religious subject and a clothed, rather than a nude figure.

11. Carlo Maderno's façade for the church of S. SUSANNA, which is believed to stand upon the site of the saint's martyrdom, was completed in 1603. The original church, in the form of a basilica, was restored in 1475 and reduced to a single nave in 1595 when the coffered ceiling was gilded and painted. The statues of the prophets Isaiah and Jeremiah in the nave are by Valsoldo.

12. Through the efforts of a force of seven hundred labourers working at full stretch, the FAÇADE OF ST PETER'S was completed in 1612, with the exception of the statues on the balustrade. The nave was finished in 1615.

13. The erection of a large canopy over the Apostle's grave at the centre of the crossing of the newly completed basilica had been considered, and designs had actually been submitted, before Cardinal Maffeo Barberini became Pope in 1623. His election ensured that the commission would be given to Bernini who began work on it before 1624. The choice of giant bronze columns, twisted as were those of the canopy in the old church, was, it seems, suggested to Bernini, but in all other respects the design of the BALDAC-CHINO was his own. It was completed in 1633.

14. Bernini's STATUE OF LONGINUS, the name tradition-ally given to the soldier who pierced the side of Christ with a spear, was finished in 1638, although

the models were prepared when the sculptor was still at work on the BALDACCHINO.

15. The TOMB OF POPE URBAN VIII, which Bernini completed in 1647, balances the earlier tomb of Pope Paul III, to the left of the CATTEDRA, by Giacomo della Porta.

16. The huge PALAZZO DORIA, whose main entrance is on the west side of the Corso, just north of Piazza Venezia, was owned by Cardinal Fazio Santorio who, when told on a visit by Julius II that the splendid palace was more suitable for a duke than a cardinal, felt compelled to make it over to the Pope's nephew, the Duke of Urbino. It subsequently passed into the hands of the Aldobrandini, then by marriage to the Pamphilj, then to the Genoese Doria. The picture gallery is open to the public. Bernini's bust of Innocent X which is on display here portrays the Pope with a much kindlier aspect than Velasquez's famous picture. The building is the work of many hands. The beautiful fifteenth-century courtyard, the older part of the building, has been attributed to Bramante. The rich, rather Rococo façade on the Corso is by the Roman architect Gabriele Valvassori and was completed about 1734; the 1740s' Via del Plebiscito front is by Paolo Ameli, while Antonio del Grande designed the fine wings overlooking the Piazza del Collegio Romano, in the seventeenth century. A nineteenth-century façade completes the west side of the palace in the Via della Gatta.

17. Begun in 1625 on the site of an old Sforza palace by Carlo Maderno, assisted by Borromini, the PALAZZO BARBERINI was completed in 1633 by Bernini who was responsible for the entrance front. At that time it stood by itself in a large park and had more the appearance of a country villa than a town palazzo.

Some of the finest rooms of the palace are occupied by the art collection of the family, among which are Raphael's renowned portrait of *La Fornarina* and Titian's *Venus and Adonis*. There are also portraits of Erasmus by Quentin Massys and of Henry VIII by Holbein. In the main hall of the palace there is a frescoed ceiling depicting the Triumph of Divine Providence. It is by Pietro da Cortona and was painted between 1633 and 1639. The collection now belongs to the Italian State.

18. The PALAZZO PAMPHILJ, built to the design of Girolamo Rainaldi between 1644 and 1650, was given by Pope Innocent X to his sister-in-law, Olimpia Maidalchini. It was acquired after the Second World War by the Brazilian government for use as its embassy. The magnificent ceiling illustrating the story of Aeneas in Borromini's gallery is by Pietro da Cortona.

19. Completed in 1657 by Borromini and Carlo Rainaldi, the church of S. AGNESE was built on the supposed site of the saint's martyrdom. The monument to Innocent X is by G. B. Maini. The Pope, together with other members of his family, is buried in the crypt. In the vaults beneath the church are the remains of the foundations of Domitian's stadium.

20. Bernini's FOUNTAIN OF THE TRITON, commissioned by Pope Urban VIII in 1632, was finished in 1637. Triton, a merman of pre-Greek mythology, was usually represented as playing on a conch. By a

brilliant combination of associated meanings Bernini has used this rather nebulous mythological figure to dominate what used to be called Piazza del Tritone and to compliment his patron. The Triton had been used as an emblem of immortality acquired through letters (Urban was a gifted Latin poet). Dolphins symbolized princely munificence (Urban was a great patron of the arts). Bees were types of divine providence (they were also the armorial decoration of the Barberini family). All are made use of in a personal allusion to the Pope. The nearby FOUNTAIN OF THE BEES, also by Bernini, was finished shortly before the twenty-first anniversary of Urban VIII's election.

21. Once considered the last work of Pietro Bernini, Gian Lorenzo's father, the BARCACCIA FOUNTAIN is now more usually attributed to the son. It was completed in 1629 almost a century before the SPANISH STEPS which now form such an elegant background to it. The fountain, for which the water of the Acqua Vergine had to be used with little pressure behind it, is ingeniously contrived to appear like a leaky boat with a cannon at either end and water seeping out of its prow and stern, in the process of sinking in a pool not much larger than itself. It is said that the idea was suggested by a boat which made a landing on the slope of the Pincian hill – where the Spanish Steps are now – during the greatest recorded flood of the Tiber which took place in 1598 when, on Christmas Day of that year, this part of Rome was submerged to a depth of between seventeen and twenty-five feet. 'The sinking ship' theme had, however, already been used for fountains by Carlo Maderno and it has also been suggested that the idea might have been inspired by the discovery of the sunken barges of Caligula in the Lake of Nemi, south of Rome, which were found in the pontificate of Eugenius IV (1431–47).

22. The PIAZZA DI SPAGNA takes its name from the Spanish Embassy which was established there in the seventeenth century and is still the Spanish Embassy to the Holy See. The building, by Antonio del Grande of Rome, was completed in 1647. Across the piazza beyond the BARCACCIA FOUNTAIN, up the slope of the Pincian hill, rise the beautiful *Scalinata della Trinità dei Monti* or the SPANISH STEPS leading up to the piazza and Church of SS. Trinità dei Monti. The staircase was built by Francesco de Sanctis between 1723 and 1726 to designs by Alessandro Specchi. It contains 138 steps of travertine stone

rising in three successive flights. The idea of building an ornamental staircase up this hill came from Cardinal Mazarin, the chief minister to Louis XIV in succession to Richelieu. His idea was to dignify the approach to the Church of SS. Trinità dei Monti which served the French community. Nevertheless, it was not until some sixty years after Mazarin's death, when the French ambassador, Etienne Gueffier, left 24,000 *scudi* in his will for a chapel in the church and a stairway leading up to it, that the decision to build was taken with the approval of Pope Innocent XIII (1721–4). The church of SS. TRINITÀ DEI MONTI was founded by King Charles VIII of France. It was begun in 1502 in a French Gothic style but the façade was not completed until about 1570. The door and towers were finished in 1587. The steps were designed by Domenico Fontana for Sixtus V. The Spanish Steps became a favourite rendezvous for artists and their models, most of them *cociari* or peasants from the Campagna south of Rome. BABINGTON'S TEA-ROOMS near the foot of the Steps, one of the most popular meeting-places in Rome for foreigners and Italians alike, was founded by an English spinster, a descendant of Anthony Babington who had been hanged, drawn and quartered for leading a conspiracy against Queen Elizabeth I. Miss Babington arrived in Rome in 1893 with £100 and a friend, Miss Cargill, who was descended from as staunch a Protestant as Anthony Babington had been a committed Catholic, a man who had been executed for high treason in the reign of Charles II for denouncing the tyranny of the King. Sharing the yearning of many other English visitors to Rome for a good cup of tea, the two friends decided to open a tea-shop in Via dei Due Macelli. The following year they moved their shop to its present site. Miss Babington retired in 1928 and the business was carried on by her partner, by then Signora da Pozzo, and afterwards by Signora da Pozzo's daughter, Contessa Bedini, who fled to Switzerland when the Germans occupied Rome. Her staff kept the tea-rooms open, however, throughout the occupation. They still thrive.

23. The FOUNTAIN OF THE FOUR RIVERS, whose water is supplied by the TREVI FOUNTAIN, was completed after four years' work in 1651. The four rivers, each represented by a stone figure, are the Nile, the Danube, the Ganges and the River Plate. The figures, designed by Bernini, were executed by his assistants. That of the Nile has its face covered as an allusion to its then unknown source; but it was said at the time that the covering was introduced by Bernini so that the statue would thus not be able to see the façade of S. AGNESE designed by his rival, Borromini. The cost of the fountain was raised by levying taxes on various commodities including bread, which naturally gave rise to widespread protest. The obelisk which rises above the rocks is a Roman copy that stood in the Circus of Maxentius.

The FOUNTAIN OF THE MOOR, which stands at the southern end of the PIAZZA NAVONA, was originally created by Giacomo della Porta in 1575. Bernini reconstructed it and himself made the central figure of the Moor.

24. First built in the fourth or early fifth century on a site belonging to a Roman matron named Lucina, the Church of S. LORENZO IN LUCINA was rebuilt by Sixtus III (432–40). During the pontificate of Pope Paschal II (1099–1118) the church was restored and the portico added. It underwent further restoration by Cosimo Fanzago in about 1650. The caissoned and gilded ceiling was restored by Pope Pius IX. The high altar, designed by Carlo Rainaldi, is surmounted by a crucifixion by Guido Reni. The bust of the painter, Nicholas Poussin, was commissioned from Lemoyne by Chateaubriand; that of Gabriele Fonseca in the Fonseca Chapel is by Bernini. The adjoining PALAZZO FIANO, which belonged in the middle of the fifteenth century to the Portuguese cardinal Giorgio da Costa and was consequently known as the Palazzo di Portogallo, was considered then to be one of the finest palaces in Rome after the VATICAN. Having passed through the hands of the Peretti, the Savelli and the Ludovisi, it was acquired by the Ottoboni. Marco Ottoboni, a nephew of Alexander VIII (1689–91), married a Boncompagni from whom he acquired the Duchy of Fiano. At the end of the nineteenth century the façade of the palace and much of the interior was completely altered for the new owners, the Almagià family, by Francesco Settimi.

25. The charming oval church of S. ANDREA AL QUIRINALE is exquisitely decorated with marbles and stucco work. Designed in 1658, it took twelve years to finish. The statue of St Andrew above the main altar, which seems to be soaring to heaven on a cloud, is by Bernini's assistant, Raggi. While work on this church was in progress the magnificent Baroque church of S. ANDREA DELLA VALLE was being completed in Corso Vittorio Emanuele. Maderno, Rainaldi and Fontana all contributed to the design of the façade.

26. The idea of a COLONNADE in ST PETER'S PIAZZA seems to have been in the minds of both Alexander VII (1655–67) and Bernini before the Pope's election. Certainly the Pope had not long been in office when he sent for Bernini and began to discuss with him and the *Fabbrica* how to achieve this great undertaking. There were a number of factors to be taken into account: the old entrance to the VATICAN PALACE, north of the portico, had to be retained, as well as the space immediately in front of the façade, known as the *piazza retta*. The Pope's window in the Vatican Palace from which papal blessings were given had to be in the sight of the largest possible number of people. So also had the loggia above the central entrance of the basilica which he used for his blessings *urbi et orbi* on ceremonial occasions. Bernini envisaged the space thus to be enclosed as a place where the faithful would receive the embrace of the Almighty. The colonnades were to symbolize the embracing arms. The geometrical centre of the whole design remained the great obelisk in the middle of the piazza. With great ingenuity Bernini managed to shrink the impression of unwieldy width left by Maderno's façade – which had to incorporate the base of Bernini's uncompleted towers at either side of the front – by throwing out two long low corridors which narrowed the space of the *piazza retta* as they advanced from the basilica. In addition he compressed the apparent width of the piazza within the colonnades by making this an oval 240 metres long. The colonnades consist of four rows of Doric travertine columns and pilasters supporting lines of gigantic angels.

27. The SCALA REGIA leads from the ceremonial entrance of the VATICAN PALACE to the papal apartments. Before Bernini completed this grand stairway in 1666, the popes had had to descend to St Peter's by a dark narrow staircase from the CAPPELLA PAOLINA past the SISTINE CHAPEL to the portico of the basilica. Having overcome the problems presented by the narrowness of the space available and the lack of light, Bernini regarded the staircase as his major technical achievement.

28. Above the altar in the apse of ST PETER'S Bernini created a scenic spectacle which, seen through the twisted columns of the BALDACCHINO, was to be the culmination of the view along the nave of the basilica. It is the CATHEDRA, a reliquary of the basilica's precious relic, a wooden chair with ivory ornamentation on which St Peter was supposed to have sat when he was a guest in the house of Pudens on his first arrival in Rome. First referred to in a written text in 1217, the chair was probably made in the eighth or ninth century. The bronze throne with gilded reliefs which encases the relic is surrounded by four large bronze statues of the great doctors of the Church, Saints Augustine, Ambrose, Athanasius and John Chrysostom.

29. The Vatican Department or Congregation of Propaganda Fide was founded in 1622 by Pope Gregory XV (1621–3) for spreading the Catholic Faith in heathen and heretic lands. It was Urban VIII, however, who decided to build a suitably large office for this important missionary organization. The main façade, on the south side of the PIAZZA DI SPAGNA, was finished by 1644. Two years later Bernini was joined by Borromini who completed the façade overlooking the Via di Propaganda in 1662.

30. When Innocent X built new prisons in Via Giulia in 1644, the site of the TOR DI NONA was cleared for the TORDINONA THEATRE, later renamed the Apollo. After being burned down, it was rebuilt by Valadier in 1830, but was later demolished once more for the Tiber embankment.

31. Originally built by the Emperor Hadrian's architect, Demetrianus, and called the Pons Aelius, the PONTE SANT' ANGELO was reconstructed in 1668. The statues of angels carry symbols of Christ's passion.

32. First built in 1231 to replace the chapel of the Hospice of St Biagio where St Francis had lodged, the church of S. FRANCESCO A RIPA was rebuilt in 1682–9 by Mattia de' Rossi. The statue of St Francis is believed to have been commissioned by his disciple, Jacopa da Settesoli, and is perhaps the work of Margaritone d'Arezzo. Bernini's statue of the Blessed Ludovica Albertoni is in the Altieri Chapel, so called because Cardinal Paluzzi degli Albertoni, who commissioned

it, took the name of Altieri when he became related by marriage to Clement X (1670–76). Ludovica Albertoni, who entered the third order of St Francis, died in Rome in 1503 and gave all her worldly goods to the poor.

33. The PALAZZO DI MONTECITORIO was built over the site of an earlier Colonna palace. Begun in 1651, it was completed in 1694. Carlo Fontana adapted the building for use as law courts in the pontificate of Innocent XII. It was enlarged at the beginning of the twentieth century by Ernesto Basile for the Lower House of the Italian Parliament which still sits here. East of the Palazzo, on the north side of the Piazza Colonna, is the PALAZZO ALDOBRANDINI-CHIGI. This was probably designed by Carlo Maderno, although it has also been ascribed to Giacomo della Porta. Having previously belonged to Cardinal Pietro Aldobrandini, it was bought in 1659 by the Chigi Pope, Alexander VII, who employed Felice Della Greca to alter it for him and to design a new façade on Piazza Colonna. It is now the seat of the Presidenza del Consiglio.

34. The PALAZZO CHIGI-ODESCALCHI in the Piazza SS. Apostoli, having belonged successively to the Colonna, the Ludovisi and the Chigi families, was rebuilt for the Odescalchi, the family of Innocent XI (1676–89), by Bernini in 1664. The courtyard is by Carlo Maderno (c. 1623); the wings were added in the middle of the eighteenth century by Nicola Salvi and Luigi Vanvitelli.

35. The small Egyptian OBELISK IN PIAZZA DELLA MINERVA, of the sixth century B.C., was found in the ruins of the Temple of Isis, a part of whose precincts formed the garden of the Dominican convent attached to the church of S. MARIA SOPRA MINERVA. The supporting elephant was sculpted in marble to Bernini's designs in 1667.

13. IL SETTECENTO

1. The confraternity which cared for the Hospice and church of S. TRINITÀ DEI PELLEGRINI was founded by St Philip Neri for the benefit of pilgrims in the Holy Year of 1550. The large hospice building was completed in 1625, thirty-three years after St Philip's death. It was converted into a foundling hospital in the nineteenth century.

2. Built in 1580–82 to serve the adjoining hospital for Polish pilgrims, the church of S. STANISLAO DEI POLACCHI, on the corner of Via delle Botteghe Oscure and Via dei Polacchi, is dedicated to the Bishop of Cracow, murdered in 1072 by King Boleslaw II whom he had rebuked for leading a disorderly life.

3. The church of S. MARIA DI MONSERRATO near the Piazza Farnese was built for the Borgia Pope Alexander VI whose remains, together with those of his fellow Spaniard, Calixtus III (1455–8), were transferred here from ST PETER'S. It was formerly attributed to Antonio da Sangallo the elder, but is now thought to be more probably the work of his nephew. Francesco da Volterra designed the portal of the façade.

4. The church of SANT' ANTONIO, whose ornate Baroque façade faces on to Via dei Portoghesi, was begun towards the middle of the seventeenth century on the site of a church built for the Portuguese colony in Rome during the pontificate of Eugenius IV (1431–47). The architects were Gaspare Guerra, Carlo Rainaldi and Cristoforo Shor, one of a family of artists from Innsbruck who completed it in 1695. The façade is by Martino Longhi the younger. The monument to Alessandro de Souza is by Canova, the Madonna and Child by Antoniazzo Romano.

5. The church of SAN LUIGI DEI FRANCESI, near the PALAZZO MADAMA, was founded by Pope Leo X, whose cousin, Cardinal Giulio de' Medici, later Pope Clement VII, laid the foundation stone. Giacomo della Porta probably designed the late-Renaissance façade which has also been attributed to Domenico Fontana. Work on the church was delayed from 1524 until 1580 when during the Regency of Catherine de Medicis, Domenico Fontana was commissioned to complete the building, which was consecrated in 1589. The frescos of the life of St Cecilia are by Domenichino, and the fine paintings in the chapel of St Matthew by Caravaggio.

6. Established in 1550 by the Portuguese St John of God, the religious order of the Fatebenefratelli founded their Roman Hospital of SAN GIOVANNI DI DIO on the Tiber Island, probably on the site of a medieval hospice. Tradition has it that Rahere, the Augustinian of Frankish descent who was a denizen of the English court of William II, came here to recover from an attack of malarial fever, and was inspired by his visit to establish St Bartholomew's,

London's oldest hospital, which was founded in 1123. The hospital of San Giovanni was rebuilt in 1930 by Cesare Bazzani. The adjoining church of SAN GIOVANNI CALABITA, which also belongs to the order, was reconstructed in 1640. The rich interior (1736–41) is by Romano Carapecchia. The church of S. BARTOLOMEO ALL' ISOLA was founded in the tenth century by the Emperor Otto III. It was rebuilt from 1583 to the designs of Martino Longhi the elder. The façade (1624–5) is probably by Orazio Torriani.

7. The Hospital of SAN GALLICANO IN TRASTEVERE off the Via Trastevere was completed by Filippo Raguzzini in 1725.

8. The Hospital of S. MARIA DELLA PIETÀ was founded in 1561 by a priest, Ferrante Ruis, who also built the church of the same name. The church, which is in the Piazza Colonna, was rebuilt by Gabriele Valvassori in 1731–5.

9. The huge OSPIZIO DI SAN MICHELE was founded in the sixteenth century on the riverside just above the Ponte Sublicio. The present building was designed in the seventeenth century by Carlo Fontana.

10. The Hospital of S. MARIA DELLA CONSOLAZIONE was attached to the church of the same name in the Piazza della Consolazione. Dedicated in 1470, the church was rebuilt to the designs of Martino Longhi the elder in 1583–1606.

11. The Hospital of SAN ROCCO, originally a hospital of fifty beds for men, was extended through the generosity of Cardinal Salviati for the pregnant wives of bargees. The care, in confidence, of unmarried mothers was sanctioned by Pope Clement XIV in 1770. The adjoining Church of SAN ROCCO in the Via Ripetta had been opened as a chapel in 1499 by the Confraternity of Innkeepers and Bargees. The chapel was rebuilt and enlarged in 1657 by Giovanni Antonio de' Rossi. The neo-classical façade was added in 1834 by Valadier.

12. The FRENCH ACADEMY was founded in 1666 by Colbert, the French finance minister, by order of Louis XIV. The students were at first lodged on the Janiculum near the Church of S. ONOFRIO which was founded in 1415 as a hermitage for monks of the Hieronymite Order. They were later housed in the Palazzo Salviati in the Corso. This palace was exchanged for the VILLA MEDICI on the Pincian hill above the SPANISH STEPS in 1803. The Villa Medici was built by Giovanni and Annibale Lippi of Florence for Cardinal Ricci of Montepulciano from 1540. It was bought by Cardinal Ferdinando de' Medici in 1580 and thereafter belonged to his family until the French Academy acquired it. Galileo was held here in 1630–33. The fountain which stands in the Viale Trinità dei Monti in front of it used to have a Florentine lily in its centre. The present stone cannon-ball is said to have hit the wall of the villa when the unpredictable Queen Christina of Sweden was unwisely invited to fire a cannon into the air from Castel Sant' Angelo. The *pensionnaires* of the Academy have included Fragonard, Ingres, Boucher, Berlioz and Debussy.

13. The TEATRO DELLE DAME was situated near the PIAZZA DEL POPOLO at the end of the Via Alibert where the Via Margutta joins the Via Babuino. It was

built by Conte Antonio d'Alibert to the designs of Ferdinando Fuga. Inaugurated for the carnival of 1717, operas were performed here as well as plays. It was also known as the TEATRO ALIBERT.

14. Designed by Marchese Girolamo Teodoli for Duke Sforza Cesarini, the TEATRO ARGENTINA was rebuilt by Pietro Camporese in 1837 and has recently been restored.

15. The TEATRO CAPRANICA was in the Palazzo Capranica which was built in the sixteenth century by Cardinal Domenico Capranica. It is now a cinema.

16. Founded in 1600 by Clement VIII, possibly as a result of the Pope's earnest hope for the conversion

of the Protestant King James I, the SCOTS COLLEGE in the Via delle Quattro Fontane was designed by Luigi Poletti who was responsible for the rebuilding of S. PAOLO FUORI LE MURA. The seminary has recently moved to Marino. The students wear a purple soutane and a red belt. The VENERABLE ENGLISH COLLEGE in the Via di Monserrato, established in 1362, was originally a hospice for English pilgrims. It became a college in 1579. The college buildings were restored in c. 1669–85. With some fifty other guests John Evelyn dined here during his visit to Rome in 1645 and 'afterward saw an Italian Comedy Acted by their Alumni before the Cardinals'.

17. The PALAZZO MUTI-PAPAZZURRI in the Piazza SS. Apostoli was completed in 1644, probably to the designs of Mattia de' Rossi.

18. The PALAZZO DEL DRAGO, formerly the Palazzo Albani, in the Via delle Quattro Fontane was begun in the seventeenth century by Domenico Fontana and finished by Alessandro Specchi who was responsible for the cornice and the tower. Since the Second World War it has provided premises for the British Council.

19. The VILLA TORLONIA, formerly Villa Albani, off the Via Salaria, was built between 1743 and 1763 by Carlo Marchionni for Cardinal Alessandro Albani. The bulk of the Cardinal's collection of classical sculpture was removed by Napoleon to Paris and recovered only in part in 1815. The villa was bought by Prince Alessandro Torlonia in 1866. The capitulation of Rome was signed here in 1870. (For the VILLA TORLONIA off the Via Nomentana see note 3, Chapter 17.)

20. The Capuchin Church of S. MARIA DELLA CONCEZIONE in Via Vittorio Veneto was built in about 1626 by Antonio Casoni of Ancona for Cardinal Antonio Barberini, a brother of Urban VIII, whose tombstone before the main altar bears the inscription in Latin, 'Hic jacet pulvius cinis et nihil', 'Here lie dust, ashes and nothing'. The face of Satan in Guido Reni's *St Michael Trampling on the Devil* is said to be a portrait of the artist's *bête noire*, Innocent X. The five chapels of the adjoining crypt are a cemetery for which the earth was brought from the Holy Land. When the cemetery was full, the bones and skulls of 4,000 friars were dug up to decorate the walls and vaults and to make room for further bodies in the earth. There are

also the skeletons of children, young sons of noble families, since burial here was considered a high honour and could be granted as a special privilege.

21. The PALAZZETTO ZUCCARI in Via Gregoriana was built as an academy of painting by the younger of the two Zuccaro brothers, Federico who spent part of his life abroad and painted both Queen Elizabeth and Mary Queen of Scots. The brothers were leaders of the Roman Mannerist school of painting. A loggia, attributed to Juvarra, was added in 1711 for Maria Casimira, Queen of Poland, who went to live here. The palazzetto later became the premises of the Hertzian library, specializing in the history of art.

22. The CAFFÈ GRECO, founded in 1760 by a Levantine, soon became the most renowned meeting-place in Rome. The American sculptor, William Wetmore Story, introduced Hans Andersen to Elizabeth Barrett Browning here in 1861. The house opposite used to be a boarding-house much favoured by English visitors, including Thackeray and Tennyson. Keats's friend, the painter Joseph Severn, who was appointed British consul in Rome in 1860, died here at the age of eighty-five in 1879.

23. The house, now known as the KEATS–SHELLEY MEMORIAL, was kept as a cheap lodging-house by a Signora Petri. The small room in which Keats died in February 1821 looks down upon the BARCACCIA FOUNTAIN in the PIAZZA DI SPAGNA. The house now contains an extensive collection of books on Keats and Shelley. On the other side of the square at No. 66 is the house where Byron lived when he was in Rome.

24. An ancient foundation, the church of S. GIULIANO DEI FIAMMINGHI or S. GIULIANO OSPITALIERO in the Via de Sudario, was remodelled at the end of the seventeenth century at the expense of a rich Flemish apothecary, Nicolaes van Haringhen, who died in Rome in 1705, having lived there most of his life. There was a hospital attached. William Kent's undistinguished ceiling was completed in December 1717.

25. The CAMPO DEI FIORI, now a fruit and vegetable market on weekday mornings and all day on Sundays, did not become a regular place of execution until after Bruno's death here in 1600. In the fourteenth and fifteenth centuries it had been celebrated for its

inns. One of these, La Vacca, on the corner of Via dei Cappellari and the Vicolo del Gallo was owned by Cardinal Rodrigo Borgia's mistress, Vanozza Cattanei, who invested her money in at least four inns in Rome. Her arms, quartered with those of her third husband as well as with those of her lover, can be seen on a shield on the wall of No. 13 Vicolo del Gallo. The statue of Giordano Bruno in the centre of the square is by Ettore Ferrari and was erected here in 1887 as a result of a political row. The mayor of that time was Duca Leopoldo Torlonia. He had been active in promoting the urban development of Rome, the street lighting of the CORSO and excavations in the FORUM. But he made the mistake, from a political point of view, of paying an official visit to the Cardinal Vicar and requesting him to express the good wishes of the Roman people to Pope Leo XIII on the occasion of his Jubilee. This provoked the instant dismissal of the mayor by the anti-clerical Prime Minister, Crispi. And, in order to scotch any notion of a closer relationship between the Roman civic authorities and the Vatican, Crispi followed up the dismissal of the mayor by the erection of the monument to Giordano Bruno and other reputed heretics whose names and likenesses are preserved in medallions around the base of the monument. Among those commemorated are Erasmus, Vanini, Pallario, Servetus, Wycliffe, Huss, Sarpi and Campanella. People standing in front of the statue on Sundays are liable to be approached by small boys with footballs who ask them to move out of the goal.

14. NAPOLEONIC INTERLUDE

1. The PALAZZO BRASCHI in Piazza di S. Pantaleo off the Corso Vittorio Emanuele II was built for the Duke Onesti-Braschi, the disagreeable nephew of Pope Pius VI, who once quelled an anti-papal demonstration in front of the palace by ordering his footmen to scatter gold coins among the mob and then belabouring the scrambling figures with a dog whip in each hand. Designed by Cosimo Morelli in the High Renaissance style, with one of the grandest staircases in Rome, the palace was completed towards the end of the eighteenth century. Formerly the Ministry of the Interior, it was converted in 1952 for use as the MUSEUM OF ROME. The works of art which the museum contains include fragments of frescos and mosaics from the old basilica of ST PETER's, busts and portraits of popes and cardinals, and paintings, water-colours and drawings of Rome

at various epochs, notably delightful views of the nineteenth-century city by Roesler Franz and Ippolito Caffi.

2. Inaugurated in 1784, the SACRISTY OF ST PETER's contains the treasure of St Peter's which, plundered by the Saracens in 846 and during the Sack of Rome in 1527, was substantially depleted by Napoleon as a result of the Treaty of Tolentino in 1797. It still, however, contains exhibits of great artistic worth and historical interest, including the Fisherman's Ring of Sixtus IV (1471–84); the jewelled cross of c. 575 which was given by the Emperor of the East, Justin II; and the so-called Dalmatic of Charlemagne which was, in fact, made no earlier than the tenth century and possibly as late as the fifteenth. The two large and lovely candelabra are by Antonio Pollaiuolo.

3. The VATICAN MUSEUMS, which are approached from the Viale del Vaticano to the north of the Belvedere and are reached and left by a beautiful and ingenious double ramp created in 1932 by Giuseppe Momo, comprise:

(i) The PINACOTECA VATICANA or VATICAN PICTURE LIBRARY. This was completed in 1932 for Pope Pius XI (1922–39) to the designs of Luca Beltrami.

(ii) The MUSEO PIO-CLEMENTINO. This collection of classical sculpture, which the popes of the sixteenth and seventeenth centuries had exhibited in the CORTILE DEL BELVEDERE, was enlarged by Clement XIV and Pius VI and displayed by them in the rooms of the PALAZZETTO DEL BELVEDERE which was built by Innocent VIII (1484–92). The palazzetto, too small for this purpose, was enlarged with new buildings by Michelangelo Simonetti who, taking the PANTHEON as his model, created the Sala Rotonda which contains, as part of the floor, a Roman mosaic discovered at Otricoli in 1780 and an immense porphyry basin from the DOMUS AUREA. Some of Rome's finest pieces of classical sculpture are to be found in this museum's salons – the bust of Jupiter from Otricoli, the Barberini Juno, the Roman copy of Scopas's Meleager, and the Venus of Cnidos and Apollo Sauroctonos, both Roman copies of works by Praxiteles. The most important exhibits of the museum, however, are to be found in the portico built into the courtyard by Simonetti in 1773. These are the Laocoön, the Hermes (formerly known as the Belvedere Antinous) and the Apollo Belvedere. Alongside these is a Perseus by Canova which replaced the Apollo Belvedere when Napoleon's troops carried it off to Paris towards the end of the century.

(iii) The MUSEO GREGORIANO EGIZIANO. The first collection of Egyptian antiquities was made by Pius VII (1800–1823) from pieces in the VATICAN, the CAPITOLINE MUSEUM and HADRIAN'S VILLA. Gregory XVI arranged for their display here in 1839. The collection has been enriched by gifts from Egypt.

(iv) The MUSEO GREGORIANO ETRUSCO. This was founded by Gregory XVI in 1837.

(v) The MUSEO CHIARAMONTI. Founded by Pius VII (1800–1823) as an additional museum of antiquities, this comprises (a) the Museo Chiaramonti proper, (b) its extension, the Galleria Lapidaria which contains some five thousand pagan and Christian inscriptions, and (c) the Braccio Nuovo (see note 5, Chapter 9), which contains a statue of Augustus, said to be the finest portrayal of the Emperor which has come down to us.

(vi) The GALLERIA DEI CANDELABRI E DEGLI ARAZZI. This is a gallery containing classical sculpture of secondary interest. Frescoed with depictions of events from the life of Pope Leo XIII (1878–1903), it takes its name from the pairs of splendid candelabra placed beneath the arches, and the Flemish tapestries which were designed by pupils of Raphael. It was originally a loggia built by Pope Clement XIII over the west wing of the CORTILE DELLA PIGNA. The loggia was enclosed by Pius VI.

(vii) The GALLERIA DELLE CARTE GEOGRAPHICHE, the walls of which are decorated with maps of all the regions of Italy painted in 1580–83 by Antonio Danti, brother of the geographer, Egnazio. The gallery was built for Pope Gregory XIII (1572–85) and has been attributed to both Martino Longhi the elder and Ottaviano Mascarino.

(viii) The MUSEO PROFANO DELLA BIBLIOTECA, a single room designed for Clement XIII in 1767 to exhibit the papal collection of medals.

(ix) The VATICAN LIBRARY (see note 7, Chapter 7).

(x) The MUSEO SACRO DELLA BIBLIOTECA. Founded in 1756 by Benedict XIV, this was rearranged in the time of Pius IX to display objects of Christian art. It contains relics and church furnishings from the SANCTA SANCTORUM. The adjoining SALA DELLE NOZZE ALDOBRANDINI takes its name from the ancient painting which represents Alexander's marriage to Roxana. Discovered on the Esquiline hill in 1605 in very good condition, it is believed to be a copy of a painting by the Greek artist, Aëtion, of the fourth century B.C.

(xi) The MUSEO STORICO. This contains a collection of papal carriages and arms and armour once used by the Papal Guards.

(xii) The former Lateran collections comprising (a) the MUSEO PIO CRISTIANO, founded by Pius IX in 1854 and notable for its collection of early Christian sarcophagi, (b) the MUSEO GREGORIANO PROFANO, founded by Gregory XVI (1831–46), containing inscriptions, mosaics and sculptures, including a room devoted to statues of women, and (c) the MUSEO MISSIONARIO ETHNOLOGICO, founded in 1926 by Pius XI, which contains a visual history of the Roman Catholic missions all over the world.

There is also an excellent, extensive and surprisingly eclectic museum of modern art, many of whose paintings were presented by the artists themselves.

4. The GABINETTO DELLE MASCHERE is part of the MUSEO PIO-CLEMENTINO. It derives its name from the mosaic floor which was found in 1780 in HADRIAN'S VILLA and which is decorated with masks.

5. The OBELISK in front of SS. TRINITÀ DEI MONTI is an imperial Roman copy of an obelisk of the period of Rameses II. It was found in the gardens of the PALACE OF SALLUST and placed here in 1789 by order of Pius VI.

6. The OBELISK OF PSAMMETICUS II in PIAZZA DI MONTECITORIO was brought from Heliopolis by Augustus who had it placed in the CAMPUS MARTIUS. It toppled over after a fire, and was raised again by Pius VI in 1792. It is fourth in size of the thirteen obelisks still remaining out of the forty-eight which stood in Rome in imperial times. It is 29 metres high.

7. The OBELISK in PIAZZA DEL QUIRINALE was brought here from the AUGUSTEUM when Pius VI rearranged the group of the Dioscuri (the two huge statues of Castor and Pollux standing by their horses) which had been found in the BATHS OF CONSTANTINE during the pontificate of Sixtus V. The obelisk was placed between the Dioscuri and the whole decorative feature was completed when Pius VII's architect, Raffaello Stern, added the fountain, using a great granite basin which had stood in front of the TEMPLE OF CASTOR AND POLLUX in the FORUM.

8. The STATUES OF THE HORSE-TAMERS in Piazza del Quirinale are Roman copies of Greek originals. They probably once stood in the BATHS OF CONSTANTINE which were built nearby towards the beginning of the Emperor's reign in about A.D. 315.

9. The impressively dignified bronze STATUE OF ST PETER, which stands on the right of the nave of the basilica near the BALDACCHINO, was long believed to have been made in the time of St Leo I (440–61) and converted from an ancient statue of the Capitoline Jupiter. Most authorities, however, now assert that it dates from the thirteenth century and believe it to be the work of Arnolfo di Cambio. The marble throne is certainly by a craftsman of the Renaissance, and the Sicilian jasper plinth with its green porphyry panels was carved in 1756–7 by Carlo Marchionni. For centuries the faithful have filed past the seated figure, whose right hand is raised in benediction and whose left clasps a large key, to kiss or rub their foreheads against the toes of the outstretched right foot. On certain festivals the statue is bedecked with fine vestments, jewels and mitre.

10. The PALAZZO FALCONIERI in the Via Giulia originally belonged to the Odescalchi. They sold it in 1606 to Pietro Farnese, Duke of Latera, from whom Orazio Falconieri bought it in 1638. In 1646, having acquired a neighbouring palace, Falconieri commissioned Borromini to design a new façade and a grand staircase. It is now occupied by the Hungarian Academy of Arts.

In 1815 Madame Mère bought the PALAZZO ASTE-BUONAPARTE (now MISCIATELLI) next to the PALAZZO DORIA. This was built in 1658–65 by Giovanni Antonio de' Rossi for the d'Aste family. From the covered balcony Madame Mère used to watch the promenade in the Corso below. The exterior was restored in 1979.

15. THE RISORGIMENTO AND THE ROMAN QUESTION

1. The VILLA CORSINI, whose celebrated salon had twelve doors and twelve windows and was known as the Casino dei Quattro Venti, was built by Simone Salvi towards the middle of the eighteenth century for the Corsini family. It was acquired in 1849 by the Prince Doria of the time who added its grounds to those of the Villa del Bel Respiro, also known as the VILLA DORIA PAMPHILJ. It was destroyed in the fighting and replaced by a triumphal arch.

2. The Casino of the VILLA DORIA PAMPHILJ was built about 1650 for Prince Camillo Pamphilj, a nephew of Pope Innocent X, by Alessandro Algardi. After the Second World War it was let to the Belgian government as a residence for their ambassador in Rome, and the surrounding extensive grounds were opened as a public park.

3. Known as del Vascello because it was shaped like a ship, the VILLA MEDICI DEL VASCELLO was designed by Basilio Bicci and built in the second half of the seventeenth century. It belonged to an agent in Rome of Louis XIV, Elpidio Benedetti, and was adorned with medallions and portraits of French royalty. Benedetti left the villa to the Duc de Nevers from whom it passed to Count Giraud whose name it bore during the events of 1849. Having been acquired by Prince Doria, its grounds were incorporated into those of the VILLA DORIA PAMPHILJ. It was later bought by the Medici family.

4. The CAFFÈ NUOVO was on the Corso on the ground floor of the PALAZZO RUSPOLI (built by Ammanati for the Rucellai in 1586). It was closed when the waiters declined to serve two French officers and later opened as the Caffè Militare Francese for the use of the French occupying forces. After the fall of Rome, it became a favourite haunt of officers in the army of King Victor Emmanuel II, and was then known as the Caffè Italia. It disappeared when the ground floor of the Palazzo Ruspoli was leased to the Banco Nazionale.

5. Paid for by the Prince Regent of England and commissioned by Pius VII on the advice of Cardinal Consalvi, who owed his advancement largely to Henry Benedict Stuart, Cardinal of York, Canova's MONUMENT TO THE STUARTS in ST PETER's was erected in 1819. It commemorates the Old Pretender, the *soidisant* 'James III', the Young Pretender, 'Charles III', and the Cardinal of York, 'Henry IX', who died in Rome in 1807.

6. Pauline Bonaparte, Napoleon's pretty and flirtatious sister, married Prince Camillo Borghese as her second husband in 1803. Canova's statue portrays her as Venus Victrix reclining on a couch with an apple in her hand. This pose and the nakedness of her breasts were her own idea and embarrassed the sculptor who had not wanted to reveal so much of his distinguished

model. When she was asked how she could have brought herself to pose almost in the nude, she replied that it had not worried her at all: there was a stove in the studio.

7. The CASINO OF THE VILLA GIUSTINIANI-MASSIMO stands just north of the Piazza San Giovanni in Laterano between the Via Tasso and the Via Boiardo with its entrance at No. 16 Via Boiardo. It was frescoed by the Nazarenes for Prince Camillo Massimo between 1821 and 1829. The reliefs, busts and medallions on the façade are in the style of Vasanzio, Pirro Ligorio and Borromini.

8. The park of the VILLA LUDOVISI covered a large part of the ancient GARDENS OF SALLUST in the area of the present Via Ludovisi between the Via Vittorio Veneto and the Via di Porta Pinciana. It was the property of Cardinal Lodovico Ludovisi, nephew of Pope Gregory XV (1621–3). The main building, by Domenichino of Bologna and Maderno, was demolished when Prince Boncompagni-Ludovisi sold most of the property for development in 1886. The palazzo by Gaetano Koch which took its place was completed in 1890. It became the residence of Queen Margherita and, after the Second World War, the AMERICAN EMBASSY. Within the present, greatly reduced, estate there still exists the Casino which contains, on the ceiling of the *gran salone*, Guercino's masterpiece, the *Aurora* of 1621.

The BRITISH EMBASSY by the Porta Pia in Via XX Settembre was designed by Sir Basil Spence after its predecessor had been blown up by Israeli terrorists in October 1946. The British ambassador's residence is the Villa Wolkonsky. Its grounds between the Via Statilia and the Via G. B. Piatti contain some fine remnants of the Neronian Aqueduct which brought the waters of the Claudian Aqueduct from Porta Maggiore to the imperial palace on the Palatine.

16. ROYAL ROME

1. The VILLA NEGRONI was situated between the VILLA MONTALTO and the BATHS OF DIOCLETIAN in the area of the present TERMINI railway station.

2. The PROTESTANT CEMETERY, or CIMITERO DEGLI INGLESI, lies close to PORTA S. PAOLO beside the PYRAMID OF CAIUS CESTIUS, a rich praetor who was buried beneath it in about 12 B.C. Until late in the eighteenth century the bodies of non-Catholics,

with the exception of Jews, were taken out of Rome for burial. Several were interred in the waste ground beneath the section of the AURELIAN WALL into which the Pyramid of Cestius had been incorporated. At the time of Keats's death in 1821, negotiations were in progress with Cardinal Consalvi, Pius VII's Secretary of State, for the creation of an enclosed cemetery. Keats's body, and, later, that of his friend, Joseph Severn, were buried in what became known as the Old Cemetery. The adjoining, cypress-shaded New Cemetery contains, among others, the tombs of Shelley and his friend, Trelawney; of Goethe's illegitimate son, Julius Augustus, who died in 1830; of the American sculptor, William Wetmore Story; of John Addington Symonds, the historian of the Italian Renaissance; of R. M. Ballantyne, the writer of boys' adventure stories. Some Italians are also buried here, including Antonio Gramsci, the first leader of the Italian Communist Party.

Beyond the Via Sabaglia is the British Military Cemetery which contains the graves of some four hundred British soldiers who died in and around Rome in the Second World War. It lies beneath MONTE TESTACCIO, a mound formed by shards of amphorae which were broken when they were unloaded from barges calling at the nearby river port, the Emporium, to discharge their contents of oil, wine and grain.

3. The PALAZZO CAETANI in the Via delle Botteghe Oscure was built in about 1564 to the designs of Bartolommeo Ammanati for Alessandro Mattei, Duke of Paganica. It was later acquired by the Negroni family before passing into the hands of the Caetani. The nearby church of S. CATERINA DEI FUNARI was founded in the twelfth century and rebuilt in the sixteenth by Guido Guidetti. The area takes its name either from a local family or from the rope-makers, *funari*, who carried on their trade here. The Via delle Botteghe Oscure is so called after the dark shops which formerly existed in the street and which medieval traders inserted into the arches of the THEATRE OF CORNELIUS BALBUS erected in 13 B.C. It was believed until recently that these shops had been built into the CIRCUS FLAMINIUS, but archaeological research has now placed the circus closer to the Tiber. The Via delle Botteghe Oscure has been considerably widened so that the name is no longer appropriate.

4. The CONVENT OF S. SILVESTRO IN CAPITE adjoined the church of S. SILVESTRO IN CAPITE.

The church was completed by Pope Paul I in 761 on the ruins of a Temple of the Sun erected by the Emperor Aurelian. It was one of Rome's ancient *diaconiae*. After the addition of the campanile in the thirteenth century, a design for a new church was submitted by Francesco da Volterra. Building began in 1593, shortly before Volterra's death. He was succeeded by Carlo Maderno who slightly modified Volterra's plans. The new church was consecrated in 1602. Redecoration began in 1680 under the direction of Carlo Rainaldi and was continued after his death by Mattia and Domenico de' Rossi and Lodovico Gimignani. The church originally contained an oratory kept by Greek monks who claimed to preserve here the head of St John the Baptist; hence the addition of *capite* to the name. In 1885 the church was handed over to English Pallottini fathers and became the church of the English Catholic community. The neo-Gothic Anglican church of All Saints, at 153 Via del Babuino, is by the English Victorian architect G. E. Street who also designed the American church of St Paul's at 58 Via Napoli. St Paul's was built in the Romanesque style in 1879 and contains mosaics by Burne-Jones.

5. The PALAZZO MADAMA was built in the sixteenth century by the Medici family and was occupied by both the Medici popes, Leo X and Clement VII, when they were cardinals as well as by Caterina de' Medici, afterwards Queen of France. It was given its present name when it was the Roman palace of Madama Margherita of Austria (see note 14, Chapter 9). The sumptuous three-storeyed Baroque façade, completed after much delay in 1649, is by Lodovico Cardi and Paolo Maruscelli. The palace has been used as the Italian Senate since 1871.

6. The buildings around the OSPIZIO DI SAN MICHELE included a housing estate, arts and crafts schools, a hospice for vagrant children and a reformatory for prostitutes.

7. The original TERMINI railway station was completed in 1876. The impressive modern building which replaced it was begun before the Second World War to the designs of Angiolo Mazzoni del Grande, who was responsible for the lateral buildings, and completed in 1950 by the construction of its striking façade and foyer by Eugenio Montuori, Annibale Vitelozzi, Massimo Castellazzi and Vasco Fadigati, assisted by the engineers, Leo Calini and Achille Pintonello.

8. Largely because subterranean springs caused protracted delays in the building operations, it was twenty-two years before the huge and ugly PALAZZO DI GIUSTIZIA, designed by Guglielmo Calderini, was completed in 1911 at the enormous cost of 40 million lire. Although the architect had declared, in response to criticism, that there was no reason why the Palazzaccio, as it had come to be called, should not stand as long as the nearby CASTEL SANT' ANGELO, it had to be abandoned temporarily in 1970 because it was considered unsafe. The three-storey building, which stands between the Piazza dei Tribunali and the Piazza Cavour, is constructed of large blocks of travertine and is surmounted by a quadriga by Ettore Ximenes. The massive statues along the façade are of renowned Roman jurists.

9. The MINISTRY OF WAR, now the MINISTRY OF DEFENCE, was built in 1876–83. The MINISTRY OF FINANCE (MINISTERI DELLE FINANZE E DEL TESORO), designed by Raffaele Canevari, was completed in 1877. The part occupied by the Treasury contains a museum of coins of the Italian mint.

10. The group of hospitals known as the POLICLINICO, designed by Giulio Podesti, was built in 1887–90.

11. Rome's monstrously conspicuous landmark the VICTOR EMMANUEL II MONUMENT, on the north slope of the Capitol overlooking Piazza Venezia, is 500 feet long and 200 feet high. The architect was Giuseppe Sacconi who chose to construct it in the glaring white *botticino* marble from Brescia that quite overpowers the lovely greys and browns, oranges and reds of the surrounding buildings. Described by Silvio Negro as 'a mountain of sugar', it was known to British soldiers in the Second World War as 'the wedding cake'. The monument contains offices, water tanks for fountains, a police station and the

archives of the Istituto per la Storia del Risorgimento Italiano. On the terrace above the lower steps is the tomb of the Unknown Soldier killed in the First World War, perpetually watched over by a guard of honour. The view of the centre of Rome from the top terrace is one of the finest in the city. To the left of the steps leading to the terraces are the fragmentary

remains of the TOMB OF C. PUBLICIUS BIBULUS, an Aedile of the first century B.C., which marked the beginning of the Via Flaminia.

12. Although the VILLA GIUSTINIANI-MASSIMO near the LATERAN has disappeared, its CASINO still remains (see note 7, Chapter 15). There is another VILLA MASSIMO at the north end of the Viale di Villa Massimo near the Via Nomentana. Its palazzina is the headquarters of the GERMAN ACADEMY.

13. The VILLA MONTALTO, once owned by Pope Sixtus V (1585–90), occupied a large area between Piazza dell' Esquilino and the TERMINI railway tracks.

14. The extensive grounds of the VILLA ALTIERI, built by G. A. de' Rossi for Cardinal Paluzzo Albertoni-Altieri in 1674, stretched from S. MARIA MAGGIORE to the CASTRO PRETORIO. Originally built by Tiberius's minister, Sejanus, for the Praetorian Guard in A.D. 23, the barracks of the Castro Pretorio were incorporated into the AURELIAN WALL and afterwards dismantled by Constantine. The buildings which replaced them were a stronghold much prized in the factional fights of the Middle Ages. The Jesuits took them over in the seventeenth century and named them after their most successful mission in the far east, Macao. They later became barracks for papal troops, and, after 1870, for the Italian army.

15. The TEATRO DELL' OPERA in the Via del Viminale was built for the hotelier, Domenico Costanzi, whose name it bore for several decades. Completed in 1880, it was acquired by the municipality of Rome in 1926. It was entirely renovated in 1956–60 by Marcello Piacentini and is now one of the world's major opera houses.

17. ROMA FASCISTA

1. The large PALAZZO DEL VIMINALE on the south-west slope of the Viminal hill was completed in 1920 to the designs of Manfredo Manfredi as the Ministry of the Interior and Health.

2. Built in 1592 for the Aldobrandini family of Pope Clement VIII, the PALAZZO CHIGI on the north side of Piazza Colonna has been ascribed to both Carlo Maderno and Giacomo della Porta. It was sold in 1659 by Donna Olimpia Aldobrandini Pamphilj to the Chigi Pope, Alexander VII, for his nephews. The palace, with its grand Baroque courtyard and façade on Piazza Colonna, was completed for the Chigi by Felice della Greca. The other façade was begun by Bernini in 1664. In 1746 the palace was bought by Prince Odescalchi who greatly extended its length to the designs of Nicola Salvi and thus deformed the effect of Bernini's work. In 1923 the palace was acquired by the Ministry of Foreign Affairs and was later taken over by the Presidenza del Consiglio.

3. The big neo-classical VILLA TORLONIA was begun in 1841 to the designs of Antonio Sarti for Prince Alessandro Torlonia on land purchased in 1825 by his father, Don Marino Torlonia. It was placed at Mussolini's disposal from 1925.

4. If the recently announced plans for a huge archaeological park in the centre of Rome are ever realized, the VIA DEI FORI IMPERIALI will disappear as the whole area between Piazza Venezia and the COLOSSEUM is uncovered.

5. After the destruction of many old buildings in the Borgo, the VIA DELLA CONCILIAZIONE was opened in 1937. The architects were Marcello Piacentini and Attilio Spaccarelli. The flow of traffic to the Vatican City was eased and the plans proposed by both Bramante and Bernini for a processional approach to the basilica were realized. But 'the whole external effect of St Peter's', which Augustus Hare considered

to depend 'upon the sudden entrance into the sunlit piazza from the gloomy street', was destroyed.

6. The area known as E.U.R. (Esposizione Universale di Roma) lies about three miles south of Rome and is reached by way of Via Cristoforo Colombo from the Porta Ardeatina. The idea for the exhibition came from Giuseppe Bottai in 1935 when he was Governor (Mussolini's substitute for Mayor) of Rome. Mussolini decided that the exhibition should be opened in 1942, the twentieth anniversary of the March on Rome. From the beginning, the dominating influence on the development and execution of the plans for E42, as the exhibition came to be called, was that of Virgilio Testa, the Secretary of the Governor of Rome's office, who retained the post until the fall of Fascism and who was recalled after the war. The supervisor of the architectural planning was one of the principal architects of the Fascist era, Marcello Piacentini, who already had some major public buildings to his credit, including the Banca d'Italia in Piazza del Parlamento (1918), the reconstructed Opera House (1928) and the Ministry of Corporations (1932). The site itself at Tre Fontane was, it seems, chosen by Mussolini himself in a reconnaissance of the area in December 1936. It was to cover (with later additions) about 1,000 acres. The exhibition was to be an 'Olympics of Civilization'. Work on the site began in 1938 and some of the larger buildings, among them the church (by A. Foschini), the Palazzo della Civiltà, the so-called 'Square Colosseum' (by G. Guerrini, E. La Padula and M. Romano), and the Palace of Congresses (by A. Libera) were completed before the outbreak of war. Thereafter work was suspended. During the war the area was occupied, first by German, then by Allied troops, and finally by refugees. The refugees burned all the floors and furniture, while gangs of robbers carried the work of demolition further until, by 1950, the site, in Guido Piovene's words, presented the aspect of a modern Pompeii. The next year Virgilio Testa was called in once again to carry out the restoration of the damaged buildings and complete those which had not been finished, including Nervi's Palazzotto dello Sport which was opened in 1958. The huge Museum of Roman Civilization by Aschieri, Bernardini, Pascoletti and Peressutti was presented to the City of Rome by the Fiat company.

7. The VILLA SAVOIA, now known as VILLA ADA, is on the northern outskirts of Rome, its grounds being bounded by the Via Salaria to the east and the Via Panama to the south. Part of the grounds are now a public park. The villa is presently occupied by the Egyptian Embassy.

8. Standing on the site of a palazzo designed for Pope Innocent XII (1691–1700), the PALAZZO WEDEKIND, on the west side of Piazza Colonna, was designed by Giuseppe Valadier and reconstructed in 1838 by Pietro Camporese who created the terrace supported by sixteen Ionic columns from Veii. It contained the famous Colonna and Fagiano restaurants on the ground floor. It was bought by the banker, Wedekind, who rebuilt it once again in 1879 to the designs of Gargiolli. The palace now provides offices for the *Tempo* newspaper.

9. Rome's main prison, the REGINA COELI, on the west bank of the river opposite the Ponte Mazzini, takes its name from a monastery which formerly occupied the site. The successor to the Carceri Nuove built by Pope Innocent X in the 1650s in Via Giulia, it was constructed on the lines of Bentham's Panopticon with cells radiating from a central warders' block.

EPILOGUE: THE ETERNAL CITY

1. Approached by way of the Via Appia Nuova and the Via Tuscolana, about ten kilometres from Rome, are the offices and studios of CINECITTÀ. Begun in 1937, to the designs of Gino Peressuti, the construction of Cinecittà was part of an attempt by the Fascist regime to develop the Italian film industry. The project was at first highly successful: in 1938–9 eighty-five films were made, whereas only twelve had been completed in 1930. For several years after the Second World War Cinecittà continued to be extremely profitable; and at one time Italy was making more money from the export of films than any country in the world other than America. Since then the industry has declined, and plans have been submitted to replace Cinecittà with suburban housing.

Sources

Ackermann, J.S., *The Architecture of Michelangelo* (1961)

Addison, Joseph, *Remarks on Several Parts of Italy* (1705)

Andrieux, Maurice, *Daily Life in Papal Rome in the Eighteenth Century* (trans. Mary Fritton, 1968)

Angeli, Diego, *Storia romana di trent' anni, 1770–1800* (1931)

Armellini, Mariano, *Le Chiese di Roma dal secolo IX al XIX* (revised by Carlo Cecchelli, 1942)

Gli antichi cimiteri cristiani di Roma e d'Italia (1893)

Ashby, Thomas, *The Aqueducts of Ancient Rome* (1930)

Baddeley, St Clair and Lina Duff-Gordon, *Rome and Its Story* (1904)

Bailey, Cyril (ed.), *The Legacy of Rome* (1923)

Baker, G.P., *Twelve Centuries of Rome* (1936)

Balsdon, J.P.V.D., *Julius Caesar and Rome* (1967)

Life and Leisure in Ancient Rome (1969)

(ed.) *The Romans* (1965)

Roman Women: Their History and Habits (1962)

Bandini, G., *Roma nel Settecento* (1930)

Barker, Ethel Rose, *Rome of the Pilgrims and Martyrs* (1913)

Barraconi, Giuseppe, *I rioni di Roma* (1974)

Barrow, R.H., *The Romans* (1949)

Belli, Giuseppe Gioachino, *Tutti i sonetti romaneschi* (1972)

Benigno, Jo di, *Occasioni mencate* (1945)

Bertolini, O., *Roma di fronte a Bisanzio e ai Longobardi* (1941)

Bianchi, Gianfranco, *Perchè e come cadde il fascismo* (1972)

Blakiston, Noel, *The Roman Question* (1962)

Bloch, Raymond, *Les Origines de Rome* (3rd edition, 1958)

Blunt, Anthony, *Borromini* (1979)

Guide to Baroque Rome (1982)

Bolton, J.R. Glorney, *Roman Century, 1870–1970* (1970)

Bonomi, Ivanoe, *Diario di un anno: 2 giugno 1943 – 10 giugno 1944* (1947)

Borsi, Franco and others, *Arte a Roma dal Neoclassicismo al Romanticismo* (1979)

Boswell, James, *Boswell on the Grand Tour: Italy, Corsica and France* (ed. Frank Brady and Frederick A. Pottle, 1955)

Bottrall, Ronald, *Rome* (1968)

Bowen, Elizabeth, *A Time in Rome* (1960)

Boyer, Ferdinand, *Le Monde des arts en Italie et la France de la Révolution et de l'Empire* (1969)

Brandi, Karl, *The Emperor Charles V* (trans. C.V. Wedgwood, 1965)

Brezzi, Paolo, *Roma e l'impero medioevale, 774–1252* (1947)

Brosses, Charles de, *Lettres historiques et critiques sur l'Italie* (3 vols., 1799)

Bryce, James, *The Holy Roman Empire* (1928)

Bull, George, *Inside the Vatican* (1982)

Burckhardt, Jacob, *The Civilization of the Renaissance in Italy* (15th edition, 1929)

Burke, Peter, *Culture and Society in Renaissance Italy, 1420–1540* (1972)

Bury, J.B., *The Invasion of Europe by the Barbarians* (1928)

History of the Later Roman Empire, 395–565 (1923)

Caesar, *The Civil War* (trans. Jane F. Gordon, 1967)

Càllari, Luigi, *I palazzi di Roma* (1932)

Le ville di Roma (1934)

Campos, Deoclecio Redig de, *I Palazzi Vaticani* (1967)

Capano, Renato Perrone, *La resistenza in Roma* (2 vols., 1963)

Caraman, Philip, *University of the Nations: The Story of the Gregorian University of Rome* (1981)

Carcopino, Jérôme, *Daily Life in Ancient Rome* (ed. Henry T. Rowell, trans. E.O. Lorimer, 1941)

Carrington, P., *The Early Christian Church* (2 vols., 1957)

Cary, Max, *A History of Rome down to the Reign of Constantine* (2nd edition, 1954)

Castagnoli, Ferdinando (with others), *Topografia e urbanistica di Roma Antica* (1969)

Catullus, Quintus Lutatius, *The Poems* (trans. Peter Whigham, 1969)

Chadwick, Owen, *The Popes and the European Revolution* (1981)

Chamberlin, E.R., *The Sack of Rome* (1979)

Chastel, André, *The Sack of Rome, 1527* (trans. Beth Archer, 1983)

Cicero, *Letters to his Friends* (trans. D. Shackleton Bailey, 2 vols., 1978)

Letters to Atticus (trans. D. Shackleton Bailey, 1978)

Clark, Eleanor, *Rome and a Villa* (new edition, 1976)

Clementi, F., *Il carnevale romano* (1939)

Collier, Richard, *Duce: The Rise and Fall of Benito Mussolini* (1971)

Cowell, F. R., *Cicero and the Roman Republic* (1948)

Crawford, Michael, *The Roman Republic* (1978)

Creighton, Mandell, *A History of the Papacy* (6 vols., 1903)

Cretoni, Antonio, *Roma Giacobina* (1971)

Cronin, Vincent, *The Florentine Renaissance* (1967)

    The Flowering of the Renaissance (1969)

D'Arrigo, Giuseppe, *Cento anni di Roma capitale, 1870–1970* (1970)

Davis, Melton S., *Who Defends Rome?* (1972)

De Felice, Renzo, *Storia degli Ebrei Italiani sotto il Fascismo* (1962)

Deiss, Joseph Jay, *The Roman Years of Margaret Fuller* (1969)

Delumeau, Jean, *Vie économique et sociale de Rome dans la seconde moitié du XVI siècle* (2 vols., 1959)

Delzell, Charles F., *Mussolini's Enemies* (1961)

De Rinaldis, Aldo, *L'arte in Roma dal Seicento al Novecento* (1948)

De Santillana, Giorgio, *The Crime of Galileo* (1956)

Dickens, Charles, *Pictures from Italy* (new edition ed. David Paroissien, 1974)

Dill, Samuel, *Roman Society in the Last Century of the Western Empire* (1910)

D'Onofrio, Cesare, *Le fontane di Roma* (1957)

    Gli obelischi di Roma (1965)

    Roma nel Seicento (1968)

Dorey, T. A. and Dudley, D. R., *Rome against Carthage* (1971)

Douglas, J. H., *The Principal Noble Families of Rome* (1905)

Ducati, Pericle, *L'arte in Roma dalle origini al secolo VIII* (1938)

Dudley, Donald Reynolds, *Urbs Roma* (1967)

Dupaty, Jean Baptiste, *Lettres sur l'Italie* (1824)

Erlanger, Rachel, *Lucrezia Borgia* (1979)

Falda, G. B., *Le fontane di Roma* (1691)

    Li giardini di Roma (1680c.)

Fermi, Laura, *Mussolini* (1961)

Ferrero, Guglielmo, *The Greatness and Decline of Rome* (trans. A. E. Zimmern, 1907)

Fischel, O., *Raphael* (2 vols., 1948)

Frank, Tenney, *A History of Rome* (1924)

    An Economic History of Rome (1927)

    Aspects of Social Behaviour in Ancient Rome (1932)

Frutaz, Amato Pietro (ed.), *Le piante di Roma* (3 vols., 1962)

Fugier, André, *Napoléon et l'Italie* (1947)

Garzetti, A., *L'impero da Tiberio agli Antonini* (1960)

Geller, H. and A., *Jewish Rome* (1970)

Gelzer, M., *Caesar Politician and Statesman* (1968)

Gianelli, G., *Roma nell' età delle guerre puniche* (1938)

Gibbon, Edward, *The History of the Decline and Fall of the Roman Empire* (edition of 1854–5)

Gill, Joseph, *Eugenius IV: Pope of Christian Union* (1961)

Giuntella, V. E., *Roma nel Settecento* (1971)

Goethe, Johann Wolfgang, *Italian Journey, 1786–1788* (trans. W. H. Auden and Elizabeth Mayer, 1962)

Golzio, Vincenzo, with Giuseppe Zander, *L'arte in Roma nel secolo XI* (1958)

    Le Chiese di Roma dal XI al XVI secolo (1963)

Grandi, Dino, *25 Iuglio: quarant' anni dopo* (1984)

Grant, Michael, *Caesar* (1974)

    The Climax of Rome (1968)

    A History of Rome (1978)

    Julius Caesar (1969)

    The Roman Forum (1970)

Gregorovius, Ferdinand, *History of the City of Rome in the Middle Ages* (1894–8, trans. Annie Hamilton, 9 vols.)

    Lucrezia Borgia (trans. J. L. Garner, 1948)

Grimal, Pierre, *La Civilisation romaine* (1968)

Grisar, Hartmann, *History of Rome and the Popes in the Middle Ages* (3 vols., 1911)

Guicciardini, Luigi, *Il Sacco di Roma* (1564)

Hales, E. E. Y., *Mazzini and the Secret Societies* (1956)

    Napoleon and the Pope (1962)

    Pio Nono (1964)

    Revolution and Papacy, 1769–1846 (1960)

Hare, Augustus, *Walks in Rome* (1878)

Harris, C. R. S., *The Allied Military Administration of Italy* (1957)

Haskell, Francis, *Patrons and Painters: Art and Society in Baroque Italy* (revised edition, 1980)

Haynes, Renée, *Philosopher King: The Humanist Pope, Benedict XIV* (1970)

Hayward, Fernand, *Pie IX et son temps* (1948)

Henig, Martin (ed.), *A Handbook of Roman Art* (1983)

Hermanin, F., *L'arte a Roma dal secolo VIII al secolo XIV* (1945)

Hibbard, Howard, *Bernini* (1965)

    Carlo Maderno (1972)

    Michelangelo (1975)

Highet, Gilbert, *Juvenal the Satirist* (1954)

    Poets in a Landscape (1957)

History of the Church (General Editor, Hubert Jedin; Translation Editor, John Dolen; 10 vols., 1980)

History of Rome and the Romans from Romulus to John XXIII (General Director, Robert Laffont; text by J. Bondet and others; trans., S. Rodway, 1962)

Hodgkin, Thomas, *Italy and Her Invaders* (8 vols., 1880–99)

Hofmann, Paul, *Rome, The Sweet Tempestuous Life* (1983)

Hook, Judith, *The Sack of Rome, 1527* (1972)

Horace, *The Complete Odes and Epodes* (trans. W.G. Shepherd, 1983)

Hülsen, Christoph, *Le chiese di Roma nel Medio Evo* (1927)

Hutton, Edward, *Rome* (1950)

Insolera, Italo, *Roma moderna* (1976)

Isbell, Harold, *The Last Poets of Imperial Rome* (1971)

Jackson, W.G.F., *The Battle for Rome* (1969)

Johnson, Paul, *Pope John XXIII* (1975)

Johnstone, R.M., *The Napoleonic Empire in Southern Italy and the Rise of the Secret Societies* (1904)

Jones, A.H.M., *Augustus* (1970)

Katz, Robert, *Death in Rome* (1967)

Kirkpatrick, Ivone, *Mussolini* (1964)

Krautheimer, Richard, *Rome, Profile of a City 312–1308* (1980)

Kristeller, Paul Oskar, *Renaissance Thought: The Classic, Scholastic and Humanist Strains* (1961)

Labat, O.P., *Voyages en Espagne et en Italie* (8 vols., 1730)

Lanciani, Rodolfo, *Ancient Rome in the Light of Recent Discoveries* (1888)

Pagan and Christian Rome (1893)

The Golden Days of the Renaissance in Rome (1906)

Larner, John, *Culture and Society in Italy, 1290–1420* (1971)

Lees-Milne, James, *Roman Mornings* (1956)

St Peter's: The Story of St Peter's Basilica in Rome (1967)

Lenkeith, Nancy, *Dante and the Legend of Rome* (1952)

Leppmann, Wolfgang, *Winckelmann* (1970)

Letarouilly, P.M., *Édifices de Rome moderne* (1869–1874)

Lewis, Naphtali and Meyer Reinhold (eds.), *Roman Civilization: Source Book 1: The Republic* (1951); *Source Book 2: The Empire* (1955)

Livy, *The Early History of Rome* (trans. Aubrey de Sélincourt, 1960)

Llewellyn, Peter, *Rome in the Dark Ages* (1971)

Low, D.M., *Edward Gibbon, 1737–1794* (1937)

Luff, S.G.A., *The Christian's Guide to Rome* (1967)

Mack Smith, Denis, *Mussolini* (1982)

Victor Emmanuel, Cavour and the Risorgimento (1971)

Madelin, Louis, *La Rome de Napoléon* (1906)

Mâle, Émile and D. Buxton, *The Early Churches of Rome* (1960)

Mallett, Michael, *The Borgias: The Rise and Fall of a Renaissance Dynasty* (1969)

Mann, H.K., *Lives of the Popes in the Early Middle Ages, 590–1304* (18 vols., 1902–32)

Martial, *The Epigrams* (trans. James Michie, 1978)

Martin, George, *The Red Shirt and the Cross of Savoy* (1970)

Masson, Georgina, *Companion Guide to Rome* (6th edition, 1980)

Courtesans of the Italian Renaissance (1975)

Italian Gardens (1961)

Italian Villas and Palaces (1959)

Queen Christina (1968)

Menen, Aubrey, *Rome Revealed* (1960)

Mitchell, R.J., *The Laurels and the Tiara: Pope Pius II, 1458–1464* (1962)

Mommsen, Theodor, *The History of Rome* (trans. W.P. Dickson, 4 vols., 1920)

Monelli, Paolo, *Rome 1943* (1954)

Morton, H.V., *A Traveller in Rome* (1957)

The Waters of Rome (1966)

Nash, Ernest, *Pictorial History of Ancient Rome* (2 vols., 1961)

Negro, Silvio, *Seconda Roma 1850–1870* (1943)

Roma non basta una vita (1962)

Nibby, Antonio, *Guida di Roma e suoi dintorni* (1894)

Nielsen, Frederick, *History of the Papacy in the Nineteenth Century* (2 vols., 1906)

Nugent, Sir Thomas, *The Grand Tour containing an exact description of most of the Cities, Towns and remarkable Places of Europe* (4 vols., 1749)

Ogilvie, R.M., *Early Rome and the Etruscans* (1976)

Pais, Ettore, *Storia di Roma* (5 vols., 1926)

Pallottino, Massimo, *Art of the Etruscans* (1955)

Paoli, Ugo Enrico, *Vita Romana* (1940)

Rome: Its People, Life and Customs (1958)

Paribeni, Roberto, *Da Diocleziano alla caduta dell' Imperio d'Occidente* (1941)

L'età di Cesare e di Augusto (1950)

La Repubblica fino alla conquista del primato in Italia (1954)

Parpagliolo, Luigi, *Italia: Volume V: Roma* (1937)

Partner, Peter, *The Lands of St Peter: The Papal States in the Early Middle Ages and the Renaissance* (1969)

Paschini, Pio, *Roma nel Rinascimento* (1940)

Pastor, Ludwig, *History of the Popes from the Close of the Middle Ages, 1305–1800* (40 vols., 1891–1953)

Payne, Robert, *The Horizon Book of Ancient Rome* (1966)

Pecchiai, Pio, *Acquedotti e fontane di Roma nel cinquecento* (1944)

Roma nel Cinquecento (1948)

Perondi, Mario, *Vatican and Christian Rome* (1975)

Pesci, Ugo, *I primi anni di Roma Capitale 1870–1878* (1971)

Petrocchi, Massimo, *Roma nel Seicento* (1970)

Petronius, *The Satyricon* (trans. J.P. Sullivan, 1965)

Piscittelli, Enzo, *Storia della resistenza romana* (1965)

Platner, S.B. and Thomas Ashby, *A Topographical Dictionary of Ancient Rome* (1929)

Plumb, J.H. (ed.), *The Horizon Book of the Renaissance* (1961)

Plutarch, *The Fall of the Roman Republic* (trans. Rex Warner, 1958)

Makers of Rome (trans. Ian Scott-Kilvert, 1965)

Ponelle, Louis and Louis Bardet, *St Philip Neri and the Roman Society of his Times* (trans. Ralph Kerr, 1932)

Pottle, Frederick A., *James Boswell: The Earlier Years* (1966)

Prescott, Orville, *Princes of the Renaissance* (1969)

Quennell, Peter, *The Colosseum* (1971)

Randall, Alec, *Discovering Rome* (1960)

Richards, Jeffrey, *Consul of God: Gregory the Great* (1980)
The Popes and the Papacy in the Middle Ages (1979)

Ridley, Jasper, *Garibaldi* (1974)

Rodd, Rennell, *Rome* (1932)

Rodocanache, E., *Le Pontificat de Jules II* (1928)
Le Pontificat de Leon X (1931)

Romano, Pietro, *Roma nelle sue strade e nelle sue piazze* (1936)

Rostovtzeff, M., *Social and Economic History of the Roman Empire* (2 vols., 1957)

Rowdon, Maurice, *A Roman Street* (1964)

Salvatorelli, Luigi and Giovanni Mira, *Storia d'Italia nel periodo fascista* (1972)

Schott, Rolf, *Michelangelo* (1963)

Scullard, H.H., *From the Gracchi to Nero* (1959)
Festivals and Ceremonies of the Roman Republic (1981)

Smollett, Tobias, *Travels through France and Italy* (1766)

Stendhal, *Promenades dans Rome* (2 vols., 1829)

Story, William Wetmore, *Roba di Roma* (8th edition, 2 vols., 1887)

Suetonius, Gaius, *The Twelve Caesars* (trans. Robert Graves, 1957)

Syme, Ronald, *The Roman Revolution* (1939)

Tacitus, Cornelius, *The Annals of Imperial Rome* (trans. G.G. Ramsay, 1952)

Tedesco, Viva, *Il contributo di Roma e della provincia nella lotta di liberazione* (1965)

Torselli, G., *Palazzi di Roma* (1965)

Toynbee, Jocelyn and J.B. Ward-Perkins, *The Shrine of St Peter and the Vatican Excavations* (1956)

Trevelyan, G.M., *Garibaldi's Defence of the Roman Republic* (1907)

Trevelyan, Raleigh, *Rome '44* (1981)

Trevor, Meriol, *Apostle of Rome* (1966)

Turchi, M., *La religione di Roma anticha* (1939)

Ullmann, Walter, *A Short History of the Papacy in the Middle Ages* (1972)

Van der Heyden, A.A.M. and Scullard, H.H., *Atlas of the Classical World* (1959)

Vasari, Giorgio, *Lives of the Artists* (trans. George Bull, 1965)

Vaughan, Herbert M., *The Medici Popes* (1908)

Vaussard, Maurice, *Daily Life in Eighteenth-century Italy* (trans. Michael Heron, 1962)

Vespasiano da Bisticci, *The Vespasian Memoirs* (1926)

Vighi, Roberto, *Roma del Belli* (1963)

Waley, Daniel, *The Papal State in the Thirteenth Century* (1961)

Wall, Bernard, *A City and a World* (1962)

Walsh, John Evangelist, *The Bones of St Peter* (1983)

Week, William Nassau, *Urban VIII* (1905)

Wickhoff, Franz, *Roman Art* (trans. Mrs A. Strong, 1900)

Wilkinson, L.P., *Letters of Cicero: A Selection in Translation* (1949)

Wittkower, Rudolf, *Art and Architecture in Italy 1600–1750* (1973)
Gian Lorenzo Bernini (1955)

Young, Norwood, *Rome and Its Story* (revised by P. Barrera, 1953)

INDEX

Page references appearing in **bold** type can be found in Part 3 of the book, under the section 'Notes on Topography, Buildings and Works of Art'.

Accademia di S. Luca, 173, **354**
Acqua Alessandrina, 173
Acqua Felice, 173
Acqua Paola, 181
Acqua Vergine, 113
Actium, battle of (31 B.C.), 34
Adam, Robert (1728–92), 222, 223
Adrian VI, Pope (r. 1522–3), 152
Agnes, St (b. c.304), 78, 337
Agrippa, Marcus Vipsanius (64 or 63–12 B.C.), 34, 38, 59
Agrippina (A.D. 15–59), 39
Alaric the Goth (c.370–410), 71, 328
Alberic I, Prince of Spoleto (d. 928), 83
Alberic II, Duke of Spoleto (d. 954), 83
Alberti, Leon Battista (1404–72), 115, 141, 345
Albertoni, Ludovica (d. 1503), 361
Albornoz, Gil Alvarez Carrillo de (1310–67), 106
Alexander II, Pope (r. 1061–73), 86
Alexander V, anti-Pope (r. 409–10), 112
Alexander VI, Pope (r. 1492–1503): ambition for his son, 133; Capello on, 136; and Charles VIII, 134; corpse, 139; death of Duke of Grandia, 137; election of 1458, 119; his election, 130; and the French, 133–4, 135; mistress, 165; personality, 133; popularity, 133; remains, 361; and Savonarola, 136; *see also* Borgia, Rodrigo
Alexander VII, Pope (r. 1655–67), 191, 193, 195, 229, 360
Algardi, Alessandro (1595–1654), 190
Ameli, Paolo, 357
Ammannati, Bartolommeo (1511–92), 172, 176, 353, 366, 367
Ampère, Jean-Jacques (1800–1864), 269
Anaclete II, anti-Pope (1130–38), 90
Anastasius, 76
Ancus Marcius, King of Rome (r. 642–617 B.C.), 5

Andersen, Hans Christian (1805–75), 222, 363
Angelico, Fra (prop. Guido di Pietro, c.1400–55), 118
Antonelli, Giacomo (1806–76), 249, 273, 274
Antoninus Pius, Emperor (86–161), 60; hall of, 200
Antonius, Marcus (c.83–30 B.C.), 26, 31, 32, 34, 59
Apollodorus of Damascus (fl. 2nd cent. A.D.), 52, 58, 323
Appian Way, *see* Via Appia
Aquinas, St Thomas (c.1227–74), 128
Ara Pacis Augustae, 35, **318**
Arcesilaus (fl. 1st cent. B.C.), 30
arches: Arch of Constantine, 69, 93, **331**; Domitian, 125; Gratian, Valentinian and Theodosius, 118, **344**; Janus Quadrifons, 69, **331**; Septimius Severus, 62, 93, 165, **221, 325**; Titus, 51, 93, 165, **322**; *see also* Arco
architecture: Baroque, 178, 181, 199; Classical, and Christian Church, 71, 73; Gothic innovations, 95; High Renaissance, 138
Arco degli Argentari, 62, **325**
Arco dei Banchi, 141, **348**
archaeology: in Fascist Rome, 291; in nineteenth century, 270–71
Aretino, Pietro (1492–1556), 151
Argiletum, **316**
Ariosto, Ludovico (1474–1533), 151
Armellini, Carlo, 252
Arnaldo da Brescia (c.1105–55), 90
Arnolfo di Cambio (c.1245–1302), 95, 339, 366
Augustus, Caesar Octavius (63 B.C.–A.D. 14), 34–6, 39, 342
Augustus, Mausoleum of, 36
arts, the: Clement VII, 152; Julius II, 143; Leo X, 151; Nicholas V, 118; portrait busts, 30; redecoration of churches in late

thirteenth century, 95–6; Scipione Borghese's collection, 183; Sixtus IV, 128
Ascaris, Giano, 151
Asprucci, Antonio (1723–1808), 357
Attila the Hun (fl. 5th cent. A.D.), 72
Augurs: duties and power of, 11–12
Aurelian, Emperor (c.215–275), 62, 326
Aurelian Walls, 71, 74, 81, 267, **326**
Avignon: anti-Pope Clement VII, 111; Clement VI, 105, 106; Cola di Rienzo, 99, 106; Gregory XI, 108; papal residence, 96; Petrarch, 97, 102; St Catherine of Siena, 110; Urban V, 108
Aventine, the: building programme under Augustus, 36; buildings on, 86, 93, 155; height, 315; plebeians march to, 9; Remus, 3
Azzolino, Decio (d. 1689), 193, 194, 195
Azzuri, Franco, 353

Badeglio, Pietro (1871–1956), 299
Balbus, Lucius Cornelius (fl. 1st cent. B.C.), 322
Ballantyne, R. M. (1825–94), 367
Baltimore, Frederick, Lord (1731–71), 217
Balzac, Honoré de (1799–1850), 222
Bande Nere, Giovanni delle (1498–1526), 154
Baraballo the priest, 150
Barberini, Maffeo, *see* Urban VII, Pope
Barbo, Pietro, *see* Paul II, Pope
Barigioni, Filippo (1690–1753), 345
Barluzzi, Giulio, 347
Barocci, Federico (1526–1612), 354
Baroncelli, Francesco, 106
Barrington's Tea-Rooms, 359
Basilica Aemilia, 36, **318**
Basilica Julia, 29–30, 36, **316**
Basilica of Maxentius and Constantine, **330**
Basilica Nova, 69
Basilica Ulpia, 52, **323**
basilicas, Christian, *see* churches

baths, 57–8, *see also* Thermae Neroniae
Baths of Caracalla, 62, 165, 221, **326**
Baths of Diocletian, 62, 217, **326**
Baths of Trajan, 41, 52, 143, **323**
Beaufort, Henry, Bishop of Winchester
   (*c.*1374–1447), 93
Belgioso, Princess, 258
Belisarius (*c.*505–65), 74
Belli, Giuseppe Gioacchino (1791–1863), 245
Belloc, Hilaire (1870–1953), 285
Beltrami, Luca (1854–1933), 364
Belvedere: Boswell at, 217; Cortile del, 142,
   172, 181, 193; Palazzetto del, 142;
   reconstruction, 167; white elephant at,
   150
Belvedere Terrace, 62, **325**
Benedict V, anti-Pope (r. 964, d. 966), 84
Benedict VI, Pope (r. 973–4), 86
Benedict VII, Pope (r. 974–83), 85
Benedict IX, Pope (r. 1032–45 *and* 1047–8),
   86
Benedict XI, Pope (r. 1303–4), 96
Benedict XII, Pope (r. 1334–42), 99
Benedict XIII, Pope (r. 1724–30), 227
Benedict XIV, Pope (r. 1740–58), 228
Benincasa, Caterina, *see* Catherine of Siena, St
Berengar II (*c.*900–966), 83
Berlioz, Hector (1803–69), 222
Bernardine of Siena, St (1380–1444), 116
Bernini, Gian Lorenzo (1598–1680): *Apollo
   and Daphne*, 183; architecture, 187, 191,
   355, 357, 360, 369; attitude to his secular
   works, 197; Borromini and, 190; Clement
   IX and, 196, 332; *David*, 183, 185;
   fountains, 181, 191, 358, 359; Fréart on,
   196–7; Innocent X and, 190; last months,
   197; marries, 189; Napoleon plunders,
   232; personality, 186, 189; and Queen
   Christina, 193, 196; Scala Regia, 360;
   sculpture, 183, 337, 356, 357, 359, 361;
   Urban VIII and, 185
Bernini, Pietro (1562–1629), 358
Bernis, François-Joachim de (1715–94), 210
Berthier, Louis-Alexandre, Prince de
   Wagram (1753–1815), 232, 234
Bertolio, Anton René (d. 1812), 235
Bisceglie, Duke of (d. 1500), 137
Bizet, Georges (1838–75), 222
Boccadifferro, Lodovico, 161
Bombace, Paolo (d. 1527), 161
Bombasi, Paolo (d. 1527), 161
Bonaparte, Caroline (1782–1839), 242
Bonaparte, Elisa (1777–1820), 242
Bonaparte, Joseph (1768–1844), 232, 242,
   347
Bonaparte, Letizia (1750–1836), 242, 366
Bonaparte, Lucien (1775–1840), 242

Bonaparte, Napoleon, *see* Napoleon I,
   Emperor
Bonaparte, Pauline, 328, 356, 366
Bonaventure, St (*c.*1217–74), 128
Boniface VII, anti-Pope (974 *and* 984–5), 85
Boniface VIII, Pope (r. 1294–1303), 95, 96,
   105, 128
Boniface IX, Pope (r. 1389–1404), 111
Bonomi, Ivanoe (1873–1951), 301
Borghese, Marcantonio, Prince of Vivaro
   (1601–58), 179, 181
Borghese, Scipione (1576–1633), 179, 181,
   183, 185
Borghesi, Giovanni Ventura (*c.* 1640–1708),
   346
Borgia, Cesare (*c.*1475–1507), 133, 135, 136,
   137
Borgia, Giovanni, Duke of Gandia (1476–
   97), 136, 137
Borgia, Lucrezia (1480–1519), 133, 136, 137
Borgia, Rodrigo (1431–1503), *later*
   Alexander VI, Pope (*q.v.*), 119
Borgo, the: attack on Otto's forces, 83;
   buildings in, 155–6; Colonna's army, 154;
   dangerous to walk in, 113; palazzi, 136,
   181; papal election of 1378, 110; protest
   march, 189; Sack of Rome, 157, 158; S.
   Spirito in Sassia, 92; Saxon schola, 79
Borromeo, St Carlo (1538–84), 338
Borromini, Francesco (1599–1667): assists
   Rainaldis, 190–91; churches, 349, 350,
   354, 356, 358; palazzi, 353, 366;
   personality, 190; Propaganda Fide, 360
Boswell, James (1740–95), 217–19
Bottai, Giuseppe, 370
Botticelli, Sandro (1445–1510), 128
Bourbon, Charles Duke of (1490–1527), 154,
   157, 161
Bramante, Donato (1444–1514):
   Michelangelo and, 169; nature, 143; S.
   Lorenzo in Damaso, 333; St Peter's
   Basilica, 141; Sistine Chapel scaffolding,
   144; Vatican Gardens, 348; years of study,
   138
Brancaleone di Andalò (d. 1258), 94
Brantôme, Pierre, Sieur de (*c.*1540–1614),
   159
Bregno, Andrea (1421–1506), 137, 345, 347
bridges (*see also* Ponte *and* Pons), **331**
Bridget, St (Bridget Godmarsson, *c.*1303–73),
   107–8
British Embassy, 367
Brosses, Charles de (1709–77): on de Bernis's
   banquet, 210; death of Clement XII, 227;
   on English Grand Tourists, 215;
   puddings, 222; on Roman palaces, 204; on
   Rome, 200–202

Browning, Elizabeth Barrett (1806–61), 363
Brunelleschi, Filippo (1377–1446), 151
Bruno, Giordano (1548–1600), 224–5
Brutus, Lucius Iunius, 7, 8
Brutus, Marcus Iunius (*c.*85–42 B.C.), 31, 32,
   34
building, *under Emperors*: Augustus, 36;
   Aurelian, 62; Caesar, 29; Constantine, 68–
   9; Hadrian, 58–60; Nero, 41; Septimius
   Severus, 62; Trajan, 52–3; Vespasian, 44
   under Popes: Alexander VI, 137–8; Clement
   VII, 152; Eugenius IV, 115; Gregory XIII,
   173; Honorius I, 78; Innocent III, 92;
   Julius II, 141–3; Leo X, 151; Martin V,
   113; Nicholas V, 115, 117, 141; Paul III,
   167, 169; Paul V, 181; Pius II, 122; Pius
   VI, 229–30; Sixtus IV, 128;
   see also Monuments
Byron, George Gordon, 6th Baron (1788–
   1824), 215, 222, 308, 363
Byzantium, 69, 78, 83

Cadorna, Count Raffaele (1815–97), 328
Caelian Hill, 221; buildings, 154–5; Golden
   House park, 41; height, 315; mansions of
   the rich, 93; S. Stefano Rotondo, 73; Villa
   Mattei, 94
Caesar Augustus, *see* Augustus
Caesar, Gaius Julius (100–44 B.C.), 23;
   abode, 319; advance to power, 26, 29;
   appearance and personality, 24;
   assassination, 31–2, 172; building
   programme, 29, 49; and Cleopatra, 29,
   30; deified, 34; Dictator, 29; early history,
   24, 26; prohibition on transport, 55;
   supposed ashes, 178; suspected of
   unbridled ambition, 30–31; Triumphs, 29
Caesarion (47–30 B.C.), 29, 30, 34
Caffè Greco, 222, **363**
Caffè Nazionale, 278
Caffè Nuovo, 268, 269, **366**
Cajetan (1468?–1534?), 159
Calderini, Guglielmo, 368
Caligula, Emperor (A.D. 12–41), 38–9, 49
Calixtus I, Pope and Saint (217/218–22), 178
Calixtus II, Pope (r. 1119–24), 90
Calixtus III, Pope (r. 1455–8), 118–19, 133,
   141
Calpurnia, wife of Julius Caesar, 26
Calvo, Fabio (d. 1527), 161
Camers, Julianus (d. 1527), 161
Camillus, Marcus Furius (d. 365 B.C.), 320
Campagna, the, 3, 74, 122, 160
Campini, Giovanni Giustino, 195
Campo dei Fiori, 123, 225, **363**
Campo Marzio, *see* Campus Martius
Campo Santo, 111

Campo Vaccino, 155

Camporese, Pietro the Younger (1792–1873), 370

Campus Martius, **315**; buildings, 212; Boswell on, 217; Romulus, 5; ruins, 111; thousandth anniversary celebrations, 62; Trajan's Column, 52; walks on, 58

Canevari, Raffaele, 368

Canina, Luigi (1795–1856), 271

Canova, Antonio (1757–1822), 222, 270, 361, 366

Capitol, the, 155; bell, 157, 205; Brancaleone's head displayed, 94; Brutus and conspirators at, 32; building programme under Augustus, 36; Cola di Rienzo, 101, 104, 105, 106; death of Berthold Orsini, 106; Gibbon on, 220; invasion of Rome, 14; *lupa*, 94; market, 93; Michelangelo's commission, 169; obelisk, 94; redevelopment under Vespasian, 44; Republicans' stronghold, 90; Temple of Jupiter, 6, 13, 36; Trees of Liberty, 234

Capitoline Museum, *see* Palazzo Nuovo

Cappella di S. Andrea, 355

Caracalla, Emperor (188–217), 61

Caravaggio, Giulio Merisi da, 353

Caravaggio (prop. Michelangelo Merisi da Caravaggio, 1573–1610), 232

Caravaggio, Polidoro da (c.1495–1543), 161

Cardi, Lodovico ('Il Cigoli', 1559–1613), 368

Cardinal Camerlengo, the, 227

Carne, Sir Edward (d. 1561), 356

Carnival: during French occupation, 238; eighteenth century, 205–7; executions, 215; in imperial Rome, 125; Innocent XI, 197; Paul III revives, 165; Pius V, 173; Queen Christina and, 193

Carracci, Agostino (1557–1602), 352

Carracci, Annibale (1560–1609), 179, 352

Carrara, 143

Carthaginian War, First (264–241 B.C.), 15

Carthaginian War, Second (218–201 B.C.), 15

Casa di Crescenzio, 94, **342**

Casanova, Giovanni Giacomo, Chevalier de Seingalt (1725–98), 202, 222

Casanova, Marcantonio (1476–c.1527), 161

Casca, Publius Longus (d. 42 B.C.), 31–2

Casino Massimo, 270

Casino Pallavicini, 356

Casino Pio, 353

Casino of the Villa Giustiniani-Massimo, 367

Casoni, Felice Antonio (1559–1634), 363

Cassius Longinus, Gaius (d. 42 B.C.), assassination of Caesar, 31, 34; suicide, 34

Castagno, Andrea del (c.1421–57), 349

Castel Sant' Angelo, Archangel Michael appears, 75; Alexander VI, 134, 135, 137; Benedict VI murdered, 85; Boniface IX, 111; Borgo, 79; building works under Eugenius IV, 115; Cellini, 160; Church treasurers in, 110; Clement VII seeks refuge in, 154, 158, 160; French Revolutionary troops in, 232, 235, 242; gallows, 137; Gregory VII occupies, 88; Hadrian's mausoleum, 60, **320**; Inquisition's prison in, 225; makeshift ammunition, 74; Otto III takes, 85; Queen Christina, 193; rebels flee to, 83

Castellesi da Corneto, Adriano (c.1460–c.1521), 136, 181

Castello, Domenico (fl. 1619–58), 320, 354

castrati, 211–12

Castro Pretorio: barracks, **369**

catacombs, **326**; bodies of saints deposited in, 64, 68; Christian cemeteries, 64; Eusebius Hieronymus describes, 64; plundered, 81; of St Sebastian, 116

Catacombs of St Calixtus, 64, 222, 271

Catherine of Siena, St (Caterina Benincasa, 1347–80), 108, 110, 111, 343

Catilina, Lucius Sergius (d. 62 B.C.), 22, 23

Cato, Marcus Porcius, 'Censorius' (234–149 B.C.), 12, 15, 17

Cato 'Uticensis', Marcus Porcius (95–46 B.C.), 23

Cattanei, Vanozza, 133, 135

Cavallini, Pietro (c.1250–c.1330), 96, 339, 340

Cavour, Count Camillo Benso (1810–61), 271

Cecilia, St, 81

Celer, *architect* (fl. 1st cent. A.D.), 41

Celestine II, Pope (r. 1143–4), 90

Cellini, Benvenuto (1500–1571), 152, 156, 160

Cencius de Praefecto, 87

Ceri, Renzo da, 156, 157

Chamberlain, Neville (1869–1940), 293

charioteers, chariot races, 49, 50

Charlemagne, Emperor (c.742–814), 79–80, 81, 83

Charles I of Anjou, King of Naples and Sicily (1246–85), 95, 96, 128

Charles IV, Emperor (1316–78), 106, 108

Charles V, Emperor (1500–1558), 153–4, 165, 168

Charles VIII, King of France (1470–98), 133–5

Chiesa Nuova: *see under* churches, S. Maria in Vallicella

Chigi, Agostino, 'Il Magnifico' (c.1465–1520), 141, 147, 150, 156

Childeric III, King (d. 755), 79

Christianity: buildings in Imperial Rome, 68–9, 70–71, 73, 76; catacombs, 64, 68; Constantine, 68; Diocletian and, 63; early community in Rome, 67; increasing conversion to, 73; persecution, 64, 66–7; Visigoths, 71

Christina, Queen of Sweden (1626–89), 362; actresses, 211; Alexander VII on, 195; amours, 194; appearance, 191, 193, 198; Bernini and, 196; death and burial, 198–9; dress, 191, 194, 198; eccentric, 191; hospitality, 197; intelligence, 193; interests, 195; in Rome, 193; place of burial, 198–9

Christopher, anti-Pope (r. 903–4), 84

Church, the: and Baroque, 181; corruption, 111; Holy Years, 95, 99, 105, 111, 137, 202; pilgrims, 116; profit from property, 91, 122; reform, 86–7, 172–3; treasures, 110; Universal Jubilee of 1450, 116; wealth, 95

Church, French: Civil Constitution of the Clergy, 230; Napoleonic regime and, 241

churches: All Saints Anglican Church, 368; Church of the Gesù, 173, 189, **354**; S.Andriano, 76, **336**; S.Agnese fuori le Mura, 78, **337**; S.Agnese in Agone, 190–91, **358**, 359; S.Agostino, 113, 155, **343**; S.Anastasia, **319**; S.Andrea al Quirinale, 191, 197, **359**; S.Andrea della Valle, **359**; S.Angelo in Pescheria, 93, 101, **341**; S.Antonio, 202, **361**; SS.Apostoli, 105, **353**; S.Bartolomeo in Isola, 92, **362**; S.Bibiana, 186, **357**; SS.Bonifacio e Alessio, 92, **340**; S.Caterina dei Funari, **340**; S.Cecilia in Trastevere, 81, 96, **338**; SS.Celso e Giuliano, 118, **344**; S.Clemente, 88, 92, **340**; S.Cosimato, 160, **351**; SS.Cosma e Damiano, 76, **321**, 335; S.Crisogno, 92, **340**; S.Croce in Gerusalemme, 68, **329**; S.Francesca Romana, 81, 110, **324**; S.Francesco a Ripa, 196, **360**; S.Giacomo degli Spagnuoli, 159, **351**; S.Giorgio in Velabro, Velabro, 75, 96, 101, **335**; S.Girolamo della Carità, **354**; S.Giovanni Calabita, **362**; S.Giovanni dei Fiorentini, 151, 155, **349**; S.Giovanni dei Genovesi, **339**; S.Giovanni a Porta Latina, 92, **340**; SS.Giovanni e Paolo, 71, **334**; S.Gregorio Magno, 183, **356**; S.Giuliano dei Fiamminghi, 222, **363**; S.Ignazio, **354**; S.Ivo, **346**; St John Lateran (*see under separate entry*); S.Lorenzo in Damaso, 71, **333**; S.Lorenzo in Lucina, 88, 191, **359**;

churches (*cont.*)

S.Lorenzo fuori le Mura, 68, 76, 92, 290,
329; S.Lorenzo in Panisperna, 107, **343**;
SS.Luca e Martina, **355**; S.Lucia, 173, **353**;
S.Luigi dei Francesi, 202, **361**; S.Marcello,
107, 211, **342**; S.Marco, 125, **344**; S.Maria
degli Angeli, **326**; S.Maria dell' Anima,
159, 202, **351**; S.Maria Antiqua, 76, **335**;
S.Maria d'Aracoeli, 105, 157, 220, 305,
342; S.Maria in Cappella, **339**; S.Maria
della Concezione, 221–2, **363**; S.Maria in
Cosmedin, 76, 92, **336**; S.Maria in
Domnica, 81, 113, 151, **338**; S.Maria sopra
Minerva, 111, 217, **343**; S.Maria dei
Miracoli, **350**; S.Maria in Monserrato, 202,
361; S.Maria di Monte Santo, **350**; S.Maria
Maggiore (*see under separate entry*);
S.Maria Nova, 81, **338**; S.Maria della Pace,
128, **346**; S.Maria della Pietà, **362**; S.Maria
del Popolo, 128, 137, 143, 155, **346**;
S.Maria Rotonda, 76, 198, **336**; S.Maria
Scala Coeli, **336**; S.Maria de Schola Graeca,
76; S.Maria in Trastevere, 92, 96, 215,
340; S.Maria in Vallicella, 173, 190, 212,
354; S.Maria in Via Lata, 75, **335**; S.Maria
della Vittoria, 181, 183, **356**; S.Martino ai
Monti, 81, **338**; SS.Nereo e Achilleo, 128,
345; S.Nicola in Carcere, **315**; S.Onofrio,
362; S.Pancrazio, 113, **336**; S.Paolo fuori
le Mura, 71, 73, 83, 95, 96, 105, 116, **333**;
S.Paolo alle Tre Fontane, **336**; St Paul's
American Church, **368**; St Peter's (*see
under separate entry*); S.Pietro in Carcere,
217, **321**; S.Pietro in Montorio, 141, 155,
348; S.Pietro in Vincoli, 71, 143, 146, **334**;
S.Prassede, 81, **337**; S.Pudenziana, 71,
333; SS.Quattro Coronati, 81, 88, 92, **338**;
S.Sabina on the Aventine, 73, **334**;
S.Sebastiano, 69, 116, 183, **330**; SS.Sergio e
Bacco, 93, **341**; S.Silvestro in Capite, 88,
94, **341**; S.Spirito in Sassia, **341**;
S.Stanislao, 202, **321**; S.Stefano Rotondo,
73, 113, 115, 207, **335**; S.Susanna, 187,
357; S.Teodoro, 115, **344**; SS.Trinita dei
Monti, 173, 183, 230, **359**; SS.Vincenzo e
Anastasio, 78, **336**; S.Zeno chapel, 81, 337
Ciano, Galeazzo, Count (1903–44), 289, 293,
295–6
Cibò, Lorenzo, Archbishop of Benevento,
134
Cicero, Marcus Tullius, (106–43 B.C.): on
Augurs, 12; attitude to Caesar, 26, 30;
Books of Fate, 13; and Cleopatra, 30;
Consul, 23; death of, 34; on gladiatorial
combat, 49; on government, 18
Cigoli, Il, *see* Cardi, Ludovico
Cimabue, (b. before 1251, d. 1302), 95

Cimber, Tullius, 31
Cinecittà, 308, **370**
Cinna, Lucius Cornelius (d. 84 B.C.), 19, 24
Circus Flaminius, 49, **322**
Circus Gaius, 49, **322**
Circus Maximus, **322**; chariot races, 73;
obelisk, 175; popularity of, 50; Tarquinius
Priscus plans, 6; Tarquin the Proud, 7;
size and capacity, 49
Circus of Nero, **355**
citizenship, Roman, 13, 19
Clark, Mark (1896–1984), 305
Claude Lorrain (prop. Claude Gellée; 1600–
1682), 222
Claudius, Emperor (10 B.C.– A.D. 54), 39
Claudius II Gothicus, Emperor (214–70), 62
Clement I, Pope and Saint (*fl. c.*96), 178, 340
Clement III, anti-Pope (r. 1080–1100), 88, 91
Clement III, Pope (r. 1187–91), 90
Clement V, Pope (r. 1305–14), 96
Clement VI, Pope (r. 1342–52), 99, 102–6
passim
Clement VII, anti-Pope (r. 1378–94), 111
Clement VII, Pope (1523–34): appearance,
152, 161; capitulates after Sack of Rome,
160; and Charles V, 153, 154; and
Colonna, 154; death, 161–2; and
Michelangelo, 151, 167; in Orvieto, 160–
61; patron of arts and scholarship, 152;
personality, 152, 153, 156; raises money,
156–7; tomb defaced, 162
Clement VIII, Pope (r. 1592–1605), 178
Clement IX, Pope (r. 1667–9), 195, 196, 205
Clement X, Pope (r. 1670–76), 196
Clement XI, Pope (r. 1700–21), 229
Clement XII, Pope (r. 1730–40), 227, 228,
229
Clement XIII, Pope (r. 1758–69), 217–18,
228
Clement XIV, Pope (r. 1769–74), 204, 226,
228–9
Cleopatra VII, Queen of Egypt (69–30 B.C.),
29, 30, 34, 59
Cloaca Maxima, 7, **316**
Clough, Arthur Hugh (1819–61), 256, 264,
265, 268–9
Collatinus, *see* Tarquinius Collatinus
Collegio Capranicense, 57, **351**
Collegio Romano, 173, 193, **353**
Colonna, Giovanni (d. 1347), 104
Colonna, Giovanni, Cardinal, 97, 99
Colonna, Marcantonio (1535–84), 342
Colonna, Pompeo, 154, 159
Colonna, Prospero, 120
Colonna, Stefanello, 106
Colonna, Stefano (d. 1347), 103, 104

Colonna family: abets French; 96; anti-papal
revolt, 123; Calixtus III, 118; Clement VII
and, 154; Cola di Rienzo and, 103; Martin
V, 112; obliged to do homage, 101–2; and
Orsini, 97; Petrarch and, 99; revolt of
1351, 106; Riario, 127, 130; *Sacro Possesso*
147
Colonna Gallery, **353**
Colosseum, **321**; Boswell at, 217, 221;
Christian persecution, 67; earthquake,
105; gladiatorial combats and other
spectacles, 45–7, 49; in late fifth century,
73; masonry from, 115, 116, 122;
popularity, 50; repaired, 73–4; Sixtus V's
plan for, 175; structure, 45; Telemachus
stoned to death, 70; wild beast shows, 47,
62, 73; work begins under Vespasian, 44
Column of Marcus Aurelius, 60, 94, 175,
211, **325**
Comitium, **317**
Commodus, Emperor (A.D. 161–93), 60
Consalvi, Ercole (1757–1824), 237, 244
Constance, Council of (1414–18), 112
Constans II, Pogonatus, Byzantine Emperor
(630–68), 78
Constantia, 78
Constantine the Great, Emperor, (c.285–
337), 67–9, 71, 158
Constantinople: anti-Pope Boniface, 85;
Constantine founds, 69; Emperors' palace
81; Gregory as papal nuncio, 75; Romans
leave for, 74; Rome and, 78, 108; Turks
take, 124
Copernicus (Nicholaus Koppernigk, 1473–
1543), 152
Cordonata, 169, 305, 342, **352**
Corelli, Arcangelo (1653–1713), 196
Corradini, Gertrude, 221
Corso, the, 212; Carnival, 125, 173, 206,
207; de Brosses on, 200–201; French
Republican envoys, 231; Pius VII, 242;
Stendhal, 243
Coscia, Niccolò, (1682–1755), 227
Counter-Reformation, Pius V and, 172–3
Crassus, 'Dives' Marcus Licinius (c.115–53
B.C.), 22, 26
Crusades, 110, 118–19, 122, 124, 165
Curia, the, 29, **317**
Curia Pompeia, 31–2
Curio, Gaius Scribonius (d. 53 B.C.), 26

Damasus I, Pope and Saint (r. 366–84), 71
Dance, Sir Nathaniel, *see* Holland
Dandolo, Emilio, 258, 264
Dante Alighieri (1265–1321), 105
Danti, Antonio, 365
David, Jacques-Louis (1748–1825), 270

David, Marco, 353
Deakin, Richard (1802–73), 322
Decius, palace of, 195
De Gasperi, Alcide, 306
Della Greca, Felice (c.1626–77)
Demetrianus (fl. 2nd century A.D.), 332
De Rossi, Giovanni Battista, 271, 327
Derry, S.I., 301
Dickens, Charles (1812–70), 321
Didius Julianus, Emperor (r. and d. A.D. 193), 60
Dio Cassius Cocceianus (c.150–c.235), 60
disabitato, 93
Diocletian, Emperor (254–316), 62–3, 67, 69
disease: Black Death, 105; leprosy, 204; malaria, 115; plague, 75, 84, 116, 117, 160, 161; syphilis, 135, 189; venereal, 58, 135, 219
Dolci, Giovannino de', 128, 345
Dolci, Mario de', 345
Domenichino (Domenico Zampieri, 1581–1641), 352, 361, 367
Dominicis, Carlo de (active 1716–70), 344
Domitian, Emperor (51–96), 51–2, 64, 67
Domitian's Palace, 52
Domus Augustana, 52, **322**, 341
Domus Aurea, 38, 41, 52, **321**
Domus Flavia, 52
Domus Tiberiana, 38, **321**
Domus Transitoria, 41
Duca, Iacopo del (fl. 1574–82), 328
Dughet, Gaspard (1615–75), 338
Dupaty, Jean Baptiste, 219
Duphot, Léon (c.1770–97), 232

earthquakes: of A.D. 508, 74; of 1044, 86; of 1348, 105
Elagabalus, Emperor, (204–22), 61
Elizabeth I, Queen of England (1533–1603), 172
Emperor, Holy Roman, 90, 91, 94
Emperors, Byzantine, papacy and, 83
Erasmus, Desiderius (c.1466–1536), 151
Esquiline, the: Golden House park, 41; height, 315; mansions of the rich, 93; obelisk, 213; S. Maria Maggiore, 73
Estouteville, Guillaume d' (d. 1483), 119, 120
Eugenius III, Pope (r. 1145–53), 90
Eugenius IV, Pope (r. 1431–47), 112, 113, 115, 123, 128
E.U.R., 290, **370**
Eusebius Hieronymus, later Jerome, St (q.v.), 64
Evelyn, John (1620–1706), 179, 183, 222, 363

Fabbri, Eduardo, Count, 249
Fabullus, artist, (fl. 1st century A.D.), 41
Fanzago, Cosimo (1591–1678), 359
Farnese, Giulia, 165
Fatebene fratelli, Order of, 202, 361
Ferdinand of Austria, later (1558) Ferdinand I, Emperor (1503–64), 154
Ferdinand II, King (1810–59), 235, 250, 252
Ferrara, Duke of, (1486–1534), 144
Ferrari, Ettore, 364
Fesch, Joseph, Cardinal (1763–1839), 242
festivals: consualia, 4; Feast of St Peter, 205; Lupercalia, 31; Madonna of the Hams, 207–8; Rappresentazione dei Morti, 207; weekly, 204–5
Fetti, Fra Mariano, 150
Filarete, Antonio (c.1400–c.1469), 115, 344
Fiorentino, Giovanni Battista Rossa, 161
Flamens, 12–13
Flaminian Way, see Via Flamina
Fonseca, Gabriele, 191
Fontana, Carlo (1638–1714): church architecture, 340, 342, 353, 356, 359; monument to Queen Christina, 199; Ospizio di San Michele, 362; Palazzo di Montecitorio, 361
Fontana, Domenico (1543–1607), 187; buildings by, 329, 330; Cappella Sistina, 355; palazzi, 355, 363; re-erection of obelisks, 176–8, 356; Sistine Loggia, 355; Spanish Steps, 359; Vatican Library, 344
Fontana, Francesco, (1668–1708), 353
Fontana, Giovanni (1540–1614), 355
fontane (see also fountains); Fontana dello Scoglio, 181; degli Specchi, 181; delle Tartarughe, **342**; delle Torri, 181; di Trevi, see Trevi Fountain
Fontanella del Facchino, 348
Fontanone dell' Acqua Paola, 181, **355**
Formosus, Pope (r. 891–6), 84
Forum Boarium, 331
Forum of Nerva, 92, **321**
Forum Olitorium, 331
Forum, the, **317**; Arch of Septimius Severus, 62; Basilica Nova, 69; Bastille anniversary, 235; Boswell at, 217; Caesar rejects laurel wreath, 31; Charles V, 165; events taking place in, 29; Gibbon on, 220; land drainage, 6, 8; market, 221; masonry from, 122; omen at, 7; position of, 6; reconstructed under Caesar, 29; Senate House, 76; temple of Vesta, 11; Trees of Liberty, 234; Twelve Tables, 9
Forum of Augustus, 36
Forum of Trajan, 52, 242, **323**
Forum of Vespasian, 44, **321**

fountains: (see also fontane, fontanella, fontanone and Trevi Fountain): 355–6; de Brosses admires, 201; Paul V, 181, **355–6**; piazza della Navicella, 338; Viale Trinità dei Monti, 362; Villa Giulia, 172
Fountain of: the Barcaccia, 191, **358**; the Four Rivers, 191, 197, **359**; Juturna, 319; the Moor, 359; the Triton, 191, **358**
Fragonard, Jean-Honoré (1732–1806), 222
France: anti-clericalism, 230; Charles Vaud, 153; Clement VII and, 153; Jesuits expelled, 228; and Kingdom of Naples, 133–5; and papal election of 1378, 111; Pragmatic Sanction of Bourges, 122
Francesca Romana, St (1384–1440), 338
Francis I, King of France (1494–1547), 153
Franco, Battista (c.1498–1561), 165
Franz, Roesler, 364
Frederick II, Emperor (1194–1250), 94
French Academy, 207, 230, 231, **362**
French Revolution: attitude of Romans to, 230–31, 234–35; envoys in Rome, 230–31; Republican army occupies Rome, 232; Roman collaboration with, 234
Freud, Sigmund (1856–1939), 285
Frundsberg, Georg von (1473–1528), 154
Fuga, Ferdinando (1699–1780), 339, 347, 355, 362
Fuller, Margaret (1810–50), 250, 262, 268
furniture: church, 81; in Imperial Rome, 54, 55

Gaiseric, the Vandal (d. A.D. 477), 72
Galba, Emperor (3 B.C.–A.D. 69), 44
Galerius Trachalus (consul A.D. 68), 30
Galilei, Alessandro (1691–1737), 330, 349
Galileo Galilei (1564–1642), 225, 362
Galleria Nazionale d'Arte Moderna, 353
Galleria Spada, 353
Gallienus, Emperor (d. A.D. 268), 62
Garibaldi, Giuseppe (1807–82): arrives in Rome, 255–6; defence of the Republic, 258–61, 263–4; leads troops out of Rome, 267–8; quarrels with Mazzini, 262, 267
Gates, see porte
Gaulli, Giovanni Battista (1639–1709), 354
Gelasius II, Pope (r. 1118–19), 89
Gerroni, Giovanni, 106
Ghirlandaio, Domenico (1449–94), 128
Gibbon, Edward (1737–94), 61, 219–20; on Elagabalus, 61; in Rome, 219–20
Giberti, Gian-Matteo (1495–1543), 154
Gigli, Beniamino (1890–1957), 303
Gimignani, Lodovico (1643–97), 368
Giotto di Bondona (d. 1337), 95
Giovanni e Paolo, SS. (martyred 361), 71
Giovo, Paolo (1483–1552), 150

Gissing, George (1857–1903), 276, 280
Giulio Romano (Giulio Pippi, c.1499–1546), 152, 349, 350, 351
gladiatorial combats, 45–7, 49, 60, 70
gladiators, in revolt, 20
Goethe, Johann Wolfgang von (1749–1832), 214, 219, 222, 226, 350
Gogol, Nikolay Vasilyevich (1809–52), 222
Golden House, see Domus Aurea
Gonzaga, Ferrante (1507–57), 159
Gracchus, Gaius Sempronius (153–121 B.C.), 18, 19
Gracchus, Tiberius Sempronius (c.163–133 B.C.), 18
Grammont, Duc de (1819–80), 273
Gramsci, Antonio (1891–1937), 367
Grand Tour: Baltimore, 217; Boswell, 217–19; Englishmen, 215–17; Frenchmen, 221; Gibbon, 219–20
Grant, Peter (d. 1784), 219
Great Schism (1378–1417), 111, 112
Grande, Angiolo Mazzoni del, 368
Grande, Antonio del, 357
Grandi, Dino, Count (b. 1895), 295–6
Greca, Felice della, 361, 369
Greece: cultural influence on Rome, 16, 36, 39; art treasures from, 40; influence on Roman architecture, 59
Gregorian University, 347
Gregorovius, Ferdinand (1821–91), 83, 85, 86
Gregory, Master (fl. 12th century A.D.), 308
Gregory I the Great, Pope and Saint (r. 590–604), 75–6, 78, 92
Gregory II, Pope and Saint (r. 715–31), 78–9
Gregory III, Pope and Saint (r. 731–41), 78
Gregory V, Pope (r. 996–9), 85
Gregory VI, Pope (r. 1045–6), 86
Gregory VII, Pope and Saint (r. 1073–85), 86–9
Gregory IX, Pope (r. 1227–41), 94, 323
Gregory XI, Pope (r. 1370–78), 108, 110
Gregory XII, Pope (r. 1406–15), 112
Gregory XIII, Pope (r. 1572–85), 173, 175
Gregory XVI, Pope (r. 1831–46), 244
Guercino, (1591–1666), 190, 367
Guerra, Gaspare (c.1560–1622), 361
Guicciardini, Francesco (1483–1540), 133, 146, 151; on Clement VII, 152, 157
Guidetti, Guido, 367
Guido Reni (1575–1642), 197, 355, 356, 359
Guy de Montpellier, 341

Hadrian I, Pope (r. 772–95), 79, 81
Hadrian's mausoleum (see also Castel Sant' Angelo), 324–5
Hadrian's Villa, see Tivoli

Hamilton, Gavin (1730–97), 219
Hannibal (247–183 or 182 B.C.), 15, 327
Hare, Augustus John (1834–1903), 274, 280
Hasdrubal (Barca, d. 207 B.C.), 15
Hazlitt, William (1778–1830), 212–3
Heemskerk, Maerten van (1498–1574), 165
Helena, St (c.248–c.328), 67, 68, 342
Henry IV, Emperor (1050–1106), 87–8, 89
Henry V, Emperor (1086–1125), 90
Hertzian Library, 363
Hildebrand, see Gregory VII
Hitler, Adolf (1889–1945), 291, 293, 302, 303
Holland, Sir Nathanial Dance (1735–1811), 219
Honorius I, Pope (r. 625–38), 76, 78
Honorius III, Pope (r. 1216–27), 92, 94
Honorius IV, Pope (r. 1285–7), 95
Horace (65–8 B.C.), 34, 49
Hortensius, Quintus (dictator, 287 B.C.), 13
hospitals: S. Gallicano in Trastevere, 204, **362**; S. Giovanni di Dio, 202, **361**; S. Maria della Consolazione, 204, **362**; S. Maria della Pietà, 204; San Michele in Trastevere, 204, 280; S. Rocco, 204, **362**; S. Spirito in Sassia, 92, 115, 158, 202, 229, **341**
Houdon, Jean-Antoine (1741–1838), 222
House of Livia, 320–21

iconoclasm: Byzantine and Roman controversy, 78
indulgences, 137; finance raised by sale of, 111; Julius II, 141; Paul III, 167 restricted, 173; Universal Jubilee of 1450, 116
Ine, King of Wessex (r. 688–726), 341
Innocent I, Pope and Saint (r. 401–17), 72
Innocent II, Pope (r. 1130–43), 90
Innocent III, Pope (r. 1198–1216), 72, 95, 96
Innocent V, Pope (r. 1276), 95
Innocent VI, Pope (r. 1352–62), 106
Innocent VII, Pope (r. 1404–6), 111
Innocent VIII, Pope (r. 1484–92), 130, 158
Innocent X, Pope (r. 1644–55), 189, 190, 191, 197, 357
Innocent XI, Pope (r. 1676–89), 197
Inquisition, 172, 173, 224, 225, 256; Galileo, 225
Insula of Felicula, 323

James Francis Edward Stewart, the 'Old Pretender' (1688–1766), 219
James, Henry (1843–1916), 274–6, 281
James, William (1842–1910), 285
Janiculum, S. Pancrazio, 78, 181, 202, 259–61, 315
Janus Quadrilous, 78

Jerome, St (348–420), 64, 70, 72
Jesuits, 167, 228, 229
Jews, 156; Carnival, 125, 173, 205; fountain for, 181; Nazi occupation, 300–301; Paul IV and, 172, 173; Sacro Possesso of Leo X, 149; Titus's treatment of, 51
John XII, Pope (r. 955–64), 83–4
John XIII, Pope (r. 965–72), 84, 85
John XIV, Pope (r. 983–4), 85
John XVI, anti-Pope (r. 997–8), 85
John XXIII, anti-Pope (r. 1410–15), 112
John XXIII, Pope (r. 1958–63), 306, 344
Joyce, James (1882–1941), 285
Judaeorum, the, 143
Julia (39 B.C.–A.D. 14), 38
Julia Maesa (d. A.D. 226), 61
Julius II, Pope (r. 1503–13): appearance, 139; lamented, 146; and Michelangelo, 144, 146; new Basilica of St. Peter, 139, 141–2, 143; personality, 139, 140; Swiss Guards, 140; tomb, 143–4, 146, 158; Vatican, 142–3
Julius III, Pope (r. 1550–55), 170, 171, 172
Justinian I, Byzantine Emperor (483–565), 74
Juvenal, (b. c.55–60, d. after 127), 55, 56–7, 58

Kappler, Colonel, 301
Kauffman, Angelica (1741–1807), 219
Keats, John (1795–1821), 222, 276, 367
Keats–Shelley Memorial, 363
Kent, William (1686–1748), 222, 363
Kesselring, Albert (1885–1960), 300, 302
Koch, Pietro, 301

Laetus, Julius Pomponius (1428–98), 125, 128
Lambruschini, Luigi (1776–1854), 245, 246
Landini, Taddeo (c.1550–96), 342
Lanfranco, Giovanni (1581–1647), 352
Lares and Penates, shrine of, 36
Largo di Torre Argentina, 291
Lateran Palace: ancient bronzes, 128; Baptistery, 73; books of magic, 86; Cavallini, 96; Constantine gives, 68; death of pontiff, 85; dining hall, 81; Emperor Henry IV in, 88; Eugenius IV renovates, 115; falling into ruin, 105; Gregory VII, 88; Innocent III renovates, 92; Leo X, 149; pagan antiquities outside, 94; reconstructed, 95; Sancta sanctorum, 68, **329**; Scala Sancta, 68, 273, **329**; Sistine Loggia, **355**; Sixtus V, 175
law, Roman: Twelve Tables, 9, 13, 56; women, 56; law courts, 29–30, 69
Laurence, St (d. 258), 68, 76

Leaping Priests (Salii), 5

Lemoyne, Jean Baptiste (1704–78), 359

Leo III, the Isaurian Emperor (c.675/80–741), 78

Leo I, the Great, Pope and Saint (r. 440–61), 72

Leo III, Pope and Saint (r. 795–816), 80, 81, 329

Leo IV, Pope and Saint (r. 847–55), 81

Leo V, Pope (r. 903), 84

Leo VIII, Pope (r. 963–5), 83, 84

Leo IX, Pope and Saint (r. 1049–54), 86

Leo X, Pope (r. 1513–21), 147–52 passim

Leo XII, Pope (r. 1823–9), 244

Leo XIII, Pope (r. 1878–1903), 278

Leonardo da Vinci, (1452–1519), 138

Leonine Wall, **337**; Borgo, 83; civitas Leonina, 92; defended, 260; encloses St Peter's, 81; Henry IV's troops through, 88; Population within, 92; reinforced, 157

Leopardi, Giacomo (1798–1837), 222

Lepidus, Marcus Aemilius, (d. 13/12 B.C.), 34

Lesseps, Ferdinand, Vicomte de (1805–94), 262

Ligorio, Pirro, (c.1500–1583), 171, 175, 353

Lippi, Filippino (1457–1504), 343

Liszt, Franz (1811–86), 222

Livia, (Julia Augusta, 58 B.C.–A.D. 29), 36, 321

Livius Andronicus, Lucius (c.284–c.204 B.C.), 50

Livy (64 B.C.–A.D. 12 or 59 B.C.–A.D. 17): on Bacchanalia, 16; history of Rome, 3, 4–5, 7; invasion of Rome by Gallic nomads, 13–14; Octavian and, 34; Romans and Sabines, 4–5; Tarquin consults the oracle, 7

Lombardi, Carlo (1554–1620), 338

Longhi, Martino, the elder (d. 1591): Borghese Palace, 181, 356; churches, 354, 362; clock tower, 342; Riario Palace, 347

Longhi, Martino, the younger (1602–60), 336, 361

Lotto, Lorenzo (c.1480–1556), 349

Louis XIV, King (1638–1715), 230

Louis Napoleon, later Napoleon III, Emperor, (1808–73), 252, 273

Loyola, St Ignatius of (1491–1556), 167, 354

Lucius II, Pope (r. 1144–5), 90

Lucretia, 7–8

Ludovisi, Prince Niccolò, 191

Lumisden, Andrew (1720–1801), 219

Lungara, the 143

Lupa, 94

Lupercal, the, 36, **319**

Luther, Martin (1483–1546), 153

Lysippus, sculptor (fl. 328 B.C.), 30

Macel' de' Corvi, 167

Macrinus, Emperor (164–218), 61

Maderno, Carlo (1556–1629): Borromini and, 190; churches, 349, 356, 359, 368; fountains, 181, 355, 356; palazzi, 181, 342, 355, 357, 361; Villa Ludovisi, 367

Maderno, Stefano (c.1576–1636), 339

Maeltzer, Kurt, 300, 303

Maidalchini, Donna Olimpia (Pamphilj), 189, 339, 358

Mamertine prison, 39, **321**

Manfredi, Manfredo, 369

Manlius, Marcus, 14

Manners, Lord John (1818–1906), 271

Mantegna, Andrea (1431?–1506), 29

Mantua, Congress of (1459–60), 123, 124

Mantua, Francesco Gonzaga, Marquis of, 135

Manzù, Giacomo (b. 1908), 344

Marcellus I, Pope and Saint (r. 308–9), 342

Marchionni, Carlo (1702–86), 229, 363, 366

Marcillat, Guillaume de (d. 1529), 161

Marcus Aurelius, Emperor (A.D. 121–80), 60, 67

Margherita, Queen of Italy (1851–1926), 278

Marius, Gaius (c.157–86 B.C.), 18–19, 24

Mark Antony, see Antonius, Marcus

Market of Trajan, 52, **323**

Marmont, Auguste de, duc de Raguse (1774–1852), 219

Marsigli, Luigi Ferdinando, Count (1658–1730), 195

Martial, Marcus Valerius (c.38/41–103), 45, 57

Martin V, Pope (r. 1414–31), 112, 113, 158

Maruscelli, Paolo (1596–1649), 368

Masaccio, Il (prop. Tommaso Guidi, 1401–28), 113

Masini, Girolamo (1840–85), 342

Maso, Angelo de (d. 1453), 123

Maso, Tiburzio and Valeriano de, 123

Matrema-non-Vuole, Clarice, 156

Matteotti, Giacomo (1885–1924), 287

Maxentius, Emperor (d. A.D. 312), 68, 69

May, Phil (1864–1903), 276

Mazarin, Jules (1602–61), 185

Mazzini, Giuseppe (1805–72): arrives in Rome, 252; inspires defence, 264; leader of Republic, 254; quarrels with Garibaldi, 262, 267; resigns and leaves Rome, 218–19

Mazzoni, Giulio (c.1525–1618), 353

Medici, Giuliano de' (1453–78), 126, 127

Medici, Ippolito de', 162

Medici, Lorenzo de', 'the Magnificent' (1449–92), 126, 127, 130, 147, 151

Medici, Maddelena de', 130

Melozzo da Forlì (1438–94), 128

Melville, Herman (1819–91), 276

Mendelssohn-Bartholdy, Felix (1809–47), 222

Mengs, Anton Raphael (1728–79), 222

Mérode, François-Xavier, 280

Messalina, Valeria (c. A.D. 22–48), 39

Metternich, Klemens, Prince von (1773–1859), 244, 246

Michelangelo Buonarotti (1475–1564), 60, 176; architecture, 169, 326, 328, 352 bis; Clement VII and, 167; death, 171; ill, 169, 170, 171; Last Judgement, 168, **352**; Leo X and, 151; Moses, 334, 349; other works, 342, 343, 352; Paul III and, 167; personality, 143, 144; physical ability, 169; Pietà, 169, **353**; Sistine Chapel, 144, 146, 147, **346**; and Sangallo's work, 169–70; tomb of Julius II, 143–4, 146, 167; unfinished work, 169; unwelcome commissions, 144

Miollis, comte de (1759–1828), 237, 238

Mithridates VI (120–63), 19

Momo, Giuseppe, 364

Monaldeschi, Gian Rinaldo, Marchese, 194

monasteries, 75, 76, 86

Moncada, Ugo de (c.1466–1528), 154

Monte Mario, 86, 152, 157

Monte Testaccio, 367

Montelupo, Raffaelo da, 165

Montesecco, Gian Battista, 126–7

Montesquieu, Charles-Louis ;(1689–1755), 204, 211–12

Montezemolo, Giuseppe, 301

monuments: Christian, 68–9, 70–1, 73; conversion for Christian uses, 76; disintegration, 78; Carolingian renaissance, 81; deplorable condition by 1300, 105; domestic, 53–4; Bramante examines, 138; nineteenth century, 280–3; protected under Eugenius IV, 115; Pius II protects, 122; Renaissance, 155–6; demolition for entry of Charles V, 165; Queen Christina, 199; Stuarts', 270, twentieth century, 307; Victor Emmanuel II, 280, **368**

Moore, Dr John (1729–1802), 216

Moravia Alberto (b. 1907), 301

Morelli, Cosimo (1732–1812), 364

Morison, Colin, 217

Moro, Aldo (1916–78), 308

Murat, Joachim, King of Naples (1767–1815), 242, 243

Museo Barracco, 352

Museo Capitolino, *see* Palazzo Nuovo
Museo Chiaramonti, 355
Museo delle Terme, 36, **320**
Museum of Rome, *see* Palazzo Braschi
Museums of the Vatican, *see* Vatican
Mussolini, Benito (1883–1945), 286, 303;
   arrest, 297–8; Dictator, 288–90; fall of
   Fascism, 299; at Grand Council meeting,
   295; and Hitler, 293; March on Rome,
   287; plans for development of Rome, 290;
   Prime Minister, 287; in Second World
   War, 195
Musuros, Markos (*c*.1470–1517), 151
Mylne, Robert (1734–1811), 222

Namatianus, Rutilius Claudius (*fl.* 412–17),
   70
Nanni di Baccio Bigio (*fl.* 16th cent.), 171
Naples, Ladislas, King of (1377–1414), 112
Napoleon I, Emperor: annexes Papal States,
   238; coronation, 237; depredations on
   Rome, 231–2; occupation of Rome, 237;
   and the Pope, 231; Napoleonic Civil Code,
   242
Narses (*c*.480–574), 74
Nazarenes, 270, 367
Nero, Emperor (37–68), 38, 39–41, 43–4;
   Christian persecution, 66–7; fire of 64
   A.D., 40–41, 66; building works, 329
Nerva, Emperor (*c*. 30–98), 52
Nicholas IV, Pope (Girolamo Masci, r. 1288–
   92), 95
Nicholas V, Pope (r. 1447–55), 112;
   appearance and personality, 113; building
   under, 115, 118; canonization of St
   Bernardine, 116; encourages the arts, 118;
   Universal Jubilee, 116; Vatican Library,
   118, **344**
Nobilior, Marcus Fulvius (*fl.* 195–179 B.C.),
   318
noble families (*see also* Colonna *and* Orsini):
   Annibaldi, 90, 94, 97, 101–2; Barberini,
   277; Boncompagni, 277, 278; Borghese,
   277; Caetani, 90, 104, 113, 277, 278;
   Conti, 97, 102; Corsi, 88, 90; Crescenzi,
   85–6, 89; Doria, 278; Farnese, 277;
   Frangipani, 90, 93, 97, 104; Normanni,
   90; Laterani, 68, 329; Massimo, 277;
   Papareschi, 90; Pierleoni, 88, 90; Ruspoli,
   278; Savelli, 90, 97, 101–2, 123; Tebaldi,
   90; Torlonia, 277; Tuscolani, 86, 90
nobles: citizens' revolts against, 90, 101, 102,
   106; Cola and, 99, 101, 103, 104; and new
   republic, 101–2; petty tyrants, 105–6
Numa Pompilius, King of Rome (trad., 715–
   673 B.C.), 5

Nugent, Sir Thomas (*c*.1700–1772), 224

obelisks: Paul VI erects, 230; Piazza della
   Minerva, 361; Piazza del Popolo, 355;
   Piazzo S. Giovanni in Laterano, 356;
   Piazza del Quirinale, 213, **365**; Piazza di S.
   Maria Maggiore, 203, Piazza di
   Montecitorio, 365; Rameses II, 175–8,
   342, **355**; SS. Trinità dei Monti, 365; Villa
   Mattei, 94, 342
Odoacer, King of Italy (r. 476–93), 73
O'Flaherty, Hugh, 301
omens: attitude of ancient Romans to, 11–
   12; Romans respect, 209; Romulus and
   Remus, 3; Tarquin the Proud, 7
Orange, Philip, Prince of (1502–30), 157,
   161
Orsini, Berthold, 106, 107
Orsini, Clarice, 147
Orsini, Giovanni Gaetano (Pope Nicholas III
   from 1227), 95
Orsini family: Calixtus III, 118; Cola di
   Rienzo and, 103, 104; and Colonna, 97;
   obliged to do homage, 101–2; power of,
   90; revolt of 1351, 106; and Riario, 128;
   Sacro Possesso, 147
Orti, Farnesiani, 38, **321**
Osborne, Sir D'Arcy, *later* 12th Duke of
   Leeds (1884–1964), 302
Ospizio di San Michele, 362
Otho, Emperor (32–69), 44
Otto I, the Great, Emperor (912–73), 83, 84,
   85
Otto II, Emperor (955–83), 85
Otto III, Emperor (980–1002), 87
Oudinot, Nicolas-Charles (1767–1847), 260,
   262, 269, 350
Ovid (43 B.C.–A.D. 17), 34, 49, 56

Pacca, Bartolomeo (1756–1844), 238
Palastrina, Giovanni Pierluigi da (1525–94),
   172
Palatine hill: Belvedere Terrace, 62; Boswell
   climbs, 217; building programme under
   Augustus, 36; buildings, 36, 38, 41, 42,
   88, 154–5; in eighteenth century, 221;
   fire on, 40–1; height, 315; House of
   Romulus, 8; location, 3; restoration work
   on, 74; Romulus and Remus, 3, 4; ruins,
   78
Palatium Sessorianum, 68
Palazzetto Venezia, **345**
Palazzetto Zuccari, 222, **363**
Palazzo della Cancelleria, 71, **345**; Bernini
   restores, 197; Giulio de' Medici, 152; Rossi
   at, 249; Sixtus IV and, 128;
   Winckelmann, 221

Palazzo Farnese, **351**; Alexander Farnese and,
   167; Carracci, 179; della Porta, 169;
   Queen Christina, 193; Salon d' Hercule,
   62
Palazzo Venezia, **345**; demonstrators burst
   into, 299; Fascist Grand Council, 295;
   fifteenth-century windows, 125;
   Mussolini in, 288, 290, 291; Sala del
   Mappamondo, 289, 290; Sala del Pappa
   gello, 295
palazzi: Palazzo Albani, 221; Aldobrandini-
   Chigi, 361; Altemps, **347**; Aste-
   Buonaparte, 366; Barberini, 190, 357;
   Borghese, 181, 204, 217, **356**; Braschi,
   229, 279, 300, **364**; Caetani, 367; della
   Cancelleria (*see under separate entry*);
   Capranica, 351; Castelli, 155; Cenci-
   Maccarani-di Brazzà, 156, **351**; Chigi, 288,
   369; Chigi-Odescalchi, 197, **361**;
   Cicciaporci, 156, **351**; Colonna, 252; dei
   Conservatori, 169, 341, **352**; Corsini, 232,
   347; Doria, 189, 237, 238, **357**; del Drago,
   221, **363**; Falconieri, 242, **366**; Farnese (*see
   under separate entry*); Fiano, 359; dei Flavi,
   322; Giraud-Torlonia, 136, 156, 181, **347**;
   di Giustizia, 280, **368**; Lante ai Caprettari,
   156, **351**; Lateran (*see under separate
   entry*); Madama, 280, **368**; Massimo alle
   Colonne, 156, **351**; Mattei di Giove, 342;
   di Montecitorio, 197, 240, 279, **361**; Muti-
   Papazzurri, 219, **363**; Niccolini-Amici,
   348; Nuovo, 128, 169, **352**; Orsini, 300,
   320; Pallavicini-Rospigliosi, 181, **356**;
   Pamphilj, 190–91, **358**; dei Penitenzieri,
   350–1; Quirinal (*see under separate entry*);
   Riario, 130, 195, **347**; Righetti, 318;
   Ruspoli, 266; dei SS. Apostoli, 159, **351**; S.
   Marco, 125, 126, 134–5; Sallust (*see under
   separate entry*); del Senatore, 94, 169, 342,
   352; Sforza-Cesarini, 133, **347**; Soderini,
   155; Spada, 172, **353**; Torlonia, 195; del
   Viminale, 288, **369**; Wedekind, 300, **370**
Pamphilj, Camillo, 191
Pamphilj, Filippo Doria, Prince, 305
Pannini, Gianpaolo (1692–1765), 343
Pantheon, **324**; Constans II plunders, 78;
   converted for Christian use, 76; Emperor
   Hadrian and, 59; Eugenius IV clears, 115;
   gold
   revetment stripped, 189; Queen Christina,
   198
papacy: Charles of Anjou and, 95; Charles V
   and, 153; in danger at Avignon, 108;
   demand for abdication of temporal power,
   90; disturbances and corruption, 84–6,
   89; election of 1378, 110–11; and
   Emperor, 83, 91, 94; Eugenius II and, 90;

financial responsibility, 122; influence and authority, 92; influence of Gregory I on, 75, 78; Julius II and temporal power of, 140–41; Lateran Pact, 290; Napoleon and, 231, 237; politics, 72, 126, 227; Republic and, 90–91; and return to Rome, 99, 108; Rome and, 94–5; rich Roman families and, 83; Second Vatican Council, 306; in Second World War, 302; Syllabus of Errors (1864), 273; Vatican Council (1869), 273; wealth, 141

Papal States: Jews expelled, 173; Julius II and, 139–40; Lombards restore, 79; Napoleon annexes, 238; in nineteenth century, 244–5; returned to Pope, 243; revenue, 122

Parione, 156

Parmigiano (prop. Girolamo Francesco Mario Mazzola, 1503–40), 161

Paschal I, Pope and Saint (r. 817–24), 81

Paschal II, Pope (r. 1099–1118), 89

Paul II, Pope (r. 1464–71), 125–6, 141

Paul III, Pope (r. 1534–49), 165–70 *passim*

Paul IV, Pope (r. 1555–9), 172, 173

Paul V, Pope (r. 1605–21), 179, 181, 185, 187

Paul, St (d. c.67), 64, 66, 71, 333

Pazzi, Francesco de' (d. 1478), 126, 127

Pecham, Robert (d. 1569), 356

Pelagius I, Pope (r. 556–61), 76

Penitenzieri, 155

Penni, Gian Francesco, 152

Pepin III, the Short, King (d. 768), 79

Peressuti, Gino, 370

Pertinax, Emperor (A.D. 126–93), 60

Perugino (prop. Pietro di Cristoforo Vannucci, c.1450–1523), 128, 349

Peruzzi, Baldassare (1481–1536), 151, 156, 161, 320, 351

Peruzzi, Salustio (d. 1573), 353

Peter the Apostle, St (d. c.64), 64, 66, 67, 69, 72

Petrarch, Francesco (1304–74), 97, 99, 102, 105, 106

Philip the Arab, Roman Emperor (202–49), 62

Philip IV, the Fair, King of France (1268–1314), 96

Philip Neri, St (1515–92), 173, 190, 354, 361

Philippi, battle of (42 B.C.), 34

Piacentini, Marcello (1881–1960), 369, 370

Piacentini, Pia, 347, 350

piazze: Piazza Barberini, 191; Branca, 135; del Campidoglio, 169, 305, **352**; Campitelli, 212; Capranica, 212; di Castello, 181; Colonna, 60, 173, 211, 231;

dei Crociferi, 113; Farnese, 62, 108; di Montecitorio, 230; Navona, 152, 159, 190, 204–5, 211, 212, **350**; Nicosia, 173; dell' Oro, 151; Palombara, 231; di Ponte di Sant' Angelo, 118; del Popolo, 151, 175, 200, 207, 215, 235, **350**; delle Quattro Fontane, 213; del Quirinale, 230; S. Giovanni, 123; di S. Giovanni in Laterano, 181, 207; S. Marco, 165; di S. Maria Maggiore, 181; S. Maria sopra Minerva, 197; S. Pantaleo, 229; S. Pietro, 165, 178, 181, 191, 201, 235; S. Salvatore in Lauro, 229; Scossa Cavalli, 181; di Spagni, 191, 204, 222, 223, **358**; Venezia, 207, 291

Piccinico, Giacomo (1420–65), 123

Piccola Farnesina, 352

Piccolomini, Aeneas Silvius, *later* Pius II, (*q.v.*), 113

Piero della Francesca (c.1420–91), 349

Pietà orphanage, 158

Pietro da Cortona (1596–1669): church architecture, 335, 338, 354; frescoed ceilings, 358; and Guernico's Holy Child, 190; S. Ivo's altarpiece, 346; pilgrims, 73, 202; Gregory I and, 75; guidebooks, 75; in Holy Years, 95, 105, 111, 116–17; largesse, 95; profitable trade, 115; robbed, 130; at St Peter's, 76, 137

Pincio, the, 213, 232, 275, 315

Pinturicchio, Bernardino (Bernardino di Betto di Biago, c.1454–1513), 128, 138, 342, 348, 349

Piranesi, Giambattista (1720–78), 222

Pisa, Council of (1409), 112

Pius II, Pope (Aeneas Silvius Piccolomini, r. 1458–64): anti-papal revolt, 123; background, 120; building under, 122; crusade, 122, 124; daily routine, 123; death of, 124; finance, 122; on Nicholas V, 113; on papal election of 1458, 119; personality, 120, 122; St Peter's, 141

Pius V, Pope and Saint (r. 1566–72), 172–3

Pius VI, Pope (r. 1775–99), 229–30, 232, 234

Pius VII, Pope (r. 1800–1823), 237, 238, 240, 242

Pius IX, Pope (r. 1846–78), 246–7, 249, 269, 271, 273

Platina, Bartolomeo de' Sacchi (1421–81), 125, 128

Plautus, Titus Maccius (c.254–184 B.C.), 50

plebeians: revolt of 494 B.C., 9; struggle for political power, 13

Pliny the Younger (61/62–c.113), 49, 59, 143

Plutarch (b. before A.D. 50, d. after 120), 20, 22, 31, 32

Poletti, Colonel, 305

Poletti, Luigi, 363

Policlinico hospital, 303, **368**

Pollaiuolo, Antonio (1429–98), 364

Pompey the Great (106–48 B.C.), 22, 26, 29, 318

Pons Cestius, 94

Ponte Molle, 152, 200, 234, 266

Ponte Sant' Angelo, 115, 117–8, 149, 196, **360**

Ponte Sisto, 128, 158, **346**

Pontelli, Baccio (c.1450–after 1492), 339, 346, 348, 353

Pontifex Maximus, 11, 26; house of, **319**

Pontine Marshes, 230, 242, 290

Ponzio, Flaminio (c.1575–1620), 330, 355, 356

population: in Trajan's time, 53; reduced by sixth-century sieges, 74; thirteenth century, 92; sixteenth century, 115; eighteenth century, 202; nineteenth century, 243, 282; twentieth century, 300, 305, 307

Porcari, Stefano (d. 1453), 123

Porta, Giacomo della (c.1537–1602): capomaestro, 175; churches, 178, 315, 336 *bis*, 354, 355, 361; fountains, 342, 354; palazzi, 169, 342, 352, 361; Sapienza, 346

porte, **327–9**; Porta Angelica, 258; Cavalleggeri, 258; Maggiore, 68; Pertusa, 157, Pia, 169, 213; del Popolo, 134, 200, 235, 237; Portese, 271; S. Giovanni, 88, 93, 235, 258; S. Pancrazio, 76, 250; San Paolo, 110; S. Sebastiano, 165; S. Spirito, 156, 157; Settimiana, 156; del Torrione, 157; Trastevere, 263

Portico d'Ottavio, 62, **325**

Poussin, Nicolas (1594–1665), Innocent X and, 190

Pozzo, Andrea (1642–1709), 354

Praetorian Guard, 36, 39, 52, 60, 61

Praz, Mario, 303

Prignano, Bartolomeo di, *later* Pope Urban VI (*q.v.*), 110

Prima Porta, 36

Propaganda Fide, 193

Protestant Cemetery, 276, **367**

Ptolemy XIII, King (63–47 B.C.), 29

Ptolemy XIV, King (c.59–44 B.C.), 29

Pyramid of Cestius, 367

Quirinal Palace, **355**; Gregory XIII begins, 173; informality at, 209; Paul V enlarges, 181; Pius VIII, 240, 242; Sixtus V, 175

Quirinal, the, 212; height, 315; Jesuit novices, 191; obelisks, 213; Servius Tullius, 6; temple of Quirinus, 36

Rabelais, François (1483–1553), 165
Rabirius, Caius (*fl.* 1st cent. A.D.), 52
Radet, Etienne, Baron (1762–1825), 238, 240
Raggi, Antonio (1642–86), 359
Raguzzini, Filippo (*c.*1680–1771), 362
Rahere (d. 1144), 361
Raimondi, Marcantonio (*c.*1480–*c.*1534), 161
Rainaldi, Carlo (1611–91): Borghese Palace, 356; churches, 190, 330, 337, 358, 359, 361, 368; high altars, 359
Rainaldi, Girolamo (1570–1655): palazzi, 342, 352, 358; S. Agnese in Agone, 190, 337
Raphael (Raffaello Sanzio, 1483–1520): Clement VII and, 152; *Fornarina*, 351, 358; Galatea, 351; Isaiah, 343; Napoleon plunders, 232; personality, 143; place of burial, 198; tapestries, 151, 161; Udine and, 161; Vatican *stanze*, 41, 151, 349; Villa Madama, 350
Reformation: Leo X and, 152; Charles V and, 153
Regina Coeli: prison, 302, 306, **370**
Regola *rione*, 156
Remus, 3–4
Renaissance: Filarete's bronze doors, 115; marble, 199; Paul IV and art of, 172; Rome and, 153
Republic, Roman: Brutus and foundation of, 8; in decline, 16; Greek cultural influence, 16; plebeians' political power, 13; political offices, 9, 11; religious offices, 11–13; structure of society, 17–18; wars, 14–15, 19; wealth, 16–17
revolts: against Otto I, 83, 84; citizens against nobility, 90, 101–2, 106; gladiators, 20; plebeians against patricians, 9; three anti-papal, 123
Riario, Girolamo, 126, 127, 128, 130
Riario, Pietro (1445–74), 126
Riario, Raffaele (1451–1521), 126, 127, 128, 133, 152
Rienzo, Cola di (1313–54), 99, 101–7 *passim*
Rioni, 339–40
Ripa *rione*, 156
Ripetta, the, 136, **347**
Rivani, Antonio, 'Cicciolino' (d. 1686), 195–6
Robert Guiscard, Duke of Apulia (*c.*1015–85), 88
Roman Academy, 125, 151
Romano, Antoniazzo, 361
Rome (*see also* Roman Society): French occupations, 232–5, 237–42; invasions, 13–14, 71–2, 84, 112; sacks, 88, 112, 154, 157–60; sieges, 74, 79, 88

Rome–Berlin Axis, 291–2
Romulus, 3–5, 36
Romulus Augustulus, Emperor (r. 475–6), 73
Rosa, Salvator (1615–73), 222
Roselli, Pietro, *architect*, 351
Roselli, Pietro, *soldier*, 266
Rossellino, Bernardo (1409–64), 141
Rossi, Domenico de', 368
Rossi, Giovanni Antonio de' (1616–95), 366, 369
Rossi, G. B. De, *see* De Rossi
Rossi, Mattia de' (1637–95), 363, 368
Rossi, Pellegrino (1787–1848), 249, 333
Rossini, Gioacchino (1792–1868), 222
Rostra, 29, 36, **317**
Rovere, Giovanni della, 126, 128
Rovere, Girolamo Basso della, 143
Rovere, Terenzio Mamiani della, 249
Rovigo, duc de (1774–1833), 242
Rucellai, Giovanni, 117
Rubicon, 26
Russell, Odo Wm., *later* 1st Baron Ampthill (1829–84), 273
Rusticus, *nephew of Gregory VII*, 88
Rusuti, Filippo, 96

Sabines, 4–5, 44
Sacre Via, *see* Via Sacra
Sacra Possesso, 147–9, 204
Saepta Julia, 58, **324**
Saffi, Aurelio (*c.*1820–90), 252
St Andrew's Monastery, 75
Sant' Angelo *rione*, 156
St John Lateran, Basilica of, **330**; Apostles' heads, 108; *cathedra*, 68; ceilings restored under Pius VI, 229; Cola di Rienzo, 101, 102; Constantine, 103; destroyed by fire, 97; mosaics, 96; pilgrims, 116; reconstructed, 95; remains of Caracallan baths, 62; Scala Regia, 191; Sistine Loggia, 175
S. Maria Maggiore, **334–5**; appointment of Rector, 106; Benedict XIV, 228; Borghese Chapel, 181; Boswell in, 217; Cappella Paolina, 179; Cappella Sistina, 175, **355**; Gregory VII kidnapped, 87; manger of baby Jesus, 76; mosaics, 73, 96; pilgrims, 116; remodelled, 95; and Trinità dei Monti, 175
St Peter's Basilica: baldacchino, 187–8, 357; Benedict XIV, 228; Bernini, 187; Bisceglie murdered, 137; Boswell at, 218; de Brosses on, 201; buildings around, 92; Campanone, 229; canonization of St Bernardine, 116; Cappella Clementina, 178, **355**; Cappella

Giulia, 172; Cappella Gregoriana, 175, 178, **355**; Cathedra of St Peter, 191, **360**; Cavallini, 96; Charlemagne, 79–80; Clement VIII, 178; Colonnade, 360; Constantine builds, 68, **330**; coronations, 80, 83, 88; crypt, 76, 198; demolition of old parts, 186–7; dome, 175, 178; Eugenius barred from, 90; façade, 357; Filarete's bronze doors, 115, **344**; Giotto, 95; Henry IV takes possession, 88; Julius II's reconstruction of, 139, 141–2; Leo X continues reconstruction, 151; Maderno, 187; *mandatum*, 218; mint near, 115; Michelangelo, 169–70; Michelangelo's Pietà, 169; new basilica built under Nicholas V, 115; Nicholas V, 115, 141; Paul VI, 229; paved, 81; Petrarch in, 99; pilgrims, 116, 137; Pius II, 122, 124; plundered, 83; Queen Christina buried in, 198–9; remodelled, 95; Sack of Rome, 158, 160, 161; sacristy, 229, **364**; St Andrew's chapel, 175; shrine of St Peter, 69; tomb of Paul III, 357; tomb of Urban VIII, 357; tribune for Papal Benediction, 122; Visigoths respect, 71; wolves and dogs, 111
S. Silvestro in Capite: convent, 279, **367–8**
S. Trinità dei Pelligrini, hospice of, pilgrims, 202, **361**
Salii (Leaping Priests), 5
Sallust (86–35/34 B.C.), 334
Sallust Palace, 71, **334**
Salvi, Nicola (1699–1751), 343, 361, 369
Salvi, Simone (*fl.* early 18th cent.), 366
Salviati, Francesco (d. 1478), 126, 127
Sanctis, Francesco de (1693–1731), 358
Sangallo the Younger, Antonio da (1483–1546): Cappella Paolina, 352; churches, 341, 349; Michelangelo and, 169–70; Palazzo Farnese, 169, 351; Paul III employs, 167; Porta S. Spirito, 329; processional route for Charles V, 165; Sala Regia, 352; Villa Madama, 350
Sangallo, Giuliana da (1445?–1516), 141, 143, 144, 350, 351
San Gimignano, Vicenzio di, 161
Sansovino, Andrea (*c.*1460–1529), 143, 151, 338, 343
Sansovino, Jacopo (1486–1570): churches, 342, 349; leaves Rome, 161; Madonna and Child, 344; palazzi, 348, 351
Santoni, G. B., 337
Sapienza, the: Leo X and, 151; Paul III restores, 167; Queen Christina, 193; Sack of Rome, 160; Sixtus IV reforms, 128, **346**
Sarti, Antonio (1797–1880), 369
Savonarola, Girolamo (1452–98), 136, 137

Scala Regia, 191

Scarampo, Lodovico, Cardinal, 123

Scarlatti, Alessandro (1659–1725), 196

Schopenhauer, Arthur (1788–1860), 222

Scipio, Publius Cornelius (d. 211 B.C.), 15

Scots College, 363

sculpture, statues: Apollo del Belvedere, 143, 232, **349**; Bernini's 'Longinus', 357; Bishop Santoni, 337; Caesar, 30; Canova's monument to Stuarts, 366; Canova's Pauline Bonaparte, 366; Castor and Pollux, 353; Claudia, 316; Cleopatra, 30; Cola di Rienzo, 342; Constantine, 94; Giordano Bruno, 364; horse-tamers, 230, **366**; Julius II, 144; Laocoön, the, 40, 143, 217, 231; Ludovica Albertoni, 360; Madonna, 107; Madonna and Child (Antoniazzo Romano), 361; Marcus Aurelius, 60, 84, 85, 94, 149, 169; Menelaus, 141; Michelangelo's Moses, 146, 167, 217, 334, **349**; Michelangelo's Pietà, 169, 353; Nero, 41, 45; Pasquino, 141, 189, **348**; Paul IV, 172; Paul IX, 335; Pius VII, 355; Pompey, 172, **353**; Ponte Sant' Angelo angels, 196, 360; S. Filippo Neri, 190; St Francis, 360; St Peter, 235, **366**; Trajan, 53; Victory, 70

Sebastian, St (d. c.288), 64, 69

Sebastiani, Antonio, 321

Sejanus, Lucius Aelius (d. A.D. 31), 38–9

Senate, the: authority of, 9; influence of rich families in, 69; and papacy, 90, 91; restoration of, 90; in Rome, 63; Trajan's Column, 94

Senate House, 20, 76

Seneca, Lucius Annaeus (d. A.D. 65), 49

Septizonium, 88, 165, 175, **340**

Sermoneta, Duchess of, 300

Sermoneta, Michelangelo Caetani, Duke of, 278

Servian Wall, 316

Servius Tullius, King of Rome, (trad. r. 578–535 B.C.), 6, 8, 316

Settini, Francesco, 359

Seven Hills of Rome, 315

Severn, Joseph (1793–1879), 276, 363, 367

Severus, Emperor (Lucius Septimius Severus, 145 or 146–211); 60, 62, 316, 319

Severus (Nero's architect, fl. 1st cent. A.D.), 41

Severus Alexander, Emperor (208–35), 62, 173

Sextus Tarquinius, 7, 8

Sforza, Ascanio Maria (1455–1505), 143

Shelley, Percy Bysshe (1792–1822), 276, 367

Shor, Cristoforo, 361

Sigismund, Emperor (1368–1437), 112

Signorelli, Luca, or Luca da Cortona (c.1445/50–1523), 128, 349

Simplicius, Pope and Saint (1468–83), 73

Sistine Chapel, 346; bequest of Sixtus IV, 128; Bourbon's body, 161; choristers, 151; Michelangelo's work in, 144, 146, 167, 168; Raphael tapestries, 151, 161

Sixtus III, Pope and Saint (r. 432–40), 73, 178, 329

Sixtus IV, Pope (r. 1471–84): appearance, 126; building works, 128; death of, 130; Medici, 126–7; nepotism, 126, 128, 130; prayer for, 346

Sixtus V, Pope (r. 1585–90): ancient buildings, 175; building programme, 173, 175; dome of St Peter's, 175, 178; Inquisitor General, 173; Maderno, 187; obelisk, 175–6, 178

slaves: attend gladiators, 46; domestic duties, 56, 57; revolt, 20, 22; seating in Colosseum, 45; transport, 55; treatment of, 17; vanquished brought to Rome as, 15

Smollett, Tobias (1721–71), 200, 223

Social War (91–87 B.C.), 19

society, Roman (see also plebeians and Rome): daily life in Imperial times, 53–8; in Middle Ages, 92–3; in eighteenth century, 209–12; organization of, 6; under Republic, 17–18; daily life of senatorial class, 55–6

Soria, Giovan Battista (1581–1651), 183, 340, 356

Spanish Steps, 222, **358**

Sparre, Ebbe, 191

Spartacus (d. 71 B.C.), 20, 22

Spechi, Alessandro (1668–1729), 358, 363

Spence, Sir Basil (1907–76), 367

Spiculus, gladiator, 43

Stahel, General, 300

statues, see sculpture

Stendhal (pseud. of Marie-Henri Beyle, 1783–1842), 222, 243

Stephen II, Pope (r. 752–7), 79

Stephen IV, Pope (r. 896–7), 84

Stern, Raffaello, 355

Story, William Wetmore (1819–95), 258, 261, 363, 367

Street, George Edmund (1824–81), 368

street-vendors, 54–5, 92, 95

Subura, the, 58

Suetonius Tranquilus, Gaius (c.69–122), 39, 43, 51

Sulla Felix, Lucius Cornelius (138–78 B.C.), 19–20, 22

Swiss Guard, 365; arrest proselytizer, 226; defence of Roman Republic, 255; Julius II founds, 140; Radet's force disarms, 240; Sacro Possesso of Leo X, 147; Sack of Rome, 157, 158

Symmachus, Quintus Aurelius (c.345–402), 70

Symonds, John Addington (1840–93), 367

Tabularium, 20, 221, **317**

Tacitus, Cornelius (c.56–c.120), 39, 40, 64, 66–7

Tarpeia, 316

Tarpeian Rock, 316

Tarpeius, Spurius, 316

Tarquin the Proud, King of Rome (trad. r. 534–510 B.C.), 6–7, 8, 316

Tarquinius Collatinus, Lucius, 7, 8

Tarquinius Priscus, King of Rome (trad. r. 616–579 B.C.), 5–6, 13

teatri (see also theatres): Teatro Argentina, 211; Capranica, 211, 212, **362**; delle Dame, 211, **362**; dell' Opera, 283, **369**

Tebaldo, Cardinal, 123

Telemachus, Christian monk, 70

temples: Temple of Apollo, 36, **319**; Caesar, 36, **318**; Castor and Pollux, 36, **319**; Claudius, 44, **321**; Concord, 36, **319**; Diana, 36, **320**; Hope, 315; Janus, 5, **315**; Juno Hospita, **315**; Jupiter Capitolinus, 6–7, 13, 18, 72, **315**; Jupiter Optimus Maximus, Minerva and Juno, see Jupiter Capitolinus; Juno Moneta, **320**; Juno Regina, 36, **320**; Jupiter Tonans, 36, **319**; Mars the Avenger, 36, **318**; Peace, 44, **321**; Quirinus, 36, **320**; Saturn, 29, 36, **319**; Trajan, **323**; Venus Genetrix, 30, **318**; Venus and Rome, 58, **324**; Vesta, 62, 70, **316**

Tennyson, Alfred, 1st Baron (1809–92), 222

Terence (186/185–159? B.C.), 50

Termini railway station, 280, **368**

Testa, Virgilio, 370

Thackeray, Wm. Makepeace (1811–63), 222

theatres (see also teatri): Theatre of Balbus, 50, **322**; of Marcellus, 36, 50, 93, 221, **320**; of Pompey, 31, 50, **318**

Theodore I, Pope (r. 642–9), 76

Theodoric the Great (Ostrogothic king, r. 493–526), 73–4, 318

Theodosius I, the Great, Emperor (347–95), 344

Theophylactus (fl. A.D. 911), 83

Thermae Neroniae, 40, **321**

Thorwaldsen, Bertel (1768/70–1844), 270, 355

Tibaldeschi, Francesco, 110–11

Tiber river: bridges, 70, 175; crossing, 3; Chigi's silver thrown into, 149; corpses thrown into, 18, 84, 136, 160; daily life on the banks of, 92–93; in flood, 81, 135, 227, 348; Gregory XI, 110, living thrown into, 158; pilgrims, 117, 118; refugees, 158; rubbish beside, 153; Saracen pirates, 83

Tiberius, Emperor (42 B.C.–A.D. 37), 36, 38; building works, 319

Titian (1488/90–1576), 167

Titus, Emperor (39–81), 51, 72

Tivoli, 59, 141, **324**, 365

Togliatti, Palmiro (1893–1964), 308

Torlonia, Leopoldo, Duca, 277

Tor de' Conti, 92, **341**

Tor di Nona, **347**; granary, 197; prison, 135; site, 360; theatre, 195, 211

Torlonia, Prince, 277

Torre delle Milizie, 323

Torriani, Orazio (fl. 1601–57), 340, 362

Torriti, Jacopo (fl. 13th cent.), 96

Totila (Ostrogothic king, d. 552), 322

Trajan, Emperor (53–117), 52–3, 58, 67, 181

Trajan's Column, 52–3, 78, 94, 175, **323**

Trastevere: during Mazzini's Republic, 263, 264; dwellings, 93, 156; Ostrogoths' fire, 74; riots in, 235; water supply, 181

Trelawny, Edward John (1792–1881), 367

Trent, Council of (1545–63), 167, 172

Trevi Fountain, 113, **343**

Tullia, 6

Tullianum, 316

Tullus Hostilius, King of Rome (r. 673–642 B.C.), 5, 317

Udine, Giovanni da (1487–1564), 41, 161, 348, 350

Umberto, Crown Prince of Italy (from May–June 1946, Umberto II, 1904–83), 306

Umberto I, King of Italy (1844–1900), 277

University of Rome, see Sapienza

Urban II, Pope (r. 1088–99), 89

Urban IV, Pope (r. 1261–4), 128

Urban V, Pope (r. 1362–70), 108

Urban VI, Pope (r. 1378–89), 110, 111

Urban VIII (r. 1623–44): and Bernini, 185–6, 187, 189; fortifications, 259; and Galileo, 225; Innocent X and, 190; personality, 185; St Peter's baldacchino, 189; tomb, 187, 190, **357**

Urbina, Gian d', 158

Urbino, Francesco Maria della Rovere, Duke of, 160, 327, 328

Valadier, Giuseppe (1762–1839), 242; piazze, 333, 350, 370; SS. Apostoli, 353; sculpture, 355; Tordinona Theatre, 360

Valerian, Emperor (r. 253–60), 62

Valeriani, Giuseppe, 354

Valvassori, Gabriele (1683–1761), 357, 362

Vansittart, 1st Baron (1881–1957), 289

Vanvitelli, Luigi (1700–1773), 343, 361

Vasanzio, Giovanni (Jan Van Senten, c. 1550–1621), 181; Borghese casino, 356; Borghese Palace, 356

Vasari, Giorgio (1511–74), 143, 168

Vassalletto, Pietro, 333

Vatican (see also Belvedere and Sistine Palace), **341**; Boniface XI, 111; Borgia Apartment, 138, **348**; Blessed Sacrament Chapel, 118; Borgia Tower, 138; Borgo Nuovo, 137; building under Innocent III, 92; Calixtus III, 119, Cappella Paolina, 167, 169, **352**; Chapel of St Nicholas, papal election, 119; Clement VII returns, 161; Cola di Rienzo at, 103–4; Cortile della Pigna, 175, 183, **355**; Court of St Damasus, 175, **355**; defensive works, 157; Fra Angelico's work in, 118; Giotto, 95; Julius II, 142, 143; latrines, 119; Lucrezia Borgia, 136; Nicholas V, 115; open galleries, 41; papal election of 1378, 110–111; Pius VI expelled, 232; Paul V, 181; private chapel, 118; Raphael Stanze, 143, 153, 161, **349**; Sacro Possesso of Leo X, 147; Sala Regia, 167, **352**; Scala Regia, 191, **360**; Sixtus V, 175; Torre dei Venti, 193; Urban V, 108

Vatican Gardens: Casino di Pio IV, 171; fountains, 181; Gardens of Julius II, 142, **348**; Giardino della Pigna, 229, **349**

Vatican Library, **344**; Benedict XIV, 228; Boswell in, 217; extended under Sixtus V, 175; in French occupation, 242; Nicholas V founds, 118; Paul III and, 167; Philip of Orange protects, 161; Sixtus IV adds to, 128

Vatican Museums, 229–30, 242, **364–5**

Velasquez, Diego Rodriguez da Silva y (1599–1660), 189

venatores, 47–9

Venerable English College, 363

Vernet, Claude-Joseph (1714–89), 222

Vespasian, Emperor (A.D. 9–79), 44, 51

Vespignani, Virginio (1802–82), 327, 333

Vestal Virgins: Elagabalus violates, 61; House of, 11, **316**; Numa Pompilius and, 5; Pontifex Maximus and, 11; seating in Colosseum, 45; unchastity, 15

Vettori, Francesco, 161–2

Vie: Via Alexandria (Borgo Nuovo), 137;

Appia (Appian Way), 22, 64, 122, 230; Ardeatina, 302; Arenula, 212; Aurelia Antica, 260; del Banco di S. Spirito, 141; delle Botteghe Oscure, 143; dei Cappellari, 212; delle Carrozze, 212; Cernaia, 181; dei Chiavari, 212; Condotti, 173, 222; della Conciliazione, 290, **369**; dei Coronari, 128, 212; Flaminia, 79, 88, 152, 232; dei Fori Imperiali, 290, **369**; Giulia, 143, 167; Gregorina, 222; Lata, 125, 152; dei Leutari, 172; Magistralis, 143; di Marforio, 165; Nazionale, 280; Nomentana, 289; Nova, 54; Panisperna, 343; Papalis, 128; dei Pellegrini, 128; IV Novembre, 52; Rasella, 287, 302; Ripetta, 151; Sacra (see under separate entry); Salaria, 8, 298; S. Celso, 143; S. Chiara, 111; Sistina, 173, 222; Trionfale, 152; Veneto, 303; delle Vite, 274

Via Sacra, 29, **318**; Arch of Titus, 51; booty carried down, 16; new pagan statues, 70; prostitutes, 58; SS. Cosma e Damiano, 76; width, 54

Vicolo dello Sdrucciolo, 231

Victor Emmanuel II, King (1820–78), 271–2

Victor Emmanuel III, King (1869–1947), 276, 293, 297–8, 306

Vida, Marco Girolamo (c. 1489–1566), 151

Vien, Joseph-Marie, Comte (1761–1848), 270

Vignola, Giacomo Barozzi da (1507–73), 175, 321, 353, 354

Villas: Villa Albani, 221, 229, 281; Altieri, 281, **369**; Borghese (see under separate entry); Caelimontana (see Mattei); Corsini, 260, 262, **366**; Doria Pamphilj, 260, **366**; Farnesina, 156, **351**; Giulia, 172, **353**; Giustianini-Massimo, 281; Ludovisi, 213, 281, **367**; Madama, 152, 160, 161, 280, **350**; Mattei, 94, **341**; Medici, 362; Medici del Vascello, 263, **366**; Mellini, 350; Montalto, 281; Negroni, 274, **367**; Pamphilj, 260, 262; Sovoia (now Villa Ada), 295, **370**; Savorelli, 267; Spada, 267; Torlonia, 221, 289, 297–8, 363; Torlonia (Via Nomentana), 369; Wolkonsky, 367

Villa Borghese, 281, **356–7**; Canova's work in, 270; Evelyn at, 183; owners of, 351; trees felled, 258

Villani, Giovanni (c. 1275–1348), 105

Viminal, the, 6, 315

Virgil, (70–19 B.C.), 34

Vitalian, Pope and Saint (r. 657–72), 78

Vitelleschi, Giovanni, 123

Vitellius, Emperor (15–69), 44

Volterra, Alessandro, 334

Volterra, Francesco da, 368

Wagner, Richard (1813–83), 222
water supply: aqueducts, 70, 81; in time of
    Trajan, 54; Paul V, 181; Sixtus V and,
    173; under Hadrian I, 81
Wilde, Oscar (1854–1900), 278
Wilkes, John (1725–97), 219, 221
Willison, George (1741–97), 219
Wilmot, Catherine, 226

Winchester, Henry Beaufort, Bishop of
    (c.1374–1447), 93
Winckelmann, Johann (1717–68), 221–2
women: attraction of eighteenth-century
    Roman, 219; Juvenal on, 56–7; and the
    law, 56; toilet and dress of Senatorial class,
    56
Worms, Concordat of (1122), 90

Wotton, Sir Henry (1568–1639), 224

Ximines, Ettore (1855–1926), 368

Zuccari (Zuccaro), Federico (c.1540–1609),
    334, 363
Zuccari (Zuccaro), Taddeo (1529–66), 334